# Introduction to Intelligence

*For the dedicated men and women of the US intelligence community.*

# Introduction to Intelligence

## Institutions, Operations, and Analysis

Jonathan M. Acuff

LaMesha L. Craft

Christopher J. Ferrero

Joseph Fitsanakis

Richard J. Kilroy Jr.

Jonathan C. Smith

FOR INFORMATION:

CQ Press
An imprint of SAGE Publications, Inc.
2455 Teller Road
Thousand Oaks, California 91320
E-mail: order@sagepub.com

SAGE Publications Ltd.
1 Oliver's Yard
55 City Road
London EC1Y 1SP
United Kingdom

SAGE Publications India Pvt. Ltd.
B 1/I 1 Mohan Cooperative Industrial Area
Mathura Road, New Delhi 110 044
India

SAGE Publications Asia-Pacific Pte. Ltd.
18 Cross Street #10-10/11/12
China Square Central
Singapore 048423

*Library of Congress Cataloging-in-Publication Data*

Names: Acuff, Jonathan M., author.

Title: Introduction to intelligence : institutions, operations, and analysis / Jonathan M. Acuff, Christopher Ferrero, Joseph Fitsanakis, Richard J. Kilroy, Jonathan Smith, Lamesha Craft, Coastal Carolina University.

Description: Washington, D.C. : CQ Press, A Division of Sage, [2022] | Includes bibliographical references and index.

Identifiers: LCCN 2020041329 | ISBN 9781544374673 (paperback) | ISBN 9781544374697 (epub) | ISBN 9781544374703 (epub) | ISBN 9781544374680 (pdf)

Subjects: LCSH: Intelligence service. | Intelligence officers. | International relations.

Classification: LCC JF1525.I6 A28 2022 | DDC 327.12—dc23 LC record available at https://lccn.loc.gov/2020041329

Acquisitions Editor:   Anna Villarruel
Editorial Assistant:   Lauren Younker
Production Editor:   Bennie Clark Allen
Copy Editor:   Melinda Masson
Typesetter:   C&M Digitals (P) Ltd.
Proofreader:   Scott Oney
Indexer:   Integra
Cover Designer:   Candice Harman
Marketing Manager:   Jennifer Jones

21 22 23 24 25 10 9 8 7 6 5 4 3 2 1

# BRIEF CONTENTS

# DETAILED CONTENTS

# PREFACE

This book is a product of the dramatic expansion of intelligence studies courses at colleges and universities over the past two decades, which itself is a result of 9/11 and the corresponding growth in the size of the US intelligence community (US IC). Accompanying this growth in intelligence programs at higher educational institutions has been a similarly rapid development of the academic discipline known as intelligence studies. The research and writing of all of the authors herein is naturally influenced by their experience in the US IC, military, and/or policy community. The text's content and methods are similarly shaped by our graduate training, for most of us as political scientists. However, intelligence studies has increasingly differentiated itself from its multidisciplinary antecedents, even as it remains shaped by them, and similarly seeks to inform practice in intelligence organizations. We see this text as part of the ongoing process of carving out a specific space for intelligence studies, balancing both scholarly rigor and practical utility. We hope the students who read this book as part of their undergraduate education will benefit from this approach.

Several analytic and empirical themes are emphasized. First, the structure and content of the text is strongly influenced by the 2019 National Intelligence Strategy, US Intelligence Community Standard (ICS) 610-3, and the International Association for Intelligence Education's (IAFIE) Standards for Intelligence Education. Comprehensive coverage of US intelligence organizations, collection, covert action, counterintelligence, cyber, inter-agency communications, oversight, intelligence analysis, professional ethics, and current and future threats is provided.

Second, although the primary focus remains by necessity on the US IC, the text is also comparative and historical. We embed more comparisons between intelligence organizations and systems in each chapter than other introductory intelligence texts. We believe more effort needs to be made to get undergraduates to see organizational and national similarities and differences in how intelligence is collected, analyzed, and disseminated. Several of the chapters devote considerable space to orienting students to intelligence organizations and practices of other countries. Understanding the nature of international threats and the role played by intelligence sharing is essential for future US intelligence officers.

Third, the text is modular. Although there is a progressive and sequential structure to the text, knowledge of one chapter is not necessary to understand later chapters. We felt this affords instructors greater thematic flexibility, as some may want to concentrate on history while others are more concerned with the contemporary agencies of the

US IC and its operations. The text accommodates a wide variety of pedagogical and content strategies.

Fourth, the focus is largely on strategic and international intelligence threats and opportunities. Although US law enforcement agencies increasingly incorporate intelligence collection and analytic methods into their day-to-day operations, the activities of civilian and military intelligence officers concerned with foreign threats remain distinct and vitally important enterprises. Although we do engage issues and organizations connected to homeland security, our book is not designed for students whose primary interest lies in domestic law enforcement, particularly at the local level. Such students would be better served by courses and texts in the US Constitution, criminology, policing, and/or public affairs.

Fifth, at the end of each chapter a list of key concepts is included. For instructors who wish to assign a research paper to students, we also include short bibliographies from the peer-reviewed and professional literatures. This material may be used as a starting point for a research project or as a resource that faculty may choose to draw on if they wish to extend discussion of the subject beyond each chapter.

Finally, the text ties content to specific career paths. In many chapters, Spotlight on Careers breakout boxes display current job advertisements in the US IC. In our experience, we have found that many students are not aware of the specific kinds of careers associated with different intelligence activities. Students' understanding of intelligence is largely based on stylized impressions derived from media. We believe it is desirable to begin to correct these misunderstandings as soon as possible, ideally when they enter an intelligence studies program. We feel these side notes will further reinforce what their professors are already trying to convey to them in class regarding the professional development and career process. Our intent here is to reinforce the in-class messaging of the dedicated faculty in intelligence studies programs, who try to encourage, cajole, and otherwise motivate the young men and women we teach to apply early and often for internships and jobs in the community. One of the major challenges faced by students in intelligence programs is the very high expectations the US IC places on them for early commitment to particular kinds of analytic and technical training. It is our hope that the Spotlight on Careers feature will help college freshmen and sophomores plan their course of study well so as to prepare them for one of the most competitive job markets out there.

Jonathan M. Acuff
Myrtle Beach, South Carolina
August 2020

# ACKNOWLEDGMENTS

My coauthors and I would like to thank our colleagues at multiple institutions who graciously provided feedback for the proposal for this book, as well as a critical reading of several early drafts of the chapters. We are also grateful for the careful shepherding of the text through various stages of publication by the SAGE/CQ team, particularly Scott Greenan, Anna Villarruel, Lauren Younker, Bennie Clark Allen, and Melinda Masson. We also appreciate the support and encouragement of our families throughout the writing process. Finally, we would like to thank the reviewers of our manuscript:

Arif Akgul, *Indiana State University*

Jason Ross Arnold, *Virginia Commonwealth University*

K. A. Beyoghlow, *American University*

Erik J. Dahl, *Naval Postgraduate School*

Nicholas Dujmovic, *The Catholic University of America*

David Hughes McElreath, *University of Mississippi*

Gregory Moore, *Notre Dame College Center for Intelligence Studies*

Brian Simpkins, *Eastern Kentucky University*

Corliss Tacosa, *Old Dominion University*

Ronald W. Vardy, *University of Houston*

# ABOUT THE AUTHORS

**Jonathan M. Acuff** is an associate professor of intelligence and national security studies at Coastal Carolina University. A former officer in the US Army Reserve, Professor Acuff has also worked as a military analyst for the National Bureau of Asian Research (NBR). While at NBR, he conducted research funded by the Department of Homeland Security evaluating the vulnerability of private sector facilities in the Pacific Northwest to terrorist attacks, as well as several projects supported by US Pacific Command (PACOM). He has published articles in *Intelligence and National Security, International Political Sociology,* and *Totalitarian Movements and Political Religions.* He is also the author of numerous book chapters and is the editor (with Brent J. Steele) of *Theory and Application of the "Generation" in International Relations and Politics* (Palgrave, 2012). Acuff has served four terms on the Executive Committee of the Ethnicity, Nationalism, and Migration (ENMISA) section of the International Studies Association. Professor Acuff previously taught at the University of Washington, Saint Anselm College, and Seattle University and was a Ford Foundation Fellow at the University of Iowa. He teaches courses on intelligence analysis, strategy, international security, terrorism, and writing in intelligence.

**LaMesha L. Craft**'s background includes 20 years of active military service in the US Army as an all-source intelligence warrant officer. Throughout her career, she provided strategic and operational intelligence analysis of nation-state and nonstate threats to US interests, policy, data, and networks in and around Asia, Europe, the Horn of Africa, the Middle East, and Southwest Asia. She has also worked overseas in Kosovo, Germany, Kuwait, and Iraq. Dr. Craft authored a comprehensive guide to conducting intelligence preparation of the battlefield (IPB) when analyzing threats in cyberspace. It was recognized as a "best practice" by the Center for Army Lessons Learned and played an integral role in developing Appendix D of Army Training Publication 2-01.3, published in March 2019. She currently serves as a faculty member of the Anthony G. Oettinger School of Science and Technology at the National Intelligence University. Dr. Craft's education includes a PhD in public policy and administration with a concentration in homeland security policy and coordination, Walden University; an MA in international relations and conflict resolution, American Military University; and a BA in international relations and international conflict, American Military University.

**Christopher J. Ferrero** holds a bachelor's degree in political science from Villanova University, a master's degree in security studies from Georgetown University, and a PhD in foreign affairs from the University of Virginia. He worked as a weapons of mass destruction analyst for the US Department of State from 2002 to 2003 and for the US Missile Defense Agency from 2003 to 2006. His areas of specialization include intelligence studies, WMD, the Middle East, and international security. He has taught courses on a range of international relations subjects at the University of Virginia, Seton Hall University, Syracuse University, and Coastal Carolina University. Dr. Ferrero is a member of US Strategic Command's Deterrence and Assurance Academic Alliance and a regular participant in the Arab Nuclear Forum at the University of Jordan in Amman.

**Joseph Fitsanakis**, PhD, is an associate professor in the intelligence and national security studies program at Coastal Carolina University, where he teaches courses on intelligence communications, intelligence operations, intelligence analysis, and human intelligence, among other topics. He has published widely on intelligence collection (communications interception and cyber espionage), intelligence reform, and transnational criminal networks. His writings also cover the evolution and practices of intelligence agencies in the United States, the Balkan region, northeast Africa, and Asia, with particular emphasis on China and North Korea. Before joining Coastal Carolina University in 2015, Dr. Fitsanakis built the security and intelligence studies program at King University, where he also directed the King Institute for Security and Intelligence Studies. He is also deputy director of the European Intelligence Academy and senior editor at intelNews.org, an ACI-indexed scholarly blog that is catalogued through the US Library of Congress.

**Richard J. Kilroy Jr.** is an associate professor in the Department of Politics at Coastal Carolina University in Conway, South Carolina, where he teaches courses in support of the intelligence and national security studies degree program and Latin America regional studies. He is also a former army intelligence and Latin America foreign area officer, having served in Germany, the US embassy, Mexico City, and US Southern Command in Panama. He holds an MA and PhD in foreign affairs from the University of Virginia. Dr. Kilroy is coauthor of *Seguridad Regional en América del Norte: Una Relación Impugnada,* published by Universidad Iberoamericana Press, Mexico (2020); editor of *Threats to Homeland Security: Reassessing the All-Hazards Perspective,* published by John Wiley and Sons, first and second editions (2008, 2018); coauthor of *North American Regional Security: A Trilateral Framework?* published by Lynne Rienner (2012); and coeditor of *Colonial Disputes and Territorial Legacies in Africa and Latin America,* published by the Northeast Asian Historical Society, South Korea (2010).

**Jonathan C. Smith** is a professor in the intelligence and national security studies program at Coastal Carolina University, which he established in 2011. He also serves as the Educational Practices Committee chairman for the International Association for Intelligence Education. In addition to his teaching activities, Dr. Smith served in the US Navy Reserve as an intelligence officer. In a 23-year career, he deployed in support of operations in Bosnia, Kosovo, Iraq, Afghanistan, and the global war on terrorism. His last assignment was as the commanding officer of Joint Intelligence Operations Center 0174 at the US Southern Command in Miami, Florida. Dr. Smith received his master of arts in international studies and his doctorate in political science from the University of South Carolina. He also earned a certificate in the Joint Professional Military Education program of the US Naval War College.

# INTRODUCTION
Jonathan M. Acuff

## WHAT IS INTELLIGENCE?

Today, most people view intelligence through the lens of pop culture. As portrayed in the Jason Bourne films and more than 50 years of James Bond novels and screen appearances, spies are heroic individuals battling against sinister adversaries with transparent plans against the free world. Yet these depictions of intelligence bear little to no resemblance to reality. Modern intelligence activities involve the planning and coordination of multiple organizations and are executed by teams, not individuals. Although the United States and its allies face real threats, who is an enemy and who is a friend are not always clear in the world of espionage. While on-screen spy gadgets often amaze, in this case reality is even more astonishing, with modern espionage employing acoustic lasers and even "Smart Dust" autonomous sensing technology.[1] Occasionally, real-world espionage resembles the implausible farce of film, as was the case with the Central Intelligence Agency's (CIA) plan to employ cats as listening devices during the Cold War, project "Acoustic Kitty."[2] But most of the time intelligence is conducted by professionals, acting on detailed, systematic plans developed as part of a bureaucratic process, not hatched over martinis in a casino.

Even after drawing a clear line between the fictional depiction of intelligence and its real-world counterpart, we must distinguish between intelligence other kinds of activities that are associated with spying. Here it is important to first draw a distinction between the scholarly study of intelligence conducted by college and university professors, which is known as **intelligence studies**, and its execution in the policy world by government officials and nongovernmental actors. Although there is some disagreement as to whether or not the academic study of intelligence is a social science or part of the humanities,[3] there is little confusion over the separate roles played by academic researchers who create knowledge that informs policy and the government

---

[1]Pister, Kris. "Smart Dust, BAA 97-43." University of California, Berkeley. DARPA/MEMS Program, 2001. https://people.eecs.berkeley.edu/~pister/presentations/Mitre0303.pdf.

[2]Edwards, Charlotte. "CIA Recruited Cat to Bug Russians." *The Telegraph*, November 4, 2001. https://www.telegraph.co.uk/news/worldnews/northamerica/usa/1361462/CIA-recruited-cat-to-bug-Russians.html.

[3]For a good overview, see Marrin, Stephen. "Improving Intelligence Studies as an Academic Discipline." *Intelligence and National Security* 31, no. 2 (2016): 266–279.

and nongovernmental leaders who act in the world of espionage. With this distinction made, let us turn to developing a definition of intelligence as it is practiced in the policy community. To do so, we must examine a number of related issues and concepts, some of which will be discussed in further detail in this chapter, while others will be covered in greater depth later in the text.

First, intelligence is often described in terms of the methods used in its **collection**, the gathering of different kinds of data through a variety of methods, principally human intelligence (HUMINT), signals intelligence (SIGINT), geospatial intelligence (GEOINT), measurement and signature intelligence (MASINT), and open source intelligence (OSINT). Second, it is also defined in terms of the **analytic process** of converting raw information collected by intelligence agencies into a finished product that decision makers use. Third, intelligence is frequently characterized in terms of different **levels** (strategic, operational, and tactical). Fourth, intelligence is classified according to different **categories of activity**, such as political, military, economic, and law enforcement intelligence. Fifth, intelligence is characterized by various kinds of **missions**, ranging from analytic activities like warning and decision support to operational endeavors such as covert action and information operations. Finally, intelligence in all its forms is **connected to politics**, though in this context there is a great deal of cross-national variation. For example, in the US intelligence community (US IC) intelligence officials are expected to remain removed from politics and do not make policy decisions, while in Great Britain politicians and intelligence officers work in tandem. In Germany, despite its close association with the office of the chancellor, intelligence plays little role in policy formulation due to the historical shadow cast by the terrible crimes perpetrated by the Nazis during World War II and the East German regime during the Cold War. In contrast, intelligence collected by the French government is used both against foreign targets and occasionally by politicians against their domestic political opponents, an activity that would be considered an unconstitutional abuse of power in most democracies. In short, providing a definition that encompasses all of the myriad activities associated with intelligence and that captures significant differences between country-specific practices is a complex issue.[4]

For the purposes of this text, we define **intelligence** as information collected, often secretly, by either governments or nongovernmental organizations that is subsequently analyzed and converted into a product used by decision makers in these organizations. However, intelligence has some additional properties that make it distinct from conventional policy analysis in several important ways. First, as noted in the definition, intelligence is frequently conducted in **secrecy**, without the targets of intelligence activities knowing about the operations against them. Secret information can

---

[4]A useful discussion may be found in Gill, Peter, and Mark Phytian. *Intelligence in an Insecure World*, 3rd ed. Cambridge, UK: Polity Press, 2018, 1–26.

make all the difference, affording consumers of the resulting intelligence product real advantages. But it is also worth noting that in the digital age most of the information collected by intelligence agencies is open source—it is generally available to all who look for it. Moreover, secrecy does not necessarily determine the usefulness of what is collected, which is dependent on collection goals and priorities. Second, intelligence often involves the use of methods that are **illegal** in the countries in which they occur. Authoritarian governments operate with little to no reference to domestic or international law and allow their intelligence services to operate in the same manner. But even democracies, which generally restrict their government's intelligence activities to conform with the law inside their borders, often allow their organizations tasked with operating overseas to violate the laws of the countries in which they work.

Although the definition we use in this book is not all-encompassing, it does cover activities undertaken by both nation-states and other organizations. Government operations constitute the bulk of intelligence activities in the world. Yet terrorist groups also use intelligence as a tool to further their causes. Al-Qaeda and the Islamic State regularly employ operational, analytic, and counterintelligence methods almost identical to those used by nation-states. Similarly, private companies regularly gather intelligence on rival businesses and use what they collect in crafting strategy, which is sometimes referred to as **competitive intelligence**. Thus, while most of this text emphasizes the intelligence activities of nation-states, other actors frequently use techniques we normally associate with states to achieve their political, economic, social, and/or religious objectives.

## THE PURPOSE OF INTELLIGENCE

Given some of the complexity involved in intelligence we've already covered, why do nation-states and nonstate actors use intelligence instead of other means of gathering and analyzing information? Simply put, intelligence offers the prospect of achieving **decision advantage** that other methods do not. Decision advantage refers to the ability to find out what an adversary plans to do, thereby enabling action to preempt or frustrate the adversary's plans. For example, interception of cell phone communications between insurgents in Afghanistan has allowed US forces to relocate away from attacks or to set up ambushes against the insurgents. While decision advantage provides prior understanding of what is planned or what is likely to happen, access to an adversary's **decision cycle** may permit an intelligence organization to affect how a state or other organization makes decisions by altering the process or procedure by which such decisions are made, shifting preferred outcomes of adversaries, or even changing the leaders of targeted organizations. For example, during the Cold War, East Germany recruited Günter Guillaume, an important staff assistant to West German chancellor Willy Brandt. From 1972 to 1974, Guillaume likely brought material to Brandt's attention that was beneficial to East German and Soviet interests. This activity may have contributed to Brandt's decision to pursue *Ostpolitik*, a dramatic policy shift aimed at reducing tensions between West Germany and the communist bloc.[5]

Depending on the adversary, gaining decision advantage can be challenging. But penetrating the decision cycle of a nation-state or other organization is an intelligence masterstroke. While gaining access to other organizations' plans and processes is desirable, it also carries potential risks and costs and should always be pursued only in light of the big picture. Decision advantage is a complex concept. Sometimes, it may involve merely determining how adversaries mean to act against us and foiling their plans. But disrupting an adversary's designs may be detected by that adversary, thereby undermining future use of the sources and methods that created decision advantage. **Sources and methods** are the people and tools used to collect information and conduct intelligence operations—protecting them so they may be used again is often just as important as the information they provide. Similarly, getting inside a target's decision cycle may result in attempts to change what an adversary wants or deems important. Yet there is no guarantee the outcome of such efforts will be an improvement, as changing the process by which decisions are made may create conditions for the emergence of new leaders or ideas that are less favorable than the prior status quo. Such was the case with the aforementioned East German agent. Although his activities may have made the emergence of the policy of *Ostpolitik* more likely, Guillaume's actions aroused the suspicion of the BfV, West Germany's domestic intelligence organization, and he was caught. Guillame's arrest forced Brandt to resign, thus removing a chancellor who was more interested in a thaw between the West and the East than his successor, Helmut Schmidt, who focused on Franco-German relations and European integration.

Weighing the balance of what might be gained versus what should be risked by attempting to gain decision advantage and/or access to an adversary's decision cycle highlights the role of intelligence in pursuit of the national interest. Intelligence activities must further the **national interest**, defined as the political, economic, and social objectives that increase a country's power relative to its international rivals and the threats it faces.[6] Effective intelligence is a force multiplier, enhancing the ability of powerful countries to advance their interests at lower cost than more conventional policy tools, such as diplomacy or military action. Intelligence operations are often **asymmetric** activities; that is, they occasionally allow weaker countries or organizations to compensate for their vulnerabilities and to "punch above their weight." Regardless as to whether it is used as a tool by the strong or the

---

[5]Sarotte, M. E. "Spying Not Only on Strangers: Documenting Stasi Involvement in German-German Cold War Negotiations." *Intelligence and National Security* 11, no. 4 (1996): 765–779.

[6]An accessible discussion of the national interest may be found in Roskin, Michael G. *The National Interest: From Abstraction to Strategy*. Carlisle, PA: Strategic Studies Institute, US Army War College, 1994.

weak, intelligence must serve the national interest—it cannot become an end that serves itself. One of the most prominent scholars of international relations, Hans Morgenthau, observed that people become beasts if the pursuit of power becomes the sole end of their actions, for the pursuit of power is moral in terms of providing security, not domination over others.[7] Intelligence officers must similarly guard against the tendency to pursue only the mission in front of them or parochial advantage for their organization, without regard as to whether either serves the higher purpose of the country.

## The Three Levels of Intelligence

How best to achieve the national interest draws us to a discussion of which organizations and resources should be used, how they should be employed, and where and when they should carry out their missions. This brings us back to the three different levels of intelligence referenced earlier (strategic, operational, and tactical). The best way to think of these levels is to view them not just as "where the action is," but also in terms of what kind of impact such action will have. So while the behavior of one person may be considered of a tactical nature in terms of the size of the unit involved (one person), if that person is the leader of the Russian Federation or a similarly powerful country, those actions probably have strategic importance. Conversely, if the intelligence refers to the behavior of the leader of a small, right-wing white supremacist organization in rural Idaho, then the issue remains tactical.

### Strategic Intelligence

The first level, **strategic intelligence**, refers to activities of a global, regional, or national scale, such as what a country wants from its neighbor or a change in policy of the world's most powerful intergovernmental organization, the military alliance known as the North Atlantic Treaty Organization (NATO). Strategic intelligence has a time frame typically measured in years. Both the National Intelligence Council and the CIA, for example, periodically produce strategic intelligence reports on global trends that attempt to forecast more than a decade into the future.[8] In addition, strategic intelligence has a specific meaning when employed in a military context. When military officers use the term, they are referring to intelligence operations supporting military activities related to altering the balance of power in the world or the survival of a state. For example, during the Cold War, one key component to US strategic intelligence involved evaluating the size and capabilities of the Soviet Union's nuclear weapons inventory.

---

[7]Morgenthau, Hans J. *Politics Among Nations: The Struggle for Power and Peace.* New York, NY: Alfred A. Knopf, 1949/1973, 14.

[8]National Intelligence Council. *Global Trends: Paradox of Progress.* Washington, DC: National Intelligence Council, 2017. https://www.dni.gov/files/documents/nic/GT-Full-Report.pdf.

# BOX 1.1

## SPOTLIGHT ON CAREERS

## CIA POLITICAL ANALYST (2019)

As a Political Analyst for the CIA, you will support policymakers by producing and delivering written and oral assessments of the domestic politics, foreign policy, stability, and social issues of foreign governments and entities. Your analysis will examine these actors' goals and motivations, culture, values, history, society, decision-making processes, and ideologies in the context of how these elements affect US interests and national security.

Opportunities exist for foreign and domestic travel, language training, analytic tradecraft and management training, training to deepen substantive expertise, and assignments to other offices in the Agency and throughout the US Government.

Location: Washington, DC, metro area

Starting salary: $55,539–$82,326

Foreign language bonus eligible

US citizenship required (dual national US citizens are eligible)

*Source:* Central Intelligence Agency.

## Operational Intelligence

At the next level down, **operational intelligence** refers to activities inside a nation-state, often directed via specific subsidiary organizations, such as the penetration of a foreign intelligence agency or the structure and function of a large government bureaucracy. Operational activities have a time frame measured in weeks to a year. It is a concept most often used by militaries, which use the term to refer to leadership, maneuver, fires, intelligence, information/cyber, and logistics supporting the conduct of a campaign in a theater of operations. Although the operational level is primarily defined by its activities rather than the size of the groups involved, it typically comprises organizations ranging in size from roughly 5,000 (a brigade, the current operational maneuver unit of the US Army) to hundreds of thousands of soldiers (armies and army groups).[9] The conduct of the US invasion of Iraq in 2003 is an example of the operational level in practice.

## Tactical Intelligence

Finally, **tactical intelligence** is defined as activities involving one person or a small organization. It may involve fine-grained detail, such as employing a low-level

---

[9]FM 3-0. *Operations.* Washington, DC: Headquarters, Department of the Army, 2017.

agent in North Korea's transportation ministry to provide information on machine parts that are being smuggled into the country in violation of international sanctions. Determining whether or not to fire a Hellfire missile from an unmanned aerial vehicle (UAV), commonly referred to as a drone, at a suspected terrorist leader is also a question of tactical intelligence. Its military usage is similarly focused on the small-scale, involving intelligence supporting the fire and maneuver of organizations ranging from a few soldiers (fire team or squad) to several hundred (a battalion).

## Three Perspectives on Intelligence

The three levels are used in the planning and execution of intelligence operations, ideally with reference to a strategy to achieve specific goals that further the national interest. The practical relationship between national strategy, these levels, and the management of intelligence and security resources is complex even in small to medium-sized states. But with 17 different agencies in the US IC and interests that span the globe, in the United States the task is more challenging than in any other nation-state. In addition to the mating of management challenges with outcomes, there is also a political dimension to deciding the role of intelligence. In the US IC, this takes the form of a debate involving three traditions or perspectives as to how intelligence should be used, the relationship between policymakers and the IC, and what kinds of missions are emphasized.

### The Kent School

The first such tradition is represented by the views of Sherman Kent, a former Yale University professor and one of the creators of modern intelligence analysis. During his long and storied career at the CIA, Kent advocated an intelligence tradition best summed up by an expression of unknown origin, that intelligence is "scholarship in service of the state." Although Kent was responsible for improving the quality of analytic products, advocating for more precise, standardized language in intelligence estimates, he is also known for keeping the Office of National Estimates, which he ran from 1952 to 1967, relatively isolated from the decision makers it served.[10] Thus the **Kent school**, as we shall call it, is defined by concern that coordination between intelligence officers and policymakers may become problematic, as politicians will attempt to politicize intelligence.[11] In order to maintain their objectivity, intelligence officers should keep policymakers at arm's length, telling them only what they need to know and nothing more. The logic underpinning this tradition is that only intelligence officers possess the specialized training and experience to evaluate and correctly

---

[10]Steury, Donald P. "Introduction." In *Sherman Kent and the Board of National Estimates: Collected Essays.* Washington, DC: Center for the Study of Intelligence, 1994.

[11]Wirtz, James J. "The Intelligence–Policy Nexus." In *Strategic Intelligence*, Vol. 1., edited by Loch K. Johnson. Westport, CT: Praeger, 2007.

employ most kinds of intelligence and should remain relatively aloof, separated from politics in the same way university professors are. Consequently, politicians should let the professionals do their job and keep their involvement in supervising intelligence agencies to a minimum.

The Kent school of thought dominated the US IC from the 1950s until the early 1970s, when the relative independence of the CIA and the Federal Bureau of Investigation (FBI) during the early Cold War and Vietnam War was halted by a series of investigations by the press that resulted in the creation of the Church Committee in the US Senate. The subsequent hearings before the committee revealed dozens of covert action programs, many undertaken with little to no notification of the White House or Congress, which many Americans found deeply disturbing. One of the key challenges with this intelligence tradition is known as the **principal–agent problem**. Specifically, the agent, in this case an intelligence service, has access to information the principal, policymakers, do not. This asymmetry in information results in different incentives, with the agent seeing reasons to act that may not be consistent with the long-term goals of the principal but nevertheless conform with the short-term interest of the agent.[12] Such was the case with the US IC running covert operations programs that furthered the near-term objectives of the IC while inhibiting the long-term goals of the political leadership of the country.

## The Gates School

The second school of thought is the dominant tradition in today's US IC. Named for Robert Gates, former director of the CIA and secretary of defense in both the George W. Bush and Obama administrations, this school of thought holds that intelligence must be actionable.[13] Intelligence must be immediately useful tactically, allowing rapid execution to maximize the decision advantage generated. Intelligence officers should work closely with the policy community, understanding and seeking to meet the objectives set by politicians. One of the results of the **Gates school** of thought has been the evolution of the CIA from a primarily strategic intelligence-focused organization into a kind of "drone kill machine." Under Gates's direction, the CIA dramatically increased its covert action capability, particularly with its leadership of the targeted drone assassination program, which has resulted in the deaths of over 3,000 suspected terrorists since 2005.

Although the Gates school offers the promise of a more rapid response to policy-makers' needs and goals, which in the information age is important, it suffers from several drawbacks. First, emphasizing the objectives of the policy community may result

---

[12]Blanken, Leo J., and Jason L. Lepore. "Principals, Agents, and Assessment." In *Assessing War: The Challenge of Measuring Success and Failure*, edited by Leo J. Blanken, Hy Rothstein, and Jason J. Lepore. Washington, DC: Georgetown University Press, 2015.

[13]Wirtz, "Intelligence–Policy Nexus."

in **politicization**, the morphing of objective intelligence into products and actions that serve the political purposes of politicians, not the national interest. Second, prioritizing operations over analysis deliberately shifts resources and attention away from long-term forecasting. This potentially reduces the decision advantage offered by intelligence, as it is less likely the US IC will be able to offer over-the-horizon predictions that allow decision makers to outwit adversaries. In this context it is somewhat ironic that Gates is associated with this school of thought, as during his first term as director of the CIA in the early 1990s he spoke with considerable pride of the lengthy research intelligence products the agency produced. Third, the drone program has resulted in some notable successes against the leadership of terrorist organizations. But it has come at the cost of thousands of civilian casualties, noncombatant men, women, and children who had no part in hostilities. Their deaths call into question the morality of the use of drones, how "targeted" UAV strikes really are, and whether or not US intelligence organizations should be in the assassination business, which is illegal under both international and US domestic law.

## The McLaughlin School

The third intelligence tradition is known as the **McLaughlin school**, named for former acting director and 30-year veteran of the CIA John McLaughlin. This third school straddles a middle position between Kent and Gates, emphasizing service to the policymaker as the primary role of the IC while reminding intelligence officers to maintain the highest professional standards in their work. McLaughlin noted the duty of intelligence officers to clarify and condense intelligence reports to maximize their usefulness to policymakers, to warn decision makers of potential threats, and to draw attention to opportunities to advance US interests.[14] Recognizing the danger of politicization, McLaughlin also emphasized the role of providing alternate views to those held by the policymakers, who are not motivated to see other perspectives on events as valid.

The McLaughlin school seems to offer an ideal balance between Kent and Gates. Yet in this strength also lies a potential weakness. By failing to take a strong position on whether the Kent or Gates school is correct in its respective view as to the proper role of the IC, it risks occupying a halfway house that rejects the risk-taking action of Gates while not going all the way toward the emphasis on detached objectivity of Kent. The danger of politicization may not in fact be reduced, as nothing guarantees politicians will listen to intelligence officers,[15] while backing off actionability as a yardstick potentially removes an important implement from the policymaker's toolbox to advance US interests.

---

[14]McLaughlin, John. "Serving the National Policymaker." In *Analyzing Intelligence*, edited by Roger Z. George and James B. Bruce. Washington, DC: Georgetown University Press, 2008.

[15]Marrin, Stephen. "Why Strategic Intelligence Analysis Has Limited Influence on American Foreign Policy." *Intelligence and National Security* 32, no. 1 (2017): 1–18.

## CONCLUSION: THE PROMISE AND
## THE LIMITATIONS OF INTELLIGENCE

As we have seen in this chapter, intelligence can be an important tool in statecraft. But significant disagreements remain as to the proper role of intelligence. In this concluding section, we shall summarize what intelligence can do when appropriately employed, as well as its limitations. Because they involve decisions regarding how national objectives are defined and provision of the resources and methods used to pursue them, deliberations as to how and when to use intelligence are often difficult. Policymakers and voting publics have distorted views regarding what intelligence can accomplish compared to making better conventional policy decisions, a process that in some ways has begun to break down in Western democracies over the past two decades.

Although intelligence can't always meet the ideal of achieving decision advantage or getting inside an adversary's decision cycle, **what intelligence can do** is create opportunities for decision makers to act. This may come as a result of excellent collection and rigorous analysis that provides warning of threats. But it may also come outside of the context of predicting the future. Intelligence can provide greater understanding of current events and processes for decision makers than their opposite numbers on the other side possess. Poor intelligence delivered to Iraqi dictator Saddam Hussein in the fall of 2002 encouraged his belief that he could minimize cooperation with United Nations weapons inspectors, just enough to satisfy the United States he did not have weapons of mass destruction (WMD) while maintaining enough doubt to deter his enemy Iran and curry domestic favor. He was wrong—the United States invaded and toppled his regime. Apart from the gains from forecasting and enhanced understanding, effective intelligence may even have the side effect of reducing tensions, often in unanticipated ways. Although the USSR's agents inflicted considerable damage to their interests, Soviet penetration of the US and British governments in the 1940s and '50s revealed to Joseph Stalin that NATO had no plans to invade the Soviet Union.[16] Consequently, Stalin saw little need to pursue plans to invade the West.

Although intelligence holds great promise in supporting the pursuit of the national interest, there are significant **limitations to intelligence** as well. Of central importance is the simple observation there are some things that are unknowable, no matter how well collection and analysis are performed. In addition, good intelligence provides a range of possibilities. But the relevant variables used to accurately forecast are neither static nor simple, as adversaries will react to US policies that build on accurate forecasting, thereby preventing predicted outcomes from happening. Moreover, unforeseen actors and events will always emerge, which suggests policymakers should

---

[16]Jervis, Robert. "Intelligence, Counterintelligence, Perception, and Deception." In *Vaults, Mirrors, and Masks: Rediscovering US Counterintelligence*, edited by Jennifer E. Sims and Burton Gerber. Washington, DC: Georgetown University Press, 2009, 77.

devote more attention to building in adaptability to institutions, rather than relying on a kind of "crystal ball" accuracy from the IC. Perhaps most frustrating is that even successes often come with hard-to-anticipate effects. For example, the 2012 raid on an Abbottabad, Pakistan, compound by SEAL Team Six resulted in the death of Osama bin Laden, the leader of al-Qaeda, and yielded an enormous trough of documents from bin Laden's computer hard drives. Yet one of the stealth helicopters that made the raid possible crashed, and its demolition by the SEALs was incomplete. Very soon after, Chinese intelligence officers had gained access to some of the undamaged components, suggesting the possibility of reverse engineering of the helicopter's carbon composite flight surfaces and stealthy paint.

Finally, intelligence is almost never decisive in foreign policy outcomes, and it cannot fix poorly conceived policies. These observations are particularly important in the context of the recurrence of **intelligence failures**, the inability of intelligence agencies to provide effective warning or to adequately respond to a threat. The lack of response by the USSR to the impending German attack against them in June 1941 and the Japanese attack on the US fleet in Pearl Harbor on December 7 that year are considered archetypical intelligence failures. The terrorist attacks of 9/11 are similarly cited as an intelligence failure, as are the inaccurate claims made by the US IC in the fall of 2002 regarding Iraqi WMD. More recently, the failure of the US IC to detect and interdict Russian cyber and information operations against the United States in 2016 to support the election of Donald Trump have also been characterized as an intelligence failure.[17]

There can be no doubt the US IC and its foreign competitors have historically failed to either accurately forecast the actions of an enemy and/or been unable to effectively intervene in a decisive manner. Intelligence is a difficult business, and failures may be part of the nature of the game. But we should be careful about assigning blame too quickly to intelligence organizations for surprise attacks, inaccurate forecasts, or other putative intelligence debacles. Politicians have strong incentives to hold intelligence organizations responsible for ill-conceived policies. In authoritarian political systems, dictators frequently blame their subordinates for intelligence failures that were in fact the product of disastrous policy decisions—their subordinates face execution if they present a more accurate account of events. In the oft-cited intelligence failure of the German invasion of the Soviet Union on June 22, 1941, Soviet dictator Stalin had been given intelligence from a source in the German embassy in Tokyo, Richard Sorge, indicating the correct date and time of the invasion. Since May, German aircraft had violated Soviet airspace and conducted high-altitude reconnaissance along the eventual route of the invasion. Moreover, German dictator Adolf Hitler had violated every international agreement he'd made, which should have given Stalin

---

[17]The US IC has determined the Russian government favored Trump over Hillary Clinton and acted to support his election. See ICA 2017-01D. "Assessing Russian Intelligence Activities and Intentions in Recent US Elections." January 6, 2017.

reason to doubt how long Hitler would honor the 1939 Nazi–Soviet nonaggression pact. Despite the excellent HUMINT available to the regime and the numerous indicators of the increasing threat posed by the Germans, Stalin's generals got the blame for their leader's incompetence.

Politicians in democracies have a similar interest in shifting blame for bad policy decisions. Although IC officials do not face death for speaking up, in many intelligence systems, including the US IC, both professional ethics and the separation of intelligence services from policy activities preclude criticizing decision makers. This allows politicians to control the writing of history in a manner that conveniently reduces their responsibility. The otherwise comprehensive *9/11 Commission Report* that examined the terrorist attacks on the United States offered some strongly worded critiques of the US IC. Yet it ignored 50 years of US foreign policy decisions in the Middle East that created conditions favorable for the rise of extremist groups like al-Qaeda. Similarly, there is some controversy concerning whether or not Iraq WMD qualifies as an intelligence failure. Regardless of the questionable quality of IC analytic products that were used to support decision makers, there is evidence the Bush administration had already made up its mind to invade Iraq, and intelligence reports did not influence this decision.[18]

Achieving the optimal balance between operational independence and political control over intelligence agencies is a constant challenge, one that no country has accomplished flawlessly. Yet for the potential advantages of intelligence over conventional policy tools to be realized, policymakers and the leaders of intelligence agencies must actively seek out ways to further the national interest while not compromising the sources and methods of intelligence operations, as well as the ethical and moral obligations both have to the publics they serve. In the information age, with increasingly complex technical collection capabilities and hard-to-anticipate threats, achieving the right balance may be more difficult than ever.

## KEY CONCEPTS

| | |
|---|---|
| intelligence studies   1 | intelligence   2 |
| collection   2 | secrecy   2 |
| analytic process   2 | illegal   3 |
| levels   2 | competitive intelligence   3 |
| categories of activity   2 | decision advantage   3 |
| missions   2 | decision cycle   3 |
| connected to politics   2 | sources and methods   4 |

---

[18]Regarding the minimal effect intelligence had on US policy formulation, see Lowenthal, Mark M. *The Future of Intelligence*. Cambridge, UK: Polity, 2018, 9.

## ADDITIONAL READING

Betts, Richard K. "Analysis, War, and Decision: Why Intelligence Failures Are Inevitable." *World Politics* 31, no. 1 (1978): 61–89.

Gioe, David V. "Cyber Operations and Useful Fools: The Approach of Russian Hybrid Intelligence." *Intelligence and National Security* 33, no. 7 (2018): 954–973.

Herman, Michael. *Intelligence Power in Peace and War.* Cambridge, UK: Cambridge University Press, 1996.

Jensen, Mark A. "Intelligence Failures: What Are They Really and What Do We Do About Them?" *Intelligence and National Security* 27, no. 2 (2012): 261–282.

Jervis, Robert. *Why Intelligence Fails.* Ithaca, NY: Cornell University Press, 2010.

Johnson, Loch K. *National Security Intelligence*, 2nd ed. Cambridge, UK: Polity Press, 2017.

Marrin, Stephen. "At Arm's Length or at the Elbow: Explaining the Distance Between Analysts and Policymakers." *International Journal of Intelligence and Counterintelligence* 20, no. 3 (2007): 401–414.

Treverton, Gregory F., and Wilhelm Agrell. *Beyond the Great Divide: Relevance and Uncertainty in National Intelligence and Science for Policy.* Oxford, UK: Oxford University Press, 2017.

Zegart, Amy. *Spying Blind: The CIA, the FBI, and the Origins of 9/11.* Princeton, NJ: Princeton University Press, 2009.

# 2

# INTELLIGENCE HISTORY

Christopher J. Ferrero

## INTELLIGENCE FROM ANTIQUITY
## TO THE WESTPHALIAN STATE SYSTEM

> And Moses sent them to spy out the land of Canaan, and said unto them, Get
> you up this way southward, and go up into the mountain. See the land, what it
> is, and the people that dwelleth therein, whether they be strong or weak, few or
> many; and what the land is that they dwell in, whether it be good or bad; and
> what cities they be that they dwell in, whether in tents or in strong holds; and
> what the land is, whether it be fat or lean, whether there be wood therein, or not.[1]

This Bible passage (Numbers 13:17–20) gives the oldest recorded account of an intelligence mission. In approximately 1300 BCE, the Israelites escaped captivity in Egypt and approached the Promised Land, which was then known as Canaan. Following God's instructions, Moses sent spies into the Promised Land to assess its value as well as the difficulty of its conquest. Moses's agents returned with stories of milk and honey, but also of Canaanites the size of giants whose defeat would be difficult. After a debate, the Israelites decided not to attack. As ostensible punishment for their lack of faith, they were forced to wander for 40 years before Joshua dispatched another reconnaissance mission and led a successful conquest of the Promised Land.

Whatever the veracity of this account, and whatever the strength of Moses's faith, the Bible shows one of humankind's earliest revered leaders seeking **decision advantage**, or the acquisition of superior knowledge and its application to optimize decision making. The value of what we today call "intelligence" has been appreciated to varying degrees for much of human history. From the ancient Middle East to ancient China, and from ancient Greece to medieval Europe, one sees the importance of intelligence for purposes ranging from military conquest to regime security. Volumes could be filled with the history of intelligence; a complete history is beyond the scope of this chapter. This chapter's more modest aims are to highlight important actors and cases from antiquity, the Middle Ages, and early modernity; to chronicle the evolution of intelligence in the United States; and to explain the role of intelligence in the major conflicts of living memory: namely World War II, the Cold War, and the 21st-century

---

[1]Numbers 13:17–20.

struggle against extremism and terrorism. Some major themes include the pivotal role that intelligence plays in the occurrence and the outcome of war, the importance of technology, the challenge of organizing and managing bureaucracies, and the tension between intelligence and democracy.

## Intelligence in Ancient Greece

Aristotelian rationality is a foundation of Western civilization, so it may surprise some that practical intelligence collection and analysis was little appreciated in ancient Greece. Aristotle's only known reference to intelligence collection is his recommendation to surveil political subversives, made in his seminal work *Politics*.[2] The use of intelligence to identify internal dangers is a feature of modern counterintelligence and policing in democracies and autocracies alike. Fixation on intelligence as a tool to identify and repress internal political dissent, however, manifests most readily and frighteningly throughout history in monarchical and autocratic governments bent on self-preservation, or **regime security**. Examples in this chapter illustrate the historic use of intelligence for regime security in England, France, and Russia.

Though the classical Greek period laid the foundation of the modern scientific method, the pillars of which are logic and evidence, superstition and divination played a dominant role in intelligence as it related to battle. Greek commanders preferred to consult oracles and dreams as opposed to tactical surveillance and reconnaissance reports. Xenophon, a soldier, historian, and philosopher, was the first to advocate for advance spies to collect tactical intelligence prior to war. But relative to divination, Xenophon acknowledged, this was of minor value. For true guidance on one's fate, one must turn to the gods. Wrote Xenophon: "In a war enemies plot against one another but seldom know whether these plans are well laid. It is impossible to find any other advisers in such matters except the gods. They know everything, and they give signs in advance to whomever they wish through sacrifices, birds of omen, voices and dreams."[3] If Xenophon had had access to space-based imagery or the U-2 spy plane, perhaps he would have been more enthusiastic about the possibility of intelligence leading to good decision making.

The theme of fate in classical Greek politics is perhaps best and most famously embodied in Thucydides's historical account and causal explanation of the Peloponnesian War in the fifth century BCE. In his account, the war is fated not by the whims or wisdom of the gods, but by practical circumstances. Wrote Thucydides: "The growth of the power of Athens, and the alarm which this inspired in Sparta, made war inevitable."[4] This dynamic about which Thucydides wrote in antiquity is known today as the **security dilemma**, a condition wherein State A's strength is

---

[2]Andrew, Christopher. *The Secret World: A History of Intelligence*. New Haven, CT: Yale University Press, 2018, 37.
[3]Ibid., 36.
[4]Quoted in Ibid., 3.

perceived as threatening by State B, leading State B to undertake defensive measures that in turn threaten the security of State A. This mutual threat perception can lead to arms races and war—even if neither side truly desires or benefits from such outcomes. The driving force of war is fear and uncertainty about the intentions of the other. The security dilemma is not unique to ancient Greece; its role in causing war is central to modern international relations theory. John Mearsheimer, a preeminent realist theorist, alludes to the tragic nature of the security dilemma in the title of his influential book *The Tragedy of Great Power Politics*.[5]

The concepts of the security dilemma and intelligence are inextricably linked. Uncertainty drives the security dilemma. Intelligence, by reducing uncertainty, can mitigate the security dilemma. Intelligence, therefore, is central to the avoidance of catastrophic war. Nearly 2,500 years after the security dilemma helped bring about the fall of Athens, intelligence on actual Soviet nuclear capabilities would reduce fear and uncertainty in the United States wrought by Soviet propaganda, forestalling an even worse Cold War arms race and perhaps nuclear war.

If the security dilemma ensured a clash between Athens and Sparta, it did *not* prescribe the war's outcome. Athens abjured secret intelligence and strategic deception to its detriment. According to Christopher Andrew, a leading historian of intelligence, "Athens's failure to 'spy out' Sparta in the way that the Israelites had been told to 'spy out' Canaan contributed to, even if it did not cause, the ultimate defeat of Athenian democracy in the Peloponnesian War."[6] Athens also failed in the realm of counterintelligence by succumbing to deception operations. Foremost among these deceptions was the appeal of a small Sicilian city-state named Egesta, which employed an elaborate ruse to fool Athens into defending it against the more powerful Sicilian city-state of Syracuse. Egesta gathered gold and other riches from surrounding towns with which it entertained Athenian diplomats, fooling them into believing that Egesta was a wealthy and worthwhile ally.[7] Athens launched an attack on Syracuse in 415 BCE, believing that it would eventually conquer all of Sicily with the help of Egesta. Besides falling for Egesta's strategic deception, Athens had no intelligence on basic factors like the size of the island or of its population. Athens's failed naval expedition against Syracuse cost it 200 ships and thousands of soldiers.[8]

The case of ancient Greece, and Athens in particular, illustrates several themes related to intelligence that reverberate across the ages: the dangers of the security dilemma, the inclination of some to give greater weight to intuition and divination than to observed fact, the strategic benefit of effective deception and the corollary need for effective counterintelligence, and the practical need for good—even if basic—tactical

---

[5]Mearsheimer, John. *The Tragedy of Great Power Politics*. New York, NY: W.W. Norton & Company, 2001.

[6]Andrew, *The Secret World*, 33.

[7]Ibid.

[8]Ibid., 33–35.

and strategic intelligence regarding enemy capabilities and intentions. A final note-worthy theme from ancient Greece concerns the tension between intelligence and democracy. It is a tension that bedevils democracies today, as seen later in this chapter and elsewhere in this textbook. What role should intelligence play in a democracy? In the 21st century, democracies have reconciled themselves to the necessity of collecting foreign intelligence. But what are the limits of domestic intelligence? At what point do openness and respect for privacy become a threat? The Athenian spokesman Pericles declared the following in a funeral oration during the Peloponnesian War. His words could be easily mistaken for those of a participant in debates about intelligence and democracy more than two millennia later:

> The freedom which we enjoy in our government extends also to our ordinary life. There, far from exercising a jealous surveillance over each other, we do not feel called upon to be angry with our neighbor for doing what he likes . . . We throw open our city to the world, and never by alien acts exclude foreigners from any opportunity of learning or observing, although the eyes of an enemy may occasionally profit by our liberality.[9]

As explained later in this chapter and elsewhere in this textbook, the United States and its fellow democracies have struggled in the 21st century to find the proper bal-ance between honoring Pericles's noble sentiments and implementing intelligence and security measures that protect the lives of citizens against hostile actors.

### The Art of War vs. On War in China

At about the same time that ancient Athenian leaders were downplaying the value of intelligence in warfare, a Chinese military strategist and philosopher named **Sun Tzu** penned one of history's most influential manuals linking intelligence to the suc-cessful conduct of war. In Sun Tzu's manual, titled *The Art of War*, intelligence is cru-cial. Sun Tzu shows awareness of both defensive and offensive counterintelligence, noting the importance of keeping one's capabilities and intentions secret and engaging in active deception.[10] *The Art of War* also devotes an entire chapter to the use of spies. In it, Sun Tzu argues that foreknowledge is the key to political and military success. How does one acquire foreknowledge? Sun Tzu's argument offers a stark contrast to his Athenian contemporaries: "Now this foreknowledge cannot be elicited from spirits; it cannot be obtained inductively from experience, nor by any deductive calculation. Knowledge of the enemy's dispositions can only be obtained from other men."[11] In other words, success requires effective collection and analysis of the enemy by human

---

[9]Ibid., 33.

[10]Sun Tzu. *The Art of War*, Chapter 1: Laying Plans.

[11]Ibid., Chapter 13: The Use of Spies.

agents. Human intelligence, or HUMINT, is an essential collection method today. Given his enthusiasm for intelligence in the fifth century BCE, one can only imagine Sun Tzu's excitement if he were alive to witness the development of modern technical means of collection.

In the early 1800s, a Prussian soldier and strategist named **Carl von Clausewitz** wrote another classic manual on the conduct of war. Its title, *On War*, is similar to Sun Tzu's *The Art of War*. Like Sun Tzu's work, Clausewitz's masterpiece is standard reading in modern military academies. Yet the two differ significantly in their appraisal of intelligence in war. Writing more than 2,000 years after Sun Tzu, Clausewitz downplayed the value of intelligence in warfare. Clausewitz's attitude shows that the influence of intelligence has been nonlinear throughout history. Capable thinkers and statesmen have assessed its value very differently throughout history, including in the United States.

Clausewitz's skepticism of intelligence in warfare is best summarized by this remark in *On War*: "Many intelligence reports in war are contradictory; even more are false, and most are uncertain."[12] One reason for Clausewitz's skepticism is the limited field of view of any single HUMINT agent. "After all, a troop's range of vision does not usually extend much beyond its range of fire . . . Enemy forces may be hidden by every wood and every fold of undulating terrain . . . Night, too, is a great source of protection."[13] Clausewitz's skepticism would likely be assuaged by modern technologies such as aerial surveillance, geospatial data, and night vision. Indeed, modern militaries do not share his skepticism. Intelligence is central to US military doctrine. Phrases like *domain awareness* and *information dominance* appear in numerous 21st-century military planning documents. High-tech intelligence capabilities are deeply interwoven with military operations. The goal is to cut through the **fog of war**, or the chance, confusion, and uncertainty that characterizes fast-paced combat.

This is not to say that Clausewitz is completely outdated, however. Modern militaries have not yet eliminated the fog of war, and timeliness remains essential. Tactical intelligence, such as intelligence regarding an enemy's position on the battlefield, can expire quickly. The temporal aspect of certain types of intelligence—specifically, the very short life span of a piece of tactical intelligence—informs Clausewitz's skepticism. Even with the benefits of 21st-century technology, ensuring the timely delivery of accurate intelligence to commanders and decision makers remains a key challenge and objective of intelligence professionals.

Clausewitz's observations on intelligence also retain relevance in the realm of analysis. He viewed skeptically people's ability to perform dispassionate analysis; he thought that intuition, emotion, and preconception beat out facts in most people's analyses.[14] Indeed, cognitive biases are an enduring challenge in the field of

---

[12]Kahn, David. "Clausewitz and Intelligence." *The Journal of Strategic Studies* 9, no. 2–3 (September 1986): 117.

[13]Ibid., 119.

[14]Ibid., 120.

intelligence analysis. To overcome these, the US intelligence community (IC) has developed **structured analytic techniques**—methods that apply the principles and best practices of the scientific method to intelligence analysis.

Finally, it must be noted that while Clausewitz was skeptical of tactical intelligence for military operations, he did recognize the value of strategic political-military intelligence. Though one must accept that the field of battle is shrouded in fog, one must still enter it with a strong grasp of the big picture:

> [We] must first examine our own political aim and that of the enemy. We must gauge the strength and situation of the opposing state. We must gauge the character and abilities of its government and people and do the same in regard to our own. Finally, we must evaluate the political sympathies of other states, and the effect that war may have on them.[15]

Despite his differences with Sun Tzu, Clausewitz finds common ground with the ancient Chinese philosopher and strategist on the value of strategic intelligence. His preceding passage echoes Sun Tzu's famous line in *The Art of War*: "If you know neither the enemy nor yourself, you will succumb in every battle."[16]

## INTELLIGENCE IN LATE MEDIEVAL AND EARLY MODERN EUROPE

The middle of the second millennium CE was formative for the practice of intelligence in major European powers, notably England, France, and Russia. The legacy of this period, which marks the transition from the medieval period to the early modern period, still shapes the culture and practice of intelligence in these countries today. (More about intelligence in these countries can be read in Chapter 4, "Comparative Intelligence Systems.")

### England

British intelligence is legendary, in part because of the fictional character James Bond, or 007. Britain has long been an intelligence powerhouse in both reality and the spy-fiction genre. Modern British intelligence traces its origins to **Elizabeth I**, who reigned from 1558 to 1603. Elizabeth employed the original 007, a spy named John Dee who signed his correspondence to the queen with the coded identifier 007. Roughly 400 years later, the author Ian Fleming drew inspiration and applied this code name to his fictional character James Bond.[17] (Few other attributes of James Bond are historically or contemporaneously accurate.)

---

[15]Ibid., 118.

[16]Sun Tzu, *Art of War*, Chapter 3: Attack by Stratagem.

[17]Alford, Stephen. *The Watchers: A Secret History of the Reign of Elizabeth I*. London, UK: Bloomsbury Press, 2012.

The Protestant Reformation of the early 16th century was the main force behind the development of an English intelligence apparatus under Elizabeth. Elizabeth was a Protestant; her throne was contested by Catholics loyal to her cousin Mary, Queen of Scots. The threat posed by Mary and the English Catholics led Elizabeth to establish a secret intelligence service known as the **Watchers**.[18] The Watchers infiltrated dissident groups with double agents, intercepted and decoded communications, and foiled assassination plots against the queen. The leader of the Watchers, **Sir Francis Walsingham**, served as the queen's chief secretary. Unfortunately, in addition to setting standards for effective spy craft in England, Walsingham presided over systematic torture of suspects. This most famously included the use of the notorious rack, whereby a prisoner's body was stretched until it tore.[19] While the professionalization of intelligence was underway, the development of ethical interrogation techniques still had a long way to go.

## France

The late medieval period also witnessed the development of a state intelligence apparatus in France. Like in England, the Reformation was a major driver. Louis XI, who reigned prior to the Reformation (1423–1483), had been the first French monarch to make regular use of intelligence, employing mathematicians to decode intercepted communications.[20] The true father of French intelligence, however, was **Cardinal Richelieu**, who served as first minister of France under King Louis XIII from 1624 to 1642. According to Henry Kissinger, Richelieu was also "the father of the modern state system."[21] "Few statesmen can claim a greater impact on history," writes Kissinger.[22]

What did Richelieu do to make such a profound impact? This can only be understood in the context of the Reformation. Richelieu served the French Crown during the Thirty Years' War, which Kissinger describes as "one of the most brutal and destructive wars in the history of mankind."[23] The Thirty Years' War was part of a Catholic backlash against the Reformation led by the Vienna-based Habsburg dynasty. The Habsburgs claimed universal authority as the Holy Roman Empire; they saw themselves as the legitimate political authority over a Catholic Europe. The Habsburg dynasty included modern Germany, Spain, and the Benelux countries at the outset of the war. France was surrounded, and though Catholic, it resisted Habsburg encroachment on its independence. Despite being an ordained high official of the Catholic

---

[18]Ibid.

[19]Ibid.

[20]Denécé, Eric. "France: The Intelligence Services' Historical and Cultural Context." In *The Handbook of European Intelligence Cultures*, edited by Bob de Graaf and James M. Nyce. Lanham, MD: Rowman & Littlefield, 2016, 135–146.

[21]Kissinger, Henry. *Diplomacy*. New York, NY: Simon & Schuster, 1994, 58.

[22]Ibid.

[23]Ibid., 59.

Church, Cardinal Richelieu pledged his primary allegiance to France and articulated the concept of **raison d'état**. According to this concept, the sovereign state is the most important political institution, and its survival and security justifies any means to safeguard it.[24]

Under the banner of raison d'état, Richelieu used state funds to build an intelligence apparatus that would protect the French Crown. He targeted internal dissidents—both Catholic and Protestant—with blackmail, intimidation, and assassination.[25] He stood up a communications interception and decryption unit known as the **Cabinet Noir**, or Black Chamber, to monitor communication between French nobles and foreign governments.[26] Richelieu also sent HUMINT agents abroad to collect secrets from European elites. Agent covers included maids, dancers, and fencers.[27] Altogether, Richelieu's intelligence apparatus pursued three goals in support of the French state: weaken the Habsburgs; prevent foreign interference in, and subversion of, France; and stamp out Protestant organizations in France.[28] It was largely successful.

The Thirty Years' War ended in 1648 with the **Peace of Westphalia**. France retained its independence and its Catholic identity. The Habsburgs ended their universalist claims. Protestantism was accepted as part of the European landscape. A new international order based on sovereign states was established. Peace would be maintained by a balance of power among sovereign states. The logic of this new order was heavily inspired by Richelieu, upon whose death Pope Urban VIII is purported to have said, "If there is a God, the Cardinal de Richelieu will have much to answer for. If not . . . well, he had a successful life."[29]

France remained active in intelligence under monarchical and republican regimes for the next two centuries. Among the most consequential examples are French intelligence support to the American revolutionaries and Napoleon's adept use of code-breaking and deception operations in building an empire.[30] "A well-placed spy is worth twenty thousand soldiers," said Napoleon.[31] France downgraded its investment in intelligence after Napoleon, contributing to its defeat in the 1870 Franco-Prussian War.[32] This highly consequential war led to the emergence of modern Germany.

---

[24]Ibid., 58.

[25]Sankey, Margaret. "Cardinal de Richelieu." In *Encyclopedia of Intelligence and Counterintelligence*, Vol. 1, edited by Rodney P. Carlisle. New York, NY: Routledge, 2005, 529–530.

[26]Denécé, "France."

[27]Sankey, "Cardinal de Richelieu."

[28]Denécé, "France."

[29]Kissinger, *Diplomacy*, 58.

[30]Denécé, "France," 135–137.

[31]Ibid., 136–137.

[32]Ibid., 138.

## Russia

The origins of Russian intelligence are generally traced to Ivan IV, or Ivan the Terrible, who reigned from 1547 to 1584. Ivan expanded Russia's borders and established himself as a powerful czar with the help of a brutal intelligence corps known as the **Oprichniki**. Ivan's agents harassed Russian nobles and confiscated their land. They enjoyed Ivan's patronage and "were encouraged to commit any crime, including mass murder, against any group suspected of disloyalty," according to Gail Nelson.[33] Ivan grew increasingly paranoid and unstable as his reign progressed. In 1572 he decided to purge the Oprickniki leaders.[34] His reasoning was unclear, but according to a historical assessment by Soviet leader Joseph Stalin, the Oprichniki should have killed more people and been more ruthless in support of Ivan.[35] Four hundred years after Ivan, Stalin presided over his own domestic reign of terror and internal purges.

Though Ivan the Terrible's royal successors did not match his brutality, they did embrace his model of maintaining a personally loyal intelligence force. These forces were known as **Okhrana** (meaning *guard* in Russian). The Okhrana's main loyalty was to regime and ruler. Their existence was officially secret until 1891. By the early 20th century, they were dreaded for their espionage throughout Europe. Principal targets included Russian emigrants to other countries whom they suspected of working to overthrow the monarchy.[36] The Okhrana was disbanded after the Russian Revolution of 1917 but was replaced by a new force that mimicked many of its behaviors: the **Cheka**. The Cheka was the first intelligence force organized by the victorious Bolsheviks. Like the Okhrana, its main purpose was regime security. To this end, official statistics suggest that the Cheka killed 12,733 people between 1918 and 1920. Some historians, however, suggest the number may exceed 300,000.[37] According to Melissa Gayan, these high numbers did not concern Lenin or Cheka leader Felix Dzerzhinsky. In their view, it was "better to overkill than be overthrown."[38]

Fortunately, contemporary Russia is not known for mass summary executions, but certain features of a 500-year-old intelligence culture remain apparent: an obsession with regime security, low tolerance of internal dissent, and the routine assassination of political opponents. In 2004, Russian president Vladimir Putin remarked

---

[33]Nelson, Gail. "Ivan IV (The Terrible)." In *Encyclopedia of Intelligence and Counterintelligence*, Vol. 1, edited by Rodney P. Carlisle. New York, NY: Routledge, 2005, 337–338.

[34]Ibid.

[35]Ibid.

[36]Kisak, Paul. "Russia (Pre-Soviet)." In *Encyclopedia of Intelligence and Counterintelligence*, Vol. 1, edited by Rodney P. Carlisle. New York, NY: Routledge, 2005, 549–551.

[37]Gayan, Melissa. "Russia (Post-Soviet)." In *Encyclopedia of Intelligence and Counterintelligence*, Vol. 1, edited by Rodney P. Carlisle. New York, NY: Routledge, 2005, 548–549.

[38]Ibid.

that "there is no such thing as a former Chekist."[39] Indeed, Putin's Russia is believed to have been behind several high-profile political assassinations or assassination attempts, two of which included using poison on Russian targets residing in England. Putin is a former agent of the **KGB**, the notorious Soviet intelligence apparatus that descended from the Cheka.

## INTELLIGENCE IN AMERICA FROM THE REVOLUTION TO PEARL HARBOR

More than 170 years would pass from the Declaration of Independence in 1776 to the establishment of a permanent, institutionalized American intelligence community in 1947. During this period, American leaders used intelligence on a sporadic and ad hoc basis. The general trend was to gather and deploy intelligence assets during times of war, and to then reduce or disband intelligence efforts during peacetime. Many American leaders associated intelligence with the tyrannical and cynical methods of European statecraft that the Founders had resisted. Intelligence was a dirty business; America would preserve democracy and moral leadership by eschewing it. This attitude is most famously and pithily captured in a remark made by Secretary of State **Henry Stimson** in 1929: "Gentlemen do not read each other's mail."[40]

Despite his foundational idealism, George Washington had no doubts or misgivings about the important role of intelligence. In this regard, Washington was the exception rather than the rule among American leaders during the country's first 171 years. According to historian Christopher Andrew, Washington became a believer in intelligence through his experience in the French and Indian War (1754–1763).[41] America's Founding Father penned a letter in 1766 in which he wrote that "there is nothing more necessary than good intelligence to frustrate a designing enemy, and nothing that requires greater pains to obtain."[42] Indeed, the United States may owe its existence to Washington's intelligence acumen. At the very least, Andrew assesses, it "hastened" victory in the Revolutionary War.[43]

---

[39]Matthews, Owen. "Vladimir Putin Resurrects the KGB." *Politico*, September 28, 2016. https://www.politico.eu/article/vladimir-putin-resurrects-the-kgb-moscow-security/.

[40]Khazan, Olga. "Gentlemen Reading Each Other's Mail: A Brief History of Diplomatic Spying." *The Atlantic*, June 17, 2013. https://www.theatlantic.com/international/archive/2013/06/gentlemen-reading-each-others-mail-a-brief-history-of-diplomatic-spying/276940/.

[41]Andrew, Christopher. *For the President's Eyes Only: Secret Intelligence and the American Presidency From Washington to Bush*. New York, NY: HarperCollins, 1995, 7.

[42]Ibid.

[43]Ibid., 1.

## The Birth of Counterintelligence

In 1775, one year before the Declaration of Independence, the Continental Congress established the **Committee of Secret Correspondence**, which built and maintained a network of human agents in foreign diplomatic circles. Washington's personal management of military intelligence was most consequential, however.[44] The Continental Army had no formal intelligence arm, but Washington recruited networks of spies that informed him of British troop movements. This tactical intelligence helped him avoid battles that would have been costly to his forces.[45] The most famous of Washington's military intelligence units was the **Culper spy ring**; it was established in 1778 to spy on British forces occupying New York City. The identities of many of Washington's other successful spy detachments remain secret to this day.[46]

Counterintelligence—specifically deception—was also central to the revolutionaries' victory. During the harsh winter encampment at Valley Forge in 1777, Washington facilitated a deception operation to make the British think his forces were stronger than they really were and to thereby stave off attack. He and his colleagues forged documents and correspondence inflating the size of the American cavalry and infantry. Washington then used double agents to make sure the documents made it into British hands. The plan succeeded; the British assessed that it would be too risky to attack the Americans at Valley Forge. Andrew assesses that were it not for this offensive counterintelligence operation, the Continental Army might not have survived the winter.[47] A deception operation would again play a role in the war's decisive battle at Yorktown. Washington once more contrived misleading correspondence indicating that he would target the British in New York—not in Virginia.[48]

## Famous Spies of the Revolution

American intelligence during the Revolutionary War is most famous for spy **Nathan Hale**'s declaration from the gallows that he regretted having only one life to lose for his country. Hale is celebrated for his patriotism, but he did his job poorly, blowing his cover very early and unnecessarily during his mission behind British lines. It is unfortunate and unfair that he is so closely associated with American intelligence during this period. While his case accurately reflects a lack of uniform professionalism

---

[44]Ibid., 7.

[45]Ibid., 7–8.

[46]Ibid., 8.

[47]Ibid., 9–10.

[48]Ibid., 10–11.

among revolutionary spies, he hardly represents the effectiveness of American intelligence overall under George Washington. Though Washington did not establish a permanent intelligence bureaucracy during his presidency, which lasted from 1789 to 1797, his administration did spend 12 percent of the federal budget annually on intelligence—the highest proportion of any American president in history.[49]

Washington's successors did not share his enthusiasm for intelligence. They did not institutionalize the profession within the new republic's government, contributing to setbacks like the British sacking of Washington, DC, in 1814.[50] By the start of the Civil War in 1861, both the Union and Confederate armies had to stand up new intelligence capabilities. President Abraham Lincoln naturally feared subversion; he thus dedicated much of his attention and resources to counterintelligence. To this end, he hired **Allan Pinkerton**, an enterprising private detective, to head the Union's intelligence effort. Pinkerton is alleged to have foiled an assassination plot against Lincoln early in the war. His agents also successfully penetrated the Confederate army for purposes of acquiring military intelligence. Another famous Union agent was **Harriet Tubman**. Though best known for her work as an abolitionist, Tubman served as a spy for the Union. She facilitated and personally participated in HUMINT collection missions involving former slaves behind Confederate lines. Their reports were known as the **Black Dispatches**. Tubman, in coordination with Union colonel William Montgomery, also led a covert action in South Carolina in 1863 resulting in the freeing of 700 slaves.[51]

## New Technologies in Intelligence

While HUMINT certainly played a role in the Civil War, the period stands out in intelligence history for the emergence of new technologies and related intelligence disciplines. The invention of the telegraph in the 1840s enabled armies and other government institutions to communicate quickly over long distances. Telegraph communications could be intercepted and read, however. Messages therefore had to be encrypted with ciphers. Naturally, the intercepting side would employ **cryptanalysts** to break the ciphers. This discipline of intercepting and decoding telecommunications is known today as COMINT, or communications intelligence, a subcategory of SIGINT, or signals intelligence. President Lincoln showed keen interest in COMINT, spending substantial time reviewing the work of telegraph operators and codebreakers at the War Department. According to Andrew, telegraph communication and decryption gave Lincoln "more detailed and up-to-date information on the war than any other source."[52]

---

[49]Ibid., 11.

[50]Ibid., 14.

[51]Office of the Director of National Intelligence. "1863: Harriet Tubman." Accessed January 5, 2020. https://www.intelligence.gov/people/barrier-breakers-in-history/454-harriet-tubman.

[52]Andrew, *For the President's Eyes Only*, 19.

Lincoln's Civil War presidency also saw the first use of overhead imagery intelligence (IMINT) to inform a policymaker. In June 1861, **Thaddeus Lowe** used a hot-air balloon to provide overhead intelligence about troop positions. Lowe telegraphed what he observed directly to Lincoln, who was at the other end of a telegraph line 500 feet below. This episode marked three firsts: the first electrical communication from an aircraft to the ground, the first real-time transmission of reconnaissance data from an aerial platform, and the first such communication of intelligence to a US president.[53]

## Institutional Support

Despite the trauma of the Civil War and the emergence of new technologies, the United States took only a couple of steps toward the institutionalization of peacetime intelligence during the period from the late 1800s to World War I. In 1882, it established the **Office of Naval Intelligence (ONI)**. The Department of the Navy's ONI remains part of the US IC today. In 1885, the Army institutionalized its own peacetime intelligence arm known as the **Military Intelligence Division**. Today, the Department of the Army's intelligence subcomponent is known as the Military Intelligence Corps.

During World War I, the military and State Department collaborated on a new, ad hoc initiative to decrypt foreign communications. The program was known informally as the **Black Chamber** (invoking the name of Cardinal Richelieu's decryption program) and was headed by a gifted cryptanalyst named **Herbert Yardley**. Yardley's program lasted from 1917 until 1929, when it was shut down by Secretary of State Stimson. The Black Chamber experienced success breaking Japanese and Latin American codes but was never able to break Soviet ciphers. It was also ineffective against the European powers' ciphers after 1921.[54]

Though the Black Chamber was shut down, the Army and Navy continued to collect and decrypt COMINT during the interwar period. The program to intercept and decrypt Japanese communications in the Pacific Theater during this period was known as **MAGIC**. If the United States had been able to gain foreknowledge of the December 7, 1941, attack on Pearl Harbor that would embroil it in the Second World War, it likely would have come through MAGIC. Though moderately successful, MAGIC was beset by challenges. President Franklin D. Roosevelt did not take an active interest in it. He tolerated disorganization and service rivalry between the Army and Navy and failed to include SIGINT in the charge of **William Donovan**, whom he appointed as **coordinator of information (COI)** in June 1941.[55] MAGIC decrypts were shared haphazardly. These themes of turf consciousness and miscommunication would reemerge more than 50 years later in the run-up to the September 11 terrorist attacks.

---

[53]Ibid., 20.

[54]Ibid., 69–70.

[55]Ibid., 119.

MAGIC also suffered from resource constraints. From 1939 to 1941, only two to five cryptanalysts were assigned to work on Japanese naval code.[56] These resource constraints slowed the Americans' efforts to decrypt a new variant of Japanese code introduced in December 1940. According to National Security Agency (NSA) historian Frederick Parker, the Navy very likely could have predicted the attack on Pearl Harbor had the US government afforded Japanese naval intercepts higher priority and more resources.[57] Instead, the intelligence failure of Pearl Harbor would galvanize the country into World War II and help ensure that it never again underestimated the importance of a strong, institutionalized intelligence community.

## WORLD WAR II AND THE BIRTH OF THE MODERN AMERICAN INTELLIGENCE COMMUNITY

US intelligence during World War II would be affected by "administrative disarray."[58] It nonetheless took important steps forward. In 1942, President Roosevelt ordered the

creation of the **Office of Strategic Services (OSS)**—widely considered the forerunner to the Central Intelligence Agency. Its head, William Donovan, gained more power in certain respects as head of the OSS. Donovan, as previously noted, had been appointed as COI a year earlier. The purpose of the COI position was to improve communication and coordination among US government entities performing intelligence functions. However, as COI, Donovan had little authority to execute intelligence operations. This changed under the OSS. The OSS performed collection, analysis, and covert action, including sabotage and support to paramilitary operations. It was still hardly Donovan's dream job, though. The military remained dominant in the realm of US intelligence. Donovan's OSS was subordinated to the Joint Chiefs of Staff. His analysts were

**PHOTO 2.1** William Donovan headed the Office of Strategic Services during World War II and was the main visionary of the modern US intelligence community.

CIA/Public domain/Wikimedia Commons

[56]Ibid., 120.

[57]Ibid., 120.

[58]Ibid., 131.

denied access to military COMINT decrypts, hampering their analysis. Turf battles between OSS and military intelligence units like the ONI were common.[59] Five years of difficult bureaucratic maneuvering would separate the birth of the OSS in 1942 and the fulfillment of Donovan's vision of a permanent, centralized intelligence apparatus in 1947.

## The US and UK Partnership

While US intelligence underwent growing pains during World War II, British intelligence proved a well-oiled machine. The two countries formed a close intelligence relationship during the war. Though the United States would eventually become the senior partner in the relationship during the Cold War, the British were more advanced in the 1940s. Britain especially excelled in codebreaking and counterintelligence during the war. Under **Project ULTRA**, Britain and the United States cracked the Nazis' military communications that were encrypted by the vaunted **Enigma machine**. The Nazis thought their code unbreakable. They were wrong. A highly classified codebreaking effort was set up at England's **Bletchley Park** to crack the Enigma code. With the help of renowned mathematician Alan Turing, the team at Bletchley produced and managed a massive mechanical computer able to run the millions of permutations necessary to crack the code. The breakthrough was pivotal to the Allied defeat of Nazi Germany.

Britain also bested the Nazis in the HUMINT field. It successfully identified and turned all of Germany's human agents in Britain in what it called the **Double-Cross System**. This system exploited British HUMINT and COMINT proficiencies, German incompetence, and Britain's isolated geographical position as an island to achieve a remarkable cooptation of the Nazis' HUMINT network. These double agents were then put to work in British and Allied deception operations—most notably, **Operation FORTITUDE**. This operation supported the June 6, 1944, D-Day invasion by tricking the Nazis into believing the Allied assault would come further to the east at Pas-de-Calais. The deception campaign employed dummy military assets for purposes of visual deception and phony radio traffic. Two British double agents turned under the Double-Cross System, code-named BRUTUS and GARBO, fed extensive false information to their Nazi superiors about the Allied order of battle.[60] A Nazi map of Allied forces captured in May 1944 showed that the deception was working. Even after the Normandy invasion began in June, the Nazis assessed it to be a diversion from the real attack to come further east. They therefore withheld reinforcements from Normandy. J. C. Masterman, a participant in and chronicler of the Double-Cross System and Operation FORTITUDE, wrote after the war that

---

[59]Ibid., 131–133.

[60]Masterman, J. C. *The Double-Cross System*. Guilford, CT: Lyons Press, 2012.

"beyond the wildest hopes of those responsible, the threat [of an Allied invasion in the east] held until the autumn."[61]

## The War's End

Despite the Allied victory, World War II exhausted Great Britain as the dominant Western power. The United States would assume the mantle as leader of the Western world. Nonetheless, it would take two years from the end of the war for the United States to finally institutionalize a peacetime, centralized intelligence apparatus. The war's end brought the disbanding of the OSS and further lobbying by William Donovan for a permanent, centralized intelligence organ reporting directly to the president. Donovan was opposed by the military service branches and the Federal Bureau of Investigation (FBI), all of which saw him as encroaching on their bureaucratic turf.[62] Members of the media also opposed Donovan for proposing a "super Gestapo agency."[63] The American aversion to tyranny was still too strong for some to accept the need for a permanent intelligence apparatus.

Over a two-year span from 1945 to 1947, President Harry Truman grew increasingly frustrated by turf battles and fragmented performance among those responsible for national security.[64] Finally, in 1947, Truman embraced Donovan's vision. The **1947 National Security Act** established the **Central Intelligence Agency (CIA)** "for the purpose of coordinating the intelligence activities of the several Government departments and agencies in the interest of national security."[65] The CIA would be headed by the director of central intelligence, or DCI, who would be dual-hatted as both head of the CIA and overseer of the broader intelligence community. The DCI would also serve as the president's principal adviser on intelligence. The National Security Act also established the Department of Defense to better coordinate the efforts of the armed forces and the National Security Council to facilitate inter-agency cooperation and coordination on issues of foreign and defense policy. The United States had learned the lessons of Pearl Harbor and of bureaucratic mismanagement. These lessons were not perfectly applied to the creation of a flawless system; the intelligence community would have to be reviewed and reorganized after the terrorist attacks of September 11, 2001, revealed flaws in its design and culture. But the United States was finally ready to embrace and excel in its role as a world power—and just in time to go head-to-head with the Soviet Union.

---

[61]Ibid., 164.

[62]Andrew, *For the President's Eyes Only*, 145.

[63]Ibid., 147.

[64]Ibid., 169.

[65]Ibid., 170.

# THE COLD WAR

The Cold War, which lasted from 1945 to 1991, provides the main framework for understanding international relations for most of the second half of the 20th century. The Cold War was a multifaceted rivalry between the United States and the Soviet Union. It was both ideological and geopolitical. The two superpowers never confronted each other in a major war, mainly due to the threat of a nuclear holocaust. But they confronted each other through political and paramilitary proxies across the world, attempted to subvert each other, and collected extensive intelligence on each other. Each side viewed the other as an existential threat. Bookshelves are filled with volumes of Cold War history. A full accounting of Cold War intelligence history is beyond the scope of this chapter. Therefore, we focus on three main themes: how the Cold War led the United States to develop a technology-centric intelligence community, how American developments in technical collection—mainly overhead imagery—may have prevented nuclear war, and the Soviet advantage in human intelligence.

## American Intelligence and the Nuclear Arms Race

The United States ended World War II in 1945 by dropping two nuclear bombs on Japan. By 1949, the Soviet Union also had nuclear weapons (due largely to successful espionage against the United States, as discussed later in this chapter). By the 1950s, the Cold War was well underway, and the United States found itself in a security dilemma. How strong and threatening was the Soviet Union? How many nuclear weapons did it have? Could it effectively attack the United States with them? A Russian military intelligence agent named Pyotr Popov volunteered to work for the CIA; Popov's information helped reduce concerns in the 1950s that the USSR was bent on America's imminent destruction.[66] But its intentions were still hostile, and Soviet propaganda and deception were designed to menace the United States and make it feel that it was losing the fledgling nuclear arms race. One famous manifestation of this was the myth of the **bomber gap**—the belief that the Soviets were outpacing the Americans in the development of bomber aircraft that could deliver nuclear weapons to the other side of the world. In one famous instance, the Soviets fostered this myth by flying bombers in wide, horizon-crossing circles at a Moscow military parade. The visual deception of onlookers made it appear that the USSR had more bombers than it really did.

To get to the bottom of Soviet military and nuclear capabilities, the United States would have to turn to the sky. The help of HUMINT assets like Pyotr Popov was the exception rather than the rule. Besides, the USSR was the largest country on Earth in terms of landmass; it covered 8 million square miles and was roughly three times the

---

[66]Ibid., 214.

size of the continental United States.[67] It was also a closed totalitarian system. Human agents did not enjoy the access or freedom of movement that democracy afforded communist agents working in the West. For these reasons, the United States focused on becoming an imagery powerhouse in the 1950s and '60s. The first—and probably most famous—imagery asset developed and deployed by the United States was the **U-2 spy plane**, which flew its first mission on July 4, 1956. The U-2 allowed the Americans to fly over Soviet territory with impunity; before 1956, American intelligence aircraft could only fly along the periphery of the country for fear of being shot down. These missions were helpful; it was aerial sampling collected by a reconnaissance aircraft off the coast of Russia that detected the Soviets' nuclear weapon test in 1949. But most of the USSR was off-limits to US aircraft until the arrival of the U-2, which flew at over 70,000 feet and outside the range of Soviet air defenses. It could fly for nine hours and cover 5,000 nautical miles.[68] This did not provide perfect coverage of the USSR but was enough to dispel the myth of the bomber gap. The last U-2 mission over Soviet territory was flown by **Francis Gary Powers** in 1960. Powers was shot down when a Soviet air defense missile detonated close enough to his U-2 to disable his aircraft's tail. Powers survived, was put on trial in the USSR, and was ultimately repatriated to the United States in a prisoner exchange. The incident was a moral and propaganda victory for the Soviets, but it was not actually very damaging to US collection efforts. By the time of Powers's trial in Russia in September 1960, the United States had deployed its first space-based imaging satellite, known as **Corona**.[69] The U-2 continued to serve important missions, but satellites would provide more comprehensive coverage of the USSR. Satellite imagery allowed American analysts to map Soviet air bases, naval stations, command centers, air defenses, critical infrastructure, and more.[70] It was also crucial to dispelling another myth about a Soviet advantage in ballistic missiles. The Soviets had beaten the United States into space with the 1957 launch of the **Sputnik** satellite. Sputnik's launch suggested the Russians would soon be capable of launching a nuclear warhead at the United States on an intercontinental ballistic missile, or ICBM. (A space-launch capability is a precursor to an ICBM capability.) Soviet premier Nikita Khrushchev played to American fears, bragging in the late 1950s that the USSR was churning out missiles "like sausages." The Soviets were indeed developing ballistic missiles, but Khrushchev was exaggerating. John F. Kennedy played to fears about the supposed **missile gap** in the 1960 presidential campaign, but upon taking the Oval Office, top-secret imagery shown to him revealed that the Soviet threat was less than he had been led to believe.

---

[67]Lindgren, David. *Trust but Verify: Imagery Analysis in the Cold War*. Annapolis, MD: Naval Institute Press, 2000, 48.

[68]Ibid., 34.

[69]Ibid., 3.

[70]Lindgren, *Trust but Verify*.

It is hard to overstate the significance of satellite reconnaissance in preventing the Cold War arms race from spiraling out of control. By reducing uncertainty, imagery intelligence on Soviet nuclear capabilities helped the United States pull its punches and avoid dangerous escalation at key points. An excerpt from David Lindgren's account of imagery and the Cold War arms race is worth consideration:

> Corona reconnaissance satellites compiled an impressive list of intelligence achievements. Because they provided photographic coverage of literally the entire Soviet Union, imagery analysts were able to amass a fairly complete inventory of all Soviet ICBM, IRBM, MRBM, and SAM complexes. Repetitive coverage of missile test centers and production facilities enables analysts to determine what was being developed, when it was being deployed, and how long it would take to become operational.[71]

Satellites were also used for the collection of signals intelligence, including long-distance telephone calls of foreign leaders. To this day, the United States leads in space-based, high-tech intelligence collection. Critics of US intelligence often suggest that it is *too* tech-centric, and that 21st-century challenges require greater investment in human intelligence. However true this may be, the United States did not become tech-centric without reason. The Cold War crucible required it.

## Avoiding Armageddon: The Cuban Missile Crisis

The **Cuban Missile Crisis** is the most famous example of how close the world came to nuclear conflict during the Cold War. The fact that this episode did *not* result in a disastrous war is due largely to good intelligence. The Cuban Missile Crisis broke in October 1962 when overhead imagery from a U-2 spy plane revealed Soviet air defense systems being constructed in Cuba. Further imagery collection helped analysts determine that additional sites under

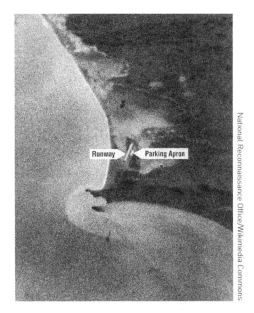

National Reconnaissance Office/Wikimedia Commons

**PHOTO 2.2** The first image ever generated by a Corona satellite in 1960. It identifies a Soviet airfield.

---

[71]Ibid., 121. (*Note:* IRBM = intermediate-range ballistic missile; MRBM = medium-range ballistic missile; and SAM = surface-to-air missile.)

construction resembled IRBM launch sites in the USSR. The Soviets were secretly trying to turn Cuba into a nuclear missile base. Ultimately, they planned to establish 40 ballistic missile launch sites in Cuba. They also planned to deploy MiG fighters and 45,000 troops to the island.[72] Why did the USSR do this? If the plan had been carried out, it would have allowed it to more quickly launch a nuclear strike on the United States. In addition to more easily threatening the United States with nuclear weapons, the Soviets also wanted to defend their ally Fidel Castro. A year earlier, the United States had supported Cuban paramilitaries aiming to overthrow the Castro regime in what became known as the **Bay of Pigs invasion**. This failed covert operation was poorly and indecisively executed. The mission was compromised by Cuban intelligence, and Kennedy refused to provide vital air support once the assault was underway. Despite this embarrassing failure, the Kennedy administration continued efforts to overthrow Castro through various covert actions organized under the code name **Operation MONGOOSE**.

If the Bay of Pigs was Kennedy's worst hour as president, the Cuban Missile Crisis was his finest. The Soviet move to deploy missiles was threatening and destabilizing, but would action against the sites in Cuba bring about the nuclear war that the Americans hoped to avoid? Kennedy had to get the missiles out of Cuba without

Kennedy Library/Public domain/Wikimedia Commons

**PHOTO 2.3** President Kennedy reviews intelligence with his special national security team, known as the ExComm, during the Cuban Missile Crisis in October 1962.

---

[72]Ibid., 68.

sparking World War III. The early warning provided by overhead reconnaissance gave the president and his advisers a week to consider options and avoid a rash and possibly disastrous countermove. Critical insight about Soviet missile operations also came from **Oleg Penkovsky**, a Soviet colonel who was probably the United States' most valuable Russian HUMINT asset during the Cold War. With help from Penkovsky, the United States was better able to assess when the Soviet missiles would become operational.

With the decision advantage provided by intelligence, Kennedy imposed a quarantine of Cuba and, after 13 days of tension, convinced Khrushchev to withdraw the missiles in exchange for a noninvasion pledge of Cuba and an unpublicized withdrawal of American missiles from Turkey. The crisis is generally considered to have ended with Khrushchev's agreement to withdraw on October 28. But the issue remained of verifying that the missiles were removed from Cuba. Castro would not consent to on-site inspection, so the United States continued its aerial reconnaissance until it was confident that the missiles were gone. It finally lifted its naval quarantine of the island on November 20, 1962.

## Soviet HUMINT Successes

Both the United States and the Soviet Union employed the full spectrum of collection methods during the Cold War. As noted, the United States enjoyed some vital HUMINT successes to supplement its focus on technical collection. Meanwhile, the Soviet Union was far from a technological backwater. It also deployed spy satellites and technical sensors. But where the Soviets really shined was in the field of HUMINT collection.

Before its deficiencies and abuses were laid bare by history, communism had substantial appeal among Westerners, including educated elites. The USSR adeptly exploited this to serve its HUMINT purposes beginning as far back as the 1930s. In America, the **CPUSA**, or Communist Party of the USA, provided especially low-hanging fruit. According to John Earl Haynes and Harvey Klehr, two leading historians of Soviet espionage in America, the CPUSA "was indeed a fifth column working inside and against the United States in the Cold War."[73] In 1995, the United States declassified a collection of 3,000 Soviet cables that it had intercepted and decoded beginning in 1943 under a SIGINT program known as **Project VENONA**. The VENONA decrypts revealed breathtakingly extensive and high-level HUMINT penetration. Haynes and Klehr note that "by 1948 . . . the Soviets had recruited spies in virtually every major American government agency of military or diplomatic importance."[74] Many of these spies had had some affiliation with the CPUSA in their past. This

---

[73]Haynes, John Earl, and Harvey Klehr. *Venona: Decoding Soviet Espionage in America.* New Haven, CT: Yale University Press, 1999, 7.

[74]Ibid., 9.

included 15 to 20 members of the OSS, such as Maurice Halperin, one of the leaders of its research and analysis division.[75] Harry Dexter White, a senior Treasury Department official, informed the Soviets on the United States' negotiating redlines for the postwar order. White, who represented the United States at the United Nations' founding conference in 1945, gave information on Truman's negotiating strategy that all but ensured Soviet annexation of the Baltic states of Latvia, Lithuania, and Estonia.[76] Similarly, Lauchlin Currie, a close adviser to President Roosevelt, provided information that proved costly to Poland's postwar independence.[77] William Perl, a government aeronautical scientist, shared jet engine technology with Moscow that undermined US-led forces in the Korean War.[78] There were many others, as well, including such famous names as Alger Hiss and Whittaker Chambers.

Of the Soviets' many HUMINT successes, perhaps none was more consequential than its penetration of the Manhattan Project—the secret American program to design the nuclear bomb. It achieved this through the **Rosenberg spy ring**, named for avowedly communist New York City couple Julius and Ethel Rosenberg. The Rosenbergs worked with Ethel's brother David Greenglass, who was a technician on the Manhattan Project, and two Manhattan Project physicists named Klaus Fuchs and Theodore Hall, to deliver to Moscow the formula for enriching uranium, the technical plans for nuclear production facilities, and engineering designs for a warhead.[79] By 1951, the United States had enough information to convict the Rosenbergs and sentence them to death. The best evidence, though, was classified and would not become public until the Venona documents were released in 1995. Their 1953 execution was therefore controversial; many Americans thought that the Rosenbergs were innocent victims of the Red Scare, and the Soviet government disseminated propaganda to support their false claims of innocence.

The Rosenbergs did not escape justice, but another notorious spy ring did—Britain's **Cambridge Five**—known to Moscow as the **Magnificent Five** for their extensive contributions to the Soviet cause. The group was known as the Cambridge Five because of its members' education and recruitment at Britain's elite Cambridge University in the 1930s. All took high-level positions in the British government, and all were apparently true believers in communism. They assisted Moscow into the 1950s. Two of the five, Guy Burgess and Donald Maclean, fled to the Soviet Union in 1951 on a tip from a third member, **Kim Philby**. Philby, an MI-6 officer, was the most infamous and devoted of the Cambridge Five. He came from a privileged pedigree that likely garnered him special treatment, helping him avoid arrest and opprobrium.

---

[75]Ibid., 331.

[76]Ibid., 140–141.

[77]Ibid., 146.

[78]Ibid., 10.

[79]Haynes and Klehr, *Venona.*

He came under suspicion in 1951 for his role in tipping off Burgess and Maclean but was allowed to continue working for the British government in various capacities until his final defection to the Soviet Union in 1963. He died there in 1988 and is still celebrated as a Russian hero. The two other members of the Cambridge Five, Anthony Blunt of MI-5 and John Cairncross of MI-6, confessed but avoided prosecution. The exploits of the Cambridge Five were a counterintelligence disaster and would place a strain on the special intelligence relationship between Washington and London for several years after.

If Philby is the best-known Brit to help the Soviets, two names deserve mention as the most notorious American traitors. Both—**Aldrich Ames** of the CIA and **Robert Hanssen** of the FBI—spied for the Russians from the late Cold War into the post–Cold War period. Ames focused on Russia and counterintelligence for the CIA. He was known at various points in his career for his middling performance, arrogance, drunkenness, and profligate lifestyle. Unlike the American spies recruited from the CPUSA in the 1930s, Ames was interested in money and ego satisfaction. In 1985, Ames walked out of CIA headquarters with files on several of the agency's HUMINT assets in Russia and sold them to the Soviets. Over the next several years, as the CIA's HUMINT network in Russia was neutralized, a counterintelligence investigation finally led to Ames. He was sentenced to life in prison in 1994. Ames, however, was not the only one providing what was now the Russian Federation with information

**PHOTO 2.4A AND PHOTO 2.4B** A Soviet postage stamp commemorates Kim Philby of MI-6 and the Cambridge Five (left). Robert Hanssen (right) is widely considered to have done the most damage among Americans who spied on behalf of Moscow. He worked for the USSR and the Russian Federation from 1979 to 2001.

on America's spies. FBI counterintelligence expert Robert Hanssen was also in on the game. He began spying for Moscow in 1979 and continued until he was caught conducting a dead drop in 2001. Hanssen's espionage was even worse than Ames's. In addition to compromising HUMINT assets, Hanssen compromised a multimillion-dollar COMINT program, military technology, and nuclear war plans. He was also sentenced to life under the 1917 Espionage Act and resides in solitary confinement in a Colorado prison.

## INTELLIGENCE IN THE 21ST CENTURY: 9/11 AND ITS AFTERMATH

Despite the continued spy games between Washington and Moscow, the end of the 20th century was marked by optimism about the future state of international relations and national security. Instead of worrying about a nuclear war with Russia, Americans grew more concerned about rogue states and terrorism—particularly radical Islamic terrorism perpetrated by an upstart group called al-Qaeda. Still, this paled in comparison to Cold War fears of nuclear annihilation, and at the turn of the millennium, the al-Qaeda threat was remote. When it attacked, it did so in parts of the world that most Americans never visited. The US intelligence community closely monitored al-Qaeda and its leader, Osama bin Laden, throughout the first nine months of 2001. But it did so in a stovepiped fashion, failing to share information that might have prevented what was to come on September 11. In some cases, the failure to share information was based on legal reasons rooted in the separation of domestic and foreign intelligence. Overall, the failure to share mainly resulted from a lack of leadership foresight and a culture of jealously guarding turf—a theme seen around the time of Pearl Harbor.

### Reorganization of the Intelligence Bureaucracy

A report by the **9/11 Commission**, which later investigated the intelligence failure leading to the attacks on New York and Washington, recommended a reorganization of the intelligence bureaucracy. This resulted in the 2004 **Intelligence Reform and Terrorism Prevention Act (IRTPA)**, which established the Office of the Director of National Intelligence (ODNI). The director of national intelligence (DNI) replaced the dual-hatted DCI as head of the US IC. The DNI was given new powers to coordinate across intelligence agencies, including both collection and analysis. The DNI also stood up new fusion centers to ensure that different agencies working on similar issues would have a mechanism to collaborate.

The National Counterterrorism Center became the principal DNI fusion center during the global war on terror of the early 2000s. Fusion centers were also set up to handle counterintelligence and counterproliferation. Improving intelligence on the proliferation of weapons of mass destruction (WMD) became a priority in the early 1990s but took on new and critical importance after intelligence agencies across the world failed to properly assess the WMD capabilities of Saddam Hussein's Iraq in the early 2000s. The belief that Iraq had a robust WMD program led to the US invasion in 2003. The next year, President George W. Bush appointed the Commission on the Intelligence Capabilities of the United States Regarding Weapons of Mass Destruction—more commonly known as the **WMD Commission**—to investigate what had happened. The commission's 600-page report, issued in 2005, uncovered several collection and analytical errors. Among these errors was the indulgence of cognitive biases and underdevelopment of HUMINT assets in Iraq.

## Adapting to New Threats

The United States has had to adapt its competencies in dealing with new threats like terrorism. Satellite imagery is less useful for gauging terrorist capabilities than for gauging Soviet missile forces. Nonetheless, advances in imagery were matched with developments in drone technology to find and kill thousands of terrorists during the first two decades of the 21st century. The United States also marshaled the extraordinary resources and technological prowess of the NSA to collect more COMINT than ever before. In the ages of terrorism and the internet, the next big attack could be planned by people using social media apps while sitting in private residences. This was a new challenge in the history of intelligence; historically, one could more confidently target the communication lines of a national leadership or target certain buildings for eavesdropping in order to collect intelligence on the next big event.

These 21st-century developments have caused problems for US intelligence. While intelligence is often good enough to identify terrorists for targeted killing, mistakes are sometimes made, and innocent people near the target also die as "collateral damage." Furthermore, the liberalization of NSA eavesdropping authority provided by the 2001 **USA PATRIOT Act** may have led to collection and privacy abuses, including eavesdropping on innocent Americans. **Edward Snowden** made this claim when he revealed the details of NSA programs in 2013 after working for the agency as a contractor. Though some celebrate Snowden as a whistleblower, he is considered a fugitive by the US government and a traitor by most intelligence professionals. As of 2020, he lives in Moscow. In 2015, Congress replaced the Patriot Act with the **USA FREEDOM Act**. The Freedom Act preserved many features of the Patriot Act but rolled back some of the intelligence community's authority to collect bulk data on American citizens.

Another difficulty wrought by the early 2000s was the collection of HUMINT from suspected terrorists. The United States came under international criticism for its use of **enhanced interrogation techniques (EITs)** during the presidency of George W. Bush. Many considered this term to be a euphemism for torture. EITs included both physical and psychological stressors such as sleep deprivation, cramped confinement, and waterboarding. In 2009, President Barack Obama ordered that interrogators revert to using the US Army Field Manual for conducting interrogations. The Army Field Manual is consistent with the Geneva Conventions on the laws of war.

Despite these difficulties associated with a new political and technological 21st-century landscape, the United States remains well positioned to maintain its status as the preeminent global power. Its continued investment in a professional intelligence bureaucracy is a key component of its continued preeminence.

## CONCLUSION: ASSESSING OVER 3,000 YEARS OF INTELLIGENCE HISTORY

From the Bible to America's 21st-century war on terror, intelligence has played a role. Its role has been nonlinear. Some leaders and societies have valued it while others have not. For the ancient Greeks, divination mattered more than surveillance and reconnaissance. For late medieval and early modern European monarchs, intelligence was essential to regime security. For a great strategic thinker of barely a century ago, Carl von Clausewitz, intelligence was a veritable waste of time. For most of America's early leaders, it was a moral anathema. In the 20th century, it was essential to defeating Nazi Germany and to preventing nuclear war with the Soviet Union.

In the 21st century, intelligence has been a source of both security and controversy for the United States. A vast, well-funded, professional intelligence bureaucracy has successfully prevented any additional major terrorist attacks on US soil since September 11, 2001. Problems associated with turf-consciousness—a condition that is apparently endemic to government by human beings—continue to be worked out. Many people fear, however, that the ubiquity of digital technology in the 21st century threatens democracy. This fear has been expressed through the revelations of Edward Snowden, but true intelligence dystopias are more likely to emerge in authoritarian states like China, were regime security is paramount and where artificial intelligence is being applied to monitor all people at all times. Throughout the world, people are spooked by the tracking algorithms that companies use to pitch products of interest. This application of such technology may be relatively harmless, but it spooks so many because it may foreshadow the use of tracking technology to monitor and enforce people's "good" political behavior. If intelligence technology served humanity well during the 20th century, it remains an open question how it will serve humanity for the balance of the 21st century.

However rapidly technology may be changing, two things remain as they have since at least the 1648 Peace of Westphalia. Sovereign states are the dominant actors in world politics, and human beings remain flawed. Under these two conditions, the security dilemma first articulated by Thucydides will persist. As long as countries are unsure whether they can trust each other, intelligence will be vital to the conduct of human affairs.

## KEY CONCEPTS

## ADDITIONAL READING

Alford, Stephen. *The Watchers: A Secret History of the Reign of Elizabeth I*. London, UK: Bloomsbury Press, 2012.

Andrew, Christopher. *For the President's Eyes Only: Secret Intelligence and the American Presidency From Washington to Bush*. New York, NY: HarperCollins, 1995.

Andrew, Christopher. *The Secret World: A History of Intelligence*. New Haven, CT: Yale University Press, 2018.

Bergman, Ronen. *Rise and Kill First: The Secret History of Israel's Targeted Assassinations*. New York, NY: Random House, 2018.

Godson, Roy. *Dirty Tricks or Trump Cards: US Covert Action and Counterintelligence*. New Brunswick, NJ: Transaction, 2001.

Haynes, John Earl, and Harvey Klehr. *Venona: Decoding Soviet Espionage in America*. New Haven, CT: Yale University Press, 1999.

Lindgren, David. *Trust but Verify: Imagery Analysis in the Cold War*. Annapolis, MD: Naval Institute Press, 2000.

Masterman, J. C. *The Double-Cross System*. Guilford, CT: Lyons Press, 2012.

# INTELLIGENCE AND SECURITY INSTITUTIONS

## Organizations and Processes

Jonathan C. Smith

## AN ILLUSTRATION OF INTELLIGENCE SUPPORT

In the fall of 1962, the Soviet Union embarked on a dangerous potential escalation of the Cold War with the United States. In response to aggressive US activities against Cuba, like the Bay of Pigs operation in 1961, the Soviet Union acceded to the request of its new ally for direct military support. Included in this support was Operation ANADYR. This was a mission to deploy nuclear-capable medium- and intermediate-range ballistic missiles to the island. Once these missiles became operational, the Soviet Union would have basic parity in the nuclear balance with the United States. However, as shown in Map 3.1, the location of these new missiles in Cuba would substantially reduce the warning time that the United States would have in the event of a Soviet first strike. Recognizing the significance of such a move, the Soviet Union began the deployment of these weapons with great secrecy. They did not want the United States to be aware of these weapons until the missiles were fully operational.

Given that the Cuban revolution in 1959 had not only disposed a US ally, but also brought to power a new government that increasingly aligned itself with the Soviet Union, understanding developments in this country was a key priority for national security decision makers; it was also expected to be an important political issue in the upcoming midterm elections for Congress in November 1962. As a result, the US intelligence community (US IC) had been tasked by policymakers with monitoring military developments on the island for some time.

A variety of intelligence collection methods were employed in support of this objective. Human sources on the island of Cuba and refugees who had fled provided a variety of information about conditions on the island. The National Security Agency monitored communications and electronic signals that indicated the deployment of Soviet military equipment, such as SA-2 surface-to-air missiles.[1] The Central Intelligence Agency and the US Air Force both conducted photo-reconnaissance missions, though they argued over which should have the lead role in the high-altitude

---

[1] Center for Cryptographic History. *The NSA and the Cuban Missile Crisis*. Fort Meade, MD: Center for Cryptographic History, 1998, 7.

**MAP 3.1    ■    Cuban Area of Operations, 1962**

*Source:* Defense Intelligence Agency, DID Graphics+1(202) 231-8601/Public domain/Wikimedia Commons.

U-2 aircraft missions.[2] On October 14, 1962, one of the U-2 aircraft took photographs of a deployment site containing the Soviet medium-range ballistic missiles near San Cristóbal in western Cuba. After the images were processed, the imagery interpreters studied the new information and assessed that the missiles were not yet operational, but would likely be so in approximately two weeks.[3] This information was briefed to President John F. Kennedy by his national security assistant McGeorge Bundy on the morning of October 16, 1962. He immediately convened an executive committee of his National Security Council to consider how the United States should respond to this new development.

---

[2]Allison, Graham. *Essence of Decision: Explaining the Cuban Missile Crisis.* Boston, MA: Little, Brown, 1971, 122.

[3]Walton, Timothy. "Cuban Missile Crisis." In *Challenges in Intelligence Analysis: Lessons From 1300 BCE to the Present,* 143–148. New York, NY: Cambridge University Press, 2011.

The new reconnaissance photographs, combined with other intelligence reporting, provided the Kennedy administration with decision advantage in two fundamental ways. First, with this advance warning of the deployment, the US military could concentrate forces in the area to provide policy options such as an invasion, airstrikes against the missile sites, or a blockade of the island. The presumption was that these military options were more likely to be successful if they were initiated before the Soviet missiles became operational. Second, since the Soviet Union was steadfast in its denials that such an operation was ongoing, the United States could utilize this information to disprove the Soviet denials and mobilize international support for the US position. This was done most famously at an emergency meeting of the United Nations Security Council on October 25, when Ambassador Adlai Stevenson presented the pictures of the Soviet missile sites in Cuba.

This case is a useful illustration of the key elements discussed in this chapter. First, the intelligence function in the United States is designed to support policymakers. As a result, it is important for students of intelligence to understand the elements of the policymaking structure, as well as how they work together (or not), and utilize intelligence information. Second, just as the national security policy process is not monolithic, neither is the US intelligence enterprise that supports it. Lastly, the development of intelligence support is a multistep process that takes the information needs of policymakers and develops finished products to address those needs.

US government, unknown photographer/Public domain/Wikimedia Commons

**PHOTO 3.1** UN Security Council meeting, 1962.

## THE NATIONAL SECURITY
## FRAMEWORK IN THE US SYSTEM

So, where did the national security policy process that President Kennedy used come from? In the mid-1780s, as the framers of the new American government were considering the structures and powers of this system, they needed to reconcile competing values. On the one hand, they were worried about the consequences of concentrations of power within the government. In *Federalist* **10**, James Madison discussed the "Mischief of Faction" and recommended that the way to avoid one of these factions gaining a dominant influence was to fragment governmental powers and make those fragments interdependent on one another. This is where the principles of separation of powers and checks and balances originate in the American system. The framers of the Constitution agreed on a system that contained three independent and coequal branches of government—Congress, the executive branch, and the judiciary. Each of these branches had specific governmental powers, but many of their key functions required the cooperation of one of the other branches. So, for example, Congress can pass a bill, but it typically requires presidential approval to become a law.

However, the framers also recognized that this new American republic, like any nation-state, needed to have the ability to protect itself. Preventing foreign invasion is one of the oldest and most fundamental objectives of any government. As Madison noted in *Federalist* 41, "Security against foreign danger is one of the primitive objects of civil society."[4] The British had withdrawn from the American colonies after the Treaty of Paris (1783), but their ongoing threat to American security brought this need into sharp relief.

So, while this new governing system fragmented power in many respects, it limited the use of this principle in some areas, such as national security. For instance, while there were some proposals in the constitutional convention to create a plural executive or attach an advisory body to the chief executive, the convention ultimately endorsed a **unitary executive model**. As Alexander Hamilton noted in *Federalist* 70, "Decision, activity, secrecy, and dispatch will generally characterize the proceedings of one man in a much more eminent degree than the proceedings of any greater number." He argued that this was an essential component to protect the new nation against foreign attack.[5]

So, as we look at the elements of the American government that are relevant to national security, it is useful to remember this dilemma of the constitutional framers regarding power. In the Constitution, many key functions related to national security are shared between the legislative and executive branches. For instance, the president is the chief executive and the commander-in-chief of the military, but Congress

---

[4]Madison, James. *Federalist* 41. Accessed July 3, 2019. https://www.congress.gov/resources/display/content/The+Federalist+Papers#TheFederalistPapers-41.

[5]Hamilton, Alexander. *Federalist* 70. Accessed July 5, 2019. https://www.congress.gov/resources/display/content/The+Federalist+Papers#TheFederalistPapers-70.

has the power to raise an army and a navy, as well as the power to declare war. Also, while the president is allowed to select the cabinet secretaries and other leadership positions of the executive branch, most of these appointments require confirmation by the Senate. However, in the years since World War II, executive power has grown relative to Congress, often under the rationale of protecting national security interests.

## BOX 3.1
### FOR EXAMPLE: WHAT IS THE IMPERIAL PRESIDENCY?

The US Constitution articulates the idea that separate institutions, such as Congress and the president, have to share power. But what if the president does not want to share? The idea of an imperial presidency was made popular by a 1973 book of the same name. Written by Arthur Schlesinger Jr., a historian who also served in the Kennedy administration, the book's premise is that the power of the presidency had grown by exceeding its constitutionally mandated authorities in the 20th century. According to Schlesinger, this undermined the ability of other elements of government, particularly Congress, to hold the president accountable.

Two national security areas are a good reflection of Schlesinger's concerns. First, with the rise of the United States as a global superpower, the president increasingly relied on making international agreements with foreign states instead of negotiating treaties. International agreements are not mentioned in the Constitution and do not require ratification by the Senate as the Constitution requires for a treaty. For instance, in the first 50 years of the republic, the United States negotiated 60 treaties and 27 international agreements. In contrast, between 1940 and 1989, the United States was a party to 759 treaties and 13,016 international agreements.[6] Similarly, the United States has only declared war (which requires a vote in Congress) in five conflicts in the history of the republic, but the number of "undeclared" wars or conflicts is in the hundreds. These include the Korean and Vietnam Wars, the Persian Gulf War, and all of the military operations since 9/11.

Keep in mind that Schlesinger wrote his book nearly 50 years ago. Since that time, do you think that the president's power relative to Congress has grown, declined, or stayed the same?

## Congress

The US Congress is a bicameral legislature that is composed of a 438-member House of Representatives and a 100-member Senate. These two chambers are charged with the research, development, and evaluation of policy. In order to fulfill this

---

[6]Justia. "International Agreements Without Senate Approval." Accessed October 2, 2019. https://law.justia .com/constitution/us/article-2/20-international-agreements-without-senate-approval.html.

mission, each chamber utilizes a committee framework where small groups of legislators focus on particular subject areas. This is where most of the real activity of Congress occurs—at the committee, and even subcommittee, level. As former US president Woodrow Wilson once wrote, "Congress on the floor is Congress on public exhibition; Congress in committee is Congress at work."[7]

There are two main types of committees in the US Congress. Authorizing committees are tasked with the mission that fits with our conventional wisdom; they create policies and programs in their given area of expertise. The organization of the authorizing committees in both chambers largely parallels the cabinet structure in the executive branch. For instance, both the House and the Senate have an Armed Services Committee to develop and monitor policy that is largely conducted by the Department of Defense. However, each chamber also has an **Appropriations Committee** to assign funding for these policies and programs. After all, a program that has no money to be implemented does not really exist. As a result, the members of the Appropriations Committees wield great power in all areas of policy. As one observer once noted,

**PHOTO 3.2** House of Representatives in session.

---

[7]Ornstein, Norman, and Thomas Mann. *Renewing Congress: A Second Report.* Washington, DC: American Enterprise Institute, 1993, 15.

"authorizers" think they are gods; "appropriators" know they are.[8] This "power of the purse" is a key lever of power for Congress over the other branches of government in any area of public policy.

The authorizing committees in the House of Representatives and the Senate that cover intelligence policy were born out of allegations of misconduct in the early 1970s. In response to allegations that national security organizations such as the Army, the Central Intelligence Agency, and the Federal Bureau of Investigation had conducted operations that violated US law, both the House and the Senate convened "select" (which typically implies that the committee is temporarily convened for this one event) committees to investigate the allegations. Each of these committees was known by the name of its chairman. The Senate committee was known as the Church Committee, as it was chaired by Idaho senator Frank Church. The House committee was led by New York congressman Otis Pike, so it was known as the Pike Committee. Over the course of 1975, these two committees researched and held public hearings on these allegations. In the aftermath, both chambers elected to continue these committees on a permanent basis. The Pike Committee was renamed the **House Permanent Select Committee on Intelligence (HPSCI),** and the Church Committee became the **Senate Select Committee on Intelligence (SSCI).** This episode represents the birth

**PHOTO 3.3** Intelligence community leadership testifying before a Senate committee.

Brian Murphy, ODNI Public Affairs

---

[8]Lowenthal, Mark. *Intelligence: From Secrets to Policy*, 6th ed. Washington, DC: CQ Press, 2015, 288.

of the permanent legislative oversight of intelligence issues in the American system. As a result, congressional hearings on intelligence issues are now commonplace.

On sensitive issues, a smaller group of congressmen, known as the **Gang of Eight**, can be notified in lieu of informing all 538 members of Congress. This "gang" is composed of the majority and minority party leadership of both institutions and their corresponding intelligence committees. So, this would include the Speaker of the House and the Minority Leader of the House, as well as the Majority and Minority Leaders of the Senate. It would also include the chairman and ranking member of both the HPSCI and the SSCI.

## Judiciary

While the judiciary is a separate and coequal branch of government as specified in the Constitution, its role in national security affairs has historically been less than the other two branches. The judiciary's role is to adjudicate disputes concerning the law. Further, if a law or governmental action is inconsistent with the court's interpretation of the Constitution, it is considered null and void under the doctrine of **judicial review**. This power is most significant with the US Supreme Court, which sits atop the federal judiciary. As one author once noted, if you lose at the Supreme Court, the only appeal is to God.[9] The Supreme Court's ability to interpret the Constitution, combined with the power of judicial review and the political insulation that comes with the lifetime appointments for the justices, is what gives the judicial branch a potentially decisive role in policy issues. As former chief justice Charles Evans Hughes once noted, "We are under a Constitution, but the Constitution is what the [justices] say it is."[10]

However, historically, the Supreme Court has refused to take on national security cases, citing the "political question" doctrine. This doctrine states that the court is reluctant to adjudicate cases that the justices believe are better handled by the elected branches of government (i.e., Congress and the president). For instance, the court has been unwilling to consider the constitutionality of the War Powers Act (1973), which passed over President Richard Nixon's veto in 1973. No US president since that time has recognized the constitutionality of the legislation, and the Supreme Court has not heard a case concerning the law. As a result, whether this law is valid or not remains unclear. However, in recent years, the Supreme Court has shown a greater willingness to consider national security–related cases as they have impacted individual rights, such as unlawful detentions and enhanced interrogation measures.

Beyond the Supreme Court, one additional area where the judiciary plays a significant role in national security is the implementation of the Foreign Intelligence Surveillance Act (FISA). First passed in 1978, this legislation was an attempt to balance

---

[9]Freer, Richard. *Civil Procedure*, 4th ed. New York, NY: Wolters Kluwer, 2017, 894.

[10]Hughes, Charles Evans. *Addresses and Papers of Charles Evans Hughes, Governor of New York, 1906–1908.* New York, NY: BiblioLife, 2009, 139.

the rights of individuals under the Constitution with the heightened secrecy and surveillance methods needed to pursue individuals committing espionage or terrorism in the United States. The FISA process parallels the search warrant process that is articulated in the Fourth Amendment, which notes that "no Warrants shall issue, but upon probable cause, supported by Oath or affirmation."[11] However, instead of this application for a search warrant taking place in a public forum that risks discovery by the suspected hostile foreign power, the FISA warrant application is presented to the members of the **Foreign Intelligence Surveillance Court (FISC)**. This court hears the warrant applications in secret in order to not alert the suspect, as well as to protect national security–protected information. The FISC is composed of 11 district court judges who are appointed to seven-year terms by the chief justice of the US Supreme Court.[12]

## Executive

The executive branch is the largest element of the federal government and is charged with the implementation of laws and policies. When one considers the nearly 4 million people who are employed by the federal government, the overwhelming majority are employees of the executive branch. As a result, most interactions that people in society have with the federal government are with members of the executive branch. From the mailman to the active-duty soldier to the person who disburses payments at the local Social Security office—all of them are a part of the bureaucracy in the executive branch. And, in accordance with the Constitution, the president sits atop this structure as the chief executive. However, this does not necessarily mean that the president has complete control of the bureaucracy. As President Harry Truman noted when his successor, President Dwight Eisenhower (a retired five-star general), was elected, being head of the executive branch is not exactly like leading a military unit. He said, "Poor Ike—it won't be a bit like the Army."[13]

Most of the personnel in the executive branch are organized within the cabinet system. In this structure, personnel are organized in cabinet departments that are tasked with executing a particular area of public policy. For instance, the State Department personnel are tasked with conducting diplomacy with foreign states and international organizations. Each of these cabinet departments is led by a cabinet secretary. These secretaries serve two primary functions: (1) manage the issues and personnel within their organization and (2) provide policy advice to the president within their given area of expertise. So, the secretary of state is expected to manage organizational issues like

---

[11]Legal Information Institute. "US Constitution: Fourth Amendment." Accessed August 1, 2019. https://www.law.cornell.edu/constitution/fourth_amendment.

[12]Foreign Intelligence Surveillance Court. "About the Foreign Intelligence Surveillance Court." Accessed July 5, 2019. https://www.fisc.uscourts.gov/about-foreign-intelligence-surveillance-court.

[13]Kelly, Jason. "OctoPOTUS?" *The University of Chicago Magazine* 105, no. 1 (September–October 2012). https://mag.uchicago.edu/law-policy-society/octopotus.

the assignment of foreign service personnel to embassies around the world, in addition to providing advice to the president on diplomatic issues. Currently, the cabinet is composed of the vice president and the 15 cabinet secretaries.

## THE GROWTH OF THE NATIONAL SECURITY BUREAUCRACY

The national security bureaucracy within the executive branch has grown substantially since the World War II era. These expansions were governmental responses to the pressing geopolitical issues of the times. However, after those issues had passed, the bureaucratic expansions remained in place with every indication that the new structures would endure. As Charley Reese, an American syndicated columnist, once noted, "Bureaucracies, once created, never die."[14] This has served to continue the growth of executive branch power relative to the other two branches of government. The two most significant historical episodes that have fueled this expansion were the Cold War and the post-9/11 security environment.

### The Cold War

While World War II was the key event that brought the United States to superpower status as a key driver of Allied victory, it was the emerging threat of the Soviet Union after 1945 that solidified the need for a more robust and permanent national security apparatus. In the wake of a nearly four-year worldwide struggle that began with the surprise attack on Pearl Harbor in December 1941, the United States looked to demobilize quickly. For instance, the Office of Strategic Services (OSS) was a robust, multifunctional intelligence organization that was created during World War II. It was formally disbanded less than three weeks after the Japanese surrendered on September 2, 1945.

However, the United States watched Soviet activities around the globe with growing alarm. In Eastern Europe, communist parties took power in Soviet-occupied countries such as Poland and Czechoslovakia. In the Middle East, Soviet reluctance to withdraw its forces from northern Iran and attempts to pressure Turkey to expand Soviet access to the Mediterranean Sea via the Turkish Straits led to American responses including a port call for the battleship USS *Missouri* at Istanbul in 1946.

The nature of this new threat was articulated by US diplomat George F. Kennan in what became known as the "Long Telegram." Writing from the US embassy in Moscow in 1946, he suggested that countering this Soviet threat was "undoubtedly [the] greatest task our diplomacy has ever faced and probably [the] greatest it will ever have to face."[15] Kennan described a Soviet Union that did not believe peaceful coexistence with

---

[14] AZ Quotes. *Charley Reese*. Accessed July 10, 2019. https://www.azquotes.com/quote/1036991.

[15] Kennan, George. "The Long Telegram." February 22, 1946. http://www.ntanet.net/KENNAN.html.

**PHOTO 3.4** USS *Missouri* in Istanbul, 1946.

the West was possible. Instead, the Soviets saw themselves in perpetual conflict with the capitalist states of the West, and their primary objective was to undermine capitalism around the world by advancing socialist causes wherever possible. Kennan's articulation of the problem, as well as Soviet actions after World War II, would lead to the United States developing a **containment strategy** that called for a US national security system that would counter any attempts at Soviet expansion around the world.

# BOX 3.2
## NATIONAL SECURITY STRATEGY

Presidents periodically submit a National Security Strategy (NSS) document to Congress. The document is intended to articulate the interests and goals of US national security, as well as the range of threats to those goals and interests. It should also assess the capability of the national security establishment to achieve these goals. For instance, if the persistent threat of terrorism is a security issue, then the ability of the US government to address that problem should be discussed in the NSS. The requirement for this strategic document was established in

*(Continued)*

(Continued)

Section 603 of the Goldwater–Nichols Department of Defense Reorganization Act in 1986. While the legislation indicates that these documents should be produced on an annual basis, current practice sees them completed approximately every two to four years.[16]

The NSS is the highest-level strategy document produced by the United States and is intended to serve as an "umbrella" document that guides lower-level strategy documents like the National Defense Strategy or the National Intelligence Strategy.[17] Whether the NSS document is driven by a top-down imperative, where the president and national security adviser dictate the structure and content, or a bottom-up approach, the document is crafted within the inter-agency structure of the National Security Council. Considering the president's priorities, the various elements of the national security establishment coordinate their views in the inter-agency policy committees, which are then consolidated by the Deputies and Principals Committees. Historically, the process takes approximately 9 to 18 months to complete.

The two most recent iterations of the US NSS were produced in 2015 and 2017. These reflect the views of two different presidential administrations—the 2015 document was produced by the Obama administration, and the 2017 document was produced by the Trump administration. To be sure, there are differences in approach. For instance, the 2015 document puts a strong emphasis on multilateralism and international institutions, whereas the "America First" theme in the 2017 document naturally leads to a stronger focus on bilateral relationships and unilateral action. That said, there is considerable overlap in how the two administrations viewed the international environment. Both documents emphasize the goal of ensuring the security of the nation from threats of terrorism or weapons of mass destruction; both documents also identify economic prosperity as a key objective for US national security.

There is always a question of how accurate these NSS documents are. After all, since they are publicly available, the adversaries of the United States can have access to them, too. It is typically not advisable to share your plan for how to overcome your adversary with that same adversary. However, while recognizing that the document is for public consumption, it is still a good general articulation of US interests and goals in the international system.

But the United States needed to strengthen its national security institutions in order to be able to compete in this new Cold War (1946–1991). Military power was a key element of this response; in his telegram, Kennan noted that the Soviet Union was "highly sensitive to the logic of force."[18] However, the Cold War would

---

[16]"Goldwater–Nichols Department of Defense Reorganization Act of 1986." Accessed November 5, 2019. https://history.defense.gov/Portals/70/Documents/dod_reforms/Goldwater-NicholsDoDReordAct1986.pdf.

[17]Stolberg, Alan. *How Nation-States Craft National Security Strategy Documents.* Carlisle Barracks, PA: Strategic Studies Institute, 2012, 71.

[18]Keenan, "The Long Telegram".

be a long-term competition that did not involve direct military conflict between the two countries. Instead, this would be a multidisciplinary competition requiring a coordinated use of all the instruments of national power—diplomacy, information, military, and economics.

## The National Security Council

The National Security Act of 1947 was the primary institutional response to the Cold War, and contained three important changes to the US national security framework. The creation of the **National Security Council (NSC)** was an essential element for presidential control of the national security bureaucracy and had two primary components. The first was the creation of a legally mandated advisory group for the president when dealing with national security issues. While the committee can be augmented by "non-statutory" members who are selected by the president, the statutory members include the vice president and the secretaries of state, defense, energy, and treasury. The chairman of the Joint Chiefs of Staff and the director of national intelligence are also statutory members, but have no voting power on the committee and are only allowed to provide advice on their area of expertise.

The second element of the NSC is a management system to improve the coordination of the various elements of the bureaucracy. Like the fingers of a musician, national security policy is more likely to be successful when the elements of the US government are working in concert as part of a larger plan. As Frederick the Great once noted, "Diplomacy without arms is like music without instruments."[19] The same is true of incorporating other elements of national power like economics and intelligence capabilities. So, as shown in Figure 3.1, below the NSC is a hierarchy of inter-agency forums to debate and develop policy options for the president. The Principals Committee is the penultimate forum and is composed of many of the same members of the NSC, but without the president. Below this, the Deputies Committee is composed of the second-in-command for the various agencies, such as the deputy secretary of state and the vice chairman of the Joint Chiefs of Staff. At the lowest level, there are interagency policy committees for specific policy areas, such as arms control, combating terrorism, and East Asian affairs. This is the action officer level of policy where the specific implementation and coordination of bureaucratic action occurs.

The national security adviser position was not specifically mentioned in the 1947 legislation, but since 1953, this has been a position of growing importance in national security affairs. In addition to managing the staff of the NSC, the national security adviser advises the president on relevant policy matters. Unlike other senior advisers, such as the secretary of defense or the director of national intelligence, this position does not require Senate confirmation. As a result, presidents have more freedom

---

[19]Goodreads. "Frederick the Great: Quotes." Accessed November 3, 2019. https://www.goodreads.com/quotes/9020207-diplomacy-without-arms-is-like-music-without-instruments.

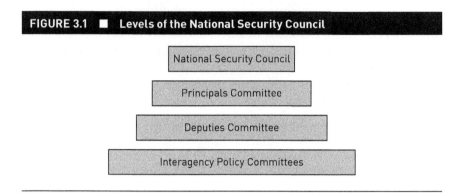

**FIGURE 3.1 ■ Levels of the National Security Council**

National Security Council

Principals Committee

Deputies Committee

Interagency Policy Committees

to select a person whom they prefer without any additional political considerations. Considering this, and the fact that this NSC adviser works in close proximity to the president, it is no wonder that this position has grown in significance. In many recent presidencies, the NSC adviser has had a more significant influence on presidential decision making than traditional advisers, such as the secretary of state.

### The National Security Act of 1947

Beyond the creation of the NSC, the National Security Act of 1947 created the nation's first peacetime strategic intelligence organization, the Central Intelligence Agency (CIA). While not a direct decedent, much of the early leadership of the CIA was drawn from veterans of the OSS. Because of concerns about how an intelligence organization might potentially harm the domestic political system, there was a clear delineation between foreign and domestic activities. The CIA's mandate specifically notes that it has no policing authority and should not conduct operations on US soil. Those operations would be managed by the Federal Bureau of Investigation (FBI). At the same time, the FBI gave up the foreign intelligence capabilities that it had cultivated primarily in Latin America.

The last major change that came from the National Security Act of 1947 was the consolidation of the National Military Establishment. Since the founding of the republic, the Department of the Navy and the Department of War had been separate organizations. In an effort to improve coordination between the military services, these organizations were united under a new Department of Defense. Additionally, the law converted the Army Air Corps into a new separate service, the Air Force. It also protected the status of the Marine Corps as a separate service within the Department of the Navy.

### The Goldwater–Nichols Act of 1986

However, the problem of inter-service cooperation continued to be an area of concern during the Cold War years. The **Goldwater–Nichols Act** of 1986 was designed to address this by streamlining the chain of command for military forces operating in the field by bypassing the four service chiefs. Prior to this, inter-service rivalries had undermined US combat operations in the Vietnam War and the aborted Iranian hostage rescue mission in 1980. Under the new system, service chiefs like the chief of naval operations or the commandant of the Marine Corps are no longer involved in the operational chain of command. Instead, they are primarily responsible for the training and equipping of their respective forces. Also, as members of the Joint Chiefs of Staff, they provide military advice to the president. Under the new Goldwater–Nichols framework, the chain of command for military operations goes from the president and the secretary of defense directly to the combatant commands. This has strengthened the role of these combatant commands, as they can more effectively integrate forces from the four services in their area of responsibility. So, the commander of US European Command has operational control of all US military forces, regardless of service, in Europe. Additionally, it has empowered these combatant commands to develop significant in-house intelligence resources to support their activities.

## The Post-9/11 Environment

It sounds cliché to say that the world changed on September 11, 2001, but for US national security, it is hard to overstate the importance of this day. The attack by 19 al-Qaeda hijackers inside the United States that left more than 3,000 people dead was a shock to the national security community for two key reasons. First, this represented the first major attack inside the United States in decades. The most comparable recent example of a similar attack was the Japanese bombing of Pearl Harbor in 1941. The United States was concerned about foreign attacks in a way that it had not had to be for most of the country's existence. While the phrase *homeland security* is commonly used in this day and age, it was rarely heard among the American public prior to this attack.

The second reason that this attack was a shock was that the US government was not very prepared to fight a nonstate actor, such as al-Qaeda. A terrorist group does not necessarily occupy a particular geographic area, does not wear a distinct uniform, and can transit national boundaries by blending in with other tourists. The United States had spent most of the past half-century preparing for the possibility of a large interstate war with the Soviet Union. This new conflict represented a qualitatively different type of conflict. The idea that the US national security community needed to adapt to this new type of threat was solidified with a series of domestic terrorist attacks that utilized anthrax in October 2001, just a month after 9/11.

### The Department of Homeland Security

Within the next three years, the national security community changed in two fundamental ways. First was the creation of the Department of Homeland Security (DHS). In the immediate aftermath of the 9/11 attacks, President George W. Bush created the DHS in the Executive Office of the President to coordinate homeland security

**PHOTO 3.5** 9/11 attacks on the World Trade Center.

strategy to prevent terrorist attacks within the United States. This served as the core element of the new cabinet-level department that was created in November 2002. However, in addition to this element, the new department consolidated 22 pre-existing federal agencies that touched on the issues of domestic security and combating terrorism. This consolidation represented the largest reorganization of the federal bureaucracy since the National Security Act (1947), and the most diverse merger ever.[20] Its elements included agencies responsible for areas such as disaster relief (Federal Emergency Management Agency), border protection (Customs and Border Protection), and protection of senior government officials (Secret Service). Notably, the FBI was not included in this merger and remains in the Department of Justice.

### The Intelligence Reform and Terrorism Prevention Act of 2004

The second structural change that occurred in the immediate post-9/11 years was reform to the US IC. Driven not just by the September 11 attacks, but also by the fallout from the US IC's Iraq weapons of mass destruction (WMD) National Intelligence Estimate in 2002, the 2004 **Intelligence Reform and Terrorism Prevention Act (IRTPA)** made two key adjustments for the leadership of the US IC. First, the leader of the US IC was previously known as the director of central intelligence, but now was designated as the director of national intelligence. Beyond a mere name change, this revised the mandate of the position from being the president's chief adviser on *foreign* intelligence matters to *national* intelligence—meaning that the scope of the position had been extended to include domestic security issues, as well. At the same time, the IRTPA legislation separated this leader of the US IC from the CIA. Prior to 2004, the director of central intelligence was dual-hatted as the leader of the US IC and the head of one of its most important elements.

[20]Perl, Raphael. "The Department of Homeland Security: Background and Challenges." In *Terrorism— Reducing Vulnerabilities and Improving Responses*. Washington, DC: Office for Central Europe and Eurasia Development, Security, and Cooperation Policy and Global Affairs, 2004, 176.

## INTELLIGENCE ORGANIZATIONS IN THE US SYSTEM OF GOVERNMENT

The US IC is a unique bureaucratic arrangement when compared to how other countries organize their intelligence apparatuses. It is composed of 17 separate organizations that are coordinated by the director of national intelligence. The system is best characterized as a decentralized arrangement that has limited centralized control.

While the US IC is the centerpiece of intelligence efforts in the American system, it is important to note that it is not the only place where intelligence occurs. The collection, analysis, and use of information to support decision advantage is used by many organizations at all levels of the US government—and even outside of the government. For instance, while we discuss the 17 elements of the US IC, there are other federal organizations that have intelligence functions that are not formally included in the US IC.

PHOTO 3.6 Intelligence community crests.

Defense Intelligence Agency

## The Intelligence Community Leadership

The **Director of National Intelligence (DNI)** is the key leader of the US IC and serves as the principal adviser to the president and the NSC on intelligence matters. Appointed by the president, but subject to Senate confirmation, the DNI's core mission is to oversee and direct the National Intelligence Program (NIP) by promoting intelligence integration among the 17 elements of the US IC. The DNI also articulates the National Intelligence Strategy to provide strategic direction for this community. However, the power to control the various intelligence agencies is limited. The DNI has no control over personnel issues in the other intelligence organizations and has limited budgetary powers. The DNI formulates the NIP budget based on inputs from the individual US IC agencies and has limited ability to reprogram funds. So, the DNI does not have the type of managerial controls over US IC assets that you might expect of a more centralized institution.

## BOX 3.3
### NATIONAL INTELLIGENCE STRATEGY

The National Intelligence Strategy (NIS) is intended to provide direction for the intelligence community (IC) over a four-year period, and should support the priorities that are outlined in the current National Security Strategy document. The legal foundation of this series is the Intelligence Reform and Terrorism Prevention Act (2004), and four versions of the NIS have been produced thus far—2005, 2009, 2014, and 2019.

Beyond a description of the current strategic environment, each NIS that has been produced thus far has been organized between mission objectives and enterprise objectives. The mission objectives focus on a "broad range of regional and functional topics facing the IC and their prioritization is communicated to the IC through the National Intelligence Priorities Framework." These objectives have been relatively stable since the 2009 NIS, focusing on areas such as terrorism, weapons of mass destruction, counterintelligence, and cyber issues.

The enterprise objectives focus on the management of the personnel and organizations within the IC, as well as the cooperation and coordination of those assets. While the specific number of these objectives has varied across the strategies that have been produced thus far, they all focus on how to promote integration and information sharing within the organization, how to attract talented people to the community, and how to improve capabilities of the IC through innovation. The more recent versions of the NIS have focused on the conduct of personnel working in the IC. Both the 2014 and 2019 documents included a statement of the Principles of Professional Ethics for the Intelligence Community. The 2019 NIS also included an enterprise objective that focused on safeguarding civil liberties and practicing appropriate transparency in order to maintain accountability and public trust in the IC.[21]

*Source: The National Intelligence Strategy of the United States (2019).*

---

[21]Office of the Director of National Intelligence. *The National Intelligence Strategy of the United States (2019)*. Washington, DC: Office of the Director of National Intelligence, 2019, 279.

However, the DNI position is a key intermediary between the policymaking world and the intelligence workforce. For instance, one task of the DNI's office is to manage the annual production of the **National Intelligence Priorities Framework (NIPF)**. This document is the primary mechanism for establishing, managing, and communicating national intelligence priorities. Departments and agencies that require intelligence support provide input, with the president and national security adviser setting the overall priorities.[22] So, the DNI solicits guidance from the national security policymakers in order to ensure that the US IC is developing information that most efficiently supports decision advantage.

The DNI may have limited powers over the entire US IC, but does have more traditional organizational authority within the Office of the Director of National Intelligence (ODNI). This includes the ability to create "centers" to advance the objectives of the organization. The **National Intelligence Council (NIC)** is the oldest of these centers, as it was created under the pre-IRTPA system in 1979. It serves as the US IC's center for mid- to long-range strategic analysis. The NIC is primarily composed of veteran analysts with extensive expertise in their areas of specialization, known as national intelligence officers (NIOs). For instance, Marten Van Heuven had a history degree from Yale and had served as a foreign service officer with several European postings before being appointed as the NIO for Eastern Europe. As Thomas Shreeve notes, "Assignment to the NIC [is] considered the mark of senior, top-gun status among analysts."[23] A summarized version of a recent job advertisement for an NIO position is listed in Box 3.4 and shows the extensive background and expertise that are required for such a position.[24] These NIOs are organized by regional and functional specialties, and they are responsible for the development of National Intelligence Estimates (NIEs). While they will produce an initial draft, their primary task is to coordinate review and revision of this analytic product among the entire US IC to ensure that it reflects the collective judgment of all 17 organizations. Beyond the production of NIEs, the NIC conducts open source, long-range estimative analysis, such as its Global Trends series.

[22]Office of the Director of National Intelligence. *Intelligence Community Directive 204—National Intelligence Priorities Framework*. Washington, DC: Office of the Director of National Intelligence, 2015. https://www.dni.gov/files/documents/ICD/ICD%20204%20National%20Intelligence%20Priorities%20Framework.pdf.

[23]Shreeve, Thomas. "The Intelligence Community Case Method Program: A National Estimate on Yugoslavia." In *Intelligence and National Security Strategist*, edited by Robert George and Robert Kline, 333. New York, NY: Rowman & Littlefield, 2006.

[24]"National Intelligence Officer for North Korea." USAJobs. Accessed August 12, 2019. www.usajobs.gov/GetJob/ViewDetails/536125300.

# BOX 3.4
## SPOTLIGHT ON CAREERS

### National Intelligence Officer for North Korea (2019)[25]

**Major Duties and Responsibilities**

- The National Intelligence Officer (NIO) for North Korea (NK) serves as the Director of National Intelligence (DNI) senior analytic manager for North Korean issues. The NIO/NK serves as the DNI's focal point for all analytic matters pertaining to North Korea and is responsible for producing finished strategic intelligence analysis in support of senior US policymakers.

- Oversee Intelligence Community (IC) wide production and coordination of the full range of analytic assessments on North Korea including strategic analysis on Korea-related issues (e.g., National Intelligence Estimates [NIE], IC Assessments, and Sense of the Community Memoranda) and, as appropriate and required, more focused, time-sensitive analysis for the most senior decision makers in the USG [government].

- Orchestrate, direct, and in some cases draft Community-wide mid- and long-term strategic analysis to support and advance senior policymaker and war fighter understanding of North Korea. Serve as subject matter expert and analytic advisor on North Korean issues in support of the DNI's role as the principal intelligence advisor to the President.

- Develop the analytic portion of the Unified Intelligence Strategy (UIS) in concert with analysts from across the IC and provide assessments of IC analytic efforts in support of the UIS. Work with the national intelligence manager to assist in ensuring that analysis and collection are fully integrated.

- Lead, manage, and direct the professional-level analytic staff of the NIO/NK Division, evaluate performance, collaborate on goal setting, and provide feedback and guidance regarding personal and professional development opportunities.

**Who May Apply**

Only Senior Service (SNIS, SES, SIS, DISES, DISEL) candidates may apply. GS [General Service] employees may not apply.

**Mandatory Experience and Educational Requirements**

- Established and recognized expertise on North Korean affairs, including political and security matters.

- Experience and expertise effectively working with senior policymakers, to include a deep and current understanding of their intelligence/analytic requirements and priorities related to North Korea.

---

[25]Ibid.

- Expertise and experience in managing analytic processes, understanding IC analytic capabilities and priorities, and working at senior levels across the community to drive analytic product.

- Demonstrated capability to direct interagency, interdisciplinary IC teams against a range of functional and/or regional analytical issues.

- Excellent communication skills, including ability to exert influence with senior leadership and communicate effectively with people at all levels, both internal and external to the organization; to give oral presentations; and to otherwise represent the national IC in interagency meetings.

*Source:* National Intelligence Officer for North Korea. USAJobs (2019).

The other four centers that are included in the ODNI are a good reflection of the intelligence priorities of the US government. In the years since 9/11, the US government has prioritized its efforts to prevent terrorism and the spread of WMD. As a result, the ODNI established the National Counterterrorism Center in 2004 and the National Counterproliferation Center in 2005. Each of these centers serves a comparable coordination function to the DNI within a specific policy area. For instance, the National Counterintelligence and Security Center (NCSC) promotes integration on key counterintelligence functions such as protecting national security information and processes. The National Insider Threat Task Force, a government-wide effort designed to detect, deter, and mitigate insider threats to the US IC, has been located in the NCSC since 2011. The newest center is the Cyber Threat Intelligence Integration Center. Created in 2015, it is designed to provide coordinated US IC analysis on foreign cyber threats and ensure that this information is coordinated and shared within the federal government's cyber community.

## The Central Intelligence Agency

The CIA is often the most well-known element of the US IC and is one of two independent agencies dedicated to intelligence in the US government (the other being the ODNI). Created in 1947, it is headquartered in Langley, Virginia. Much of the initial design was heavily influenced by the experiences of the Office of Strategic Services, with approximately one-third of the initial personnel being OSS veterans.[26] Like the OSS, the CIA is a multifunctional organization that conducts intelligence collection and analysis. Also like the OSS, it conducts counterintelligence and covert action functions outside of the United States.

---

[26]Central Intelligence Agency. "History of the CIA." Accessed July 13, 2019. www.cia.gov/about-cia/history-of-the-cia.

While the CIA is organized into five directorates, the Directorate of Analysis and the Directorate of Operations have historically been the most significant elements of the organization. The Directorate of Analysis is tasked with providing timely and objective all-source analysis to all levels of government, though its primary focus is on serving senior policymakers. Indeed, a 2011 report by the DNI indicated that the CIA was the largest producer of all-source intelligence for national security issues in the entire US IC.[27]

The Directorate of Operations (DO), previously known as the National Clandestine Service, is the CIA's primary resource for conducting intelligence collection, counterintelligence, and covert action missions. With regard to collecting intelligence information, the DO is focused on the clandestine collection of human intelligence information. Given this person's resources and expertise in this area, the director of the CIA is the functional manager for human intelligence collection for the entire US IC, leading the effort to coordinate and de-conflict this type of collection for all 17 intelligence organizations in the US system. While little is officially known of the CIA's covert action capability, it is widely reported that this part of the DO expanded greatly in the years after 9/11 in order to prosecute the campaign against terrorist organizations such as al-Qaeda.

The Directorates of Support (DS) and Science and Technology (DS&T) are not as well known but are still important to the functioning of the organization. The DS provides a wide array of administrative and logistical services to support CIA missions. These include functions such as acquisitions, personnel recruiting, medical services, and site security. The DS&T develops and applies new technologies to collect and process intelligence information. In some ways, it is like the character Q in the James Bond movies. As the directorate's website notes, "To spend a day with the DS&T is to spend a day inside the imagination of the CIA."[28] Indeed, the inspiration for In-Q-Tel, the private venture capital firm that develops information technology solutions for the CIA, came out of the DS&T leadership in the late 1990s.[29]

The newest directorate was created in 2015. The Directorate of Digital Innovation was the first organization added to the CIA in nearly 50 years, and is an institutional reflection that issues related to information technology and computer networks are a growing national security priority. Its primary focus is modernizing information technology assets for the CIA and operationalizing cyber capabilities in support of CIA missions. The Open Source Center, which is the lead open source intelligence

---

[27]Director of National Intelligence. *US Intelligence: IC Consumer's Guide.* Washington, DC: Office of the Director of National Intelligence, 2011, 18.

[28]Central Intelligence Agency. "Science and Technology." Accessed July 13, 2019. https://www.cia.gov/offices-of-cia/science-technology.

[29]Yannuzzi, Rick. *In-Q-Tel: A New Partnership Between the CIA and the Private Sector.* Washington, DC: Joint Military Intelligence College, 2000. http://www.cia.gov/library/publications/intelligence-history/in-q-tel.

FIGURE 3.2 ■ 2015 CIA Organization Chart

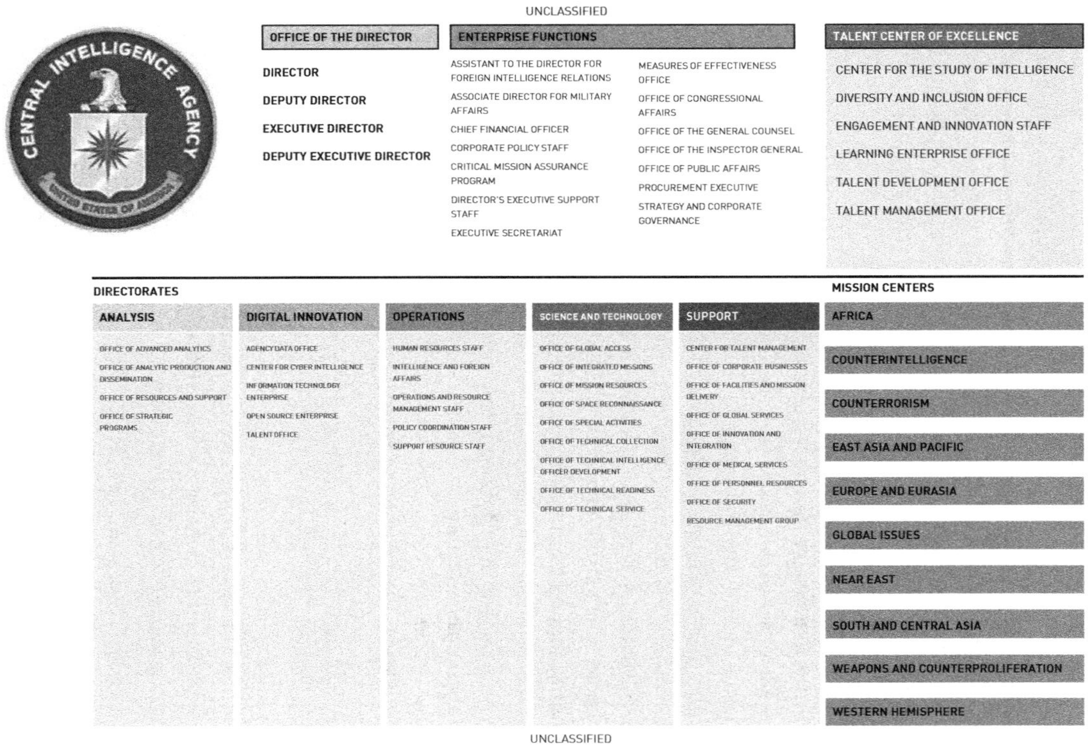

UNCLASSIFIED

**OFFICE OF THE DIRECTOR**

DIRECTOR

DEPUTY DIRECTOR

EXECUTIVE DIRECTOR

DEPUTY EXECUTIVE DIRECTOR

**ENTERPRISE FUNCTIONS**

ASSISTANT TO THE DIRECTOR FOR FOREIGN INTELLIGENCE RELATIONS

ASSOCIATE DIRECTOR FOR MILITARY AFFAIRS

CHIEF FINANCIAL OFFICER

CORPORATE POLICY STAFF

CRITICAL MISSION ASSURANCE PROGRAM

DIRECTOR'S EXECUTIVE SUPPORT STAFF

EXECUTIVE SECRETARIAT

MEASURES OF EFFECTIVENESS OFFICE

OFFICE OF CONGRESSIONAL AFFAIRS

OFFICE OF THE GENERAL COUNSEL

OFFICE OF THE INSPECTOR GENERAL

OFFICE OF PUBLIC AFFAIRS

PROCUREMENT EXECUTIVE

STRATEGY AND CORPORATE GOVERNANCE

**TALENT CENTER OF EXCELLENCE**

CENTER FOR THE STUDY OF INTELLIGENCE

DIVERSITY AND INCLUSION OFFICE

ENGAGEMENT AND INNOVATION STAFF

LEARNING ENTERPRISE OFFICE

TALENT DEVELOPMENT OFFICE

TALENT MANAGEMENT OFFICE

**DIRECTORATES**

| ANALYSIS | DIGITAL INNOVATION | OPERATIONS | SCIENCE AND TECHNOLOGY | SUPPORT |
|---|---|---|---|---|
| OFFICE OF ADVANCED ANALYTICS | AGENCY DATA OFFICE | HUMAN RESOURCES STAFF | OFFICE OF GLOBAL ACCESS | CENTER FOR TALENT MANAGEMENT |
| OFFICE OF ANALYTIC PRODUCTION AND DISSEMINATION | CENTER FOR CYBER INTELLIGENCE | INTELLIGENCE AND FOREIGN AFFAIRS | OFFICE OF INTEGRATED MISSIONING | OFFICE OF CORPORATE RESOURCES |
| OFFICE OF RESOURCES AND SUPPORT | INFORMATION TECHNOLOGY ENTERPRISE | OPERATIONS AND RESOURCE MANAGEMENT STAFF | OFFICE OF MISSION RESOURCES | OFFICE OF FACILITIES AND MISSION DELIVERY |
| OFFICE OF STRATEGIC PROGRAMS | OPEN SOURCE ENTERPRISE | POLICY COORDINATION STAFF | OFFICE OF SPACE RECONNAISSANCE | OFFICE OF GLOBAL SERVICES |
|  | TALENT OFFICE | SUPPORT RESOURCE STAFF | OFFICE OF SPECIAL ACTIVITIES | OFFICE OF INNOVATION AND INTEGRATION |
|  |  |  | OFFICE OF TECHNICAL COLLECTION | OFFICE OF MEDICAL SERVICES |
|  |  |  | OFFICE OF TECHNICAL INTELLIGENCE OFFICER DEVELOPMENT | OFFICE OF PERSONNEL RESOURCES |
|  |  |  | OFFICE OF TECHNICAL READINESS | OFFICE OF SECURITY |
|  |  |  | OFFICE OF TECHNICAL SERVICE | RESOURCE MANAGEMENT GROUP |

**MISSION CENTERS**

AFRICA

COUNTERINTELLIGENCE

COUNTERRORISM

EAST ASIA AND PACIFIC

EUROPE AND EURASIA

GLOBAL ISSUES

NEAR EAST

SOUTH AND CENTRAL ASIA

WEAPONS AND COUNTERPROLIFERATION

WESTERN HEMISPHERE

UNCLASSIFIED

*Source:* Central Intelligence Agency.

(OSINT) collection organization for the US IC's Open Source Enterprise, is also housed within this directorate.

In an effort to foster integration of activities within the organization, the CIA instituted a mission centers structure to augment the directorates in 2015. This system functions much like the military after the Goldwater–Nichols reforms mentioned earlier. The directorates provide the training and resources to develop their personnel expertise in their respective skill sets. Then, these personnel are integrated with CIA personnel from the other directorates in a mission center that focuses on a particular geographic area or functional issue. As of 2015, there were 10 mission centers focusing on issues such as Africa, global issues, counterterrorism, and counterproliferation.[30] The expectation is that this will improve integration and interoperability, and mitigate traditional bureaucratic problems such as "stovepiping."

As is common in organizations that have a diverse collection of missions, competing cultures can develop within the structure. In the CIA, the most prominent cultural fault line is between operators and analysts. The operations staff see themselves as doing the real work of the CIA—running HUMINT and covert action operations overseas. Historically, these operators have populated the upper leadership of the organization. Indeed, the current director of the CIA, Gina Haspel, spent most of her career in the National Clandestine Service (now known as the Directorate of Operations).[31] In contrast to these "cool kids" in operations, analysts are generalized as brainy, introverted, and sensitive about their independence. Some agency veterans saw the 2015 reforms as favoring the analysts, dubbing the plan "the revenge of the nerds."[32] Regardless of the validity of that claim, it suggests that the historic cultural divide within the CIA continues to endure on some level.

## The Pentagon and Defense Intelligence

The Pentagon is the proverbial 800-pound gorilla in the US IC. As Mark Lowenthal notes, "The Secretary of Defense controls much more of the intelligence community on a day-to-day basis than does the DNI."[33] For instance, of the 17 organizations that the DNI is charged with coordinating, almost half of them are managed by the Department of Defense (DOD). Also, while official numbers are not available, most estimates suggest that approximately 80 percent of the budget and manpower of the US IC resides within the Pentagon's control.

[30]Central Intelligence Agency. "CIA Organization Chart." Accessed July 11, 2019. https://www.cia.gov/about-cia/leadership/cia-organization-chart.html.

[31]Central Intelligence Agency. "Gina Haspel, Director." Accessed July 13, 2019. https://www.cia.gov/about-cia/leadership/gina-haspel.html.

[32]Ignatius, David. "Will John Brennan's Controversial CIA Modernization Survive Trump?" *The Washington Post*, January 17, 2017. https://www.washingtonpost.com/opinions/will-john-brennans-controversial-cia-modernization-survive-trump/2017/01/17/54e6cc1c-dcd5-11e6-ad42-f3375f271c9c_story.html.

[33]Lowenthal, *Intelligence*, 41.

However, the defense secretary's concern for intelligence issues is not typically as strong as the DNI's. Comparing the size of the organizations reveals this dynamic. When you include all of the civilian and military personnel who work in the DOD, you find that there are approximately 2.8 million people in the organization. There is no official statement on the size of the US IC, but according to a *New York Times* article from 2015, there are approximately 180,000 intelligence personnel in the DOD.[34] That would represent less than 7 percent of the Pentagon's personnel. So, while the DNI may view the Pentagon as a dominant force in its field, intelligence is not necessarily a dominant concern in the DOD. One manifestation of this was the creation of the **undersecretary of defense for intelligence (USDI)** position in 2002. This third-tier leadership position in the Pentagon is limited to management and oversight issues like budgets and policies regarding defense intelligence. Still, while the USDI has no operational control of intelligence functions, many argue that this position has more power in the US IC than even the DNI.

Each of the uniformed military organizations has an attached intelligence organization to support its service. The oldest intelligence organization in the US IC is the Office of Naval Intelligence, which was founded in 1882 and focuses on maritime intelligence issues. The National Ground Intelligence Center is located in Charlottesville, Virginia, and is the premier provider of intelligence products for the US Army. The 25th Air Force and the Marine Corps Intelligence Activity perform comparable functions for their respective services. These four organizations are managed by their respective service secretaries and are typically focused on operational-level intelligence issues.

The Defense Intelligence Agency (DIA) is separate from the military services and focuses on strategic-level defense issues in addition to supporting deployed military forces. Created in 1961, the DIA is primarily composed of civilian personnel, with only 30 percent coming from the uniformed military. Beyond its all-source analytic production, there are three key intelligence areas where the DIA plays an important role. First, it manages the Defense Attaché Office (DAO). The DAO program places military personnel in US embassies overseas in order to serve as a liaison to the host country's military forces and report back on their findings. In that capacity, they serve as one of the largest sources of overt human intelligence collection for the US IC. The second area where the DIA plays a significant role is in the functional management of measurement and signature intelligence (MASINT). In this capacity, DIA staff play a leading role in the development and coordination of MASINT capabilities for the US IC. Lastly, like the CIA's DO, the DIA has a new organization that develops clandestine human intelligence collection. While little is known about the Defense

---

[34]Shanker, Thom. "A Secret Warrior Leaves the Pentagon as Quietly as He Entered." *The New York Times,* May 1, 2015. https://www.nytimes.com/2015/05/02/us/a-secret-warrior-leaves-the-pentagon-as-quietly-as-he entered.html.

Clandestine Service (DCS), former USDI Michael Vickers noted in 2015 that while this organization does not rival the CIA in size, it is growing.[35]

The DIA also plays a role in managing the intelligence personnel who are assigned to the intelligence sections, typically known as the J2, for the combatant commands (COCOMs). Currently, as can be seen on Map 3.2, there are six geographically based COCOMs.[36] There are also five functionally based COCOMs. The intelligence personnel at these organizations are not typically counted as members of the US IC. However, they provide significant intelligence collection and analysis for their assigned geographic or functional area of responsibility.

Along with the DIA, the remaining DOD intelligence organizations are typically referred to as combat support agencies. This includes the National Geospatial-Intelligence Agency (NGA), the National Reconnaissance Office (NRO), and the National Security Agency (NSA). The NGA is the lead organization in the US IC for geospatial intelligence. Beyond just the analysis of imagery, the NGA focuses on cartography, or mapmaking.

In recent years, in addition to its mission to support national security, the NGA has provided support to disaster relief efforts inside the United States by providing imagery and mapping support to government response and recovery plans.

Headquartered at Fort Meade, the NSA is the lead organization in the US IC for signals intelligence. Given its role in the encryption of national security information and decryption of adversary communications, it is the largest employer of mathematicians in the country. Widely believed to be the largest (by both manpower and budget) organization within the US IC, this organization also has a substantial connection to cyber intelligence issues. Indeed, US Cyber Command was created at the NSA in 2009. The director of the NSA is dual-hatted as the commander of this COCOM, and it is a sign that the NSA will likely become more powerful within the US IC. As one observer noted, "Cyber will become as important to the IC as overhead [satellite] systems became a half century ago."[37]

However, as important as the NGA and NSA are to US national security, much of their work would be impossible without the NRO. A joint DOD-CIA staffed organization whose existence was not publicly acknowledged until 1992, the NRO is a

---

[35]Pavgi, Kedar. "Former Pentagon Intel Chief Says Military's Clandestine Service Is Growing." *Defense One*, July 23, 2015. https://www.defenseone.com/threats/2015/07/former-pentagon-intel-chief-says-militarys-clandestine-service-growing/118537/.

[36]As of 2018, US Pacific Command was renamed US Indo-Pacific Command due to the growing importance of South Asia. See "US Indo-Pacific Command Holds Change of Command Ceremony." US Indo-Pacific Command. Public Affairs Communication & Outreach, May 30, 2018. https://www.pacom.mil/Media/News/News-Article-View/Article/1535776/us-indo-pacific-command-holds-change-of-command-ceremony/.

[37]Kojm, Christopher. "Global Change and Megatrends: Implications for Intelligence and Its Oversight." *Lawfare Blog*, May 12, 2016. https://www.lawfareblog.com/global-change-and-megatrends-implications-intelligence-and-its-oversight.

## MAP 3.2 ■ US Regional Combatant Commands

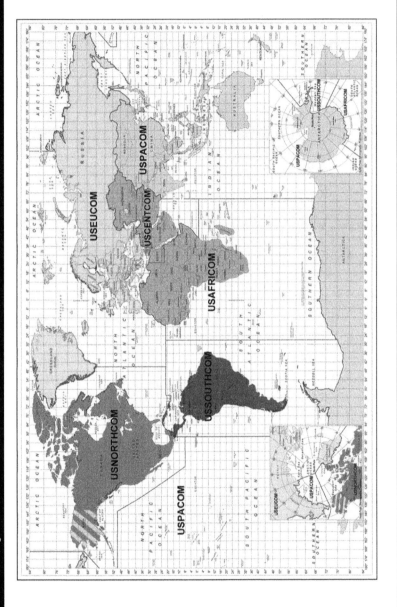

*Source:* National Geospatial-Intelligence Agency/Public domain/Wikimedia Commons.

National Security Agency/Public domain/Wikimedia Commons

**PHOTO 3.7** NSA headquarters at Fort Meade.

primary enabler for technical intelligence collection operations. Its mission is essentially to design, build, and fly the satellites that provide for the collection of technical intelligence information, such as imagery and communications intercepts. Typically, when you hear an official referring to **national technical means**, they are referring to intelligence gathered by the NRO. The organization was created in 1961 in order to improve coordination between the imagery collection functions of the CIA and the US Air Force. However, in contemporary times, private contractors play a significant role in the operations of the NRO. According to one 2009 book, nearly 88 percent of the organization's budget went to private corporations.[38]

These combat support agencies are one of the key points in the debate over whether the DOD has too much influence on intelligence issues in the US system. For instance, in the debate regarding the IRTPA reforms in 2004, one proposal was to transfer management of the NRO, NGA, and NSA from the Pentagon to the DNI. While this would have greatly strengthened the power of the DNI by giving the position a substantial role in the collection of intelligence information, the DOD resisted this move and was ultimately able to persuade its allies in Congress to reject this proposal.

---

[38]Paglen, Trevor. *Blank Spots on the Map: The Dark Geography of the Pentagon's Secret World*. New York, NY: Dutton, 2009, 178.

So, the defense sector is a dominant element in the US IC. The fact that the Pentagon already controls a vast majority of the IC has traditionally raised concerns about the **"militarization" of intelligence**. Indeed, the rise of new elements, such as the DCS, has further spurred this debate. Critics of this growth cite their concern that the DOD-controlled intelligence organizations might focus too much on intelligence issues directly related to military security. This is essentially the "law of the instrument"—if you are a hammer, every problem is a nail. Conversely, some embrace this "militarization." They contend that military security is the primary concern of national security, and therefore, it is appropriate for there to be greater focus in this domain.

## The Rest of the Intelligence Community

Like the military service intelligence components of the DOD, many nonmilitary intelligence organizations are elements of an established cabinet department and are primarily charged with supporting that policy area. Hence, their specializations are connected to the organization that they serve. For instance, the Bureau of Intelligence and Research (INR) at the State Department provides all-source intelligence analysis and reporting in support of US diplomacy. Many of these organizations are believed to be relatively small compared to more prominent US IC members, such as the CIA. For example, the INR is reported to have approximately 300 personnel in its organization.

While the State Department's INR was established after World War II, the need for intelligence in support of diplomacy is certainly not new. Indeed, the Black Chamber operated by Herbert Yardley collected communications intercepts to support US diplomatic efforts in the 1920s. And while the Black Chamber was disbanded in 1929 because Secretary of State Henry Stimson famously noted that "gentlemen do not read each other's mail," the INR was created out of another intelligence organization that was being disbanded—the Office of Strategic Services. In September 1945, as President Truman was closing out the OSS, the State Department recruited the Office of Research and Analysis Branch to form its new intelligence component.

While the mission of the INR is to provide all-source intelligence support to US diplomats, the bulk of its work utilizes reports from foreign service officers serving overseas. These "cables" are very similar to the overt human intelligence reports produced by defense attachés. However, the insights and assessments that are contained in these cables can be very sensitive. For instance, in "Cablegate," the disclosure of more than 250,000 State Department cables by WikiLeaks in 2010 was damaging to US diplomatic efforts in the Middle East.[39]

The Office of Intelligence and Counterintelligence of the Department of Energy was created in 1977 and focuses on technical analysis on foreign intelligence issues.

---

[39]Welch, Dylan. "US Red-Faced as 'CABLEGATE' Sparks Global Diplomatic Crisis, Courtesy of WikiLeaks." *Sydney Morning Herald*, November 29, 2010. https://www.smh.com.au/technology/us-redfaced-as-cablegate-sparks-global-diplomatic-crisis-courtesy-of-wikileaks-20101128-18ccl.html.

Financial Crimes Enforcement Network

**PHOTO 3.8** FinCEN crest.

Primarily, it focuses on assessing the nuclear weapons programs of foreign actors, making them a key component of the US IC's counterproliferation intelligence efforts. However, it also looks at other issues in the area of energy security, including the security of radioactive waste sites.

While the Department of the Treasury has maintained a foreign intelligence function since the early 1960s, its Office of Intelligence and Analysis was created in the Intelligence Authorization Act of 2004. Believed to be one of the only national finance ministries with an indigenous intelligence capability, it provides both analytic and counterintelligence support to Treasury Department missions. This means it specializes in the subject area of financial intelligence (FININT). It is supported in this effort by another element within the Treasury Department, the Financial Crimes Enforcement Network (FinCEN). Using the motto "follow the money," this organization coordinates with domestic and foreign partners to develop intelligence to combat money laundering and other financial crimes.

There are two agencies within the Department of Justice (DOJ) that are members of the US IC, the Drug Enforcement Administration (DEA) and the FBI. Unlike the CIA and the intelligence organizations within the DOD, the missions of these organizations are more likely to involve them in domestic security operations that would relate to homeland security issues.

The DEA joined the US IC in 2006. Its Office of National Security Intelligence is charged with facilitating coordination and information sharing with other elements of the national government in counterdrug activities. One of its most visible activities is its participation in the El Paso Intelligence Center (EPIC), which is focused on identifying and monitoring drug trafficking operations along the US–Mexico border.

The FBI is the other element of the DOJ that is included in the US IC. While it serves in both a law enforcement and intelligence capacity, the FBI is mandated by federal law as the lead agency in domestic intelligence collection.[40] As a result, in addition to pursuing traditional law enforcement missions like major thefts, white-collar crime, and corruption, the FBI pursues foreign espionage assets, subversives, and terrorists.

---

[40]Carter, David. *Law Enforcement Intelligence: A Guide to State, Local, and Tribal Law Enforcement Agencies.* Washington, DC: US Department of Justice, Office of Community Oriented Policing Services, 2004, 16.

In the balance between law enforcement and intelligence, the recent emphasis on counterintelligence and combating terrorism has shifted the focus of the FBI toward intelligence-related operations.[41]

Initially created as the Bureau of Investigation (BOI) by Attorney General Charles Joseph Bonaparte in 1908, it was renamed as the Federal Bureau of Investigation in 1935. The focus of the early years was primarily on law enforcement issues, such as bank robberies and kidnappings. For instance, the FBI killed or apprehended several high-profile criminals in the 1930s such as Machine Gun Kelly, Baby Face Nelson, and John Dillinger. While not as prominent, the FBI also worked to combat foreign espionage threats during World War II and the Cold War years. It even ran foreign collection and counterintelligence operations in Latin America up to the creation of the CIA in 1947.

One critical driver of the FBI's development was J. Edgar Hoover. Initially appointed as the director of the BOI in 1924, he would continue to serve as the head of the FBI until his death in 1972. During his 48-year tenure, the FBI grew in prominence as the nation's lead law enforcement agency, as well as a robust domestic counterintelligence organization. However, Hoover's aggressive, and sometimes illegal, use of intelligence collection methods raised concerns about his power within the political system. Specifically, Hoover was known to have "files" on government leaders giving him the potential to intimidate elected officials, including the president.

The organization's intelligence mission was substantially impacted by the September 11 attacks. Beyond the concerns of the 9/11 Commission that the FBI had not effectively coordinated with the CIA on the threat posed by al-Qaeda prior to the 2001 attacks, it was recognized that the intelligence function within the FBI required enhanced capabilities. The threat of violent nonstate actors attempting to conduct large-scale terrorist attacks within the United States represented a different type of security threat. As a result, the Intelligence

**PHOTO 3.9** Joint Terrorism Task Force.

FBI/Public domain/Wikimedia Commons

---

[41]Smith, Jonathan. "Homeland Security Intelligence." In *Threats to Homeland Security*, 2nd ed., edited by Richard Kilroy. New York, NY: John Wiley & Sons, 2018, 418.

Branch was established in 2005, and a surge of intelligence analysts flowed into the FBI. Indeed, according to one 2012 book, the intelligence workforce grew by 200 percent in the years after 9/11.[42]

Outside of the headquarters element in Washington, there are 56 FBI field offices located throughout the United States. Each of these offices has an associated Field Intelligence Group (FIG) to support operations and investigations within its jurisdiction. These sections use linguists, analysts, and special agents to gather and assess intelligence information from their area to support the national headquarters. Additionally, each of the FBI field offices manages at least one **Joint Terrorism Task Force (JTTF)** to promote collaboration with other government organizations at the federal, state, and local levels.

As with the DOJ, there are two US IC members within the DHS. Coast Guard Intelligence was created in 1915 as an office serving the assistant commandant. It was initially a small office but grew substantially during the period of Prohibition and, later, World War II. Currently, the organization focuses on supporting the range of maritime security issues that the Coast Guard conducts, including counternarcotics, port security, and interdicting alien migration. The newest member of the US IC is the DHS Office of Intelligence and Analysis, which joined the US IC in 2012. Beyond coordinating the efforts of the non–US IC intelligence offices within the subelements of the department, such as the Secret Service, the Office of Intelligence and Analysis provides training and assistance to the intelligence organizations that are operated by the states.

## Intelligence Outside of the Intelligence Community

While many discussions of intelligence in the American system focus on the 17 organizations that comprise the US IC, it is important to note that intelligence work is done by other elements of the federal government, as well as by private organizations and other levels of government. It is also important to note that this non–US IC intelligence presence is increasing. Given its focus on gathering and interpreting information to help improve decision making, the field of intelligence is a growth industry.

In their 2011 book, *Top Secret America*, Dana Priest and William Arkin found that there were 854,000 people in the United States with a top-secret security clearance.[43] This likely reflects that there are a number of federal organizations that utilize classified information but are not included in the US IC. For instance, we noted that the DHS has both its resident Office of Intelligence and Analysis and the Coast Guard's intelligence office as elements of the US IC. However, there are several other agencies within the DHS that have a resident intelligence operation, including Customs and Border Protection, the Secret Service, and the Transportation Security Administration. Even organizations like the Centers for Disease Control and Prevention and the Internal Revenue Service utilize intelligence professionals to support their missions.

---

[42]Priest, Dana, and William Arkin. *Top Secret America: The Rise of the New American Security State*. New York, NY: Little, Brown, 2011, 151.

[43]Ibid., 10.

Another element of intelligence support that occurs at the federal level is the use of private contractors. Private contractors are companies that have negotiated a contract with the government to provide a specified service. In order to fulfill that contract, they must hire personnel for their company who have the requisite expertise. Many large defense companies such as General Dynamics, L3, and SAIC provide intelligence support to the US government in this manner. This reliance on private contractors is not a new phenomenon and is a common practice across the federal government. For instance, Paul Light noted that there were approximately 3.7 million private contractors working on federal government programs in 2015.[44]

Private contracting organizations may also provide intelligence support to the growing number of intelligence operations that are emerging at the state and local level. In the aftermath of the attacks of September 11, all of the states have developed an intelligence capability. The overwhelming majority of the states established **fusion centers**. As can be seen in Map 3.3, some states have more than one. Currently, there are 79 fusion centers in operation around the country. These organizations are designed to promote information sharing between different levels of government, particularly with the Office of Intelligence and Analysis at the DHS. However, these fusion centers

**MAP 3.3  ■  Fusion Centers in the United States**

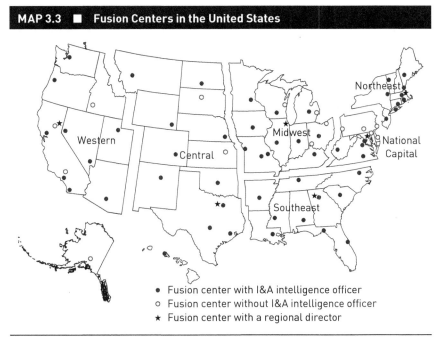

- ● Fusion center with I&A intelligence officer
- ○ Fusion center without I&A intelligence officer
- ★ Fusion center with a regional director

*Source:* US Government Accountability Office from Washington, DC, United States/Public domain/ Wikimedia Commons.

[44]Light, Paul. "Issue Paper: The True Size of Government." *The Volker Alliance*, October 5, 2017. www .volkeralliance.org/publications/true-size-government.

often coordinate with the intelligence organizations of local law enforcement departments, which are increasingly incorporating these functions in support of crime analysis and intelligence-led policing initiatives.

## THE INTELLIGENCE CYCLE AND ITS CRITICS

### Origins of the Intelligence Cycle

The modern intelligence cycle is an attempt to visualize the process by which intelligence information is produced, but it was not the first attempt. In the early 20th century, some of the elements of the intelligence process were noted as important in the craft of intelligence, but there was no real discussion of the coordination of these elements. For instance, while US Army regulations from World War I noted that the collection, collation, and dissemination of intelligence are "essential functions," there was no indication of these steps being coordinated in a larger process.[45]

The concept of an intelligence cycle became more prominent in the years around World War II. As the size of intelligence bureaucracies grew, the need to develop processes and training for new personnel became manifest. One of the first mentions of an "intelligence cycle" was by Phillip Davidson and Robert Glass in their 1948 book, *Intelligence Is for Commanders*. The cycle that they articulated in their book is not as

**FIGURE 3.3  ■  Current Version of the Intelligence Cycle**

---

[45]Wheaton, Kristopher. "Thinking in Parallel: A 21st Century Vision of the Intelligence Process." *Sources and Methods Blog*, June 6, 2014. https://sourcesandmethods.blogspot.com/2014/06/thinking-in-parallel-21st-century.html.

specific on the steps as modern variations of the intelligence cycle, but it does follow the concept that intelligence production is a sequential process designed to facilitate information support to decision makers. As Davidson and Glass note, "This relationship may be said to constitute the basic principle of intelligence."[46]

The ODNI identifies the current **intelligence cycle** as incorporating six steps in the process. These include (1) planning and direction, (2) collection, (3) processing and exploitation, (4) analysis and production, (5) dissemination, and (6) evaluation. Certainly, there are more steps in this model than the earlier versions. However, the organizing principle that the process of intelligence is a cycle that is designed to support policymakers remains. When the US IC Consumer's Guide describes the intelligence cycle process as "highly dynamic, continuous, and never-ending," earlier scholars such as Davidson and Glass would likely be in complete agreement.[47]

## Overview of the Elements

### 1. Planning and Direction

Given that intelligence is fundamentally designed to provide information advantage to policymakers, it is reasonable to assume that the process would start with an articulation of requirements by the policymakers. Requirements are a statement of information needs. They commonly identify the gaps in the knowledge base that decision makers currently possess in order to improve their awareness of the situation. These requirements are designed to drive the rest of the intelligence cycle process by determining what to collect, how to analyze it, and how to answer the requirement back to policymakers. Unfortunately, policymakers frequently are not energetic or enthusiastic participants in the process.

The lack of participation in the intelligence cycle process by senior decision makers likely stems from two issues. First, many senior policymakers lack an understanding of national security process in general and the role of intelligence support in particular. Consider the background of US presidents before they were elected. Of the last seven occupants of the White House, only two had served in elected office at the national level; four had been state governors. The current president came to the White House with no prior experience in government at all. Indeed, of these seven men, only President George H. W. Bush (1989–1993) came to the office with any experience in the business of intelligence; he served as the director of central intelligence from 1976 to 1977. As a result of this limited experience, these policymakers may come to the office with a limited understanding of how intelligence works and how it can serve their interests.

A second reason for the limited participation of senior policymakers in the White House is that the business of intelligence and national security is only one area

[46]Davidson, Phillip, and Robert Glass. *Intelligence Is for Commanders*. New York, NY: Military Services, 1948, 6.

[47]Office of the Director of National Intelligence. *US National Intelligence: An Overview*. Washington, DC: Office of the Director of National Intelligence, 2011, 10.

**PHOTO 3.10** Director of Central Intelligence George H. W. Bush.

of concern among many. If you consider the range of other priorities they may come to the office with—domestic policy issues, appointments to the federal judiciary, reelection, and others—it can be easier to see how these policymakers may not value and drive the intelligence cycle process as they perhaps should.

An illustration of this lack of senior policymaker participation was seen with the creation of the Intelligence Committee for the National Security Council in 1971. This body was organized in response to the findings of an Office of Management and Budget study that found that the IC was getting almost no guidance from senior officials in the Nixon administration. The inaugural meeting lasted 30 minutes. Its second meeting did not take place for another two and a half years![48] While other presidents have attempted to address this issue with different structures, they were all facing a similar dynamic. As Richard Betts notes in his book, *Enemies of Intelligence*, for senior policymakers, "attention is a scarce resource."[49]

Traditionally, the main types of intelligence requirements were either standing or ad hoc. Standing requirements reflect intelligence issues that are of continual importance, and therefore, intelligence activities to study these questions can be planned well in advance. For instance, the United States was concerned about Soviet nuclear capabilities during the Cold War. Intelligence products on this topic could be planned

---

[48]Betts, Richard. *Enemies of Intelligence*. New York, NY: Columbia University Press, 2009, 71.

[49]Ibid., 68.

and developed along a regularized schedule. As another example, when Fidel Castro rose to power in Cuba in 1959 and began to develop an alliance with the Soviet Union, the US IC was continually monitoring military developments on the island. The July 1962 NIE, "Situation and Prospects in Cuba," was an update to a previous NIE on the same topic.

In contrast, ad hoc requirements are often developed in response to unanticipated events. Oftentimes, these ad hoc requirements can be viewed as urgent issues that require immediate attention. For instance, when the United States discovered the SS-4 ballistic missile sites in Cuba on October 14, 1962, the question of Soviet intentions became an ad hoc requirement. From President Kennedy's perspective, assessing whether the Soviet deployment was a prelude to World War III and how the Soviets would likely respond to US policy responses was not a requirement that could wait until next year. The Special NIE on this issue, "Soviet Reactions to Certain US Courses of Action in Cuba," was completed within a week of the discovery.

This tension between standing and ad hoc requirements stems from the fact that there are always more requests for collection than there are resources to answer them. This dynamic is known as a **zero-sum game**. In this context, there are a fixed amount of resources in a given system. So, if additional resources are needed in one area, by definition, the other areas must lose an equivalent amount of resources. A game of tug of war is a good visual analogy of the zero-sum game. If one team gains a foot of rope in the struggle, then you can say with certainty that the other team has lost a foot of rope. So, bringing this back to the world of intelligence, if new ad hoc requirements emerge that must be addressed, then other standing collection requirements are going to suffer. This is sometimes referred to as the **tyranny of the ad hocs**.

The most recent attempt to resolve the issue of policymaker input is the creation of the National Intelligence Priorities Framework. Developed by Director of Central Intelligence George Tenet in 2003, the system is essentially a spreadsheet of intelligence topics rather than a listing of complete intelligence requests. The NIPF is intended to capture the priorities of senior policymakers within the NSC, and is managed by the DNI who ensures that policymakers review the document on an annual basis.

The construction of the NIPF helps to identify actor-issue concerns, as well as how important the issue is viewed by policymakers. To do this, the spreadsheet has two axes. One axis identifies all possible intelligence actors—both state and nonstate. The other axis covers a range of substantive topics. Then, the areas that are of concern to national security policymakers are identified and ranked with a priority number from 1 to 5, with 1 as the top priority. As the hypothetical illustration in Figure 3.3 notes, policymakers are interested in monitoring North Korea's ballistic missile technology, but they are not concerned with the Philippines' capability in this area. Similarly, counternarcotics issues are a bigger area of concern for US policymakers when considering the Philippines than when considering North Korea.

**FIGURE 3.4 ■ NIPF Hypothetical Example**

| | Counterintelligence | Counternarcotics | Cyber Threats | Regime Stability | Terrorism | WMD Chemical | WMD Nuclear | Ballistic Missiles |
|---|---|---|---|---|---|---|---|---|
| Japan | | | 4 | 5 | | | | |
| North Korea | 2 | 5 | 2 | 3 | | | 1 | 1 |
| Philippines | | 2 | | | 4 | | | |
| South Korea | 5 | | | 4 | | | | |
| Taiwan | 4 | | | 4 | | | | |

## 2. Collection

If policymakers have questions that the current information holdings cannot answer, then the intelligence function must have a mechanism for gathering new information to support this effort. This is where the collection process begins. The initial step will involve the management of the requirements that came from the first step in the process. This would involve such questions as which requirements are most important, what method of collection is most appropriate for the requirement, and what collection resources are actually available for the mission. Unfortunately, in the US IC, the management of requirements is decentralized with several discipline-specific systems, such as the National SIGINT Requirements Process and the MASINT Requirements System, concurrently managing their respective areas of the collection process.[50]

The ability to collect information is typically premised on having two key elements, a sensor and a platform. The sensor refers to the mechanism that gathers the information that is of intelligence value. For instance, in the Cuban Missile Crisis, the images showing the Soviet missile sites west of Havana were derived from a geospatial collection sensor (i.e., a camera). However, that camera required some mechanism to get it to the right place in space and time to gather that information. If the camera noted in this example was not installed on the U-2 aircraft that was flying over Cuba on October 14, we would not have collected this vital intelligence information. Indeed, for the month prior to the discovery, the United States had a "photo gap" because it stopped

---

[50]Clark, Robert. *Intelligence Collection*. Washington, DC: CQ Press, 2014, 461.

flying U-2 missions over Cuba, thereby keeping the camera sensors out of position to collect the needed intelligence. So, a collection sensor must be paired with a **collection platform**. These platforms are typically some type of transportation mechanism—a satellite, an aircraft, or otherwise. However, not all platforms have

US Air Force photo

**PHOTO 3.11** Camera installation on U-2 reconnaissance aircraft.

to be mobile. Closed-circuit television cameras and other surveillance sensors are typically, and increasingly, mounted on poles, buildings, or other stationary objects.

The sensors that collect information are typically described as the five collection disciplines. HUMINT is the oldest form of intelligence collection. It is even referenced in the Bible. In the Book of Numbers, when Moses directs his spies to infiltrate Canaan to gather information on the quality of the land and the strengths of its people that lived there, he was conducting HUMINT collection. However, in spite of the popular notion that all HUMINT is clandestine HUMINT (also known as espionage), there are other types of collection operations that involve direct human interaction. For instance, defense attachés or foreign service officers report on their activities within a foreign country typically with the full knowledge of that country—this would be called overt HUMINT. The debriefing of refugees and defectors, as happened in the years after the Cuban revolution, would also be categorized as overt HUMINT. Another form of HUMINT collection is interrogation, where the information source is typically being detained (and potentially coerced) by the organization that is seeking the information.

Intelligence derived from unclassified sources is typically referred to as open source intelligence (OSINT). While the growth of the internet and social media has greatly expanded the volume of potential OSINT collection, the use of this collection method has been around for some time. In 1948, Roscoe Hillenkoetter, the first director of central intelligence, noted, "80 percent of intelligence is derived from such prosaic sources as foreign books, magazines, and radio broadcasts, and general information from people with a knowledge of affairs abroad."[51]

The technically driven methods of collection are the most recent additions to intelligence collection with most of the methods associated with geospatial intelligence

---

[51]Richelson, Jeffrey. *The US Intelligence Community*, 5th ed. New York, NY: Routledge, 2008, 318.

**PHOTO 3.12** Image of missile site during the Cuban Missile Crisis.

(GEOINT), signals intelligence (SIGINT), and measurement and signature intelligence (MASINT) being developed within the last 200 years. Many of these collection methods are driven by the concept of **remote sensing**. This is a concept that suggests that it is possible to gather information without directly touching the target. So, while HUMINT typically requires a personal interaction, a geospatial sensor might be mounted on a satellite platform that is hundreds of miles above Earth—and the collection target.

These technical collection disciplines are a key driver in the issue of storing material gathered in the collection process. Whether it is due to the sheer volume of collection targets or the size of the data files, the storage of intelligence collection data is a perennial and growing problem. Intelligence organizations continue to develop additional storage facilities to manage this issue. For instance, the NSA created a massive data storage facility in Utah in 2012. Known as the Bumblehive, one report notes that it has a storage capacity of over 500 billion gigabytes.[52] However, as large as that is, it is still finite. The continuing flow of collection data and the growing capacity to store that information resembles the dilemma of "the immovable object and the unstoppable force."

## 3. Processing and Exploitation

In this age of multisensor platforms and growing technological sophistication, the volume of information that is gathered in the collection process far exceeds what is needed. For instance, a newer version of the MQ-9 Reaper unmanned aerial vehicle (UAV) is capable of continuously collecting data from its sensors over a period of 37 hours.[53] While that is potentially valuable surveillance data, there has to be a process in place for separating the useful information from the collected data that are not

---

[52]Goodwin, Bill. "Interview: James Bamford on Surveillance, Snowden and Technology Companies." *Computer Weekly*, January 5, 2016. https://www.computerweekly.com/feature/Interview-James-Bamford-on-surveillance-Snowden-and-technology-companies.

[53]Szondy, David. "MQ-9 Reaper Big Wing Sets Predator Flight Endurance Record." *News Atlas*, June 1, 2016. https://newatlas.com/predator-b-mq-9-endurance-record/43620/.

relevant to the intelligence process. For every image of an adversary's military facility, there will be hundreds or thousands of images of vacant terrain as the collection platform conducts its mission. As one intelligence analyst noted, "I leave more than 90 percent of my collection on the cutting room floor."

This process of separating the relevant from the irrelevant data is frequently referred to as **separating the wheat from the chaff**, which harkens back to the process of harvesting grain. Farmers must separate the wheat, which they value, from the protective husk (the chaff), which is not of any further use. The intelligence process, much like those farmers in the fields, must have the resources to not only gather all of the data, but also sort the data into the appropriate categories.

The processing and exploitation of intelligence collection can take different forms, depending on the type of collection. For instance, SIGINT intercepts of phone conversations in a foreign country will likely require a translation to know whether the call contained relevant information or not. It may also require decryption if the adversary has used a system to encode the communications. HUMINT often requires an evaluation of the source's credibility. For instance, before January 1962, there had been more than 200 HUMINT reports from Cuba regarding the presence of atomic weapons and ballistic missiles on the island.[54] However, since the Soviet operation to deploy these systems did not start until the summer of 1962, these reports were not credible.

There is oftentimes an imbalance between the resources dedicated to the collection and processing phases of the intelligence cycle, and the growth of technology compounds the problem. As one senior military official noted regarding the growth of UAVs using full-motion video collection, "We are swimming in sensors and drowning in data."[55] This creates a potential information choke point where information of critical intelligence value may have been collected, but may be delayed in getting to the later stages of the intelligence cycle. Or, worse still, the collected information is never processed. After all, information that is collected but never processed will likely never be seen, raising the question of why it was collected at all. Intelligence organizations have responded to this challenge by researching technological solutions like image recognition software and artificial intelligence that can assist in managing the processing workload.

Another potential issue in the processing and exploitation phase is whether the system is using the appropriate filter to evaluate the information. That is, if you are asking the wrong question, you may inadvertently confuse what counts as "wheat" and what counts as "chaff." Intelligence failures can sometimes be the result. For instance,

---

[54]Caddell, Joseph. "Discovering Soviet Missiles in Cuba." *War on the Rocks*, October 19, 2017. https://warontherocks.com/2017/10/discovering-soviet-missiles-in-cuba-intelligence-collection-and-its-relationship-with-analysis-and-policy/.

[55]Magnuson, Stew. "Military Swimming in Sensors and Drowning in Data." *National Defense Magazine*, January 1, 2010. http://www.nationaldefensemagazine.org/articles/2009/12/31/2010january-military-swimming-in-sensors-and-drowning-in-data.

the US IC largely missed the fall of the Soviet Union because it did not attach as much importance to data that were collected on economic and social conditions in that country as it did to military issues.

It's also possible that the processing and exploitation phase can simply make a mistake. The United States received a warning from the Peruvian embassy in Tokyo in January 1941 that indicated the Japanese government intended to go to war with the United States, but it was dismissed because the State Department believed the Peruvians were not credible.[56] Similarly, the evaluation of the Iraqi defector code-named **CURVEBALL** as credible added support to the assessment that the Iraqi government was maintaining a secret bioweapons program—an assessment that turned out to be wrong. Curveball admitted that he lied to US personnel about this in a 2011 article that was published in the British newspaper *The Guardian*.[57]

## 4. Analysis and Production

While raw intelligence typically refers to single-source information, most analysts strive to incorporate all-source analysis for finished intelligence products. This means that the analysis is derived from many different sources of intelligence collection. For instance, in the Cuban Missile Crisis, when the U-2 aircraft imaged the missile trailers, that provided useful—but limited—analysis on Soviet capabilities. However, once that information was combined with intelligence gathered from human and open source collection methods, as well as the education and expertise that the analysts brought to the issue, a much better sense of the gravity of the situation was possible.

Finished intelligence analysis can address of a variety of needs for decision making. It can be descriptive in nature, such as the CIA's World Factbook, which provides basic context on foreign countries around the world. In other cases, the analysis might focus on understanding and explaining current issues, such as the President's Daily Briefs (PDBs). Other analytic products are estimative in nature, meaning that they are an attempt to forecast the future (e.g., NIEs). Additionally, analysis might focus on providing advanced warning of adversary actions that would affect the country or its vital interests—what is known as **indications and warning (I&W)**. Ultimately, the types of intelligence analysis should be driven by the logic of what knowledge can facilitate decision advantage.

Regardless of the variety of topics and formats that can be considered intelligence analysis, they all share a common sense that there are multiple challenges to providing high-quality analysis. First, there is almost always some evidence that is not available. This uncertainty is akin to trying to solve a jigsaw puzzle when many of the pieces

---

[56]Walton, Timothy. "Pearl Harbor." In *Challenges of Intelligence Analysis: Lessons From 1300 BCE to the Present*, 89–98. New York, NY: Cambridge University Press, 2011.

[57]Chulov, Martin, and Helen Pidd. "CURVEBALL: How US Was Duped by Iraqi Fantasist Looking to Topple Saddam." *The Guardian*, February 15, 2011. https://www.theguardian.com/world/2011/feb/15/curveball-iraqi-fantasist-cia-saddam.

are missing. What is more, adversaries often are aware that you are trying to analyze their operations and so will take measures to make this harder. This might include denial operations, such as the use of camouflage, or deception operations where they actively mislead. For instance, when the Allies conducted Operation FORTITUDE to deceive the Germans regarding the location of the D-Day landings in 1944, they did not completely deny the Germans information on the invasion; they simply provided false information to undermine the analytic efforts of German intelligence. In the Cuban Missile Crisis, the Soviet attempts to deny the United States any indication of the missile deployment went to great lengths, including withholding knowledge of the operation from several key senior Soviet leaders, including their ambassador to the United States.[58] Lastly, perhaps no one is better at deceiving us than ourselves. To that end, analysts must beware of cognitive biases and other flaws in critical thinking when they are developing their analytic products.

Additionally, since intelligence analysis is often premised on incomplete information and assumptions, it must effectively communicate to decision makers both what it knows and what it does not know. So, given that there can be some degree of uncertainty about the collection material that was incorporated in the analytic product, many will include a confidence level to communicate the strengths and weaknesses of the material that was used to develop the analysis. Similarly, since analysts often reach their conclusions based off of some combination of evidence, assumptions, and inference, they will often incorporate estimative language in their judgments. For instance, in the 2002 Iraq NIE, they did not say that Iraq would have nuclear weapons in the coming decade. Given that there were pieces of information that they were lacking, such as what might happen in the future, they assessed that Iraq would *probably* have nuclear weapons in the coming decade.[59]

### 5. Dissemination

Dissemination is driven by the concept of effective communication. For analysts to have the information is not enough; they must also be able to communicate that information to decision makers. The absence of the ability to communicate effectively has largely the same effect as having no information at all—the intelligence process will have no value for the decision maker. One way to think about this is that analysis and dissemination are the two numbers contained in a multiplication equation. Anything times zero equals zero.

Beyond quality analysis and effective communication skills, it is vital that the analytic community has access to the decision makers. Many analysts worry that they might suffer the same fate as **Cassandra** from ancient Greece. According to legend,

---

[58]Caddell, "Discovering Soviet Missiles in Cuba."

[59]National Intelligence Estimate. *Iraq's Continuing Program for Weapons of Mass Destruction.* Washington, DC: National Intelligence Council, Key Judgements Section, 2002.

US Air Force photo by Master Sgt. Beth Holliker/Released

**PHOTO 3.13** Intelligence briefer.

Cassandra was a princess of Troy who promised herself to the god Apollo in exchange for the gift of foresight. However, when she broke her word to Apollo, he gave her both the gift of prophecy and the curse that no one would believe her. The idea that the intelligence function could have important information for decision makers, but that they could not present it (or were not believed), is a nightmare scenario for intelligence analysts.

Presuming that the access exists, the methods of disseminating intelligence analysis and products to the decision makers can be as varied as the types of intelligence products themselves. The main distinction is between written products and oral intelligence briefings. To be sure, written products require the active participation of the decision makers since they have to read the product in order to gain any value from it. These products can be quite short like a PDB or quite long like an NIE. Most products, like the PDBs and NIEs, are one-off affairs where they are requested, produced, and disseminated. However, some products, like an I&W matrix, are more like a "living document" where they are constantly updated. The oral dissemination of intelligence products primarily engages the auditory and visual senses of the consumer. It is common for these briefings to be accompanied by presentation slides that are projected on a screen and/or included in a book or computer tablet.

Dissemination requires an awareness of who the audience is. The main generalization about decision makers is that they are severely short on time. Hence, intelligence dissemination focuses on the **Bottom Line Up Front (BLUF)** format in constructing analytic products. However, beyond this, it is important to have an awareness of the background of the specific individual who is receiving the intelligence analysis. A case of two presidents and how they preferred to receive the PDB is instructive. It has been reported that President George W. Bush (2001–2009) preferred to receive the PDB in a traditional oral briefing and ask questions of the briefer. However, his successor, President Barack Obama (2009–2017), apparently preferred to receive a written copy of the PDB, which he would review, and then submit written questions.[60] The point is

[60]Theissen, Marc. "Why Is Obama Skipping More Than Half of His Daily Intelligence Meetings?" *The Washington Post*, September 10, 2012. https://www.washingtonpost.com/opinions/why-is-obama-skipping-more-than-half-of-his-daily-intelligence-meetings/2012/09/10/6624afe8-fb49-11e1-b153-218509a954e1_story.html.

not that one is inherently preferable to the other, only that members of the US IC will more effectively communicate if they have an understanding of the background and learning preferences of their customer.

## 6. Evaluation

If the intelligence process is truly a cycle, then feedback from the decision makers is vital to improving the process. If nothing else, if the final analytic product that is disseminated to the decision makers does not adequately address their needs, then the process should begin again in an attempt to address the deficiency. As the US IC Consumer's Guide in 2011 noted, "Constant evaluation and feedback are extremely important . . . to adjust and refine their activities and analysis to better meet consumers' changing and evolving information needs."[61]

Unfortunately, just as decision makers are not always enthusiastic participants in the development of intelligence requirements, providing critique and feedback to improve the process has not typically been a driving priority. If the generalization that policymakers are severely time constrained and focused on immediate decisions is accurate, then it is understandable that their ability to stop and reflect on larger issues is limited.

However, evaluation and feedback may be gathered by interpreting the response of decision makers when the intelligence analysis is delivered. This is one potential benefit to oral briefings over disseminating intelligence analysis via written products. Since briefings involving oral communication with decision makers are "live" (and, typically, in-person), the decision maker may ask questions or provide comments that implicitly provide evaluation and feedback to the intelligence briefer. It is also possible to get some evaluation and feedback by assessing the nonverbal communication of the decision maker during the brief. To be sure, this is less than what intelligence professionals typically hope for.

## CONCLUSION: CRITIQUES AND ALTERNATIVE APPROACHES

While the intelligence cycle is a common framework to understand the process of how intelligence is created, it certainly has its share of critics. Many critique it for being out of date. The intelligence cycle was developed before the information age and, thus, may not reflect changes in organizational theory. For instance, Robert Clark attempts to explain the process as target-centric, where integration and networks create a very different method for producing intelligence than is described by the traditional model.[62]

---

[61]Director of National Intelligence. *US Intelligence: IC Consumer's Guide*. Washington, DC: Office of the Director of National Intelligence, 2011, 12.

[62]Clark, Robert. *Intelligence Analysis: A Target-Centric Approach*, 3rd ed. Washington, DC: CQ Press, 2010, 13.

Many scholars focus on the critique that the intelligence cycle is not an accurate description of how the intelligence process works in reality. Arthur Hulnick notes that the intelligence cycle does not incorporate two of the main areas of intelligence, counterintelligence and covert action, in its description.[63] Many of these critiques also note that many of the steps in the process are occurring simultaneously, and that the intelligence cycle's depiction of a sequential process does not reflect actual practice. Indeed, Mark Lowenthal's depiction of the intelligence process incorporates a multilayered approach where multiple cycles are occurring concurrently and feedback is ongoing throughout the process.[64]

Winston Churchill once famously noted that "it has been said that democracy is the worst form of Government except for all those other forms that have been tried from time to time."[65] Perhaps, the same can be said regarding the intelligence cycle as an explanation of how intelligence is produced. As a description of the process, it clearly has limits. Yet, it does identify the basic elements that are involved in the process of creating intelligence products to support decision advantage. Particularly for new personnel who are joining the intelligence profession, this is an important first step. And thus far, no other alternative model has gained enough support to supplant the intelligence cycle.

## KEY CONCEPTS

*Federalist* 10   46
unitary executive model   46
Appropriations Committee   48
House Permanent Select Committee on
    Intelligence (HPSCI)   49
Senate Select Committee on Intelligence
    (SSCI)   49
Gang of Eight   50
judicial review   50
Foreign Intelligence Surveillance Court
    (FISC)   51
containment strategy   53
National Security Council (NSC)   55
Goldwater–Nichols Act   56

Intelligence Reform and Terrorism
    Prevention Act (IRTPA)   58
director of national intelligence
    (DNI)   60
National Intelligence Priorities
    Framework (NIPF)   61
National Intelligence Council
    (NIC)   61
undersecretary of defense for intelligence
    (USDI)   67
national technical means   70
"militarization" of intelligence   71
Joint Terrorism Task Force (JTTF)   74
fusion center   75

---

[63]Hulnick, Arthur. "What's Wrong With the Intelligence Cycle?" *Intelligence and National Security* 21, no. 6 (2006): 961.

[64]Lowenthal, *Intelligence*, 85.

[65]Churchill, Winston. "The Worst Form of Government." International Churchill Society. Accessed September 30, 2019. https://winstonchurchill.org/resources/quotes/the-worst-form-of-government/.

## ADDITIONAL READING

Best, Richard. "Intelligence and US National Security Policy." *International Journal of Intelligence and Counterintelligence* 28, no. 3 (2015): 449–467.

Bolton, Kent. *US National Security and Foreign Policymaking After 9/11: Present at the Re-creation.* New York, NY: Rowman & Littlefield, 2007.

George, Roger. *Intelligence in the National Security Enterprise.* Washington, DC: Georgetown University Press, 2020.

Kennedy, Robert. *Of Knowledge and Power: The Complexities of National Intelligence.* New York, NY: Praeger Security International, 2008.

Matthais, Willard. *America's Strategic Blunders: Intelligence Analysis and National Security Policy, 1936–1991.* State College, PA: Penn State University Press, 2001.

Phythian, Mark. *Understanding the Intelligence Cycle.* London, UK: Routledge, 2014.

Quigley, Michael. "Revitalizing Intelligence: The History and Future of HPSCI, the IAA, and Congressional Oversight." *Harvard Journal on Legislation* 56, no. 2 (2019): 341–353.

Tropotei, Teodor. "Criticism Against the Intelligence Cycle." *Scientific Research and Education in the Air Force* (May 2018): 77–88.

Wolfensberger, Donald. "The Return of the Imperial Presidency." *The Wilson Quarterly* 26, no. 2 (2002): 36–41.

Zegart, Amy. *Eyes on Spies: Congress and the United States Intelligence Community.* Stanford, CA: Hoover Institute Press, 2011.

# 4 COMPARATIVE INTELLIGENCE SYSTEMS

Jonathan M. Acuff

## CASES IN INTELLIGENCE STUDIES

After completing our discussion of US intelligence and national security institutions and processes, we now turn to examining the intelligence systems of other nation-states. But which countries will we select to study? Should we evaluate them in isolation or compare them with each other? What are the best ways to analyze these countries? These are the kinds of questions political scientists and historical sociologists working in the interdisciplinary field of study known as comparative politics have dealt with for over 100 years.[1] After largely ignoring the social sciences in favor of historical narrative, biography, and primitive case study methods from business schools, scholars working in intelligence studies have finally started to employ more rigorous research methods.[2] In this chapter, we shall draw on some of these insights as we compare the intelligence systems of six important nation-states.

In comparative politics, the countries we examine are referred to as **cases**. In a broader context, cases refer to any object of a study, be it a political leader, terrorist group, or corporation. A **case study** is what we call analysis of a case or cases using a particular framework to evaluate the empirical evidence. The use of an analytic, explanatory framework distinguishes case studies from mere journalistic description and can be qualitative in nature, quantitative, or both. In comparative politics, case studies have five primary functions: creating theories, testing theories, determining which factors affect the case, weighing the relative importance of these factors, and explaining cases that are important in their own right.[3] Both in the practice of intelligence and in the academic discipline of intelligence studies, we rarely use or

---

[1] In the early 20th century, the German sociologist Max Weber pioneered the comparative social scientific study of different political and economic systems. See Weber, Max. *Economy and Society*, Vols. 1 and 2, edited by Guenther Roth and Claus Wittich. Berkeley: University of California Press, 1978.

[2] When the US IC frequently uses case studies, it often does not follow basic social scientific methods. Compare the internal training document by Shreeve, Thomas W. "Experiences to Go: Teaching With Intelligence Case Studies." Discussion Paper Number 12. Washington, DC: Joint Military Intelligence College, 2004, with the scholarship of Davies, Philip H., and Kristian C. Gustafson, eds. *Intelligence Elsewhere: Spies and Espionage Outside the Anglosphere*. Washington, DC: Georgetown University Press, 2013.

[3] Van Evera, Stephen. *Guide to Methods for Students of Political Science*. Ithaca, NY: Cornell University Press, 1997, 55.

test theories. We are, however, interested in factors derived from theoretical frameworks that shape the current makeup of cases and may influence their future activities and interests, which are frequently referred to in intelligence as **drivers**. Finally, both intelligence officers and academics are more interested in some cases than others. The desire for complete coverage must be balanced by focusing on cases that directly affect the work of intelligence officers in advancing the national interest or ones with particular scholarly importance in the study of intelligence.

## Case Selection

The process by which we choose countries to analyze is known as **case selection**. The first and most important criterion in choosing a case or cases is determining whether this will be a comparative study that examines more than one case or a single-case study. In this chapter, we will analyze six cases, which is a form of **cross-national comparison**, a comparison of multiple countries or international organizations. This kind of case study is useful because it involves **variation** across cases—that is, the characteristics of the individual cases differ. Cross-national comparison allows us to use the cases as a kind of natural laboratory to determine which characteristics tend to matter in intelligence activities. But one need not look solely at multiple cases to achieve sufficient variation to reach general conclusions. Examining a single case over time may also yield within-case variation, achieving much the same effect as cross-national comparison.[4]

The second criterion used in the selection of cases directly relates to one of the core functions of case studies—examining cases that are important. In this context, importance is a relative quality, such as the role of the USSR in defeating Nazi Germany in World War II versus the part played by Greece. Importance may also be measured in terms of the relative size of a country's economy, its diplomatic influence, and/or its geographic location, all of which determine whether or not the country is of strategic importance. We are also interested in how representative the case is of a broader group of cases. For example, a case study of the United States would not only be important in terms of the analysis of the United States in and of itself; such a study would also be more generally applicable to a larger group of countries that historically have influenced world politics, the Great Powers. When we select a country or countries that have some variation but generally conform to a set of shared characteristics of a larger group of nation-states than we will analyze, we have a **representative sample**.

The third criterion often employed in case selection is to what extent a case reflects the subject of interest. For example, we might conduct a cross-national study as to how

---

[4]Dover, Robert, and Michael S. Goodman, eds. *Learning From the Secret Past: Cases in British Intelligence History*. Washington, DC: Georgetown University Press, 2013; and Blanken, Leo J., Hy Rothstein, and Jason J. Lepore, eds. *Assessing War: The Challenge of Measuring Success and Failure*. Washington, DC: Georgetown University Press, 2015.

militaries have been integrated into counternarcotics operations. Despite its location in a region where drug trafficking is a major challenge, we would probably not choose Costa Rica, as it abolished its military in 1948.[5] In this chapter, the focus is on intelligence organizations, how they operate within the political system in which they are embedded, and the manner in which they are used to advance the national interest. Thus we would not choose a country with no military and little to no intelligence capability, as that would not tell us much about the political role of intelligence in a broader sense.

With these criteria in mind, which countries were selected? We derived the sample for our cross-national comparison based on factors derived from the aforementioned criteria. First, we chose cases based on variation in **regime type**, the form of government of a country. Specifically, the sample included countries that are democracies (United States, Great Britain, France, Germany, and Israel), as well as some that are authoritarian (Russia and China). But regime type goes beyond this relatively straightforward distinction. One of the key findings from comparative politics is that countries with presidential political systems tend to be less democratic than countries with parliamentary forms of government, even if their political institutions are formally democratic.[6] This variation may have important implications for how intelligence operations are conducted, the role of oversight, and the degree of influence of intelligence on politics more broadly. Thus, our sample included a mix of both democratic and authoritarian regimes, as well as presidential and parliamentary political systems.

In addition to variation in regime type, we sought variation in terms of both the importance of the countries in our sample and their relative intelligence capabilities. Several of the countries we selected are powerful states with global influence, such as the United States, Russia, and China. Other countries in our sample are less powerful but nevertheless use their power to influence politics outside of their region. France, for example, has security relationships with many of its former colonies in Africa and has been willing to deploy its military to support these countries in their struggle against radical Islamic terrorism. Great Britain is one of the world's largest economies and regularly executes intelligence operations far from its shores. But neither of these countries is a world power on the same scale as the United States, Russia, or China. We also chose several countries that have considerable intelligence capabilities but, for various reasons, have generally not utilized them outside of the region in which they are located, specifically Germany and Israel. Finally, cases were selected with an eye toward regional variation, with cases from Europe, Asia, and the Middle East.

---

[5]Students of comparative politics will note that Costa Rica might be selected as a control case to evaluate the implied null hypothesis, that militaries have little to no effect on the effectiveness of counternarcotics operations. But for simplicity's sake, we will not examine the issue here.

[6]Linz, Juan. "The Perils of Presidentialism." *Journal of Democracy* 1, no. 1 (Winter 1990): 51–69.

## Theoretical Lenses for Analysis

Now that case selection is complete, how should we analyze the countries in our sample? The field of comparative politics generally follows three research traditions: culture, structuralism, and rational choice theory.[7] In this context, **culture** refers to looking to a case's identities, norms, symbols, and practices, all of which are historically derived and are used to explain the goals and actions of the country in question. Culture has been used by scholars in intelligence studies to explain cross-national variation in intelligence organizations—there are distinctly American or Russian ways of conducting intelligence activities.[8] Conversely, **structuralism** focuses on the institutional architecture of a society, how its various political, economic, and social institutions are arranged and interact. Descriptions of how government agencies are organized and interact and how the resulting structures have affected political objectives have long dominated the study of intelligence. Finally, **rational choice theory** emphasizes rational calculation by individuals weighing their interests against the costs of pursuing them. Rational choice theory has had little role in intelligence studies or its practice. When rationality has been referenced by students or practitioners of intelligence, it often takes the mistaken form of determining whether a political leader is rational or not, a classic **false dichotomy**. One may be perfectly rational in the pursuit of one's breakfast but at the same time decidedly irrational in making foreign policy decisions. This is neither representative of rational choice theory as it is used in comparative politics nor useful in forecasting future events.

As theory has been used only sparingly in the practice and study of intelligence, we shall employ an amalgam of these traditions, noting cultural variation in intelligence activities while paying attention to the institutions and interests of each nation-state. As we examine the cases, we will look at the **structure and function** of intelligence organizations and the relevant domestic political institutions overseeing them. The effects of culture, structure, and interests will be blended into this description. By examining the structure and function of each case, we draw on the strengths of each tradition without committing ourselves to one.

## THE UNITED KINGDOM

A political union of England, Scotland, Wales, and Northern Ireland, the United Kingdom, often referred to as Great Britain, has historically been one of the most powerful nation-states in the world. At its height, the British Empire encompassed over

---

[7]Lichbach, Mark Irving, and Alan S. Zuckerman, eds. *Comparative Politics: Rationality, Culture, and Structure.* Cambridge, UK: Cambridge University Press, 1997.

[8]De Graaf, Bob, and James M. Nyce, eds. *The Handbook of European Intelligence Cultures.* Boulder, CO: Rowman & Littlefield, 2016; and Willmetts, Simon. "The Cultural Turn in Intelligence Studies." *Intelligence and National Security* 34, no. 6 (2019): 800–817.

400 million people and one-quarter of the world's territory. A Great Power since the 16th century, the United Kingdom (UK) fought for the Allied side during both world wars, with World War II nearly bankrupting the country. During the Cold War, the United Kingdom gradually lost almost all of its former colonies, retaining only a few territories. Economic decline in the 1970s resulted in dramatic cuts to the British intelligence community's budget. Secession movements in Scotland, Ireland, and Wales have recently begun in earnest again, and the United Kingdom's probable departure from the European Union (EU) presents considerable challenges. Although it remains the world's fifth-largest economy and holds a permanent seat on the United Nations Security Council, the United Kingdom's military power lags considerably behind both its historical status and the most powerful states in the contemporary international system. It has, nevertheless, retained considerable intelligence capabilities relative to most states, allowing it to frequently "punch above its weight" in world politics.

## MI-5, Security Service

Unlike some democracies, intelligence has always played an important role in British foreign policy decision making and strategic thinking. The United Kingdom is one of the most important countries in the history of intelligence. The structure of many nation-states' intelligence institutions more or less derives from the British system, which from its origin emphasized functional differentiation between domestic and internationally focused intelligence agencies. Although English spies regularly operated to great effect in the court of Elizabeth I, the British intelligence community was only formally established in 1909 with the creation of **MI-5** (Military Intelligence, Section 5), aka the "Security Service," then known as the Secret Service Bureau. Falling under the responsibility of the Home Office, MI-5 is the lead domestic intelligence agency for the United Kingdom, responsible for counterintelligence and counterterrorism, the latter supervised by MI-5's Joint Terrorism Analysis Centre, which also pulls officers from other UK intelligence agencies. Although MI-5's area of responsibility is similar to that of the Federal Bureau of Investigation (FBI), unlike its US counterpart the Security Service is not a law enforcement agency. Freed from a constant focus on arresting subjects and trying them, MI-5 enjoys the advantage of being able to flip foreign penetrations and use these agents for years against their ostensible masters. While lack of a law enforcement purview carries with it the potential for abuse of power, historically MI-5 has been able to turn foreign agents back on their handlers to great effect, as was the case when it co-opted all of Nazi Germany's British assets during World War II.

MI-5 is not the only organization in the United Kingdom with a domestic intelligence-related mission. The recently created **National Crime Agency (NCA)**, which like MI-5 is part of the Home Secretary's purview, is a law enforcement organization responsible for combating organized crime, human trafficking, cybercrime, weapons smuggling, and any other serious cross-border crimes it is tasked with investigating. In addition, London's **Metropolitan Police Service (MPS, aka Scotland Yard)** employs its intelligence capability to protect the British royal family, Parliament, and Heathrow Airport, as well as support efforts against the significant counterterrorism threats faced by the capital. As the United Kingdom is a **unitary form of government**—that is, all government agencies are controlled and regulated by the national government—coordination between these organizations is easier than it is in **federal systems**, which cede much of their authority to regional and/or local jurisdiction. Agency heads also answer directly to members of Parliament (MPs), who run the ministries in which the agencies are housed.

## MI-6, Secret Intelligence Service

Also founded in 1909, **MI-6**, or the Secret Intelligence Service (SIS), answers to the Foreign Secretary and is responsible for intelligence operations overseas. It is perhaps the most well-known intelligence organization in the world through its association with the fictional character James Bond, who in between his martini-soaked liaisons with all manner of female agents somehow maintains active employment in the SIS. As is the case with its sister organization, MI-6's primary focus is human intelligence (HUMINT) collection and covert action. With a greater focus on language education in its universities and recruitment practices emphasizing these skills, British intelligence has historically enjoyed significant advantages over its American and other foreign rivals in HUMINT activities. This remains largely the case today, although one should be careful not to overemphasize British reliance on HUMINT, as one of the oldest signals intelligence (SIGINT) organizations is also British. Originally founded in 1919 as the Government Code and Cypher School, **Government Communications Headquarters (GCHQ)** is one of the world's leading SIGINT and cryptographic agencies. During World War II, the forerunner of GCHQ operated a communications interception and decryption facility at Bletchley Park. Code-named Project ULTRA and aided by early work from Polish intelligence, these operations allowed the British government to read all German signals traffic encrypted on the supposedly unbreakable Enigma machines, giving the Allies a tremendous advantage over their opponent. Contemporary GCHQ surveillance of known Russian spies also detected suspicious interactions between them and figures tied to Donald Trump as early as 2015, long before US intelligence agencies were aware of Russian attempts to penetrate the presidential candidate's campaign.[9]

## The Joint Intelligence Committee

Drawing on both its HUMINT and SIGINT strengths, the British intelligence community has enjoyed a high level of access to policymakers and a great deal of

---

[9]Harding, Luke, Stephanie Kirchgaessner, and Nick Hopkins. "British Spies Were First to Spot Trump Team's Links With Russia." *The Guardian*, April 13, 2017. https://www.theguardian.com/uk-news/2017/apr/13/british-spies-first-to-spot-trump-team-links-russia.

**PHOTO 4.1** "The Doughnut," GCHQ building, Cheltenham, Gloucestershire, United Kingdom.[10]

influence on the diplomatic and strategic direction of the country. In 1936, the **Joint Intelligence Committee (JIC)** centralized intelligence analysis and management of information flow across the various agencies. The JIC remains the primary vehicle through which strategic intelligence assessments are generated and the British government manages its intelligence community, while analytic missions specific to the military are handled by the **Defence Intelligence Staff (DIS)** as part of the Ministry of Defence. One important function of the JIC is to set collection requirements and priorities, much the same as the US National Intelligence Priorities Framework. Paradoxically, although it centralized intelligence management long before the United States' comparatively much weaker director of national intelligence, the United Kingdom recently determined the JIC alone was not adequately coordinating defense and intelligence activities. In 2010, the first British **National Security Council (NSC)** was formed, an organization that brings together the prime minister (PM) and several ministers; the chair of the JIC; the heads of MI-5, MI-6, and GCHQ; and the chief of the defense staff. At first glance, the creation of the NSC seems to add an additional bureaucratic layer to decision making, thereby slowing the process. In fact, the NSC has the power to rapidly shift resources across agencies in a way that the JIC does not, enhancing crisis response and the efficient direction of security and

[10]British Ministry of Defence. Accessed September 12, 2020. http://www.defenceimagery.mod.uk/.

intelligence affairs.[11] The NSC is a marked improvement over previous attempts at gaining input from the ministries, most notably the Ministerial Committee on the Intelligence Services, which did not even meet for four years during the 1990s.[12]

Although it has seen its role diminished somewhat by the NSC, the JIC also plays a vital role in coordinating UKUSA, more commonly known as **Five Eyes**, the most important multilateral intelligence agreement in the world. Five Eyes provides a framework for broad and deep intelligence cooperation between the United States, the United Kingdom, Canada, Australia, and New Zealand, including the direct sharing of classified material via the communications network known as **STONEGHOST**. The success of Five Eyes has provided the basis for an expansion in intelligence cooperation beyond just the "Anglophone" members. Dubbed "14 Eyes," SIGINT Senior Europe, or **SSEUR**, has broadly expanded intelligence sharing between the Five Eyes countries and Germany, Italy, Sweden, Belgium, and Spain.

## Oversight of the UK Intelligence Community

Despite the early operational advantages created by the JIC and the good working relationship between government and the intelligence community, oversight of intelligence in the United Kingdom has been weak. Failure by British political leaders to exercise adequate supervision led to a series of scandals regarding domestic surveillance abuses by MI-5 during the Cold War, which was nearly as broad in scope as the FBI's COINTELPRO, generated hundreds of thousands of files on British citizens, and included surveillance of several serving MPs. UK intelligence organizations also participated in widespread human rights abuses both in the former overseas colonies and against members of the Irish Republican Army terrorist group in Northern Ireland.[13] Throughout this period, the House of Commons, Britain's lower house of Parliament, had no authority or capability to supervise intelligence operations—the British PM enjoyed unchecked power over the activities of the intelligence community. Finally, a legal framework was established with the **Security Service Act of 1989** (for MI-5) and the **Intelligence Services Act of 1994** (for MI-6 and GCHQ), with the first oversight committee created in 1993. Although the **Intelligence and Security Committee (ISC)** has statutory authority, something most parliamentary committees lack, the ISC's members are chosen by the PM, and it seems largely limited to producing an annual report, the timing and contents of which are also controlled by the PM. Although there is an Investigatory Powers Tribunal to handle complaints by British

[11]Goodman, Michael S. "The United Kingdom." In *Routledge Companion to Intelligence Studies*, edited by Robert Dover, Michael S. Goodman, and Claudia Hillebrand, 135–144. Oxford, UK: Routledge, 2014.

[12]Phytian, Marky. "The British Experience With Intelligence Accountability." *Intelligence and National Security* 22, no. 1 (2007): 88.

[13]Walton, Calder. *Empire of Secrets: British Intelligence, the Cold War, and the Twilight of Empire*. London, UK: Harper, 2013.

citizens, the doctrine of "parliamentary supremacy" ensures the British courts have little say over regulation of the intelligence community's actions. Moreover, the United Kingdom's possible exit from the EU (Brexit) means the end of the external jurisdiction of the European Court of Human Rights, one of the key motivations in the push for oversight in the 1970s and '80s.[14] Although British intelligence officers are prohibited from engaging in activities supporting any political party and are broadly tasked with "defending the realm," intelligence oversight in Parliament remains anemic. UK intelligence officers are largely subject to the discipline of their own conscience, not supervision by democratically elected MPs who, unless they are willing to challenge the PM, have little input into the actions of the intelligence services.

## Performance of UK Intelligence

Although the UK intelligence community has demonstrated strengths in HUMINT and SIGINT collection and close coordination with policymakers, its history is also marked by significant intelligence failures. The inability to forecast likely Egyptian, US, and Soviet reactions to the **Suez Crisis** of 1956 proved disastrous. Although British intelligence efforts to halt the various anticolonial insurgencies enjoyed some minor successes in Malaysia and Yemen, overall they had little effect on arresting the United Kingdom's slow decline. And there was an extraordinarily damaging counterintelligence failure. During the 1930s, five Cambridge University students were recruited by the Soviet Union to spy on their homeland by pursuing careers in the intelligence and diplomatic services. Several of these students came from upper-class families and as a result were able to quickly acquire positions of influence in these organizations. The **Cambridge Five**, as they became known, operated undetected for several decades. Although several were unmasked and arrested or fled to Moscow, perhaps the most important, MI-6's Kim Philby, steadfastly denied any affiliation with the Soviets and, rather than face criminal prosecution from treason, was allowed to resign from MI-6. Other Soviet assets repeatedly penetrated UK intelligence institutions during the Cold War. But the protection of Philby, the son of a prominent professor and diplomat, by his erstwhile colleagues at MI-6 against the well-founded suspicions of MI-5 put the widespread practice of recruiting from only the "right families" in stark relief.[15] The subsequent 1963 defection of Philby; the revelation that the curator of the queen's art collection, Anthony Blunt, was one of the Cambridge Five; and the suppression of this fact from public knowledge by PM Margaret Thatcher until 1990 did little to bolster public confidence in the intelligence services. These failures also undermined cooperation between the United Kingdom and the United States, which grew understandably wary of sharing material that might be compromised by more

---

[14]Phytian, "The British Experience With Intelligence Accountability," 77.

[15]Macintyre, Andrew. *A Spy Among Friends: Kim Philby and the Great Betrayal.* New York, NY: Broadway Books, 2014.

penetrations. Later claims that the head of MI-5, Sir Roger Hollis, was a Soviet agent were probably false. But the combination of amateurish recruiting practices and weak counterintelligence left damage that lasted for decades.

More recently, the UK intelligence community was ensnared in the same analytic failures as the US intelligence community (IC) in the run-up to 2003's Iraq War. Although the United Kingdom had better source reporting than was suggested in the media,[16] JIC analysis nevertheless grotesquely exaggerated the threat posed by Iraq, which in fact had no weapons of mass destruction (WMD) program. UK PM Tony Blair also erroneously claimed the Iraqis were capable of executing a WMD strike within 45 minutes of it being ordered. Sources in the UK intelligence community later told reporters JIC assessments had been "sexed up"—made to sound more convincing than they were as part of a process of politicization by Blair and his ministers. The intelligence postmortem that followed, the **Butler Review**, found that JIC analysts were not made aware of significant weaknesses in MI-6's collection.[17] With the war already deeply unpopular with the British public, these revelations created the impression the decision to invade Iraq by Blair was not made in good faith and contributed to the limited duration of the deployment of British forces to Iraq.

Although weak oversight and repeated intelligence failures have dogged the UK intelligence community, it remains both a vital tool of state and a force to be reckoned with in world politics. The United Kingdom faces a number of threats in the 21st century requiring effective intelligence. A resurgent Russia now menaces the country's North Atlantic Treaty Organization (NATO) allies in Europe. Although the British Empire is long gone, the United Kingdom's relationship with most of the Commonwealth states, its former colonies, remains strong. British intelligence resources are deployed to Pakistan and several West African nations to aid in the struggle against radical Islamic terrorist groups that are destabilizing these states. The United Kingdom also faces a significant domestic terrorism threat from Islamic terrorist groups, which executed bombings in London in 2005, Glasgow in 2007, and Manchester in 2017 that killed dozens of people and wounded hundreds. More recent terrorist attacks have even included the driver of a van running over people on the iconic London Bridge, with a similar attack on pedestrians in front of Westminster Abbey, the home of Parliament. Finally, the United Kingdom faces a rising China, which has executed sustained intelligence campaigns against Commonwealth states Australia and New Zealand and has violated several of the provisions of the 1997 treaty that returned the British colony Hong Kong to Chinese rule.

---

[16]Davies, Philip H. J. "A Critical Look at Britain's Spy Machinery." *Studies in Intelligence* 49, no. 4 (2005). https://www.cia.gov/library/center-for-the-study-of-intelligence/csi-publications/csi-studies/studies/vol49no4/Spy_Machinery_4.htm.

[17]Report of a Committee of Privy Counsellors. *Review of Intelligence on Weapons of Mass Destruction*. London, UK: The Stationery Office, 2004. news.bbc.co.uk/nol/shared/bsp/hi/pdfs/14_07_04_butler.pdf.

# FRENCH REPUBLIC

France occupies a similar position in the international system to the United Kingdom. Much like its European neighbor, France was a Great Power for centuries. But defeat in World War II and the loss of its colonial empire in costly conflicts during the Cold War greatly reduced French power. As in the case of Great Britain and the Commonwealth countries, France does, however, maintain good relations with many of its former colonies in East Africa and Asia and will use its military to protect them. In 2014, France deployed military forces to assist Chad, Mali, Burkina Faso, Mauritania, and Niger in counterterrorism efforts in the region. Also a top-10 economy, prominent NATO member, and permanent member of the United Nations Security Council, France has unfortunately much like the United Kingdom also underfunded both its military and intelligence organizations as part of fiscal retrenchment following the end of the Cold War. But the French Republic retains some intelligence capabilities that allow it to operate globally. Recent efforts at reform and modernization are suggestive of the future French ambition to remain relevant in the emerging pattern of competition between the United States, Russia, and China.

## The Early French Intelligence Community

French espionage activities date to at least the court of King Louis XIII, during whose reign Cardinal Richelieu operated a network of spies that supported his efforts at centralizing power, thereby creating the modern French state. Numerous leaders and institutions built on the legacy of Richelieu, most notably during the early 19th century with the establishment of the **Gendarmerie Nationale**, a national police force with a military intelligence support role; creation of the national police, the Sûreté, one of the forerunners of Scotland Yard and the FBI; and the surveillance activities of Joseph Fouché, Napoleon's secret policeman. However, the emergence of a more permanent French intelligence system is best defined by the 1874 creation of the military's Second Bureau of the French General Staff (Deuxième Bureau).[18] The Deuxième Bureau possessed strong cryptographic capability and excellent HUMINT, operating agents inside the German General Staff in the late 1930s until the defeat of France in June 1940. After the conquest of France by Germany, the Deuxième Bureau continued to operate inside the puppet Vichy government in France and in its colonies.[19] Following World War II, the French military retained second departments in its individual services. But the larger Deuxième Bureau morphed into the contemporary

---

[18]The Second Bureau was subdivided into several organizations. However, for simplicity's sake not all names and iterations of French intelligence organizations are covered in this chapter.

[19]Denécé, Eric. "France: The Intelligence Services' Historical and Cultural Context." In *The Handbook of European Intelligence Cultures,* edited by Bob de Graaf and James M. Nyce. Boulder, CO: Rowman & Littlefield, 2016, 139.

**Directorate of Military Intelligence (DRM)**, which is responsible for military attachés, geospatial intelligence (GEOINT) collection, and coordinating the individual branch's intelligence output. The dramatic success enjoyed by US electronic warfare in the Gulf War prompted creation of the Intelligence and Electronic Warfare Brigade (BRGE). Finally, the Directorate for the Protection and Security of Defense (DPSD) is the military's counterintelligence organization, responsible for the protection and security of French military personnel and critical infrastructure.

## The General Directorate for External Security

Since 1946, strategic intelligence functions have been handled primarily by the **General Directorate for External Security (DGSE)**. After the founding of the Fourth Republic in the wake of the return of sovereignty at the end of World War II, the previous concentration of foreign intelligence activities in the Deuxième Bureau was overhauled. Although it operates under the umbrella of the Ministry of Armed Forces (known as the Ministry of Defense until 2017), the DGSE is a civilian intelligence organization that reports directly to the French president or PM, providing strategic intelligence and support to the French military. The DGSE is a skilled HUMINT organization. It also has considerable covert action capability in its Action Division, which it operates in close coordination with special operations forces in the French military. In addition, after GCHQ, the DGSE has the most significant SIGINT capability in Europe. During the Cold War, the DGSE focused its collection activities in Eastern Europe, where France had previously enjoyed security relationships. Hopes that these past associations could be converted into an intelligence gold mine proved false, as despite better HUMINT sourcing than other NATO countries, the DGSE consistently failed to anticipate important events, including the Soviet and client regime crackdowns in Hungary (1956), Czechoslovakia (1968), and Poland (1981). Deficiencies in strategic forecasting continue to plague the DGSE in its support of French diplomacy and military action.

## Intelligence Reform in France

The 1907 creation of what would eventually be called the **General Information Directorate (RG)** saw the emergence of an expanded domestic intelligence capability. Supervised by the national police under the Ministry of the Interior, the RG was responsible for domestic security, with its early activities emphasizing operations against anarchists, communists, and fascists opposed to the French Third Republic. As part of its dual law enforcement and counterintelligence roles, RG also went after organized crime. Another prominent, domestically focused intelligence service, the **Directorate of Territorial Surveillance (DST)**, was founded in 1946. For over 60 years until the intelligence reform of 2008, the DST was responsible for counterintelligence, counterterrorism, and border security, the latter entailing some overlap with the duties of the *Gendarmerie*. During the Algerian War for independence (1954–1962), along with the French military DST officers were deeply involved in the brutal counterinsurgency methods used in this conflict, employing torture against suspected insurgents and conducting information operations against more moderate voices calling for a peaceful settlement. More recently, the **National Directorate of Intelligence and Customs Investigations (DNRED)** and the **Intelligence Processing and Action Against Illicit Financial Networks Unit (TRACFIN)** have been established to, respectively, counter trafficking and money laundering activities.

The end of the Cold War and the emergence of new threats have resulted in significant changes to the structure of the French intelligence community. The most significant reforms were the result of a 2008 policy paper, following which the **General Directorate for Internal Security (DGSI)** was created, merging the DST and RG. In 2014, the **General Secretariat for Defense and National Security (SGDSN)** emerged, expanding interministerial powers under the French PM over the DGSE, DRM, and DPSD. Additionally, the **National Security and Defense Council (CDSN)** was established under the direction of the French president and including the PM and relevant French ministries to establish operational parameters for the intelligence community. Finally, the position of **national intelligence coordinator (CNR)** was created, answering directly to the French president.

## Oversight of the French Intelligence Community

Although management of the French intelligence community has improved in recent years, it labors under leadership and oversight issues. Although the CDSN and CNR are meant to reduce this problem, due to the constitutional structure of the Fifth Republic direction of the community has shifted abruptly from one administration to the next. France is formally a mixed presidential system—the president is head of state, while the prime minister manages the government. However, political power is concentrated in the hands of the president, who appoints the PM, determines the nature of the PM's portfolio that may or may not place the PM in the position of managing intelligence activities, and can also remove the PM once during the five year presidential term, triggering new elections in the National Assembly. Oversight has been largely nonexistent. Although there is now a standing committee in the National Assembly, its role is limited to receiving testimony and writing summary reports—it has little authority. Politicization of intelligence has also been a consistent problem. Domestic intelligence gathering has been used in French election campaigns, while a scandal involving favoritism in the promotion of younger recruits with political ties to President François Hollande over more experienced officers undermined morale at the DGSI in 2011.

## Performance of French Intelligence

The historical performance of French intelligence organizations has been mixed. One can make a case for a long record of disaster, beginning with the anti-Semitic campaign against Captain Alfred Dreyfus in 1894 drummed up by the French military to cover up military intelligence's incompetence in detecting German agents among French forces. During the Cold War, repeated Soviet penetration of the DGSE in the 1950s, paired with recent allegations that the DGSE began actively *helping the USSR against its ally the United States* in the 1970s, cast a shadow over French strategic intelligence.[20] The DGSE also presided over several disastrous covert action operations, fomenting rebellion in French Quebec and civil war in Biafra (Nigeria), the latter of which cost approximately 500,000 lives and still simmers today. The 1985 bombing of Greenpeace's *Rainbow Warrior*, bugging operations against foreign businessmen on transatlantic Air France flights during the 1990s, and the ease by which both were linked to the DGSE suggest long-standing deficiencies in covert operations capabilities, as well as questionable political judgment regarding the obvious blowback risks involved with such operations promising marginal returns. However, the record of French intelligence disasters may be overexaggerated. Prewar French intelligence efforts against Nazi Germany were superior to their British rivals, and the Deuxième Bureau should not be blamed for the subsequent defeat in 1940.[21] More recently, in 2012 the DGSE detected the US National Security Agency's (NSA) efforts to penetrate the Élysée Palace to spy on the French president, a considerable technical achievement. Nevertheless, ongoing structural weaknesses remain with regard to analysis in general, technical collection, operational redundancies in domestic security, and an overly complex system of management.

With regard to international interests, France has long guarded its freedom of action, withdrawing from NATO in 1966 after objecting to a joint command structure that privileged the largest contributor to the alliance, the United States. Although France finally returned to NATO as a full member in 2009, French nuclear doctrine is still not coordinated with the alliance. Noting the relatively weak quality of the intelligence regarding WMDs in Iraq, France also refused to participate in the invasion in 2003, a decision vindicated by subsequent events. However, France has frequently deployed forces to counterterrorism and stabilization operations, including several thousand troops as part of the NATO mission to Afghanistan from 2001 to 2012. France faces one of the severest domestic threats from radical Islamic terrorism in the developed world, with a tragic record of dozens of attacks and hundreds of fatalities over the last several decades. From 2015 to 2018, France was in a continuous state of emergency, with its security resources fully deployed. Whether the recent decline in incidence of terror attacks is due to this increased operational tempo, organizational reforms in intelligence, or simply the destruction of the Islamic State's territorial base of operations in Syria is unclear. As

---

[20]Poirier, Dominique. *Napoleon's Spies: Revelations From a Spy Who Came in From France*. CreateSpace, 2018.

[21]Schuker, Stephen A. "Seeking a Scapegoat: Intelligence and Grand Strategy in France, 1919–1940." In *Secret Intelligence in the European State System, 1918–1989*, edited by Jonathan Haslam and Katrina Urbach. Palo Alto, CA: Stanford University Press, 2014.

a member of NATO, France faces a resurgent Russia, including cyber attacks on the 2017 presidential elections that, while ineffective due to the news blackout required by French law just prior to voting, still point to the long-term threat posed by the Kremlin. Unlike some NATO members, France has been reluctant to ban Chinese telecom giant Huawei from developing fifth-generation (5G) networks, despite the company's close association with the communist government and the resulting security risk. Finally, France has sought increased SIGINT cooperation with Germany, which may be viewed as part of a wider French plan to foster ever-greater political integration in the European Union. Broader security and intelligence cooperation with fellow NATO members the United Kingdom and the United States is hampered by Brexit and the policies and behavior of President Trump, whose approval rating hovers around 10 percent in France.

## FEDERAL REPUBLIC OF GERMANY

In sharp contrast with fellow NATO allies Great Britain and France, Germany has an ambivalent relationship with intelligence activities. Since the creation of the first unified German nation-state in 1871, Germany participated in World War I as a member of the Central Powers and, under the leadership of the Nazis, launched the most destructive war in human history, World War II. The legacy of Nazi tyranny, the resultant horrors of the Holocaust, and the unprecedented level of surveillance conducted during the communist German Democratic Republic's (DDR) existence have caused Germany to greatly de-emphasize the role of intelligence in politics. An economic power since the 19th century, Germany's gross domestic product (GDP) is the fourth largest in the world and remains the driving force of the European economy. Since the end of the Cold War, however, Germany has cut its defense budget to levels that have resulted in massive personnel and equipment shortfalls. Although German troops were deployed in support of the NATO mission to Afghanistan, lack of political will severely curtailed participation of these troops in combat operations.[22] At home, revelation of US surveillance of long-serving chancellor Angela Merkel and the cooperation of some German intelligence organizations with the NSA have undermined efforts to enhance transatlantic intelligence cooperation against Islamic terrorism. Similarly, Germany has been reluctant to openly confront Russian aggression against NATO due to its long-standing natural gas agreements with the Russians. Yet much like France, Germany faces a variety of domestic, regional, and international threats that necessitate effective intelligence operations.

---

[22]Rid, Thomas, and Martin Zapfe. "Mission Command Without a Mission: German Military Adaptation in Afghanistan." In *Military Adaptation and the War in Afghanistan*, edited by Theo Farrell, Frans Osinga, and James Russell. Palo Alto, CA: Stanford University Press, 2013.

## The Federal Intelligence Service (BND)

Following its defeat in World War II, Germany was split in two, with the Federal Republic (West Germany) part of NATO and the DDR (East Germany) as a member of the Warsaw Pact in the communist bloc. The lead strategic intelligence organization of both West Germany and the post-1990 reunified Germany is the **Federal Intelligence Service (BND)**. During the final days of the Nazi regime, the former head of the German Army's Foreign Armies East intelligence organization, Reinhard Gehlen, hid a vast trove of files and retained his network of contacts in Eastern Europe. Gehlen parlayed these files and his agents into monetary and logistical support from the United States, which he used to build the infrastructure of what eventually became the BND in 1956. Unfortunately, all of his foreign assets had been detected and turned by the Soviets, a problem compounded by Gehlen's willingness to hire former Nazis, some of whom had already been co-opted. The BND was fundamentally handicapped by the compromise of its networks, Gehlen's poor leadership, and several moles in its headquarters, including the head of Soviet counterintelligence, Heinz Felfe. Gehlen was forced into retirement in 1968, and the BND began the slow process of becoming a professional intelligence organization worthy of the name.

The modern BND is far more effective, albeit limited by the political environment in which it operates. Reporting directly to the office of the chancellor, the Chancellery (*Kanzlei*), on paper the BND appears to be ideally placed to influence policy. But due to the history of Nazi and communist oppression in Germany, intelligence plays little role in either foreign or domestic policy decisions. Nonetheless, the BND has officers in all German embassies, operating "residences" in much the same manner as the US Central Intelligence Agency's (CIA) overseas operations. The BND has excellent SIGINT capability and is part of the SSEUR agreement. The BND also conducts briefings on strategic intelligence for periodic meetings of government principals, a structure similar to the US National Security Council.

# BOX 4.1

## FOR EXAMPLE: BND HEADQUARTERS

Spy agencies have sought to construct increasingly sophisticated buildings in which to conduct their operations. Germany's BND is no exception. Its sprawling headquarters building in the heart of Berlin is a far cry from the comparatively modest complex it used for five decades in Pullach, a sleepy suburb of Munich. The new BND building has several steel "palm trees" scattered at various points, as well as a massive sculpture in its courtyard, both of which are meant to somehow humanize the imposing concrete, steel, and glass structure. After 12 years of construction and more than $1.2 billion, the building opened to its approximately 4,000 occupants in early 2019.[24]

Apart from serving as bureaucratic centers and showcases for advanced architecture, spy headquarters often have symbolic roles, with their design echoing larger political principles. The new BND building has 14,000 windows, a move reminiscent of the reconstructed dome of the *Reichstag*, the home of Germany's

**PHOTO 4.2** BND Headquarters, Berlin, Germany.[23]

Olaf Kosinsky/CC BY-SA 3.0 DE (https://creativecommons.org/licenses/by-sa/3.0/de/deed.en)/Wikimedia Commons

parliament, which has mirrors in it that allow any viewer to look down directly at the activities of the *Bundestag*. Both buildings emphasize glass in their construction, symbolizing transparency in postwar German government—never again will its security services be allowed to abuse human rights or assist in compromising democracy. Yet advanced technology invariably accompanies such symbolism, as the windows are designed to inhibit laser microphones or other sophisticated listening devices.

The new BND headquarters is impressive. But it is not without its problems. Delivered five years late and 42 percent over budget, the building had to be completely redesigned after its original blueprints were stolen.[25] In a 2015 incident the German press humorously dubbed "Watergate," unauthorized intruders snuck into the construction site and vandalized toilets, causing significant flooding and construction delays.[26] Germany's Watergate illustrates the enormous challenges involved in building a secure facility, which has been a consistent problem that has bedeviled spy agencies in the past. During the Cold War, the US embassy in Moscow was purpose-built by the US government at great expense. Yet before it was occupied, the KGB had found a way to plant listening devices in its very walls by secreting the devices in the concrete as it was poured. The US government rejected the building, and it wasn't used for more than a decade. Finally, US intelligence agencies found a way to defeat the Soviet-era surveillance technology in a move code-named "Operation TOP HAT"—they sliced off two floors from the top of the building and replaced them with new ones.[27]

[23]Kosinsky, Olaf. "BND Headquarters in Berlin." Created August 30, 2019. https://en.wikipedia.org/wiki/Headquarters_of_the_Federal_Intelligence_Service#/media/File:2019-08-30_BND_Zentrale_Berlin_OK_0318.jpg.

[24]Schultheis, Emily. "World's Biggest Intelligence Headquarters Opens in Berlin." *The Guardian*, February 8, 2019. https://www.theguardian.com/world/2019/feb/08/worlds-biggest-intelligence-headquarters-opens-berlin-germany-bnd.

[25]Scally, Derek. "Mockery Greets Berlin's 'Megalomaniacal' New Spy HQ." *The Irish Times*, February 8, 2019. https://www.irishtimes.com/news/world/europe/mockery-greets-berlin-s-megalomaniacal-new-spy-hq-1.3787280.

[26]Schultheis, "World's Biggest Intelligence Headquarters Opens in Berlin."

[27]Stanley, Alessandra. "In Moscow, US Hushes Walls That Have Ears." *The New York Times*, May 4, 1997. https://www.nytimes.com/1997/05/04/world/in-moscow-us-hushes-walls-that-have-ears.html.

Although the BND has historically provided strategic intelligence for the German military (*Bundeswehr*), several intelligence organizations are under the command of the Federal Ministry of Defense. The **Strategic Surveillance Command (KSA)** of the *Bundeswehr* collects SIGINT, with particular attention to electronic warfare, and GEOINT. The KSA is also Germany's primary cyber organization. Counterintelligence for the military is provided by the **Military Counterintelligence Service (MAD)**. All German military intelligence organizations are directed by the Federal Ministry of Defense.

Under the authority of the Federal Ministry of the Interior, the lead domestic intelligence agency for Germany is the **Federal Office for the Protection of the Constitution (BfV)**. As its name suggests, Germany takes the delicate balancing act of protection of civil liberties and intelligence very seriously. BfV is primarily a HUMINT collector, with responsibilities including counterintelligence and counterterrorism. In contrast with the unitary political systems of the United Kingdom and France, Germany is a federal system, with similar domestic intelligence organizations at the level of the 16 *Länder* (lands/states). Dubbed State Offices for the Protection of the Constitution (LfV), these state-level organizations function in a manner analogous to state- and local-level law enforcement and intelligence agencies in the United States, such as the New York Police Department's intelligence branch or the Kansas Bureau of Investigation. Two additional domestic intelligence and security organizations operate within the German intelligence system, both of which are also part of the Ministry of the Interior and handle various aspects of cybersecurity. The **Federal Office for Information Security (BSI)** deals with cybersecurity at the federal level, while the **Central Office for Information Technology in the Security Sphere (ZITiS)** handles cryptanalysis and digital support needs for law enforcement and domestic security organizations. As has been the case with the United States' federal system, coordinating the activities of these various federal- and state-level agencies has not been easy.[28]

## Oversight and Performance of German Intelligence

Oversight of German intelligence organizations has also become more difficult as the number of agencies has grown and the missions they address have become more complex. The BND is under the direct supervision of the *Kanzlei*, while the 16 LfVs are directed by the states, a division of power that is a direct result of the federal system. Since 2009, the German parliament (*Bundestag*) has had more effective oversight over federal-level agencies, specifically delineating their roles and powers. This enhanced supervision is a significant improvement over the limitations imposed on intelligence agencies due to the aforementioned history of intelligence in the country. However, additional work remains to be done in this area.

---

[28]Krieger, Wolfgang. "Germany." In *The Handbook of European Intelligence Cultures*, edited by Bob de Graaf and James M. Nyce, 155–156. Boulder, CO: Rowman & Littlefield, 2016.

Germany has had trouble balancing the demands of its political culture and legal structure with the requirements of intelligence and counterterrorism missions. The BfV experienced significant difficulties during the Cold War dealing with the complexity of domestic terrorism and intelligence threats. The massacre of Israeli athletes by the Palestinian Black September terrorist group in 1972 was a black eye for the organization. Subsequent attacks during the 1970s by the Baader–Meinhof Group or the Red Army Faction, among others, included aircraft hijackings, bombings, and assassination of the West German attorney general. Germany's intelligence services also failed to detect the activities of the Hamburg cell of al-Qaeda, which launched the 9/11 terrorist attacks. Given this tragic history, by now Germany should be familiar with combating terrorism. However, both the BfV and the MAD have come under significant criticism recently in the *Bundestag* for failing to detect neo-Nazi infiltrators in the ranks of both domestic security agencies and the *Bundeswehr*. Several low-impact attacks by Muslim terrorists in the wake of the admission into Germany of nearly 1 million refugees by Chancellor Merkel have gotten much more attention in the press. However, as in the United States the data suggest Germany's homegrown far right poses a much greater threat than Islamic radicals among its recent immigrants. Regardless, the dangers posed by both suggest Germany still has a long way to go in improving domestic surveillance.

While the country faces the same threat from a newly assertive Russia as the rest of NATO, German efforts against Russia have been tepid. Until recently, the *Bundesrepublik* had a limited intelligence-sharing agreement with the Russians, directed primarily at reducing the activities of Russian organized crime in Western Europe. Moreover, Germany is the largest purchaser of natural gas from Russia, carried to it via a growing system of pipelines across Eastern Europe and under the Baltic. Both Merkel and her predecessor, Gerhard Schröder, who inexplicably sits on the board of Gazprom, the Russian natural gas conglomerate, have been loath to disrupt this relationship. German willingness to ignore legitimate security concerns regarding Huawei's plans to build its 5G network in Europe is similarly alarming. Finally, since the end of the Cold War, Germany has consistently underfunded both its military and its intelligence services. Budget cuts grew so pronounced under Merkel that Germany cannot send its small submarine fleet to sea, conduct logistical support for its forces overseas, or operate a division-sized tank force.

## ISRAEL

Intelligence agencies enjoy a level of respect and deference in Israel unparalleled among democracies in the developed world. Possessing a modern, technologically sophisticated economy, Israel is a leader in information technology and one of the world's largest arms exporters. Almost from the establishment of the state in 1948, Israeli intelligence organizations have been aggressive, conducting covert operations to reduce the incessant border attacks sponsored by neighboring Arab states. The conviction that the country must destroy its adversaries before they overcome it is arguably hardwired into Israel's intelligence community.[29] Despite the battlefield dominance of the **Israel Defense Forces (IDF)** over the course of four wars from 1948 to 1973, the widely acknowledged superiority of its intelligence services, and the ready willingness to use both, Israel has achieved neither victory nor peace. Israelis continue to live under the constant threat of attack by the Palestinian terrorist group Hamas, operating out of the Gaza Strip, and Hezbollah, the Iranian-sponsored Shiite terrorist group based in Lebanon. Although Israel has concluded peace agreements with Egypt and Jordan, the collapse of the 1993 Oslo Accords and several failed efforts sponsored by Presidents Bill Clinton and George W. Bush have all but ended hope for peace between Israel and the Palestinians.

The creation of the state of Israel was largely due to the effectiveness of several Jewish terrorist groups that drove out the colonial British administration.[30] Some of the members of two of these terror groups, Lehi and Irgun, along with the Jewish militia, the Haganah, were later folded into Israel's early intelligence organizations. Much like their counterparts in France, these agencies would undergo a number of different configurations and name changes. However, the general architecture of the Israeli intelligence system includes military intelligence organizations, domestic security agencies, and foreign intelligence and analytic support groups that provide strategic political and military intelligence. One of the key distinguishing features of the Israeli community is the high level of coordination between these agencies relative to other intelligence systems in the world. In Israel, military–civilian and domestic–international organizations and processes are closely integrated.

## Mossad and Partner Organizations

The most prominent of these organizations is **Mossad**, which serves as Israel's principal foreign intelligence agency. Mossad has world-class collection capabilities in almost all areas of intelligence. It also operates two very effective covert action groups, Kidon and Metsada. While both have participated in targeted assassination programs, Kidon is the better known of the two, as its officers probably ran Operation WRATH OF GOD, Israel's assassination campaign against the Black September terrorists and their supporters responsible for the murder of Israeli athletes at the 1972 Summer Olympics in Munich. Although primarily focused on the Middle East, Mossad has conducted operations in all corners of the globe, from the prominent capture of Nazi war criminal Adolf Eichmann in Argentina to contemporary coordination with its

---

[29]See Bergman, Ronen. *Rise and Kill First: The Secret History of Israel's Targeted Assassinations*. New York, NY: Random House, 2018.

[30]Pedahzur, Ami, and Arie Perliger. *Jewish Terrorism in Israel*. Cambridge, UK: Cambridge University Press, 2009.

former enemy, Pakistan's Inter-Services Intelligence, against Islamic militants. Mossad also operates a financial intelligence unit tasked with combating money laundering, as well as an extensive technology research department with much the same capability as its counterpart at the CIA. Like the BND and the German Chancellery, Mossad's director reports to the PM, not a cabinet ministry.

Strategic intelligence is also provided by other civilian and military organizations. The Foreign Ministry operates the **Center for Political Research (CPR)**, which provides the PM with assessments of global and regional political events and decision support. Although it does collect some intelligence, its operational capabilities are much lower than Israel's other agencies. The **Directorate of Military Intelligence (AMAN)** is the IDF's intelligence agency. AMAN is an all-source collector that also conducts analysis. AMAN's cryptology section (Unit 8200) is comparable in capability to the US NSA and the UK GCHQ. Although both the French and British systems pride themselves on close coordination with special operations forces (SOF), AMAN takes this a step further, with both the land- and sea-based SOF units under its command. AMAN also manages the Israeli military attaché program (Unit 504).

The Israel Security Agency, more commonly referred to as **Shin Bet**, is the system's lead counterintelligence agency. As is the case with both Mossad and AMAN, Shin Bet's operations exhibit close cooperation between agencies. In addition to its counterintelligence and domestic security duties, Shin Bet has provided targeting intelligence for both IDF and Mossad assassination programs. This cooperation from an ostensibly domestic security agency again demonstrates that while other countries pay lip service to breaking down the foreign–domestic intelligence distinction in a globalized world, Israel puts this concept into practice. Like Mossad, Shin Bet reports directly to the PM.

## Israeli Intelligence Oversight and Performance

Although formally a mixed presidential system, much like Germany and in contrast with France, the position of president in the Israeli system is largely symbolic. Real power resides with the PM. Israel is also a unitary system, with no distinction between local, regional, and national security organizations and activities. Thus the intelligence branch of the Israeli police, the counterterrorism group Yamam, and its border security forces all readily coordinate with Shin Bet and the rest of the intelligence community, making homeland security operations much easier than in federal systems. Oversight in the Israeli system is accomplished via three mechanisms. First, the PM supervises the performance of the individual agencies, through both their ministers and the Committee of the Heads of Service, which is chaired by the head of Mossad. Second, the Israeli parliament (*Knesset*) exercises some oversight through the Subcommittee for Intelligence, Secret Services, Captives, and Missing Soldiers supervision that as with the British system is largely limited to what the PM will permit. Finally, Israel has appointed different independent commissions to evaluate the performance of its intelligence agencies. The Landau Commission had a more significant impact than the leadership of the PM or the *Knesset*. The commission drew attention to the torture of Palestinian prisoners by Shin Bet, which is now required to obey the Israeli constitution and not engage in such activity. Whether or not this is in fact the practice on the ground is unclear, as the government of PM Benjamin Netanyahu has shown little interest in following the prohibitions of the constitution.

Israel has repeatedly penetrated hostile governments and intelligence services, assassinated enemy bomb makers and scientists, and collected technical intelligence in friendly countries, including operations against the United States that greatly aided Israel's nuclear weapons program.[31] Its intelligence operations have been both varied and, mostly, successful. But the very success of these activities has also antagonized other states, and not just regional competitors. Israel's use of one of its American agents, US naval intelligence civilian Jonathan Pollard, to obtain extremely sensitive material on surveillance and communication programs has been a problem for US–Israeli diplomacy over the course of five presidential administrations. Similarly, Israel's willingness to conduct assassinations in neutral or friendly countries soured relations with much of Western Europe during Operation WRATH OF GOD, while the more recent killing of a Hamas leader in Dubai in 2011 has had much the same impact. There has also been controversy over the foreign sale of Israeli intelligence information technology and contracting services, including to clients in Mexico to spy on opponents of the sale of sugary drinks contributing to the obesity epidemic in that country. Several of the targets of these efforts have gone missing after their phones were hacked by Black Cube. A case can also be made that the willingness of Israel's intelligence and security services to use force against Palestinian and Arab targets greatly contributed to the outbreak of the First and Second Intifadas (1987 and 2000), the suppression of which increased the militarization of Israeli politics and further reinforced the cycle of violence. Alternatively, the willingness of Israel's Arab opponents to target civilians as a first resort since 1948 leaves Israeli intelligence agencies with little choice but to kill terrorists and their supporters before they attack. Yet the inability of Israeli intelligence services to create the conditions for peace via "'arranging meetings with God'"[32] is a tragic reminder that intelligence cannot make up for policy failures.

Additional challenges remain. As with some notable operational shortcomings, the analytic capabilities of the Israeli intelligence community have occasionally come into question. In 1973, Israel was nearly destroyed by a synchronized attack from the Egyptian Army across the Suez Canal and the Syrian Army in the Golan Heights. Failure to detect the preparations for this attack or to accurately predict the Arab states' intentions has been frequently cited as an intelligence failure. Although more recent scholarship has noted intelligence analysts accurately predicted the invasion, predictions

---

[31]Thomas, Gordon. *Gideon's Spies: The Secret History of the Mossad.* New York, NY: St. Martin's Press, 2009, 87–104.

[32]Bergman, *Rise and Kill First*, 39.

that were neither believed by the senior leadership of AMAN nor reported to Israeli policymakers,[33] the Israeli intelligence system failed. Similarly, Shin Bet performed poorly both in its interpretation of the intentions of Israel's far right and in the resultant lax protective measures for PM Yitzhak Rabin, who was assassinated in 1995 by a radical Jewish settler opposed to peace with the Palestinians. Finally, close coordination between Israel's intelligence agencies has served the country well. But it also points to redundancy across intelligence agencies, which operate in each other's regions and technical areas of responsibility, thereby wasting resources.

## RUSSIAN FEDERATION

Almost since the inception of modern Russia, espionage, surveillance, covert action, and propaganda have been defining features of the Russian state. Following the assassination of Alexander II in 1881, the czarist empire relied on its secret police, the Okhrana, to monitor dissidents, infiltrate political groups, and murder or imprison its domestic opponents. With the rise of the Soviet Union after the Russian Revolution of 1917, a massive apparatus of secret police and prisons was established, with domestic and international intelligence organizations that enforced the will of the Communist Party at home and fomented revolution abroad. These intelligence agencies, or **organs** as the Soviets referred to them, formed the core of the communist state, existing to protect the Communist Party's monopoly on power and to enforce the political ideals of Marxism–Leninism. Following the collapse of the USSR in 1991, the Russian Federation retained much of its intelligence capability during its brief flirtation with democracy under Boris Yeltsin. Yet the rise of Vladimir Putin in 1999 saw Russia return to authoritarian rule and a resurgence of both domestic and foreign intelligence operations. With a moribund economy, low technological innovation, and a shrinking population, Russia faces a grim future of declining global status. Nevertheless, from his earliest days in office ex-KGB lieutenant colonel Putin has attempted to reverse the downward slope of Russian power, stating openly that the collapse of the USSR was a mistake and Russia should attempt to reincorporate the 14 countries that achieved independence in 1991. Although it is a shadow of the former USSR in terms of its economic and military power, the Russian Federation devotes a disproportionate amount of resources toward its security and intelligence organizations. As was the case with the USSR, this spending is meant to protect the Putin regime and further Russian territorial ambitions. With the suppression of political opposition, corrupt enrichment of himself and his oligarch cronies, and the invasion of Georgia in 2008 and Ukraine in 2014, Putin has made Russia an international pariah, resulting in a punishing

---

[33]See Bar-Joseph, Uri. "Intelligence Failure and the Need for Cognitive Closure: The Case of the Yom Kippur War." In *Paradoxes of Strategic Intelligence*, edited by Richard K. Betts and Thomas G. Mahnken. London, UK: Frank Cass, 2003.

sanctions regime that has hobbled the already-weak Russian economy. Recent information operations and elections meddling have sown chaos in the democracies of the West and undermined the confidence of citizens in their institutions.

Analyzing the Soviet and Russian intelligence systems has been a challenge. A classic "denied area," restrictions on the free movement of foreigners make both scholarly study and intelligence operations difficult. The constant flow of disinformation and propaganda by both regimes ensures that no information coming from government sources or their proxies in the private sector can be trusted. Finally, limited resources for language training at US universities make Russia a hard target to analyze. Western intelligence agencies had such difficulty in penetrating the Soviet system that at the height of the Cold War analysts were reduced to assessing the relative influence of political figures in the Politburo by measuring their physical proximity to the Soviet premier on the podium during the annual May Day parade in Moscow's Red Square.

## The KGB and Partner Organizations

During the Cold War, the Soviet Union's primary intelligence organ was the **KGB**, the "Committee for State Security," which was an all-source agency combining both vast domestic surveillance and counterintelligence capabilities with extensive technical collection and HUMINT activities abroad. Following the collapse of the USSR, the KGB splintered into two agencies, nominally divided along foreign and domestic missions in much the same manner as the US and UK systems. The **Foreign Intelligence Service (SVR)** is the direct descendant of the KGB's First Chief Directorate, responsible for intelligence operations outside of Russia's borders. The SVR employs all-source collection combined with analysis, espionage, and covert action capabilities. The second agency rising out of the ashes of the KGB is the **Federal Security Service (FSB)**, the principal mission of which is counterintelligence and domestic security and counterterrorism. The FSB is massive, employing approximately 70,000 officers and 100,000 border guards, and also engages in some law enforcement activities, including counternarcotics operations and efforts against Russian organized crime. However, the apparently neat division of the organs into international and domestic missions is belied by the involvement of the FSB in Russian efforts to undermine the 2016 US presidential election. There are two reasons for this blurring of the lines between domestic and international missions. First, the FSB is also responsible for supervision of the Russian SIGINT service, the **Federal Agency for Government Communications and Information (FAPSI)**. As the Russian efforts against the United States occurred primarily as cyber and information operations, FAPSI was integral to these actions. Second, the FSB's primary mission is suppressing dissent and undermining the exercise of political activities against President Putin. As it has all but eliminated organized political opposition to Putin at home and regularly secures the sham elections of the Russian Federation, it has expertise that could be readily applied toward undermining democracy in the West.

The SVR and FSB are supported by several comparatively lesser players in the Russian intelligence system. The Federal Customs Service (FTS) provides technical counterintelligence against foreign intelligence services and is also a direct descendant of a KGB suborganization. The FTS enjoys good relations with several successor intelligence agencies in the former republics of the Soviet Union. The Federal Protective Service (FSO) and the President's Main Directorate of Special Programs (GUSP) are also organizations derived from former KGB sections. The FSO and GUSP are responsible for the security of Russian military bases and the personal protection of key politicians, including Putin himself at his offices in the Kremlin.[34]

There is a great deal of continuity between military intelligence in the USSR and the Russian Federation. Russian military intelligence, the **Main Intelligence Directorate (GRU)**, is unique in the Russian system as it is the only organization that did not have to change its name or mission following the demise of the Soviet regime. The GRU is part of the Russian Army's General Staff, providing both battlefield intelligence to the Russian armed forces and strategic intelligence services as well. As with the SVR and FAPSI, the GRU has powerful SIGINT capabilities, and as with the FSB, these capabilities were deployed against the United States in 2016. Sections of two GRU units, 26165 and 74455, were organized into **Fancy Bear**, a unit dedicated to cyber operations against the US presidential campaign in 2016. GRU efforts were

**PHOTO 4.3** Internet Research Agency, St. Petersburg, Russia.[35]

---

[34]Pringle, Robert W. "The Intelligence Services of Russia." In *The Oxford Handbook of National Security Intelligence*, edited by Loch K. Johnston, 784. Oxford, UK: Oxford University Press, 2010.

[35]Maynes, Charles. "Inside the Internet Research Agency: A Mole Among Trolls." *Voice of America*, April 17, 2018. https://www.voanews.com/a/inside-the-internet-research-agency-a-mole-among-trolls/4352107.html.

further augmented by the so-called **Internet Research Agency**, a troll farm with thinly concealed connections to Russian intelligence activities.

Both 26165 and 74455 have also been linked to cyber activities undermining international investigations regarding blood doping by Russian athletes and the shooting down of a Malaysian Airlines jetliner over Ukraine in 2014 by insurgents linked to the Russian government.[36] GRU units were previously tied to cyber operations in Estonia in 2007 and against the government of Georgia during the Russian invasion of that country in the summer of 2008.

## Oversight and Performance of Russian Intelligence

Although on paper Russia is a mixed system with the president as head of state and a PM as head of government, in practice this terminology is meaningless. Since his appointment as PM by President Yeltsin in 1999, Putin has worked to eliminate organized political opposition to his regime. Although the Russian parliament, the Duma, has five political parties represented, all of them support Putin, ensuring no legislative opposition to his rule. Consequently, there is no system of intelligence oversight in the Russian Federation. Just as they did during the USSR, Russia's organs exist to protect the power of the head of state.

Current operations of the Russian organs are widespread, spanning domestic threats from Islamic separatists in Chechnya to international covert action in Syria. SVR headquarters nearly doubled in size between 2007 and 2016, with a corresponding increase in personnel likely. During the Cold War, the KGB operated an espionage training facility called "Little Kansas" to train its **illegals**, what it called its officers who would pass as foreign nationals and infiltrate key institutions. The illegals program placed KGB officers in a position to influence the political and economic decisions of several US allies.[37] Although not all Russian illegals are trained in such a manner today, the placement of sleeper agents has continued. In 2010, Anna Chapman and nine other Russian illegals were rounded up by the FBI. The daughter of a former KGB officer, Chapman was tasked with infiltrating US financial institutions with an eye toward finding a way to engineer a financial crisis. Through connections she made via her marriage to her British husband, she gained employment at the prestigious Barclays investment bank before forming her own consulting firm, based a stone's throw away from Wall Street. Several of her fellow SVR officers caught in 2010 were able to gain employment at universities, a US think tank, and a telecommunications firm. Although the 2010 ring of illegals was almost completely ineffective and its tradecraft shoddy, the breadth of the operation was surprising. More recently, Maria Butina infiltrated several

---

[36]Oliphant, Roland. "What Is Unit 26165, Russia's Elite Hacking Centre?" *The Telegraph*, October 4, 2018. https://www.telegraph.co.uk/news/2018/10/04/unit26165-russias-elite-military-hacking-centre/.

[37]Andrew, Christopher, and Vasili Mitrokhin. *The Sword and the Shield: The Mitrokhin Archive and the Secret History of the KGB*. New York, NY: Basic Books, 1999.

conservative groups in the United States, including the National Rifle Association. She was subsequently able to gain access to several US Republican politicians associated with these groups. Although Butina was never charged with espionage, her activities bore some of the hallmarks of Russian HUMINT operations.

The Russian intelligence community has also recently engaged in covert operations using private sector corporations. These companies serve as fronts to conceal their direction by Russian intelligence officers, thereby maintaining plausible deniability. During the 2014 seizure of Crimea, Russia deployed what the international press soon dubbed "Little Green Men," Russian special forces (*Spetsnaz*) and intelligence officers in military uniforms without identifying insignia. The Little Green Men posed as local "militia" supporting the "return to the Motherland," ostensibly enjoying wide support among the Ukrainian population. In fact, they seized key government installations and communication centers, making organized opposition by the Ukrainian government impossible. Russia has similarly employed private military contractors, the personnel of which are a mix of former Russian military and current soldiers and intelligence officers. To support the Assad regime in Syria, its last ally in the Middle East, Russia has deployed the Wagner Group, a shadowy paramilitary organization. However, such front organizations are not limited to military contractors. The English-language news service **RT (formerly Russia Today)** is in fact a front for Russian intelligence agencies' agitation and propaganda (AGITPROP) operations. This affiliation is barely denied by RT, with its editor-in-chief once proclaiming she was "'waging the information war against the entire Western world.'"[38]

Although the murder campaign and mass incarceration of the Soviet gulag system is long over, the Russian intelligence community has also regularly engaged in extrajudicial killings domestically and in an assassination campaign against its critics abroad. A partial list of the documented killings by Russian intelligence officers produces an appalling range of crimes perpetrated in Russia and abroad. Pro-Western Ukrainian politician Viktor Yushchenko was horribly disfigured after being poisoned by Russian intelligence. In one of the most brazen examples of Russian ruthlessness, former SVR officer and Putin critic **Alexander Litvinenko** was murdered in 2006 in the United Kingdom by poisoning via polonium, a radioactive substance likely administered by the SVR in his tea. Investigators into the Litvinenko killing fared little better, with a former US Senate staff member mysteriously shot in 2007 and a researcher into polonium poisonings committing suicide in 2015. In 2012, the Russian banker turned whistleblower Alexander Perepilichny was murdered after helping Swiss authorities with a money laundering investigation into people tied to Putin. Former deputy PM and Putin critic Boris Nemtsov was mysteriously murdered in Moscow in 2015. In 2018, former GRU officer and Western agent Sergei Skripal and his daughter nearly

---

[38]Nimmo, B. "Question That: RT's Military Mission." Atlantic Council, Digital Forensics Lab, January 8, 2018. https://medium.com/dfrlab/question-that-rts-military-mission-4c4bd9f72c88.

died after being poisoned by a rare nerve agent. In 2019, a witness to former Italian PM Silvio Berlusconi's sexual encounter with an underage prostitute was murdered. Berlusconi had reversed decades of Italian wariness of ties with Russia in favor of a provocatively pro-Putin stance.

## The Future of Russian Intelligence

Given its reliance on oil and arms exports and a complete inability to compete in the modern global economy, Russia faces a deeply uncertain future. While on the surface Putin seems to have reinvigorated the Russian state and its organs, the long-term consequences of his aggressive foreign policy and the use of the intelligence services to achieve it may hasten, not postpone, Russia's decline. Employing disinformation and cyber hacking in the Brexit vote in the United Kingdom and in elections in France, Germany, and the United States may harden, not soften, attitudes in these countries toward the Russians. Putin's probable attempt to co-opt Trump and key figures in the American conservative movement may have produced a president who is far friendlier toward the dictator than the previous three US chief executives. But it is likely to be a temporary victory and revealed the Russian playbook to Western intelligence agencies. It has not broken the sanctions regime or addressed any of the problems facing Russia, almost all of which are internal. During the Cold War, the KGB consistently generated intelligence coups. It repeatedly penetrated the highest echelons of the US IC through agents like Aldrich Ames and Robert Hanssen, senior counterintelligence officers in the CIA and FBI. Although these assets allowed Russia to roll up US spy rings and dramatically impeded US HUMINT activities, it did not prevent the collapse of the USSR or meaningfully increase the successor Russian regime's relative power. It is worth considering whether the effectiveness of information and cyber operations and the ruthless assassination of Putin's critics are similarly papering over the fundamental weaknesses of Russia.

## PEOPLE'S REPUBLIC OF CHINA

With the world's second-largest economy, a population of 1.4 billion people, and a rapidly modernizing military, the People's Republic of China (PRC) is perhaps the only current world power with the potential to rival the United States. The PRC is an authoritarian state, with the **Communist Party of China (CPC)** deploying its vast intelligence apparatus to advancing China's interests abroad with aggressive espionage efforts against the West, as well as monitoring the Chinese public for any signs of dissent against the regime. China has the most extensive and intrusive system of domestic surveillance in the world, devoted to preventing the creation of any civic organizations independent from the CPC and suppressing the rights of ethnic and religious minorities, such as the Muslim Uighurs and the people of Tibet.

Since reducing some of the communist state's role in the economy in the 1980s, China has become the center of much of the world's foreign direct investment, with US, European, and East Asian companies relocating much of their manufacturing base to China in search of cheap labor. Over the course of a generation, China moved almost 300 million people into the middle class, an astonishing feat without historical precedent. In addition to this massive growth in national wealth, as China's economy has matured in recent years it has also employed its large industrial base to modernize the PRC's armed forces. Much of this modernization effort has been abetted by long-term industrial espionage against US and European defense companies.[39]

Although Chinese officials frequently reference international norms and treaties and vacillate between accommodation and aggression as diplomatic strategies, the primary focus of the CPC is regime survival—all other considerations are secondary. Cooperation with foreign countries and firms serves the purpose of increasing the state's power, not the furtherance of modern free market capitalism, which was the world's clear expectation of China when it acceded to the World Trade Organization in 2001. The PRC is a permanent member of the United Nations Security Council and frequently uses this position to block any efforts to promote democracy and human rights or to increase multilateralism at the expense of Chinese sovereignty. China also routinely ignores the sovereign borders of other countries bordering the South China

MSgt John Nimmo Sr./Public domain/ Wikipedia Commons

Danny Yu/CC BY-SA (https://crea- tivecommons.org/licenses/by-sa/4.0)/ Wikimedia Commons

**PHOTO 4.4** Chinese industrial espionage: Can you identify which one is the US F-35[40] and which one is the Chinese J-31?[41]

---

[39]Lindsay, Jon R., and Tai Min Cheung. "From Exploitation to Innovation: Acquisition, Absorption, and Application." In *China and Cybersecurity: Espionage, Strategy, and Politics in the Digital Domain*, edited by Jon R. Lindsay, Tai Min Cheung, and Derek S. Reveron. Oxford, UK: Oxford University Press, 2015.

[40]Nimmo, John, Sr. "F-35A Moving Into Position to Refuel." Created May 16, 2013. https://en.wikipedia .org/wiki/Lockheed_Martin_F-35_Lightning_II_development#/media/File:A_U.S._Air_Force_pilot_navi- gates_an_F-35A_Lightning_II_aircraft_assigned_to_the_58th_Fighter_Squadron,_33rd_Fighter_Wing_ into_position_to_refuel_with_a_KC-135_Stratotanker_assigned_to_the_336th_Air_Refueling_130516-F- XL333-505.jpg.

[41]Yu, Danny. "J-31 at Zhuhai." Created November 7, 2014. https://commons.wikimedia.org/wiki/ Category:Shenyang_FC-31#/media/File:J-31.Jpg.

Sea, with territorial claims directed at Vietnam, Malaysia, the Philippines, and Taiwan that are illegal under international law.

China's recent rise to Great Power status has been remarkable. But long before Europe and the United States become world players, China was a powerful and advanced state throughout premodern and early modern history. However, the country withdrew inward just as Europe began to reject the religious superstition of the Middle Ages and embrace science and technology. The resultant Age of Discovery saw the European Great Powers expand their power and influence across the globe, forging large empires at the expense of developing countries like China. Following the Opium Wars of the mid–19th century, Great Britain humiliated China by forcing it to cede Hong Kong and offer terms of trade favorable to its interests. Much as Britain consistently recalls the British empire and the United States similarly references the "American century," the Chinese remember this period of Western domination, which they see as a historical aberration that unjustly impeded their country's natural course of development. From the Chinese perspective, China would have become similarly positioned on the world stage much sooner were it not for active European efforts to suppress its modernization.

With the 100-year anniversary of the founding of the CPC rapidly approaching in 2021, contemporary PRC politics is a blend of the Maoist authoritarianism of the CPC and the renewal of Chinese nationalism. Both historical legacies shape the organizational culture of the Chinese intelligence community. But we must be careful so as not to reduce contemporary PRC intelligence strategy, operations, and organizational structure to history alone. China is just as capable of using sophisticated SIGINT, measurement and signature intelligence (MASINT), and cyber capabilities to advance its interests as its Western rivals.

# BOX 4.2
## FOR EXAMPLE: SUN TZU

As one of the world's oldest civilizations, China appreciated the relationship between politics, strategy, and intelligence far sooner than its rivals, particularly its eventual antagonists in the West. The sixth-century BCE general and strategist **Sun Tzu** is often cited as the first person to grasp the potential role of effective intelligence operations. In what has come to be known as the "indirect approach," in his timeless treatise *The Art of War* Sun Tzu emphasized outthinking and outmaneuvering opponents, thereby maximizing economy of force and coercing opponents without having to fight major battles. Sun Tzu viewed the *chang* method of using massive force to be foolish, as it destroyed cities and undermined the political objectives of military campaigns. Instead, Sun Tzu advocated the *chi* approach—understanding the adversary's leadership and attacking his purpose or strategy, thereby subduing him with a minimum of conflict.

Alongside Carl von Clausewitz's *On War*, *The Art of War* remains required reading for any student of war and politics both at military staff colleges and in university courses on strategy and international relations. Some of Sun Tzu's principles continue to influence contemporary Chinese thinking regarding intelligence, particularly the tenet of "'Know the Enemy and Know Yourself,'" which anticipates much of today's information warfare.[42] However, we must be careful to not reduce Chinese strategic thinking and intelligence activities to being merely the legacy of Sun Tzu.[43] To do so represents falling victim to what one expert on Chinese intelligence calls the "area studies trap."[44] It essentializes Chinese intelligence as reliant on Sun Tzu mentality and methods, suggesting it is frozen in time and does not evolve like its more technically rational Western counterparts. Contemporary PRC intelligence operations encompass a wide range of activities, some of which are just as technically sophisticated as their Western counterparts, while others rely on the Chinese cultural legacy of Sun Tzu and Maoist ideology.

## The Ministry for State Security

Founded in 1983 as the result of the merging of several intelligence functions of other PRC intelligence organizations, the Chinese intelligence agency charged chiefly with providing strategic intelligence is the **Ministry for State Security (MSS)**. The MSS has over 100,000 officers, almost half of whom are stationed overseas. As is the case with many intelligence agencies around the globe, MSS officers serve in a variety of covers, concealing their espionage activities as diplomats, journalists, college students, businessmen, and employees of nongovernmental organizations. Structured in a manner very similar to the US CIA, the MSS has operations, analysis, counterintelligence, and administrative bureaus. Also like the CIA, the MSS operates the University of International Relations and research and development think tanks, and is organized both geographically and functionally. The MSS similarly has departments with regional foci, such as its North American operations bureau and divisions with responsibilities for Taiwan, Hong Kong, and Macau, and divisions focused on issue areas, such as political and economic intelligence and science and technology.

---

[42]Blasko, Dennis J. *The Chinese Army Today*, 2nd ed. London, UK: Routledge, 2012, 127.

[43]See, for example, Sawyer, Ralph D. "Subversive Information: The Historical Thrust of Chinese Intelligence." In *Intelligence Elsewhere: Spies and Espionage Outside the Anglosphere*, edited by Philip H. J. Davies and Kristian C. Gustafson. Washington, DC: Georgetown University Press, 2013. This chapter provides a very useful survey of ancient Chinese strategy, then claims without providing any empirical evidence this historical legacy still dominates the thinking of contemporary Chinese intelligence leaders.

[44]Mattis, Peter L. "Assessing Western Perspectives on Chinese Intelligence." *International Journal of Intelligence and Counterintelligence* 25, no. 4 (2012): 678–699.

Yet in one notable difference between the structure of the two agencies, the MSS has satellite imaging capability, a responsibility that the CIA handed off to the National Geospatial-Intelligence Agency decades ago. In another sharp distinction between the adversary organizations, the MSS also keeps some of its personnel and their families in a secure compound, with self-contained facilities providing education, medical services, and housing. Finally, the most important difference between the CIA and the MSS is that the Chinese intelligence agency operates both abroad and domestically, whereas the CIA is forbidden by law from operating inside US borders. Despite its strategic purview, like all other Chinese intelligence organizations, the MSS's primary mission is protection of the CPC's power. Both its foreign and domestic intelligence activities must always be viewed in this light.

Combining both battlefield tactical support and strategic intelligence, the **People's Liberation Army (PLA)** has historically been China's all-source intelligence organization. Spanning several departments that are functionally differentiated, PLA activities span a wide range of intelligence enterprises. Employing more than 100,000 people, the **Second Department's** primary responsibility is overseas technical and military intelligence collection. It also manages the military attaché system in China's embassies overseas and staffs the National Watch Center. As with all other PRC intelligence organizations, the Second Department is likewise concerned with protecting the regime. As part of an operation dubbed "AUTUMN ORCHID," the Second Department operates HUMINT assets to infiltrate pro-democracy, religious, and university student groups in Hong Kong and Macau.

The PLA's Third and Fourth Departments are technical in orientation. The **Third Department** manages the PLA's foreign SIGINT and cyber capabilities, including Unit 61398. Operating out of a nondescript office tower in Shanghai, Unit 61398 is one of the most active cyber espionage organizations in the world, constantly attempting to penetrate Western governments and private sector businesses. The **Fourth Department** runs electronic countermeasures and possesses MASINT capabilities via its extensive radar network.

The **Political Education Department** of the PLA is responsible for serving as the CPC's eyes and ears in the military, as well as serving as a counterintelligence organization. It supervises political education in the ranks. But it also manages the interface between the Chinese private sector and military industrial base, infiltrating companies to maintain control over militarily sensitive technology.

Although primarily a law enforcement organization, with 1.6 million officers the **Ministry for Public Security (MPS)** is also the world's largest intelligence organization. Although seemingly eclipsed by the MSS, which took over many of its domestic surveillance functions in 1983, the MPS's capabilities and duties have recently expanded again. The MPS has enormous cyber and surveillance capabilities. It also manages the forced reeducation and work camps to which Chinese dissidents and significant numbers of China's ethnic and religious minorities are consigned. Finally, the

MPS handles the public identity card and census programs—a staggering task considering China's 1.4 billion citizens.

The MPS may be the world's leading manager of "public security intelligence"—that is, a wide variety of data that are used to identify, monitor, and forecast the behavior of Chinese citizens.[45] The MPS is responsible for securing and monitoring Chinese civilian computer systems. It also collects imagery intelligence (IMINT) data from Chinese surveillance video. More recently, the MPS has collected the DNA of approximately 36 million Chinese, with particular focus on the Muslim Uighur minority population that the government has brutally oppressed for decades. The MPS has been able to accomplish this largely by contracting American researchers working at Yale University.[46] Taken together, the combination of facial, electronic signature, and now even DNA identifiers is the most extensive and intrusive surveillance database in human history.

A subsidiary organization of the MPS is the **People's Armed Police (PAP)**. Commanded by the Central Military Commission (CMC) and senior CPC leaders, the PAP is a 600,000-person heavily armed paramilitary force, with responsibility over critical infrastructure protection and the security of China's borders. The PAP is tasked with putting down large public disturbances, and with its own mechanized infantry formations it may also be called upon to put down a possible mutiny within the PLA.

## Oversight of Chinese Intelligence

Since 1949, control and supervision of China's formidable state security and intelligence apparatus has resided with the CPC. However, that control has not always been held directly by the general secretary of the CPC and the Chinese president. In the early 2000s, command over the PLA was exercised by Jiang Zemin, the former president, via the party's CMC. During this period, it seemed as if political power was divided into several spheres between former president Jiang and the new president, Hu Jintao. However, Jiang was ultimately forced to relinquish this position.

When **Xi Jinping** assumed the presidency and general secretary positions in 2013, he prevented a repeat of the CMC leadership division by immediately assuming control over the CMC himself. Xi's consolidation of power over the military may be seen as the logical outgrowth of "creeping *guojiahua* . . . the gradual process of transforming the PLA from a purely party-army into a more party-state military."[47] Moreover, he has

[45]Schwarck, Edwards. "Intelligence and Informatization: The Rise of the Ministry of Public Security in Intelligence Work in China." *The China Journal* 80 (2018): 1–23.

[46]Wee, Sui-Lee. "China Uses DNA to Track Its People, With the Aid of US Expertise." *The New York Times*, February 21, 2019. https://www.nytimes.com/2019/02/21/business/china-xinjiang-uighur-dna-thermo-fisher.html.

[47]Scobell, Andrew. "China's Evolving Civil-Military Relations: Creeping *Guohiahua*." In *Chinese Civil-Military Relations: The Transformation of the People's Liberation Army*, edited by Na Li, 31. London, UK: Routledge, 2006.

reformed the Chinese state via a program of centralization that has concentrated power in his hands. Xi also removed Politburo member Zhou Yongkang from his position of managing China's police and domestic security and transferred its powers to a new committee that he chaired. Xi has directed a massive propaganda campaign that has attempted to re-create the Maoist "cult of personality," with Xi cast as the new Maoesque prophet figure. This campaign has been accompanied by a cell phone surveillance app that Chinese citizens have been pressured to put on their phones, with approximately 100 million people downloading the app by 2019. The app has been integrated into a system of mandatory testing on "Xi Jinping Thought," further bolstering a system of surveillance and penalties for failing to evince sufficient enthusiasm for Xi and the CPC's stranglehold on Chinese society.[48] In keeping with his uncontested leadership of China, in 2018 Xi abolished term limits, making him by default president for life.

The breadth and pace of China's rise has been staggering. In three decades, China moved 500 million people from its rural interior into urban spaces. During the early 2000s, China was creating an urban space the size of Manhattan every three to four months. The corresponding growth in national wealth and power has moved China from economic and political backwater to the center of the world stage. However, the country faces significant challenges that may upend the PRC economic miracle.

China is ringed by hostile states, and its foreign policy is engendering international resistance. Although the Democratic People's Republic of Korea is a client state and Sino-Russian relations have grown warmer in recent years, India, Vietnam, South Korea, and Japan are hostile states. With the 2016 election of President Rodrigo Duterte in the Philippines, China gained a temporary respite in the growing antagonism between the two states over Chinese incursions into the South China Sea. But the construction of permanent Chinese military bases on man-made islands in the region has laid bare Chinese ambitions to the region's states, which are already not predisposed toward Chinese interests. In an attempt to buy influence globally, China created the **Belt and Road Initiative**, a massive infrastructure development assistance program that promises Chinese funds for the construction of ports, rail lines, and airports to foster increased economic integration with the Chinese market. Yet the loan terms for these construction projects have been onerous, causing some countries to have to trade access to these new capital assets to reduce the interest rate or payments. This was probably China's plan all along—saddle developing countries with unpayable debts and then obtain access and control of strategically important infrastructure. Case in point has been the construction of a world-class airport in Sri Lanka, an airport that the government could not pay for, causing the country to allow access to important ports as a potential strategic block on the Indian Navy. China's drive to obtain more and more natural resources to fuel its industrial base has been viewed as similarly coercive, particularly in Africa.

---

[48]Hernandez, Javier. "The Hottest App in China Teaches Citizens About Their Leader—and, Yes, There's a Test." *The New York Times*, April 7, 2019. https://www.nytimes.com/2019/04/07/world/asia/china-xi-jinping-study-the-great-nation-app.html.

The PRC's use of infrastructure development to further its strategic ambitions is not limited to concrete and steel manifestations. Often with the tacit encouragement or even under the direct supervision of the state, Chinese private sector technology companies have increasingly sought access to Western markets with similar goals to the Belt and Road Initiative. Of particular importance has been **Huawei**, an acknowledged leader in 5G wireless technology that has launched low bids to create 5G cellular networks in Europe. Such bids have garnered positive attention from strong US allies, such as Germany, France, and even Great Britain. The concern has been that Huawei will build 5G in such a manner so as to allow PRC intelligence organizations access to Western secure networks, something that critics of Huawei have pointed out the company is required to do under a 2017 Chinese law.[49] The Chinese government has been even more brazen with its use of so-called Confucius Institutes. The PRC offers sometimes millions of dollars to US colleges and universities to establish centers to foster Sino-American relations and language instruction. Yet the Confucius Institutes are in fact part of longer-term Chinese efforts to infiltrate American think tanks and higher educational institutions to shape US public opinion and to conduct espionage.[50]

## Performance of Chinese Intelligence

Increased Chinese assertiveness abroad is in part due to the growth in the PRC's power over the past 30 years. But it is also in a sense due to **China's growing domestic problems**, which incentivize overseas ventures to foster Chinese nationalism and divert attention from the regime's failures at home. China's population is aging rapidly, and the country is in demographic decline. Decades of the CPC's "one-child policy" and traditional Confucian emphasis on male children has left tens of millions of Chinese men in their 30s with no marital prospects. Despite its rapid GDP growth rate, Chinese labor productivity remains low, and the country faces long-term problems with innovation. Much of its technological prowess is purchased via contracting or, more often, stolen through cyber theft. This is not a sustainable strategy. Massive corruption at the heart of the state severely limits technological innovation. Although President Xi has prosecuted over 1 million Chinese officials for corruption, there is little sign this has done much to persuade the average person corruption is not systemic.[51] After all, Xi's family is worth hundreds of millions of dollars, wealth that in the Chinese system cannot have been acquired without some graft.

[49]Kharpal, Arjun. "Huawei Says It Would Never Hand Data to China's Government. Experts Say It Wouldn't Have a Choice." CNBC, March 4, 2019. https://www.cnbc.com/2019/03/05/huawei-would-have-to-give-data-to-china-government-if-asked-experts.html.

[50]Poreba, John. "Neutralizing China's Spy Network." *International Journal of Intelligence and Counterintelligence* 25, no. 2 (2012): 260–291.

[51]Bloomberg News "Cash-Stuffed Secret Hideaway Discovered in Chinese Banker's Apartment." January 13, 2020. https://www.bloomberg.com/news/articles/2020-01-14/cash-stuffed-hideaway-revealed-in-confession of-chinese-banker.

Endemic corruption is also accompanied by structural problems with the Chinese economy. Poor rates of domestic consumption have also led to continued reliance on foreign consumers of its products, a weakness highlighted by President Trump's recent trade war with China. There are also huge off-the-book debt obligations—trillions of dollars in bad loans that will never be repaid, with some estimates that Chinese municipalities alone are $10 trillion in debt.[52] In order to clear the new cohort of labor market entrants and avoid large-scale unemployment, China must maintain GDP growth rates of around 7 percent per year, which has historically been impossible once developing countries transition to mature economies. Since the late 1980s, the Chinese social contract has been an avowed disinterest by the majority of the population in politics so long as the CPC could guarantee employment, growth, and rising living standards.

Centralization of political power may be following the same logic of state development as "creeping *guojiahua*" for the PLA—it is a sign of the increasing sophistication and rationalization of the Chinese state. But although the logic of state reform may work well with regard to the military, in a broader context it may also be a sign the CPC is increasingly concerned it is losing control over the population and must tread carefully. Since the early 2000s, there have been between 23,000 and 87,000 public disturbances a year in China.[53] The refusal of protesters in Hong Kong to accept Beijing's continued violation of the 1997 treaty that reunited the former British territory with the mainland may be a sign of further trouble down the road for the Chinese state. Concentration of power in the hands of a Maoist figure may be the CPC's strategy to maintain control when economic growth inevitably declines and the Chinese social contract evaporates. But there is no guarantee that it will work.

## CONCLUSION: SIMILARITIES AND DIFFERENCES OF FOREIGN INTELLIGENCE SYSTEMS

In this chapter, we examined the intelligence systems of six important nation-states. Utilizing a framework commonly employed in the comparative study of political systems, we analyzed the structure and function of these organizations, how culture and history affect their operations, and the interests and policy preferences of the politicians and intelligence organizations in these systems. We also assessed how well these organizations were managed, particularly regarding political oversight. We found some commonality across systems, most significantly in the general division of domestic versus international intelligence activities and missions. But we also

---

[52]Stevenson, Alexandra, and Cao Li. "'China's Manhattan' Borrowed Heavily. The People Have Yet to Arrive." *The New York Times*, April 10, 2019. https://www.nytimes.com/2019/04/10/business/china-economy-debt-tianjin.html.

[53]Pike, John. "Ministry of Public Security." Accessed January 10, 2020. https://www.globalsecurity.org/intell/world/china/mps.htm.

noted considerable differences between intelligence systems, variation that was not always explained by regime type. As they begin their own research into how intelligence organizations operate and are embedded within larger political structures and processes, students should consider employing a similar approach to the comparative study of intelligence systems.

## KEY CONCEPTS

case   91

case study   91

drivers   92

case selection   92

cross-national comparison   92

variation   92

representative sample   92

regime type   93

culture   94

structuralism   94

rational choice theory   94

false dichotomy   94

structure and function   94

MI-5   95

National Crime Agency (NCA)   95

Metropolitan Police Service (MPS, aka Scotland Yard)   95

unitary form of government   96

federal system   96

MI-6   96

Government Communications Headquarters (GCHQ)   96

Joint Intelligence Committee (JIC)   97

Defence Intelligence Staff (DIS)   97

National Security Council (NSC)   97

Five Eyes   98

STONEGHOST   98

SSEUR   98

Security Service Act of 1989   98

Intelligence Services Act of 1994   98

Intelligence and Security Committee   98

Suez Crisis   99

Cambridge Five   99

Butler Review   100

Gendarmerie Nationale   101

Directorate of Military Intelligence (DRM)   102

General Directorate for External Security (DGSE)   102

General Information Directorate (RG)   102

Directorate of Territorial Surveillance (DST)   102

National Directorate of Intelligence and Customs Investigations (DNRED)   103

Intelligence Processing and Action Against Illicit Financial Networks Unit (TRACFIN)   103

General Directorate for Internal Security (DGSI)   103

General Secretariat for Defense and National Security (SGDSN)   103

National Security and Defense Council (CDSN)   103

national intelligence coordinator (CNR)   103

Federal Intelligence Service (BND)   106

Strategic Surveillance Command (KSA)   108

Military Counterintelligence Service (MAD)   108

Federal Office for the Protection of the Constitution (BfV)   108

## ADDITIONAL READING

Aldrich, Richard J. *GCHQ: The Uncensored History of Britain's Most Secret Intelligence Agency.* London, UK: Harper, 2011.

Andrew, Christopher. *Defend the Realm: The Authorized History of MI-5.* New York, NY: Vintage, 2010.

Andrew, Christopher, and Oleg Gordievsky. *KGB: The Inside Story.* New York, NY: HarperCollins, 1990.

Barsky, Jack. *Deep Undercover: My Secret Life and Tangled Allegiances as a KGB Spy in America.* New York, NY: Tyndale Momentum, 2018.

Dahl, Erik J. "Getting Beyond Analysis by Anecdote: Improving Intelligence Analysis Through the Use of Case Studies." *Intelligence and National Security* 32, no. 5 (2017): 563–578.

Dietrich, Jan-Hendrik. "Of Toothless Windbags, Blind Guardians, and Blunt Swords: The Ongoing Controversy About the Reform of Intelligence Services Oversight in Germany." *Intelligence and National Security* 31, no. 4 (2016): 397–415.

Funaiole, Matthew P., and Jonathan E. Hillman. "China's Belt and Road Initiative Turns Five." *CSIS Briefs*, Center for Strategic and International Studies, April 2, 2018. https://www.csis.org/analysis/chinas-maritime-silk-road-initiative-economic-drivers-and-challenges?gclid=EAIaIQobChMI2KfY0bGV5wIVy5-zCh0sBggDEAAYAiAAEgLcofD_BwE.

Garthoff, Raymond L. *Soviet Leaders and Intelligence: Assessing the American Adversary During the Cold War.* Washington, DC: Georgetown University Press, 2015.

Gazit, Shlomo. "Intelligence and the Peace Process in Israel." *Intelligence and National Security* 12, no. 3 (2008): 35–66.

Hayez, Philip. "'*Renseignement*': The New French Intelligence Policy." *International Journal of Intelligence and Counterintelligence* 23 (2010): 474–486.

Krier, Wolfgang. "The German *Bundesnachrichtendienst* (BND): Evolution and Current Policy Issues." In *The Oxford Handbook of National Security Intelligence*, edited by Loch K. Johnson. Oxford, UK: Oxford University Press, 2010.

Mattis, Peter, and Matthew Brazil. *Chinese Communist Espionage: An Intelligence Primer.* Annapolis, MD: Naval Institute Press, 2019.

Pascovich, Eyal. "Military Intelligence and Controversial Political Issues: The Unique Case of Israeli Military Intelligence." *Intelligence and National Security* 29, no. 2 (2013).

Ragin, Charles C., and Howard S. Becker, eds. *What Is a Case? Exploring the Foundations of Social Inquiry.* Cambridge, UK: Cambridge University Press, 1992.

# 5 INTELLIGENCE OPERATIONS

Richard J. Kilroy Jr.

## HOW DO WE COLLECT INTELLIGENCE?

In 2012, Edward Snowden, a defense contractor at the National Security Agency (NSA), revealed that the **US intelligence community (IC)** had been conducting intelligence collection on US citizens. For many older-generation Americans, such revelations harkened back to the 1960s and 1970s, when intelligence agencies were investigated for targeting student groups on college campuses, particularly those opposed to the Vietnam War. For younger Americans, who had grown up since the terrorist attacks of September 11, 2001, and had been living under the USA PATRIOT Act, there was very little reaction. It was simply viewed as the price to be paid in an age of terror, where security trumped liberty. The NSA's domestic surveillance program, as well as the Central Intelligence Agency's (CIA) use of enhanced interrogation techniques and its extraordinary rendition program targeting suspected terrorists, was viewed by many Americans as the necessary means by which the IC was actively supporting both international and domestic counterterrorism operations.[1]

This chapter looks at intelligence operations by first examining the complexity and challenges of intelligence given the contemporary security environment and the adversaries nations face today. Second, it discusses collection planning and how intelligence sources and methods are used to gather information of intelligence value. Third, it examines the five principal intelligence collection disciplines: human intelligence (HUMINT), signals intelligence (SIGINT), geospatial intelligence (GEOINT), measurement and signature intelligence (MASINT), and open source intelligence (OSINT), as well as new domains, such as cyber. Fourth, it looks at military intelligence, to include the defense intelligence structure, service intelligence agencies, roles and missions, and scientific and technical intelligence.

---

[1] Kilroy, Richard J., Jr. "Terror and Technology: Domestic Intelligence Collection and the Gossamer of Enhanced Security." *Journal of Policing, Intelligence and Counter Terrorism* 12, no. 2 (2017): 119–141.

# COMPLEXITY AND CHALLENGES OF CONTEMPORARY INTELLIGENCE OPERATIONS

## What Are Intelligence Operations?

When asked to define intelligence operations, many people naturally think of spying or espionage. While both of these are activities conducted by intelligence organizations, intelligence operations are much broader. The *Dictionary of Military and Associated Terms* defines intelligence operations as

> the variety of intelligence and counterintelligence tasks that are carried out by various intelligence organizations and activities within the intelligence process [which includes] analysis and production; collection; dissemination; evaluation and feedback; planning and direction; [and] processing and exploitation.[2]

Embedded in that definition is what has also been called the intelligence cycle (see Chapter 3). In other words, intelligence operations are considered to be the entire process of collecting intelligence information, analyzing it, and producing intelligence products. However, many intelligence organizations do make a distinction between the analytical and operational functions. For example, the CIA has five organizational directorates, which include a Directorate of Analysis and Directorate of Operations, with the operations directorate focused on foreign intelligence collection activities and the analysis directorate focused on the production of intelligence products.[3]

In addition to collection activities, intelligence operations include counterintelligence and covert operations, which are addressed, respectively, in Chapters 6 and 7. These can also be viewed as either subsets of intelligence operations or stand-alone functions. For example, when John Brennan became the director of the CIA in 2013, he created eight centers, which were organized primarily geographically, but also topically, one of which is focused on counterintelligence. The purpose of the centers was to facilitate communication and coordination between analysts and collectors, an idea that was developed first with the formation of the **Counterterrorism Center (CTC)** at the CIA before 9/11, and later with the stand-up of the **National Counterterrorism Center (NCTC)** under the Office of the Director of National Intelligence (ODNI) in 2003.

---

[2]Department of Defense. "Intelligence Operations." In *Dictionary of Military and Associated Terms*, 108. As of June 2020. https://www.jcs.mil/Portals/36/Documents/Doctrine/pubs/dictionary.pdf.

[3]Central Intelligence Agency. "Organizational Chart." Last updated October 9, 2015. https://www.cia.gov/about-cia/leadership/Org_Chart_Oct2015.pdf.

## The Evolving Operational Environment

Throughout history, intelligence operations have been considered the domain of states in their quest for gaining an advantage over other states. To this end, we often associate intelligence operations during wartime as the function of military organizations seeking to defeat an adversary on the battlefield with superior weaponry and better tactics and strategy. Yet, in many conflicts, the country with better intelligence has been victorious on the battlefield, despite having fewer combatants and resources. Sun Tzu, the ancient Chinese military strategist, summed it up this way: "The supreme art of war is to subdue the enemy without fighting."[4] In other words, superior intelligence can identify an adversary's center of gravity, which, if neutralized, will prevent that nation from even having the capacity to fight a war. For example, during the Vietnam War, the center of gravity for the United States was public opinion and the will to fight. Although North Vietnam did not defeat the United States militarily, it did eventually win the war due to the loss of public support for war and the public's mistrust of the Johnson administration.[5]

During the Cold War, the focus of US intelligence operations was the former Soviet Union. Billions of dollars were spent developing intelligence capabilities to counter the Soviet military, to include fielding satellites, planes, and ships with sophisticated radar and other collection means. Intelligence was critical in determining the adversary's strengths and weaknesses in the event that the Cold War turned hot at any moment. Due to the difficulty of penetrating the "denied areas" of a totalitarian state with HUMINT collection efforts, the use of **national technical means (NTM)** by the CIA and military intelligence agencies was paramount in intelligence collection.[6]

The restrictive operational environment during the Cold War determined the need for the development of sophisticated technology by the US IC. One specific intelligence agency at that time, the National Reconnaissance Office, was created in 1961 and tasked with developing and fielding what were called spy satellites, the first being CORONA, developed by the CIA in 1960. By launching a camera into space on a satellite, the CIA was able to receive images of parts of the Soviet Union that had previously been inaccessible. The problem was the film bucket had to be jettisoned from the satellite and recovered by an airplane.[7] This was not a very timely means of gaining

---

[4]Giles, Lionel. *Sun Tzu on* The Art of War: *The Oldest Military Treatise in the World*. London, UK: Luzac, 1910, 19.

[5]See Sheehan, Neil. *A Bright Shining Lie: John Paul Vann and America in Vietnam*. New York, NY: Vintage Books, 1988.

[6]Smith, Clarence E. "CIA's Analysis of Soviet Science and Technology." In *Watching the Bear: Essays on CIA's Analysis of the Soviet Union*, edited by Gerald K. Haines and Robert E. Leggett. Washington, DC: CIA Center for the Study of Intelligence, 2003. https://www.cia.gov/library/center-for-the-study-of-intelligence/csi-publications/books-and-monographs/watching-the-bear-essays-on-cias-analysis-of-the-soviet-union/article04.html.

[7]Jensen, Carl, David McElreath, and Melissa Graves. *Introduction to Intelligence Studies*. New York, NY: CRC Press, 2013.

photographic intelligence products and would later be replaced by satellites that could provide near-real-time imagery digitally from space.

After the end of the Cold War, the operational environment changed significantly. Intelligence collection platforms that had previously only been used to collect on the Soviet Union were now being used by the IC to surveil other countries to assist with nontraditional military missions, such as counterdrug operations in Latin America and later with counterterrorism and counterinsurgency operations in Afghanistan and Iraq. Due to the need for actionable intelligence to support tactical operations on the battlefield, intelligence collection resources needed to be placed more directly into the hands of deployed forces. The use of drones, in particular, became more widespread, providing real-time collection for **reconnaissance, surveillance, and target acquisition (RSTA)**. Drones also facilitated the shortening of "sensor-to-shooter" capability, thus providing an intelligence collection platform the means by which it could engage with a target. This capability would become more pronounced in the use of covert operations to target suspected terrorists.

## Assessing the Adversary

One of the key functions of intelligence operations has been assessing adversaries or threats and responding to them. When making a threat assessment, the criteria used by the IC are often capability plus intent. In other words, states may possess military capabilities that can cause harm to the United States; however, these states—for example, North Atlantic Treaty Organization (NATO) allies Great Britain, France, and Germany—do not possess the intent to do so. On the other hand, a number of states and nonstate actors clearly have an intent to do harm to the United States, but do not have the capability to be considered a serious threat (e.g., Venezuela, Syria, the Islamic State, and al-Qaeda).

During the Cold War, intelligence analysts were adept at assessing Soviet military weapons, capabilities, doctrine, and tactics due to the emphasis placed on intelligence operations to gather information on this threat. This helped US military forces train for a potential conflict with the Soviets, as well as their proxies (other countries' militaries that employed Soviet weapons and tactics, like Iraq). When the Berlin Wall fell and many former Soviet Warsaw Pact satellite states became democratic in the 1990s, their militaries still retained mostly Soviet-era equipment and trained using Soviet-era tactics and thus had a capability to threaten US interests. As these nations began to integrate with NATO nations and replace their Soviet-era weapons with those of other nations, both the capability and intent changed. Some NATO-member states do have US military equipment, but also are considering purchasing Russian military equipment. This creates an operational challenge due to the fact that some weapons systems are incompatible, and providing the technical details to overcome these technical issues creates an intelligence problem of compromising US weapons systems that were designed to defeat certain Russian capabilities.

## BOX 5.1
### FOR EXAMPLE: TURKEY'S PURCHASE OF RUSSIAN S-400 AIR DEFENSE MISSILE SYSTEM

In December 2018, Turkey stated it was going through with plans to purchase the Russian S-400 surface-to-air missile system, despite already having contracted to purchase the new F-35 stealth fighter from the United States. The two weapons systems are meant to defeat each other. Also, the S-400 cannot be integrated with other NATO air defense systems to support the concept of a theater air defense system in southern Europe. The United States proposed selling Turkey the Patriot air defense missile system; however, the cost is twice that of the Russian system. If Turkey were to fly the F-35 and employ the S-400, the manufacturer of the F-35 would need to provide technical details to the S-400 that would preclude that system from being able to engage the F-35, which would create a compromise of intelligence collection efforts against the S-400 to exploit its vulnerabilities.[8]

When the Cold War ended, the IC still considered threats posed by nation-states (Russia, China, Iran, and North Korea), but also expanded its focus on assessing threats from nonstate actors such as terrorist groups, drug traffickers, and international criminal organizations. After 9/11, the primary focus shifted to the threat of terrorism and intelligence operations focused on providing direct support to military commanders on the ground in Afghanistan and Iraq fighting against al-Qaeda and its affiliated movements. Military intelligence agencies always had such a mission, providing tactical and operational intelligence support to forces in contact with an adversary; however, the strategic intelligence organizations (NSA, CIA, Defense Intelligence Agency [DIA], National Geospatial-Intelligence Agency [NGA], etc.) became more engaged with supporting these military units. These agencies always had representatives at the theater-level commands (US European Command, US Central Command, etc.) who provided linkages back to those agencies for both operational and collection support, along with analytical support. These were sometimes referred to as forming a **National Intelligence Support Team (NIST),** and US military intelligence officers could reach out to their intelligence colleagues for intelligence support through a program called **Tactical Exploitation of National Capabilities (TENCAP).**[9]

[8]Macias, Amanda A. "A Messy Multibillion-Dollar Weapon Sale Between Turkey, Russia and the US Just Got More Complicated." *CNBC*, December 9, 2018. https://www.cnbc.com/2018/12/19/a-messy-multi-billion-dollar-weapon-sale-between-turkey-russia-and-the-us-just-got-more-complicated.html.

[9]Federation of American Scientists. "TENCAP (SIGINT and IMINT)," Accessed May 5, 2019. https://fas.org/spp/military/program/sigint/tencap.htm#N_44_.

As a result of the George W. Bush administration's global war on terrorism in 2001, national intelligence agencies increased their responsiveness to military commanders directly confronting terrorist organizations overseas. The CIA had operational teams in Afghanistan before the US Special Operations Command sent troops to that country to fight al-Qaeda, as well as defeat the ruling Taliban party, which harbored terrorists there. Once the US military expanded its base of operations throughout the country, the CIA also sent both analysts and operators to these locations to help provide timely, actionable intelligence against potential targets. One such location employed as a CIA operating base was Camp Chapman in 2009 in eastern Afghanistan close to the Pakistani border, where US intelligence collectors were targeted by al-Qaeda with a deep-cover operation.

## BOX 5.2

### FOR EXAMPLE: KHOST BOMBING, CAMP CHAPMAN, AFGHANISTAN

On December 30, 2009, the CIA suffered its worst loss of personnel on a single day, when an al-Qaeda terrorist detonated a suicide vest, killing seven US intelligence personnel, a Jordanian intelligence officer, and the terrorist. Camp Chapman was located in Khost, Afghanistan, close to the border with Pakistan and an area called the FATA (Federally Administered Tribal Areas), where intelligence agencies thought Osama bin Laden was hiding. Humam Khalil Abu-Mulal al-Balawi was a Jordanian militant who Jordanian intelligence officials believed had been turned into a principal agent against al-Qaeda. Since he was believed to have firsthand knowledge of bin Laden's second-in-command, Ayman al-Zawahiri, the CIA welcomed the opportunity to debrief him. The CIA was desperate for intelligence that could lead to the capture of bin Laden and was willing to forgo normal security checks and precautions in allowing al-Balawi access to the base and contact with the CIA officials.[10]

In the 19 years since 9/11, the United States has been engaged in a war against terrorist groups throughout the world. These nonstate actors pose significant challenges to intelligence operations since they defy many of the traditional, technical means of intelligence collection used during the Cold War. A former senior military intelligence officer, Brigadier General Wayne Michael Hall, characterized the adversary today as

---

[10]Young, Steve. "Using a Principal Agent in Intelligence Collection in Afghanistan." In *Critical Issues in Homeland Security: A Casebook*, edited by James D. Ramsay and Linda A. Kiltz. Boulder, CO: Westview Press, 2014.

having unique capabilities that make intelligence operations particularly challenging. These include invisibility (ability to blend into the population), mental and organizational agility (ability to adjust quickly to changing conditions in the operational environment), secrecy and operations security (excellent use of OPSEC to protect themselves from observation), use of networks (which are difficult to penetrate), a will and motivation to achieve their goals (to include conducting acts of suicide), ability to take the initiative (freedom of movement and action), intelligence collection through extensive HUMINT, support of the populace (through either coercion or sympathy to the cause), and effective use of both low- and high-technology capabilities (for communication, command and control, etc.).[11]

## INTELLIGENCE COLLECTION PLANNING

### Developing a Collection Plan

The first step in the intelligence cycle is planning and direction. The saying "garbage in, garbage out" is very appropriate in understanding how effective the IC is in responding to consumers' demands. If the consumers of intelligence products (Congress, the president, National Command Authority, etc.) cannot articulate their specific needs to the IC in terms of validated intelligence production requirements with specific questions to be addressed (or intelligence gaps identified), then the collectors of intelligence are left guessing what the analysts, and ultimately the consumers, need.

Prior to 9/11 and the subsequent formation of the ODNI as a result of the Intelligence Reform and Terrorism Prevention Act of 2004, the **National Foreign Intelligence Program (NFIP)** was developed by the director of central intelligence, who was dual-hatted as the director of the CIA. The military intelligence agencies contributed to the NFIP by developing the **General Defense Intelligence Program (GDIP)** as a guideline for articulating the specific intelligence resources, budget, and personnel requirements necessary for the Department of Defense (DOD) to be able to collect the intelligence to produce intelligence products required by the consumers of intelligence.[12] The NFIP and GDIP provided the framework for developing collection plans based on collection resources available to the different intelligence agencies. For example, the CIA was designated the primary functional manager for HUMINT collection, the NSA for SIGINT collection, the NGA for GEOINT collection, and so on.

---

[11]Hall, Wayne Michael, and Gary Citrenbaum. *Intelligence Collection: How to Plan and Execute Intelligence Collection in Complex Environments.* Santa Barbara, CA: Praeger Security International, 2014.

[12]Department of Defense. *General Defense Intelligence Program (GDIP) Management.* Department of Defense Directive No. 3305.5. Washington, DC: Defense Technical Information Center (AD-A270-423), May 9, 1986.

Collection requirements have to be first validated and prioritized through the **National Intelligence Priorities Framework (NIPF)**. The NIPF emerged after 9/11 under the George W. Bush administration in February 2003. With the creation of the ODNI in 2004, the NIPF fell under the deputy director of national intelligence for intelligence integration for oversight and management.[13] The consumers of intelligence products (the White House, Congress, National Security Council, military, etc.) make their requirements known to the ODNI directly, or through the **National Intelligence Managers (NIMs)** and the functional managers within the IC. The ODNI validates the requirements and then determines priorities and the resources available to respond to those requirements through the development of collection requirements. The NIPF, however, is not static. It is updated quarterly, to include responding to ad hoc requirements as they develop, based on changing international political and security developments. Since these new ad hoc priorities must compete with the existing priorities, some intelligence analysts refer to this as the "tyranny of the ad hocs" since they can take away from other collection needs.[14]

## Role of the Collection Manager

In the business world, the term *middleman* connotes an individual who stands between the producer of a product and the consumer, often contributing to increased costs to the consumer. Some businesses champion "cutting out the middleman" and letting the consumer go directly to the producer for the product. In the intelligence world, the "middleman" between the producers of intelligence products (analysts) and the operators (collectors of intelligence) is the collection manager. The collection manager plays a critical role in communicating the needs of the analyst to the collector through the generation of collection requirements that respond to intelligence gaps identified by the analyst. These collection requirements are written by the collection manager in the format required by each of the functional managers (HUMINT collection requirements sent to the CIA or DIA, SIGINT requirements sent to the NSA, GEOINT requirements sent to the NGA, etc.). Collection managers are trained in understanding the capabilities of the collectors, as well as the needs of the analysts. They play a crucial role in being able to discern which intelligence discipline is most likely capable of satisfying an analyst's need for the type of intelligence collected.

---

[13]Director of National Intelligence. *Intelligence Community Directive 204: National Intelligence Priorities Framework*. Washington, DC: Office of the Director of National Intelligence, January 2, 2015.

[14]Lowenthal, Mark. *Intelligence: From Secrets to Policy*, 7th ed. Washington, DC: CQ Press, 2017, 79.

## BOX 5.3

### SPOTLIGHT ON CAREERS

### INTELLIGENCE COLLECTION MANAGER (2019)

Defense contractor at Shaw Air Force Base, Charleston, South Carolina

Assist the USAF [Air Forces] and other government agencies in the creation and development of combat capability documents, presentations, formal messages, background papers, items of interest, and staff summary packages for USAFCENT [Central Command] Senior Management review.

The Collection Manager shall coordinate and schedule video teleconferences with military and associated partnering units upon request.

The Collection Manager shall provide training to junior intelligence analysts through informal and formal training sessions within each perspective function performed within the PWS [Performance Work Statement].

The Collection Manager shall provide air intelligence support to USCENTCOM forces and support USAFCENT's interface with national agencies, USCENTCOM, and component elements.

The collection manager provides two-way communication between the analysts and the collectors. Not only does the manager generate collection requirements on behalf of the analysts; the manager also facilitates feedback to the collectors to let them know whether the information they have collected satisfies the analysts' need or whether additional collection may be necessary. In some cases, such as in HUMINT reporting, a collector may have a continuing intelligence requirement from an analyst to collect information on a foreign military's artillery systems, and will apply those standing questions to any source that is debriefed who may have had access to such information. After the report is generated and the analyst receives it, the analyst may have additional questions for the collector to follow up on through a specific source-directed collection requirement, which the collection manager generates. Since that collector may no longer have access to the source, the collection manager may have to request a follow-up debriefing of the source by another service or agency through the collection requirements process. The feedback the collection manager provides to the collector is critical in helping the collector "tweak" the process of asking the right questions of a source to respond to the analyst's needs.

After the 9/11 attacks, during the George W. Bush administration's global war on terrorism, the intelligence community was under much pressure to identify sources who could lead US forces to capture or kill the leader of al-Qaeda, Osama bin Laden. As a result of the time-sensitive nature of gaining actionable intelligence necessary to find key leaders of al-Qaeda, such as bin Laden, there was an increase in direct analyst-to-collector communication, where instead of waiting for a debriefing to be processed and disseminated to the analyst through the collection manager, the analyst would deploy to Afghanistan to facilitate the debriefing and be present during the questioning of sources.[15] This created a security challenge for collectors and analysts, often working on the front lines of the war where they were exposed to the threat of terrorist attacks, as occurred with the CIA operating out of Camp Chapman in Khost, Afghanistan, in 2009.

## The Collection Requirements Process

Intelligence collection requirements generally fall within two categories: tasking to lower, organic resources belonging to the organization, or requests for information (RFIs) to higher agencies outside of that particular organization's chain of command. For example, in a combat situation, an army intelligence officer (S-2) on a battalion staff would have a number of organic "collectors" within the unit, such as a scout platoon, or deployed forces directly in contact with the enemy. Since the S-2 belongs to the unit, the S-2 would generate collection taskings to the subordinate elements. If the commander of that battalion needed additional intelligence on a region or area outside of the current operating area due to future combat operations, the S-2 would create RFIs to the higher headquarters (brigade, division, or higher) for collection support from their units (e.g., long-range reconnaissance patrols, drones, or other collection platforms). At times, a unit may actually need strategic intelligence collection from one of the functional managers, such as the CIA, DIA, or NSA, possibly involving national technical means of collection. To facilitate the process, those agencies may already have liaison officers at the unit, referred to as a NIST, who can generate collection requirements on behalf of the supported unit and provide them directly to the agency.

## BOX 5.4
### FOR EXAMPLE: US SOUTHERN COMMAND AND MEXICO

In 1996, the commander of the US Southern Command (SOUTHCOM) in Panama, US Army general Barry McCaffrey, was selected to be the new "drug czar" leading the Office of National Drug Control Policy for President Bill Clinton. He was scheduled to visit Mexico with then secretary of defense William Perry to meet with his Mexican counterparts. Since Mexico was not within SOUTHCOM's area of responsibility, the J2 section did not have biographical information on the military officers that General McCaffrey would be meeting with during his visit, to include the Mexican "drug czar" Army General José de Jesús Gutiérrez Rebollo. An RFI was provided to the DIA liaison

---

[15] Hall and Citrenbaum, *Intelligence Collection*.

officer at SOUTHCOM, who was able to obtain biographical information on these key officials in order to support General McCaffrey's visit. Ironically, 11 weeks after the visit, General Rebollo was indicted for drug trafficking with Mexican cartels.[16]

Figure 5.1 portrays a generic collection requirements management process. Although this example is from a US Army Field Manual, each IC member agency will

**FIGURE 5.1  ■  Generic Collection Requirements Management Process**

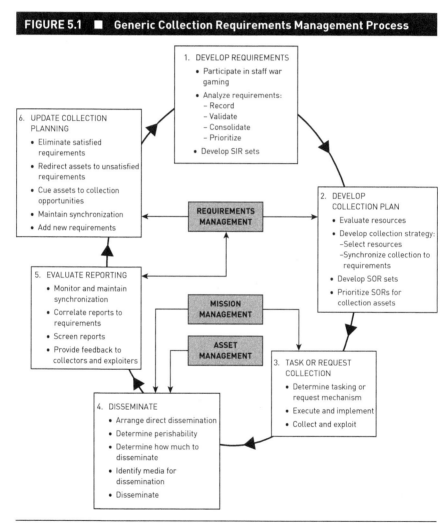

*Note:* SIR = specific information requirements; SOR = specific orders and requests.

*Source:* Department of the Army 2003.

[16]Wilkinson, Tracy. "Jose de Jesus Gutierrez Rebollo Dies at 79; Disgraced Mexican General." *Los Angeles Times,* December 20, 2013. https://www.latimes.com/local/obituaries/la-xpm-2013-dec-20-la-me-jose-gutierrcz-rebollo-20131221-story.html.

have its own collection management procedures that are germane to that agency. The process, however, is very similar between intelligence agencies and collection managers.

## THE FIVE PRINCIPAL INTELLIGENCE COLLECTION DISCIPLINES AND BEYOND

### Human Intelligence (HUMINT)

When people think of **human intelligence (HUMINT)**, they often think of James Bond, spies, and espionage. While spying and espionage are part of intelligence collection using human sources covertly or clandestinely, much of HUMINT is actually conducted overtly. Defense attachés (DATT) are one example of overt intelligence collection that all countries conduct at their embassies overseas. In the United States, DATT work for the ambassador; however, they are assigned to their duty stations through the DIA Defense Attaché System. DATT go through a rigorous training program through the Joint Military Attaché School and the Defense Language Institute.

The functional manager for both covert and clandestine HUMINT is the CIA. The CIA runs the **National Clandestine Service (NCS)**. Clandestine HUMINT is conducted by operations officers under official cover. What this means is that if they were discovered conducting espionage in a foreign country, they would likely be determined to be persona non grata and sent home. Covert HUMINT would be conducted by a principal agent or foreign national overseas who does not have official cover, which means if discovered the agent would be subject to the laws of the foreign country and detained, or even executed in wartime.

## BOX 5.5

### FOR EXAMPLE: MARTI PETERSON, WIDOW SPY

During the Cold War, one of the first women arrested for spying for the United States in the Soviet Union was Martha (Marti) Peterson. Marti was a CIA operations officer working under official cover in the US embassy in Moscow in 1975. She was assigned as the case officer for handling Aleksandr Ogorodnik, a mid-level official in the Soviet Ministry of Foreign Affairs, code name TRIGON. Marti and TRIGON never met. Through a series of dead drops, they passed information to each other, until TRIGON was discovered by the Soviet intelligence service (KGB), and Marti was arrested during a dead drop. She was declared persona non grata and returned to the United States. Ogorodnik committed suicide during questioning, using a pen issued by the CIA that contained a cyanide pill.[17]

---

[17]Peterson, Martha D. *The Widow Spy: My CIA Journey From the Jungles of Laos to Prison in Moscow.* Wilmington, NC: Red Canary Press, 2012.

Although HUMINT has existed for millennia, in the United States its origins date from the Revolutionary War. The first "spy" to be executed for his actions was Nathan Hale. Hale was part of General George Washington's "Culper spy ring," which conducted espionage operations against the British Army. Hale was a patriot, but not a very good spy, failing to use known tradecraft at the time, such as invisible ink. Once caught, he also readily confessed that he was a soldier in the Continental Army. Since he was apprehended behind enemy lines, in civilian clothes, posing as schoolteacher, he was hanged as a spy.[18]

During the Civil War, HUMINT was employed by both the North and the South in support of their military operations. Major General Grenville Dodge was General Ulysses S. Grant's chief of intelligence, running a spy network of over 100 agents behind Confederate lines. He practiced good tradecraft, protecting the identities of his agents, as well as disguising how they were paid. He also employed the use of cryptography in using coded messages when communicating with his agents. Dodge's intelligence was key to Grant's victory over Lt. General John Pemberton at Vicksburg, Mississippi, in 1863, by conducting an economy of force operation.[19] Another Union army spymaster was Allan Pinkerton, who supported Union general George McClellan's campaigns. After the Civil War, he gained fame for his "Pinkerton National Detective Agency," which helped break up the Molly Maguires and other trade unions.[20] The Pinkerton agency still exists today. The Union army also used women as spies. Elizabeth Van Lew was a Richmond abolitionist who ran a spy ring in the Confederate capital in support of her cause, ending slavery and keeping the United States unified. After the war, she was ostracized by her neighbors, such that she was quoted as saying when her mother passed away in 1875 that there were not friends enough to serve as pallbearers at her burial.[21]

On the Confederate side, women also played a prominent role in supporting the South. Rose O'Neal Greenhow was a socialite who used her political connections in Washington, DC, to provide intelligence to the Confederate army. General P. G. T. Beauregard credits the intelligence provided by Greenhow for his victory at the First Battle of Bull Run in 1861. "One of her couriers, a young woman named Bettie Duvall, dressed as a farm girl in order to pass Union sentinels on the Chain Bridge leaving Washington, then rode at high speed to Fairfax Courthouse in Virginia to deliver her message to Confederate officers stationed there."[22] One of the most enigmatic characters

---

[18]Rose, Alexander. *Washington's Spies: The Story of America's First Spy Ring.* New York, NY: Random House, 2006.

[19]Lotter, David. "Grenville Dodge (1831–1916)." *Signal Corps Association 1860–1865.* Accessed May 9, 2019. http://www.civilwarsignals.org/pages/spy/pages/dodge.html.

[20]Civil War Academy. "Alan Pinkerton 1819–1884." Accessed May 9, 2019. https://www.civilwaracademy.com/allan-pinkerton.

[21]Schoof, Heidi. *Elizabeth Van Lew: A Civil War Spy.* North Mankato, MN: Capstone, 2005, 88.

[22]History Editors. "Spying in the Civil War." *History*, February 3, 2019. https://www.history.com/topics/american-civil-war/civil-war-spies.

of this period was Mary Surratt, who was arrested as a Confederate spy and accused of being one of the conspirators who planned the assassination of President Abraham Lincoln. Her Washington, DC, boarding house was used by Confederate agents, to include her son, John Surratt Jr. Although she maintained her innocence throughout her trial, she was convicted of conspiracy and was the first woman to be hanged by the federal government in 1865.[23]

HUMINT operations were conducted extensively during both World War I and World War II in Europe. One of the most famous spies during the Great War was Mata Hari, a Dutch exotic dancer. She used one of the oldest "tricks" of the trade to seduce her victims to reveal secrets. She was eventually captured and executed in 1917 for spying for Germany. A Polish baker, living in Moscow, spied for the Germans by using bread displays in his bakeshop window display to send coded messages. A number of German and British agents posed as businessmen to gain access to each other's countries, passing messages through their "wares" such as cigars and sardines.[24]

US HUMINT came of age during World War II, under the leadership of General William Donovan's Office of Strategic Services (OSS). Donovan ran a sophisticated espionage network, which also conducted sabotage operations behind enemy lines. The OSS is considered to be the precursor to both the CIA and the military's Special Operations Command, due to their involvement in both intelligence collection and covert operations (Donovan's statue is in the lobby of the CIA headquarters in Langley, Virginia). The British also ran successful espionage operations during the war, through the Special Operations Executive (SOE) and the Secret Intelligence Service (SIS), also known as MI-6. These agencies were often at odds with each other and with the OSS during the war, yet their goals were the same: defeat of Nazi Germany through espionage, sabotage, disinformation, deception, and counterintelligence. One of the most successful spies working for the SOE during the war was Vera Atkins, a Romanian émigré to France who was recruited by Britain's most famous spymaster, William Stephenson (*A Man Called Intrepid*). General Dwight Eisenhower credited Atkins and her network of French resistance forces as crucial in supporting the Normandy invasion and shortening the entire war effort.[25]

Throughout the Cold War, HUMINT was a valuable source of intelligence from both the United States and the Soviet Union, which ran successful espionage

---

[23]Blakemore, Erin E. "The Enduring Enigma of the First Woman Executed by the US Federal Government." *Time*, June 30, 2015. http://time.com/3935911/mary-surratt/.

[24]King, Melanie. "Thanks for the Spycraft, World War I: The Fight That Launched an Explosion of Espionage Innovation." *Boston Globe*, August 3, 2014. https://www.bostonglobe.com/ideas/2014/08/02/thanks-for-spycraft-world-war/lrjmteHDfRevXdP9qGACHN/story.html.

[25]Stephenson, William. *Spymistress: The True Story of the Greatest Female Secret Agent of World War II*. New York, NY: Arcade, 2011.

operations against each other and their allies. During World War II, the Soviets recruited Kim Philby and the Cambridge Five, Communist sympathizers who spied against the British and Americans, passing information on Allied intelligence operations against Germany and, later, the Soviet Union. One of the most successful HUMINT operations was Soviet military intelligence (GRU) colonel Oleg Penkovsky, code name HERO, who provided critical information on the placement of nuclear-capable missiles in Cuba, which helped the United States develop policy options (to include a naval blockade) during the Cuban Missile Crisis in October 1962.[26] One of the most influential spies in terms of his impact on military weapons capabilities was Adolf Tolkachev, a Soviet electronics engineer. Code-named SPHERE, Tolkachev was a dissident who was disillusioned with the corrupt Soviet system. His access to sensitive military technology information provided to the United States earned him the name "the billion dollar spy" in terms of the value of the intelligence he provided in the 1970s and 1980s.[27]

With the end of the Cold War in the 1990s, HUMINT operations did not go away. If anything, they expanded as many nations turned their attention toward economic espionage. In 2020, China is considered to be the single greatest threat to the United States in terms of its extensive espionage operations, directed at gaining technological, as well as commercial, intelligence.[28] The Federal Bureau of Investigation extends a significant amount of its counterintelligence resources targeting Chinese espionage activities, to include recruiting US students studying in China to work for the CIA or State Department, as well as tracking Chinese students studying at US universities.[29]

## Signals Intelligence (SIGINT)

While **signals intelligence (SIGINT)** can be considered a more modern, technical form of intelligence collection, the origins can be seen in the use of some very nontechnical means of sending and receiving information. Native North American peoples used smoke signals to send coded messages, while naval ships used semaphore flags and signal lights (Aldis lamps) to communicate and avoid adversary collection. SIGINT really began as codebreaking, which goes back several millennia. During World War II operations in the Pacific Theater, the US Marines used Navajo code

---

[26]Suvorov, Viktor. *Soviet Military Intelligence*. London, UK: Grafton Books, 1986, 155.

[27]Hoffman, David E. *The Billion Dollar Spy: A True Story of Cold War Espionage and Betrayal*. New York, NY: Doubleday, 2015.

[28]Viswanatha, Aruna A., and Dustin Volz. "China's Spying Poses Rising Threat to US." *The Wall Street Journal*, April 28, 2019. https://www.wsj.com/articles/chinas-spying-poses-rising-threat-to-u-s-11556359201.

[29]Federal Bureau of Investigation. "Advice for US College Students Abroad: Be Aware of Foreign Intelligence Threat [Game of Pawns Video: The Glenn Duffie Shriver Story]." FBI News, April 14, 2014. https://www.fbi.gov/news/stories/advice-for-us-college-students-abroad.

talkers to confuse Japanese SIGINT with their unique language. Germany and Japan used complex cypher machines (such as Enigma), which were eventually broken.[30]

Intercepting communications through intelligence collection is one example of SIGINT called **communications intelligence (COMINT)**. As telegraphs, telephones, radio, and later the internet created new means of communication, intelligence collection by the use of COMINT also adapted. During the Cold War, communications done by virtue of microwave antennae could be intercepted using space-based systems through satellites. When undersea cables were developed, such collection was not possible. Instead, intelligence agencies developed sophisticated operations to try and tap into those cables to collect COMINT.

## BOX 5.6

### FOR EXAMPLE: OPERATION IVY BELLS

In 1972, the United States and the Soviet Union were involved in diplomatic efforts to reduce the number of nuclear weapons each country had in its arsenal. The first Strategic Arms Limitation Talk (SALT I) had just concluded; however, the United States sought to verify Soviet compliance through intelligence collection. A CIA-led operation, called IVY BELLS, successfully tapped undersea cables in the Sea of Okhotsk for over 10 years, gathering unencrypted message traffic, since the Soviets believed their transmissions to be secure. Intelligence gained through this classified SIGINT operation was instrumental in supporting the US position in the 1979 SALT II negotiations.[31]

Another form of SIGINT involves **electronic intelligence (ELINT)**, which is the collection of noncommunications electronic signals, such as radar and other emitters. ELINT is primarily used at the tactical and operational level of warfare, such as in electronic warfare, to include radio jamming and detecting air defense or artillery radar sites. At the strategic level, another form of SIGINT called **foreign instrumentation**

---

[30]"Codes generally operate on *semantics*, meaning, while ciphers operate on *syntax*, symbols. A code is stored as a mapping in a codebook, while ciphers transform individual symbols according to an algorithm" (see Khan Academy. "Ciphers vs. Codes." Accessed September 14, 2020. https://www.khanacademy.org/computing/computer-science/cryptography/ciphers/a/ciphers-vs-codes). The National Cryptologic Museum at Fort Meade, Maryland, displays the history of codebreaking and cryptanalysis to include the Navajo code talkers, as well as Germany's use of the Enigma machine and Allied efforts to break the German (Ultra) and Japanese (Magic) cyphers. See National Security Agency Central Security Service. "National Cryptologic Museum." Accessed September 14, 2020. https://www.nsa.gov/about/cryptologic-heritage/museum/.

[31]Blitz, Matt. "How Secret Wiretapping Helped End the Cold War." *Popular Mechanics*, March 30, 2017. https://www.popularmechanics.com/technology/security/a25857/operation-ivy-bells-underwater-wiretapping/#.

**signals intelligence (FISINT)** was extremely important during the Cold War, due to the threat of nuclear warfare. The United States collected emissions signals from Soviet missile sites to detect possible testing or launching of intercontinental ballistic missiles that could reach the United States.

In the 1960s, the first SIGINT satellites "were intended to detect and locate air defense radars, to determine the electronic order of battle (EOB, which listed the types and locations of Soviet defense system radars), and thus to assist American bombers to pass through Soviet defenses to military targets in the event of war."[32] Since these collection requirements required COMINT, ELINT, and FISINT signals collection, the satellites designed by the **National Reconnaissance Office (NRO)** were multi-purpose platforms, which posed significant challenges, including the need for multiple antennae to be able to pick up communications, radar, and telemetry data over different frequencies.

The NSA was created in 1952 to be the functional manager for COMINT collection. In 1958, ELINT was added to its responsibilities. Today, the NSA/CSS (Central Security Service) operates out of Fort Meade, Maryland. The NSA has responsibility for the collection of foreign SIGINT as well as the information assurance role to protect DOD information systems against foreign intelligence agencies, nonstate actors, and other threats to the nation's security.[33] The NSA runs the National Security Operations Center, which provides 24/7 operational support to the National Command Authority. The director of the NSA (DIRNSA) is an active-duty military-flag-grade (three-star) officer who responds directly to the secretary of defense and the director of national intelligence. In 2009, with the stand-up of the US Cyber Command at Fort Meade, the DIRNSA is dual-hatted as commander of the US Cyber Command.

## Geospatial Intelligence (GEOINT)

While many may consider **geospatial intelligence (GEOINT)** to be a relatively new intelligence discipline, its origins go back centuries. Before it was called GEOINT, maps, charts, and cartography products; aerial photography; and other graphic images provided decision makers knowledge of terrain, topography, climate, and weather conditions that impacted military operations, exploration, and navigation. As one example, in the United States, President Thomas Jefferson commissioned the Lewis and Clark expedition in January 1803 to map the territory later known as the Louisiana Purchase (acquired from France), which doubled the landmass of the new nation.[34]

---

[32]Bradburn, David D., John O. Copley, and Raymond B. Potts. *The SIGINT Satellite Story.* Washington, DC: National Reconnaissance Office, 1994 (Declassified February 10, 2016), 5.

[33]Office of the Director of National Intelligence. *Intelligence Consumer's Guide.* Washington, DC: Office of the Director of National Intelligence, 2013.

[34]Thomas Jefferson's Monticello. "Thomas Jefferson: Louisiana and Lewis and Clark." Accessed July 3, 2019. https://www.monticello.org/thomas-jefferson/louisiana-lewis-clark/the-louisiana-purchase/.

The US Navy also depended on the use of hydrographic products in the early 1800s to map the country's new territorial seas and international waterways, which facilitated commerce and transportation.[35]

Aerial photography dates from the end of the 18th century in Europe with the use of observation balloons. These were used by the Union army during the US Civil War; however, being tethered they had limited observation range. With the advent of the airplane in World War I, aerial photography literally took flight with its use in support of battlefield operations. **Photographic intelligence (PHOTINT)** expanded greatly during World War II, with the use of dedicated photo-reconnaissance aircraft providing both tactical and operational support. However, it wasn't until the Cold War that the expanded use of **imagery intelligence (IMINT)** came into its own, with the emergence of sophisticated manned and unmanned collection platforms.

In 1956, the United States deployed the U-2, a dedicated "spy plane" with the ability to fly at 70,000 feet and take high-resolution photographic images deep inside the Soviet Union in an attempt to determine the extent of Soviet nuclear capabilities and defenses. The Soviets countered the US intelligence collection capabilities by developing longer-range surface-to-air missiles (SA-2), which shot down a U-2 piloted by Air Force captain Francis Gary Powers in 1960. As a result, the United States moved to the

**PHOTO 5.1** SR-71 Blackbird on display at the Udvar-Hazy Center, National Air and Space Museum, Chantilly, Virginia.

---

[35]Lowenthal, Mark, and Robert M. Clark. *The 5 Disciplines of Intelligence Collection.* Washington, DC: CQ Press, 2015, 116.

use of a new generation of spy planes that could fly at altitudes much higher (80,000 feet) and faster (Mach 3) than the U-2 to avoid Soviet air defense systems.[36]

In the 1960s, the United States also developed its first imagery satellite, code-named CORONA, which still used film and aerial photography, but now from outer space. The CORONA used a film canister system that would be ejected from the satellite, and then the bucket (carried by parachute) would be retrieved by an air force plane upon reentry into Earth's atmosphere. The film would then be sent to the new **National Photographic Interpretation Center (NPIC)** in Washington, DC (jointly run by the CIA and the DOD), to be analyzed by imagery analysts (called "squints") using the latest light table technology to enhance the images' quality. In the late 1970s, the United States launched the first satellites with near-real-time electro-optical imagery. These high-resolution images could be downloaded directly to a satellite ground station and provided to intelligence analysts, who could then develop new collection requirements for imagery products in a more responsive means available versus the older photographic products.

Today, the National Geospatial-Intelligence Agency, located in Springfield, Virginia (East Campus), and St. Louis, Missouri (West Campus), serves as the functional manager for the intelligence community's need for GEOINT. The NGA was created in 2003 by then director of the Air Force lieutenant general James Clapper (who went on to become the director of national intelligence under President Barack Obama). The NGA evolved from the National Imagery and Mapping Agency, which itself was a merger of the Defense Mapping Agency and the NPIC in 1996. Today, the NGA provides GEOINT support to all of the intelligence community, although the operational control resides under the DOD. Future challenges to GEOINT and the intelligence community include the rise of commercial satellite imagery, which will be covered in the section on OSINT.

## Measurement and Signature Intelligence (MASINT)

One of the challenges intelligence analysts face is determining the weapons capabilities of their adversaries. This was particularly critical during the Cold War in being able to maintain the balance of military power between NATO countries and Warsaw Pact countries. Since most scenarios of potential conflict between the two sides began as a conventional conflict in Europe, where the Warsaw Pact countries had a quantitative advantage in military forces, NATO countries counted on having a qualitative advantage in weapons systems and military capabilities.

---

[36]Jensen, McElreath, and Graves, *Introduction to Intelligence Studies*, 96. The CIA's A-12 spy plane was already in development before 1960, but not fielded until 1962. It was later followed by the Air Force's SR-71 in 1964, which could fly longer with more fuel and included a reconnaissance assistance officer aboard (see Lockheed Martin. "Creating the Blackbird." Accessed September 14, 2020. https://www.lockheedmartin.com/en-us/news/features/history/blackbird.html).

**Measurement and signature intelligence (MASINT)** can be defined as "technically derived information that provides distinctive characteristics of a specific event such as a nuclear explosion, or locates, identifies, and describes distinctive characteristics of targets through such means as optical, acoustic, or seismic sensors."[37] In other words, MASINT can be viewed as "the CSI of the US IC" due to the forensic nature of the analysis involved.[38] Military intelligence analysts often used the term *technical intelligence* (TECHINT) to describe their work to determine foreign military equipment capabilities using different types of collection platforms, to include HUMINT to acquire actual samples (e.g., a piece of the collective protection liner in a Soviet T-80 main battle tank to determine its ability to withstand radiological, biological, or chemical weapons).

Today, MASINT incorporates many of the tools used in TECHNINT to include the six main subdisciplines shown in Figure 5.2.

Electro-optical includes ultraviolet, visible, and infrared images and signatures. Radar includes imaging, synthetic aperture (SAR), over the horizon (OTH), and laser. Radiofrequency (RF) includes directed energy (DE), electromagnetic pulse (EMP), unintentional radiation, and lightening. Geophysical includes acoustic, seismic, and magnetic. Nuclear radiation includes X-ray, gamma ray, and neutron. Material sampling includes effluents, particulates, and debris; chemical; and biological.[39]

**FIGURE 5.2  ■  MASINT Subdisciplines**

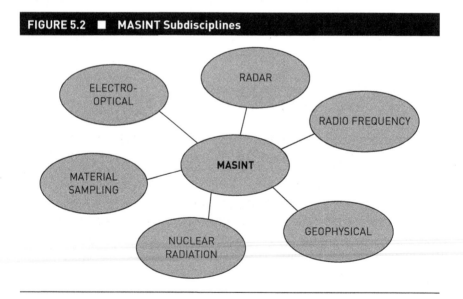

[37]Reagan, Mark L., ed. "Measurement and Signature Intelligence." In *Terms and Definitions of Interest for Counterintelligence Professionals*, 212–213. Washington, DC: Federation of American Scientists, June 9, 2014. https://fas.org/irp/eprint/ci-glossary.pdf.

[38]Lowenthal and Clark, *The 5 Disciplines of Intelligence Collection*, 163.

[39]Ibid., 177.

Since MASINT is not collected by any single intelligence agency (e.g., there is no national MASINT agency), functional management has fallen to the DIA, since much of the analysis involves scientific and technical (S&T) intelligence. Each of the military services has its own S&T intelligence centers (which will be discussed in the "Military Intelligence" section of the chapter). For example, the US Navy is the primary collector of acoustic intelligence involving foreign navies and understanding the signatures of their ships, submarines, and underwater weapons systems.

## BOX 5.7
### FOR EXAMPLE: *THE HUNT FOR RED OCTOBER*

In 1990, the Tom Clancy book *The Hunt for Red October* was made into a movie, staring Sean Connery as renegade Soviet submarine captain Ramius and Alec Baldwin as a naval intelligence analyst (Jack Ryan) trying to figure out his intentions. A key piece of evidence used in determining whether the Soviet submarine was defecting was the acoustic intelligence obtained by the US submarine's sonar technician "Jonesy" (played by Courtney B. Vance) who detected a unique nautical maneuver by the Red October known as a "crazy Ivan," which Ramius was known for conducting.[40]

## Open Source Intelligence (OSINT)

Although **open source intelligence (OSINT)** is considered to be a new intelligence discipline, open sources of information have always been used by intelligence analysts. Typically, these sources are *unclassified* since they are often coming from non-intelligence sources and methods (e.g., news reports, academic research). However, to be considered OSINT, they need to meet three tests: the sources of information need to be publicly available; the sources must also be lawful; and, finally, the sources need to be properly vetted to ensure reliability.[41]

During the Cold War, OSINT provided a much-needed source of information for intelligence analysts on what was being reported in foreign press and media in countries behind the Iron Curtain. The CIA, through the use of the Foreign Broadcast Information Service (FBIS), provided translations of both print and broadcast media (television and radio) in communist countries. FBIS products were are also available to intelligence analysts, as well as academia and particularly the State Department,

[40]IMDb. "*The Hunt for Red October* (1990)." Accessed July 5, 2019. https://www.imdb.com/title/tt0099810/fullcredits?ref_=tt_ql_1.

[41]Jardines, Eliot A. "Open Source Intelligence." In *The Five Disciplines of Intelligence Collection*, edited by Mark M. Lowenthal and Robert C. Clark. Washington, DC: CQ Press, 2016, 5.

providing keen insights on media, communications, and government actions in these countries to control information and public awareness. The US Information Agency's Voice of America (created during World War II as the Office of War Information) sought to counter the propaganda of state-run media in these countries, providing accurate information to people living under communist governments.

The advent of the internet and social media brought a plethora of new OSINT to the IC; however, the ability to "separate the wheat from the chaff" became more difficult due to the number of sources of information and the challenge of vetting those sources. In the 2016 US presidential election, the charge of "fake news" by the Trump administration to discredit any media source that challenged the administration's narrative was particularly vexing. The IC was not excluded, as the president himself questioned his own IC's assessments on the threat posed by Russian intelligence agencies in influencing social media (particularly Facebook) to support his election.[42]

One of the most significant contributions OSINT has made to intelligence analysis has been in the area of GEOINT, with availability of commercial satellite imagery that often rivals the capabilities of the IC's satellite platforms. In 1972, the launch of the first Landsat promised the availability of satellite imagery for users outside the IC, such as the US Geological Survey, to map land usage, environmental and climate change, forest fire damage, surface water extent, and so on. However, the earlier products did not have the level of resolution needed by the IC for distinguishing between a tank and a commercial truck. Newer commercial imagery providers, such as France's SPOT, Maxar (DigitalGlobe), and Planet, have increased resolution and accessibility, such that the IC now considers open sources of satellite imagery viable collection platforms for satisfying its collection requirements.[43]

Although any intelligence agency can acquire OSINT, the ODNI established the Open Source Center in 2005 to serve as a source of materials from "the Internet, databases, press, radio, television, video, geospatial data, photos, and commercial imagery. This also includes translated material from foreign source."[44] The Open Source Center falls under the CIA as functional manager for OSINT within the IC, coming full circle from its ownership of the FBIS during the Cold War. In 2015, the Open Source Center changed its name to Open Source Enterprise.[45]

---

[42]Davis, Julie Hirschfeld. "Trump, at Putin's Side, Questions US Intelligence on 2016 Election." *The New York Times*, July 18, 2018. https://www.nytimes.com/2018/07/16/world/europe/trump-putin-election-intelligence.html.

[43]Werner, Debra. "NRO Shares Plans for Commercial Imagery Acquisition." *Science News*, June 9, 2019. https://spacenews.com/nro-shares-plans-for-commercial-imagery-acquisition/. For additional information on the use of OSINT by the intelligence community, see Olcott, Anthony. *Open Source Intelligence in a Networked World*. New York, NY: Bloomsbury, 2012.

[44]Jensen, McElreath, and Graves, *Introduction to Intelligence Studies*, 103.

[45]Kringen, John. "Rethinking the Concept of Global Coverage in the US Intelligence Community." *Studies in Intelligence* 59, no. 3 (September 2015): 3.

## Cyber Threat Intelligence

Some intelligence literature has posited that intelligence gathered in cyberspace should be considered a new intelligence discipline called "cyber intelligence."[46] At one point, the use of the term *computer intelligence* (COMPUINT) was bantered about in the IC due to the proliferation of the internet. Most analysts, however, do not consider the domain in which intelligence is gathered to be the source (e.g., SIGINT or GEOINT from space is not considered space intelligence). Rather, the use of the term *cyber threat intelligence* has come into vogue in the IC, when the focus of the threat is to the specific collection platform in cyberspace. Thus, when the ODNI established the **Cyber Threat Intelligence Integration Center (CTIIC)** in 2015, it was considered not a functional manager for "cyber intelligence," but rather a fusion center to integrate intelligence collection on specific threats to the nation's information systems that controlled critical infrastructure.[47]

Intelligence collection remains one of the principal aspects of intelligence operations since intelligence analysis is dependent on collection of information. As this section points out, collection takes place across a number of domains, all of which support analysis. One domain is not more dominant than any other, and the production of intelligence products depends on access to sources of information from "all sources" of intelligence collection. Since most of the platforms and sources of intelligence collection are owned by the military and half of the IC agencies fall under the DOD, military intelligence is addressed as a separate section of this chapter.

## MILITARY INTELLIGENCE

### Defense Intelligence Structure

Of the 17 agencies that are members of the IC, 8 of these are part of the DOD. Each of the four armed services (Army, Navy, Air Force, Marines) has its own intelligence organization, while the other four are national-level agencies (DIA, NSA, NRO, and NGA). While the US Coast Guard is also considered an "armed service," it does not come under the DOD. Rather it is part of the Department of Homeland Security, yet is considered a separate agency under the IC. Given its maritime security and intelligence role, its Intelligence Coordination Center is actually co-located with the Office of Naval Intelligence (ONI) National Maritime Intelligence Center (NMIC) in Suitland, Maryland.

---

[46]Mattern, Troy, John Felker, Randy Borum, and George Bamford. "Operational Levels of Cyber Intelligence." *International Journal of Intelligence and CounterIntelligence* 27, no. 4 (2014): 702–719. doi: 10.1080/08850607.2014.924811.

[47]Stroebel, Warren. "US Creates New Agency to Lead Cyberthreat Tracking." *Reuters*, February 10, 2015. https://www.reuters.com/article/us-cybersecurity-agency/u-s-creates-new-agency-to-lead-cyberthreat-tracking-idUSKBN0LE1EX20150210.

The national intelligence agencies run by the DOD support a wide range of intelligence operations, to include collection, analysis, and even covert operations. The DIA, located at Joint Base Anacostia–Bolling in Washington, DC, provides intelligence support to each of the armed services, as well as combatant commands located throughout the globe. For example, the DIA runs the Defense HUMINT Service, which includes both overt (defense attachés, etc.) and clandestine collection. DIA liaison officers at each regional combatant command provide reach-back capabilities for the command to tap into the DIA's collection and analytical sources, which are often beyond the scope of the military commands. The NSA, located at Fort Meade, provides SIGINT support to the military commands also through liaison officers and collection sites located throughout the globe, which are manned by the military services intelligence agencies. For example, the NSA field site in Hawaii has both military personnel and civilians (to include contractors like Snowden) who work at the site, providing "tailored SIGINT and cyber security support to the Warfighter."[48] The NGA, located at Fort Belvoir in Springfield, Virginia, and in St. Louis, Missouri, provides GEOINT support, through tasking authority of national technical means of collection controlled by the NRO, which is located at Chantilly, Virginia.

## Service Intelligence Agencies

Each of the armed services intelligence agencies is organized to support the needs of the individual military services. The US Army Intelligence and Security Command (INSCOM), located at Fort Belvoir, is comprised of military intelligence units that provide direct support to Army units deployed throughout the globe. For example, the 500th Military Intelligence Brigade (MIB) is located at Schofield Barracks, Hawaii, providing dedicated intelligence support to the US Army Pacific, which supports the US Indo-Pacific Command. Under the 500th MIB are military intelligence battalions, such as the 311th located at Camp Zama, Japan, that support US Army units with multidiscipline intelligence operations in the Asia/Pacific Theater.[49] The Army deploys tactical and operational collection platforms, such as RC-12X Guardrail fixed-wing aircraft (primarily SIGINT); AN/TYQ-224 Ground Station, Operational Intelligence (OGS) (multisource); Distributed Common Ground System–Army (DCGS-A) Enterprise; and a number of drone and helicopter-based systems, as well as Manpack and portable collection systems.

The ONI provides intelligence support to the US Navy's fleets stationed throughout the globe, through its four centers: Nimitz Operational Intelligence Center, Farragut Technical Analysis Center, Kennedy Irregular Warfare Center, and Hopper

---

[48]National Security Agency Central Security Service. "NSA/CSS Hawaii." Accessed July 9, 2019. https://www.nsa.gov/about/cryptologic-centers/hawaii/.

[49]US Army. "500th Military Intelligence Brigade-Theater: Units." Accessed July 9, 2019. https://www.inscom.army.mil/MSC/500MIB/Units.html.

Information Services Center.[50] The Navy also has deployed intelligence platforms to include USNS *Observation Island* (T-AGM-23) (MASINT), P-3 Orion aircraft (SIGINT),[51] and drone platforms, such as the MQ-4C Triton and MQ-8 Fire Scout. Marine Corps Intelligence Command, located at Quantico, Virginia, provides direct support to Marine forces, but also comes under the Department of the Navy. Thus its intelligence support roles are primarily at the tactical level of operations, supporting deployed Marines with organic intelligence collection capabilities, such as dedicated **intelligence, surveillance, and reconnaissance (ISR)** resources (e.g., the Tactical SIGINT Collection System).[52]

---

## BOX 5.8
### FOR EXAMPLE: EP-3 INCIDENT WITH CHINA

In April 2001, a US Navy EP-3 ARIES II aircraft was collecting SIGINT in international waters off China. It was being observed by a Chinese F-8 fighter aircraft, which challenged the Navy reconnaissance aircraft by flying close to the plane and eventually making contact. The Chinese fighter pilot, Wang Wei, was killed, while the EP-3 was forced to make an emergency landing on China's Hainan Island. While the crew was able to destroy some of the intelligence collection systems and information it was collecting prior to landing, the Chinese still gained insight on US intelligence capabilities. The Chinese also won the propaganda war by getting the story out first about how the US "spy" plane had violated China's airspace and caused the death of its pilot, requiring an apology from the United States before releasing the crew members.[53]

---

Air Force intelligence support is provided by the 25th Air Force, located at Lackland Air Force Base in Texas. It is comprised of six wings and a technical applications center. The 9th Reconnaissance Wing operates out of Beale Air Force Base in California and controls a number of reconnaissance squadrons on the West Coast and in the Pacific area of operations. Airborne collection platforms controlled by the 9th Reconnaissance

---

[50]Office of Naval Intelligence. "Centers of Excellence." Accessed July 9, 2019. https://www.oni.navy.mil/.

[51]The older P-3 Orion aircraft are being replaced by the Navy's P-8 Poseidon aircraft, which in addition to the intelligence, surveillance, and reconnaissance capabilities can also conduct antisubmarine warfare.

[52]US Marine Corps. *Marine Corps Intelligence Reconnaissance and Surveillance Enterprise Plan 2015–2020.* Arlington, VA: US Marine Corps, September 2014. https://www.hqmc.marines.mil/Portals/133/Docs/MCISRE_Final_Sept2014.pdf.

[53]Donnelly, Eric. "The United States–China EP-3 Incident: Legality and Realpolitik." *Journal of Conflict and Security Law* 9, no. 1 (2004): 25–42.

**PHOTO 5.2** RC-135V/W Rivet Joint.

Wing include U-2 Dragon Lady, T-38 Talon, and RQ-4 Global Hawk.[54] The Air Force owns most of the airborne intelligence collection platforms used by the military. Examples include the RC-135V/W Rivet Joint (multispectral), RC-135U Combat Sent (strategic communications), MQ-9 Reaper (tactical drone), OC-135B Open Skies (treaty verification), and E-3 Sentry (battle management), as well as fixed phased-array radar sites in Shemya, Alaska (missile tracking).

## Military Intelligence Roles and Missions

The military conducts intelligence operations at the tactical, operational (theater), and strategic levels of warfare. Each of the armed services has a dedicated intelligence staff at the different levels to coordinate intelligence missions for the supported command. In the US Army, the lowest tactical-level intelligence staff officer assigned to a military unit is the battalion S-2 (section 2, intelligence). The S-2 officer and the intelligence staff section are responsible for providing intelligence support to the commander. For example, in an armor battalion, the intelligence staff section would include an officer (captain or lieutenant), a noncommissioned officer in charge (typically a staff sergeant E-6), and three or four additional enlisted personnel with military intelligence occupational specialties. A similar structure would also be at the brigade level (also S-2). At the division and corps levels, it would be called a G-2 (since these organizations are commanded by general officers). A battalion intelligence staff section would have organic collection resources, such as a scout platoon and other combat sections. A brigade intelligence staff section would be able to task the organic elements of the brigade from all battalions and would also be augmented with military intelligence battalion resources at the division level. Any additional intelligence collection requirements would be forwarded to the G-2 staff for support with their organic intelligence resources at the division level, or sent to the corps (or higher headquarters).

The Marines have similar S-2 organizational structures to the Army for their ground combat forces, except they do not have brigades or divisions. The Marines are organized into battalions and then into Marine expeditionary units (MEUs) and Marine expeditionary forces (MEFs). The MEF (like the Army division) is where the Marine military intelligence battalions are located that provide intelligence support to the warfighters. For example, the 1st Military Intelligence Battalion is located at Camp Pendleton, California, to support the MEF that deploys with the Navy's Pacific Fleet.

The Navy has the N-2 as its intelligence staff section. The Navy uses the N staff system for operational levels of command (e.g., squadrons, strike groups, and fleet levels). At a ship level there are two forms of staff structure: the fighting organization and the administrative organization. With the advent of new Navy doctrine in the early 2000s, called **Network Centric Warfare (NCW),** the Navy changed its staff structure to combine the N-2 with the N-39 (information operations) in order to coordinate intelligence and information operations to support NCW. The doctrinal change reflected the rise of computer network operations in the military, which combined offensive computer network attack with defensive computer network defense and intelligence-gathering computer network exploitation functions.

The Air Force's intelligence section, A-2, is located at the squadron, group, wing, and numbered air force levels of organization, as well as higher headquarters staffs. The squadron would be the equivalent of an Army or Marine battalion; a group, consisting of two or three squadrons, would be similar to a brigade; a wing would be the equivalent of a division; and a numbered air force would be similar to a corps or higher. Air Force intelligence officers and noncommissioned officers can also serve as members of a flight crew on an intelligence collection platform, such as the RC-135V/W Rivet Joint, with as many as 14 intelligence operators on board.[55]

The Pentagon's Joint Staff and the theater- and strategic-level regional and functional combatant commands (US Central Command, etc.) are joint commands, and thus their intelligence sections would be coded J-2. The joint commands include personnel from all military services who bring knowledge of their respective service intelligence organizations to support the joint command's mission. For example, in US Southern Command's area of operational responsibility (AOR), intelligence support would include providing knowledge of each of the region's armed forces, to include doctrine, tactics, weapons systems, and key leaders. When a border skirmish between Peru and Ecuador in 1995 turned into a protracted conflict, the J-2 deployed personnel to the war zone to aid in demobilization of forces and identification of weapons systems used by the belligerents (many of which were of vintage Soviet-era design).

Most intelligence sections at all levels of command (tactical, operational, and strategic) are involved in similar missions. These include knowing the threats to friendly military forces in the area (both adversarial state and possibly nonstate actors, such

---

[55]US Air Force. "RC-135V/W Rivet Joint." May 23, 2012. https://www.af.mil/About Us/Fact-Sheets/Display/Article/104608/rc-135vw-rivet-joint/.

as terrorists), developing collection requirements based on the commander's priority intelligence requirements (PIR), understanding the AOR through a process called **Intelligence Preparation of the Battlespace (IPB)**, and providing intelligence support to combat operations and covert operations when necessary. The commander expects the staff section intelligence officer to be able to provide a threat order of battle, to include size, composition, and capabilities of all those potential threats in the AOR. If the intelligence officer does not have the organic collection capabilities that can be tasked to respond to the commander's PIR, then the officer generates requests for information to the next higher level of command. Most of the theater combatant commands also have representatives from the national-level agencies (CIA, NSA, DIA, NGA, etc.), which form a NIST to reach out to their organizations to satisfy the collection requirements.

## Scientific and Technical Intelligence

Three of the military services (Army, Air Force, and Navy) have dedicated scientific and technical intelligence agencies that provide assessments of other nations' military forces. The Army's National Ground Intelligence Center (NGIC) located in Charlottesville, Virginia, focuses on foreign army capabilities, to include assessing doctrine, order of battle, and military weapons systems. It was formed in 1994 out of a merger of the Foreign Science and Technology Center and the Intelligence Threat Analysis Center. One of its key functions is gaining intelligence through foreign material exploitation from equipment captured on battlefields or through acquisition programs. The Air Force has a similar center at Wright–Patterson Air Force Base in Dayton, Ohio, called the National Air and Space Intelligence Center (NASIC). The NASIC focuses on gaining intelligence on the technical capabilities of foreign military aircraft and air defense systems. Whereas the Army's NGIC comes under Army INSCOM, the NASIC no longer comes under the 25th Air Force, but rather has reported directly to the headquarters US Air Force air staff in the Pentagon since 2014. The Navy's scientific and technical intelligence functions are performed by the ONI's Farragut Technical Analysis Center, located within the NMIC in Suitland, Maryland. It assesses the technical capabilities of foreign navies and conducts foreign material exploitation of foreign naval systems.

## CONCLUSION: INTELLIGENCE OPERATIONS SUMMARY

This chapter looked at intelligence operations by examining the complexity and challenges of intelligence given the contemporary security environment and the adversaries faced today. It also discussed collection planning and how intelligence sources and methods are used to gather information of intelligence value. It also examined the five principal intelligence collection disciplines: human intelligence (HUMINT), signals intelligence (SIGINT), geospatial intelligence (GEOINT), measurement and signature intelligence (MASINT), and open source intelligence (OSINT), as well as cyber threat intelligence. Finally, it looked at military intelligence, to include the defense intelligence structure, service intelligence agencies, roles and missions, and scientific and technical intelligence. Two areas not covered in this chapter, which could also be included in intelligence operations, are counterintelligence and covert operations. The authors decided these two topics deserve to be covered in separate chapters due to the complexity and breadth of each. We provide a more in-depth examination of counterintelligence in Chapter 6, and covert operations in Chapter 7.

## KEY CONCEPTS

US intelligence community (IC)   131
Counterterrorism Center (CTC)   132
National Counterterrorism Center (NCTC)   132
national technical means (NTM)   133
Reconnaissance, Surveillance, and Target Acquisition (RSTA)   134
National Intelligence Support Team (NIST)   135
Tactical Exploitation of National Capabilities (TENCAP)   135
National Foreign Intelligence Program (NFIP)   137
General Defense Intelligence Program (GDIP)   137
National Intelligence Priorities Framework (NIPF)   138
National Intelligence Managers (NIMs)   138
human intelligence (HUMINT)   142
National Clandestine Service (NCS)   142
signals intelligence (SIGINT)   145

communications intelligence (COMINT)   146
electronic intelligence (ELINT)   146
foreign instrumentation signals intelligence (FISINT)   146
National Reconnaissance Office (NRO)   147
geospatial intelligence (GEOINT)   147
photographic intelligence (PHOTINT)   148
imagery intelligence (IMINT)   148
National Photographic Interpretation Center (NPIC)   149
measurement and signature intelligence (MASINT)   150
open source intelligence (OSINT)   151
Cyber Threat Intelligence Integration Center (CTIIC)   153
intelligence, surveillance, and reconnaissance (ISR)   155
Network Centric Warfare (NCW)   157
Intelligence Preparation of the Battlespace (IPB)   158

## ADDITIONAL READING

Hall, Michael, and Gary Citrenbaum. *Intelligence Collection: How to Plan and Execute Intelligence Collection in Complex Environments.* Santa Barbara, CA: Praeger Security International, 2014.

Hoffman, David. *The Billion Dollar Spy: A True Story of Cold War Espionage and Betrayal.* New York, NY: Doubleday, 2015.

Jensen, Carl, David McElreath, and Melissa Graves. *Introduction to Intelligence Studies.* New York, NY: CRC Press, 2013.

Kilroy, Richard J., Jr. "Terror and Technology: Domestic Intelligence Collection and the Gossamer of Enhanced Security." *Journal of Policing, Intelligence and Counter Terrorism* 12, no. 2 (2017): 119–141.

Lowenthal, Mark. *Intelligence: From Secrets to Policy*, 7th ed. Washington, DC: CQ Press, 2017.

Lowenthal, Mark, and Robert C. Clark. *The 5 Disciplines of Intelligence Collection.* Washington, DC: CQ Press, 2015.

Olcott, Anthony. *Open Source Intelligence in a Networked World.* New York, NY: Bloomsbury, 2012.

Peterson, Martha D. *The Widow Spy: My CIA Journey From the Jungles of Laos to Prison in Moscow.* Wilmington, NC: Red Canary Press, 2012.

Rose, Alexander. *Washington's Spies: The Story of America's First Spy Ring.* New York, NY: Random House, 2006.

Schoof, Heidi. *Elizabeth Van Lew: A Civil War Spy.* North Mankato, MN: Capstone, 2005.

Sheehan, Neil. *A Bright Shining Lie: John Paul Vann and America in Vietnam.* New York, NY: Vintage Books, 1988.

Smith, Clarence E. "CIA's Analysis of Soviet Science and Technology." In *Watching the Bear: Essays on CIA's Analysis of the Soviet Union*, edited by G. K. Haines and R. E. Leggett. Washington, DC: CIA Center for the Study of Intelligence, 2003.

Stephenson, William. *Spymistress: The True Story of the Greatest Female Secret Agent of World War II.* New York, NY: Arcade, 2011.

Suvorov, Viktor. *Soviet Military Intelligence.* London, UK: Grafton Books, 1986.

Young, Steve. "Using a Principal Agent in Intelligence Collection in Afghanistan." In *Critical Issues in Homeland Security: A Casebook*, edited by J. D. Ramsay and L. Kiltz. Boulder, CO: Westview Press, 2014.

# 6 COUNTERINTELLIGENCE

Richard J. Kilroy Jr.

## THE WORLD OF ESPIONAGE AND INTRIGUE

In 1998, Ali Mohamed, a member of the Egyptian Islamic Jihad (EIJ) and al-Qaeda, was arrested for espionage in the United States. Mohamed was actually a triple agent who had been a member of the US Army Special Forces, an informant for the Federal Bureau of Investigation (FBI), and a Central Intelligence Agency (CIA) recruit. While US intelligence agencies thought they had "turned" Mohamed into a US intelligence asset, he had, in fact, continued to spy for the EIJ and al-Qaeda, providing intelligence to support the 1993 World Trade Center bombing.[1] While Sun Tzu's maxim points out the important work of counterintelligence to "seek out" enemy agents, it also alludes to the potential damage that can occur if the agent continues to work for the adversary.

Counterintelligence is considered a part of intelligence operations (Chapter 5), although the topic is dealt with as a separate chapter in this text in order to provide more depth in coverage and understanding of its importance. Having the most sophisticated intelligence collection capabilities in order to gather intelligence on one's adversaries is of little use if an equally sophisticated counterintelligence effort is not employed to protect against intelligence operations conducted against the state.

## COUNTERINTELLIGENCE ROLES AND MISSIONS

### Defining Counterintelligence

The *Dictionary of Military and Associated Terms* defines counterintelligence (CI) operations as "proactive activities designed to identify, exploit, neutralize, or deter foreign intelligence collection and terrorist activities directed against the United States."[2] While the military focuses its CI efforts on the battlefield tactically and operationally, the FBI and CIA also have responsibility for conducting CI at the strategic level.

---

[1] Combating Terrorism Center at West Point. "Ali Mohamed: A Biographical Sketch." June 2011. https://ctc.usma.edu/app/uploads/2011/06/Ali-Mohammed.pdf.

[2] Department of Defense. "Counterintelligence Operations." In *Dictionary of Military and Associated Terms*, 52. As of June 2020. https://www.jcs.mil/Portals/36/Documents/Doctrine/pubs/dictionary.pdf.

The FBI primarily operates domestically, focused on adversary intelligence operations conducted within the United States. Its missions include the following:

- Protect the secrets of the US intelligence community (IC), using intelligence to focus investigative efforts, and collaborating with our government partners to reduce the risk of espionage and insider threats.

- Protect the nation's critical assets, like our advanced technologies and sensitive information in the defense, intelligence, economic, financial, public health, and science and technology sectors.

- Counter the activities of foreign spies. Through proactive investigations, the FBI identifies who they are and stops what they're doing.

- Keep weapons of mass destruction from falling into the wrong hands, and use intelligence to drive the FBI's investigative efforts to keep threats from becoming reality.[3]

The CIA conducts foreign CI operations by "analyzing the capabilities, intentions, and activities of foreign intelligence services" through its **Counterintelligence Mission Center (CIMC)**.[4] Former CIA director Mike Pompeo elevated the role of the CIMC within the agency so that its director reported directly to him. Also, to prevent repeating some of the CI failures of the past, like Ali Mohamed, much of the work of the CIMC is to conduct better vetting of those agents the CIA is recruiting for its espionage activities.[5] It also works to prevent foreign intelligence agencies from discovering those agents that the CIA has recruited within their intelligence organizations. A failure by the CIA to protect its communications with such agents operating in China led to the disruption of a spy network in 2010.

## BOX 6.1

### FOR EXAMPLE: CHINA'S MSS ROUNDUP OF CIA SPIES

Beginning in 2010, China's **Ministry of State Security (MSS)** began rounding up and executing a number of Chinese nationals identified as spies as a result of the CIA's failure to protect sensitive communications with its agents. The CIA had been

---

[3]Federal Bureau of Investigation. "What We Investigate: Counterintelligence." Accessed July 15, 2019. https://www.fbi.gov/investigate/counterintelligence.

[4]Gertz, Bill. "CIA Director Seeks Stronger Counterintelligence Against Spies and Leakers." *The Washington Free Beacon*, January 18, 2018. https://freebeacon.com/national-security/cia-director-seeks-stronger-counter intelligence-spies-leakers/; Central Intelligence Agency. "Counterintelligence at the CIA: A Brief History." As of March 23, 2018. Accessed September 23, 2020. https://www.cia.gov/news-information/featured-story-archive/2018-featured-story-archive/counterintelligence-at-cia-a-brief-history.html.

[5]Gertz, "CIA Director."

using a communications system developed for operations in the Middle East, which it thought was impenetrable. The agency failed to take into account China's more sophisticated means of conducting cyber operations and breaking the codes being used by the IC to communicate with its agents. A total of 30 agents were suspected of being executed. Once the penetration had been detected, the CIA reportedly conducted an exfiltration operation to try to bring some of its assets out of China before they were arrested.[6]

## Counterintelligence Officers

Within the military, CI officers are assigned to tactical and operational units to provide CI support to the military commands. At the brigade level, a CI officer is often a warrant officer who works closely with the S-2 intelligence officer on the brigade staff. The CI officer helps to assess the level of training of personnel in the unit to identify threats to the mission and protect sensitive information. In Germany, during the Cold War, the CI officer would operate under cover, in civilian clothes, and visit local bars to engage service members in conversation to see what information about the unit they were willing to reveal. The CI officers would also conduct "dumpster diving" by sifting through office trash to see what had been thrown away and whether any of the information discovered could provide details on unit readiness. During exercises, CI officers would also visit unit deployment sites to see what had been left behind once a unit departed, to include codebooks, keys, and even weapons or other sensitive items.

## BOX 6.2

### SPOTLIGHT ON CAREERS
INTELLIGENCE OPERATIONS
SPECIALIST (COUNTERINTELLIGENCE)

**GS 0132-13 (2019)**

**Summary**

This position is located in Department of Homeland Security, United States Coast Guard (USCG), Assistant Commandant for Intelligence and Criminal Investigations, Counterintelligence Service (CIS), OPS and Investigation Division, Boston, Massachusetts.

*(Continued)*

[6]Dorfman, Zach. "Botched CIA Communications System Helped Blow Cover of Chinese Agents." *Foreign Policy*, August 18, 2018. https://foreignpolicy.com/2018/08/15/botched-cia-communications-system-helped-blow-cover-chinese-agents-intelligence/.

(Continued)

**Responsibilities**

You will serve as an Intelligence Operations Specialist (Counterintelligence CI) and as the Resident-Agent-in-Charge at the USCG First District (D1). You will be responsible for executing CI activities and CI investigations and maintaining responsibility for CG Human Intelligence (HUMINT) missions throughout the D1 and for coordinating those associated activities with internal and external partners.

**Typical work assignments include:**

Executing the CGCIS mission within the Boston area, including management of CGCIS activities conducted by other CGCIS agents assigned or supporting the CGCIS D1.

Within intelligence agencies, CI officers investigate insiders for potential recruitment by adversary intelligence services. Probably the most famous CI officer was the CIA's James Angleton, who considered CI work "a wilderness of mirrors" as he sought out Soviet moles within the agency during the Cold War. Angleton was a controversial character, much feared within the IC, due to his support of questionable tactics to target suspected adversary agents. His efforts, along with the CIA's Operation MHCHAOS (targeting student dissident groups), led to charges of infringement of civil liberties of US citizens. CI operations conducted by the CIA, as well as the **Counter Intelligence Program (COINTELPRO)** conducted by the FBI (targeting suspected Communist Party members), eventually led to investigations by the US Congress (Church and Pike Committee hearings in the 1970s), which had a major impact on IC agencies' ability to operate within the United States.[7]

Today, due to the increasing threat of economic espionage, many US corporations, particularly those involved in the defense industries, have dedicated CI personnel working in the private sector to detect adversary intelligence agencies targeting their companies and employees for recruitment. The FBI has a dedicated Economic Espionage Unit to assist those CI personnel in US corporations to prevent the theft of trade secrets. Operating under the authority of the 1996 Economic Espionage Act, the FBI works to protect trade secrets from foreign espionage activities, advocating that US companies take the following actions to protect against penetration:

- Recognize the threat.

- Identify and value trade secrets.

---

[7]Robarge, David. "The Angleton Phenomenon." *CIA Studies in Intelligence* 53, no. 4 (December 2009). https://www.cia.gov/library/center-for-the-study-of-intelligence/csi-publications/csi-studies/studies/vol53no4/201ccunning-passages-contrived-corridors201d.html.

- Implement a definable plan for safeguarding trade secrets.

- Secure physical trade secrets and limit access to trade secrets.

- Provide ongoing security training to employees.

- Develop an insider threat program.

- Proactively report suspicious incidents to the FBI before your proprietary information is irreversibly compromised.[8]

## Insider Threats

The most damaging cases of espionage to the United States have historically been insiders who are US citizens who work for the different IC organizations. Due to their access to classified information about intelligence operations being conducted by the agency against adversaries, such as the Soviet Union during the Cold War, these individuals have often compromised those operations and, more importantly, risked the lives of agents recruited by those agencies.

## BOX 6.3
### FOR EXAMPLE: ALDRICH AMES AND ROBERT HANSSEN

Two of the most notorious spies in US history are Aldrich Ames (CIA) and Robert Hanssen (FBI). Ames spied for the Soviet Union from 1985 to 1993, while Hanssen's spying took place from 1979 to 2001, long after the end of the Cold War. What made Hanssen's spying so egregious was that his position within the FBI was CI, which provided him access to information about Soviet, and later Russian, intelligence activities in the United States and abroad. "Together, their leaks resulted in the exposure of hundreds of U.S. assets in the Soviet Union, but their most direct damage to the U.S. military was from exposing one high-level asset. Gen. Dmitri Polyakov was the head of Soviet intelligence and a major spy for the U.S., providing information on Soviet anti-armored missile technology, the Cuban Missile Crisis, and China. That fountain of military intelligence shut down when Polyakov was revealed by Ames and Hanssen, leading to Polyakov's execution in 1988."[9]

---

[8]Department of Justice, Federal Bureau of Investigation. "Economic Espionage: Protecting America's Trade Secrets." Accessed July 15, 2019. https://www.fbi.gov/file-repository/economic-espionage-1.pdf.

[9]Nye, David, "11 Spies Who Did the Worst Damage to the US Military." *Real Clear Defense*, June 3, 2015. https://www.realcleardefense.com/articles/2015/06/04/11_american_spies_who_did_the_worst_damage_to_the_us_military_108022.html.

In order for CI officers to be able to detect potential threats to their agencies, they need to understand what motivates an individual to conduct espionage and be willing to conduct treason against one's own country. The traditional motivations have been **money, ideology, compromise (or blackmail), and ego (MICE)**.[10] Aldrich Ames was primarily motived by money, while Robert Hanssen's motivation was mostly ego and excitement. Ana Montes, an intelligence analyst at the Defense Intelligence Agency (DIA), was convicted of spying for Cuba in 2001. Her motivation was ideological, having developed a sympathy for revolutionary movements in Latin America during her college education at the University of Virginia and Johns Hopkins University, where she openly criticized US foreign policy in the region.[11] US Marine Corps sergeant Clayton Lonetree was a Marine security guard at the US embassy in Moscow in 1985 when he was seduced by Violetta Seina, a Russian woman employed at the US embassy who was actually a source for the KGB (Soviet intelligence agency). Due to his being compromised by violating US policy against fraternization with Russian nationals, he was blackmailed by the KGB into committing espionage and providing the Soviets with information on the US embassies and personnel stationed in Moscow and later in Vienna, Austria.[12]

Although the MICE acronym does help to understand the motivation for many spy cases, it doesn't capture all the reasons someone might commit espionage and challenge CI officers in today's contemporary security environment, dealing with both state and nonstate actors. Robert Cialdini proposed the acronym RASCLS as a "weapon of mass influence" in trying to understand the complexity of human motivations through his study of psychology and marketing. It stands for **reciprocation, authority, scarcity, commitment (and consistency), liking, and social proof (RASCLS)**.[13] Intelligence officers looking to recruit spies are moving beyond the traditional motivations, captured by the MICE acronym, to look at multiple factors in order to understand human behavior. Understanding such "weapons of mass influence" developed by Cialdini can also help CI officers understand human vulnerability and susceptibility to being targeted for recruitment by adversary intelligence agencies and nonstate actors, such as terrorist and criminal organizations.

---

[10]Burkett, Randy. "An Alternative Framework for Agent Recruitment: From MICE to RASCLS." *Studies in Intelligence* 57, no. 1 (March 2013). https://www.cia.gov/library/center-for-the-study-of-intelligence/csi-publications/csi-studies/studies/vol.-57-no.-1-a/vol.-57-no.-1-a-pdfs/Burkett-MICE%20to%20RASCALS.pdf.

[11]Patterson, Thom. "The Most Dangerous US Spy You've Never Heard Of." *CNN*, August 8, 2018. https://www.cnn.com/2016/07/06/us/declassified-ana-montes-american-spy-profile/index.html.

[12]History of Spies. "Clayton Lonetree." Accessed July 23, 2019. https://historyofspies.com/clayton-lonetree/.

[13]Burkett, "Alternative Framework," 7.

## DEFENSIVE COUNTERINTELLIGENCE

### Fundamentals

CI is inherently defensive by nature, since its goal is to prevent an adversary from collecting information of intelligence value. Hank Prunckun notes that the fundamental tenets of defensive CI include detection and deterrence.[14] Yet, being defensive does not mean being passive. In other words, defensive CI can also involve more active measures to be able to both detect the threat and deter that threat. In order to detect a threat, any organization can apply some basic principles to identify threats, assess risk, and determine vulnerabilities in order to shore up its defenses. A **threat assessment** follows the simple formula threat (T) = capability (C) + intent (I). Capability can further be assessed as knowledge (K) + resources (R), and intent can further be assessed as desire (D) + expectations (E). Once the threats are evaluated, a **risk assessment** then determines the likelihood (L) or probability of the threats targeting that organization and the consequences (C) if they are successful. A **vulnerability assessment** can then determine the weaknesses of the organization by the formula vulnerability (V) = target information attractiveness (A) + ease of penetration (EP) + impact (I).[15] Noting these vulnerabilities can then enable an organization to take effective measures to deter a threat by looking across a number of security domains.

### Security Domains

Conducting these types of assessments enables the CI professionals to offer reasonable recommendations on defensive countermeasures to protect an organization based on the most likely threats, risks, or vulnerabilities it faces. In other words, if an organization assesses its most likely threat is an insider, rather than someone attempting to gain access to the organization from outside, then it will focus on different measures to detect and deter that type of threat, looking across five security domains: physical, personnel, information, cyber, and communications.

Physical security is the domain where the IC puts much of its attention to threats by taking defensive measures such as erecting barriers (walls), locking doors, positioning security cameras, hiring security guards, and installing intrusion detection systems. Anyone who has visited one of the intelligence agencies can attest to the strict security measures in place to gain access to the facility. Once inside, there are also levels of security access based on compartmentalization of data and "need to know."

---

[14]Prunckun, Hank. *Counterintelligence: Theory and Practice.* Lanham, MD: Rowman & Littlefield, 2013, 25.
[15]Ibid., 54–69.

Personnel security is also extremely tight within the IC to ensure that those being hired to work in the organization are not adversary agents. Gaining a security clearance (depending on the level of clearance and sensitivity of the organization's work) can take up to one year or longer. Typical personnel security measures include background checks (criminal, financial, medical, etc.), investigations (interviews, employment history, residences, foreign contacts, social media, etc.), and in some cases a polygraph (lie detector test). Employees with security clearances are also required to sign a **nondisclosure agreement (NDA)**, which commits them to protecting the classified information they have access to in their job and not releasing it to unauthorized persons.

Information security involves all measures taken to protect classified or sensitive information from disclosure, through proper handling, marking, storage, and destruction of such material. Before the advent of computing technology, classified information was almost always in printed documents, which required the use of special containers, such as safes or large rooms or facilities called **Sensitive Compartmented Information Facilities (SCIFs)**. Since most classified information today exists in digital format on computer drives, that information still needs to be protected in similar facilities where those computers and databases reside.

Cybersecurity involves the transmission of classified information over secure networks and ensuring that top-secret information is not sent over an unclassified computer system. The military uses three networks to separate classified information: the Joint Worldwide Intelligence Communications System (JWICS; top secret/code word), the Secret Internet Protocol Router Network (SIPRNet; secret/not code word), and Non-classified Internet Protocol Router Network (NIPRNet; unclassified/for official use only). A more recent development is the use of Intellipedia, a classified version of Wikipedia, which allows intelligence analysts to share intelligence products across agencies, although it never quite caught on as the collaborative tool imagined for creating and sharing National Intelligence Estimates.[16]

Communications security (COMSEC) was historically how radio or telephone conversations were protected from communications intelligence collection. While there is still a need to protect sensitive communications and avoid discussing classified information over nonsecure telephones, much of the focus of COMSEC today is in cyberspace and monitoring what IC employees are discussing in email, on social media, in chat rooms, in text messages, on Snapchat, and so on. Adversary intelligence agencies still use different communications means to gain access to sensitive information through social engineering, spearfishing, and other means. Despite all the advancements in encryption of data today, it only takes someone carelessly revealing a password over the phone to an unauthorized individual belonging to a foreign intelligence service to gain access to a secure network.

---

[16]Dreyfuss, Emily. "The Wikipedia for Spies and Where It Goes From Here." *Wired*, March 10, 2017. https://www.wired.com/2017/03/intellipedia-wikipedia-spies-much/.

## BOX 6.4

### FOR EXAMPLE: DEPARTMENT OF JUSTICE ATTACK IN 2016

"The United States Department of Justice fell for a social engineering attack that resulted in the leak of personal details of 20,000 FBI and 9,000 DHS employees. The hacker claimed that he downloaded 200 GB of sensitive government files out of a terabyte of the data to which he had access.

The attack began with the hacker gaining access to the email account of a DOJ employee through unknown means. After this, he attempted to access a web portal that required an access code that he didn't have. Rather than give up, the attacker called the department's number and, claiming to be a new employee, asked for help, resulting in them giving him their access code to use. With this code, he was able to access the DOJ intranet using his stolen email credentials, giving him full access to three different computers on the DOJ network as well as databases containing military emails and credit card information. He leaked internal DOJ contact information as proof of the hack, but it is unknown what else he had access to and might have stolen off of the DOJ intranet."[17]

## OFFENSIVE COUNTERINTELLIGENCE

### Fundamentals

There is an axiom that the best defense is a good offense. In other words, don't wait for the adversary to come to you, but rather be proactive in taking the fight to your adversaries, particularly when it comes to CI operations. Thus, as Hank Prunckun notes, the fundamental tenets of offensive CI include detection, deception, and neutralization.[18] Detection would be the same as for defensive CI, understanding the threat, risk, and vulnerabilities. Deception includes actions taken to deliberately mislead adversaries by throwing them off track in their collection efforts expending an inordinate amount of time or resources. Neutralization involves much more direct actions to thwart collection by using counterespionage, traps, double crosses, and other methods.

Any offensive CI operation must work hand-in-hand with defensive CI operations. Otherwise, the effort will be counterproductive and, at worst, allow adversaries to focus on the most lucrative targets. For example, if a deception story is that the

[17]Poston, Howard. "The Top Ten Most Famous Social Engineering Attacks." Infosec Security Awareness, July 26, 2018. https://resources.infosecinstitute.com/the-top-ten-most-famous-social-engineering-attacks/#gref.

[18]Prunckun, *Counterintelligence*, 25.

main military action will be an amphibious assault, then the Marines preparing for the assault need to train and practice for the assault as if it will be the main attack (and should not be told they are part of a deception operation). Likewise, offensive CI must work with intelligence collection operations to ensure that the message being communicated to the adversaries on intelligence gaps also dovetails with the deception or neutralization operation (e.g., focusing collection on the beachhead for the amphibious assault, as if it is the main attack).

## Deception Operations

Winston Churchill is credited with saying that "in wartime the truth is so precious that it must be protected by a bodyguard of lies."[19] The success of the D-Day invasion of France in June 1944 lends credence to what many consider to be the most successful large-scale theater-level wartime deception operation ever conducted.[20] Yet, in order to create such an elaborate deception story and make it believable to the Germans, it took a significant amount of planning, from the use of inflatable tanks and fake communications to soldiers wearing fake unit patches and creating vehicle tracks on the ground to convince any aerial imagery that the vehicles were real. It even involved the creation of an entire fake army, the First US Army Group, under the command of Lieutenant General George Patton, to convince Hitler that the main invasion would still take place at Pas-de-Calais, rather than Normandy, and thus keep his reserve forces tied down to support the defense of that part of the French coastline.[21]

Military deception involves the use of very simple techniques, such as decoys and camouflage, to disguise actual unit locations or create a false narrative of weapons capabilities. From the ground these may not look very realistic, but from the air or from

PHOTO 6.1 Russian S-300 surface-to-air missile decoy.

Xabier Eskisabel/CC BY-SA (https://creativecommons.org/licenses/by-sa/2.0)/Wikimedia Commons

---

[19]International Churchill Society. "Correct Attributions or Red Herrings?" Spring 2006. https://winston-churchill.org/publications/finest-hour/finest-hour-130/correct-attributions-or-red-herrings/.

[20]Brown, Anthony Cave. *Bodyguard of Lies: The Extraordinary True Story Behind D-Day*. New York, NY: Harper Collins, 1975.

[21]Ibid.

reconnaissance satellites they can be very effective at causing the enemy to attack the suspected target.

Military deception can also involve more complex operations, such as feints, displays, demonstrations, and ruses (trick of war). These are all considered lawful in wartime to deceive an adversary. What is not lawful under the Law of Armed Conflict are "perfidious acts" or perfidy, which is a manipulation of existing laws of warfare designed to protect noncombatants or medical units. An example would be putting a red cross on a military building to trick an adversary into believing it was a hospital, so as to avoid being targeted. Similarly, a troop transport vehicle cannot cover its movements by placing a red cross (or crescent) to disguise actual military operations.[22]

## BOX 6.5

### FOR EXAMPLE: THE HAVERSACK RUSE

During World War I, the British were at a stalemate in their operations in Palestine, having been unsuccessful in defeating the German-Turkish forces along the Gaza-Beersheba line. After two failed attacks on Gaza, General Sir Archibald Murray was replaced by General Sir Edmund Allenby. Allenby decided to use a deception plan to convince the Germans that an attack on Beersheba was only a feint and the main attack would once again be at Gaza. Allenby's new intelligence officer, Major Richard Meinertzhagen, devised a ruse, or trick of war, in the form of a lost haversack during a reconnaissance patrol. The haversack contained details of the war plans that the attack on Beersheba was only a feint. To convince the Germans that it was real, it also contained personal items belonging to the officer who "lost" it, to include a letter from his wife about their newborn son (written by an Army nurse at a hospital in Egypt). Meinertzhagen supported the deception story with intercepted signals intelligence, as well as human intelligence, by having British and Australian soldiers "gossip" about the intelligence officer who lost important documents. The result was a successful main attack on Beersheba and later defeat of the German and Turkish forces at Gaza.[23]

[22]Joint Forces Staff College, National Defense University. "Joint Publication 3-13-4: Military Deception." January 26, 2012. https://jfsc.ndu.edu/Portals/72/Documents/JC2IOS/Additional_Reading/1C3-JP_3-13-4_MILDEC.pdf.

[23]Eddow, Andrew W. *The Haversack Ruse, and British Deception Operations in Palestine During World War I.* Unpublished master's thesis. Newport, RI: US Naval War College, June 17, 1994. https://apps.dtic.mil/dtic/tr/fulltext/u2/a279574.pdf.

## Neutralization

In CI, the term *neutralization* refers to the ability to render an adversary's intelligence collection operations as useless or to actually defeat adversaries' efforts by frustrating their activities. It is different from deception in that with deception, you want the adversary's intelligence operation to believe the information you want the adversary to collect, reinforcing any perception biases the adversary may have already formed. Neutralization seeks at the least to make adversary collection efforts ineffective, and at the worst to actually disable a collection platform (or agent) from performing the mission. An example of neutralization would be capturing a suspected spy or breaking up a spy network (such as the Walker family spy ring in the US Navy in the 1980s). It could also include jamming adversary radar to prevent it from identifying a potential target on the battlefield. For aerial reconnaissance platforms, neutralization could include engaging the platform (e.g., shooting down a drone or aircraft) or limiting the ability to overfly a position by taking threatening actions (such as China did with the EP-3 incident mentioned in Chapter 5, Box 5.8).

Efforts to neutralize an adversary's intelligence operations can also involve the diversion of resources by creating a false narrative or potentially lucrative target so as to draw out the threat and make it easier to defeat the adversary. Shortly after the terrorist attacks on 9/11, the Department of Defense (DOD) was tasked with providing homeland defense in support of other federal agencies involved in the new homeland security mission area to protect potential targets in the United States. One example was the Salt Lake City Winter Olympics, which took place in February 2002. Large-scale sporting events like the Olympics were considered lucrative targets for terrorist attacks (like that which occurred at the Munich Summer Olympics in 1972). The military provided increased security and intelligence support to law enforcement agencies, to include identifying any potential intelligence collection efforts and devising means to neutralize the threat's ability to gain intelligence on the security efforts in place in Utah.

## CONTEMPORARY CHALLENGES FOR COUNTERINTELLIGENCE

### Cyber Domain

Today, operations to counter adversary intelligence collection are much more difficult given the large amount of information that is available in cyberspace. As mentioned in Chapter 5, open source intelligence has been a boon for intelligence collectors who are able to access large amounts of information via the internet. On the flip side, this means that adversary intelligence organizations also have access to such information, which challenges the CI and security community. Just as cybercrime has become much more lucrative and profitable, rather than breaking into banks or robbing stores, cyber intelligence threats are expanding significantly, as more and more nations are developing cyber intelligence collection capabilities and even cyber warfare units able to target critical infrastructure, as well as government agencies.

Countering adversary intelligence collection in cyberspace falls to federal, state, and local government agencies and the private sector, which work together to face these threats. In the 1990s, the FBI stood up the **National Infrastructure Protection Center (NIPC)**, together with the CIA and DOD. The NIPC tracked cyber intrusions into the nation's power grid, telecommunications, water, financial, and transportation sectors. After the attacks on 9/11, the functions of the NIPC were transferred to the new Department of Homeland Security, today residing in its **Cybersecurity and Infrastructure Security Agency (CISA)**. CISA works with the private sector through a series of **Information Sharing and Analysis Centers (ISACs)** across 21 critical infrastructure sectors to help those industries detect cyber espionage activities and potential cyber attacks.[24]

The National Security Agency (NSA) has the mission of computer network defense through information assurance, protecting the DOD agencies from intrusions into their information systems. According to the NSA, what are commonly referred to as cyber attacks on DOD systems are often "cyber reconnaissance" by adversary intelligence agencies searching for access to classified information by seeking vulnerabilities that can be exploited. These vulnerabilities can also be used as staging for the delivery of a malicious code to be used to conduct an actual cyber attack at a later date.[25]

## National Counterintelligence and Security Center

Within the IC, "the **National Counterintelligence Executive [NCIX]** under section 902 of the Counterintelligence Enhancement Act of 2002 [50 U.S.C. 3382] is a component of the Office of the Director of National Intelligence [ODNI]."[26] In 2014, the DNI merged the NCIX with other functions under the DNI, such as the Center for Security Evaluation, the Special Security Center, and the National Insider Threat Task Force, in order to better coordinate all the CI functions being performed by the agency. Today, the **National Counterintelligence and Security Center (NCSC)** exists "to protect and defend U.S. infrastructure, facilities, classified networks, information and personnel."[27]

[24]National Council of ISACs. "About NCI." Accessed July 19, 2019. https://www.nationalisacs.org/about-nci.

[25]National Security Agency. "Cyber Security Report: NSA/CSS Technical Cyber Threat Framework v2." A Report From Cybersecurity Operations, the Cybersecurity Products and Sharing Division, November 13, 2018. https://www.nsa.gov/Portals/70/documents/what-we-do/cybersecurity/professional-resources/ctr-nsa-css-technical-cyber-threat-framework.pdf.

[26]US Code, Title 50: War and National Defense, Chapter 44, Section 3031, National Counterintelligence Executive, 2015: 502.

[27]Office of the Director of National Intelligence. "History of NCSC." Accessed July 19, 2019. https://www.dni.gov/index.php/ncsc-who-we-are/ncsc-history.

To perform this mission, the NCSC is responsible for creating the **National Threat Identification and Prioritization Assessment (NTIPA)**, which develops priorities for CI collection, investigations, and operations. The NCSC is also responsible for program budgets and evaluations that reflect the DNI's strategic priorities. It also conducts damage assessments for espionage cases within the various intelligence agencies, which includes the impact on sources and methods, as well as associated costs in remediating the effects. Depending on the case, the impact of an espionage case can last for years, damaging national security and even putting the IC's own collection platforms or agents at risk. The NCSC has an educational mission to enhance CI awareness, outreach, and training for all 17 agencies in the IC. It also supports other federal agencies within the US government, as well as the private sector.

## CONCLUSION: COUNTERINTELLIGENCE SUMMARY

Counterintelligence is a critical component of intelligence operations. It runs throughout all steps of the intelligence cycle, impacting planning and direction, collection, processing and exploitation, analysis, dissemination, and feedback, all of which are susceptible to adversary intelligence operations. Yet, CI is also critical to the nation's federal, state, and local government agencies and private sector, which are increasingly becoming targets of adversary intelligence. The recent investigations into Russian interference in the 2016 presidential elections demonstrate the extent to which foreign intelligence agencies will go to impact the United States' democratic institutions by compromising the integrity of the electoral process. The threat to the nation is so significant that in 2019 members of the US Senate petitioned to have funding for protecting state and local electoral processes included in the National Defense Authorization Act.[28]

Detecting intrusions by adversary intelligence agencies in the private sector is also a growing concern, since economic espionage can be a national security threat. Countries such as China, Russia, and Iran have sophisticated intelligence collection operations targeting US technology and industry constituting an advanced persistent threat in cyberspace.[29] Stealing trade secrets is estimated to cost the US economy $450 billion annually, with most of the spying being done by China.[30] In 2019, FBI director Christopher Wray stated that China constituted the most significant CI threat to the United States, noting the vulnerabilities of US universities in particular to Chinese espionage activities.[31]

[28]Personal observations of the author in the Senate gallery on June 25, 2019.

[29]National Counterintelligence and Security Center. *Foreign Economic Espionage in Cyberspace, 2018.* Accessed July 19, 2019. https://www.dni.gov/files/NCSC/documents/news/20180724-economic-espionage-pub.pdf.

[30]Staff. "Stolen Secrets." *Full Measure*, December 2, 2018. http://fullmeasure.news/news/terrorism-security/stolen-secrets.

[31]Fischer, Karen. "American Universities Are Called Vulnerable to China Threat." *Chronicle of Higher Education*, July 24, 2019. https://www.chronicle.com/article/American-Universities-Are/246762.

CI efforts to detect, deter, and, when necessary, deceive and neutralize foreign intelligence operations did not decrease with the end of the Cold War. If anything, they have increased as the number of state and nonstate actors conducting espionage has grown significantly. Understanding the threats posed by adversary intelligence agencies and the risks or vulnerabilities intelligence agencies (as well as other government organizations and private sector businesses) face can help these agencies and organizations develop appropriate CI policies, procedures, and strategies.

## KEY CONCEPTS

Counterintelligence Mission Center (CIMC)   162
Ministry of State Security (MSS)   162
Counter Intelligence Program (COINTELPRO)   164
money, ideology, compromise (or blackmail), and ego (MICE)   166
reciprocation, authority, scarcity, commitment (and consistency), liking, and social proof (RASCLS)   166
threat assessment   167
risk assessment   167
vulnerability assessment   167
nondisclosure agreement (NDA)   168

Sensitive Compartmented Information Facilities (SCIFs)   168
National Infrastructure Protection Center (NIPC)   173
Cybersecurity and Infrastructure Security Agency (CISA)   173
Information Sharing and Analysis Centers (ISACs)   173
National Counterintelligence Executive (NCIX)   173
National Counterintelligence and Security Center (NCSC)   173
National Threat Identification and Prioritization Assessment (NTIPA)   174

## ADDITIONAL READING

Barker, Rodney. *Dancing With the Devil: Sex, Espionage and the US Marines: The Clayton Lonetree Story.* New York, NY: Simon & Schuster, 1996.

Brown, Anthony Cave. *Bodyguard of Lies: The Extraordinary True Story Behind D-Day.* New York, NY: HarperCollins, 1975.

Burkett, Randy. "An Alternative Framework for Agent Recruitment: From MICE to RASCLS." *Studies in Intelligence* 57, no. 1 (March 2013). https://www.cia.gov/library/center-for-the-study-of-intelligence/csi-publications/csi-studies/studies/vol.-57-no.-1-a/vol.-57-no.-1-a-pdfs/Burkett-MICE%20to%20RASCALS.pdf.

Dorfman, Zach. "Botched CIA Communications System Helped Blow Cover of Chinese Agents." *Foreign Policy*, August 18, 2018. https://foreignpolicy.com/2018/08/15/botched-cia-communications-system-helped-blow-cover-chinese-agents-intelligence.

Grimes, Sandra, and Jeanne Vertefeuille. *Circle of Treason: CIA Traitor Aldrich Ames and the Men He Betrayed.* Annapolis, MD: Naval Institute Press, 2012.

Jensen, Carl, David McElreath, and Melissa Graves. *Introduction to Intelligence Studies.* New York, NY: CRC Press, 2013.

Lowenthal, Mark. *Intelligence: From Secrets to Policy*, 7th ed. Washington, DC: CQ Press, 2017.

Olson, James M. *To Catch a Spy: The Art of Counterintelligence.* Washington, DC: Georgetown University Press, 2019.

Prunckun, Hank. *Counterintelligence: Theory and Practice.* Lanham, MD: Rowman & Littlefield, 2012.

Robarge, David. "The Angleton Phenomenon." *CIA Studies in Intelligence* 53, no. 4 (December 2009). https://www.cia.gov/library/center-for-the-study-of-intelligence/csi-publications/csi-studies/studies/vol53no4/201ccunning-passages-contrived-corridors 201d.html.

Vise, David A. *The Bureau and the Mole: The Unmasking of Robert Philip Hanssen, the Most Dangerous Double Agent in FBI History.* New York, NY: Atlantic Monthly Press, 2002.

# 7 COVERT ACTION

## Christopher J. Ferrero

Sometimes neither overt diplomacy nor the overt use of military force can help a country achieve its national security and foreign policy objectives. Under such circumstances, leaders often seek a **third option**. This third option is covert action. **Covert action** is fundamentally different from other, more common intelligence activities. The primary mission of intelligence agencies is to collect, process, analyze, and disseminate information in order to give policymakers decision advantage. Their role is to provide objective support to decision making—not to make or carry out foreign and national security policy. Covert action is the exception to this rule. In covert action, an intelligence agency helps to design and execute foreign and national security policy. This policy is carried out in a disguised manner—or covertly—to conceal the involvement of one's government and produce **plausible deniability**. The 1947 National Security Act defines covert action as "an activity or activities of the United States Government [USG] to influence political, economic, or military conditions abroad, where it is intended that the role of the USG will not be apparent or acknowledged publicly."[1]

Readers should notice a few things about this official definition. First, covert action seeks to influence conditions and outcomes. This is distinct from the routine collection and analysis performed by intelligence agencies. In covert action, which is relatively rare, the intelligence community moves from being an observer and analyst of world affairs to a participant in shaping events. As explained later in this chapter, this cannot happen in the United States without strict oversight and presidential direction. Second, the official definition states that covert action targets conditions and events *abroad*; it is illegal for the US government to perform covert action against domestic targets. Third, the official definition does not specify the agency or agencies responsible for covert action. In the United States, the Central Intelligence Agency (CIA) is the de facto lead agency for covert action, but the president is legally permitted to delegate responsibility for covert action to other agencies. Military entities are a common alternative executor of covert action. In many cases, militaries and intelligence agencies cooperate or pursue parallel activities that constitute covert action. Since the terrorist attacks of September 11, 2001, the line between CIA covert action

---

[1]Office of the Director of National Intelligence. "1947 National Security Act." Accessed January 4, 2020. https://www.dni.gov/index.php/ic-legal-reference-book/national-security-act-of-1947.

and military special operations has become blurred. The gray area between covert action and military operations is explained later in this chapter. Finally, readers may note the nuance in the words "apparent or acknowledged publicly." The *ideal* covert action will not be apparent—meaning clear or obvious. Sometimes, however, it *is* clear or obvious that a covert foreign effort is driving events, such as when insurgents acquire advanced weaponry unavailable on the black market. In some cases, it may even be largely attributable—or apparent who the source is—such as when the United States supplied the Afghan mujahedeen with Stinger antiaircraft missiles during their resistance against Soviet occupation in the 1980s, and in the case of CIA drone strikes on terrorists in Pakistan since the 9/11 attacks. In such instances, use of the term *covert* strains credulity. Yet the government will still not acknowledge these actions publicly or officially. Doing so maintains at least a thin veneer of plausible deniability. Denying responsibility serves a face-saving political purpose for the target. Public acknowledgment may make the target feel that it has no choice but to retaliate. Keeping activity in the shadows can prevent a simmering conflict from escalating to a boil. When covert action is apparent but not publicly acknowledged, one might label it with the oxymoron **overt–covert action**.[2] Overt–covert action has become increasingly common in recent years. Governments perform actions that they officially deny but that are often clearly attributable to them.

## BOX 7.1
### CLANDESTINE VS. COVERT

It is a common mistake to use the words *clandestine* and *covert* interchangeably. There is an important distinction. *Clandestine* implies that a given action may be *attributable, but not detectable.* For example, the United States knows that Russia is trying to collect intelligence on it; it can attribute intelligence collection to Russia. It knows, for example, that certain Russian diplomats posted to the United States are truly spies operating under official cover. But if these Russian agents are effective at acting clandestinely, the United States does not know specifically what they have collected or how or when they have done so. Their specific acts of spying cannot be detected. As such, we use the word *clandestine* mainly to describe *hidden collection efforts.*

When one acts covertly, the action taken *may be obvious or detectable.* What remains secret is the *sponsorship* of the activity. In other words, *the actor is disguised.* For example, imagine that Iran is pursuing a covert action to arm an insurgent group that is fighting Saudi Arabia. The Saudis may notice that the

[2]Wettering, Frederick. "(C)overt Action: The Disappearing 'C.'" *International Journal of Intelligence and Counterintelligence* 16, no. 4 (2003): 570.

insurgent group they are fighting has acquired new and advanced weapons. This fact can hardly remain secret once the insurgent group begins using these weapons. What remains unknown—or covert—is the source of these weapons. Where did the insurgents' weapons come from? If Iran can successfully disguise or plausibly deny its involvement in providing these weapons, it has waged a successful covert action.

While it may take some time to appreciate the distinction between *clandestine* and *covert*, remember this cardinal distinction: covert action is *not* a collection operation—it is disguised action taken to achieve a specific foreign policy goal.

## TYPES OF COVERT ACTION

Covert action can manifest in several ways. Often, a country pursuing a covert action strategy will employ a combination of tactics to achieve its policy objective. The most common categories of covert action are as follows:

- Information operations

- Political activity

- Economic activity

- Sabotage

- Coups

- Support to paramilitary operations

- Secret participation in combat

- Targeted killing/assassination

### Information Operations

Information and ideas are powerful. They are major currencies of world politics. It is thus not surprising that governments attempt to harness and shape the information environment in order to protect or further the national interest. Not all such efforts are covert. Governments routinely issue public statements, and many overtly sponsor some form of state media. When states seek to shape the information environment in a secret, nonattributable manner, however, they enter the realm of covert action. Such activities are often referred to as propaganda operations. *Merriam-Webster* defines propaganda as "the spreading of ideas, information, or rumor for the purpose of helping or injuring an institution, a cause, or a person."[3] Though this definition allows for

---

[3] *Merriam-Webster*. "Propaganda." Accessed June 11, 2019. https://www.merriam-webster.com/dictionary/propaganda.

propaganda to include accurate, truthful information, the word **propaganda** has a negative connotation and is often used to dismiss or discredit information with which one disagrees. The term **information operations** is more neutral and thus more useful for discussing how governments shape the information environment. Such operations are also sometimes called **psychological operations**.[4] Regardless of the term that one uses, the purpose of these operations is to influence the thinking and the beliefs of a target audience in order to achieve a national objective.

Covert information operations—whether they spread truth or falsehood—conceal the source of information. They can vary, however, in the extent to which they are covert. Gray information operations possess limited deniability.[5] An example of a gray information operation is the work of Radio Free Europe and Radio Liberty (RFE/RL). These entities broadcast American propaganda behind the Iron Curtain during the Cold War. A person of average intelligence could surmise that these broadcasts had at least some degree of US government backing. Leaks confirmed in the mid-1960s that the broadcasts were part of a covert CIA program.[6] The broadcasts nonetheless continued. Congress removed the radio stations from CIA control in 1972 and made them overt tools of the US government under the direction of the Broadcasting Board of Governors. By 1999, the Broadcasting Board of Governors had assumed responsibility for all US government–sponsored international broadcast outlets, including the consolidated RFE/RL, Voice of America, Radio Sawa (focused on the Middle East), Radio Martí (focused on Cuba), and Radio Free Asia. Though these stations put a pro-American spin on the news, they are legally forbidden from broadcasting **disinformation**.[7]

Black information operations are thoroughly concealed. Often, full concealment is essential to the success of the operation because the messenger's identity could undermine the message.[8] Consider a scenario in which the United States wants to disseminate truthful information inside of Iran that supports US interests. Because many Iranians are socialized to distrust the United States, because the Iranian government would dismiss the information as the malicious fabrications of an enemy, and because knowledge of the United States as the source might instead *harm* any intended beneficiaries inside of Iran, the information may be best disseminated in a manner that removes any American fingerprints.

Full concealment may also be critical to the success of a disinformation campaign. Russian trolls have successfully stirred social and political tensions in the United States

---

[4]Stempel, John. "Covert Action and Diplomacy." *International Journal of Intelligence and Counterintelligence* 20, no. 1 (2007): 122–135.

[5]Ibid.

[6]Wettering, "(C)overt Action," 562.

[7]Ibid., 566.

[8]LeGallo, Andre. "Covert Action: A Vital Option in US National Security Policy." *International Journal of Intelligence and Counterintelligence* 18, no. 2 (2005): 354–359.

by posing as Americans and posting inflammatory material online. Any given post would presumably have less impact if a reader knew that a Russian troll was the source. In the early 1980s, the Soviet Union planted a fake story in India's news media claiming that the United States had created AIDS in a military laboratory at Fort Detrick, Maryland. The purpose of this covert action was to undermine global opinion of the United States by making it appear that Washington had designed a biological weapon with which it was targeting Africans and homosexuals. The story gained such traction globally that, once US counterintelligence identified Moscow as the source, President Ronald Reagan demanded that Soviet premier Mikhail Gorbachev disavow the rumor and set the record straight (Gorbachev obliged).[9] Had the fake story first appeared in the Communist Party's newspaper *Pravda*, it would have been less plausible to the global masses.

## Political Activity

A second category of covert action is **political activity**. This includes a broad range of actions that go beyond information operations to support preferred political actors and outcomes. For example, a government performing covert political activity might provide technical, logistical, and financial assistance to a group that it wants to see win an election or otherwise gain or maintain power. Examples of logistical and technical assistance are facilitating communication among members of a political movement and training political actors to run effective campaigns. Financial assistance can be used to cover the routine costs of political organization and advocacy, like producing campaign literature, or for less savory purposes, like paying bribes and buying votes.

The first major post–World War II US covert action sought to influence elections in Italy, where the increasingly powerful Italian Communist Party threatened the Christian Democratic government of Prime Minister Alcide De Gasperi. According to former CIA officials involved in the operation, communist and left-wing political parties in Italy were receiving up to $10 million per month from foreign sponsors, and communists were overtaking Italian labor unions.[10] A joint effort of the State Department and the fledgling CIA provided countervailing aid and funding to the Christian Democrats and other anticommunist political groups, many of which were also supported by the Vatican. Some of the funds were raised by appeal to the Italian American community and anticommunist labor unions. Additionally, the United States organized a letter-writing campaign through which Italian Americans wrote to their Italian brethren assuring them of their quality of life in the capitalist United

---

[9]Qiu, Linda. "Fingerprints of Russian Disinformation: From AIDS to Fake News." *The New York Times*, December 12, 2017. https://www.nytimes.com/2017/12/12/us/politics/russian-disinformation-aids-fake-news.html.

[10]Mistry, Kaeten. "Approaches to Understanding the Inaugural CIA Covert Operation in Italy: Exploding Useful Myths." *Intelligence and National Security* 26, no. 2–3 (June 2011): 253.

**PHOTO 7.1** Italian prime minister Alcide De Gasperi graces the cover of *Time* magazine in 1953. In 1948, De Gasperi was the first beneficiary of a CIA covert action to influence an election in support of a pro-Western candidate.[12]

States and urging them to resist communism.[11] This case illustrates how political activity and information operations often coincide.

Notably, this all occurred with the knowledge and consent of Prime Minister De Gasperi, who sought the American assistance. De Gasperi requested even more than covert political support; he also sought military assistance because he feared left-wing guerrilla subversion or a Soviet-sponsored coup. At his request, the United States secretly conveyed military aid to his government. De Gasperi agreed that both political and military assistance should remain secret to deny the Italian Communist Party the opportunity to paint the Christian Democrats as Western imperialist stooges.[13] The Italian prime minister's initiative demonstrates an important feature of most covert action. Despite myths of an all-powerful CIA, covert action does not create agents and outcomes from thin air. In the case of political activity—as well as other variants of covert action explained as follows—success requires that the covert action support the independent and preexisting interests of like-minded actors in the target country.

Political activity is usually nonviolent. One occasional exception to the nonviolent character of political activity is the use of **agents-provocateurs**. The United States employed agents-provocateurs in Iran in 1953 to create the impression that Prime Minister Mohammad Mossadegh, whom the United States and Great Britain wanted to overthrow, could not control an emerging communist threat. Agents in Iran were paid to behave as unruly communist street mobs. They vandalized national and religious monuments, and their presence led to some violent encounters. So effective were these agents-provocateurs that actual Iranian communists joined the demonstrations, not realizing that they were part of a CIA plot.[14] Ultimately, the covert action to overthrow Iran's prime minister succeeded (a fuller account of this case appears later in this

---

[11]Ibid.

[12]Chaliapin, Boris. "Alcide De Gasperi on Time Magazine Cover, 1953." Wikimedia Commons. Last updated July 5, 2020. https://commons.wikimedia.org/wiki/File:Alcide_De_Gasperi-TIME-1953.jpg.

[13]Mistry, "Approaches to Understanding the Inaugural CIA Covert Operation in Italy," 264–265.

[14]Gasiorowski, Mark. "The 1953 Coup D'etat in Iran." *International Journal of Middle East Studies* 19, no. 3 (1987): 261–286.

chapter). Agents-provocateurs are not always violent. The internet trolls employed by Russia to influence the 2016 US presidential election are a modern example of agents-provocateurs. And while generally nonviolent, covert political activity of any sort can have unintended violent consequences.

American democracy promotion has become more overt over the years, particularly since the end of the Cold War.[15] In 1983, President Reagan established the National Endowment for Democracy (NED). The NED and its subsidiary organizations are sometimes called quasi-NGOs (nongovernmental organizations) because they are private and independent but receive federal funding. Moreover, their missions align with long-standing US grand strategy to promote democracy. Though they conduct their operations openly, authoritarian regimes threatened by their activities often accuse them of being fronts for the CIA. Unfortunately, savvy governments around the world are increasingly using government-organized nongovernmental organizations (GONGOs) as fronts for political activity and information operations.[16] The existence of GONGOs increases the danger to legitimate, independent NGOs operating in hostile environments; NGO personnel are often viewed as spies. Russia has taken steps in recent years to restrict the operation of foreign NGOs on its soil for fear that they are vehicles of foreign meddling. Democracy promotion in Russia by American NGOs is believed to have played a role in President Vladimir Putin's decision to interfere in US elections.

The NED played a role in securing post–Cold War democratic governments in Lithuania, Slovakia, Romania, and Bulgaria. It also supported efforts to defeat Serbian strongman Slobodan Milošević in Yugoslav elections in 2000. The NED's activities in Yugoslavia, though done openly, resembled classic covert political activity. It provided financing and training for the campaigns of democratic candidates; distributed posters, stickers, and T-shirts; and organized rock concerts to promote enthusiasm and civic engagement.[17] Subsidiary bodies of the NED include the International Republican Institute; the Center for International Private Enterprise, which is located in the US Commerce Department; and the Solidarity Center, which focuses on labor unions and is named for the Solidarity movement that won the first free Polish elections in 1989.

## Economic Activity

A third category of covert action is **economic activity**. Economic activity involves action taken to disrupt a target's economy. Examples include inciting labor strikes, manipulating currencies and commodity prices, sabotaging economic infrastructure,

---

[15]Wettering, "(C)overt Action."

[16]Vojtíšková, Vladislava, Vít Novotný, Hubertus Schmid-Schmidsfelden, and Kristina Potapova. *The Bear in Sheep's Clothing: Russia's Government-Funded Organisations in the EU.* Brussels, Belgium: Wilfried Martens Centre for European Studies, 2016. https://www.martenscentre.eu/publications/bear-sheeps-clothing-russias-government-funded-organisations-eu.

[17]Wettering, "(C)overt Action," 567.

and spreading disinformation to undermine consumer or investor confidence in a country or market. For example, the United States is believed to have facilitated strikes and worked to depress world copper prices as part of a covert action strategy to overthrow the socialist Chilean leader Salvador Allende in the early 1970s.[18] The idea behind economic activity is that leaders' political support often depends on their ability to provide an acceptable standard of living. If the economy suffers, political leaders will lose support and thus power. Covert economic activity is constrained, however, by ethical concerns about harming innocent people. It is one thing to try to topple a foreign leader by providing covert political aid to his opponents; it is another thing entirely to cause economic pain for a population in order to undermine that leader. Most economic coercion occurs overtly; economic sanctions have become a favored foreign policy tool of the United States since the 1990s. Yet ethical concerns about harming innocent people have led the United States over the last two decades to tailor "smart" sanctions that reduce the impact on innocent people and target only those groups and individuals that threaten American interests.

## Sabotage

A fourth category of covert action is **sabotage**. Broadly speaking, the word *sabotage* can be used to describe virtually any type of disruption, including that of a nonviolent nature. For example, information operations can be construed as sabotage if they sow instability. Russian covert action in 2016 aimed to "sabotage" Hillary Clinton's presidential campaign as well as American national unity. Yet a more common and precise meaning of sabotage is *the waging of physical harm or destruction upon a target's material assets.* Covert physical attacks against key economic infrastructure, such as factories, crops, transportation nodes, and computer networks, would constitute the merging of economic activity and sabotage. Sabotage is more commonly used against military targets, however, and has been particularly helpful in slowing the proliferation of weapons of mass destruction (WMD). The United States is believed to have remotely sabotaged certain North Korean missiles.[19] Several media accounts also suggest that the United States has slowed Iran's nuclear and missile programs by infiltrating and introducing defective parts into Tehran's WMD supply chains.

The most famous and well-documented case of covert sabotage in recent history was a **computer network attack (CNA)** against Iran's uranium enrichment facility at Natanz in 2010. The covert operation, conducted jointly by the United States and Israel, introduced malicious code into the software that controlled Iran's uranium enrichment centrifuges. Centrifuges spin at very high speed; they employ

---

[18]Stempel, "Covert Action and Diplomacy," 126.

[19]Sanger, David E., and William J. Broad. "Hand of US Leaves North Korea's Missile Program Shaken." *The New York Times*, April 18, 2017. https://www.nytimes.com/2017/04/18/world/asia/north-korea-missile-program-sabotage.html.

centrifugal force to isolate the uranium-235 isotope that can be used in a nuclear weapon. The malware, which became known as Stuxnet, caused the centrifuges to lose control, break down, and explode. According to *New York Times* reporter David Sanger, who was given breathtaking insight into the operation for his book *Confront and Conceal,* the operation affected roughly one-fifth of the centrifuges at Natanz and set back Iran's nuclear program by two or three years.[20] This covert action, code-named OLYMPIC GAMES, was the first known use of malware to cause physical sabotage. Though it was conducted under President Barack Obama, the covert action originated with George W. Bush, who demanded of his advisers a third option between allowing Iran to continue enriching uranium and using military force to stop it. The operation's cover was blown when the malware escaped the control of its handlers and began to affect computers worldwide.

## Coups

A fifth category of covert action is support to coups. **Coup d'état** is a French word that refers to the removal and replacement of a leader or governing regime. Coups differ from revolutions in that they preserve institutions and replace elites; revolutions, by contrast, seek to replace an entire system of institutions. Coups, by necessity, catch their victims by surprise. Otherwise, the target of a coup is likely to arrest the coup planners and purge suspected traitors before being overthrown. Militaries are frequently involved in coups because they control the instruments of force, but political and "palace" coups can occur in which wily political actors outmaneuver each other for power while the military remains a bystander. A country concerned about the policies and direction of another country under a certain leader may consider covert support to a coup as a policy option. After all, the covert removal of a dangerous leader or regime is probably better than all-out war. Though coups may sound good in theory, America's experience with covert support to coups suggests that they are far from a panacea.

The United States covertly supported about a half-dozen coups during the Cold War, chiefly targeting leaders for their communist sympathies. The most high-profile coups had several negative effects and remain stains on the Cold War legacy of US intelligence. For example, a socialist politician named Salvador Allende won the presidency of Chile in 1970 through a democratic election. Though the CIA denies involvement, the United States is widely believed to have supported a military coup against Allende in 1973. Allende committed suicide, and his replacement, coup leader Augusto Pinochet, presided over a brutal military junta until 1990. Pinochet persecuted thousands and came to be viewed as a criminal for his regime's numerous human rights–related crimes. He died in 2006 before he could face justice.

Two decades before the coup in Chile, the United States facilitated its first coup against a socialist Latin American leader, Jacobo Árbenz of Guatemala. Árbenz won a

---

[20] Sanger, David. *Confront and Conceal,* 206–207. New York, NY: Broadway Paperbacks, 2012.

democratic election and became Guatemala's president in 1951. Árbenz showed communist sympathies that concerned American Cold Warriors, and his domestic agenda threatened the interests of the largest American corporation in Latin America, United Fruit Company. Inspired in part by the lobbying of United Fruit, the Eisenhower administration authorized a joint CIA–State Department covert action to help coup plotters overthrow Árbenz in 1954. The operation, known as PBSUCCESS, is chronicled in an official CIA history released in 1994.[21] The multifaceted operation combined support to paramilitary operations with black information operations. Covert radio broadcasts from Miami spread disinformation throughout Guatemala about Soviet infiltration and stoked fear of a communist takeover. More importantly, the broadcasts inflated the strength and success of the US-backed rebel fighting forces under the command of Carlos Castillo Armas. Armas's forces experienced initial military setbacks and likely would not have defeated the pro-Árbenz forces. PBSUCCESS radio broadcasts reported the converse—that Armas was on the doorstep of the capital. The disinformation demoralized and deceived both the Guatemalan military and Árbenz, leading them to stand down from the fight.[22] Árbenz was ultimately replaced by a right-wing authoritarian regime. The coup against Árbenz later fed the socialist narrative about imperialism and inspired left-wing actors, notably Che Guevara (who was in Guatemala at the time), to take up arms.[23]

Perhaps the most consequential US-supported coup of the Cold War was the 1953 coup against Iranian prime minister Mohammad Mossadegh. Mossadegh, among other goals, sought to wrest power from the shah (Iran's king). His removal paved the way for a quarter-century of repressive rule by the shah, which ended with the 1979 Iranian Revolution and the rise of the theocratic Islamic Republic of Iran. Had Mossadegh not been overthrown in 1953, it is possible that Iran would be a very different country today—and much less hostile toward the United States.

Though a monarchy for most of the 20th century, Iran also had a parliament, known in Farsi as the *Majlis*. Mossadegh's popularity all but forced the shah to appoint him prime minister in 1951. At the top of Mossadegh's agenda was to nationalize the Iranian oil industry. The British-owned Anglo-Iranian Oil Company (AIOC) made extraordinary profits on Iranian oil; under terms agreed to between London and the former Qajar dynasty of Iran, most of the profit from Iranian oil went to the AIOC—not to Iran. Mossadegh's National Front—a loose coalition of parties and political leaders united by the same goal of nationalizing the oil industry—succeeded in passing

---

[21]Cullather, Nicholas. *Operation PBSUCCESS: The United States and Guatemala, 1952–1954*. Washington, DC: Central Intelligence Agency, 1994.

[22]Ibid.

[23]Kurtz-Phelan, Daniel. "Big Fruit." *The New York Times*, March 2, 2008. https://www.nytimes.com/2008/03/02/books/review/Kurtz-Phelan-t.html.

**PHOTO 7.2** Iranian prime minister Mohammad Mossadegh visits the Liberty Bell in Philadelphia during a trip to the United States in 1951. He would be overthrown two years later in a CIA covert action.[24]

a nationalization law in the Majlis in 1951. A furious Great Britain brought international political pressure to bear on Iran, threatened an invasion, and activated a pair of covert agents in Iran to engage in political activity and information operations to undermine the Mossadegh government. The British effort enjoyed little sympathy in the United States until President Dwight D. Eisenhower entered office in 1953.

By 1953, several members of the National Front had defected from their alliance with Mossadegh and sought to replace him. Iranian politics were divided. This was due, in part, to anti-Mossadegh information operations waged by both Britain and the United States. Iranian political unrest, however, had its deepest roots inside of Iran itself. Sensitive to the wishes of its ally in London, wary of an independently minded Mossadegh, and fearful that the large Iranian communist party known as Tudeh might exploit conditions in Iran to seize power, Eisenhower authorized by covert action to support an anti-Mossadegh coup. The covert action included information operations

---

[24]Harry S. Truman Library and Museum. "Prime Minister Mohammed Mossadegh Examining the Famous Liberty Bell." Wikimedia Commons. Last edited August 9, 2020. https://commons.wikimedia.org/wiki/File:Mossadegh_US02.jpg.

to undermine Iranian faith in Mossadegh, political activity to turn additional members of the military and National Front against him, and logistical aid to the coup plotters, including a safe house for the coup's leader, General Fazlollah Zahedi. It finally succeeded on August 19, 1953.[25]

According to Mark Gasiorowski, the leading scholar on US covert action in Iran during the early Cold War, it is unlikely that the coup was necessary to prevent an imminent rise to power of Iranian communists. It is also unlikely the coup would have succeeded when it did were it not for the role played by the CIA.[26] That does not mean, however, that Mossadegh would have remained in power indefinitely and that Iran would have been guaranteed a prosperous future were it not for American interference. As noted, Mossadegh was a divisive figure within Iran. The contemporary Iranian narrative that the CIA spoiled a peaceful, consensus move toward national self-determination is oversimplified. Nonetheless, the United States officially apologized for its role in the coup during a thaw in relations in the late 1990s. The apology did little to improve relations. To this day, the legacy of the 1953 coup remains an important consideration for, and constraint upon, any American strategy to influence Iranian politics.

## Support to Paramilitary Operations

A sixth category of covert action is **support to paramilitary operations**. This involves the provision of weapons or other military aid to foreign clients. In some cases, the clients may have tenuous control of the government and require military assistance outside of normal channels to prepare for civil conflict. The covert military aid to De Gasperi's anticommunist Italian government in 1948 fits the bill. Paramilitary support was given to several Cold War clients, including in Western Europe and Iran, to use in insurgencies should their governments fall to communists. Such insurgent paramilitary forces were known as **stay-behind networks** because they would remain and fight any new communist regime.[27] In other cases, support to paramilitary operations helps clients that seek to violently overthrow an existing regime or defeat an occupying force.

Support to paramilitary operations is more common than support to coups. In recent years, Russia has provided matériel to pro-Russian separatists in Ukraine; the United States, Saudi Arabia, Turkey, Qatar, and the United Arab Emirates have provided support to various paramilitary groups in Syria; and Iran has provided aid to paramilitary clients in Iraq, Yemen, Lebanon, and the Palestinian territories. These are only the most high-profile and public examples. Where violence and weak governance beset a country of strategic importance, one might possibly find external paramilitary

---

[25]Gasiorowski, "1953 Coup D'etat in Iran."

[26]Ibid.

[27]Ganser, Daniel. "The CIA in Western Europe and the Abuse of Human Rights." *Intelligence and National Security* 21, no. 5 (October 2006): 760–781.

support for some warlord or faction. This is particularly true in the 21st century where major powers are concerned about Islamist insurgencies and terrorist safe havens.

The United States has experienced some of its greatest success in this category of covert action in—of all places—Afghanistan. The ground war to remove the Taliban from power in Afghanistan after the terrorist attacks of September 11, 2001, was primarily waged by an Afghan resistance movement known as the Northern Alliance. The CIA leveraged long-standing relations with Northern Alliance members to facilitate the defeat of the Taliban. The CIA's Operation JAWBREAKER distributed millions of dollars to Northern Alliance leaders to purchase weapons and ammunition and to provide food and salaries for troops. It also provided essential communication and logistical support. Critically, the CIA won over a Pashtun tribal leader named Hamid Karzai, bringing him into the war and airdropping weapons and supplies to his troops. Karzai would become Afghanistan's first post-Taliban president.

This post-9/11 operation was not the CIA's first success in Afghanistan. It built on a previous success from the 1980s. The Soviet Union invaded and occupied Afghanistan in 1979. President Jimmy Carter immediately authorized a covert action to help the Afghan resistance, known as the mujahedeen. Operating out of a CIA station in Pakistan, the United States initially provided the mujahedeen with small weaponry that the Afghans could have plausibly acquired on the black market. The purpose of starting small was to conceal American involvement and avoid a direct confrontation with Moscow. By the mid-1980s, the Soviets were wearing down the Afghan resistance. Under the direction of President Reagan, the CIA increased its support to include heavier and more advanced weaponry, including massive mortars that could destroy entire Soviet barracks. The CIA also provided training in more effective guerrilla tactics, such as hit-and-run operations and remote bomb detonation. The Soviets responded by marshaling air power against the mujahedeen. In response, the CIA provided its Afghan clients with a cutting-edge, heat-seeking, shoulder-fired antiaircraft missile known as the Stinger. The Stinger was a game-changer. Though US involvement was now fully apparent, the operation succeeded. The Soviets withdrew in defeat in 1989.

The decision to escalate involvement to the point at which it became apparent illustrates a trade-off that must sometimes be made in covert action, most notably in support to paramilitary operations. Sometimes secrecy must be compromised to ensure success. The US decision to risk the program's covert nature helped ensure its military success. Fortunately, the Soviet Union was in decline by 1989, so there was little risk of Soviet retaliation. At an earlier point in the Cold War, however, a different calculation helped ensure the failure of a covert paramilitary operation. In 1961, the Kennedy administration supported a covert paramilitary operation against Cuba known as the Bay of Pigs invasion. The operation was a catastrophic failure for several reasons. One reason was President John F. Kennedy's refusal to send air support for fear that it would compromise the covert nature of the operation. Critics charged that US involvement was barely concealed, anyway, and that successfully removing Castro was more important than maintaining a pretense of noninvolvement.

## Secret Participation in Combat

A seventh category of covert action is **secret participation in combat**. This goes a step beyond providing support to paramilitary operations and involves inserting one's own troops into battle under a false flag. This remains a rare type of operation but may constitute an emerging trend in a world increasingly marked by **gray zone conflict**, or informal warfare that skirts international law and obscures the role of governments and militaries.

The presence of unmarked Russian troops in Ukraine illustrates secret participation in combat. A 2014 political crisis in Ukraine led to separatist sentiment among its ethnic Russian population in the east, namely in Crimea and the region known as Donbas. Russia quickly seized Crimea, but initially claimed that the troops who militarily occupied key offices were just well-armed, well-organized, pro-Russian Ukrainian separatists. Russia then admitted that some of the troops may have been Russian soldiers volunteering their time to the Crimean cause while on holiday. The Russian troops wore plain green uniforms with no national insignia, garnering the name **Little Green Men**. Given the very thin veneer of deniability, President Putin eventually admitted that he had sent a small detachment of special forces into Crimea, but he never admitted to the scale of the covert operation.[28] Little Green Men also appeared in the Donbas region of eastern Ukraine, especially after Ukrainian security forces made gains against separatists in 2015. A monitoring mission of the Organization for Security and Co-operation in Europe observed a minimum of 30,000 Little Green Men crossing the border from Russia into Ukraine to fight alongside the Ukrainian separatists.[29] Though apparent, the operation has not been acknowledged by Moscow. On one occasion, 10 Russian paratroopers were captured in Ukraine. The Russian government said that they had accidentally crossed the border during a training mission.[30]

## Assassination and Targeted Killing

An eighth category of covert action is **assassination**, or covert murder of political leaders. The United States attempted to assassinate Cuban leader Fidel Castro in the 1960s under a series of covert actions known as Operation MONGOOSE, but ultimately outlawed assassination in 1976. The ban on assassinations remains in place under Executive Order 12333, but it does not restrict the United States from targeting a foreign leader in case of open and acknowledged warfare. In the 21st-century war against terrorists, the United States engages in what it calls **targeted killings**. These killings are

---

[28]Freedman, Lawrence. *Ukraine and the Art of Strategy.* New York, NY: Oxford University Press, 2019.

[29]Baer, Daniel B. "Response to Chief Observer of the Observer Mission at the Russian Border Checkpoints Gukovo and Donetsk: Statement to the PC." US Mission to the OSCE, November 17, 2016. https://osce .usmission.gov/response-chief-observer-observer-mission-russian-border-checkpoints-gukovo-donetsk-statement-pc/.

[30]Freedman, *Ukraine and the Art of Strategy*, 114.

often done by drone and target terrorist leaders—not the leaders of recognized, sovereign states. The January 2020 assassination via drone strike of Iranian general Qassim Soleimani marked a potential inflection point in the American use of targeted killings. For the first time since World War II (Japanese admiral Isoroku Yamamoto), the United States deliberately killed the

**PHOTO 7.3** Probable Russian troops at an airport in Crimea, Ukraine, in February 2014. Their lack of identifying insignia provided the thinnest layer of plausible deniability for the Russian Federation.[31]

top military official of a sovereign state. Soleimani headed the Islamic Revolutionary Guard Corps' Quds Force, which US law designates as a terrorist organization. In this legal sense, he was a terrorist; and under US law, terrorists are legitimate combat targets. But Soleimani was also a major official in the Iranian government—by many accounts, even more powerful than Iran's president. Notably, the United States did not try to hide its responsibility for the killing. As such, the drone strike was *not* a covert action. The Soleimani killing illustrates the nuanced and sometimes murky legal and political nature of lethal operations against individual enemies.

Other states more regularly use assassination as an instrument of statecraft. Israel is believed responsible for the covert assassination of a handful of Iranian nuclear scientists in 2010 and 2011. Israel also has an extensive history of assassinating Palestinian political leaders whom it considers to be terrorists. For example, in 2004 Israel assassinated Sheikh Ahmed Yassin, the founder of Hamas. Yassin was elderly, blind, and wheelchair-bound, but was still considered dangerous as a political figure. Like the Soleimani killing, this operation was not denied by its sponsor, and thus should not be considered a covert operation. Most assassinations, however, are conducted covertly.

More authoritarian states tend to use assassination against internal political enemies—particularly those that have moved abroad and may participate in antiregime resistance. Iran assassinated several regime opponents in Europe during the 1980s, contributing to its reputation as a sponsor of terror. It most notably assassinated Shapour Bakhtiar, the shah's former prime minister, in Paris in 1991. The assassination dissuaded

President George H. W. Bush from engaging in diplomacy with Tehran.[32] Russia has also been implicated in recent years in the assassination of those deemed to be political opponents or traitors. In the highest-profile political assassination, Boris Nemtsov, a liberal political opponent of Putin, was gunned down in front of the Kremlin in 2015. Russia has also notably targeted former spies in the United Kingdom. Alexander Litvinenko was assassinated by radiological poisoning in London in 2006, and Sergei Skripal was (unsuccessfully) targeted in Salisbury in 2018 with a potent chemical nerve agent. Both men were former intelligence officers who had defected to the United Kingdom.

Assassination may be a good idea in theory if it eliminates a specific danger while sparing innocent people the depravities of war. But it remains a rarely used instrument in the modern state system. Revelation of an operation to assassinate a leader of a sovereign state would likely constitute *casus belli*, or an act justifying war. Moreover, normalizing assassination would go against the interests of leaders due to the adage that "what goes around comes around."

## OVERSIGHT OF COVERT ACTION IN THE UNITED STATES

The United States is governed by the rule of law. This includes covert action. The idea of the CIA as a "rogue elephant" is at best outdated, and at worst a dangerous myth. Covert action is subject to extensive oversight to prevent the abuse of power or the violation of law, including international treaties to which the United States is party. As stated at the beginning of the chapter, covert action is a method of executing foreign and national security policy. As such, covert action must originate with the president in a document known as a **Presidential Finding**. A Presidential Finding is a written and signed document that outlines the president's justification for a covert action. It identifies the legal authority for the operation (**Title 50** outlines the role of US intelligence agencies), the target, the foreign policy objectives to be served, and the lead agency (usually the CIA). Appendices provide a plan of action outlining the methodology of the covert action, a statement of required resources, and a risk assessment.[33] This report must be submitted to the House and Senate Intelligence Committees of the US Congress before the covert action can begin. In rare and compelling circumstances, the operation can begin prior to notification of Congress, but the Presidential Finding must be delivered to Congress within 48 hours. Congress has no veto power. If it disapproves of a covert action, it can try to persuade the president to change course, it can deny funding, or—as a last resort—it can leak knowledge of the action to stop it from proceeding. If the proposed covert action violates the law, Congress can bring especially powerful pressure to bear to stop the covert action.

---

[32]Pollack, Kenneth. *The Persian Puzzle*. New York, NY: Random House, 2004.

[33]Daugherty, William. "Approval and Review of Covert Action Programs Since Reagan." *International Journal of Intelligence and Counterintelligence* 17, no. 1 (2004): 75.

Covert action did not always require a Presidential Finding. From the late 1940s to the early 1970s, US presidents preferred not to know the details of covert actions in order to preserve their own plausible deniability. They mainly gave general direction and expected their intelligence leaders to perform actions that supported US policy goals. The **1974 Hughes-Ryan Amendment** required presidents to affix their names to covert action and vastly improved oversight. The **1991 Intelligence Authorization Act** updated the 1974 Hughes-Ryan Amendment and remains the legal framework for covert action oversight. US law forbids the US government from targeting its own country and people with covert action and from engaging in activities that might produce blowback.

Before a Presidential Finding reaches Congress, it typically goes through an interagency planning and review process at the National Security Council. National security officials and staff look at the planned covert action's goals, compatibility with overt policy, methodology, resource requirements, operational security requirements, chances for success, overall benefits, and operational and political risks. Some of the risks examined include the risk to human life, the risk of failure, and the risk of the operation's cover being blown.[34] Once the Presidential Finding reaches Capitol Hill, Congress's intelligence committees maintain oversight throughout the life of the operation. The House and Senate Intelligence Committees conduct quarterly reviews of all covert action programs and can call for briefings and updates at any time.[35]

## THE US MILITARY AND COVERT ACTION

The post-9/11 security environment has blurred the line between traditional military activity and covert action. Covert action is understood to be the bailiwick of intelligence agencies, but the need to kill terrorists, to combat shadowy nonstate actors, and to wage counterinsurgency has caused the US armed forces and the Department of Defense to engage in more special operations and activities that resemble covert action, even if they are not by the same name. Special Operations Command (SOCOM) and Joint Special Operations Command are the tip of the Pentagon's spear in conducting what it calls "special activities." These are special operations in which the Pentagon wishes its involvement to be nonapparent and unacknowledged.[36] While the specifics of the Pentagon's "special activities" remain necessarily vague, one can surmise their general nature from the legal authority for SOCOM, which defines special operations as including "direct action, strategic reconnaissance, unconventional warfare, foreign internal defense, civil affairs, psychological operations, counterterrorism, humanitarian

---

[34]Ibid.

[35]Ibid.

[36]Kibbe, Jennifer. "Covert Action and the Pentagon." *Intelligence and National Security* 22, no. 1 (2007): 65.

assistance, theater search and rescue, and such other activities as may be specified by the Secretary of Defense."[37]

Many special operations are made public, but Pentagon "black ops" are understood to exist. Though these do not require a Presidential Finding or undergo the same oversight process as covert action, the president is kept in the loop as the commander-in-chief of the armed forces, and Congress holds routine closed hearings on sensitive Pentagon operations.[38] Skeptics, however, worry that legally classifying so many special operations as "traditional military activities" under **Title 10**—the section of the US legal code that covers the role of the armed forces—constitutes an end run around the strict oversight of covert action delineated in the Hughes-Ryan Amendment and the Intelligence Authorization Act.

## CONCLUSION: CONSIDERATIONS IN COVERT ACTION

This chapter has alluded to several considerations that go into any plan for covert action. In this section, we address them more deeply and directly. One issue of which national security planners must remain cognizant is **blowback**, or the possibility that a covert action could have negative, unintended consequences that harm rather than serve the national interest. US law prohibits the use of disinformation in covert action if there is a reasonable expectation that that disinformation could find its way into American media and discourse. This might be called "propaganda blowback." Another type of blowback occurs when arms or other forms of paramilitary assistance are redirected for use against the covert action sponsor or its allies and interests. An example of this occurred in the United States' short-lived effort to arm and train anti-Assad militants in Syria. Many of the trainees defected and used their US-supplied weapons and training on behalf of jihadist groups.[39] A third type of blowback is political. Political activity or coups may not yield the precise political results that the covert action planners intend. Or the covert action planners may lack foresight and fail to consider the long-term political repercussions of the covert action—particularly if its cover is blown. The case of the 1953 coup in Iran is instructive. In the short term, the covert action succeeded. Mossadegh was removed, and the shah returned to power. Oil markets stabilized, and Iran remained in the US camp in the Cold War. Yet the long-term costs were profound. The shah alienated his people, leading to the 1979 Iranian Revolution and the rise of the theocratic Islamic Republic, which is hostile toward the United States and many of its allies. Iranians cite the 1953 coup and American support for the shah as key reasons for their revolution and hostility. Though it is possible

---

[37]Ibid., 59.

[38]Ibid., 67.

[39]Krishnan, Armin. "Controlling Partners and Proxies in Pro-Insurgency Paramilitary Operations: The Case of Syria." *Intelligence and National Security* 34, no. 4 (2019): 544–560.

that Iran would have gone in a theocratic and/or hostile direction even without CIA involvement in 1953, one cannot fully discount the possibility that blowback from 1953 complicates US-Iran relations and broader Middle East politics today.

Closely linked to the concept of blowback is the concept known as **agency loss**. Agency loss derives from principal–agent theory. In short, when a principal contracts with an agent to perform a task or mission, the agent retains free will. If the agent's interests diverge from the principal's, the agent may behave in ways that deviate from—or completely undermine—the goals of the principal with whom the agent has contracted. When this happens, the contract is effectively broken, and the principal experiences agency loss. Agency loss is a risk in sponsoring covert action. Agents—such as Syrian militants who dislike President Bashar al-Assad—may opt to defect to a terrorist group like al-Nusra. Similarly, leaders installed in a covertly assisted coup may disagree with their sponsor on important political issues once they are securely in command of the country.

Beyond blowback and agency loss, a third consideration concerns the practical ability to carry out the covert mission. As noted, covert actions do not produce results from thin air. Like-minded clients, or agents, are required. So, too, is an operational support structure. Former CIA official Mark Lowenthal refers to this support structure as **plumbing**.[40] Plumbing is the human and matériel infrastructure that empowers an intelligence agency to carry out a successful covert action. It includes contacts, false documents, communication protocols, meeting places and safe houses, means of transportation, and more. The need to routinely cultivate and maintain the plumbing of covert action is a reason that covert action is housed within intelligence agencies such as the CIA. Even when no covert action is occurring, intelligence agencies must be in the business of laying the groundwork should policymakers request or order a covert action.

**Ethics** constitute another consideration. Is it ethical, for example, to attempt to influence a foreign election or to overthrow a democratically elected leader? Are assassinations ever ethical? What about economic activity, which could harm several innocent people and use them as pawns to undermine a target regime?

A final consideration is risk—specifically of two types.[41] First is the **risk of failure** to achieve your operational objective. What if supported paramilitary forces fail to push the Soviets out of Afghanistan or to remove Assad from power in Syria? Do you escalate to overt military conflict? Do you accept the status quo? The risk of failure, which is inherent in any covert operation, reinforces the point that covert action must be part of a broad, coherent strategy for dealing with a national security or foreign policy challenge. One should never undertake a covert action with the attitude of "it will work, and if not, we'll see what happens."

---

[40]Lowenthal, Mark. "Covert Action." In *Intelligence: From Secrets to Policy*, 7th ed., edited by Mark Lowenthal, 250–251. Washington, DC: CQ Press, 2017.

[41]Ibid.

The second type of risk is **risk of exposure**. Regardless of the success or failure of the operation, what could happen if the sponsor's involvement is revealed? In some cases, exposure could be fatal, or at least produce blowback. In other cases, countries willingly risk exposure to ensure success, as in the case of the US delivery of Stinger missiles to the Afghan mujahedeen in the 1980s. Tolerance of exposure has, by necessity, increased since the early days of the Cold War. The reform of oversight in the United States in the 1970s and the worldwide proliferation of independent media, camera-equipped smartphones, and the internet have made it increasingly difficult to completely conceal certain operations. The counterintelligence departments of intelligence agencies across the world face several new challenges, including how to keep their government's covert operations truly covert. Yet the value of the third option is unlikely to disappear, and even increasingly overt–covert operations are likely to feature in international politics for a long time to come.

## KEY CONCEPTS

third option   177
covert action   177
plausible deniability   177
overt–covert action   178
propaganda   180
information operations   180
psychological operations   180
disinformation   180
political activity   181
agents-provocateurs   182
economic activity   183
sabotage   184
computer network attack (CNA)   184
coup d'état   185
support to paramilitary operations   188
stay-behind networks   188
secret participation in combat   190

gray zone conflict   190
Little Green Men   190
assassination   190
targeted killings   190
Presidential Finding   192
Title 50   192
1974 Hughes-Ryan Amendment   193
1991 Intelligence Authorization
   Act   193
Title 10   194
blowback   194
agency loss   195
plumbing   195
ethics   195
risk of failure   195
risk of exposure   196

## ADDITIONAL READING

Bergman, Ronen. *Rise and Kill First: The Secret History of Israel's Targeted Assassinations.* New York, NY: Random House, 2018.

Cullather, Nicholas. *Operation PBSUCCESS: The United States and Guatemala, 1952–1954.* Washington, DC: Central Intelligence Agency, 1994.

Daugherty, William. "Approval and Review of Covert Action Programs Since Reagan." *International Journal of Intelligence and Counterintelligence* 17, no. 1 (2004): 62–80.

Gasiorowski, Mark. "The 1953 Coup D'etat in Iran." *International Journal of Middle East Studies* 19, no. 3 (1987): 261–286.

Gasiorowski, Mark. "The CIA's TPBEDAMN Operation and the 1953 Coup in Iran." *Journal of Cold War Studies* 15, no. 4 (2013): 4–24.

Gasiorowski, Mark. "The US Stay-Behind Operation in Iran, 1948–1953." *Intelligence and National Security* 34, no. 2 (2019): 170–188.

Kibbe, Jennifer. "Covert Action and the Pentagon." *Intelligence and National Security* 22, no. 1 (2007): 57–74.

Krishnan, Armin. "Controlling Partners and Proxies in Pro-Insurgency Paramilitary Operations: The Case of Syria." *Intelligence and National Security* 34, no. 4 (2019): 544–560.

Lowenthal, Mark. "Covert Action." In *Intelligence: From Secrets to Policy*, 7th ed., edited by Mark Lowenthal, 249–273. Washington, DC: CQ Press, 2017.

Mistry, Kaeten. "Approaches to Understanding the Inaugural CIA Covert Operation in Italy: Exploding Useful Myths." *Intelligence and National Security* 26, no. 2–3 (June 2011): 246–268.

Sanger, David. *Confront and Conceal*. New York, NY: Broadway Paperbacks, 2012.

Stempel, John. "Covert Action and Diplomacy." *International Journal of Intelligence and Counterintelligence* 20, no. 1 (2007): 122–135.

Wettering, Frederick. "(C)overt Action: The Disappearing 'C.'" *International Journal of Intelligence and Counterintelligence* 16, no. 4 (2003): 561–572.

# 8 CYBERSPACE OPERATIONS AND THE INFORMATION ENVIRONMENT

LaMesha L. Craft

Cyberspace and threats in the cyberspace domain are not new. However, since the early 2000s, nation-states (from the most powerful to the less influential) have experienced the impact of poor cybersecurity, underdeveloped cyber threat intelligence analysis, and the general lack of imagination when considering *how* offensive cyberspace capabilities could be used by nation-states and nonstate actors to achieve strategic objectives. The aftermath of several cyberspace incidents led to increased demand by policymakers and decision makers to understand the premise of this domain.[1]

Likewise, anyone pursuing a career in the intelligence or national security field should seek to understand the tactics, techniques, and procedures of cyberspace operations. However, one can do this without being what is often referred to as a "1s and 0s person." In other words, a degree in computer science or data analytics is not mandatory to provide valuable threat analysis of cyberspace activity. Nevertheless, understanding key terms and techniques used in cyberspace operations and the information environment, the magnitude of cyber threats, and how this domain impacts globalization and geopolitics is paramount to intelligence analysis and national security studies. This chapter will explain key concepts, examine the information environment and subsequent impact of information operations, describe international efforts in cyberspace operations, explain the current US cyberspace strategy, and demonstrate the relevance of cyber threat intelligence in assessing the current and future threats to US strategic interests and data.

## CONVERGENCE OF TECHNOLOGY

The **Internet of Things (IoT)** is a concept that highlights the increasing interconnectivity of data and electronics to our everyday lives, from cellular phones and home

---

[1]Department of Defense. "Summary: Department of Defense Cyber Strategy, 2018." Accessed July 31, 2019. https://media.defense.gov/2018/Sep/18/2002041658/-1/1/1/CYBER_STRATEGY_SUMMARY_FINAL .PDF; White House. "National Cyber Strategy of the United States of America, 2018." Accessed July 31, 2019. https://www.whitehouse.gov/wp-content/uploads/2018/09/National-Cyber-Strategy.pdf; Coats, D. R. "Statement for the Record: Worldwide Threat Assessment of the US Intelligence Community." Office of the Director of National Intelligence, February 13, 2018. https://www.dni.gov/files/documents/Newsroom/ Testimonies/2018-ATA---Unclassified-SSCI.pdf.

security services to coffee pots, headphones, home lighting systems, vehicle emergency services, and wearable devices that enable us to send and receive data through the internet.[2] In 2016, information technology specialists estimated the proliferation of IoT would encompass between 25 and 50 billion objects by 2020 (including mobile devices, artificial intelligence, home automations, and medical devices), and 2020 projections estimate 75 billion objects will be connected via IoT by 2025.[3]

Furthermore, one need only pull out one's smartphone to appreciate the **convergence of technology** (see Figure 8.1). The opportunity to streamline and increase the amount of data and information that can be shared has expanded our capabilities across many sectors. For example, we can operate and maintain critical infrastructure such as energy, water, agriculture, and transportation through the automated use of **industrial control systems (ICSs)** and **supervisory control and data acquisition (SCADA)** systems. ICSs and SCADA systems are prevalent in the day-to-day operations and maintenance of critical infrastructure. ICSs enable the command and control of networks to support all types of industrial processes. SCADA systems are computerized

**FIGURE 8.1 ■ Convergence of Technology**

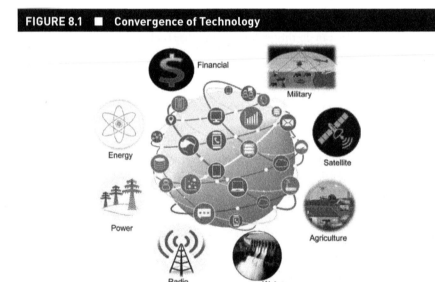

[2]Gery, William, SeYoung Lee, and Jacob Ninas. "Information Warfare in an Information Age." *Joint Force Quarterly* 85, no. 2 (2017): 22–29. https://ndupress.ndu.edu/Portals/68/Documents/jfq/jfq-85/jfq-85_22-29_Gery-Lee-Ninas.pdf; National Security Agency. "Internet of Things." *The Next Wave* 21, no. 2 (2016). https://www.nsa.gov/Portals/70/documents/resources/everyone/digital-media-center/publications/the-next-wave/TNW-21-2.pdf.

[3]Georgia Institute of Technology. "Emerging Cyber Threats Report: 2016." Accessed July 31, 2019. http://iisp.gatech.edu/sites/default/files/documents/threats_report_2016.pdf?_ga=2.130111311.1313428773.1558042325-1113364069.1558042325; Statista Research Department. "Internet of Things (IoT) Connected Devices Installed Base Worldwide From 2015 to 2025." Accessed September 23, 2020. https://www.statista.com/statistics/471264/iot-number-of-connected-devices-worldwide/.

systems that gather and process data to control and monitor physical processes over long distances. Examples of SCADA systems that enable day-to-day activities include traffic lights, water distribution plants, the regulation of water in dams, the transmission of electricity, and the transportation of gas and oil in pipelines.[4]

The convergence of technology also promotes global economic growth via the SWIFT banking network. The Society for Worldwide Interbank Financial Telecommunication (SWIFT) is a global messaging network used by banks and other financial institutions to efficiently and securely send and receive information such as money transfers and online payments.[5] Technology has also improved the US Department of Defense's ability to apply combined arms tactics in conflict.

While the convergence of technology provides opportunities across many sectors, the interconnectivity also increases the vulnerability of countries, organizations, and people because malicious cyber actors often exploit this growing dependence on technology.[6] Furthermore, the convergence of technology has decreased the level of expertise required to launch an effective cyber incident. In essence, a cyber actor does not have to be a computer expert to perform sophisticated cyber activity, which significantly increases our risks in the cyberspace domain. Information technology also provides an extensive platform to broadcast grievances as well as develop followers, sympathizers, and supporters. This spans beyond geographic boundaries and makes it increasingly difficult to tangibly identify *who* is leading *what* initiatives and *how* they may impact current and future relationships.[7]

## PEELING BACK THE LAYERS OF CYBERSPACE

**Cyberspace** is defined as "a global domain within the information environment that consists of the interdependent network of information technology infrastructures and resident data, including the internet, telecommunications networks, computer systems, and embedded processors and controllers."[8] There are three main layers of cyberspace: the social layer (sometimes called the "persona layer"), the logical network layer, and

---

[4]Department of Homeland Security, Cybersecurity and Infrastructure Security Agency. "Overview of Cyber Vulnerabilities." Accessed July 31, 2019. https://www.us-cert.gov/ics/content/overview-cyber-vulnerabilities#under.

[5]Seth, Shobhit. "How the SWIFT System Works." Investopedia, February 11, 2020. https://www.investopedia.com/articles/personal-finance/050515/how-swift-system-works.asp.

[6]Yampolskiy, Roman, and M. S. Spellchecker. "Artificial Intelligence Safety and Cybersecurity: A Timeline of AI Failures." Accessed July 31, 2019. https://arxiv.org/pdf/1610.07997.pdf; Warner, Michael. "Intelligence in Cyber and Cyber in Intelligence." In *Understanding Cyber Conflict in 14 Analogies*, edited by George Perkovich and Ariel Levite, 17–29. Washington, DC: Georgetown University Press, 2017.

[7]National Intelligence Council. "Global Trends: Paradox of Progress." Accessed July 31, 2019. https://www.dni.gov/files/documents/nic/GT-Full-Report.pdf.

[8]Department of Defense. "Cyberspace." In *Dictionary of Military and Associated Terms*, 55. As of June 2020. https://www.jcs.mil/Portals/36/Documents/Doctrine/pubs/dictionary.pdf.

the physical layer (see Figure 8.2). These layers, and the nature of cyberspace, increase the difficulty of analyzing who or what entity was responsible for a cyber incident. For the purpose of explanation, these three layers are further dissected into sub-layers.[9]

## FIGURE 8.2 ■ Layers of Cyberspace

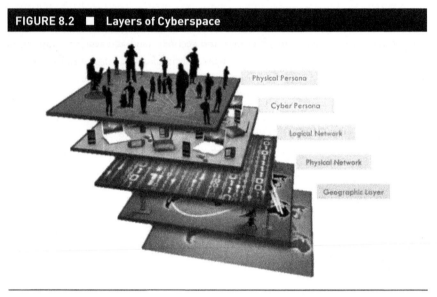

Physical Persona

Cyber Persona

Logical Network

Physical Network

Geographic Layer

*Source:* Adapted from Joint Publication 3-12, Cyberspace Operations, 8 June 2018.

Within the **social layer** are the physical persona layer and the cyber persona layer. The **physical persona layer** is the human (flesh and bones). So, let's use a female named Jane Doe as an example. The **cyber persona layer** is the assumed identity used by a human. In Jane's case, she has two social media accounts, she owns a spin bike that provides virtual classes and requires a profile, and she is a blogger on two websites. Essentially, Jane (one person) has five cyber personas. The **logical network layer** consists of virtual parts of the network, like internet protocol (IP) addresses, internet domains, and cloud services. If Jane primarily uses the internet at her home office and at work, then she will have the corresponding IP addresses and internet domains. Within the **physical layer** are the physical network layer and the geographic layer. The **physical network layer** includes components such as the computer, the cables connected to the computer, and the modem and routers that enable Wi-Fi. The **geographic layer** is the actual terrain where the physical network resides such as a city, a neighborhood, or a specific house or building.

---

[9]Department of Defense. "Joint Publication 3-12: Cyberspace Operations." Last modified June 8, 2018. https://fas.org/irp/doddir/dod/jp3_12.pdf.

Now, let's assume that Jane has a career but also moonlights as a nefarious cyber-criminal and two of her five cyber personas are aliases for her nefarious activity; her profile is *not* "Jane Doe" but rather "Suzy Que" in one account and "John Doe" in the other. Because she is conducting criminal activity, her IP addresses and internet domains are spoofed to impersonate a legitimate user or account and conceal her true identity, activity, and geographic location. So, as illustrated, the structure of this domain creates challenges in knowing not only *what* entity is truly responsible for actions but also *where* that entity is physically located. Moreover, when attempting to attribute activity to a nefarious cyber activity (by a lone cyber actor or a group), these methods of concealment make that process difficult—but not impossible.[10]

## The Information Environment and Information Operations

It is important to note that the manipulation of information to achieve effects is not a *new* concept. America's use of information to influence the enemy dates back to the Revolutionary War when American agents used forged documents to convince the British that George Washington's army possessed greater capability than it actually did.[11] However, the changing dynamics of cyberspace operations has led to the examination of terms such as *information environment, information warfare,* and *information operations*. The following discussion acknowledges the ongoing debates on the terms, but focuses on the most up-to-date doctrinal and practical application. Despite the debate on terminology, the general international consensus remains that the changing dynamics of cyberspace operations has expanded the elements that one must consider when analyzing the environment. Those elements make it difficult to identify what entities are responsible for creating and disseminating a particular narrative, the authenticity of the information, and the secondary and tertiary impacts of the information on social, economic, and political stability.

The **information environment** is "the aggregate of individuals, organizations, and systems that collect, process, disseminate, or act on information."[12] This environment consists of three interrelated dimensions (physical, informational, and cognitive), which continuously interact with individuals, organizations, and systems. The **physical dimension** is composed of command and control systems, key decision makers, and supporting infrastructure that enable individuals and organizations to create effects. The **informational dimension** specifies where and how information is collected, processed, stored, disseminated, and protected. The **cognitive dimension**

[10]For a more in-depth discussion about the challenges and process for cyber attribution, see *A Guide to Cyber Attribution* available from the Office of the Director of National Intelligence at https://www.dni.gov/files/CTIIC/documents/ODNI_A_Guide_to_Cyber_Attribution.pdf.

[11]Hutcherson, Norman B. *Command and Control Warfare: Putting Another Tool in the War-Fighter's Data Base.* Maxwell Air Force Base, Montgomery, AL: Air University Press, September 1994.

[12]Department of Defense. "Information Environment." In *Dictionary of Military and Associated Terms*, 104. As of June 2020. https://www.jcs.mil/Portals/36/Documents/Doctrine/pubs/dictionary.pdf.

encompasses the minds of those who transmit, receive, and respond to or act on information. We largely cannot physically touch the information environment because the objectives include impacting human perceptions or behaviors. In this environment, the goal is to influence the will to act, which is often accomplished by manipulating information and subsequently altering ideas, perceptions, and judgments of people.[13] **Information operations,** then, is the employment of information to influence, disrupt, corrupt, or usurp the decision making of the enemy, all the while protecting the integrity of our own information. In this sense, information is both a resource and an instrument of power.[14]

## Impacts of Cyberspace and the Information Environment on Geopolitics

Cyberspace capabilities have changed the dynamics of geopolitics. As noted in the 2017 Global Trends: Paradox of Progress, the rapid advancement of technology and cyberspace capabilities is changing the nature of conflict and power.[15] Likewise, Richard Andres, a scholar of US national security policy, noted that technology can change the status quo when its use alters how nations compete for security, generate wealth, and exert military power.[16]

Since at least the late 1990s, a variety of **cyber incidents** and **cyber attacks** targeting multiple countries have had global impacts (see Table 8.1). Distinguishing between what constitutes a cyber incident (or event) and a cyber attack is an important aspect in the relationship between cyberspace operations and geopolitics. As noted in the Australian Cyber Security Centre 2016 Threat Report, the term *cyber attack* has been sensationalized to describe a variety of malicious cyber activities (e.g., cybercrime and intellectual property theft), and the term is frequently used within the information security community when describing malicious activity against a computer network or system. However, the term has greater consequences if a nation, when discussing potential red lines in cyberspace, says it has been subjected to a cyber attack (with the same connotation as an armed attack).[17] As of September 2020, there is not an international

---

[13]Paul, Christopher, Colin P. Clarke, Bonnie L. Triezenberg, David Manheim, and Bradley Wilson. "Improving C2 and Situational Awareness." Santa Monica, CA: RAND Corporation, 2018. https://www.rand.org/pubs/research_reports/RR2489.html.

[14]Department of Defense. "Strategy for Operations in the Information Environment." Last modified June 2016. https://dod.defense.gov/Portals/1/Documents/pubs/DoD-Strategy-for-Operations-in-the-IE-Signed-20160613.pdf; Department of Defense. "Joint Concept for Operating in the Information Environment." Last modified July 25, 2018. https://www.jcs.mil/Portals/36/Documents/Doctrine/concepts/joint_concepts_jcoie.pdf?ver=2018-08-01-142119-830; Iasiello, Emilio J. "Russia's Improved Information Operations: From Georgia to Crimea." *Parameters* 47, no. 2 (2017): 51–64. https://www.hsdl.org/?view&did=803998.

[15]National Intelligence Council, "Global Trends."

[16]Andres, Richard B. "Cyber Conflict and Geopolitics." *Great Decisions* (2019): 69–78.

[17]Australian Government. "Australian Cyber Security Centre 2016 Threat Report." Accessed July 31, 2019. https://www.cyber.gov.au/sites/default/files/2019-04/ACSC_Threat_Report_2016.pdf.

definition of what constitutes a cyber attack, in part due to the challenge of identifying what cyberspace operations are considered *armed attacks* as defined in international law. Moreover, the question of what constitutes an act of war in cyberspace is one that international organizations such as the North Atlantic Treaty Organization (NATO) struggle to answer. Article V of NATO elicits a response from the 28 nations of NATO following an armed attack against one of the countries. However, Article V does not explicitly address the criteria of an armed conflict in cyberspace.[18] One of the challenges is the fact that not all events conducted by a cyber actor, such as cybercrime, intellectual property theft, cyber espionage, and hacktivism, meet the threshold of an armed attack.[19]

| TABLE 8.1 ■ Example Cyber Incidents, 1998–2018 | |
| --- | --- |
| **When*** | **Synopsis of Event*** |
| **1998** | Russian hackers stole information on sensitive US projects, weapons-guidance systems, critical infrastructure, and naval intelligence codes. Systems within the Pentagon, NASA, and the Department of Energy were affected. |
| **2007** | Russian actors launched distributed denial of service and website defacements against government, financial, and telecommunications companies in response to Estonia's relocation of a Soviet-era statue in Tallinn. |
| **2007–2009** | The United States and Israel are suspected of developing and employing the Stuxnet malware to sabotage Iranian nuclear equipment. |
| **2008** | Russian actors intruded into US military classified and unclassified networks and attempted extraction of military plans, weapons systems, and capabilities. |
| **2009** | China conducted a cyber espionage operation dubbed GHOSTNET that infiltrated computer systems in 103 countries—targets included embassies, ministries of foreign affairs, international organizations, nongovernmental organizations, and news media. |
| **2011–2017** | Iran conducted a series of social engineering campaigns using social media accounts to target high-ranking military and political figures from several countries, including the United States. |
| **2012, 2016, and 2017** | Iranian Shamoon and Shamoon 2.0 malware destroyed data on computer systems of Saudi Aramco oil company and RasGas natural gas company. |

*(Continued)*

---

[18]Sanders, Christopher M. "The Battlefield of Tomorrow, Today: Can a Cyberattack Ever Rise to an 'Act of War'?" *Utah Law Review* 2 (2018): 503–522. doi: https://dc.law.utah.edu/ulr/vol2018/iss2/6.

[19]For a further explanation, see Schmitt, Michael. *Tallinn Manual 2.0 on the International Law Applicable to Cyber Operations.* Newport, RI: Cambridge University Press, 2017, 25–30.

| TABLE 8.1 ■ (Continued) | |
| --- | --- |
| **When*** | **Synopsis of Event**** |
| **2014–2015** | Chinese cyber espionage was committed against the US Office of Personnel Management; sensitive information from 21.5 million people was stolen. |
| **2016** | Russian cyber espionage and information influence operations targeted the US Democratic National Convention to interfere with the 2016 presidential election. |
| **2017** | Cybercriminals stole data from Equifax Inc., possibly affecting over 145 million US consumers. |
| **2018** | Cybercriminals stole personal information from nearly 14 million Facebook users. |

*The dates reflect when the events were discovered—oftentimes cyber actors gain access months or years before discovery.

**This is not an all-inclusive list of cyber incidents from 1998 to 2018 (see the Council on Foreign Relations Cyber Operations Tracker for more events).

Absent an international definition, some nations have established their own definition of a cyber attack. For example, in 2011 Australia defined a cyber attack as a "deliberate act through cyberspace to manipulate, disrupt, deny, degrade or destroy computers or networks, or the information resident on them, with the effect of seriously compromising national security, stability, or economic prosperity."[20] Although the intent to protect US interests against cyber attacks is discussed in several US documents, policies, directives, and strategies, they stop short of defining a cyber attack.[21] However, the Department of Defense[22] defines a cyber attack as "actions taken in cyberspace that create noticeable denial effects (i.e., degradation, disruption, or destruction) or manipulation that leads to denial that appears in a physical domain, and is considered a form of fires."[23]

Throughout a brief examination of this history, it becomes apparent that several countries have been both the victim and the perpetrator of cyber activity. Nations have observed and/or experienced significant cyber incidents that have had secondary and

[20]Australian Cyber Security Centre. "Cyber Attack." Accessed September 23, 2020. https://www.cyber.gov.au/acsc/view-all-content/glossary/cyber-attack.

[21]The following are examples of documents that do not define cyber attacks: Presidential Policy Directive (PPD) 21, PPD-41, the 2018 National Cyber Strategy, the 2018 Department of Defense Cyber Strategy, the 2019 National Intelligence Strategy, and the 2019 Worldwide Threat Assessment.

[22]Department of Defense. "Cyberspace Attack." In *Dictionary of Military and Associated Terms*, 55. As of June 2020. https://www.jcs.mil/Portals/36/Documents/Doctrine/pubs/dictionary.pdf.

[23]"Fires" means the use of weapon systems or other actions to create specific lethal or nonlethal effects on a target.

tertiary impacts across the political, military, economic, social, information, and infrastructure operational variables.[24] In that same vein, the use of **social engineering** campaigns,[25] ransomware, and malicious software (malware) has spread globally and has changed the concept of power and influence among nation-states as well as nonstate actors.[26] For example, cyber incidents and influencing operations have discredited the effectiveness of infrastructure, election systems, and election processes, as well as the dissemination of accurate and unbiased news. Russia, China, North Korea, and Iran are currently the most prominent examples of countries that are building and integrating cyberspace capabilities to advance their national security interests, influence competitors, and deter adversaries. However, the proliferation of cyberspace capabilities has changed the landscape of potential threats; the number of nation-states with offensive cyberspace capabilities doubled from 15 to 30 in only three years (see Figure 8.3).[27]

**FIGURE 8.3 ■ Countries With Offensive Cyberspace Capabilities**

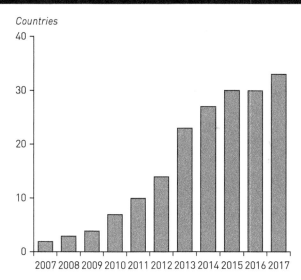

*Source:* Worldwide Threat Assessment, 2018.

---

[24]Coats, Dan R. "Statement for the Record: Worldwide Threat Assessment of the US Intelligence Community." Office of the Director of National Intelligence, January 29, 2019. https://www.dni.gov/files/ODNI/documents/2019-ATA-SFR---SSCI.pdf.

[25]In cybersecurity, social engineering is the act of manipulating people into performing actions or divulging information. Common examples include phishing, spear phishing, and watering holes.

[26]National Intelligence Council, *Global Trends*.

[27]See Coats, "Statement for the Record," 2019; and Coats, "Statement for the Record," 2018.

## THE US CYBER STRATEGY

Simply put, the convergence of technology and the strategic competition in cyberspace has increased threats to the United States, leading to the development of the US cyber strategy. The 2018 strategy consists of four pillars: (1) protect the American people, the homeland, and the American way of life; (2) promote American prosperity; (3) preserve peace through strength; and (4) advance American influence. The pillars reinforce the significance of the reliance on computer-driven and interconnected information technologies. Nation-states and nonstate actors have used cyberspace technology to steal information, influence citizens, and disrupt critical infrastructure.[28] The US cyber strategy emphasizes building and strengthening US cyber capability to maximize flexibility and **decision advantage** during conflicts, while also protecting US national interests by deterring malicious cyber activities that target critical infrastructure.

### Cyber Threats to Critical Infrastructure

**Critical infrastructure** is physical or virtual systems and networks that are vital to day-to-day operations.[29] The 2013 Presidential Policy Directive 21: Critical Infrastructure Security and Resilience legislation identified 16 critical infrastructure sectors including food and agriculture, water and wastewater systems, energy, transportation systems, dams, communications, health care and public health, and emergency services.[30] The exploitation, degradation, or destruction of critical infrastructure sectors would have a debilitating effect on the economic security, social well-being, and public health of the United States.

According to the US Cybersecurity and Infrastructure Security Agency, the energy infrastructure fuels the economy, the public health sector, and the general way of life.[31] Several vulnerabilities and threats to the energy sector were highlighted on December 23, 2015, when the Ukrainian government experienced an unprecedented cyber attack on its energy infrastructure. Starting at approximately 3:35 p.m. local time, three Ukrainian electricity distribution companies suffered widespread power outages that impacted approximately 225,000 customers over approximately six hours. The cyber actors demonstrated a variety of capabilities when they synchronized and coordinated the remote hijacking of ICSs across multiple facilities within 30 minutes

---

[28]White House, "National Cyber Strategy."

[29]Department of Defense, "Summary: Department of Defense Cyber Strategy."

[30]Federal Emergency Management Agency. "Critical Infrastructure and Key Resources." Accessed July 31, 2019. https://emilms.fema.gov/IS520/PAN0101400text.htm.

[31]Cybersecurity and Infrastructure Security Agency. "Energy Sector." Accessed July 31, 2019. https://www.dhs.gov/cisa/energy-sector.

of each other.[32] These actors also used the BlackEnergy3 malware as well as malicious firmware to escalate their privileges, establish persistent access to the network, and prevent operators from manually controlling the systems.[33] The Ukrainian government blamed Russia for the attack; however, the international investigative team stopped short of directly attributing it to Russian cyber actors.

The attack on Ukraine was the first known cyber-enabled disruption of electricity service and served as a reality check to other countries that needed to improve their security, test their infrastructure, and establish processes to respond to a cyber attack on the energy sector. In the United States, historic concerns about the infrastructure[34] and the subsequent blackout in Ukraine elevated efforts to secure the electric grid and ensure domestic access to energy.[35] One such event occurred in late 2018 when the Department of Energy's Office of Cybersecurity, Energy Security, and Emergency Response conducted "Liberty Eclipse 2018," a two-phase exercise to test and evaluate US capabilities to respond to and recover from a cyber attack against the power grid.[36] Exercises like "Liberty Eclipse 2018" highlight the importance of collaboration, coordination, and communication across government agencies at all levels. As noted in the 2018 National Cyber Strategy, protecting US interests requires the sharing of actionable intelligence of adversary intent, tactics, and activities to enable a whole-of-government response.

## Cyber Threat Intelligence

When discussing the premise of cyber threat intelligence, it is paramount to make a distinction between cyber threat intelligence and the sometimes misused term *cyber intelligence*—which is not an intelligence discipline or a recognized doctrinal intelligence process within the intelligence community. The 2019 National Intelligence

---

[32]National Cybersecurity and Communications Integration Center. "ICS Alert (IR-ALERT-H-16-056-01): Cyber-Attack Against Ukrainian Critical Infrastructure." Last modified August 23, 2018. https://www.us-cert.gov/ics/alerts/IR-ALERT-H-16-056-01.

[33]SANS Industrial Control Systems, Electricity Information Sharing and Analysis Center. "Analysis of the Cyber Attack on the Ukrainian Power Grid: Defense Use Case." Last modified March 18, 2016. https://ics.sans.org/media/E-ISAC_SANS_Ukraine_DUC_5.pdf.

[34]Wilshusen, Gregory C. *Cybersecurity: Actions Needed to Strengthen US Capabilities* (GAO-17-440T). Washington, DC: US Government Accountability Office, February 14, 2017. https://www.gao.gov/assets/690/682756.pdf.

[35]US Department of Energy. *Valuation of Energy Security for the United States: Report to Congress.* Washington, DC: US Department of Energy, January 2017. https://www.energy.gov/sites/prod/files/2017/01/f34/Valuation%20of%20Energy%20Security%20for%20the%20United%20States%20%28Full%20Report%29_1.pdf.

[36]US Department of Energy. "National Cybersecurity Awareness Month: DOE Conducts Cyber-Attack Exercise on Electricity, Oil, and Natural Gas Infrastructure." Last modified October 26, 2018. https://www.energy.gov/articles/national-cybersecurity-awareness-month-doe-conducts-cyber-attack-exercise-electricity-oil; Sobczak, Blake. "DOE to Vet Grid's Ability to Reboot After a Cyberattack." *E&E News*, August 3, 2018. https://www.eenews.net/stories/1060092675.

Strategy defines **cyber threat intelligence** as the "collection, processing, analysis, and dissemination of information from all sources of intelligence on foreign actors' cyber programs, intentions, capabilities, research and development, tactics, targets, operational activities and indicators, and their impact or potential effects on US national security interests."[37] As demonstrated in this definition, when analyzing the threat, all-source intelligence analysts must determine if and how nation-state or nonstate entities have the capability and intent to utilize cyberspace operations to achieve strategic, operational, or tactical effects. Maintaining situational understanding of adversary activities is the first step in developing indications and providing warning of malicious cyber activity.

## BOX 8.1

### SPOTLIGHT ON CAREERS

### CYBER THREAT ANALYST, CENTRAL INTELLIGENCE AGENCY (2019)

Langley, Virginia

### Description

As a Cyber Threat Analyst for the CIA, you will conduct all-source analysis, digital forensics, and targeting to identify, monitor, assess, and counter the threat posed by foreign cyber actors against US information systems, critical infrastructure, and cyber-related interests. You will support the President, the National Security Council, and other US policymakers with strategic assessments and provide tactical analysis and advice for operations.

Cyber Threat Analysts apply their scientific and technical knowledge to solving complex intelligence problems, produce short-term and long-term written assessments, and brief US policymakers and the US cyber defense community. This work demands initiative, creativity, analytic skills, and technical expertise.

You will also have the opportunity to maintain and broaden your professional ties throughout your career through academic study, collaboration with Intelligence Community peers, and attendance at professional meetings.

Opportunities exist for foreign and domestic travel, language training, analytic tradecraft and management training, training to deepen substantive expertise, and assignments to other offices in the Agency and throughout the US Government.

---

[37]Office of the Director of National Intelligence. "National Intelligence Strategy of the United States of America: 2019." Accessed July 15, 2019. https://www.dni.gov/files/ODNI/documents/National_Intelligence_Strategy_2019.pdf.

## Qualifications

US citizenship required (dual-national US citizens eligible). All positions require relocation to the Washington, DC, metro area.

## Minimum Qualifications

- Bachelor's or Master's degree in one of the following fields or related studies:
  - o Computer Science
  - o Computer Engineering
  - o Digital Forensics
  - o Cybersecurity
  - o Telecommunications
  - o Information Assurance
  - o Security Studies
  - o Or, a mix of international and technical studies

- GPA of at least 3.0 on a 4-point scale is preferred
- Ability to work under tight deadlines
- Excellent analytic abilities and relevant experience
- Strong ability to think creatively when approaching issues
- Strong critical thinking and problem-solving skills

## Desired Qualifications

- Interest in international affairs
- Awareness of US national security interests
- Foreign language proficiency
- Strong verbal presentation skills
- Demonstrated ability to write clear, concise text
- Research experience in international affairs
- Ability to work in a team environment
- Interest in a career that requires regular writing assignments

## All applicants must successfully complete:

- A thorough medical and psychological exam
- A polygraph interview
- A comprehensive background investigation

*(Continued)*

[Continued]

To be considered suitable for Agency employment, applicants must generally not have used illegal drugs within the last 12 months. The issue of illegal drug use prior to 12 months ago is carefully evaluated during the medical and security processing.

*Source:* Central Intelligence Agency, https://www.cia.gov/careers/opportunities/science-technology/cyber-threat-analyst.html.

Over the years, various intelligence or cybersecurity experts have established or adopted at least eight cyber threat frameworks to assess malicious cyber activity,[38] to include the Adversary Lifecycle Analysis and Lockheed Martin's Cyber Kill Chain.[39] In addition to the frameworks, intelligence analysts developed analytical models, such as the A.C.A.R.E.+I model, to help prioritize research and resources against the perceived primary cyber threat(s). The model A.C.A.R.E.+I stands for activity, capability, access, resources, expertise, and intent. Sometimes threat prioritization can be subjective; however, the A.C.A.R.E.+I model combines the tenets of good analytic tradecraft by providing a means of challenging hypotheses with quantifiable data, based on established criteria, that can be supported by evidence.[40]

## ANALYZING CYBER THREATS

The following anecdotes demonstrate how cyber actors with varying degrees of expertise conducted notable cyber incidents that in some cases changed the international prioritization of cyber threats. They also illustrate the application of cyber threat intelligence analysis when assessing cyber activity.

---

[38]Since 2012, the Office of the Director of National Intelligence has worked with interagency partners to build and refine a "Common Cyber Threat Framework" to serve as a "universal translator" among the various threat models—not to displace or replace an organization's existing model. Further discussion can be found at https://www.dni.gov/files/ODNI/documents/features/ODNI_Cyber_Threat_Framework_Overview._UNCL._20180718.pdf.

[39]A guide to applying Lockheed Martin's Cyber Kill Chain methodology can be found at https://www.lockheedmartin.com/content/dam/lockheed-martin/rms/documents/cyber/Gaining_the_Advantage_Cyber_Kill_Chain.pdf.

[40]The A.C.A.R.E.+I model was developed by all-source intelligence analysts working in the US Army Cyber Command Intelligence Directorate between 2015 and 2017. The model was effectively applied during real-world heightened tensions with nation-state and nonstate actors to prioritize threats and facilitate decision advantage.

## Using Destructive Malware to Protest Freedom of Expression

Experts have long debated whether or not the Democratic People's Republic of Korea (North Korea) has cyber expertise or infrastructure (given most of its internet is routed through China). However, over the last few years, Pyongyang has increased its frequency and complexity of cyber activity. Since 2009, North Korea primarily targeted the Republic of Korea with distributed denial of service (DDoS) attacks against the websites of government organizations and financial institutions—including the 2013 incident that used "Dark Seoul" malware to cripple the networks of three major banks and two television broadcast companies in South Korea. North Korea has also regularly launched cyber espionage campaigns against prominent South Korean government officials.[41]

However, in late 2014, a cyber group[42] backed by North Korea marked a change in **access**, **capability**, and **intent** when it targeted Sony Pictures Entertainment (SPE) in response to the pending release of a movie, *The Interview*. This US movie is a comedy in which the Central Intelligence Agency orchestrates the assassination of Kim Jong-un. Shortly after the June 2014 release of the first trailer, North Korea vehemently protested to the United Nations secretary-general, claiming the movie was a form of terrorism and an act of war.[43] Despite North Korea's public condemnation, Sony continued with plans to release the movie in December 2014. In November 2014, North Korean cyber actors infiltrated Sony's networks and used malware to destroy proprietary data and corrupt disk drives. They also extracted information such as private corporate emails, unreleased Sony films, and the personally identifiable information of Sony employees.

In the grand scheme of national security, targeting a private entertainment company may not seem significant. However, this incident increased US and international concern for North Korea's willingness to employ offensive cyber capabilities to target a company in response to insulting North Korean government officials.[44] In addition

---

[41]Feakin, Tobias. "Playing Blind-man's Buff: Estimating North Korea's Cyber Capabilities." *International Journal of Korean Unification Studies* 22, no. 2 (2013): 63–90.

[42]The initial text on the hacked websites included #GOP suggesting a cyber group by the name of Guardians of Peace was responsible for the hack. However, after further technical analysis the advanced analytics company, Novetta, attributed the SPE cyber incident to the Lazarus Group, while the cybersecurity company, FireEye, attributed the incident to Advanced Persistent Threat (APT) 38. Technical analysis is primarily the result of assessing signatures, tactics, techniques, and procedures. Despite a difference in attribution, both organizations agree that Guardians of Peace, the Lazarus Group, and APT 38 are supported by and affiliated with the North Korean government.

[43]Ja Song Nam. "Letter Dated 27 June 2014 From the Permanent Representative of the Democratic People's Republic of Korea to the United Nations Addressed to the Secretary-General" (A/68/934–S/2014/451). United Nations General Assembly Security Council, June 27, 2014.

[44]Novetta. "Operation BLOCKBUSTER: Unraveling the Long Thread of the Sony Attack." Accessed July 31, 2019. https://www.operationblockbuster.com/wp-content/uploads/2016/02/Operation-Blockbuster-Report.pdf.

to the SPE incident, from 2014 to 2018, state-sponsored cyber actors effectively countered United Nations sanctions by stealing approximately $670 million in foreign and virtual currency by infiltrating the computer systems of banks in over 16 countries.[45] Given the SPE and cyber theft incidents, when studying the North Korean threat (e.g., nuclear ambitions), intelligence analysis should include an assessment of potential catalysts for offensive cyberspace operations during heightened tensions with North Korea.

## Malicious Software to Wipe Away the Competition

Iran's offensive cyberspace capabilities are similar to North Korea's in most experts' assessments. Iran has primarily focused on regional competitors. However, the alleged use of destructive software to target competitors in the oil and natural gas sector has enabled Tehran to modestly project itself as a notable cyber threat because it has successfully exploited vulnerabilities abroad.[46] In August 2012, suspected Iranian-sponsored cyber actors targeted the Saudi Arabian Oil Company (also known as Saudi Aramco) with malware that wiped data from approximately 30,000 computers. Later that month, RasGas, a Qatari natural gas company, also fell victim to a deliberate virus that shut down its website and email servers. Similarly, in 2016 and 2017, Saudi Aramco was targeted with Shamoon 2.0, a new variant of the 2012 wiper malware.[47] While the incidents successfully hit the targets and disrupted day-to-day operations, they did not significantly impact oil and natural gas production. Some experts, after reviewing forensic evidence, opined that Iran exercised restraint when employing the malware.[48] In other words, Iran wanted to demonstrate its offensive capabilities while avoiding an escalated conflict in the region.

## Using Cyber to Shape Political-Military Objectives

Russia's use of cyberspace operations in conjunction with military operations in the 2008 conflict with Georgia and the 2014 annexation of Crimea drove international discourse of whether Russia was outpacing its competitors (including the United States) in the use of cyber to achieve effects in support of geopolitical objectives. Russia

---

[45]Center for Strategic & International Studies. "Significant Cyber Incidents Since 2006." Accessed July 23, 2019. https://csis-prod.s3.amazonaws.com/s3fs-public/190523_Significant_Cyber_Events_List.pdf.

[46]Fixler, Annie, and Frank Cilluffo. "Evolving Menace: Iran's Use of Cyber-Enabled Economic Warfare." Foundation for Defense of Democracies, November 2018. https://carnegieendowment.org/files/Iran_Cyber_Final_Full_v2.pdf.

[47]Bronk, Christopher, and Eneken Tikk-Ringas. "The Cyber Attack on Saudi Aramco." *Survival* 55, no. 2 (2013): 81–96. doi: 10.1080/00396338.2013.784468; and Alelyani, Salem, and Harish Kumar. "Overview of Cyberattack on Saudi Organizations." *Journal of Information Security and Cybercrimes Research* 1, no. 1 (2018): 42–50. doi: 10.26735/16587790.2018.004.

[48]Anderson, Collin, and Karim Sadjadpour. "Iran's Cyber Threat: Espionage, Sabotage, and Revenge." Carnegie Endowment for International Peace, January 4, 2018. https://carnegieendowment.org/files/Iran_Cyber_Final_Full_v2.pdf.

employed several types of cyberspace operations during these conflicts that impacted Georgian and Crimean citizens, respectively. For example, the DDoS attacks in Georgia and Crimea impacted the citizens' ability to access financial and government websites, which prevented citizens from getting accurate and timely information from their government. Also, during the conflict in Crimea, cyber actors shut off the telecommunications service preventing citizens and government officials from accessing the internet and mobile phone service. This significantly limited government communication internally and externally.[49] Russia also enjoyed support from pro-Russian hacktivists to manipulate information—in some cases they controlled which information citizens could access, and in other cases they posted incorrect information for public consumption.[50]

The cyber attacks did not significantly impact the respective conventional forces or determine the outcome of the conflicts; however, they were significant because they forced scholars and practitioners to redefine the character of modern warfare.[51] For example, in 2008, although Russia initiated the propaganda, information control, and disinformation campaigns, Georgia actually outmaneuvered Russia by responding with an effective counterinformation operations campaign.[52]

This is another example of why and how intelligence analysts should include cyber-related indicators when assessing the capabilities of a nation-state. Research should include whether or not a nation-state has resources such as proxy groups (hacktivists or cybercriminals) that will support its objectives. If so, how many cyber actors—fewer than 20, a few hundred, or thousands? What level of cyber activity are they capable of conducting—social engineering, disinformation, or controlling the narrative to bolster international support? In essence, to provide thorough situational understanding of the environment, assessing the composition and disposition of the adversary must now include cyber actors.

## Holding Information and Infrastructure at Risk

Whether it is a nation-state like China conducting cyber espionage (such as the 2015 Office of Personnel Management breach), a hacktivist group (such as Anonymous) protesting perceived wrongs, or unknown cybercriminals using ransomware to disrupt operations of municipalities (like Baltimore, Maryland), the sophistication and

[49]Iasiello, Emilio J. "Russia's Improved Information Operations: From Georgia to Crimea." *Parameters* 47, no. 2 (2017): 51–64. https://www.hsdl.org/?view&did=803998.

[50]Gery, William, SeYoung Lee, and Jacob Ninas. "Information Warfare in an Information Age." *Joint Force Quarterly* 85, no. 2 (2017): 22–29. https://ndupress.ndu.edu/Portals/68/Documents/jfq/jfq-85/jfq-85_22-29_Gery-Lee-Ninas.pdf.

[51]White, Sarah. "Understanding Cyberwarfare: Lessons From the Russia-Georgia War." *Modern War Institute*, March 20, 2018. https://mwi.usma.edu/understanding-cyberwarfare-lessons-russia-georgia-war/.

[52]Wilby, Peter. "Georgia Has Won the PR War." *The Guardian*, August 17, 2008. https://www.theguardian.com/media/2008/aug/18/pressandpublishing.georgia.

frequency of cyber incidents have increased, and cyber actors have demonstrated malicious intent and capability to hold governments and infrastructure at risk. In addition to the aforementioned events, it is important to acknowledge that at least 20 countries (including the United States) are suspected of sponsoring and/or conducting offensive cyberspace operations against regional competitors and at times nonstate actors to further strategic objectives.

## BOX 8.2

### SPOTLIGHT ON CAREERS

### CYBER MITIGATIONS ENGINEER/SYSTEM VULNERABILITY ANALYST ENTRY TO EXPERIENCED LEVEL, NATIONAL SECURITY AGENCY (2019)

System Vulnerability Analysts identify vulnerabilities and attacks to the design and operation of a system (H/W, S/W, personnel, procedures, logistics, and physical security). They compare and contrast various system attack procedures and develop effective defensive mitigations. Additionally, system vulnerability analysts produce formal and informal reports, briefings, and perspectives of actual and potential attacks against the systems or missions being studied. They perform a broad spectrum of duties that may include critical infrastructure defense, control system security, wired and wireless network security, vulnerability analysis and research, scalable defensive mitigation development, perimeter/boundary defense, malware analysis, web and cloud security, mobile network security (LTE, Baseband), tailored security solution and methodology automation, and researching emerging network industry technologies and solutions. If you routinely visit network security websites or attend network security conferences or maintain your own network, we would like to talk to you! If you are a computer hobbyist, enjoy setting up new networks, love the Black Hat/DEFCON briefings, and capture the flag events, then you need to talk to us!

The optimal candidate is someone with strong problem-solving, analytical, communication, and interpersonal skills and who has knowledge or experience in several of the following areas: defending against and/or mitigating system vulnerabilities, including at the infrastructure, host, and enterprise levels; intrusion detection and incident response; network operating systems and network data/traffic analysis; scripting languages (e.g., Power Shell, Python), software reverse engineering; fuzzing; virtualization; penetration testing; ports, protocol, and services analysis; vulnerability detection and analysis; network security devices (e.g., firewalls, intrusion and detection systems); packet analysis; malicious code analysis; [and] SCADA and Control Systems Devices.

### Qualifications

The qualifications listed are the minimum acceptable to be considered for the position. Salary offers are based on candidates' education level and years of experience relevant to the position and also take into account information provided by the hiring manager/organization regarding the work level for the position. Entry is with a Bachelor's degree and no experience. An Associate's degree plus 2 years of relevant experience may be considered for individuals with in-depth experience that is clearly related to the position. Degree must be in Computer Science or a related field (e.g., General Engineering, Computer Engineering, Electrical Engineering, Systems Engineering, Mathematics, Computer Forensics, Cybersecurity, Information Technology, Information Assurance, and Information Security). Relevant experience must be in computer or information systems design/development, programming, information/cyber/network security, vulnerability analysis, penetration testing, computer forensics, information assurance, and/or systems engineering. Network and system administration may account for some, but not all, of the experience. Completion of military training in a relevant area such as JCAC (Joint Cyber Analysis course), Undergraduate Cyber Training (UCT), Network Warfare Bridge Course (NWBC)/Intermediate Network Warfare Training (INWT), [or] Cyber Defense Operations will be considered toward the relevant experience requirement (i.e., 20–24 weeks course will count as 6 months of experience, 10–14 weeks will count as 3 months of experience).

Salary Range: $70,519–$87,868 (entry), $81,571–$108,643 (full performance)

In the 2015 Department of Defense Cyber Strategy, the Director of National Intelligence (DNI) named the cyber threat as the number-one strategic threat against the United States, placing it ahead of terrorism for the first time since 9/11. Since 2015, the 2018 Worldwide Threat Assessment of the US Intelligence Community and the 2019 National Intelligence Strategy, both published by the Office of the DNI, underscored the sign of the times where malicious cyber actors will use the information environment and cyberspace operations as strategic tools to shape the political, economic, and social climate to their advantage.

## CONCLUSION: THE COMPLEXITY OF THREATS IN THE CYBERSPACE DOMAIN

Today, the convergence of technology has facilitated the global spread of knowledge and ultimately changed the concept of "borders." It has also made partners and adversaries more diverse and interconnected. Technology is literally changing at the speed of light, and professionals in the intelligence or national security field will need to leverage critical and creative thinking skills to effectively analyze threats in this complex environment. Analysts not only need to think *outside* of the proverbial box; they must think *beyond* the box as offensive cyberspace capabilities increase globally. It is likely that covert activity in cyberspace will increase, and if operations are publicized, nation-states and nonstate actors will likely deny involvement while exploiting the lack of an international consensus on what constitutes "an act of war in cyberspace." In Chapter 14, we discuss the current trajectory and implications of artificial intelligence, quantum computing, and telecommunications. The future is plural, and many potential game-changers of global trends involve the application or exploitation of technology to solve some of the world's problems or exacerbate them.

## KEY CONCEPTS

Internet of Things (IoT)   199
convergence of technology   200
industrial control systems (ICSs)   200
supervisory control and data acquisition (SCADA)   200
cyberspace   201
social layer   202
physical persona layer   202
cyber persona layer   202
logical network layer   202
physical layer   202
physical network layer   202
geographic layer   202
information environment   203

physical dimension   203
informational dimension   203
cognitive dimension   203
information operations   204
cyber incident   204
cyber attack   204
social engineering   207
decision advantage   208
critical infrastructure   208
cyber threat intelligence   210
access   213
capability   213
intent   213

## ADDITIONAL READING

Brantly, Aaron F. "A Fierce Domain: Conflict in Cyberspace, 1986 to 2012," edited by Jason Healy. *American Foreign Policy Interests* 36, no. 5 (2014): 334–335. doi: 10.1080/10803920.2014.976111.

Clarke, Richard, and Richard Knake. *Cyber War: The Next Threat to National Security and What to Do About It.* New York, NY: HarperCollins, 2010.

DeSimone, Antonio, and Nicholas Horton. *Sony's Nightmare Before Christmas: The 2014 North Korean Cyber Attack on Sony and Lessons for US Government Actions in Cyberspace.* National Security Report, John Hopkins Applied Physics Laboratory (2017). Accessed July 31, 2019. https://www.jhuapl.edu/Content/documents/SonyNightmareBeforeChristmas.pdf.

Holt, Thomas J. "Regulating Cybercrime Through Law Enforcement and Industry Mechanisms." *The Annals of the American Academy of Political and Social Science* 679 (2018): 140–157. doi: 10.1177/0002716218783679.

Koppel, Ted. *Lights Out: A Cyberattack, A Nation Unprepared, Surviving the Aftermath.* New York, NY: Broadway Books, 2015.

Lynn, William J., III. "Defending a New Domain: The Pentagon's Cyberstrategy." *Foreign Affairs* 89, no. 5 (2010): 97–108. https://www.foreignaffairs.com/print/1113238.

McDonough, Bart R. *Cyber Smart: Five Habits to Protect Your Family, Money, and Identity From Cyber Criminals.* Indianapolis, IN: John Wiley & Sons, 2019.

# 9 INTELLIGENCE REGULATION AND GOVERNANCE

## Joseph Fitsanakis

From the moment of its birth, the United States has engaged in wartime intelligence activities. But the nation traversed the first 170 years of its history without a permanent **peacetime intelligence** institution. This is often attributed to its relatively serene geographical neighborhood, which kept it at a safe distance from the political turmoil of the so-called old world of Europe, Asia, and Africa. But it is also the case that Americans have tended to treat the very idea of a government-run security force, whether military or civilian, with skepticism. During the Revolutionary War, many American rebels refused to use militarized insignia and uniforms, and for nearly a century police officers in cities like Philadelphia, Boston, and New York patrolled in civilian clothes and operated more like traditional community watchmen, rather than members of formal law enforcement agencies.[1] It was only as a result of the Civil War that police departments across America adopted a more militarized organizational model—a move that caused considerable controversy at the time.[2] The National Security Act of 1947, which created the Central Intelligence Agency (CIA), America's first permanent peacetime intelligence agency, proved equally controversial. During the congressional debate to discuss the government's proposal, some members of Congress warned that the new intelligence organization seemed reminiscent of Nazi Germany and could become an "American Gestapo."[3] Similar concerns have reverberated throughout the decades, as Americans have largely remained protective of their **civil liberties** and highly skeptical of expanding governmental powers. Ever since 1947, therefore, the evolution of the US intelligence community (IC) has been a delicate balancing act between the need to protect national security and respecting constitutionally protected freedoms. This balancing act has historically leaned on the side of protecting civil liberties, though there have been times in the nation's history when civil liberties were severely curtailed, ostensibly to protect loosely defined national security goals.

---

[1]Caiden, Gerald E. *Police Revitalization*. Lexington, KY: Lexington Books, 1977, 22. See also Fuld, Leonhard F. *Police Administration*. New York, NY: Patterson Smith, 1909, Chapter 1.

[2]Leonard, Vivian A. *Police Organization and Management*. Brooklyn, NY: The Foundation Press, 1964, 18.

[3]Theoharis, Athan G. "A New Agency: The Origins and Expansion of CIA Covert Operations." In *The Central Intelligence Agency: Security Under Scrutiny*, edited by Athan G. Theoharis et al. Westport, CT: Greenwood Press, 2006, 156.

## MCCARTHYISM AND THE SECOND RED SCARE

The balance between the mission of the IC and the rights of a free citizenry proved especially fragile during the Cold War—a period in which domestic politics were largely shaped by America's confrontation with the Soviet Union. A major theme in American political life at the time revolved around real or imaginative fears that key government positions were secretly occupied by pro-Soviet **communists**. These were individuals of all backgrounds who tended to favor Soviet, rather than American or Western European, models of social and economic organization. The growing political anxiety about communism gave rise to a sociopolitical phenomenon known as the **Second Red Scare**, which emerged in the second half of the 1940s and lasted for most of the 1950s. The Second Red Scare was marked by almost daily media headlines alleging that clandestine communist networks were trying to overthrow the government of the United States and institute a Soviet-like system of rule. During that time, several public figures emerged in the public consciousness as guarantors of security, by cultivating popular fears of an imminent communist takeover of America. Among them was Joseph McCarthy, a Republican senator from Wisconsin, who in many ways became the face of American **anti-communism**. McCarthy's decade-long campaign rested on the claim that the American film industry, academia, government agencies, the military, and even the White House were secretly penetrated by communists. The fiery and sensationalized rhetoric of the senator from Wisconsin gave him nationwide media attention, which he visibly relished. Over time, however, in an attempt to stay in the media limelight, McCarthy began to voice increasingly wild conspiratorial claims, which were as sensational as they were unsubstantiated. For example, he alleged that the government was placing fluoride in the water system so as to brainwash Americans in a secret communist plot, and he even accused the leadership of the Department of Defense—which was composed largely of World War II heroes—of communist sympathies. McCarthy was eventually abandoned by all but his most zealous supporters, and fell spectacularly from grace in 1957. By that time, however, the term **McCarthyism** had come to describe the most polarizing phase of the period that became known as the Second Red Scare.

## DOMESTIC INTELLIGENCE AND COINTELPRO

Another public figure who used the Second Red Scare for his personal benefit was Federal Bureau of Investigation (FBI) director J. Edgar Hoover. By the 1940s, when anti-communism became a recognizable force in American politics, Hoover was already a powerful figure in the US IC. He was feared and respected in equal measure by the American political class. He eventually died in office in 1972, having led the FBI with an iron fist for 48 years. Although he secretly loathed McCarthy, whom he saw as an attention-seeking narcissist, Hoover cleverly exploited the Wisconsin senator's anti-communist campaign to enhance the FBI's counterintelligence role. He also encouraged suspicions about the presence of communist sympathizers in the ranks of the CIA, in an attempt to subvert the then-young intelligence agency, which he viewed as a major bureaucratic rival to his power. In 1956, as part of his anti-communist campaign, and in an attempt to respond to popular fears about communism, Hoover launched a new covert FBI effort, code-named Counter Intelligence Program. Referred to in internal FBI documents simply as **COINTELPRO**, the program was aimed at disrupting the work of political groups that were deemed subversive. Its initial targets were the pro-Soviet Communist Party USA and several smaller left-wing and ultra-liberal political groups. The program gradually expanded to incorporate organized **white supremacists**, many of whom were members of the Ku Klux Klan. Eventually, the FBI relied on substantial resources that were contributed to COINTELPRO by other members of the IC, including the National Security Agency (NSA) and some military intelligence units. Other **domestic intelligence** programs were launched in parallel by the CIA and the NSA. These were smaller in scope but equally intrusive, and focused on an ever-expanding list of political groups that were deemed extremist. By 1960, the growing list of targets incorporated numerous nonviolent and wholly law-abiding groups, such as trade unions, religious associations, and gay-rights campaigns. These were targeted by the IC under the often-false pretext that they were led by communists or had members with communist sympathies.

By 1960, COINTELPRO's primary targets included the **civil rights movement** and its principal leader, Martin Luther King Jr., who was ruthlessly and unjustly vilified by Hoover as an un-American subversive. Under the personal direction of Hoover and the senior leadership of the Department of Justice, the FBI installed wiretaps on the telephone lines in King's home and office. Moreover, the FBI employed technical experts to surreptitiously place listening bugs at the civil rights leader's home and church, as well as at the homes and offices of nearly every one of his close aides and associates. As King's reputation grew across the nation, FBI special agents were sent out to bug many of the hotel rooms in which the civil rights leader stayed during his numerous speaking tours.[4] After King's assassination in 1968, COINTELPRO's primary focus shifted to **anti–Vietnam War** protest groups. For the most part, these groups—led primarily by college students or recent college graduates—did nothing more than exercise their members' constitutionally protected right to publicly challenge the government's policies in Vietnam, Laos, and Cambodia. However, they were systematically targeted by several domestic intelligence programs. At least two of these programs, code-named **MERRIMAC** and **MHCHAOS**, were run by the CIA. Under the patently false pretext that antiwar groups were guided by foreign enemies, the CIA employed human intelligence (HUMINT) operatives to infiltrate their ranks. In some

---

[4]Donner, Frank J. *The Age of Surveillance: The Aims and Methods of America's Political Intelligence System*. New York, NY. Alfred A. Knopf, 1980, 244.

cases, the CIA and other member agencies of the IC waged psychological operations against individual antiwar activists, for example by sending anonymous letters to their spouses claiming that they had been unfaithful, or by pressuring their university professors to give them failing grades in class. In one instance, a senior official in the **Black nationalist** group Nation of Islam, who had no criminal record, had his personal telephone constantly wiretapped for eight years by the FBI, without any effort by the FBI to prosecute him for criminal activity.[5]

## THE WATERGATE SCANDAL

This period of highly intrusive domestic surveillance operations by the IC culminated in the early 1970s, with an event known as the **Watergate scandal**. The incident took its name from the Watergate Complex, a group of six buildings located in the Foggy Bottom area of Washington, DC. The Watergate Complex housed the headquarters of the Democratic National Committee (DNC), which is the main governing body of the Democratic Party. A group of senior aides in the reelection campaign of President Richard Nixon—a Republican—employed former intelligence practitioners with experience in nondestructive entry operations. They tasked these men with secretly entering the DNC headquarters and wiretapping the telephones in the office. The purpose of that illegal act was to sabotage the Democratic Party's electoral campaign, thus helping to reelect Nixon for a second term in the White House. Things, however, did not go as planned by the president's aides. In the early-morning hours of June 27, 1972, five burglars were arrested by police in the DNC office as they were attempting to reinstall a malfunctioning wiretap device that they had concealed there at an earlier date. Over the next 18 months a trail of evidence was uncovered, which connected the burglary to core members of the president's reelection effort. On August 9, 1974, Nixon resigned from office in disgrace, having first tried to cover up his personal connection to the dirty-tricks campaign against the Democratic Party. The president also tried on multiple occasions to obstruct a number of investigations into the Watergate scandal, often with the help of members of the IC, including officials in the CIA. In addition to the president's resignation, the Watergate scandal resulted in the indictment of 69 individuals, most of whom were found guilty of various offenses, such as conspiracy, perjury, and obstruction of justice.

President Gerald Ford, who succeeded Nixon in the White House, eventually pardoned his predecessor, in a move that relieved some voters while infuriating others. But the Watergate scandal marked an unprecedented period in American political history and continues to have a chilling effect on American politics to this

---

[5]Diffie, Whitfield, and Susan Landau. *Privacy on the Line: The Politics of Wiretapping and Encryption*. Cambridge, MA: MIT Press, 2007, 184.

day. It also prompted a radical redefinition of the concept of **intelligence oversight**. The term refers to the supervision of the activities of the IC by the elected and appointed representatives of the American people. Unlike countries such as Egypt or North Korea, the United States is not a **security state**. This means that its intelligence and security agencies are subject to a set of parameters that are determined by the three branches of power, namely Congress, the Executive Office of the President (EOP), and the judiciary. An example of the latter is the **Foreign Intelligence Surveillance Court**, a group of 11 federal district court judges who consider requests by federal law enforcement and intelligence agencies to issue surveillance warrants in compliance with the Foreign Intelligence Surveillance Act (FISA). **FISA warrants** are used to facilitate intelligence collection operations against suspected foreign spies who operate on US soil. But the FISA system did not exist in the pre-Watergate period. The latter was characterized by the absence of concrete measures to protect the civil liberties of Americans from unreasonable government intrusion. Indeed, the Watergate scandal demonstrated beyond a reasonable doubt that the uses to which the IC had been put by those in power had at times directly subverted the constitutional rights and freedoms of American citizens and permanent residents.

## THE CHURCH AND PIKE COMMITTEES

In 1975, two Democratic congressmen, Senator Frank Church (Idaho) and Representative Otis Pike (New York), led exhaustive congressional investigations into prior activities of the IC going back many decades. These committees, which became known by the names of their chairmen as the **Church Committee** and **Pike Committee**, uncovered a record of reprehensible abuse that included COINTELPRO, MHCHAOS, and MERRIMAC. These revelations shocked many Americans and prompted lengthy public discussions about the reasons that led to such extensive abuses of power by the IC. It was clear that officials in the White House and the IC had exploited the tense political atmosphere of the Cold War to break the law. Successive administrations in the White House had viewed the right of Americans to disagree with their government as political subversion. In other words, by the early 1970s it had become apparent that senior officials in intelligence agencies like the CIA, the FBI, and the NSA were systematically viewing lawful political dissent as un-American. By doing so, they deliberately ignored the wise words of Senator George Mitchell that, "in America, disagreement with the policies of the government is not evidence of lack of patriotism."[6] Intelligence observers generally agree that the pressures of the Cold War, and the fear that the United States

---

[6]Cited in Walsh, Lawrence E. *Firewall: The Iran-Contra Conspiracy and Cover-Up*. New York, NY: Norton, 1997, 133.

could be defeated in its confrontation with the Soviet Union, encouraged an environment of permissiveness in the sphere of domestic intelligence activities. Within that environment, the American IC developed an operational culture that evolved in what may be described as the shadows of democracy. This lack of accountability was multiply reinforced by a strong ethos of secrecy, which is understandably endemic in the business of intelligence. Ultimately, the prevailing atmosphere of permissiveness of the Cold War allowed American intelligence agencies to operate with what at times seemed to be a complete disregard for the law.

The seriousness of this illegality cannot be understated. Indeed, at times the modus operandi of domestic intelligence operations targeting Americans came uncomfortably close to the kinds of abuses that took place behind the Iron Curtain by the likes of the East German Stasi and the Soviet KGB. This negated the very mission of the US IC, which is to protect the country and its system of governance, not subvert it in the interests of politically dubious definitions of national security. Perhaps the most disturbing revelation of the post-Watergate investigations concerned the so-called **Huston Plan**, which took its name from Tom Huston, a White House aide to Nixon, who also served as the president's speechwriter. In 1970, Huston, a lawyer by training, drafted a proposal to repurpose the methods of collection that the IC used against foreign targets, and employ them against American citizens. Huston's report argued that there were connections between foreign enemies of the United States and "domestic radicals," such as antiwar groups. In Huston's mind, these connections—which were wholly unsubstantiated—justified the full use of the resources of the IC against American citizens. This domestic intelligence effort, argued Huston, should be led by agencies such as the CIA and the NSA, which are not legally permitted to spy on Americans. The report proceeded to detail ways in which intelligence collection methods, such as nondestructive entry, warrantless electronic surveillance, mail opening, and HUMINT operations, should be employed against large numbers of Americans. Remarkably, the president asked Huston to draft a more detailed report, and when it was completed, he forwarded it to the directors of the CIA, NSA, FBI, and Defense Intelligence Agency, asking them to take immediate steps toward its implementation. A few days after authorizing the Huston Plan, Nixon changed his mind and backed away from its application. By that time, however, the IC was already using several of the Huston Plan's methods against American citizens.[7] Once the Huston Plan was reported in the press, it became clear that the Watergate scandal involved the application of intelligence collection techniques that had been used on antiwar activists, but this time against the American political establishment—namely the Democratic Party. The chilling effect of these activities, coupled with the president's attempts to cover them up, led to his dramatic fall from power under the threat of imminent impeachment.

---

[7]Theoharis, Athan G. *Spying on Americans: Political Surveillance From Hoover to the Huston Plan*. Philadelphia, PA: Temple University Press, 1978, 30ff.

# INTELLIGENCE OVERSIGHT AFTER WATERGATE

## The Role of Congress

The revelations of the post-Watergate investigations convinced lawmakers that they needed to exercise stricter oversight into the activities of the IC. Therefore, Congress decided to turn the Church and Pike Committees into permanent efforts. Today these are known as the **Senate Select Committee on Intelligence** and the **House Permanent Select Committee on Intelligence**. They are an embodiment of the belief that the executive should never again be trusted to operate as the sole overseeing authority on matters of intelligence.

Today the Senate Select Committee on Intelligence consists of 15 members, of which 8—7 members and the committee chair—represent the majority party. The House Permanent Select Committee on Intelligence consists of a varying number of members, usually totaling over 20. As in the case of the Senate Intelligence Committee, most of the House Intelligence Committee members represent the majority party. Both committees employ several dozen **intelligence committee staff**—known informally as *staffers*—whose job is to review copious amounts of written material from the IC, which relates to analysis, operations, and budget. These staffers also help prepare legislation and are typically present during briefings given by the IC. Their role in the efficient running of the committees is critical, because it is they—and not the elected senators—who conduct **daily oversight** of the activities of the IC and alert committee members of issues that require immediate attention. Unlike other members of Congress, intelligence committee members are able to access information relating to intelligence programs and operations, budgetary details, and even intelligence sources and methods. When an intelligence operation requiring covert action is deemed too sensitive by the president, the president has the right to restrict access to just the chair and vice chair of the intelligence committees. In such instances, however, the president is not relieved of the obligation to provide a broad description of the topic to the remaining members of the intelligence committees.

A major regular duty of the intelligence committees is to consider every piece of stand-alone legislation that governs, or in any way affects, the activities of the IC. But the most powerful aspect of their regular functions is undoubtedly that which relates to budgetary issues. In accordance with the constitutionally mandated requirement for congressional approval of all government expenditures, the intelligence committees provide the two chambers of Congress with the **annual intelligence authorization bill**, which sets funding limits for every one of America's intelligence agencies. The committees can even authorize funds for individual intelligence programs if they so choose. These bills must then undergo a process of **appropriation**, which means that Congress must essentially approve them by allocating specific dollar amounts to cover the authorized funding. It is possible—and indeed a frequent occurrence—for a bill to be authorized but then be dropped in the appropriation stage of the process, if the

**PHOTO 9.1** Director of National Intelligence Daniel R. Coats testifying before the Senate Select Committee on Intelligence, May 11, 2017.

relevant committees refuse to allocate sufficient funds for it. Intelligence agencies are fully cognizant of the fact that a budgetary authorization means nothing in Congress until it is successfully appropriated. They also know that an authorized bill may be appropriated, but with such limited funds that it is rendered essentially meaningless. Congress often treats these legislative provisions as weapons that allow it to place limits on—or even terminate—intelligence operations or initiatives that it objects to. For example, from 2010 to 2012, the Republican-controlled House sought persistently to defund the CIA's Center on Climate Change and National Security. It was a short-lived analytical initiative that the CIA had established in order to study the national security implications of climate change. These include the desertification of the planet and the rising cost of food production, which arguably contributes to increasing of poverty, mass immigration, and rapid population shifts that affect the United States and its interests around the world. This effort was strongly resisted by many Republican members of Congress, who rejected the scientific evidence on climate change. Eventually, the lack of sufficient funding appropriation from Congress contributed to the CIA's decision to shut down the center in 2012.

As part of their duties, the intelligence committees also conduct **congressional briefings and hearings**. These are regular committee sessions that include oral and written testimony by witnesses, such as senior intelligence officials and outside experts. Witnesses are called to provide oral and written testimony and are then questioned by the members of the committees. Briefing and hearing sessions can turn combative and are at times extremely adversarial, depending on the subject under discussion. A significant number of briefing and hearing sessions concern **legislative hearings**, which are designed to allow the intelligence committees to consider the ramifications of various measures that have the potential to become public law. Others are **oversight hearings** that center on reviewing or evaluating the lawfulness or efficacy of an intelligence program or function. These hearings often have an investigative feel and concern topics such as the usefulness of routine intelligence collection programs or highly sensitive covert action operations. On occasion, the intelligence committees conduct oversight hearings that relate to a specific **congressional inquiry** that has been issued on behalf of individual American citizens or groups who have been affected by intelligence policy or operations (see the case of the 2001 Peru shoot-down later in this chapter). During what are known as **confirmation hearings**, the committees evaluate the suitability of individuals who are nominated by the president to serve in intelligence positions. They subsequently make recommendations to their respective chambers of Congress, which are taken into consideration when these appointments require congressional approval. The intelligence committees also conduct **ratification hearings**, which concern the endorsement and approval of treaties that the executive branch negotiates with foreign governments, as well as **field hearings**, which are rare occasions when hearings take place outside of Washington.

The majority of the sessions described in the previous paragraph are **closed hearings**, which means that they are not open to the public because they involve national security information. This is in stark contrast to congressional hearings other than those held by the intelligence committees, the vast majority of which are held in open session. In the case of the intelligence committees, open-session meetings are only occasional occurrences. They are usually annual hearings that feature highly **redacted** and abstract testimony by senior intelligence officials about current and prospective threats to the national security of the United States.

## The Role of the President

In the post-Watergate oversight model, Congress shares the oversight of the IC with the president, who is the foremost representative of the executive branch of government. No covert action or classified mission can be carried out by the IC without the expressed approval of the president. The latter is also able to appoint members of the various intelligence oversight councils that operate as part of the executive branch of government, and can also establish special commissions to investigate or otherwise evaluate intelligence programs or activities. The president also chairs the **National Security Council (NSC)**, which advises the president on pressing matters of national security and foreign policy. To properly perform their duty, the members of the NSC—including the vice president; the secretaries of state, defense, energy, and treasury; and the assistant to the president for national security affairs—are required to remain informed at all times of intelligence operations, analyses, and major findings.

In addition to the NSC, the president supervises and coordinates the activities of the IC with the help of the **President's Intelligence Advisory Board (PIAB)**. The mission of the PIAB is to assess the degree to which the activities and output of the IC are meeting the requirements of national security, and to provide these assessments to the commander-in-chief. The PIAB consists of no more than 16 members who are directly appointed by the president. They usually come from professional fields other than government—though many tend to have prior intelligence experience. The PIAB includes a standing committee—that is, a permanent committee that meets on a regular basis—which is known as the **President's Intelligence Oversight Board (PIOB)**. The PIOB consists of up to 4 members of the PIAB, who have the primary task of ensuring that the IC operates in accordance with the law of the land, including

Pete Souza, the White House

**PHOTO 9.2** President Barack Obama meeting with the National Security Council in the White House Situation Room, March 2009.

the Constitution and all executive orders and presidential directives. To accomplish its mission, this board works closely with the **inspectors general** of the IC. There are inspectors general in every member agency of the IC. Their mission is to ensure that the law is being observed at all times within their respective agencies. However, neither the inspectors general nor the PIOB have the ability to initiate investigations or hold hearings. They simply notify the EOP in the event of legal breaches; additionally, the inspectors general are required by law to notify Congress.

Since 2007, presidents have also received consultation and advice from the **Privacy and Civil Liberties Oversight Board (PCLOB)**. The PCLOB's five members are tasked with reviewing intelligence policies that relate to terrorism, with an eye to ensuring that these policies do not negatively impact the civil liberties of Americans. They also advise the EOP and other executive branch bodies on how to formulate intelligence policies in such a way that they do not subvert or otherwise threaten existing civil liberties. In addition to the PCLOB, the EOP rests on the advice of the **Office of Management and Budget (OMB)**, whose overall mission is much broader than just intelligence matters, but overlaps with a host of managerial and financial aspects of intelligence work. The OMB helps to execute the president's budget priorities by ensuring that federal agencies comply with it in accordance with existing regulations. It also coordinates these budgetary priorities with Congress while taking into consideration **executive orders** and **presidential memoranda**—legal directives issued by the president. In all matters that relate to its mission, therefore, the OMB has supervisory power over the IC.

## INTELLIGENCE OVERSIGHT IN PRACTICE

The methods of intelligence oversight described in the previous section are in many ways abstract and idealized. In practice, the process of intelligence oversight is highly contentious, messy, and at times problematic. For example, the aforementioned FISA court, which issues surveillance warrants to be used in counterintelligence operations against foreign spies operating on American soil, is often accused of being a **rubber stamp** system. The term refers to a largely automated procedure that provides a semblance of lawfulness to an administrative process, without properly considering its legal parameters. Indeed, studies show that FISA court judges denied only 11 of nearly 44,000 requests for surveillance warrants between 1979 and 2012, a number that amounts to an approval rate of 99.97 percent.[8] Another example of the muddled landscape of intelligence oversight is the institution of the inspectors general, which was discussed earlier. After 2015, when the CIA's inspector general David Buckley resigned following four years on the job, the Obama administration did not nominate a replacement. Following several months of inaction, the chair of the Senate Intelligence Committee sent a letter to the White House expressing "mounting concerns" about the president's failure to nominate a replacement for Buckley and urging him to do so "as soon as possible." But the president did not even respond to the committee's request, let alone propose a nominee.[9] By 2020, a full five years after Buckley's resignation, the CIA's Office of the Inspector General continued to be led by Christopher Sharpley, a government lawyer who worked under Buckley and agreed to serve temporarily in an acting capacity. The next White House administration did not do much better: by 2018, two years after President Donald Trump assumed office, there were no fewer than 12 vacant inspector general positions across the federal government. A similar situation transpired in the aforementioned PCLOB, which practically ceased to exist from 2007 to 2012, as Congress refused to approve successive presidential nominees for the board.

Why is the intelligence oversight process so chaotic at times? The answer is complicated. As with everything else in Washington, the inconstancy and unevenness of human relationships can impede the effectiveness of intelligence oversight. When it comes to Congress, much depends on whether the intelligence committees operate in a spirit of collaboration and bipartisanship, not only between their members, but also between them and other congressional committees that have a say on matters of intelligence. Some aspects of the relationship between the various committees are enforced by law. For instance, the Senate Select Committee on Intelligence is required by law to include in its ranks two members (one Republican and one Democrat) from the

---

[8]Clarke, Conor. "Is the Foreign Intelligence Surveillance Court Really a Rubber Stamp? Ex Parte Proceedings and the FISC Win Rate." *Stanford Law Review* 66, no. 125 (2014): 125–133.

[9]Isikoff, Michael. "White House Criticized for Not Filling Watchdog Post at CIA." *Yahoo News*, August 5, 2015. https://www.yahoo.com/news/white-house-criticized-for-not-filling-watchdog-125876527661.html.

Senate Judiciary, Foreign Relations, Appropriations, and Armed Services Committees. Moreover, the chair and ranking members—the senior representative from the minority party—of the Senate Armed Services Committee are legally required to serve in the Senate Intelligence Committee in an *ex officio* capacity, which means that they are members by right of office or by virtue of holding another office. The same applies for the Senate's majority and minority leaders. The purpose of the *ex officio* measure is to facilitate—albeit forcibly—close coordination between the intelligence committees and several other congressional posts or committees that have an interest in intelligence matters. But such measures are not in themselves sufficient to ensure a conflict-free oversight environment. There is often tension between the Senate and House Intelligence Committees, especially when they are chaired by members of opposite political parties. There are also territorial antagonisms between the intelligence committees and other committees in Congress—for instance between the intelligence committees and the armed services committees in both chambers. The Senate and House Armed Services Committees see themselves as overseers of matters relating to military intelligence. That is a function that inevitably conflicts with the supervisory role of the intelligence committees, which see it as their mission to supervise both civilian and military intelligence agencies. There are also recurring tensions between members of Congress who are involved in the authorization of intelligence bills, as is the case with intelligence committee members, and those who serve in appropriations committees. The latter have the right to allocate specific funds that render authorized bills feasible, or to limit funding and—in some cases—deny it altogether, thus effectively killing previously authorized bills.

## THE SEPARATION OF POWERS IN INTELLIGENCE OVERSIGHT

The relationship between the legislative and executive powers on matters of intelligence is invariably strenuous and thorny. Ever since Watergate, these two centers of power have been engaged in a seemingly endless struggle for control of the intelligence process, with victories and defeats shared by both sides in almost equal measure. Members of the congressional intelligence committees—irrespective of political affiliation—demand to be treated by the executive as equal partners in intelligence oversight. This demand, which strongly echoes the spirit of the post-Watergate investigations, is truly ever-present and can be described as the only constant feature of intelligence oversight in today's Congress. Recent years have witnessed numerous conflicts between congressional committees and the White House on matters relating to intelligence. One such conflict erupted in 2018, following the brutal murder of Jamal Khashoggi by an assassin unit of the Saudi Arabian General Intelligence Directorate. Khashoggi, a Saudi former government adviser turned critic of the regime, was killed inside Saudi Arabia's consulate in Istanbul, Turkey, where he had gone to receive a set of divorce documents that he needed in order to marry his Turkish fiancée. Despite strong evidence that Khashoggi's murder was preplanned and ordered by the highest echelons of the Saudi government, the White House refused to assume a critical stance on the matter. In December 2018, the Senate Select Committee on Intelligence helped facilitate a closed-door briefing by CIA director Gina Haspel on the Khashoggi case. Following the briefing, several Republican senators fingered the Saudi government as the culprit of Khashoggi's murder and later voted to end American weapons sales to Saudi Arabia. This forced Trump—a fellow Republican—to veto Congress's decision. It was President Trump's first-ever veto, and it infuriated Congress. The congressional committees later responded by limiting funds for several presidential budget requests for intelligence programs.

A major complaint that Congress often levels against the White House and the IC at large is that they frequently fail to comply with core statutory procedures of the National Security Act of 1947. The act stipulates that the congressional intelligence committees must be kept "fully and currently informed," in writing, of all intelligence activities. This includes anticipated intelligence operations, which are to be communicated to Congress for informational purposes, rather than for approval. Rare exceptions can be made in "extraordinary circumstances affecting vital interests" in order to safeguard intelligence sources and methods. Broadly speaking, however, Congress cannot be kept in the dark, even on matters of covert operations or intelligence disasters and failures. However, as is the case with much of the National Security Act, the phrase "extraordinary circumstances affecting vital interests" is not precisely defined. In the past, this has permitted the White House and the IC to apply it liberally to intelligence activities, thus withholding a significant number of them from Congress. The act also permits the president to severely limit congressional access to covert action information, by making the latter available only to the leadership of Congress and to the two ranking members of each of the intelligence committees. This type of notification is typically communicated to no more than eight members of Congress, which is why it is often referred to as a **gang of eight notification**. Over the years, Congress has attempted to limit the president's use of gang of eight notifications to specific aspects of covert action operations. But the White House, and in some cases the IC, continues to resist congressional attempts to exercise stricter oversight over intelligence activities.

An example of a seemingly major intelligence program that was kept secret from Congress was the so-called executive assassination squad. This secret group was reportedly set up within a special unit of the Joint Special Operations Command (JSOC). Headquartered in Fort Bragg, North Carolina, JSOC operates under the US Special Operations Command. It is tasked with planning and conducting highly specialized training aimed at developing tactics that can be successfully shared and implemented across all Special Operations commands. In March 2009, Pulitzer Prize–winning journalist Seymour Hersh alleged that the administration of President George W. Bush had set up a special JSOC wing that carried out assassinations of terrorism suspects around the world, and was expected to report directly to Vice President Dick Cheney.

Hersh also claimed that the White House had kept the program secret from Congress for eight years. Throughout that time, the highly secret unit reportedly received orders directly and solely from the offices of the president and vice president.[10] Immediately upon learning of Hersh's allegations, the congressional intelligence committees threatened to launch closed-door investigations into the matter. In June of that year, CIA director Leon Panetta, an appointee of the Obama administration, reportedly terminated the program and sent letters of apology to the intelligence committees, in which he admitted that the congressional oversight mechanism had been wrongfully abandoned by his predecessors. He also promised that the CIA would not repeat such a blatant violation of the National Security Act under his tenure.[11]

Another controversy that stigmatized relations between the congressional committees and the IC relates to an incident that became known as the Peru shoot-down. It involved the CIA's Air Bridge Denial program, a counternarcotics operation that the CIA undertook in support of the governments of Peru and Colombia. Its goal was to detect and stop—using lethal force if necessary—aircraft that were used to facilitate the trafficking of illicit narcotics. In April 2001, a Peruvian Air Force fighter jet, which was being assisted by a CIA reconnaissance airplane, shot down an unarmed Cessna aircraft that was flying over the jungle of northeastern Peru. It soon emerged that the downed aircraft was not trafficking illicit narcotics, but was instead carrying an American missionary family. Two members of the family, Veronica Bowers and her six-month-old daughter Charity, were killed in the attack. In a surveillance video released by the CIA, at least one member of the agency's reconnaissance team is heard expressing doubts that the airplane fit the profile of a renegade drug-trafficking aircraft. But the CIA team did not attempt to prevent the Peruvians from opening fire. A subsequent investigation by the CIA's inspector general concluded that the agency had deliberately lied to Congress about the nature and operational details of the Air Bridge Denial program, which was run with "routine disregard of [required] procedures." It also criticized the CIA's general counsel—the agency's senior lawyer—who allegedly advised the officers involved in the shoot-down to avoid writing anything down so as not to further incriminate themselves. In short, the CIA was caught trying to cover up and misrepresent its role in the killing of two innocent Americans. The incident gave rise to severe criticism of the CIA by senior members of the Senate and House Intelligence Committees and led to the temporary termination of the Air Bridge Denial program.[12] At one point during the probe, a closed-door briefing held

---

[10]Shah, Naureen. "A Move Within the Shadows: Will JSOC's Control of Drones Improve Policy?" In *Drone Wars: Transforming Conflict, Law and Policy*, edited by Peter L. Bergen and Daniel Rothenberg. New York, NY: Cambridge University Press, 2015, 177n13.

[11]Gorman, Siobhan. "CIA Had Secret al-Qaeda Plan." *The Wall Street Journal*, July 13, 2009. https://www.wsj.com/articles/SB124736381913627661.

[12]Colvin, Ross. "CIA Faulted in Shooting Down of Missionary Plane." *Reuters*, November 20, 2008. https://www.reuters.com/article/us-usa-cia-report/cia-faulted-in-shooting-down-of-missionary-plane-idUSTRE4AJ9AX20081120.

by the Oversight and Investigations Subcommittee of the House Permanent Select Committee on Intelligence was reportedly canceled, after government officials refused to testify under oath about whether the Justice Department was prepared to file charges on the Bowers case. That incident, which occurred eight years after the Peru shoot-down incident, is indicative of the tension that often arises between the IC and Congress in the course of the latter's constitutionally mandated oversight activities.

Arguably one of the most scarring oversight battles between Congress, the White House, and the IC centers on the so-called enhanced interrogation program, which was approved in 2002 by the administration of President George W. Bush. The program involved the use of torture on terrorism suspects for purposes of intelligence collection. It was utilized by both civilian and military intelligence agencies in response to the attacks of September 11, 2001. It eventually emerged that the CIA had taken the controversial measure of destroying nearly 100 videotapes that contained recorded enhanced-interrogation sessions, despite having been instructed by members of the congressional intelligence committees not to do so. The leadership of the CIA claimed that the tapes were destroyed in order to safeguard sources and methods, but many in Congress accused the agency of trying to evade oversight. The Senate Intelligence Committee did not forget that incident, and in 2014 it launched an investigation into whether the use of torture in interrogations helped safeguard national security. In the course of that probe, relations between the committee and the CIA sunk into what one Department of Justice lawyer described as "the most acrimonious public moment between the CIA and a Senate committee [in] nearly 40 years."[13] The committee publicly accused the CIA of illegally spying on its computers and withholding vital documents. In turn, the CIA asked the FBI to investigate whether the committee's staffers illegally removed from the agency's archives a number of classified documents that were beyond the scope of the investigation. At the height of the dispute, Republican senator Lindsey Graham (South Carolina) said that the time had come for "the legislative branch [to] declare war on the CIA."[14] In July 2014, an investigation by the CIA's own Office of the Inspector General found that the agency had indeed spied on the Senate Intelligence Committee. According to the inspector general's report, a number of CIA officers created fake online identities in order to surreptitiously access computers used by congressional staffers who were involved in the committee's torture probe. The findings of the investigation were communicated to the ranking members of the Senate Intelligence Committee by then CIA director John Brennan, who proceeded to apologize for the agency's conduct. He also offered to take "steps to address systemic issues" within the agency, such as establishing "an internal accountability

---

[13]Harris, Shane, and John Hudson. "Rock Bottom." *Foreign Policy*, March 11, 2014. https://foreignpolicy.com/2014/03/11/rock-bottom.

[14]Correra, Gordon. "Senate Intelligence Head Says CIA Searched Computers," *BBC*, March 11, 2014. https://www.bbc.com/news/world-us-canada-26533323.

board" chaired by a former senator, which would further investigate the CIA officers' conduct and "recommend potential disciplinary measures."[15]

## CONCLUSION: AN IMPERFECT BUT INDISPENSABLE SYSTEM

The fact that the IC is regulated by the executive, legislative, and judicial centers of American power is a good thing. The opposite would mean that Americans would be subjected to a largely unregulated—and therefore unaccountable—intelligence apparatus, whose members would almost certainly exercise unyielding power. This does not mean that our current system of oversight is efficient, or even functional. As was shown by the experience of the Cold War, intelligence oversight is crucially shaped by the broader sociopolitical context in which it takes place. Furthermore, it suffers from the same deficiencies that are endemic in all Western democracies, such as political partisanship and bureaucratic turf wars. Ultimately, America's intelligence oversight remains a work in progress, and its evolution continues to shape much of the country's civil rights and civil liberties landscape.

| KEY CONCEPTS | |
|---|---|
| peacetime intelligence   219 | Foreign Intelligence Surveillance Court   223 |
| civil liberties   219 | |
| communism   220 | FISA warrants   223 |
| Second Red Scare   220 | Church Committee   223 |
| anti-communism   220 | Pike Committee   223 |
| McCarthyism   220 | Huston Plan   224 |
| COINTELPRO   221 | Senate Select Committee on Intelligence   225 |
| white supremacy   221 | |
| domestic intelligence   221 | House Permanent Select Committee on Intelligence   225 |
| civil rights movement   221 | |
| anti–Vietnam War movement   221 | intelligence committee staff   225 |
| MERRIMAC   221 | daily oversight   225 |
| MHCHAOS   221 | annual intelligence authorization bill   225 |
| Black nationalism   222 | |
| Watergate scandal   222 | appropriation   225 |
| intelligence oversight   223 | congressional briefings and hearings   226 |
| security state   223 | |

[15]Mazzetti, Mark, and Carl Hulse. "Inquiry by CIA Affirms It Spied on Senate Panel." *The New York Times*, July 31, 2014. https://www.nytimes.com/2014/08/01/world/senate-intelligence-commitee-cia-interrogation-report.html.

## ADDITIONAL READING

Diffie, Whitfield, and Susan Landau. *Privacy on the Line: The Politics of Wiretapping and Encryption.* Cambridge, MA: MIT Press, 2007.

King, David C. *Turf Wars: How Congressional Committees Clam Jurisdiction.* Chicago, IL: University of Chicago Press, 1997.

Medsger, Betty. *The Burglary: The Discovery of J. Edgar Hoover's Secret FBI.* New York, NY: Vintage Books, 2014.

Schmidt, Regin. *Red Scare: FBI and the Origins of Anticommunism in the United States, 1919–1943.* Copenhagen, Denmark: Museum Tusculanum Press, 2000.

Theoharis, Athan G. *The Central Intelligence Agency: Security Under Scrutiny.* Westport, CT: Greenwood Press, 2006.

Theoharis, Athan G. *Spying on Americans: Political Surveillance From Hoover to the Huston Plan.* Philadelphia, PA: Temple University Press, 1978.

Zegart, Amy B. *Eyes on Spies: Congress and the United States Intelligence Community.* Stanford, CA: Stanford University Press, 2011.

# 10 INTER-AGENCY COMMUNICATIONS

Joseph Fitsanakis

Much of the American scholarship on intelligence has traditionally focused on three highly studied aspects of intelligence work, namely collection, analysis, and operations. Intelligence operations appeal to scholars because they attract more media attention than any other aspect of intelligence work. Thus the visibility of intelligence operations in the unclassified domain encourages open research and helps facilitate scholarly work on the topic. Collection—often described as the "bread and butter"[1] of intelligence—is equally fascinating and provides a hands-on approach to the intelligence cycle. Lastly, the process of analysis is instinctively attractive to scholars because it highlights the intellectual qualities of the intelligence profession. There is also something uniquely satisfying about turning raw information into intelligence through methodical processing, contextualization, and interpretation. Much of this involves a peer-review-like process that most academics find both familiar and appealing.

But the overwhelming emphasis of intelligence scholarship on these topics tends to overlook the fact that the US intelligence community (IC) exists for one primary reason: to communicate effectively its findings to policymakers and decision makers, thus enabling them to take action that will protect national security and preserve the country's way of life. It follows that a crucial and inseparable aspect of the IC's central mission involves **intra-** and **inter-agency communication**, namely the exchange of information within and between intelligence agencies in the interests of promoting collaboration. It also involves the effective **dissemination of intelligence**, which is the efficient transmission of finished—and in rare cases raw—intelligence products from intelligence producers to intelligence consumers. Fascinating though they are, therefore, intelligence collection and analysis amount to nothing if they are not appropriately and effectively communicated to those who make decisions in the interests of national security. It is true that effective communication requires effort from at least two parties—something that is highly applicable to the dissemination portion of the intelligence cycle. But in reality, the establishment and maintenance of effective modes of intelligence communications are responsibilities that fall primarily on the shoulders of the IC.

---

[1]Mickolus, Edward. "Peasant at the Creation: The Agency's First Terrorism Analyst and Beyond." In *Stories From Langley: A Glimpse Inside the CIA*, edited by Edward Mickolus. Omaha: University of Nebraska Press, 2014, 159.

To fulfill these responsibilities, the member agencies of the IC have devised elaborate mechanisms, which some experts call **intelligence maintenance** or **intelligence management** systems.[2] These terms allude to the methods by which intelligence agencies systematize and standardize the processing and storing of collected information, as well as their methods for retrieving and disseminating intelligence products. These processes can be as esoteric and secretive as any other aspect of the intelligence cycle, which means that there are inherent restrictions in discussing them in an unclassified environment such as this. It is possible, however, to draw a number of important observations about the communicative aspects of intelligence work.

## THE INHERENT TENSIONS IN INTELLIGENCE COMMUNICATIONS

One must first acknowledge the presence of a number of inherent tensions that inform the process of intelligence communications. There is no doubt that the administrative structure of intelligence agencies is based on the principle of **compartmentalization**. This is a counterintelligence term that is derived from the field of information security. It describes systems and processes that are designed with reference to deliberately partitioned components. In intelligence systems, compartmentalization rests on the—usually correct—belief that restricting classified information to a small number of individuals tends to limit the risk that this information will be compromised by falling into the hands of adversaries. Information restriction forms the basis of the IC's **need-to-know** method of information management. Put simply, classified information is communicated to intelligence practitioners on a need-to-know basis. This is regardless of an intelligence practitioner's level of security clearance, or of the level of classification—confidential, secret, or top secret—of a certain piece of information. The ensuing information structure prevents individuals from accessing large data sets, or information that is above and beyond the scope of their level of clearance. This means that individual intelligence practitioners are unable to deliberately or unconsciously divulge to a potential adversary broad or deep knowledge on classified topics. This system of intelligence management unquestionably promotes **information security**. At the same time, however, it promotes a **culture of secrecy** that discourages **information sharing** and collaboration within agencies—let alone between them. The principle of compartmentalization is so engrained in the modus operandi of intelligence work that practitioners will often avoid prolonged discussions with each other at the workplace in fear that they might unintentionally infringe information security boundaries.

It is easy to see how compartmentalization encourages fragmentation—with both positive and negative aspects. It also promotes competitiveness, which is

---

[2]Jensen, Carl J., David H. McElreath, and Melissa Graves. *Introduction to Intelligence Studies*. Boca Raton, FL: CRC Press, 2013, 8–10.

arguably a central cultural pillar of the gargantuan apparatus that we have come to call the US IC. The proverbial "rugged individualism" of the American psyche informs the "endless succession of contests" that the educationalist Alfred Kohn calls "the common denominator of American life."[3] Inevitably, the competitiveness of American culture also infuses its institutions, including its intelligence agencies. The nature of relationships of America's intelligence agencies is to a large extent competitive. They compete for funding, for bureaucratic dominance, and for attention from intelligence consumers. In the words of the National Commission on Terrorist Attacks Upon the United States—better known as the 9/11 Commission—American intelligence agencies fight "ferociously over roles and missions" in times of war and "over budgets and posts of leadership" in times of peace. Contemporary American intelligence organizations follow proud traditions of agency-specific customs, rituals, and conventions that go back several decades. They have grown accustomed to distinguishing themselves by virtue of being different, bigger, or better than other agencies in the IC. They have, in short, developed a highly bureaucratic **culture of demarcation**. The latter rests on a set of complex inter-agency dynamics that are fundamentally competitive in character. It can therefore be difficult for these agencies to engage in collaborative relationships with each other in the interests of national security. This is not because they are unwilling to do so, but because they do not know how. They tend to behave like extremely shy teenagers during the opening minutes of their high school prom.

## COMMUNICATIONS CHALLENGES IN INTRA-AGENCY SETTINGS

The challenges of intelligence communications arise primarily in inter-agency settings—that is, they are most noticeable in systems of communications between agencies. But some of their complex aspects have their roots in relations *within* agencies—thus in intra-agency settings.

### Highly Hierarchical

In addition to compartmentalization, which, as discussed earlier, is a structural feature of information security in the IC, intelligence agencies are highly **hierarchical**. This means that their personnel are arranged on the basis of administrative ranking and are expected to operate with reference to status, seniority, or various other elements of authority. This model of organization is not unique to the United States. Indeed, all nation-states have historically sought to legitimize their power by organizing their administrative components into hierarchical systems of information flow and

---

[3]Kohn, Alfred. *No Contest: The Case Against Competition*. Boston, MA: Houghton Mifflin, 1992, 1.

decision making. In fact, the top-down structure of organizations, with its sequential layers of status-conscious officialdom, is arguably *the* defining characteristic of state-run Western bureaucracies. Therefore, in the words of security scholar Peter Gill, it is "entirely appropriate" to explain the policies of intelligence agencies "in terms of hierarchies."[4]

Americans often take pride in seeing their system of social organization as less rigid than those of many other Western—primarily European—countries. There is a general informality in American life, which is coupled with the idea that socioeconomic mobility—the speed with which individual income and social status fluctuate—is more fluid in America than elsewhere in the world. Such perceptions contribute to the widespread belief that organizational hierarchy is less rigid in American bureaucratic systems. In reality, however, American intelligence agencies have always been, and remain, highly hierarchical. They are arguably less so today than in the previous century, when they were known for what Central Intelligence Agency (CIA) official Victor Marchetti and diplomat John D. Marks described as their "concentration of Eastern Establishment, Ivy League types."[5] But they continue to be militarized in both structure and culture. Accordingly, they feature pyramidal hierarchies with strong elements of disjunction—some would say ghettoization—between operational, analytical, and administrative personnel. In his study of American national security institutions, titled *Enemies of Intelligence*, Columbia University professor and former congressional intelligence staffer Richard K. Betts supports the view that a strict hierarchy continues to dominate the US IC of today. This, he says, is despite the onset of the computer revolution, which has infused daily life with the concept of horizontal, peer-to-peer communication networks.[6] Indeed, studies show that traditional bureaucracies do not become less hierarchical when they begin to employ computer networks. Instead, they tend to use them to reproduce, rather than challenge, the hierarchical channels of communications they are accustomed to.[7] This is applicable almost universally to American intelligence agencies in our time.

An exception to this rule is represented by the example of Intellipedia, a classified collaborative online information-sharing platform that is built in the style of Wikipedia. It was established in 2005 by the Office of the Director of National Intelligence (ODNI) with the expressed purpose of promoting information sharing and collaboration across the IC.

---

[4]Gill, Peter. "Security and Intelligence Services in the United Kingdom." In *Democracy, Law and Security*, edited by Jean-Paul Brodeur, Peter Gill, and Dennis Töllborg. New York, NY: Routledge, 2016, 266.

[5]Marchetti, Victor, and John D. Marks. *The CIA and the Cult of Intelligence*. New York, NY: Dell Books, 1974.

[6]Betts, Richard K. *Enemies of Intelligence: Knowledge and Power in American National Security*. New York, NY: Columbia University Press, 2007, 28.

[7]Oberg, Achim, and Peter Walgenbach. "Hierarchical Structures of Communication in a Network Organization." *Scandinavian Journal of Management* 24, no. 3 (2008): 183–198.

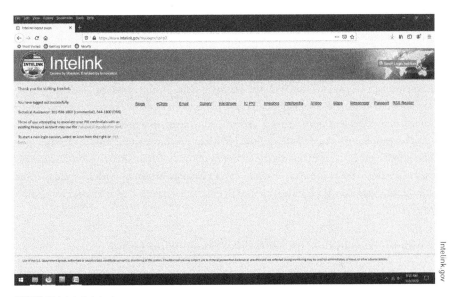

**PHOTO 10.1** Intelink login.

Intellipedia contains articles on over a million topics that can be edited by all users with access to classified government information. Intellipedia articles can be accessed on three separate wikis (online communications platforms that allow collaborative editing by their users) based on each article's level of classification. According to media reports, the Intellipedia model has been utilized as a collaborative platform to produce National Intelligence Estimates (NIEs, discussed later in this chapter) and is now increasingly employed to facilitate collaborative intelligence analyses across different member agencies of the IC.[8] It can be argued, however, that the Intellipedia model is the exception—not the norm—in communications within the US IC.

It must be noted that, whether computer-mediated or not, hierarchical communication is not inherently problematic for institutions. It helps create coherent structures of management based on clear rules and procedures. It also helps establish well-defined expectations that are commensurate to one's rank within a larger hierarchy of responsibility. While solving some problems, however, hierarchical models of communication generate other sets of challenges. In his relentless critique of military intelligence in the United States, David Thomas lambasts the "inflexible, ponderous, and short-sighted bureaucratic behavior of hierarchical . . . organizations that can impede creative, forward-leaning . . . analysis and prevent proper dissemination of controversial

---

[8]Dreyfuss, Emily. "The Wikipedia for Spies—and Where It Goes From Here." *Wired*, March 10, 2017. https://www.wired.com/2017/03/intellipedia-wikipedia-spies-much/.

assessments."[9] He makes a good point: rigid hierarchical systems of intelligence communications encourage models of top-down information exchange and tend to disinvest individual analysts from the core mission of helping protect national security. In other words, they encourage a philosophy of intelligence work that can be summarized in the proverbial phrase "this is above my pay grade." In the words of Peter Gill, intelligence practitioners who operate in hierarchical systems become accustomed to simply following intelligence policy that is determined almost exclusively at the top and then "implemented downwards through the hierarchy."[10] At the same time, as former CIA operations officer Charles Faddis illustrates in his book *Beyond Repair: The Decline and Fall of the CIA*, those who wish to challenge traditional hierarchy with imaginative and contrarian operational planning or intelligence assessments find it almost impossible to prevail.[11]

## Allegations Against the Defense Intelligence Agency

An example of the challenges that intelligence practitioners can face while working in rigid hierarchical systems can be seen in a series of allegations made in 2015 by analysts in the Defense Intelligence Agency (DIA). In August of that year, media reports claimed that as many as 50 DIA intelligence analysts alleged that their counterterrorism assessments had been deliberately tweaked by officials at the US Central Command (CENTCOM), the Pentagon body that directs and coordinates American military operations in Egypt, the Middle East, and Central Asia. Some of the reports related to al-Qaeda activity in Iraq and Syria, but most were about the Islamic State group, which at that time controlled large swathes of territory in the area of the Middle East known as the Levant. The analysts reportedly filed complaints with the Pentagon's Office of the Inspector General, claiming that their reports were altered in order to give a falsely positive projection of American policy in CENTCOM's operational region. One source, who spoke anonymously to the media, described the situation as "a revolt" by intelligence analysts. Another described the altering of the intelligence reports as a "cancer . . . within the senior level of the intelligence command." The source, identified only as "a defense official," said that the analysts' "revolt" was prompted by the experience of the US invasion of Iraq in 2003. At that time, "poorly written intelligence reports suggesting Iraq had weapons of mass destruction, when it did not, formed the basis of the George W. Bush administration's case for war," said the defense official, who continued by noting that the analysts

---

[9]Thomas, David. "US Military Intelligence Analysis: Old and New Challenges." In *Analyzing Intelligence: Origins, Obstacles and Innovations*, edited by Roger Z. George and James B. Bruce. Washington, DC: Georgetown University Press, 2008, 140.

[10]Gill, "Security and Intelligence Services in the United Kingdom," 266.

[11]Faddis, Charles. *Beyond Repair: The Decline and Fall of the CIA*. Guilford, CT: Globe Pequot Press, 2010, 13ff.

"were frustrated because they didn't do the right thing then and speak up about their doubts on Iraq's weapons program."[12]

The analysts' allegations prompted two separate classified investigations, one by the Department of Defense's Office of the Inspector General and one by a task force consisting of members of three committees in the House of Representatives— the Committee on Armed Services, the Permanent Select Committee on Intelligence, and the Committee on Appropriations. The ensuing congressional report—the precise content of which remains classified—concluded that "intelligence products approved by senior CENTCOM leaders typically provided a more positive depiction of United States counterterrorism efforts than was warranted by facts on the ground, and were consistently more positive than analysis produced by other elements of the intelligence community."[13] In February of the following year, however, the inspector general's report concluded that "allegations of intelligence being intentionally altered, delayed, or suppressed by top CENTCOM officials . . . were largely unsubstantiated."[14] At the same time, the report did note the "widespread perception among many intelligence analysts" that CENTCOM leaders were deliberately attempting to distort intelligence on counterterrorism. CENTCOM commanders said that the report's findings pointed to problems of communication in CENTCOM's organizational hierarchy, which were being addressed. Sadly, the CENTCOM analyst controversy is not unique; but it provides an illustrative case study of the problems with synergy that can result from overly hierarchical and centralized systems of intelligence communications.

## COMMUNICATIONS CHALLENGES IN INTER-AGENCY SETTINGS

One of the defining features of the US IC is its sheer size and scope. It is comprised of 17 agencies with areas of intelligence work, capabilities, and needs that sometimes diverge and other times overlap. To make this arrangement even more complicated, the IC has to coordinate its activities with a host of other federal, state, and local agencies that have intelligence or security functions. Providing these agencies with direction and synchronization, while at the same time averting conflict and discord, is a major operational objective that requires an **inter-agency approach** to problem solving. The term *inter-agency* refers to a formal structure of deliberation on the policymaker level, which aims to coordinate multiple agencies of the government to assist in decision making at the executive

---

[12]Harris, Shane, and Nancy A. Youssef. "50 Spies Say ISIS Intelligence Was Cooked." *The Daily Beast*, September 5, 2017. https://www.thedailybeast.com/exclusive-50-spies-say-isis-intelligence-was-cooked.

[13]Cooper, Helene. "Military Officials Distorted ISIS Intelligence, Congressional Panel Says." *The New York Times*, August 11, 2016. https://www.nytimes.com/2016/08/12/us/politics/isis-centcom-intelligence.html.

[14]Cohen, Zachary. "Report: CENTCOM Leaders Didn't Cook ISIS Intelligence." *CNN*, February 1, 2017. https://www.cnn.com/2017/02/01/politics/report-centcom-intelligence/index.html.

level. The most senior inter-agency organization is the National Security Council (NSC), which relies heavily on what are known as **inter-agency working groups (IWGs)**. The job of IWGs is to frame policy topics that require coordination between government agencies, encourage harmony between them, and help implement executive decisions that require inter-agency action. Official structures aside, the term *inter-agency* also implies a process of coordination that is applicable to different levels of cross-agency communications. Some of these processes are formal, while most are informal and operate strictly on the personal level. The IC's ability to contribute to the inter-agency process on the policy-maker level depends on the efficiency with which it coordinates its various components. This is precisely where the notion of inter-agency communications comes into play.

## Institutionalization

At this point a distinction must be made between two equally important terms that affect how the IC communicates within itself, namely **organizations** and **institutions**. Most organizations tend to have temporary existences and be limited in scope. They also tend to be informal and highly shaped and influenced by the individuals who establish and lead them. Institutions, on the other hand, project an appearance of durability and permanence. Furthermore, they are governed by sets of rules, laws, and conventions that are significantly more established than those of organizations, and require more than the influence of a single leader or leadership group to change. Institutions are, in fact, more likely to disappear, as a result of revolutionary upheaval, than to change radically. It is possible for organizations to be transformed into institutions through a process of **institutionalization**—namely a gradual entrenchment of strong norms (beliefs, clerical roles, and modes of operation) into their administrative structure. All institutions begin their existence as organizations. The resulting firmness that is projected by an institution is so powerful that it makes it difficult for people to imagine their society without it.

Societies tend to welcome institutionalization because it reduces uncertainty and unpredictability, which is, of course, a major aspect of the IC's mission. Institutionalization also brings with it more defined—and therefore more accountable—administrative structures and a higher professionalism among staff. At the same time, however, institutionalization comes with drawbacks, such as a higher degree of operational rigidity and distinct administrative cultures that may seem esoteric and at times incomprehensible to outsiders. The term used in organizational theory to describe such structures is **bureaucracy**. Scholars of social organization broadly agree that bureaucracies fulfill useful functions in complex systems of social and economic organization like ours. They represent a rational method of systematizing human activity in a way that usually ensures order and balance. At the same time, the term *bureaucracy* bears an unmistakably negative connotation. It refers to leviathan-like government agencies with overly convoluted organizational cultures that impede the efficient administration of government. In assessing the less desirable aspects of bureaucracy, traditional organizational theory usually concentrates on three of its major features, namely **noncanonical practices, displacement**, and **bureaucratic cultures**. Noncanonical practices refer to the tendency of bureaucrats to develop informal workarounds to deep-rooted problems, instead of trying to fix them once and for all. Displacement occurs when a bureaucracy stops serving the government under which it operates, or the people that it was initially designed to serve, and chooses instead to prioritize its own interests. A bureaucratic culture consists of a set of practices, norms, symbols, rituals, or beliefs that are distinct to an institution and are used as a means of providing continuity, identity, and meaning to its day-to-day practices.

Inter-agency communications in the IC display all of the aforementioned phenomena. For instance, as discussed earlier, there are bureaucratic impediments to inter-agency communications that arise from compartmentalization. Theoretically it would be possible to preserve compartmentalization while promoting inter-agency communication. This could be governed by a sophisticated auditory system of checks and balances. Admittedly, such a change would require a radical transformation of the system; therefore, many intelligence practitioners tend to work around it by employing noncanonical practices. Take, for instance, an informal oral chat on a topic of common interest between intelligence practitioners from different agencies. That would be part of **inter-agency networking**—building capital by seeking mutually beneficial relationships with members of other intelligence agencies—and could largely be described as a noncanonical workaround designed to circumvent the inherent rigidity of bureaucratic systems.

## Displacement in Practice

One can also observe elements of displacement in the practices of intelligence agencies. For example, in 2019 the *Washington Post* published a profile of Gina Haspel, the CIA's first female director. The article noted that President Donald Trump was known for his "uniquely volatile" relationship with the IC. It explained that, having derided American intelligence agencies before he even took office, Trump took the unprecedented step of ridiculing his intelligence chiefs in public after they issued intelligence assessments that contradicted his pronouncements about Iran, North Korea, and other foreign-policy topics. The president reacted by calling intelligence chiefs "extremely passive and naïve" and suggested that they "go back to school." Surprisingly, however, Haspel had managed to escape the president's ire despite the fact that she served in a highly visible intelligence post, the article said. How did she do it? The answer was that she kept a low profile and was "careful not to contradict the president or argue with him about his opinions." In doing so, Haspel seemed to possess some of the "key qualities you need in that job," current and former intelligence insiders were quoted as saying. Chief among them, said an "anonymous former senior intelligence official," was this: "Your first responsibility as director is to protect your organization."[15]

[15]Harris, Shane. "How Gina Haspel Manages the CIA's Volatile Relationship With Trump." *The Washington Post*, July 30, 2019. https://www.washingtonpost.com/world/national-security/the-quiet-director-how-gina-haspel-manages-the-cias-volatile-relationship-with-trump/2019/07/30/c54cae04-9920-11e9-830a-21b9b-36b64ad_story.html.

That quote is a classic example of displacement—the tendency of bureaucracies to prioritize their narrow institutional interests over the needs of the state or the people whom they serve. The anonymous former intelligence official was describing an accepted dogma in the IC: that the primary responsibility of each agency's leadership is not to further the overall national security mission, but to "protect your organization." These types of attitudes are largely responsible for the entrenchment of intelligence agencies and the fragmentation of inter-agency communications. They result in the **stovepipe** phenomenon of isolated bureaucratic units that resist the open flow of information within and between agencies. The result of stovepiping is **communication silos**, which occur when these isolated bureaucratic units communicate mostly internally at the expense of agency- or community-wide coordination. This phenomenon inevitably impedes information sharing and prevents the IC from achieving unity of effort.

## Rivalry and Infighting

Distinct bureaucratic cultures can sometimes result in **inter-agency antagonisms**, which are informally known as **turf wars**. These are rancorous and sometimes prolonged disputes between intelligence agencies over influence, authority, or other measures of administrative power. In addition to the tensions that are inherent in the high-pressure and high-stakes work of intelligence, **inter-agency rivalry** is triggered by the temptation of agencies to alleviate themselves of responsibility for intelligence failures, for which they blame other elements of the IC. Size and resources are also important here, as intelligence agencies with a large personnel base and funds tend to throw their weight around. For instance, the National Security Agency (NSA)—the largest and wealthiest American intelligence agency—insists on maintaining its own in-house clearance process and does not rely on those that are followed by most of the other members of the IC. Some believe that the intelligence wing of the Department of Homeland Security (DHS) will take its cue from the NSA and increasingly dominate the IC in the future, owing to the sheer size of the DHS's personnel base.

Rivalries between intelligence agencies are as old as the IC itself, with some of them going back decades. In the 1940s, the Federal Bureau of Investigation (FBI) led an extensive campaign to prevent the creation of the CIA and the NSA, which it saw as potential rivals. When they were established, the FBI's longtime director, J. Edgar Hoover, refused to cooperate with them for many years. The rivalry between those three agencies often descended into **inter-agency infighting**, as their directors refused to even speak to each other. Relations between them improved considerably after longtime director Hoover died in 1972. But some bitterness remains. In more recent years, the FBI's efforts to further its global reach following the 1998 bombings of the US embassies in Kenya and Tanzania have caused the CIA considerable consternation. Another lengthy dispute broke out between the CIA and the Drug Enforcement Administration (DEA) during the Central American wars of the 1980s. Under the direction of the White House, the CIA supported numerous right-wing armed groups in Central America. However, while furthering the goals of the administration of President Ronald Reagan, these groups also trafficked illicit narcotics. Most of these narcotics ended up in the streets of the United States. The DEA, a federal law enforcement agency tasked with combating drug trafficking and distribution on American soil, was incensed by the situation and partly blamed the CIA for turning a blind eye to it.[16] Some authors have even suggested that the two agencies were engaged in a low-level ground war in Central America, where they maintained a separate and distinct presence with explicitly contradictory goals.[17]

## The War on Terror

In some ways, the most recent reincarnation of the war on terrorism, declared by the United States in response to the attacks of September 11, 2001, has intensified bureaucratic infighting among members of the IC. The conflict blurred the traditional distinction between intelligence collection and counterterrorism operations. In turn, this resulted in a prolonged turf war between civilian and military intelligence agencies for control of the post-9/11 intelligence landscape. This has been especially notable in relation to covert action and counterterrorism. It is worth remembering that the Department of Defense is in charge of a much larger portion of the IC than all other government departments combined. It is also by far the largest consumer of intelligence products, and at times demands to be treated as such. The war on terrorism has also been a point of contention between the CIA and America's newest intelligence agency, the ODNI. Upon its formation in 2005, the new agency took over the CIA's role of central coordinator of the IC, a change that did not sit well at Langley. The CIA's worst fears were confirmed in the summer of 2009, when the ODNI issued a directive in which it argued that it should have a say in appointing **chiefs of station (COSs)** in foreign countries. Since the 1940s, COS posts have been held by the senior American intelligence officer in a foreign country or region. These officers have traditionally come from the ranks of the CIA. As can be expected, the CIA fought back ferociously against the ODNI's recommendation. A number of former CIA officers penned press editorials denouncing the ODNI's proposal as "sheer insanity."[18] Meanwhile, the CIA demanded that the Senate Intelligence Committee look into the matter. The committee held a closed-door hearing. However, much to the CIA's chagrin, it sided with the ODNI, arguing that "some locations may give rise to circumstances where th[e station

---

[16]Scott, Peter Dale, and Jonathan Marshall. *Cocaine Politics: Drugs, Armies and the CIA in Central America.* Berkeley: University of California Press, 1998, xviii–xix.

[17]Cockburn, Alexander, and Jeffrey St. Clair. *Whiteout: The CIA, Drugs and the Press.* New York, NY: Verso, 1999, 95ff.

[18]Smith, Haviland. "CIA Director Should Name Station Chiefs." *The Baltimore Sun*, July 6, 2009. https://www.afio.com/sections/wins/2009/2009-25.htm#haviland.

chief's] responsibility is best met by an official with expertise derived from another element" of the IC.[19] But the CIA had the last word in November 2009, when the White House reportedly issued a sharply worded memorandum that "asserted the [CIA's] direct authority" over COS posts, as well as over paramilitary and human intelligence (HUMINT) operations abroad.[20]

At times, the Department of State has also kicked back against COS offices. It is customary for the CIA to use the Foreign Service of the Department of State to embed its official-cover officers who are stationed abroad. These officers essentially masquerade as diplomatic personnel, but are in fact performing a secret intelligence function. Moreover, the CIA will occasionally conduct intelligence operations—including covert action—that make use of the resources available at its stations in American diplomatic facilities. This is not always pleasing to the Department of State, which is not an intelligence agency and sees itself as performing a function that is very different to that of the CIA. The latter is technically required to keep the Department of State leadership at different embassies appraised of its clandestine activities through the COS. But this does not always occur, and CIA stations have been known to refuse to comply with the directives of ambassadors, even though they are technically in charge of CIA personnel—including COSs—masquerading as Foreign Service officers.

## PRODUCTS FOR INTELLIGENCE CONSUMERS

Intelligence is primarily a consumer-driven process. This means that it is led by the needs of **intelligence consumers** or **intelligence customers**—individuals, agencies, or departments who are involved in policymaking or decision making. Consumers use intelligence products to reduce the degree of uncertainty that is inherent in the decision-making process on the tactical or strategic levels. In the federal sphere, intelligence consumers generally fall within five categories. They are led by the offices of the president and vice president, which include their senior aides. Congress—especially the intelligence and armed services committees—is also a major consumer of intelligence products. The IC also serves the members and staff of the NSC, which operate as the president's primary advisers on national security issues. Lastly, intelligence products are communicated to government departments—including the Departments of Defense and State—and to other intelligence agencies. These customers are part of the same broad effort to safeguard and promote national security. At the same time, they are all more different from each other than similar, and have varying priorities and agendas. Therefore, communicating with them requires the dissemination of a wide variety of intelligence products.

---

[19]Pincus, Walter. "Senate Panel Backs DNI in Turf Battle With CIA." *The Washington Post*, July 23, 2009. https://www.washingtonpost.com/wp-dyn/content/article/2009/07/22/AR2009072202979.html.

[20]Mazzetti, Mark. "White House Sides With CIA in Turf Battle." *The New York Times*, November 12, 2012. https://www.nytimes.com/2009/11/13/us/politics/13intel.html.

Whether oral or written, intelligence products are highly standardized and generally fall into seven categories. The first category of intelligence products is **current intelligence**. Current intelligence products consist of descriptive snippets of recent events and concentrate on ongoing challenges and concerns to policymakers and decision makers. An example of a current intelligence product is *Executive Highlights*. This top-secret daily edition is produced by the DIA and contains brief reports on ongoing issues from around the world that are of concern to the United States. The CIA disseminates a similar product in the form of a classified website, which is called the *Worldwide Intelligence Review*, or *WIRe*. The second category of intelligence products is **trend analysis**, which is also known as **second-phase reporting**. Instead of just providing basic facts, as is the case with current intelligence products, trend analysis products typically provide context and an assessment of the factual evidence of the reporting, which is the product of vetting. The third category of intelligence products is known as **long-term assessment**, otherwise referred to as **third-phase reporting**. The main difference between it and second-phase reporting is that third-phase reporting also provides projections of future developments on a topic or a series of topics. The fourth category of intelligence products is **estimative intelligence**, which evaluates the projected strategic development of current challenges and anticipates future threats. The aforementioned NIEs, which are produced collaboratively under the supervision of the National Intelligence Council, are prime examples of estimative intelligence, because they constitute collaborative efforts to assess the trajectory of events concerning various regions or topics. They are thus anticipatory in character, and their judgments represent various gradations of analytical consensus between agencies. The fifth type of intelligence product is known as **warning intelligence**. It provides policymakers and decision makers with information on an issue of imminent concern that may not be on their radar. The sixth category of intelligence products is **research intelligence**, which tends to go into depth in analyzing current challenges. By utilizing the dynamism of the online format, *WIRe* editions, which generally contain short articles, often contain links to in-depth reports that could be described as research intelligence. Research intelligence products can be requested by individual consumers on a case-by-case basis, and may take several months to complete. Finally, the seventh category of intelligence products is known as **technical intelligence**. These products provide policymakers and decision makers with technical analyses of topics of concern, which rest on information from highly specialized scientific and technological fields.

Intelligence products have two things in common: First, all of them contain almost exclusively **finished intelligence**. In other words, these products have been disseminated after going through the appropriate stages of the intelligence cycle and after having been subjected to a rigorous process of peer-reviewed vetting, validation, and verification. The opposite of finished intelligence is **raw intelligence**, which senior policymakers and decision makers rarely see. Second, all types of intelligence products are generally devoid of operational details that relate to the collection aspects of the intelligence cycle. Such details usually contain information about sources and methods and are communicated to customers on extremely rare occasions—for instance when their disclosure may constitute a source of deep embarrassment for the highest echelons of government.

## GETTING THE ATTENTION OF INTELLIGENCE CONSUMERS

A basic axiom of government is that the higher the seniority of policymakers or decision makers, the less time they have to devote to those who want to speak with them. It follows that senior members of the executive, such as the president or the secretary of defense, are the most difficult intelligence customers to secure access to. Intelligence agencies and their representatives should not assume that they have priority access to the Oval Office or any other decision-making or policymaking center of government. On the contrary, whether they like it or not, intelligence agencies are among literally thousands of actors that vie for the attention of people in executive power. Moreover, senior government figures are almost invariably suffering from **information overload**, a phenomenon that appears to have grown significantly in our digital age. To make things even more challenging, when they do get access to people in power, intelligence briefers often find them distracted by fleeting concerns that have little to do with national security—for instance, getting reelected to office. Nevertheless, intelligence agencies need to be heard by those in power, however difficult that may be. They have therefore developed elaborate methods of disseminating their products to policymakers and decision makers, which take into consideration the numerous practical barriers that litter the process.

For example, intelligence agencies try to assess the psychology of their consumers and carefully listen to them so as to understand their information priorities, as well as the communication format that they prefer. Some consumers have a preference for short daily meetings with intelligence briefers. Others opt for more irregular, but longer and more substantial, briefing sessions. Additionally, some consumers prefer text-based products, while others—most of them, in fact—opt for oral briefs. The latter are generally seen as less time-consuming and requiring less energy to digest by those on busy schedules. Whether written or oral, intelligence products rely on brevity and display a **bottom-line approach** to communication. This is so because their authors rely on the assumption that intelligence consumers are pressed for time and will not hesitate to request elaboration if one is needed. The president, who is the ultimate consumer of intelligence products, receives most information from the IC through a format that has come to be known as the **President's Daily Brief**, or **PDB**. The PDB is a classified daily compendium of intelligence products from across the IC. Its all-source briefs address ongoing worldwide developments that are of concern to the United States. From 1946 to 2013, the PDB was supplied to the White House in hard-copy format. Since 2014, following a request by President Barack Obama, the PDB was converted into an online edition. Today the PDB is provided to the White House by the ODNI, which took this responsibility from the CIA in the post-9/11 era. When the president requires third-phase, estimative, or even research analyses of articles included in the PDB, the president's aides file a **PDB memorandum**, which is a request for elaboration of one or more articles in the PDB.

### Bin Ladin Determined To Strike in US

*Clandestine, foreign government, and media reports indicate Bin Ladin since 1997 has wanted to conduct terrorist attacks in the US.* Bin Ladin implied in US television interviews in 1997 and 1998 that his followers would follow the example of World Trade Center bomber Ramzi Yousef and "bring the fighting to America."

After US missile strikes on his base in Afghanistan in 1998, Bin Ladin told followers he wanted to retaliate in Washington, according to a ▓▓▓▓▓▓▓▓▓ service.

An Egyptian Islamic Jihad (EIJ) operative told an▓▓▓▓▓ service at the same time that Bin Ladin was planning to exploit the operative's access to the US to mount a terrorist strike.

*The millennium plotting in Canada in 1999 may have been part of Bin Ladin's first serious attempt to implement a terrorist strike in the US.* Convicted plotter Ahmed Ressam has told the FBI that he conceived the idea to attack Los Angeles International Airport himself, but that Bin Ladin lieutenant Abu Zubaydah encouraged him and helped facilitate the operation. Ressam also said that in 1998 Abu Zubaydah was planning his own US attack.

Ressam says Bin Ladin was aware of the Los Angeles operation.

*Although Bin Ladin has not succeeded, his attacks against the US Embassies in Kenya and Tanzania in 1998 demonstrate that he prepares operations years in advance and is not deterred by setbacks.* Bin Ladin associates surveilled our Embassies in Nairobi and Dar es Salaam as early as 1993, and some members of the Nairobi cell planning the bombings were arrested and deported in 1997.

*Al-Qa'ida members—including some who are US citizens—have resided in or traveled to the US for years, and the group apparently maintains a support structure that could aid attacks.* Two al-Qa'ida members found guilty in the conspiracy to bomb our Embassies in East Africa were US citizens, and a senior EIJ member lived in California in the mid-1990s.

A clandestine source said in 1998 that a Bin Ladin cell in New York was recruiting Muslim-American youth for attacks.

*We have not been able to corroborate some of the more sensational threat reporting, such as that from a* ▓▓▓▓▓▓▓▓▓ *service in 1998 saying that Bin Ladin wanted to hijack a US aircraft to gain the release of "Blind Shaykh" 'Umar 'Abd al-Rahman and other US-held extremists.*

*continued*

For the President Only
6 August 2001

**PHOTO 10.2** Presidential Daily Brief, August 6, 2001.

## RETAINING THE ATTENTION
## OF INTELLIGENCE CONSUMERS

The nature of the relationship between intelligence consumers and their briefers varies. The best producers never forget that consumers rarely have a background in intelligence and are thus strangers to the language, conventions, and methodologies of the profession. This means that the communication process between intelligence producers and consumers is characterized by the absence of a shared vocabulary. It is also characterized by the absence of a shared mindset and approach to problems. It has been acutely observed that policymakers and decision makers are by nature optimistic, because they believe that problems are ultimately solvable.[21] In contrast, intelligence practitioners are taught to question and express skepticism, and are trained to always anticipate the worst possible outcome. They are also trained to think in degrees of probability and to avoid providing categorical responses to questions, no matter how simple. In his book *Enemies of Intelligence*, former congressional staffer Richard K. Betts quotes Ray Steiner Cline, a longtime CIA analyst, who once said with reference to estimative intelligence that, "unless something is totally conclusive, you [as an intelligence analyst] must make an inconclusive report. [Inevitably, b]y the time you are sure it is always very close to the event."[22] It is also important for intelligence agencies to continue to tweak their intelligence output in accordance with the changing requirements of their consumers. Mark Lowenthal notes that, as they gain more experience, intelligence consumers tend to become more familiar with topics that concern them, and therefore develop higher expectations of intelligence products.[23] In some cases, there may be a complete breakdown between an intelligence producer and a consumer—for instance, if the latter loses confidence in the intelligence product. In such cases, it is always up to the producer to mend the relationship, for example by improving the quality of the intelligence output or by changing the method or speed of delivery.

Policymakers and decision makers are under no obligation—legal or otherwise—to utilize intelligence products. It is therefore up to the IC to convince them that doing so is to their benefit. This is best done in two interrelated ways. First, intelligence communicators must take into account the time limitations of policymakers and decision makers. They therefore have to **prioritize** their intelligence dissemination. This means that they must provide consumers with the types of intelligence products that are relevant to them—that is, products that reflect their policy priorities and assist them in making decisions. It is often the case that the customer appears to have no clear priorities, or is not particularly effective in articulating those priorities to the IC. Even worse, there are times when outright arrogant customers are not convinced that intelligence

---

[21]Lowenthal, Mark M. *Intelligence: From Secrets to Policy*. Washington, DC: CQ Press, 2009, 186.

[22]Cited in Betts, *Enemies of Intelligence*, 27.

[23]Lowenthal, *Intelligence*, 185.

will assist their decision making on a given subject. In such cases, it is up to the IC to discern the customers' policy priorities and to do its best to mirror them in its output. A major way of gaining a customer's trust is by effectively utilizing warning intelligence. Such products can potentially provide customers with the ability to anticipate emerging threats, the existence of which they would otherwise have been unaware. However, the marketing of intelligence products as early-warning systems must be judiciously utilized to ensure that no **false alarms** are issued in the process. This is because, unsurprisingly, false alarms tend to make customers lose their faith in intelligence products.

One of the main differences between politicians and intelligence practitioners is that politicians are often guided by ideologies. In contrast, intelligence practitioners are supposed to be guided by evidence or, in the absence of evidence, by measurable probability. Consequently, many politicians—and many voters—will selectively search for evidence to justify their fixed views on a topic. Intelligence practitioners, on the other hand, are obligated by the conventions of their profession to form their analyses on the basis of evidence or probability. Given this major difference, there will be times when intelligence consumers will consciously or unconsciously seek specific intelligence that supports their preconceived political preferences. Such attempts are corrupting influences in the intelligence business and must be resisted at all cost by the IC. Rather, intelligence judgments must be relayed in pure form without regard to the wishes or preferences of intelligence consumers. The latter must be told the facts, no matter how ugly or disappointing, and must be given analyses that rest on nothing except facts or probability. Intelligence consumers must not be told what they like to hear in fear that if they do not they will stop relying on intelligence products. Losing a customer's faith on the intelligence product is preferable to deliberately altering the product in order to retain access to the customer. Additionally, there will be times when consumers will seek policy advice from producers of intelligence. Such requests should be graciously deflected and, if need be, forcefully declined. It is not the task of the IC to formulate policy options for its customers.

## CONCLUSION: MAKING INTELLIGENCE USEFUL

Intelligence products assume meaning only by being useful to policymakers and decision makers. This happens through communication. However, the consumers of intelligence are far from identical. They are guided by different intelligence requirements and wildly divergent modalities of consumption. For instance, a military commander's interest in intelligence may reflect an urgent need to make tactical decisions affecting real-time hostile situations on the ground during an armed engagement. In contrast, a policymaker may request an analysis of the long-term strategic consequences of a planned treaty between the United States and a foreign power. Such varied requests come with varying degrees of exigency and tension. They also come with differing challenges that require diverse approaches in communication. The task of developing and refining these communication approaches rests almost exclusively on the shoulders of the IC. The latter is always in a weaker position in relation to its customers. As Lowenthal astutely remarks in his *Intelligence: From Secrets to Policy*, "policy and policy makers can exist and function without the Intelligence Community, but the opposite is not true."[24]

## KEY CONCEPTS

## ADDITIONAL READING

Arcos, Ruben, and Randolph H. Pherson. *Intelligence Communication in the Digital Era: Transforming Security, Defence and Business.* Basingstoke, UK: Palgrave Macmillan, 2015.

Betts, Richard K. *Enemies of Intelligence: Knowledge and Power in American National Security.* New York, NY: Columbia University Press, 2007.

---

[24]Lowenthal, *Intelligence*, 194.

Jones, Ishmael. *The Human Factor: Inside the CIA's Dysfunctional Intelligence Culture*. New York, NY: Encounter Books, 2008.

Major, James S. *Communicating With Intelligence: Writing and Briefing in the Intelligence and National Security Communities*. Lanham, MD: Scarecrow Press, 2008.

Priest, Dana, and William M. Arkin. *Top Secret America: The Rise of the New American Security State*. New York, NY: Little, Brown, 2011.

# 11 INTELLIGENCE ANALYSIS

Jonathan M. Acuff

As discussed in Chapter 3, the creation of finished intelligence products in the form of classified memoranda or briefings requires completion of the intelligence cycle. In this chapter, we examine the activity that follows the planning, collection, and processing phases—intelligence analysis. We will discuss basic terminology and concepts involved in the conversion of raw data into a product, which is connected to the broader enterprise of making knowledge claims. In the next chapter, we will cover the specific analytic techniques regularly used in the US intelligence community (IC) and other intelligence systems. These methods allow intelligence analysts to gain greater understanding of current trends, possible future activity of nation-states or nonstate actors, and how to mitigate potential threats. However, our immediate focus is on the thinking processes and cognitive pitfalls that affect the enterprise of intelligence analysis, an activity that can only be effectively executed with an understanding of the core concepts of epistemology.

## EPISTEMOLOGY AND INTELLIGENCE ANALYSIS

How do we know something is true or false? What kind of confidence should we have in our beliefs about the world? How can we communicate this information in a manner that clearly distinguishes between opinion and fact? These are the kinds of questions every intelligence analyst confronts on a regular basis. Moreover, they are related to larger philosophical and methodological discussions in the natural and social sciences. If we are serious about correctly interpreting the meaning of the actions of intelligence targets or making accurate predictions about the future, we cannot avoid the difficult challenge of examining the nature of knowledge itself. We must engage in a discussion of **epistemology**, the concepts and tools we use to warrant knowledge. Put more simply, epistemology is how we know what we know. Epistemology is connected to a broader field of inquiry known as the **philosophy of science**, which examines the nature of concepts and the conduct of inquiry. Epistemology is the real-world application of often very old arguments among philosophers of science, some of which remain unsettled.

We begin our brief foray into these issues by distinguishing between several types of knowledge in the world. **Opinions** are beliefs about the truth or falsehood of an event, whether something is good or bad, or the relative merits of different choices. They are heavily influenced by a person's prior beliefs, hereafter referred to as one's **priors**, which may or may not be empirically accurate perceptions about the world. Opinions may relate to tastes or personal preferences, such as whether or not it is acceptable to put ketchup on a hot dog. Opinions can also be value judgments, such as whether or not abortion is morally permissible. Contrary to conventional wisdom in contemporary American culture, not all opinions are equal. We can judge the quality of opinions based on the degree to which they are logically consistent, rely on factual information, or, in the case of values, connect to broader moral belief systems. But opinions cannot be **falsified**—that is, we cannot gather observable evidence about the world to determine whether or not the Mona Lisa is the greatest painting of all time or whether mustard or ketchup is best on a hot dog. In contrast, **facts** are either true or false—they are not dependent on people's beliefs about them. Because facts can be falsified, as a form of knowledge they are superior to opinions. As New York senator Daniel Patrick Moynihan is reputed to have put it, "everyone is entitled to his own opinion, but not his own facts." Obtaining accurate information about intelligence targets other people or states do not have access to allows our leaders to advance the nation's interests. Validating this information and interpreting its meaning is the purpose of intelligence analysis. It is vitally important intelligence analysts always distinguish between their opinions and the facts about a target or subject of analysis.

Although we have now distinguished between two kinds of knowledge and established that facts are better than opinions, we have not stated the conditions under which we know something is true or false. The manner in which we do this relates to various **warrants**, which define the quality of empirical evidence on a subject. The first such warrant is personal experience. Although many people weight this category of evidence highly, it is actually quite poor as a warrant, as we have no way of knowing from a single person's observations whether or not the person's experiences are indicative of a larger category of events, limited to the one instance, or even accurately perceived by the observer. Such knowledge claims are **anecdotal**, limited to one person's experiences, and generally a low-quality form of warrant for a knowledge claim. Second, we have **corroborated observation**, a warrant commonly used in the newspaper industry. For example, the *New York Times* will not report on a subject until the empirical claims made in the article have been verified by at least two, oftentimes three or more independent sources, a process supervised by one or more editors and further guaranteed by an ombudsman, who responds to internal or external concerns about the veracity of a story. Because the information is corroborated in high-quality papers like the *Times* or the *Wall Street Journal*, the knowledge contained therein is higher in quality than blog postings by individuals or other forms of anecdotal observation. Corroboration can be obtained through verification by additional observers. But it can also be achieved via technical or scientific means, a common practice in the IC. From an epistemological perspective, intelligence analysts should generally view an asset's personal observations more favorably if they are buttressed by additional collection via signals intelligence (SIGINT), geospatial intelligence (GEOINT), and/or measurement and signature intelligence (MASINT) that supports their claims. Similarly, technical collection methods acquire more credibility if human intelligence (HUMINT) gives them meaning and context.

**Scientific warrants** are the third and most rigorous form of knowledge. Scientific warrants involve the precise measurement of the characteristics of phenomena, from the effectiveness of a vaccine in preventing the onset of disease to the growing frequency and intensity of heat waves and storms caused by climate change. Some forms of intelligence data are intrinsically scientific in nature, such as SIGINT, GEOINT, and MASINT collection. However, not all inferences intelligence analysts have to make about targets can be reduced to scientific measurement. Indeed, if technical collection platforms could tell us everything about a target, intelligence analysis would be unnecessary.

One important feature of scientific knowledge that distinguishes it from corroboration alone is the peer review process, which is central to the enterprise of validating knowledge claims in science. **Peer-reviewed research** occurs when scholars subject their substantive claims and the methods by which they arrived at their conclusions to external, anonymous review by recognized experts in the field of study. Peer-reviewed research comprises a vast array of subjects and methods, from the laboratory experiments of chemists or biologists to archival research by historians or political scientists, all of which generate findings that are reviewed by anonymous experts on behalf of university book presses, grant administrators, or academic journal publishers. Peer review is also used in the arts and humanities, though as we discussed earlier, the work of painters and sculptors resides in the realm of aesthetic taste and opinion, not science. Although no process or procedure can ever guarantee knowledge claims are always true, peer review is the most rigorous warrant of knowledge we have. Intelligence officers often use peer-reviewed sources as a starting point for strategic intelligence assessments, research intelligence, and other long-term projects, which is why the Central Intelligence Agency (CIA) has one of the largest libraries in the world and operates its own peer-reviewed scholarly journal, *Studies in Intelligence*. However, for more immediate analytic missions, the most commonly used knowledge warrant is corroboration, ideally across different collection disciplines and platforms.

Although the three knowledge warrants seem relatively straightforward and are used in a wide variety of private sector and academic enterprises, intelligence analysis occupies a difficult position in this hierarchy of knowledge. It is not an art—that is, an activity in which opinion and anecdotal observation govern judgments of quality—as in sculpture or literature. Intelligence analysis is also not a science, as unlike physics or chemistry we cannot falsify every knowledge claim and warrant all of our evidence via the peer review process, a time-consuming activity that would make it impossible for intelligence officers to provide prompt support for policymakers. It is also not entirely a social science either, as some of the data gathered via the collection process are secret and the knowledge claims of intelligence analysts are rarely subjected to external review by the open source community.[1] Nevertheless, much like natural and social scientists, intelligence analysts deal with problems of incomplete information and making judgments under uncertainty. They also strive for precision, use standardized methods that can be evaluated apart from their utility for one project, and state the conditions under which their knowledge claims can be falsified. All of these characteristics make intelligence analysis far closer to a science than an art. Consequently, intelligence analysts regularly import many concepts and methods from the social sciences, albeit in a carefully controlled manner.[2]

One of the areas of strong overlap between the sciences and intelligence analysis is the need to distinguish between **correlation** and **causation**. Correlation refers to two or more events occurring at roughly the same time and place that may or may not be related causally. For example, a student may notice a flamingo in a pond on his walk across campus just before the first exam in an introduction to intelligence studies course. The student then earns an A on the exam. Just prior to taking the second exam, the student sees the same flamingo and again scores an A. However, just prior to taking the third exam, the student misses sighting his feathered friend on the walk across campus and earns a C on that exam. Change in exam scores is correlated with variation in the presence of a pink bird. But without an explanation as to *how* something about the bird so dramatically affects cognition that exam scores soar by 20 points, there is no causal link. For a variable to be causal, it must have at least four characteristics.[3] First, it must occur chronologically prior to the effect. Second, it must be distinct from other candidate causes. Third, there is a necessary connection between the cause and its effect; when the cause happens, the effect happens. Moreover, the connection must be plausible—that is, it should conform with both general experience and what makes sense intuitively. Fourth, it must continue to have the same effect over time.

In the campus flamingo example, we can see how the proposition that variation in bird sightings causes exam performance to vary meets some, but not all, of the requisite conditions. Although bird-watching does occur prior to taking the exams, there is no certainty that other factors aren't affecting exam performance more directly. In addition, both the third and fourth causal conditions suggest variation in seeing the

---

[1]Some scholars believe intelligence analysis is analogous to medicine, as it involves analyzing collected data that may be scientific and technical in nature, but also has input from people. Both medicine and intelligence have human observers who engage in deception or self-deception regarding the evidence they report, be it from patients who believe they are in better health or sicker than they really are versus foreign intelligence agents who mislead or withhold information from their handlers. See Marrin, Stephen, and Efren Torres. "Improving How to Think About Intelligence and Medicine." *Intelligence and National Security* 32, no. 5 (2017): 649–662.

[2]Former CIA analyst and scholar John Gentry argues intelligence analysis is almost identical to social science research. See Gentry, John A. "The 'Professionalization' of Intelligence Analysis: A Skeptical Perspective." *International Journal of Intelligence and Counterintelligence* 29, no. 4 (2016): 643–676.

[3]This discussion is informed by Hume, David. *An Enquiry Concerning Human Understanding*, 2nd ed., edited by Eric Steinberg. Indianapolis, IN: Hackett, 1993.

flamingo and exam performance is a coincidence and not a causal relationship. Minor brain chemistry changes caused by variance in bird viewing are unlikely to have a dramatic effect on exam performance. Other factors, such as whether or not a student completes the course readings when they are assigned, takes good notes, and studies enough, are far more likely explanatory variables.

Although correlation is defined only as a close connection in terms of time and space between events, causation may take several forms. First, causality can be **probabilistic**, an expression of the likelihood of event B occurring if cause A happens, or **deterministic**, where event B always occurs when cause A happens. Second, causation can be **monocausal**, where event B happens as a result of cause A; **multicausal**, where event B happens as a result of causes A and A'; or **conjunctural**, where event B occurs because a cluster of seemingly unrelated causes coalesce. For example, some scholars argue revolutions are caused by charismatic leaders. Others claim revolutions are the product of a permissive international environment combined with a revolt by rural peasants. Finally, revolutions may also be caused by the conjunctural combination of increases in population precipitating state crisis, inclusionary pressures on elites, rising state expenditures, unrest from inflation, and the mobilization of marginalized groups.[4]

This example of scholarly analysis of the causes of revolution directs our attention to the next subject in understanding knowledge claims—how candidate causal variables are identified. In the natural and social sciences, there are three statements of causality that direct researchers as to which factors come to bear on a given phenomenon. **Laws** are the broadest statements of causality, highlighting an unvarying, deterministic relationship between a cause and its effects. The law of gravity is the most famous law, establishing the relationship that objects of larger mass always attract objects of smaller mass. **Theories** are also broad statements of cause and effect. But unlike laws, multiple theories compete to explain the same categories of events. For example, in the field of international relations (IR), the theories of realism, liberalism, and constructivism offer very different explanations as to what causes war. No one theory has prevailed because each provides a plausible account, much how physicists continue to contest which theory—wave, quantum, or electromagnetic—best explains the existence of light. Finally, **hypotheses** are specific explanations of cause and effect. Commonly derived from the broader causal statements provided by theories, hypotheses explain individual events. For example, a scholar using the IR theory known as liberalism would draw on the theory's general claim that domestic politics tends to drive foreign policy to derive the hypothesis that Austria-Hungary started World War I to stave off revolution.

---

[4]The three different causal explanations of revolution are from, respectively, Weber, Max. "Charismatic Authority." In *Economy and Society*, Vol. 1, edited by Guenther Roth and Claus Wittich. Berkeley: University of California Press, 1979; Skocpol, Theda. *States and Social Revolutions: A Comparative Analysis*. Cambridge, UK: Cambridge University Press, 1979; and Goldstone, Jack A. *Revolution and Rebellion in the Early Modern World*. Berkeley: University of California Press, 1993.

## FORECASTING AND THE CHALLENGES OF PREDICTION

As we can see from the previous discussion, the natural and social sciences have coherent bodies of theory from which to derive hypotheses to explain current events and make predictions about the future. However, intelligence studies as an academic discipline has no laws and very little by way of theories to generate hypotheses.[5] The situation is even bleaker with regard to the practice of intelligence analysis, which often out of necessity generates hypotheses in an ad hoc, case-by-case manner.

Nevertheless, several concepts from the sciences that help us judge how well a theory or hypothesis explains an event are directly applicable to intelligence analysis. Recall that causation can be expressed in three different ways: probabilistically, deterministically, or conjuncturally. Because the very nature of intelligence is to deal with uncertainty, employing a deterministic model of causation in intelligence analysis can be problematic. When US IC officers present intelligence as certain, they undermine the very nature of the enterprise, as was the case when CIA director George Tenet referred to evidence of Iraq possessing weapons of mass destruction (WMD) as a "slam dunk case" at a 2002 meeting at the White House. This was neither an accurate representation of the quality of the evidence the IC possessed regarding Iraqi WMD nor

US Department of State

**PHOTO 11.1** President George W. Bush in the Oval Office with Vice President Dick Cheney, CIA director George Tenet, and Chief of Staff Andy Card on March 20, 2003.

---

[5]See Gill, Peter, Stephen Marrin, and Mark Phytian, eds. *Intelligence Theory: Key Questions and Debates.* London, UK: Routledge, 2009.

an appropriate way to frame an intelligence assessment. As Iraq had in fact destroyed almost all of its chemical weapons and ended its WMD programs in the late 1990s, Tenet's boastful claim turned into a costly embarrassment for the administration and the US IC.

In lieu of using deterministic language more suited to physics or chemistry, intelligence analysts often express causality in probabilistic terms. But because they do not have the same kind of evidence or bodies of theory to draw on that one finds even in the social sciences, expressions of likelihood in the US IC are not observed probability—that is, probabilities derived from empirically observable events. Instead, the term **estimative probability** is used, which refers to the beliefs of analysts in the likelihood of an event occurring based on the available information. In another important difference with the sciences, estimative probability is not expressed numerically to policymakers, even if it is produced using analytic methods that are quantitative in nature. Instead, estimates are given using specific words covering ranges of likelihood. The Office of the Director of National Intelligence has standardized the meaning of these terms, which are used across the entire IC.

**TABLE 11.1 ■ Estimative Language of the US IC[6]**

| Almost no chance | Very unlikely | Unlikely | Roughly even chance | Likely | Very likely | Almost certain(ly) |
|---|---|---|---|---|---|---|
| Remote | Highly improbable | Improbable (improbably) | Roughly even odds | Probable (probably) | Highly probable | Nearly certain |
| 1%–5% | 5%–20% | 20%–45% | 45%–55% | 55%–80% | 80%–95% | 95%–99% |

*Source:* Office of the Director of National Intelligence, 2015.

Looking at Table 11.1, several questions may arise as you think critically about the language and its referent probability ranges. One question frequently expressed by people outside of the IC is "Why not just give decision makers the raw numbers?" There are several reasons for this. First, simple language that is used in all intelligence forecasts is more readily understood by policymakers, very few of whom have had any training in either probability or intelligence analysis. There have been several prominent instances in which politicians have drawn incorrect conclusions when the terminology used in briefings was inconsistent or when numerical probabilities were offered

[6]Office of the Director of National Intelligence. "Intelligence Community Directive 203: Analytic Standards." January 2, 2015. https://www.dni.gov/files/documents/ICD/ICD%20203%20Analytic%20Standards.pdf.

by intelligence officers.[7] Using plain language that is consistent for all intelligence estimates reduces the likelihood of misunderstandings.[8] Second, the expectation that intelligence officers can offer a specific point estimate (e.g., 74%) is unrealistic given the nature of estimative probability. Rather, estimative probability is best thought of as Bayesian in nature. Named for the 18th-century theologian and mathematician Thomas Bayes, this kind of probability reflects shared beliefs about likelihood, not observed (empirical) probability, and is thus very sensitive to new information. Empirical probability is more precise because it refers to real, observed events, not beliefs *about* events. Moreover, using "74%" instead of "Likely" logically leads to the follow-up question from the recipient of such a report or briefing, "So how or when would it increase to 75%? 76%? 77%?" Again, an intelligence estimate cannot offer that level of precision. Using language instead of specific numbers keeps expectations realistic regarding what intelligence can and cannot do. Finally, using plain language emphasizes the differences in likelihood between ranges, thereby making it easier for policymakers to make a decision, rather than introducing additional uncertainty and hesitation on their part by having choices hinge on the difference between 79% and 81% for a potentially very complex, important decision. Expressing those same probabilities as "Likely" versus "Highly likely" more accurately captures the analytic distinction intelligence officers are trying to make between those two categories and simplifies the choices politicians face.

Estimative probability is an expression of the likelihood of an event occurring. But it is not a statement that evaluates the quality of the diagnostic information used to make this prediction. In both the natural and social sciences, when researchers evaluate the data they have gathered and the degree to which they have used methods that can be replicated, they refer to this as **reliability**. For US IC intelligence analysts, reliability is expressed in the form of **confidence levels**. Whenever they make a forecast, IC analysts characterize their confidence in the quality of the collected data used in making this prediction as either high, medium, or low. Although it may seem like they are connected, estimative probability and confidence *are not related to each other*. A claim about whether or not something is going to happen is a separate issue from how confident one is in making that claim. Analysts must not "hedge" an estimate by

---

[7]During the Cuban Missile Crisis, despite being present in all of the same briefings it was clear that President John F. Kennedy, cabinet officials, and intelligence briefers all had very different understandings of the likelihood of Soviet military action. More recently, the 2012 raid on Osama bin Laden's Abbottabad house revealed a similar communications gap. See Friedman, Jeffrey A., and Richard Zeckhauser. "Handling and Mishandling Estimative Probability: Likelihood, Confidence, and the Search for Bin Laden." *Intelligence and National Security* 30, no. 1 (2015): 77–99.

[8]Recent research challenges this claim. Some scholars have found that exposing policymakers to numerical estimates makes them more careful in making decisions and prone to seek out more information on a subject. See Friedman, Jeffrey A., Jennifer S. Lerner, and Richard Zeckhauser. "Behavioral Consequences of Probabilistic Precision: Experimental Evidence From National Security Professionals." *International Organization* 71 (Fall 2017): 803–826.

claiming something is highly likely but then assigning a low confidence level because they feel uncertain about making what they might see as a bold claim. Analysts almost always make forecasts with incomplete information—that is the nature of intelligence. If the information used in constructing the estimate is limited, then that is an issue of confidence, not probability.

Estimative language is not used in all analytic products. As discussed in Chapter 10 intelligence analysis has several functions in addition to forecasts about the future. For example, current intelligence describes what is happening, not what is likely to occur. Estimates, however, provide what the US IC calls **anticipatory intelligence**, judgments about the likelihood of future events presented in a context that allows decision makers to make choices to avoid or shape these outcomes. The term was adopted ostensibly because the world has become more complex. By referring to forecasts as anticipatory, intelligence analysts are attempting to use terminology to reinforce the point that policymakers can make choices to influence future events if they choose to act promptly.

However, there may be an additional, perhaps more cynical reason for the use of the term anticipatory intelligence. After two prominent negative events that were popularly understood to be intelligence failures (9/11 and Iraq WMD), the term may also have come into use because the leadership of the IC did not want to be perceived as being in the business of predicting the future. Predicting the future is hard, and making inaccurate forecasts is part and parcel of the enterprise. Intelligence officers are understandably resistant to use "batting average"—the percentage of correct predictions ("hits") versus attempts ("at bats")—as a metric of the effectiveness of the analytic products they generate.[9] But resistance to predicting the future is also an old problem in the US IC that is perhaps part of its organizational culture. In a famous incident, one of the most influential figures in the history of intelligence analysis, Sherman Kent, sought to make estimative language a requirement during the 1960s, for which he was ridiculed. During a heated discussion about this reform effort, one of Kent's colleagues derisively implied intelligence analysts were not in the same business as Vegas oddsmakers, to which Kent replied with characteristic aplomb, "'I'd rather be a bookie than a fucking poet!'"[10] Despite the US IC's historical and contemporary reluctance to characterize intelligence estimates as attempts to predict the future, make no mistake, that is exactly what intelligence estimates are. Much as social scientists try to predict election outcomes, the likelihood of war breaking out in a given region, and a host of other possible events, intelligence analysts use both classified and unclassified data to predict the future.

---

[9]Marrin, Stephen. "Evaluating the Quality of Intelligence Analysis: By What (Mis)Measure?" *Intelligence and National Security* 27, no. 6 (2012): 896–912.

[10]Quoted in Davis, Jack. "Sherman Kent and the Profession of Intelligence Analysis." Sherman Kent Center for Intelligence Analysis, Central Intelligence Agency. *Occasional Papers* 1, no. 5 (2002). https://www.cia.gov/library/kent-center-occasional-papers/vol1no5.htm.

The track record of prediction in the US IC is mixed. The CIA, for example, has made a number of highly accurate forecasts since its inception, from arguing before the deployment of combat troops that US efforts in South Vietnam were likely to fail to drawing attention to the rising threat to the US homeland posed by al-Qaeda prior to 9/11. But the CIA has also failed to predict some of the most important events of the past 75 years, from the collapse of the Soviet Union to recent Russian election interference in Western democracies. What role this "batting average" of predictive success/failure should play in evaluating the quality of intelligence produced for our nation's leaders is debatable. The very act of successful prediction and the resultant alteration in US policy may cause adversaries to change their plans, thereby rendering an accurate prediction inaccurate because the predicted outcome did not happen. Prediction is also only one of several purposes of intelligence.[11] Providing objective, enhanced understanding of complex events and choices facing policymakers may be more important. Nevertheless, forecasting is one of the primary missions of intelligence analysis, and if the US IC's ability to do so is deficient, examining why this is the case is important.

First, a *perfect track record* of prediction is simply impossible due to the **butterfly effect**. In complex systems, small variations in seemingly unlinked conditions can still produce large impacts, effects that are impossible to model. For example, hurricane forecasting has improved significantly over the past 25 years, reducing errors in the monitoring of storms from 415 to 135 kilometers. But the science of hurricanes is now approaching the limits of its ability to predict storm paths with greater precision.[12] Yet unlike the targets of intelligence analysis, weather conditions are not thinking systems that change their behavior when they believe they are being monitored. In this important aspect, intelligence analysis is thus more complex than the extremely rigorous science of hurricane prediction, which draws on the disciplines of meteorology, physics, chemistry, and computer science. If hurricane forecasting has likely reached its limits in terms of accuracy, it is unreasonable to believe that forecasting in intelligence will surpass it.

Second, failure to achieve better forecasting accuracy may also relate to poor leadership and institutional incentives that have resulted in what one scholar has termed the **professionalization of analysis**, attempts to transform intelligence analysis into a kind of pseudo or dumbed-down version of social science in lieu of hiring people with advanced degrees in the social sciences from the best universities in the world. A direct consequence of this educational decline has been a reduction in the intellectual abilities of analysts.[13] Although additional investigation of these claims is warranted,

---

[11]Marrin, "Evaluating the Quality of Intelligence Analysis."

[12]Berger, Eric. "Hurricane Forecasts May Be Running Headlong Into the Butterfly Effect." *Ars Technica*, August 12, 2019. https://arstechnica.com/science/2019/08/hurricane-forecasters-may-be-reaching-the-limits-of-predictability.

[13]Gentry, "'Professionalization' of Intelligence Analysis."

this hypothesis is supported by a recent series of experiments in which IC analysts with access to classified material performed poorly relative to amateurs who used a few simple statistical techniques to improve how they made predictions using only open source information.[14]

Finally, analytic failures may be the product of problems in perception. In this context, **perception** is defined as both correctly viewing the world via sensory data and making accurate inferences as to how others will perceive the world.[15] The former is hard enough—consider how heated air over asphalt creates the appearance of water, or the strange echoes produced in canyons that make it all but impossible to determine the origin of a gunshot. But the latter is significantly more complicated. Our adversaries will do everything they can to deceive us, while the incentives to deceive oneself into believing that things are worse or better than they really are can be just as pernicious.[16] It is to these perceptual challenges we now turn.

## PSYCHOLOGICAL BIASES AND INTELLIGENCE ANALYSIS

In previous chapters, a variety of organizational impediments to the production of effective intelligence products were discussed, from cultures of secrecy to inter-agency rivalries. Organizational problems with intelligence are the result of group behavior, often without awareness of the barriers to effective intelligence created by such activities. Moreover, these problems are often the result of the organizational structure of the IC itself. For example, the division of intelligence collection into specialized categories (HUMINT, SIGINT, etc.) may result in **stovepiping**, the separation of intelligence from a larger context that prevents the analysts and consumers of such information from seeing the "big picture." Organizational barriers can reduce the accuracy or quality of analytic products. These problems are pernicious. However, they can be addressed by organizational reform, changes in procedures, and improvements in the quality of the leadership of these organizations and their oversight by Congress.

In contrast, psychological barriers to effective analysis exist in the minds of individual analysts and are not group properties. Because they are part of human nature, specifically the brain mechanisms that govern perception, they are very difficult to address. Although they take many forms, these barriers are collectively referred to as **biases**, problems with perception that cause people to view the world inaccurately and/or make erroneous inferences regarding what others perceive. In this context,

---

[14]See Tetlock, Philip E., and Dan Gardner. *Superforecasting*. New York, NY: Broadway Books, 2015.

[15]Jervis, Robert. *Perception and Misperception in International Politics*. Princeton, NJ: Princeton University Press, 1976.

[16]This is particularly difficult in counterintelligence. See Jervis, Robert. "Intelligence, Counterintelligence, Perception, and Deception." In *Vaults, Mirrors, and Masks: Rediscovering US Counterintelligence*, edited by Jennifer E. Sims and Burton Gerber. Washington, DC: Georgetown University Press, 2009.

biases are not pejorative. In colloquial speech, many people interpret the word *bias* as if the people with biases are deliberately dishonest or underhanded. But this is not the case with psychological biases, which often exercise their influence over our minds even when we make sincere efforts to control or reduce the effects they have on perception. Moreover, people with perceptual biases are psychologically healthy—they are not mentally ill.

All of us are at one time or another affected by such biases. Yet it took several decades before the IC began to appreciate the role of the psychology of perception in intelligence analysis. During the late 1970s, retired CIA analyst Richards Heuer developed an interest in emergent work in the field of cognitive psychology that focused attention on the importance of perceptual biases in decision making. In 1979, Heuer wrote a primer on the importance of this research for intelligence analysis that remains influential in the US IC.[17] Over 30 years later, Heuer and coauthor and fellow CIA veteran Randolph Pherson composed a manual of analytic techniques designed to reduce the effects of some of the biases we will examine in the next section.[18]

## Cognitive Biases

The first psychological category of misperception is **cognitive bias**, errors in perception stemming from the sources of information we draw on to make judgments about the world. Cognitive biases are often the result of difficulty in updating one's priors. The world is complex and constantly changing. Tracking every event and issue from medically sound dietary advice to the current location of active Islamic State cells is very time-consuming. It also requires careful selection of media sources to ensure consumption of accurate information. Fortunately, because cognitive biases are the result of how information is processed in the human brain, they can be reduced. Shifting away from a deficient source of information to one that is more accurate will reduce bias. For example, as Figure 11.1 demonstrates, people who rely on CNN or MSNBC as their primary source of information are likely to have much more accurate views about climate change compared with people who watch Fox News. If some of the viewers of Fox were to consume other media, it is likely their perceptions about the world would be more accurate.

In addition, using relatively simple techniques to improve how we process information can reduce the effects of cognitive biases. Many of these techniques will be covered in more detail in the next chapter. The bottom line concerning cognitive biases is that if we want to do something about them, we can. But they are nonetheless very common and present constant challenges for intelligence analysts.

---

[17]Heuer, Richards J., Jr. *Psychology of Intelligence Analysis*. Langley, VA: Center for the Study of Intelligence, 1979.

[18]Heuer, Richards J., Jr., and Randolph H. Pherson. *Structured Analytic Techniques for Intelligence Analysis*, 2nd ed. Los Angeles, CA: CQ Press, 2015.

**FIGURE 11.1  ■  Cognitive Bias, Climate Science, and Cable News[19]**

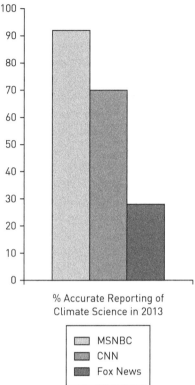

% Accurate Reporting of
Climate Science in 2013

- MSNBC
- CNN
- Fox News

*Source:* Union of Concerned Scientists, 2014.

In order to understand their effects and how to mitigate them, we need to examine some of the more important cognitive biases in more detail. One of the most common is **confirmation bias**, which is the tendency to seek out only information that supports prior beliefs. Confirmation bias is particularly challenging with regard to previous knowledge, learning that has led to accurate perceptions about the world in the past. For example, the manner in which many people become familiar with terrorist suicide bombers is in the context of Islamic extremists from al-Qaeda or the Islamic State. The frequency with which both groups have used this tactic in the Middle East and Southwest Asia would seem to suggest that it is a technique germane to religious fanatics. Thus, if such an attack were to occur again, it would seem rational for intelligence analysts to focus their attention on information about the attack that suggested connection to these two terrorist organizations, such as attempting to deduce motive

[19]Union of Concerned Scientists. "Science or Spin? Assessing the Accuracy of Cable News Coverage of Climate Science." April 8, 2014. https://www.ucsusa.org/resources/science-or-spin.

or the purpose of the target based on the strategic objectives of al-Qaeda or the Islamic State. Yet other kinds of terrorist groups have also used suicide bombers to advance their goals, such as the secular Palestinians of the al-Aqsa Martyrs' Brigades or the Buddhist Tamil Tigers of Sri Lanka. What appears rational from one's past experience, education, and training may in fact be confirmation bias.

Another cognitive bias that frequently affects analysts is **vividness of personal experience**, a bias that causes people to believe impactful anecdotal events are broadly generalizable to circumstances that in fact have little to do with personal experience. Both in prior service in the military and in intelligence operations, many intelligence officers have been forward-deployed over the past several decades. Similarly, analysts with prior service or who have supported tactical analytic missions may have been in close proximity to combat or other dangerous situations, be it from evaluating linkages between militias in Baghdad by studying the patterns of insurgent graffiti or from analytic support for drone targeting. Such visceral experiences often shape broader perceptions about the world, leading to beliefs that other, less austere or risk-prone operational environments such as the urban United States have analogous threat profiles when they clearly do not. Similarly, research by cognitive psychologists has suggested that presentations by a briefer who emphasizes audiovisual material over substantive information have more impact on recipients than presentations that focus on content. This issue is particularly salient for the US IC, as the manner in which it has presented information graphically has shaped how private industry has conducted briefings as well.[20] Recipients of such vivid briefings may come to believe inaccurate information because it was presented in a creative or otherwise appealing manner. Despite the vast differences between being under fire and enduring "death by PowerPoint," both kinds of experiences can be vivid and thus distort perception.

One particularly troublesome cognitive bias for intelligence analysts is **mirror imaging**. It presents such problems because it arises from an impulse or predisposition that is otherwise enormously useful—empathy. One of the most important attributes of intelligence analysts is empathy, the ability to see how someone who is not like you may interpret the world. But empathy sometimes leads to a willingness to believe adversaries or allies have the same kind of reasoning ability, access to information, or decision-making capacity the analysts and their organization possess. Individuals "look in the mirror," so to speak, and see they are "just like us." Yet sometimes our opponents or friends are wilier or more intelligent than we are. Other times they are not. This is an empirical, not methodological, question. Mirror imaging often starts with an analyst asking, "What would I do in their shoes?" This kind of reasoning can be useful, though only to the extent the analyst remembers such deductions may have nothing to do with the actual thought process of the target.

Reliance on deduction as a baseline can significantly distort perception. And the effects are not limited to mirror imaging. **Fundamental attribution error** is a cognitive bias in which individual analysts view their country's actions as a product largely of

[20]Saval, Nikil. "The Curious Case of the US Government's Influence on 20th Century Design." *The New York Times*, December 18, 2019. https://www.nytimes.com/2019/12/11/t-magazine/us-government-20th-century-design.html.

the situation or environment. In contrast, the same analysts see an adversary's actions or decisions as a dispositional feature of that country—the nature of the adversary is to act this way. Fundamental attribution error is deductive, as it depends on prior assumptions about the nature of intelligence targets as fundamentally different from the nature of the analyst. It is an inversion of the logic of mirror imaging that can be just as damaging, particularly with regard to conflict.

For example, in January 2016, two small US Navy patrol boats accidentally strayed into Iranian territorial waters. Noting this violation of their sovereignty, the Iranians seized the vessels and their crews. The reaction by some members of the US Senate clearly exhibited fundamental attribution error, with Republican senator Tom Cotton characterizing Iran's conduct as "an unending series of provocations."[21] Yet Cotton and others failed to note either the 2003 US invasion and occupation of Iraq, an illegal act under international law and something that could be considered provocative by Iran, or that the US vessel had been seized in Iranian waters, which also could be considered a "provocation." For Cotton and other saber-rattlers, any US action was explainable by unfortunate mistakes (i.e., the context), while Iranian actions were always the result of the nature of Iran, which in their minds is evil. Noting Turkey's destruction of a Russian fighter that had strayed into its airspace during the same time period, Tufts University professor Dan Drezner observed that "fortunately, Iran did not respond to this incident in the same way that, oh, I don't know, a NATO ally recently responded to an aerial incursion. They seized the ships, did not harm any of the sailors and eventually returned both the crew and the ships."[22] Recognizing the effect of fundamental attribution error on perception is not to diminish pervasive violation of human rights by the Iranian regime, or its support for terrorism. But Iran's improper or threatening behavior in some areas of international politics does not guarantee that *all* of its actions are wrong, any more than the fact that the United States is the most war-prone nation since World War II makes it inherently aggressive.

In contrast with the deduction-influenced biases of mirror imaging and fundamental attribution error, **anchoring** is a bias caused by a problem with induction. Anchoring is a bias in which an analyst focuses on an initial piece of information, establishing a baseline that may not be representative of the target. Subsequent information on the subject is interpreted through the prism of the anchoring baseline. Another perceptual bias that is similarly influenced by induction is **oversensitivity to consistency**, a bias in which the analyst either focuses on an established pattern holding or, paradoxically, believes that a pattern must be breaking precisely because it has been consistent for so long. Oversensitivity to consistency can cause analysts to believe a pattern break is also a new baseline condition, a phenomenon known as the **normalization of deviance**. Although there is still some controversy regarding how much Israeli intelligence

---

[21] *Morning Joe.* "Iran Holds America Hostage." MSNBC, January 13, 2016. https://www.msnbc.com/morning-joe/watch/iran-holds-america-hostage--says-gop-senator-601028675899.

[22] Quoted in Bender, Bryan. "The Iranian Hostage Crisis That Wasn't." *Politico*, January 13, 2016. https://www.politico.com/story/2016/01/iran-hostage-crisis-that-wasnt-217729.

analysts were influenced by psychological biases in the 1973 Yom Kippur War, one argument for the Israeli Defense Forces' surprise was that the Egyptian Army staged a series of mobilization drills during the spring and summer of 1973. Initially, Israeli analysts believed that the mobilization of the Egyptian Army was an indicator of war, a reasonable inference given both past patterns from history and the threat posed. But after the Egyptians mobilized several times and did not invade, the analysts adjusted their baseline expectations as to what constituted "normal" behavior by the Egyptian Army so much that they failed to provide adequate warning just prior to the October attack by the Egyptians—they normalized deviance.

The final two cognitive biases we shall examine involve beliefs in actors and events as more impactful or planned than they necessarily are. The **fallacy of centralized direction** is a bias in which the analyst believes that a country or nonstate actor is governed by one leader or group at the top, when in fact leadership is divided and/or many different subgroups compete for control over the country or nongovernmental organization. For example, the manner in which al-Qaeda was reported in the press following the 9/11 attacks made it seem as if the leader of the terrorist group, Osama bin Laden, had direct command over all aspects of the organization. In fact, al-Qaeda had several suborganizations that exercised influence, including the Shura Council, a group of religious figures whose purpose was ostensibly to evaluate the acceptability of al-Qaeda's operations from an Islamic perspective, and a number of different subordinate leaders, such as Khalid Sheik Mohammed, the architect of the 9/11 attacks, and bin Laden's eventual successor, Ayman al-Zawahiri. The already fragmented leadership was further divided as al-Qaeda morphed into "franchises" following the destruction of its base of operations in Afghanistan in 2001–2002. In this case, the fallacy of centralized direction encouraged the belief that if bin Laden were to be killed or captured, al-Qaeda's ability to operate would be severely impeded. Unfortunately, al-Qaeda has proven to resemble the many-headed hydra of Greek mythology more than it does a military organization or even a Mafia family.

Similarly, the belief that big effects must have big causes is also a form of cognitive bias. The **fallacy of big causes and big effects** explains many cases of misperception in foreign policy. One of the most prominent examples is World War I, which was such a devastating conflict that people believed its cause or causes must be similarly titanic in proportion. Yet the proximate cause of the war that killed almost 20 million people and reshaped the maps of Europe and the Middle East was the murder of the successor to the Austro-Hungarian throne by a 19-year-old member of an obscure Serbian terrorist group. This is not to minimize the other, very complex forces at work in Europe at the time, such as the European alliance system, the rivalry between Germany and Great Britain, or the nature of German war plans. But what started the chain of events in motion were the actions of a person the same age as many college freshmen.

## Motivated Biases

In addition to cognitive biases, human perception is shaped by what are known as **motivated biases**. As the word *cognitive* emphasizes the thinking component to cognitive biases, *motivated* draws our attention to the driver of motivated biases—people actively want to believe certain things. Moreover, this motivation to believe is both emotional and cognitive, connecting a person's identity to the belief. Motivated biases are almost impossible to alter because of the deep commitment people have to them. Because people with motivated biases do not respond to new information by altering their beliefs, people with such biases make poor intelligence officers. Although there are multiple sources of motivated bias, political ideology and religion are the two most prominent causes.

In addition to their professional duties, intelligence officers have obligations as citizens. Many political philosophers have argued one of the obligations of citizens in democracies is to participate in the political process. Having a preference for political candidates or parties and exercising one's right and obligation as a citizen is appropriate for intelligence officers, perhaps even a duty as a politically active citizen. But identifying with a party or political ideology so strongly that it determines the choice sets of intelligence officers suggests motivated bias. For intelligence to serve the national interest, intelligence officers must be able to recognize differences of opinion regarding policy choices as being a fundamental part of a functioning democracy. Fellow citizens with different opinions are not "enemies," language that has increasingly crept into political discourse in the United States in recent years. Moreover, motivated biases based on ideology cause people with them to disregard factual evidence for a host of challenges facing the country, from denial of climate change science to the belief that anyone who crosses the US border illegally is entitled to a green card. Even when confronted with empirical facts, people with motivated biases find new ways to rationalize their beliefs.[23] They simply do not want to update their priors, regardless of the evidence.

Much as one has a civic duty in a democratic society, if one is a true believer in a religion, that too carries with it obligations. But as is the case with politics, faith cannot be allowed to influence perception in intelligence analysis to the point at which its adherents deny the legitimacy of the beliefs of their coworkers or to the point where it shapes views about intelligence targets. Since the 9/11 attacks, there has been a growing tendency in the US Department of Defense for unit leaders to openly emphasize Christianity, a clear violation of the First Amendment's establishment clause and one of the most basic principles of modern democracies: the separation of church and state. This has presented problems for maintaining professional standards of conduct

---

[23]Bisgaard, Martin. "How Getting the Facts Right Can Fuel Partisan-Motivated Reasoning." *American Journal of Political Science* 63, no. 4 (2019): 824–839.

and reducing religious and gender discrimination.[24] It has also made the battle of ideas more difficult, as such episodes reinforce the perception of many in the Muslim world that Western counterterrorism activities are really a thinly disguised attack on Islam itself.

Both ideology and religion tell us what is right or wrong—they constitute our value systems. This is psychologically healthy, as it allows us to make choices based on principle and gives purpose to our actions. But when personal beliefs prevent us from recognizing facts about the world, they undermine our ability to serve as intelligence officers. The US IC has been slow in recognizing the potential influence of motivated biases on intelligence analysis. A prominent article by a veteran intelligence officer noted the emergent problem of "Blue and Red" analysts, reflecting too close of an affiliation with the worldviews of the Democratic (Blue) and Republican (Red) Parties.[25] But this paper failed to use the appropriate terminology from psychology and demonstrated little awareness of what constitutes a motivated bias. Moreover, the author's suggestion for addressing the problem was to ensure analytic teams have a balance of Blue and Red analysts, a cure probably worse than the disease. People with motivated biases do not change their minds when confronted with new information, particularly if it is presented by a known affiliate of the opposite worldview. This poor understanding demonstrated by a senior intelligence official concerning the problems presented by motivated biases points to the difficulty the US IC has had remaining current with developments in the field of psychology. Although path-breaking at the time they were introduced, Heuer's views continue to dominate thinking on the subject in the US IC long after the field of psychology has moved on from his purely cognitive perspective on bias.[26] As the Western democracies become more polarized, motivated biases will present an increasing problem for effective intelligence analysis.

## CONCLUSION: FROM THE PHILOSOPHY OF SCIENCE TO PRACTICE

In this chapter, we have discussed basics of epistemology and social science terminology. Being familiar with these concepts is essential in the successful execution of analytic missions. So too is consciousness of cognitive and motivated barriers to accurate analysis. But the nuts and bolts, as it were, of intelligence analysis have yet to be discussed. Now that you are familiar with the epistemological foundations and

---

[24]See Levy, Yagil. "Desecularization of the Military: The United States and Israel." *Armed Forces and Society* 46, no. 1 (2018): 92–115; and Pendlebury, Jarrod. "'This Is a Man's Job': Challenging the Masculine 'Warrior Culture' at the US Air Force Academy." *Armed Forces and Society* 46, no. 1 (2018): 163–184.

[25]Muller, David G. "Intelligence Analysis in Red and Blue." *International Journal of Intelligence and Counterintelligence* 21, no. 1 (2007): 1–12.

[26]See Mercer, Jonathan. "Emotional Beliefs." *International Organization* 64 (Winter 2010): 1–31.

psychological challenges inherent to intelligence analysis, we turn to analytic methods, specific procedures and tools used to investigate the raw data collected from both human and technical platforms.

## KEY CONCEPTS

## ADDITIONAL READING

Bar-Joseph, Uri, and Rose McDermott. "The Intelligence Analysis Crisis." In *The Oxford Handbook of National Security Intelligence*, edited by Loch K. Johnston. Oxford, UK: Oxford University Press, 2010.

Bruce, James B. "Making Analysis More Reliable: Why Epistemology Matters to Intelligence." In *Analyzing Intelligence: Origins, Obstacles, and Innovations*, edited by Roger Z. George and James B. Bruce. Washington, DC: Georgetown University Press, 2009.

Kent, Sherman. "Words of Estimative Probability." Central Intelligence Agency. Historical document, last updated July 7, 2008. https://www.cia.gov/library/center-for-the-study-of-intelligence/csi-publications/books-and-monographs/sherman-kent-and-the-board-of-national-estimates-collected-essays/6words.html.

Kerbel, Josh. "Coming to Terms With Anticipatory Intelligence." *War on the Rocks*, August 13, 2019. https://warontherocks.com/2019/08/coming-to-terms-with-anticipatory-Intelligence/.

Klemke, E. D., Robert Hollinger, and David Wÿss Rudge, eds. *Introductory Readings in the Philosophy of Science*. Amherst, NY: Prometheus Books, 2012.

Marrin, Stephen. "Understanding and Improving Intelligence Analysis by Learning From Other Disciplines." *Intelligence and National Security* 32, no. 5 (2017): 539–547.

Phytian, Mark. "Intelligence Analysis and Social Science Methods: Exploring the Potential for and Possible Limits of Mutual Learning." *Intelligence and National Security* 32, no. 5 (2017): 600–612.

# 12 ANALYTIC METHODS

Jonathan M. Acuff

I n this chapter we will examine some of the methods used in the US intelligence community (IC) to analyze raw data that have been gathered and vetted during the collection process. We will discuss some of the traditional techniques that have been used for decades, such as scenarios, case studies, Analysis of Competing Hypotheses (ACH), network analysis, route analysis, and Red Teams. But we will also cover some analytic methods of a more recent vintage, such as Structured Analytic Techniques (SAT) and several quantitative approaches. We will describe how and when such methods are used and evaluate the strengths and weaknesses of each. Although a wide variety of approaches will be discussed, this is far from a comprehensive list. There is a large and growing literature on intelligence analysis that is impossible to cover in its entirety here. We continue with a discussion of the basics of intelligence writing, the means by which we translate the findings of these analytic techniques into a language that is both precise and easily understood by decision makers. The chapter concludes with a brief assessment of hiring trends in the US IC as they relate to analytic training and standards.

## THE CONTEMPORARY CONTEXT OF INTELLIGENCE ANALYSIS

All intelligence analysis is a form of **risk management**. Analysts must balance the nature of the target, judge its capabilities and intentions, and determine possible end states that may result from what the target plans to do and how the United States and its allies might react. Although they should not make policy recommendations, analysts must also constantly keep in mind the national interest and resources available to achieve it. As Roger George succinctly puts it, analysts are "enablers," not creators, of national security strategy.[1] The ability of analysts to provide effective warning and to shape outcomes is guided by priorities set by the National Command Authority and the senior leadership of the intelligence and national security communities. Analysts should think about how the threat or problems presented by the target of

---

[1]George, Roger Z. "The Art and Strategy of Intelligence." In *Analyzing Intelligence*, edited by Roger Z. George and James B. Bruce. Washington, DC: Georgetown University Press, 2008, 108.

analysis relate to the National Security Strategy, the National Intelligence Strategy, the National Intelligence Priorities Framework, and the Office of the Director of National Intelligence's (ODNI) Worldwide Threat Assessment. It is also worth keeping in mind that the most precious of resources is time, particularly with regard to how much time analysts can devote to producing a finished product. The timeliness of analysis is often just as important as its accuracy in creating decision advantage.

Effective analysis is also shaped by several important changes in the current context in which it is produced. The intelligence cycle portrays the process by which intelligence is collected, processed, analyzed, and disseminated as linear, with one step leading sequentially to the next. In practice, there is a reciprocal relationship between the types of collection platforms and the analytic methods that are used to evaluate them. Similarly, the types of analytic methods used may also have an effect on collection. Although this reciprocal relationship has many dimensions, there are two trends in collection affecting analysis that are particularly important. As collection platforms have grown increasingly sophisticated, more technical data are collected than ever before. This is particularly true with regard to measurement and signature intelligence (MASINT). At the same time, more open source intelligence (OSINT) is being utilized than at any previous time in the US IC's history, largely because of the sheer size of the World Wide Web. Both trends may necessitate structural changes in how we think about the relationship between what is collected and the analytic techniques used to produce a finished intelligence product. As both involve more information than has been previously available, this presents problems in determining which data are most important or relevant for the problem at hand. It may also incentivize attempts to narrow the question being asked, which can easily lead to oversimplification or analytic traps such as mirror imaging.[2]

Several implications follow from these two trends. First, it may be difficult to use some qualitative analytic methods when the data being analyzed were derived from scientific forms of collection, as it is difficult to translate some of the data into a form amenable to these techniques. This is the **problem of commensurability**, the ability of analysts to deploy an analytic vocabulary similar enough to the manner in which the technical intelligence is collected so that these data can be analyzed. Second, as collection increasingly draws on OSINT, it will be increasingly difficult for analysis to provide the **"value added"** it has historically offered when most of what was collected was secret.[3] One corollary to the changing nature of what is collected is that it would be prudent for intelligence organizations to draw on expertise in the academy and the private sector.[4] The private sector increasingly employs innovative syntheses

---

[2]Gill, Peter, and Mark Phythian. *Intelligence in an Insecure World*, 3rd ed. Cambridge, UK: Polity Press, 2018, 95.

[3]Lowenthal, Mark M. *The Future of Intelligence*. Cambridge, UK: Polity Press, 2018, 55.

[4]Ibid., 57–58.

of technical collection and analysis to forecast a wide variety of events. For example, some financial services firms use geospatial intelligence (GEOINT) tracking changes in traffic flow in Walmart parking lots to predict growth in gross domestic product (GDP)—more cars in the lot compared to the previous quarter suggests an uptick in consumer spending. During the late 1990s and early 2000s, the Central Intelligence Agency (CIA) increased its outreach to the academy and think tanks as part of its Open Source Initiative, which was institutionalized as the Open Source Center, and later as the Open Source Enterprise. Drawing on the intellectual power of both scholars and the private sector may facilitate how the US IC adapts to these difficult-to-manage trends.

Another implication of these structural changes in intelligence collection is the use of more rigorous methods in the analysis of intelligence. Naturally, this requires higher expectations for potential job candidates regarding technical training, a trend that is already becoming noticeable in job advertisements for positions at the CIA, the National Security Agency (NSA), and the National Geospatial-Intelligence Agency. Increasingly, the US IC expects its analysts to be able to handle both the traditional techniques that have been used to great effect in the past and the more cutting-edge, methodologically sophisticated methods of today and tomorrow.

## BOX 12.1

### SPOTLIGHT ON CAREERS

### ANALYTIC METHODOLOGIST, NATIONAL GEOSPATIAL-INTELLIGENCE AGENCY (2019)

**Wright–Patterson Air Force Base**

**Position Summary**

Analytic Methodologists develop and apply quantitative and qualitative techniques to enhance the analysis of complex national security problems. They apply knowledge of analytic tools to develop models, visualize data, and perform a range of analyses (e.g., systems analysis, comparative analysis). They provide technical consultation and input into the development, evaluation, use, and deployment of solutions to optimize GEOINT analysis and production. Additionally, they educate analysts, management, and customers on solutions and methodologies as they apply to GEOINT analysis.

**Education Requirements**

Education: Bachelor's degree from an accredited college or university in Operations Research, Geographic Information Systems (GIS), Geography, or at least 24 semester

*(Continued)*

(Continued)

hours in a combination of Operations Research, Mathematics, Probability, Statistics, Mathematical Logic, Science, or subject-matter courses requiring substantial competence in college-level Mathematics or Statistics. At least 3 of the 24 semester hours must have been in coding, data analysis, or data science. -OR- Combination of Education and Experience: A minimum of 24 semester (36 quarter) hours of coursework in any area listed in option A, that included at least 24 semester hours in a combination of Operations Research, Mathematics, Probability, Statistics, Mathematical Logic, Science, or subject-matter course substantial competence in college-level mathematics or statistics. At least 3 of the 24 semester hours must have been in coding, data analysis, or data science plus experience that required development and application of quantitative and qualitative techniques to enhance intelligence analysis or a related field that demonstrates the ability to successfully perform the duties associated with this work. As a rule, every 30 semester (45 quarter) hours of coursework is equivalent to one year of experience. Candidates should show that their combination of education and experience totals 4 years.

Salary: $89,762–$137,897.

*Source:* https://apply.intelligencecareers.gov/job-description/20200075

Finally, massive growth in the volume of data collected and the increasingly technical nature of much of this information make the ability to distinguish what is useful from what is not and to identify potential sources of adversary deception even more important. Both activities relate directly to **critical thinking**, which is vital in intelligence analysis. Although broad disagreements remain as to the definition of critical thinking, most scholars describe critical thinking as reflexivity regarding how one thinks about subjects—that is, thinking about thinking—and the ability to interrogate the possible hidden motives behind the truth claims of others, to discern the origins of ideas.[5] Some scholars argue that critical thinking is an attribute that is almost impossible to acquire—most people simply don't see the world in this manner. Others assert it is a trainable skill. Regardless as to where one stands in this debate, there is strong consensus regarding the role of critical thinking in intelligence analysis. Analysts who can't think critically are not as effective as analysts who can.

## METHODS USED TO ANALYZE INTELLIGENCE TARGETS

There are many ways to define different kinds of analytic techniques. Recently, the US IC has employed a typology consisting of seven categories. The first such category is

[5]Cf. Moore, David T. "Critical Thinking and Intelligence Analysis." Occasional Paper 14. Washington, DC: Center for Strategic Intelligence Research, National Intelligence University, 2007; and Hendrickson, Noel. "Critical Thinking in Intelligence Analysis." *International Journal of Intelligence and Counterintelligence* 21, no. 4 (2008): 679–693.

**decomposition and visualization**, which allows analysts to break down intelligence taskings into manageable segments, graphically represent how the relevant issues relate to each other, and task-organize how they will structure the time they have available for the project. Second, **idea generation** involves consideration of as wide a universe of concepts as possible given the time available. The third category, **scenarios and indicators**, encourages analysts to think about different outcomes that may result from current trends and to identify measurable drivers affecting the multiple possible outcomes. **Hypothesis generation and testing** forces analysts to specify relationships between drivers and outcomes so as to make them empirically testable and thus **falsifiable**. One of the hallmarks of both good social science and effective intelligence analysis is being able to state under what conditions a claim is not true. In both endeavors, more information is found to be false than true. The fifth category, **assessing cause and effect**, is also directly related to social science. Identifying causes of phenomena allows us to predict future events. It also enhances understanding of the nature and importance of these events. **Challenge analysis** plays an important role in reducing cognitive and group biases that may have skewed analysis. Finally, **conflict management** allows analysts who continue to disagree with each other at the end of the analytic process to either resolve their differences or find a way in which their competing findings can be usefully presented in the intelligence product. Depending on the nature of the target and the purpose of the intelligence tasking, some or all of these kinds of analytic methods may be used. Let's look at some examples of different kinds of techniques.

## Decomposition

As noted in the previous section, **decomposition** is a means by which analysts break down intelligence taskings into smaller, more manageable parts. This process increases the precision by which relevant factors can be assessed. But it also serves as a potential brake on perhaps inflated expectations of what can and cannot be accomplished by an analytic team during the time available, thereby necessitating further taskings.

# BOX 12.2
## FOR EXAMPLE: DECOMPOSITION

Let's say a group of analysts has been directed to answer the following question: "What will be the effects of a collapse of the Chinese stock market?" At first glance, this seems to be a straightforward strategic intelligence question. However, if we break apart "effects" into different potential subcategories, the tasking quickly becomes more complicated. What will be the effects on the Japanese economy, one of China's trading partners? How will the collapse affect the regional economies

*(Continued)*

(Continued)

as a whole? What will be the effect on the US economy? What are the potential domestic political effects for China? If the collapse signals a long-term shift in Chinese GDP growth, how will this affect military readiness and procurement? Will the collapse halt the Chinese Belt and Road Initiative? Will it change the global balance of power? These are just some of the potential dimensions of "effect." What is affected? Where are the effects felt? We could also do the same in terms of time as a factor—that is, near-, medium-, and long-term effects. Subdividing the broad question into a series of more focused categories in time and space helps analysts rank-order questions in terms of importance and their relation to the educational background and training of team members.

Decomposition can play a vital role in task management for analysts, allowing analysts to attack the most important issues first. Complex questions can be reduced to smaller puzzles that can be addressed in sequence. These advantages are particularly important when requests for intelligence are initiated by political appointees or other leaders who may not be well acquainted with the relevant issues or the nature of the problem. However, analysts need to be careful not to dilute the original question too much, rendering their approach too narrow to be of much use for decision makers. Decomposition combines well with other techniques that ensure the original research question is being adequately addressed, such as customer checklists.

## Network Analysis

**Network analysis** is used to graphically represent relationships between the intelligence target and other actors and institutions. It has been successfully employed to study the internal makeup and relationships of organized crime families, arms traffickers, and terrorists. Hollywood films often portray this method in the form of pictures of Mafia leaders attached to a wall or butcher board, depicted in hierarchical chain of command over the group's soldiers. Drawing such relationships by hand using colored markers to denote different kinds of relationships remains a useful exercise in visualizing connections, particularly when the intelligence target is a group that is unfamiliar to members of the analytic team or difficult to understand with verbal or written descriptions alone.

# BOX 12.3
## FOR EXAMPLE: NETWORK ANALYSIS

In this example (Figure 12.1), we will graphically represent the network relationship between different subcommanders in a notional Islamic State cell. The thicker lines reflect a relationship by marriage between the cell leader and his subordinates, while thinner lines reflect no such relationship, only network ties through the cell.

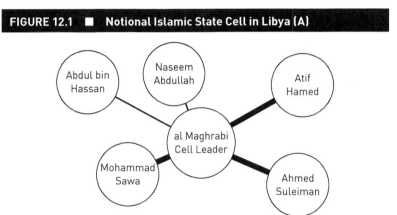

**FIGURE 12.1 ■ Notional Islamic State Cell in Libya (A)**

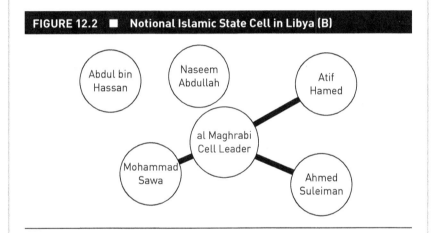

**FIGURE 12.2 ■ Notional Islamic State Cell in Libya (B)**

Next (Figure 12.2), we will model the men in the cell who have actually carried out terror attacks. In this network illustration, the lines represent men in the cell who have participated in attacks.

Via network analysis, we now have a clearer view of this terrorist cell. It seems that marital ties suggest greater levels of trust, more secure personal communications, or other reasons as to why the cell leader has only used men with whom he has such ties. However, to determine the specific reasons for this and to rule out the possibility it is merely a coincidence requires more rigorous methods that determine causal relationships.

However, the US IC also employs a variety of different software packages to more formally analyze networks, which provides both the aforementioned visual representation of complexity and a ready pathway to other methods that can be used to make inferences about the organization and its decision-making process. Network analysis may be combined with other techniques to help establish causal relationships between network nodes. Case studies of an organization's leadership are one such method. Via Palantir or other software, more formal methods such as decision trees or impact models can establish chains of events originating with specific actors. Statistical analysis identifying correlations between when actors communicate and subsequent operational activities can also reveal who may have authority in the organization to direct specific kinds of actions, a method similar to signals intelligence (SIGINT) traffic analysis.

## Brainstorming

Most of us are familiar with **brainstorming** as a technique to pick a paper topic or similar academic activity. However, in the US IC, brainstorming serves a different function. Although it does foster creativity, brainstorming's primary function is to reduce the effects of participants' prior mindsets. One's priors can cause one to not consider the full range of options or to dismiss outright an idea or approach without giving it due consideration. Brainstorming can take many forms. Unstructured brainstorming works well when group members have already worked well together and have developed group norms that ensure the fair and equal participation of each group member. More structured approaches may be required if group members don't have much experience working with each other, if the nature of the intelligence tasking is particularly complex, or if there is a limited amount of time to accomplish the intelligence assessment. In more structured approaches, a group moderator may keep time as participants contribute, ensuring that no group member tends to dominate the conversation or takes time away from others. The moderator may also keep a record of the different ways of thinking about the problem. Brainstorming can be entirely verbal or can take more graphical forms, with participants writing out ideas on a dry-erase board or even placing sticky notes on a wall.

## Scenarios

Also referred to as alternate futures analysis, **scenarios** are different causal pathways for future events. Scenarios are particularly useful during a period when large-scale changes are occurring and there is a high degree of uncertainty about the future. For example, during the months just before the collapse of the Soviet Union in 1991, intelligence analysts developed several scenarios covering a wide range of potential end states.[6] Scenarios are particularly useful in dealing with complex intelligence targets. Many strategic intelligence taskings expect analysts to forecast the policy choices of nation-states or large organizations associated with states, such as militaries. This

---

[6]Director of Central Intelligence. Special National Intelligence Estimate 11-18.2-1991. Washington, DC: September 1991.

is intrinsically a challenging undertaking, with many moving parts. In this context, it is also worth remembering the choices made by other states are in part conditioned by the choices the United States makes, a situation that rapidly grows in complexity if we consider that policymakers may adjust US decisions to anticipate the adversary actions, and vice versa. What quickly develops is a series of alternate pathways to the future. Some nonstate actors are similarly difficult to forecast, as their decision-making processes are sometimes more opaque, as is the case with terrorist groups. Scenario analysis can help us understand the future implications of various decisions taken by such groups as well.

Scenarios are created by identifying specific drivers of the intelligence target that shape its decision making. For example, in the context of the aforementioned collapse of the USSR, one of the primary drivers was increasing nationalism among the subject peoples of the Soviet Union. Once drivers are identified, specific assumptions are made as to how those drivers might function in combination with each other to shape future events. This is accomplished by assigning different values or levels to each driver, resulting in several sets of assumptions and multiple resulting future pathways.

The use of scenarios as a method is a useful reminder of the contingent nature of social systems. In one of the most quoted passages in social science, Max Weber noted that "'world images' created by 'ideas' have, like switchmen, determined the tracks along which action has been pushed by the dynamic of interest."[7] Scenarios help us identify what those "switchmen" are, the ideas that determine choice sets for leaders. In addition, when using scenarios, we must be sensitive to the fact that when confronted with unfamiliar or particularly fluid environments, people tend to reason by analogy. It is rational for them to do so, and it can help organize their thinking. However, one must be cautious—analogies are only helpful if they are the right ones. For example, during conversations that resulted in the deployment of US ground forces to South Vietnam in 1965, policymakers and their advisers constantly invoked the Munich analogy, that to not use force to stop communism was the same thing as Britain and France's policy of appeasement toward Hitler in 1938. Yet far better analogies for potential future pathways of US involvement in Vietnam were left largely unexamined, including the Korean War and France's disastrous recent war to retain its colonies in Indochina.[8] Analysts must be cautious when using analogical reasoning both in the development of drivers and assumptions for the case being studied and in determining potential pathways of events. Indeed, if analysts find themselves leaning on analogies too much in the development of scenarios,

---

[7]Weber, Max. *From Max Weber: Essays in Sociology*, translated and edited by H. H. Gerth and C. Wright Mills. New York, NY: Oxford University Press, 1946, 280.

[8]Khong, Yuen Foong. *Analogies at War: Korea, Munich, Dien Bien Phu, and the Vietnam Decisions of 1965*. Princeton, NJ: Princeton University Press, 1992.

they should consider shifting from scenarios to the use of Structured Analogies as an analytic technique.

## Indicators

**Indicators** are drivers of events used to track changes and the corresponding effects of these drivers over time. One of the ways to think about indicators is as a kind of thermometer. As the temperature increases outside, a host of different implications tend to arise. People tend to go outside more, attendance at sporting events rises, and people tend to travel more. But several less obvious trends are associated with a change in this indicator. As temperatures soar, so too does crime, with gun violence spiking during the summer months. When the temperature falls, a whole host of other human behaviors are associated with this change in the indicator as well.

In order to be useful for intelligence analysts, indicators must have several characteristics. First, they must be specific regarding what is being measured. Second, they must be reliable, meaning their use must be relatively interchangeable between different analysts and across analytic teams. Third, they must be useful over time, allowing comparison over multiple years, even decades. Finally, they should be nonreducible. Although indicators tend to be associated with each other as they are related to the same phenomenon they seek to represent, their attributes should bleed over into other indicators as little as possible.

Indicators allow us to observe changes in various obvious and less intuitive behaviors over time. However, it is important to note here that indicators are not direct causes—they influence behaviors and magnify the impact of other factors. Indicators may also be observable representations of much deeper or concealed activities. It is best to see them as suggesting the terms, characteristics, or range of activity of social phenomena, not determining outcomes or discrete decisions by individuals or groups. Nation-states, private firms, and nongovernmental organizations (NGOs) employ a wide variety of quantitative indicators to assess the performance of states, from rating agencies evaluating risk via credit scores to corruption indicators being used by states to guide the distribution of foreign aid. Indicators are common metrics of state power and shape the reputation of states.[9] Intelligence agencies use them in a wide variety of analytic missions. One of the most prominent is strategic warning, with political and military indicators used in an effort to reduce surprise.[10]

---

[9]Kelley, Judith G., and Beth A. Simmons. "Introduction: The Power of Global Performance Indicators." *International Organization* 73 (Summer 2019): 491–510.

[10]Grabo, Cynthia M. *Anticipating Surprise: Analysis for Strategic Warning*. Bethesda, MD: Joint Military Intelligence College, Center for Strategic Intelligence Research, 2002.

# BOX 12.4

## FOR EXAMPLE: INVASION INDICATORS, GERMAN ATTACK ON THE USSR, JUNE 22, 1941

- Increase in high-altitude overflights by German reconnaissance aircraft, March–June 1941
- German troops begin to concentrate in Poland, March 1941
- Movement of German troops into Hungary and Rumania, May–June 1941
- Germans slow down their delivery of industrial machinery to the USSR, May 1941
- Reports of draft-age German men in civilian clothes improving roads and bridges in occupied Poland near the Soviet border, June 1941
- Increasing volume and frequency of sounds of heavy vehicle movement on German side of the border, June 1941
- During meeting with Soviet foreign minister on June 21, German ambassador is evasive when asked about increasing rumors of pending conflict

Note that this list of relevant indicators is independent from the very specific human intelligence the Soviet leader Joseph Stalin received from sources inside the German military and diplomatic establishment, as well as multiple reports submitted to the USSR by both the US State Department and the British ambassador warning of an attack. Even without the excellent intelligence collection that Stalin ignored and the attempts by the US and British governments to alert the Soviets to the growing threat, the aforementioned indicators demonstrate a pattern of German conduct consistent with imminent attack. Given the quality of these indicators, the Germans should not have been able to achieve tactical surprise along a 1,500-mile border and successfully deceive the senior leadership of the Soviet state.

Although indicators can be qualitative in nature, as in the previous example, many commonly used indicators are expressed quantitatively. Slowing GDP growth, increasing unemployment, and a decline in consumer confidence are indicators associated with a potential recession. Indicators are also used to evaluate potential relationships that are not as obvious as economic metrics, such as the relationship between a growth in draft-age males and conflict propensity, a sharp increase in the volume of US currency in a country and the presence of drug trafficking, or a demographic bulge of people under the age of 30 and the emergence of social movements. The data tracked and measured by individual indicators can also be integrated into a variety of other analytic methods or models, such as the historical model used by the CIA to measure state power.

## BOX 12.5

### FOR EXAMPLE: INDICATORS AND THE CIA'S MODEL OF STATE POWER[11]

$Pp = (C + E + M) \times (S + W)$

> $Pp$ stands for power potential
>
> $C$ represents critical mass, calculated as territory + population
>
> $E$ is economy, calculated as natural resources + economic system
>
> $M$ stands for military power, calculated as on-hand forces + potential – time
>
> $S$ is strategic purpose, including cultural factors, presence of factions in government, alliances, intelligence capabilities, etc.
>
> $W$ evaluates will, a very complex metric involving leadership, a country's history or relations/conflict, etc.

This is the model the CIA used during the 1980s to assess a country's power. Note how it draws on several indicators, such as on-hand and potential military forces, combining them with other factors that are not easily represented as indicators, such as cultural factors and leadership.

## Systems Analysis

This technique originated as a product of an increase in methodological rigor in the sciences following World War II, during which time social scientists began importing and synthesizing concepts from other disciplines. Originating as a reaction by biologists against too much focus on individual organisms, systems theory grew of a desire to view species as linked together in interacting groups. Systems analysis has enjoyed widespread application in a wide variety of disciplines, including biology, computer science, mathematics, political science, organizational economics, sociology, and business. All forms of **systems analysis** have several key foci. First, there is an emphasis on holism—the entirety of the different constitutive parts of a system. Second, there is the interaction of the different parts of the system, which produces greater effects overall than simply adding the effects of each individual component of the system. Former senior analyst with the CIA Robert Clark captures these foci well by measuring three interdependent factors: structure, function, and process. As Clark puts it, "structure is defined by a system's components and the relationships among them. Function

---

[11]Jordan, David C. Former US ambassador to Peru. Personal communication. University of Virginia, 1997.

involves the systems effects or results produced, that is, the outputs. Process refers to the sequence of events or activities that produce results."[12]

# BOX 12.6
## FOR EXAMPLE: SYSTEMS ANALYSIS

Systems range in size from the smallest form of life (protists) to the international system (all intergovernmental organizations, nation-states, and NGOs operating at the system level). We can analyze the structure, function, and process of each system to identify how a system increases the power and/or efficiency of its constitutive parts, as well as key system vulnerabilities. Let's examine several examples in more detail.

### Micro Level: M1-A2 Abrams Main Battle Tank

When they look at a large tank like the M1, people tend to think of it as a single object. In reality, large weapons like tanks, fighters, and warships are systems, with the various components of structure, function, and process. In the case of the M1, its structure consists of its 120 mm main gun, different kinds of ammunition for that weapon (high explosive, depleted uranium armor piercing, and anti-infantry canister), its mixed ceramic/steel armor, auxiliary armament (.50 caliber and 7.62 mm machine guns), its 1,500 horsepower turbine engine, a sophisticated infrared targeting system, onboard computers, and the crew. The function of this system ties together these various components to effect various combat missions, from tank-on-tank combat to support of accompanying infantry, even a limited antiaircraft capability. The process element of the system unifies the various components of the structure, such as the link between the crew's training and the operation of the weapons and movement of the tank during battle. Analyzing the Abrams is an excellent example to illustrate how systems are more than the sum of their parts. Despite being a 40-year-old design, the M1 remains a world-class weapon system because of its superior unity of structural form, battlefield function, and process of operation.

### Meso Level: Russia's Air Defense System

Protection of a country's airspace is not limited to patrolling fighter aircraft. Instead, most advanced industrialized countries have some form of air defense, typically integrating a variety of different detection technologies and defense assets into a system. Although some components of Russia's air defense system rely on decades-old technology, it remains one of the most sophisticated in the world and, consequently, one of the hardest for attacking aircraft to penetrate.

*(Continued)*

---

[12]Clark, Robert M. *Intelligence Analysis: A Target-Centric Approach*, 5th ed. London, UK: SAGE, 2017, 39.

(Continued)

As with other systems, the Russian air defense combines structure, function, and process. The structural elements of the system include a variety of interceptor aircraft, including the SU-27, MIG-25, MIG-29, MIG-31, and, eventually, SU-57 stealth fighters. These fighters are guided by air-based radar tracking aircraft, the *Beriev* A-50 early-warning radar aircraft, and fixed ground-based systems, capable of tracking targets hundreds of kilometers away. Ground-based tracking systems include the advanced "Sunflower" low-frequency, over-the-horizon radar system that has a limited capability to detect stealth aircraft. The tracking radars are linked to a variety of surface-to-air missile (SAM) platforms, arranged in a series of layers, with the outer rim guarded by S-200 and S-400 SAMs reaching out to 800 km and more localized weapons designed to protect fixed positions, such as the *Pantsir* S-1, which has both antiaircraft guns and missiles. Sea-based *Sovremenny* class guided missile destroyers also contribute to both tracking and SAM operations, albeit with much less sophistication than US Aegis-equipped missile cruisers and destroyers. In this context, the function of the Russian air defense system would describe how the many components of the system are deployed against different kinds of threats. The process element of the system would emphasize how the system is managed via its computer and communications components, referred to as C⁴ISR by the US military—command, control, communications, computers, intelligence, surveillance, and reconnaissance.

## Macro Level: International Market for Mortgage-Backed Securities

One of the most complex systems ever devised is the international market for mortgage-backed securities (MBS), which were valued at more than $9.7 trillion in 2019.[13] But this figure belies the total amount of money tied to MBS, which due to the derivatives market associated with it is probably greater by many factors. The mortgage markets collapsed as a result of these financial instruments, known as collateralized debt obligations (CDOs), triggering the Great Recession in 2008.

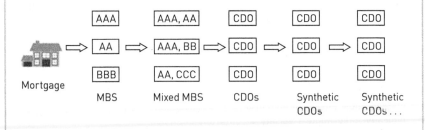

---

[13]Trefis Team. "Mortgage Backed Securities Held by US Commercial Banks Surpasses $2 Trillion Cause for Concern." *Forbes*, December 9, 2019. https://www.forbes.com/sites/greatspeculations/2019/12/09/mortgage-backed-securities-held-by-us-commercial-banks-surpasses-2-trillion-cause-for-concern/#48cd524f4358.

An individual buyer purchases a home by obtaining a mortgage from a bank. After the purchase, thousands of home mortgages are bundled together by banks into "tranches," which are then evaluated for their risk by credit-rating agencies such as Standard & Poor's and Moody's. These ratings range from AAA, the best, to CCC, junk. These tranches are then sold as securities (MBS) that may be purchased by large institutions, such as other banks, or by individuals. As the mortgage market expanded in the early 2000s, more people bought homes who would not normally qualify for a loan. To increase profits, banks increasingly mixed homes with different ratings into tranches so as to make more MBS products—AAA mortgages were mixed with AA and even CCC mortgages. But the ratings agencies made no effort to evaluate these mixed tranches differently, granting MBS products with large blocks of CCC mortgages an AAA rating. Moreover, because mortgages were considered one of the safest forms of investments, MBS products became highly leveraged, with banks creating CDOs, essentially bets by investors on what the value of an MBS truly was, and then other banks buying these CDOs and repackaging them for subsequent sale, "synthetic CDOs," bets on the investor bets. This CDO chain often exceeded by many factors the original face value of the MBS, which itself was overvalued because of the mixed tranches. Thus, an MBS bond might have a face value of $25 and result in synthetic CDOs with a price of $300 or more.

Large banks and financial services firms such as Lehman Brothers and Goldman Sachs bought and sold hundreds of billions of dollars of MBS and CDOs, often with little to no attention as to the attendant risk they were assuming. Moreover, they kept increasing their lending to homebuyers in an effort to keep increasing their pool of MBS, frequently lending to buyers with inadequate income to meet their payments. As the riskier mortgages in the MBS tranches failed because homebuyers could not make their mortgage payments, this started a cascading chain of failures that made it impossible for some firms, such as Lehman, to meet their obligations to investors who had purchased MBS and CDOs. Several very large lending institutions went bankrupt, others were purchased at bargain-basement prices, and thousands of small regional banks failed. The systemic collapse of the lending sector triggered a massive global recession, and millions of people lost their jobs and homes.

Although the MBS market lacks the main gun of the M1 or the fleet of advanced fighter aircraft in the Russian air defense system, it nevertheless has more destructive power than either. The damage inflicted on the world economy totaled in excess of $15 trillion, making financial systems like MBS worth analyzing as intelligence targets because of their potential to alter the global power structure.

Systems analysis has many advantages. Because it forces analysts to consider group and individual actors as part of larger, synthetic wholes, we are more likely to include relevant drivers for behavior than if we approached them as atomistic or self-contained factors. Moreover, systems analysis also allows us to view effects caused by

Staff Sgt. Austin Berner, US Army, January 29, 2020

**PHOTO 12.1** M1-A2 Main Battle Tank.[14]

the interaction of such factors in the system that make the system as a whole greater than the sum of its parts. This allows us to explain why some militaries are able to prevail over opponents with better weapons and greater numbers, as was the case with the German Army against the French in 1940. German tanks had less armor and lower-powered guns than those of the French, while the French Army had more tanks, artillery, and men than the Germans as well. The *Wehrmacht* prevailed because its men and weapons platforms were part of a much better system—it fought using combined arms tactics that integrated air power, armor, and artillery using modern radio. Conversely, systems analysis can also explain why complex, modern systems fail to prevail over less sophisticated adversaries.[15] Finally, systems analysis can draw our attention to the potential risks involved in catastrophic system failures, such as accidents at nuclear power plants or the destruction of several US space shuttles.[16]

---

[14]Berner, Austin, Army Staff Sgt. "Tank Trail." US Department of Defense, January 29, 2020. https://www.defense.gov/observe/photo-gallery/igphoto/2002243698/.

[15]Connable, Ben, et al. *Will to Fight: Analyzing, Modeling, and Simulating the Will to Fight of Military Units.* Santa Monica, CA: RAND, 2018.

[16]See Perrow, Charles. *Normal Accidents: Living With High-Risk Technologies.* Princeton, NJ: Princeton University Press, 1999.

## Case Studies

Although social scientists and intelligence officers have historically understood this technique very differently, one of the oldest analytic methods used by intelligence officers is the **case study**. More recently, the US IC has shown greater interest in applying the approaches used by social scientists. This technique can be useful in hypothesis testing and generation as well as evaluating cause and effect. Case studies examine one or more instances of a phenomenon in depth, describing and probing the case's various components. When more than one case is examined, cross-case comparisons are performed to reveal shared patterns in the features of the cases, significant pattern breaks across cases, and potential causes for different outcomes. Case studies can be used to analyze large transformations, such as the collapse of an empire or the evolution of an economic system.[17] Conversely, the case study method can be applied to analyzing a single nation-state, a business, a terrorist organization, or even an individual person. In the US IC, case studies of prominent political, military, economic, and cultural leaders are often conducted to evaluate medical and/or psychological issues that may affect how they make decisions and the potential impact on US interests.

Case studies can be performed in several different ways. In the case of the CIA's Medical and Psychological Analysis Center, evaluating the health and psychology of leaders involves technical methods specific to the fields of medicine and psychology.[18] However, analysis of states or other organizations is more directly related to conventional tools used by social scientists and intelligence analysts. In a seminal chapter, prominent political scientist Harry Eckstein identified five different kinds of case studies presented as narratives.[19] Idiographic case studies are rich descriptions of the configuration of a case. The second kind of case study, disciplined configurative, applies findings from previous case studies to look for continuity or discontinuity across cases. Heuristic case studies are exploratory in nature, intended to probe a case to generate new insights for other subsequent researchers to follow up on with more rigorous methods. A plausibility probe is an attempt to apply a new concept to a case, to ask "What if?" Finally, critical case studies involve testing concepts or patterns on a case that is fundamentally important to the research question. For example, if an analyst was attempting to forecast the likelihood of a war breaking out between several very powerful states, studying the two world wars—the archetypal examples of Great Power wars—might reveal potential causal drivers and crisis dynamics in the present case.

---

[17]See, for example, Pierson, Paul. "Big, Slow-Moving, and . . . Invisible: Macro-Social Processes in the Study of Comparative Politics." In *Comparative-Historical Analysis in the Social Sciences*, edited by James Mahoney and Dietrich Rueschemeyer. Cambridge, UK: Cambridge University Press, 2003.

[18]Clemente, Jonathan D. "CIA's Medical and Psychological Analysis Center (MPAC) and the Health of Foreign Leaders." *International Journal of Intelligence and Counterintelligence* 19, no. 3 (2006): 385–423.

[19]Eckstein, Harry. "Case Study and Theory in Political Science." In *Handbook of Political Science*, edited by Fred Greene and Nelson Polsby. Reading, MA: Addison-Wesley, 1975.

Eckstein's case study typology remains useful. However, more recent work in qualitative methods in the social sciences has yielded additional ways to perform case studies, from the causal mechanisms approach, which identifies environmental, cognitive, and relational drivers, to process tracing, a form of temporal sequencing at the micro level that reveals causes of macro-level events.[20] Of particular importance to intelligence analysts is the method of **nominal comparison** developed by University of Chicago sociologist Charles Ragin, as it anticipated the approach used in many SATs by more than 30 years.[21] Ragin applied a nominal coding scheme to the case study method, entering a 1 for "present" and 0 for "not present" for candidate causes of events across several different cases. The resulting table reveals potential configurations or combinations of causes that make an event more likely to happen.

# BOX 12.7

## FOR EXAMPLE: THE METHOD OF NOMINAL COMPARISON

Let's take a closer look at Charles Ragin's method of controlled cross-case comparison. The nominal method of comparison can serve a heuristic function, as it is utilized in Table 12.1, or to evaluate causality, albeit with a larger sample population. Cases are compared using a common set of potential causal variables, which are coded using a Boolean method, "1" for present and "0" for not present. For the research question "What causes revolution?" three important cases are examined. Relevant variables to be tested are derived from scholarly research trends on the subject. For example, the hypothesis that revolutions are liberal in nature derives

**TABLE 12.1 ■ Causes of Revolution: A Nominal Comparison**

| | Peasant revolt? | Liberal? | War? | Relative deprivation (poverty)? | Ethnic conflict? | Elite led? |
|---|---|---|---|---|---|---|
| American Revolution (1775–1783) | 0 | 1 | 1 | 0 | 0 | 1 |

[20]Tilly, Charles. "Mechanisms in Political Processes." *Annual Review of Political Science* 4 (2001): 21–41; and Checkel, Jeffrey T. "Process Tracing." In *Qualitative Methods in International Relations: A Pluralist Guide*, edited by Audie Klotz and Deepa Prakash. New York, NY: Palgrave Macmillan, 2008.

[21]Ragin, Charles C. *The Comparative Method: Moving Beyond Qualitative and Quantitative Strategies*. Berkeley: University of California Press, 1987.

| | Peasant revolt? | Liberal? | War? | Relative deprivation (poverty)? | Ethnic conflict? | Elite led? |
|---|---|---|---|---|---|---|
| French Revolution (1789–1799) | 1 | 1 | 1 | 1 | 0 | 1 |
| Russian Revolution (1917–1923) | 1 | 0 | 1 | 1 | 1 | 1 |
| Score | 2 | 2 | 3 | 2 | 1 | 3 |

from Hannah Arendt's *On Revolution*, while the argument that mass peasant revolts cause revolutions comes largely from Theda Skocpol's *States and Social Revolutions*, one of the most widely cited books in the history of social science.

As we can see, several patterns emerge. For the majority of these three cases, ethnic conflict does not seem to play much of a role. However, both war and leadership by elites are potential causes that are present in all three. Subsequently, investigation can be performed to tease out the specific dynamics via process tracing or another method to more directly tie causes to outcomes. Similarly, a larger universe of cases can be evaluated using the nominal method. Analysis of a dozen or more cases will probably yield much greater variation in the summary scores, lending greater validity to any causal inferences made from the resultant patterns.

Ragin's Boolean method has the virtue of simplicity and ease of use. Yet unlike coding schemes that have more than two values for each variable, Ragin's model does not handle ambiguity very well. For example, in the table, "war" is coded as present in all three important historical examples of revolution. But in the case of the American Revolution, France and Spain did not declare war on Great Britain until 1778 and 1779, respectively. Thus "war" as a variable might be better measured in a coding scheme with more than two values—that is, as ordinal data. Nevertheless, familiarity with Ragin's model allows for easy transition to the use of SATs, some of which draw on outside experts to build a knowledge base and use a similar coding scheme.

## Quantitative Approaches

As you have learned from previous chapters, intelligence involves the conversion of information that is collected into a finished product disseminated to decision makers. This process is distinguishable from conventional policy analysis in several ways. First, it involves some information that is secret. Second, the question being asked may involve a level of uncertainty and/or risk that is different from regular policy issues.

Third, and most importantly, if the question being asked can be answered via conventional analytic tools from the social and/or natural sciences, then tasking the US IC is unnecessary. Every time an intelligence organization employs its assets, be they human or technical, it runs the risk of revealing sources and methods to adversaries.

All of these considerations relate to the analytic tools commonly used to evaluate data that are collected. Statistical analysis requires large volumes of information involving many cases, commonly referred to as large-$N$ research, with $N$ representing the number of cases in a sample of a population. The smallest $N$ from which we can make inferences that are generalizable to a larger population from which the sample was derived is 30. Even then, having hundreds, if not thousands, of observations is preferable, as both the internal and external validity of findings are greatly enhanced by larger samples. From these large samples, researchers can run bivariate analysis (chi-square), logit, probit, linear regression, time-series, and other statistical methods to estimate relationships between variables. Some of these techniques have been used to support the analysis of elections, conflict dynamics, content analysis of speeches, and other political intelligence at the CIA for nearly 50 years.[22] However, for some questions related to intelligence, we simply cannot achieve a sample size of 30, let alone hundreds. These kinds of topics often necessitate the use of qualitative analytic methods. Yet as noted at the outset of this chapter, intelligence collection has evolved over the past several decades, magnifying the role of **quantitative techniques** some agencies have been using for decades. The volume and the nature of data have changed significantly, with many more indicators of social behavior being used to derive inferences about general populations and to predict the behavior of individuals. These changes mean that quantitative methods are being applied to many more analytic activities in the US IC than they have been in the past.

## BOX 12.8
### FOR EXAMPLE: THE GERMAN TANK PROBLEM[23]

When US crews began encountering the German *Panzerkampfwagen* V, "Panther," they found their Shermans were markedly inferior to the German machine in terms of both firepower and armor. There was concern that if they could field the Panther

---

[22]Heuer, Richards J., Jr., ed. *Quantitative Approaches to Political Intelligence: The CIA Experience.* New York, NY: Routledge, 1978.

[23]See Statistics How To. "German Tank Problem." Accessed September 27, 2020. https://www.statisticshowto.com/german-tank-problem/; and Wikipedia. "German Tank Problem." Last edited September 3, 2020. https://en.wikipedia.org/wiki/German_tank_problem.

in sufficient numbers, US casualties would rise, and the Germans might even achieve a stalemate on the Western front. If the Panther became the dominant tank on the battlefield, this would require design of an entirely new US main battle tank to match it. Consequently, estimating production figures for the Panther became a critical task for intelligence analysts. But since they would not necessarily be able to obtain this information via human or technical collection, a basic method of statistical inference was used. Using the serial numbers from a sample population of knocked-out or captured Panthers, analysts were able to estimate German tank production as follows:

$$N = m + (m / n) - 1$$

$N$ represents the population maximum, $m$ stands for the sample maximum, and $n$ is the sample size. Let's say we have 10 captured Panthers with the serial numbers 9, 23, 44, 52, 64, 88, 91, 103, 176, and 200. This results in $N = 200 + (200/10) - 1$, yielding 219. Thus from our sample we can conclude that the population maximum (i.e., the total estimated Panthers produced) is 219.

In the historical case, Allied intelligence officers estimated that the Germans could produce approximately 1,400 Panthers a month if they devoted the entirety of their tank production capacity to the Panther. However, after collecting battlefield serial number data for several months, intelligence analysts used the equation to generate an estimate. The result was a production estimate of a maximum of 246 Panthers per month. After the war, data obtained from German armaments records indicated the actual figure was 245 machines per month, remarkably close to the statistical estimate.

One area in which quantitative methods are increasingly applied is **"Big Data,"** the accumulation of enormous amounts of information about individuals, including consumer purchases, tax payments, marital and dating history, friends, professional connections, internet browsing history, arrest record, travel, and thousands of other data points. Integrating these data and converting them into predictive models is a complex undertaking. Several examples of the US IC's adaptation to Big Data include the ODNI's Disruptive Technologies Office, the National Counterterrorism Center's Terrorist Identities Datamart Environment, the NSA's Special Source Operations collection program, the Federal Bureau of Investigation's Terrorist Screening Database, and the CIA's recent establishment of the Directorate of Digital Innovation. Moreover, increasing receptivity on the part of the IC to new methods has resulted in improvements in analysis derived from the decision sciences. The IC now has two well-funded programs it can draw on that directly engage advances made by academics, think tanks, and the private sector. The Department of Defense (DOD) runs the Minerva Research Initiative, which supports research by civilian academics and scholars at military-run educational institutions to advance analytic methods used to support security policy.[24] Similarly, the ODNI sponsors the Intelligence Advanced Research Projects Activity (IARPA), which looks for ways to apply the latest advances in the social and natural sciences, as well as technical developments in the private sector.[25] Case in point is the IARPA-supported **Good Judgment Project (GJP)**. Created and managed by University of Pennsylvania psychology professor Philip Tetlock, GJP teaches people from a wide variety of backgrounds how to become "Superforecasters." Utilizing a few simple techniques from statistics, psychology, and economics, Tetlock's students have competed in analytic forecasting tournaments with members of the US IC with access to top-secret/sensitive compartmented information. Using only OSINT and Tetlock's techniques, the Superforecasters have consistently outperformed IC-trained analytic teams.[26] Moreover, Tetlock's students have methods to analyze where they went wrong and to improve their forecasting accuracy over time, again relying on insights from statistics. As Tetlock cheekily puts it, "Superforecasters are perpetual beta."[27]

Some scholars of intelligence are worried that the leadership of the US IC has embraced Big Data too readily and may be easily persuaded that quantitative approaches to intelligence analysis should supplant extant analytic tools. As Gill and Phythian succinctly put it, "data evangelism, if it may be called that, is potentially dangerous."[28] Their skepticism is well founded. In the years immediately following the 9/11 attacks, retired admiral and former national security adviser during the Reagan administration James Poindexter attempted to create the Total Information Awareness (TIA) Program under the auspices of the NSA. TIA was intended to integrate *all* of the information in a given country—every consumer purchase, every email, every phone call. It was data mining in the furtherance of surveillance that was unprecedented in scale. It was also completely beyond the capabilities of the US IC to integrate all of the data in a society, which requires a digital infrastructure that essentially duplicates the computing capacity of every private sector and government terminal. TIA was also a surveillance program way beyond the legal structure of the US Constitution, a program that paid no attention to the Bill of Rights.

However, if one looks carefully at many of the legal surveillance programs that have been introduced by the US IC over the past two decades, many integrate all kinds of collection activities that were never considered before. IC programs analyze how people walk in public places, facial recognition software, and other biometric indicators

[24]Minerva Research Initiative. Accessed September 27, 2020. https://minerva.defense.gov/.

[25]See Office of the Director of National Intelligence. "IARPA." Accessed September 27, 2020. https://www.dni.gov/index.php/careers/special-programs/iarpa.

[26]Tetlock, Philip E., and Dan Gardner. *Superforecasting: The Art and Science of Prediction*. New York, NY: Broadway Books, 2015. For more information on how you can become a Superforecaster, see Good Judgment Inc. "Public Superforecasts." Accessed September 27, 2020. https://goodjudgment.com/.

[27]Tetlock and Gardner, *Superforecasting*, 174.

[28]Gill and Phythian, *Intelligence in an Insecure World*, 70.

that relate to predicting behavior. In a sharp break from prior wartime analytic methods, Task Force 714 employed integrated databases that tied everything from vehicle license plates to geospatial data to uncover hidden terrorist networks in Iraq.[29] Several IC activities attempt to integrate artificial intelligence with human analysis, such as the DOD-funded Semantic Web program at the University of Maryland, a terrorist database system that combines data visualization with machine learning functions.[30] "Crisis informatics" has been deployed by scholars at both universities and think tanks to analyze a wide variety of subjects, from how social media activity affects responses to natural disasters to how Russian information operations involving 66,000 tweets across 8,500 accounts exploited existing divisions in US society during the 2016 election campaign.[31] Agent-based modeling is being used to improve forecasting in strategic intelligence via computer simulations.[32]

Quantitative methods have been used for decades in the US IC—from large-$N$ work at the CIA in the 1960s to game theoretic models that accurately predicted the Soviet invasion of Afghanistan in 1979 when no country expert in the IC believed such an attack was likely. More recent applications of these methods show how useful they can be, and the emergence of Big Data has amplified the role quantitative methods will play in the community. In one sense, the legacy of TIA lives on, albeit in a greatly disaggregated form. Moreover, the enormous analytic gains derived from such methodological advances should not be ignored out of a misplaced belief that intelligence cannot use some of the more advanced data analysis techniques from the social sciences. Students interested in working in the IC in the future had best prepare themselves to master a wide variety of analytic skills, from traditional techniques to the latest quantitative approaches.

## Red Teams

**Red Teams** are a form of challenge analysis, sometimes referred to as "alternative analysis."[33] Red Teams have been around in the US military for a long time, employed

---

[29]Schultz, Richard. "Post-9/11 Wartime Intelligence." *Intelligence and National Security* 33, no. 7 (2018): 974–998.

[30]Manes, Aaron, Jennifer Golbeck, and James Hendler. "Semantic Web and Target-Centric Intelligence: Building Flexible Systems That Foster Cooperation." Accessed September 27, 2020. https://citeseerx.ist.psu.edu/viewdoc/download?doi=10.1.1.80.8050&rep=rep1&type=pdf.

[31]Palen, Leysia, and Kenneth M. Anderson. "Crisis Informatics—New Data for Extraordinary Times." *Science* 353, no. 6296 (July 15, 2016): 224–225. https://science.sciencemag.org/content/353/6296/224; and Starbird, Kate. "The Surprising Nuance Behind the Russian Troll Strategy." *Medium*, October 20, 2018. https://medium.com/s/story/the-trolls-within-how-russian-information-operations-infiltrated-online-communities-691fb969b9e4.

[32]Frank, Aaron. "Computational Social Science and Intelligence Analysis." *Intelligence and National Security* 32, no. 5 (2017): 579–599.

[33]George, Roger Z. "The Problem of Analytical Mindsets: Alternative Analysis." *International Journal of Intelligence and Counterintelligence* 17, no. 3 (2004): 385–404.

to use an enemy's tactics and equipment in war games against American soldiers. Red Teams are still used at places like the National Training Center at Fort Irwin, California, where the 11th Armored Cavalry Regiment plays the role of the "opposing force" to help prepare US soldiers for war. However, in contemporary parlance in the US IC, adopting the mindset or mentality of an adversary, in essence to become the enemy, is an SAT called Red Hat analysis. Red Teams are used in the US IC to criticize intelligence assessments by employing the Red Team's knowledge of adversary cultural and organizational practices without necessarily assuming the role of the adversary. Although it requires some knowledge of an adversary, it is not a form of role-playing and therefore can be accomplished without necessarily having years of education covering the enemy country. Red Teams try to think like the enemy without submerging themselves completely in the role.

Like all challenge analysis techniques, Red Teams reduce the effect of prior mindsets or beliefs about how adversaries think, what they want, and the means by which they will try to achieve their objectives. Red Teams are a brake on cognitive biases and can help detect errors in measurement or emphasis in techniques previously used by an analytic team as it reaches the end of the assessment process. They are used by a wide variety of organizations and in a similarly diverse set of contexts. Red Teams have been employed to check for vulnerabilities in nuclear power plants, as a critical thinking activity by senior military leaders, and to test the rollout of complicated government programs.[34] Although Red Teams can be very useful, as is the case with all analytic techniques the users must believe in their efficacy and accept their findings. This can result in analysts returning to the drawing board, discarding days, even months, of work. Moreover, the senior leadership of organizations must also be invested in challenge analysis, creating an environment in which analytic teams are encouraged to use Red Teams and allowed to "fail." However, it has historically been difficult both for analytic teams to accept the findings of challenge analysis and for upper management to afford them time to fix problems or shortcomings identified by Red Teams or other techniques.

## Structured Analytic Techniques and Their Critics

During the 1990s, analysts at the CIA and DOD began working on reforming the methods used to produce intelligence assessments. Following 9/11, the passage of the Intelligence Reform and Terrorism Prevention Act (IRTPA) in 2004, and the establishment of community-wide analytic standards by the ODNI, these efforts accelerated. By 2010, **Structured Analytic Techniques (SAT)** had become commonly used across the community, first in the form of analyst training at the CIA's Sherman Kent School and the subsequent publication of the CIA's 2009 *Tradecraft*

---

[34]Zenko, Micah. *Red Team: How to Succeed by Thinking Like the Enemy.* New York, NY: Basic Books, 2015, xxiv–xxv.

*Primer*, then eventually via a book by Randolph Pherson and Richards Heuer that is required reading throughout the US IC.[35] Several of the methods described earlier predate SATs by decades, such as scenarios and Red Teams, yet have been incorporated into the broader SAT family. Other SATs are of very recent vintage, designed specifically to tie together other methods. The purpose of SATs is to formalize the process of intelligence analysis. SATs create a structure that forces analysts to clearly state their ideas and to evaluate them in a consistent, measurable format. SATs are an interlinked family of techniques, with idea generation techniques designed to fit in with specific hypothesis-testing methods, reducing the rate of error in shifting from one method to the next. They are easy to understand and learn, using vocabulary that is simple and straightforward. Their widespread adoption makes inter-agency analytic cooperation much more effective, reducing the impact of different organizations' analytic cultures. Because they are systematic, they may also help reduce the effects of cognitive and organizational biases. A perfect example of how SATs are intended to function is **Analysis of Competing Hypotheses (ACH)**, a method designed to eliminate less plausible explanations for events.

## BOX 12.9
### FOR EXAMPLE: ANALYSIS OF COMPETING HYPOTHESES

ACH allows us to probe the plausibility of different hypotheses. Consider the following hypothetical scenario and the associated known facts.

1. The US secretary of state (SECSTATE) collapses at a 2022 United Nations conference on nuclear disarmament. SECSTATE is taken to a hospital, lingers in agony for 24 hours, then dies of total system failure. Assume relative continuity between the current world situation and 2022.

2. Cause of death is determined to be poison, specifically the radioactive metal polonium.

3. Russia has used polonium as a poison to kill its political opponents, including the prominent assassination of former FSB officer Alexander Litvinenko in Great Britain in 2006.

4. Russia, China (PRC), Israel, North Korea (DPRK), and Iran were all opposed to US proposals fielded at this conference.

*(Continued)*

---

[35]Heuer, Richards J., Jr., and Randolph H. Pherson. *Structured Analytic Techniques for Intelligence Analysis*, 2nd ed. Los Angeles, CA: CQ Press, 2015.

(Continued)

5. The polonium was of a type much less refined than the Russian material that was used to kill Litvinenko.

6. Department of Energy radiological scans indicated polonium was most likely administered to SECSTATE at a formal dinner the evening before. Attending legations included France, the United Kingdom, Russia, China, India, Israel, and Japan.

| TABLE 12.2 ■ ACH of SECSTATE Poisoning | | | | | | | | | |
|---|---|---|---|---|---|---|---|---|---|
| Evidence | Credibility | Relevance | H1 | H2 | H3 | H4 | H5 | H6 | H7 |
| E1: Has previously used polonium to kill opponents | High | High | CC | N/A | N/A | N/A | N/A | N/A | N/A |
| E2: Polonium administered during state dinner | Medium | Medium | C | C | C | C | C | C | C |
| E3: Attended state dinner | High | Medium | C | C | C | I | I | II | II |
| E4: Under US-led sanctions regime | High | Medium | CC | II | II | CC | CC | N/A | N/A |
| E5: Opposed to US proposals | Medium | Medium | CC | CC | C | CC | CC | C | C |
| E6: Willing to risk consequences of such aggression | Low | High | C | II | II | C | CC | C | I |
| E7: Lacks ability to influence US with other methods | Low | High | C | II | II | C | CC | CC | C |
| E8: Willing to make appear other state did it | Low | High | I | II | II | C | CC | II | C |

H1: Russia killed SECSTATE

H2: China killed SECSTATE

H3: Israel killed SECSTATE

H4: Iran killed SECSTATE

H5: DPRK killed SECSTATE

H6: Nonstate actor killed SECSTATE

H7: Other state killed SECSTATE

Credibility and relevance weights are assigned to each piece of evidence, assessed in terms of its quality and relationship to different hypotheses. For example, in Table 12.2, weights of "High" were assigned to E1, E3, and E4, which are known facts. However, weights of "Low" were assigned to E6, E7, and E8 because these are assumptions, not empirically observed data. The degree to which each piece of evidence comports with a given hypothesis is measured as CC (*strongly consistent*), C (*consistent*), I (*inconsistent*), II (*strongly inconsistent*), or N/A (*not applicable*). Evaluating various hypotheses in this manner allows us to graphically see in one place the relative likelihood of hypotheses alongside each other. ACH software also automatically generates inconsistency scores, allowing us to dismiss hypotheses that are comparatively weak. ACH should result in most hypotheses being discarded, leaving a relatively narrow band of possible explanations for an event that can be further explored using other analytic techniques. For example, even though the Chinese legation attended the state dinner, the likelihood that China killed SECSTATE is low. The PRC is not under a US sanctions regime, has other means to influence US policy that are less risky and aggressive, and would not want to make it appear as if another state carried out this crime if it wanted to change US policies toward it. Given these scores, analysts should dismiss the other hypotheses and further investigate potential explanations involving Russia, the DPRK, and Iran.

Many of these techniques similar to SATs have been used for years in contexts far removed from intelligence analysis. Ragin's Boolean approach to comparative case studies discussed earlier anticipated SATs like ACH and Paired Comparison by more than three decades. Budding intelligence officers would do well to acquaint themselves with these diverse applications, particularly with regard to their relative efficacy.[36] This is particularly important, as some scholars have noted that SATs tend to water down the rigor of the social science methods from which they are derived—they are in effect "'social science for dummies.'"[37]

Moreover, even as they have enjoyed widespread adoption in the US IC, SATs have been subject to sustained criticism from a variety of sources. Despite their ostensible

---

[36]Coulthart, Stephen. "An Evidence-Based Evaluation of 12 Core Structured Analytic Techniques." *International Journal of Intelligence and Counterintelligence* 30, no. 2 (2017): 368–391.

[37]Quoted in Gentry, John A. "The 'Professionalization' of Intelligence Analysis: A Skeptical Perspective." *International Journal of Intelligence and Counterintelligence* 29, no. 4 (2016), 648.

utility in improving analytic acuity, SATs might result in the paradoxical effect of *less* diagnostic accuracy. Analysts' awareness of the restraining effect of SATs may cause them to exaggerate the values of relevant drivers or indicators, much as consciousness of the devil's advocate at the end of analysis may cause analysts to "take uncalculated risks in formulating their intelligence assessments."[38] Similarly, SATs that reduce one bias may at the same time cause other biases to become more prominent. Citing the **"bipolar nature"** of cognitive biases, several prominent researchers note SATs could reduce the problem of overconfidence and just as readily replace that bias with underconfidence.[39]

Even more damning, the central premise of SATs is that they reduce what Heuer and Pherson call "system 1 thinking" in lieu of "system 2 thinking." In this context, system 1 represents "fast, unconscious, and intuitive thinking," while system 2 represents "thoughtful reasoning."[40] For Heuer and Pherson, the primary source of error in intelligence analysis is system 1 thinking. However, because intuition and imagination are closely related, if SATs do indeed actively suppress analyst reliance on system 1 thinking, then they are also probably reducing the ability of analysts to be creative. But if we are to anticipate attacks by adversaries against the United States and its allies, **analyst creativity** is fundamentally important. As the 9/11 Commission put it, the success of al-Qaeda's operation was the result of a "failure of imagination." One might consider the failure of the IC to forecast the rise of the Islamic State or Russian information operations against the US election system in a similar light.

Although many of these critiques are quite strong, for a variety of reasons SATs appear to be here to stay. First, they were designed by several figures who were senior members of the US IC, and these techniques have had broad support from the IC leadership since their introduction. As a result, 16 of 17 agencies have adopted them, with only the Bureau of Intelligence and Research (INR) holding out. Second, in the IRTPA, Congress made the use of some of these methods mandatory, specifically challenge analysis. Third, the massive crisis in confidence in intelligence analysis that made analytic reform possible was 9/11 and Iraq weapons of mass destruction, both of which highlighted analytic weaknesses many SAT supporters had been drawing attention to for decades. It may take another exogenous shock, with SATs failing to perform adequately, to precipitate rethinking their use. Finally, although some of these techniques are of dubious value for ostensibly sophisticated analysts (Venn diagrams are a product of elementary school math curricula), other SATs seem to provide value added—they work well compared to their predecessors.

---

[38]Pascovich, Eyal. "The Devil's Advocate in Intelligence: The Israeli Experience." *Intelligence and National Security* 33, no. 6 (2018): 856.

[39]Chang, Welton, Elisabeth Berdini, David R. Mandel, and Philip E. Tetlock. "Restructuring Structured Analytic Techniques in Intelligence." *Intelligence and National Security* 33, no. 3 (2018): 337–356.

[40]Heuer and Pherson, *Structured Analytic Techniques for Intelligence Analysis*, 5.

## PRESENTING FINDINGS: THE STRUCTURE AND VOICE OF WRITTEN ANALYTIC PRODUCTS

All forms of writing have a style and structure that reflect the norms and expectations of the larger field of inquiry, academic discipline, or profession to which they are connected. Intelligence analysis is no exception. In this section, we will review some of the characteristics of effective writing for intelligence officers. Both internally circulated classified reports and material distributed to policymakers follow these standards. Students who wish to work in the US IC must learn how to write using this style and structure.

### Voice

Intelligence reports are in the **active voice**. Subjects and verbs are directly connected. Qualifying language or modifiers are kept to minimum. In contrast, **passive voice** employs language that indirectly describes action. Passive voice frequently includes qualifiers or other expressions that writers may think makes their prose more precise. In reality, it tends to reduce the clarity of the claims and the reader's confidence in the knowledge of the writer. For example, an intelligence analyst might start an estimate with the phrase "it can be assessed." This seems straightforward enough. However, the addition of "can" logically leads to the question "But is it?" The phrase "we assess" is much clearer and reflects the proper tone of intelligence writing, which is clinical, unadorned, and active voice. Subjects are treated objectively, using only modifiers that impart precise meaning. When modifiers are used, they should include the specific phrases commonly used in intelligence writing, not colloquial speech.

Figure 12.3 identifies some phrases that commonly appear in student intelligence reports or assessments. The language is passive and imprecise. Intelligence officers must not write using this style, which is unsuitable for communicating analytic findings.

**FIGURE 12.3  ■  Inappropriate Language for Intelligence Writing**

| | |
|---|---|
| "It can be assessed" | "In this assessment we will discuss" |
| "This can occur" | "I want to approach this paper" |
| "It should be estimated" | "I might assess" |

In contrast, Figure 12.4 provides a set of terms frequently mentioned in stylebooks used in the US IC to teach analysts how to present their findings in intelligence assessments.[41] The language used is active voice, distinguishes between what is known and

---

[41]For example, see Directorate of Intelligence. *Style Manual & Writer's Manual for Intelligence Publications.* Langley, VA: Central Intelligence Agency, 2011. https://fas.org/irp/cia/product/style.pdf.

what is unknown, and clearly identifies what is being predicted or interpreted. Writers using this style convey both confidence and precision, important qualities for products read by policymakers and used to make decisions.

| FIGURE 12.4 ■ Language Used in Intelligence Writing | |
|---|---|
| "We estimate that" | "We cannot judge confidently that" |
| "We judge that" | "In our judgment, if X happens, Y will result" |
| "We assess that" | "Country X's decision suggests that" |
| "We predict that" | "Country X's change in behavior indicates" |
| "We cannot dismiss" | "We cannot rule out" |

## Structure

In addition to employing a distinct voice, intelligence is organized in a manner that is different from other forms of writing. Intelligence products must follow the maxim of **BLUF**—bottom line up front. The central finding or conclusion of the product is presented in the first paragraph, ideally the first sentence. Moreover, the first section of the report summarizes all of the relevant findings, allowing consumers to understand the critical information as quickly as possible. In the digital age, decision makers are confronted with more information than ever before, as well as many more demands on their time. Although some intelligence problems are irreducibly complex, such as how to achieve peace in the Middle East, intelligence officers must do their best to reduce many of their products to a manageable length for consumers. BLUF helps achieve this. However, we must also keep in mind that some analytic products are by design lengthy, in-depth analyses of complex issues. For example, research intelligence may be used to support the production of subsequent intelligence products, such as estimates. But research intelligence is not necessarily reducible to a short report. For some intelligence research questions, to force complex findings into too short of a package may oversimplify some issues and serve to undermine decision makers' appreciation of the associated policy challenges.

In addition, written intelligence products are organized in a manner that ensures readers know the relevant time period covered in each section. Expressions such as "near- to medium-term" and "long-term" are used to identify whether the scope conditions of the report are weeks, months, or years. Moreover, effective intelligence writing specifies **information gaps**, issues in which there was insufficient collection or the nature of the target made it impossible to determine something with much certainty in the time available. Identifying information gaps is important for policymakers, as it both reduces the perception of the omniscience of intelligence and draws attention to issue areas that may require follow-up investigation, perhaps via a new venture that requires additional appropriations. Information gaps also allow intelligence analysts who inherit the project a clearly defined place to pick up where their predecessor left off. The days of intelligence officers occupying a single "desk" or area of responsibility for the duration of their careers are long over. Consequently, including information gaps reduces analytic errors due to personnel rotation. Finally, effective intelligence products specify how changes in conditions would cause a shift in the report itself. This is particularly important for intelligence estimates, as forecasts should be responsive to new information.

Intelligence writing is a delicate balance of producing material that meets the demands and time constraints of consumers while preserving analytic rigor. Intelligence officers must constantly strive to communicate their findings in a manner accessible to people unfamiliar with the subject matter and the methods used to analyze it. Effective writing is fundamentally important in intelligence products. As one former senior intelligence officer put it, "Good writing is not simply a matter of grammar, syntax, vocabulary and spelling. It reflects the quality of thinking going on inside the analyst's head better than any other measure."[42]

## CONCLUSION: PATTERNS OF RECRUITMENT AND TRAINING OF INTELLIGENCE ANALYSTS IN THE US INTELLIGENCE COMMUNITY

Following 9/11, there was an enormous increase in hiring in the US IC. Although this hiring surge declined sharply as the United States withdrew from Iraq and reduced its footprint in Afghanistan, it reinforced a previous trend emphasizing more current intelligence and less work on strategic issues. It also left in its wake a generation of analysts with considerably less experience and education than their predecessors.[43] Even intelligence analysts with doctorates were increasingly drawn from online, for-profit institutions with degrees in subjects like homeland security and education administration, not the social sciences or STEM (science, technology, engineering, and mathematics).[44] However, judging by recent job advertisements in the IC, this trend is reversing, with many analyst jobs at a variety of agencies with educational requirements one would find in a social science or intelligence studies course of study.

As we have seen in this chapter, effective intelligence analysis requires a combination of skills, ranging from specific analytic techniques to high-quality writing.

---

[42]Former national intelligence officer and CIA branch chief. Private communication with the author, July 2, 2013.

[43]Gentry, "'Professionalization' of Intelligence Analysis," 650.

[44]Arkin, William H., and Alexa O'Brien. "Doctors of Doom: What a Ph.D. Really Means in the US National Security Community." *Vice*, January 27, 2016. https://www.vice.com/en_us/article/8x3mpz/doctors-of-doom-what-a-phd-really-means-in-the-us-national-security-community-1.

However, we must be careful not to overemphasize process and methods over substantive knowledge of important regional or functional areas, such as expertise in Russian politics or missile technology. Prospective analysts need to prepare for the analytic tools of tomorrow, not just previous practices. Higher expectations may require increased "analytic agility."[45] This may take the form of increased cross-training between operations personnel and analysts, something that is already happening at the Sherman Kent School at the CIA. In this context, it is also worth noting that the majority of US IC officers do not major in intelligence studies. While the degree of study you have embarked on gives you certain advantages, intelligence studies students must also face the fact they are forgoing other programs of study that may be important in their future career. Therefore, carefully choose your minor—consider complementing a degree in intelligence with a minor in a foreign language, economics, political science, or STEM. Better yet, consider double-majoring in intelligence and a subject that will give you the substantive area studies or functional knowledge of an intelligence analyst assigned to a desk focused on that subject.

## KEY CONCEPTS

risk management   277
problem of commensurability   278
value added   278
critical thinking   280
decomposition and visualization   281
idea generation   281
scenarios and indicators   281
hypothesis generation and testing   281
falsifiable   281
assessing cause and effect   281
challenge analysis   281
conflict management   281
decomposition   281
network analysis   282
brainstorming   284
scenarios   284
indicators   286

systems analysis   288
case studies   293
nominal comparison   294
quantitative techniques   296
Big Data   297
Good Judgment Project (GJP)   298
Red Teams   299
Structured Analytic Techniques
    (SAT)   300
Analysis of Competing Hypotheses
    (ACH)   301
bipolar nature of cognitive biases   304
analyst creativity   304
active voice   305
passive voice   305
BLUF   306
information gaps   306

---

[45]Lowenthal, *Future of Intelligence*, 80.

## ADDITIONAL READING

Dahl, Erik J. "Getting Beyond Analysis by Anecdote: Improving Intelligence Analysis Through the Use of Case Studies." *Intelligence and National Security* 23, no. 5 (2017): 563–578.

Fingar, Thomas. *Reducing Uncertainty: Intelligence Analysis and National Security.* Stanford, CA: Stanford University Press, 2011.

George, Alexander L., and Andrew Bennett. *Case Studies and Theory Development in the Social Sciences.* Cambridge, MA: MIT Press, 2004.

Major, James S. *Communicating With Intelligence: Writing and Briefing for National Security,* 2nd ed. London, UK: Rowman & Littlefield, 2014.

Marrin, Stephen. "Understanding and Improving Intelligence Analysis by Learning From Other Disciplines." *Intelligence and National Security* 32, no. 5 (2017): 539–547.

National Research Council. *Intelligence Analysis for Tomorrow.* Washington, DC: National Research Council, 2011.

Omand, David. "Understanding Bayesian Thinking: Prior and Posterior Probabilities and Analysis of Competing Hypotheses in Intelligence Analysis." In *The Art of Intelligence: Simulations, Exercises, and Games,* edited by William J. Lahneman and Rubén Arcos. Lanham, MD: Rowman & Littlefield, 2014.

Prunckun, Hank. *Scientific Methods of Inquiry for Intelligence Analysis.* Lanham, MD: Rowman & Littlefield, 2014.

Sinclair, Robert S. *Thinking and Writing: Cognitive Science and Intelligence Analysis.* Washington, DC: Center for the Study of Intelligence, 2010.

# 13 THE ETHICS OF INTELLIGENCE

Jonathan M. Acuff

Following the 9/11 attacks, Vice President Dick Cheney famously remarked that the fight against al-Qaeda and other Islamic extremists would require operating "through sort of the dark side . . . spend[ing] time in the shadows."[1] Yet apart from the halting attempt by the Clinton administration to limit recruitment of assets to people without ties to criminal organizations, US intelligence officers have always operated with their peers and competitors close in the "shadows" of international politics. As former secretary of state Dean Rusk appropriately characterized the nature of the Cold War, "'it was a mean, back-alley struggle.'"[2] One of the missions of intelligence officers operating overseas is to cultivate assets in target countries, convincing them to spy for the United States and thus commit one of the worst crimes possible—treason. And such activities are not limited to betrayal of one's country, with violations of the domestic laws of most states running from signals intelligence (SIGINT) surveillance to the US and Israeli drone assassination programs. Indeed, the purpose of intelligence collection and covert operations is explicitly to violate the laws of other countries. As one former head of MI-6 put it, "'we act within our own law. Our relationship with other people's laws is . . . interesting.'"[3] But if this is the core purpose of many, if not most, intelligence activities overseas, how, then, can we as citizens in democratic societies governed by the rule of law tolerate such behavior? Is it possible to justify such actions morally?

In this chapter we shall examine some of the ways in which we can evaluate the actions of intelligence officers from an ethical and moral perspective. As we begin this discussion, it is important to note the intrinsic complexity of examining intelligence through a moral lens. Intelligence activities can bring out the best and the worst in people, sometimes even from the same person. For example, former director of the Central Intelligence Agency (CIA) Richard Helms is rightly lauded for his refusal to cooperate with Richard Nixon's attempt to cover up the Watergate break-in, a courageous act for which he was fired. But Helms also lied under oath to Congress regarding

---

[1] eMediaMillWorks. "Vice President Cheney on NBC's 'Meet the Press.'" *The Washington Post*, September 16, 2001. https://www.washingtonpost.com/wp-srv/nation/specials/attacked/transcripts/cheney091601.html.

[2] Quoted in Gaddis, John Lewis. *George F. Kennan: An American Life*. New York, NY: Penguin, 2011, 319.

[3] Quoted in Corera, Gordon. *The Art of Betrayal: The Secret History of MI6*. New York, NY: Pegasus Books, 2012, 3.

the CIA's role in the violent overthrow of the democratically elected Chilean president Salvador Allende in 1973.[4]

In this context, note that we will focus on the ethical choices made by individuals, not determining which nation-states are "good" or "evil." Both political philosophers and scholars of international relations have long noted the difficulty in defining states as good or evil, noting that ostensibly liberal republics are guilty of egregious acts of imperialism and are no less war-prone than authoritarian states, albeit not against each other.[5] Moreover, the unit of analysis in moral philosophy is the individual, not the state, a disciplinary norm reinforced by the requirement enshrined in the 2019 National Intelligence Strategy that all intelligence officers follow ethical standards of conduct in the course of their duties.[6] One of the core ethical challenges facing intelligence officers is the **politicization** of intelligence. Politicization takes several forms, from misrepresentation of intelligence by politicians to support a particular policy choice to the biasing of intelligence analysis by an analyst to favor a particular policy. It is difficult to prevent politicians from abusing their power and politicizing intelligence. But intelligence officers as individuals have a professional ethical obligation both not to support such efforts by politicians and to provide unbiased, objective work in the service of the US national interest.

Ethics as a professional demand for the US intelligence community (IC) is all the more important because of the inherent limitations of the judicial oversight process over the intelligence community. Although the Foreign Intelligence Surveillance Court ostensibly prevents illegal intelligence collection in the United States, from 1979 to 2017 it rejected less than 1 percent of the applications solicited by the US IC, suggesting the court acts more like a rubber stamp than a protector of the Constitution. Recent revelations concerning sloppy procedure by agents of the Federal Bureau of Investigation (FBI) in their applications for Foreign Intelligence Surveillance Act authorization are similarly troubling.[7] Such challenges are not surprising for scholars of administrative law, who have long noted consistent problems with judicial oversight of government agencies.[8] In short, we must have a basis for legitimating intelligence activities that goes beyond simplistic characterizations of good or evil and reliance on US courts. This is particularly important for strategic intelligence operations, which

---

[4]Herken, Gregg. *The Georgetown Set: Friends and Rivals in Cold War Washington*. New York, NY: Vintage Books, 2015, 375.

[5]See Arendt, Hannah. *The Origins of Totalitarianism*. New York, NY: Harcourt Brace, 1948; and Doyle, Michael W. "Liberalism in World Politics." *American Political Science Review* 80, no. 4 (December 1986): 1151–1169.

[6]Office of the Director of National Intelligence. *National Intelligence Strategy of the United States*. Washington, DC: Office of the Director of National Intelligence, 2019, 31.

[7]Savage, Charlie. "Problems in FBI Wiretap Applications Go Beyond Trump Aide Surveillance, Review Finds." *The New York Times*, March 31, 2020. https://www.nytimes.com/2020/03/31/us/politics/fbi-fisa-wiretap-trump.html.

[8]Shapiro, Martin. *Who Guards the Guardians? Judicial Control of Administration*. Athens: University of Georgia Press, 1988.

take place outside of US borders and are thus not always subject to federal law. Morality and the law are related, but not equivalent, domains.

We proceed in the following manner. First, we examine several traditions in moral and political philosophy of potential relevance to analyzing the conduct of intelligence officers. Next, we apply these tools to analyze several examples of such activities with potential moral challenges. We conclude with a brief discussion of the ethical demands on intelligence officers with regard to conduct, requirements that far exceed those of most professions.

## OF ETHICS AND MORAL SYSTEMS

Before we dive too deeply into philosophy, we must make an important terminological distinction between *morality* and *ethics*. **Morality** refers to a system of values with requirements for the individual to follow to be a good person. **Ethics** is the application of these moral principles in specific contexts. For example, almost all moral systems hold that lying is wrong. However, there are situations in which lying is ethical, such as when undercover police officers interact with the criminals they are surveilling and must lie to preserve their cover and/or to elicit information of probative value. In this chapter, we will examine only secular moral systems, as almost all religions are exclusionist—their demand for adherence requires rejection of competing religions. In a secular democracy, the only legitimate means by which conduct can be evaluated ethically is through a secular moral system, as most secular systems allow adherents of many religious faiths to follow their principles without demanding the exclusion of other faiths. Since the 18th-century period known as the Enlightenment, a time marked by philosophers who strongly influenced Thomas Jefferson and the other founders of the United States, ethicists have focused on the use of rationalism, not religion, to examine and weigh moral and ethical questions. Consequently, this is the approach we will follow, without dismissing the value of any specific religious belief system in informing the moral conduct of its adherents.

One of the most common secular justifications given for conduct in the intelligence and national security communities is **patriotism**, loyalty to one's nation. However, patriotism as a moral justification and ethical guide is in itself insufficient. Although patriotism plays a vital role in the recruitment of new officers and getting them to serve in often austere conditions for little pay and with punishing hours, "for country" cannot be the sole moral backbone of an IC. All countries demand loyalty and invoke a higher purpose or justification for the actions of their agents. Even in Nazi Germany, its soldiers marched into battle with belt buckles emblazoned with the words *Gott mit uns* ("God is with us").[9] If all countries invoke patriotism as justification,

---

[9] On the efforts of ordinary Germans to see their country's actions as moral, even after the horrors of the Holocaust were laid bare, see Koonz, Claudia. *The Nazi Conscience*. Cambridge, MA: Harvard University Press, 2003; and Stargardt, Nicholas. *The German War*. New York, NY: Basic Books, 2015.

then it is a form of moral relativism. Moreover, invoking patriotism does not relieve individuals of responsibility for their ethical choices. Many countries, including the United States, have invoked devotion to the nation as the basis for horrific policies, including mass discrimination against ethnic and religious minorities, deportation of people from these same groups, and even genocide. The individuals who carried out these acts at the behest of their governments did not act ethically—patriotism is not a kind of moral car wash.

Alternatively, the substantive content of the beliefs of some national identities may distinguish them from others, and this plays a role in providing moral justification for intelligence. The liberal principles of freedom of speech, conscience, and religion undergird US collective identity, and actions in their defense may be more justifiable than actions undertaken with the explicit intent of oppressing others. However, in this context, students of intelligence must be cautious. By many measures, the United States is not the most democratic country in the world. Several Western democracies are much freer, less corrupt, and more devoted to protecting the health, well-being, and rights of all of their citizens than the United States.[10] The "exceptional nation" justification is poorly supported by empirical evidence, and the claim "the United States is different" is not in and of itself a convincing basis by which to justify intelligence operations.

A more sophisticated version of acting on behalf of one's state may be found in the work of Niccolò Machiavelli, author of *The Prince* and one of the founders of the modern theory of politics known as **political realism**. In his seminal work that is often misrepresented as justifying all manner of barbarity, Machiavelli draws our attention to immoral actions being potentially legitimate only in the case of service to a higher purpose, *virtu*. From Machiavelli's perspective, the highest form of *virtu* was the defense of the nation. Machiavellian logic has informed much historical and contemporary statecraft. Acting in furtherance of the state, raison d'état, guided the decisions of Cardinal Richelieu in 17th-century France and German chancellor Otto von Bismarck in the 19th century, two of the leading historical figures associated with the application of political realism to Great Power politics.[11] However, as is the case with patriotism, political realism also ultimately offers a weak case for justifying intelligence. Realism relies exclusively on the judgment of Machiavellian princes—figures unchecked by political institutions, domestic or international—to determine what is virtuous conduct. Moreover, one of the core tenets of political realism is that men are corruptible by nature, thus necessitating the guiding, ultimately manipulative figure of the prince to govern them. However, it is logically incoherent to assert that princes are somehow different—they are men, and thus they too will abuse their power in the absence of courts or legislatures that may circumscribe their efforts. Consequently, political realism is more useful as a theory of international relations—that is, in offering social

---

[10]See the annually produced report by the nongovernmental organization Freedom House, *Freedom in the World*, available from https://freedomhouse.org/report/freedom-world.

[11]See Chapter 2.

scientific predictions and explanations about individual and state behavior—than it is as a moral theory justifying that behavior.[12]

Another prominent candidate belief system for justifying intelligence activities is **Just War theory**. Associated primarily with Augustine of Hippo's 5th-century-CE formulation, a distinction is made between conduct *jus ad bellum*, the rules governing what is a legitimate reason to go to war, and *jus in bello*, the rules determining how war may be fought. For example, *jus ad bellum* holds that wars of aggression are immoral, while *jus in bello* dictates that combatants make every effort to spare innocent civilians. Just War theory is the touchstone of much discussion at US service academies and in other professional military and intelligence *fora*. It provides a useful framework for evaluating whether or not it is proper for a country to enter into war and the ethical practices for waging such a conflict in a just manner. However, Just War theory is not a useful means by which to evaluate intelligence activities for several reasons. First, most intelligence activity takes place in peacetime. The philosophical boundaries of the run-up to a war and then conduct of said war are problematically stretched when discussing peacetime operations, something that was never anticipated or intended by Just War theory's progenitors. Second, trying to stretch Just War theory into a peacetime context runs the risk of **securitizing** the relevant ethical issues, something that must be avoided in moral systems intended to govern ethical conduct that may involve violence or coercion, as in the case of a system meant to guide intelligence operations. The distinction between war and peace has blurred a great deal in recent years; an effective moral theory should not exacerbate this problem. Finally, Just War theory was formulated in a Christian context, making its transposition into a secular ethical guide problematic.[13] It was explicitly concerned with creating a moral framework specifying the conditions under which faithful Christians could engage in war.

## BOX 13.1

### FOR EXAMPLE: SECURITIZATION

Developed in the late 1990s by international relations scholars Barry Buzan, Ole Wæver, and Jaap de Wilde, securitization is the attempt to refocus a subject from its normal, nonmilitary context to the realm of security.[14] Problems are shifted

*(Continued)*

---

[12]For a discussion of the moral complexity of realism, see Williams, Michael C., ed. *Realism Reconsidered: The Legacy of Hans J. Morgenthau in International Relations*. Oxford, UK: Oxford University Press, 2007.

[13]Hatfield, Joseph M. "An Ethical Defense of Treason by Means of Espionage." *Intelligence and National Security* 32, no. 2 (2017): 198.

[14]Buzan, Barry, Ole Wæver, and Jaap de Wilde. *Security: A New Framework for Analysis*. Boulder, CO: Lynne Rienner, 1998.

(Continued)

from normal policy debates into questions of vital national security, even existence. Securitization has been a rhetorical move frequently employed by US politicians to prevent the public from learning the specifics about the consequences of policy choices or even to forestall any public debate about a policy choice. For example, in the United States, international terrorism has become thoroughly securitized, with the threat posed by al-Qaeda and the Islamic State cast in terms of the very survival of the country. However, although they can inflict harm on unarmed civilians, terrorists do not threaten the existence of powerful nation-states like the United States. Indeed, the very use of terrorism as a tactic indicates weakness on the part of the group perpetrating such acts—they cannot stand in conventional battle against the armed might of uniformed militaries. Moreover, as John Mueller and Mark Stewart have noted, US citizens are far more likely to die in accidents involving household appliances than at the hands of an attack by the Islamic State.[15] Yet these facts are belied by the consistent securitization of the term in the United States by a variety of politicians since 9/11.

Having dispensed with three common means used to justify intelligence activities, where does this leave us? Three traditions in moral and political philosophy offer less flawed, and thus more useful, perspectives: deontology, consequentialism, and critical theory. No moral philosophy is without its critics. But these three traditions offer better prospects than patriotism, realism, and Just War theory in serving as a moral basis for identifying and guiding ethical action. We will now examine each in turn. In the next section, we will analyze a sample of different intelligence activities through these three lenses.

## Deontology

**Deontology** is a philosophical system in which the moral principles that constitute it must be obeyed as a duty without exception. The primary progenitor of this moral system was the Prussian philosopher Immanuel Kant. In his *Groundwork of the Metaphysic of Morals*, Kant argued that the motive of duty matters—people should act in a moral manner not out of self-interest but out of interest in doing good in itself. Our intent should be to do good things, not the incidental by product of other motivations.[16] In addition, Kant explicitly rejected evaluating moral action in terms of outcomes—"an action done from duty has its moral worth, *not in the purpose* attained

---

[15]Mueller, John, and Mark G. Stewart. "Hardly Existential: Thinking Rationally About Terrorism." *Foreign Affairs*, April 2, 2010. https://www.foreignaffairs.com/articles/north-america/2010-04-02/hardly-existential.

[16]Kant, Immanuel. *Groundwork of a Metaphysic of Morals*, translated by H. J. Patton. New York, NY: Harper, 1956, 64–66.

by it, but in the maxim in accordance with which it is decided upon."[17] Kant also claimed that "I should never act except in such a way that I can also will that my maxim should become a universal law," which he labeled the "categorical imperative."[18] In other words, one should act in a manner that all rational people would recognize as correct independent of variations in their experiences or desires. One of the key extensions of the categorical imperative is Kant's view that individual human beings have intrinsic dignity and thus cannot be used as a means to another end. It is also important to note here the impact deontology had on the Founding Fathers—Jefferson's argument in the *Declaration of Independence* "we hold these truths to be self-evident, that all men are created equal" is a deontological claim.

The deontological moral system sets a very high bar for intelligence operations to meet. Indeed, it might seem as if intelligence per se is impermissible from a Kantian perspective. In a later essay, Kant even argues that "no nation shall forcibly interfere with the constitution and government of another," which would seem to forbid all manner of coercive activities from information operations to covert action.[19] Kant goes on to argue that no state may use methods of war during a conflict that would make "future trust impossible," including assassins, poison, and "instigation of treason," including "the use of spies," as "such activities will carry over to peacetime and will thus undermine it."[20]

However, Kant's framing of espionage as impermissible follows from the mutual condition of law between states, including universal application of civil rights, mutual respect of sovereignty, and "world citizenship."[21] Although the post–World War II international system exhibits an unprecedented body of international law, it is nonetheless clear that these three conditions are not and have never been universal. International relations scholars have subsequently softened the logic of the "zone of peace" that Kant describes to relations between liberal democracies as one of peace. Indeed, much of the Democratic Peace research program is predicated upon a Kantian framework.[22] Consequently, we can deduce from Kant's original deontological system and its subsequent contemporary extension that intelligence operations are circumscribed to the use of methods that do not erode trust between friendly nations and will not increase enmity between adversaries. Again, this may seem as if all intelligence operations are banned. However, even while the United States and USSR were waging

---

[17]Ibid., emphasis in original, 66–67.

[18]Ibid., 70.

[19]Kant, Immanuel. *Perpetual Peace and Other Essays*, translated by Ted Humphrey. Indianapolis, IN: Hackett, 1983, 109.

[20]Ibid., 109–110.

[21]Ibid., 111–112.

[22]See Doyle, "Liberalism in World Politics"; and Maoz, Zeev, and Bruce Russett. "Normative and Structural Causes of Democratic Peace, 1946–1986." *American Political Science Review* 87, no. 3 (September 1993): 794–807.

a very coercive intelligence battle against each other, they came to accept a common normative framework at the highest levels of government.[23] Their espionage activities did not undermine this reduction in tensions, known as détente, and thus did met the Kantian condition of not undermining future good will. Nevertheless, we should proceed from the position that deontology is more likely to prohibit intelligence activities than permit them. Kant viewed the gradual, consistent expansion of lawful relations between states to be the ultimate logic of state power that was moral.[24] Thus even when intelligence activities are deemed ethical from a deontological perspective, this is a diminishing property.

## Consequentialism

In contrast with deontology's emphasis on the ethical nature of acts themselves, **consequentialism** reverses the emphasis, placing the focus of moral evaluation on outcomes. Conduct is judged moral if the consequences produce an improvement in people's circumstances. As noted earlier, this kind of cost-benefit analysis has been the focus of realism, with raison d'état used to justify actions that would be immoral were they carried out by individuals in service of their own ends, not the ends of the polity. However, consequentialism as a moral system breaks with realism in that the focus on measuring the value of outcomes resides in what maximizes the good not for one state, but for all states and peoples.[25]

Although there are a variety of frameworks employing a logic of consequences, the most common manifestation in modern philosophy is **utilitarianism**. The product of late-18th-century English philosopher and contemporary of Kant Jeremy Bentham, utilitarianism holds that moral evaluation of conduct should be based on which decisions produce the greatest amount of happiness for the most people. The subsequent elaboration of the theory by John Stuart Mill, a student of Bentham's, established a hierarchy for evaluating people's interests. Like Bentham, Mill argued "the greatest happiness principle holds that actions are right in proportion as they tend to promote happiness, wrong as they tend to produce the reverse of happiness. By 'happiness' is intended pleasure, and the absence of pain; by 'unhappiness,' pain and the privation of pleasure."[26] However, Mill did not measure "greatest happiness" solely in terms of quantity produced. The quality of pleasure and pain was also important, suggesting that some kinds of pleasure were superior while some varieties of pain were similarly distinguishable.[27] Although he repeatedly asserted that the interests of individual

[23]Thomas, Daniel. *The Helsinki Effect*. Princeton, NJ: Princeton University Press, 2001.

[24]Huntley, Wade L. "Kant's Third Image: Systemic Sources of the Liberal Peace." *International Studies Quarterly* 40, no. 1 (March 1996): 45–77.

[25]Ronn, Kira Vrist. "Intelligence Ethics: A Critical Review and Future Perspectives." *International Journal of Intelligence and Counterintelligence* 29, no. 4 (2016): 770.

[26]Mill, John Stuart. *Utilitarianism*. Buffalo, NY: Prometheus Books, 1987, 16–17.

[27]Ibid., 18.

people "must be regarded equally," Mill also attempted to establish a kind of hierarchy of wants, claiming that selfishness and "want of mental cultivation" are the primary things that "make life unsatisfactory."[28]

While deontological ethics makes for an uncomfortable fit with intelligence operations, so too does utilitarianism. If the categorical nature of moral rules in deontology presents a difficult ethical standard to meet, Mill's utilitarianism rejection of ethical motivations stemming from a sense of duty, which Mill likened to the ineffectiveness of religious sentiments in restraining immoral conduct, is an awkward basis for determining ethical choices for intelligence professionals steeped in a sense of duty.[29] There is a kind of core cultural friction between intelligence officers, who are motivated by service to country, and Mill's dismissal of service to others as an ethical expectation.[30] Although utilitarianism may make for an uncomfortable fit with intelligence officers, it establishes clear ethical criteria by which to evaluate intelligence operations. Actions that maximize happiness while minimizing pain are ethical. While clearly many intelligence activities may not meet this standard, others certainly do.

## Critical Theory

Emerging from the late-19th-century writing of Karl Marx and Friedrich Nietzsche, **critical theory** examines the origins of ideas, institutions, and power relations. As one of its leading scholars in international relations, Robert Cox, succinctly put it, "theory is always for someone and some purpose."[31] Drawing a distinction between critical theory and what he called empirically focused, ostensibly scientific "problem-solving theory," Cox noted,

> It is critical in the sense that it stands apart from the prevailing world order and asks how that order came about. Critical theory, unlike problem-solving theory, does not take institutions and social power relations for granted but calls them into question by concerning itself with their origins and how and whether they might be in the process of changing. It is directed toward an appraisal of the very framework for action, or problematic, which problem-solving theory accepts as its parameters.[32]

Thus critical theory is used to examine specific discourses that suggest choices are incontestable, that the current state of affairs is inevitable and/or unchanging, and the

---

[28]Ibid., 24–25, 45.

[29]Ibid., 29, 42–43.

[30]Ibid., 26–27.

[31]Cox, Robert W. "Social Forces, States, and World Orders: Beyond International Relations Theory." In *Neorealism and Its Critics*, edited by Robert O. Keohane. New York, NY: Columbia University Press, 1986, 206.

[32]Ibid., 208.

"assumption that there is a single ideal model for thinking about politics."[33] Critical theorists interrogate language that suggests human relations are naturalistic or fixed, such as claims about human nature or the imposition of rigid behavior qualities to masses of people. Similarly, critical theorists draw attention to how public rituals and practices serve to reproduce the power of the state.[34] Critical theorists also note the negative effects modernity has had on humanity, reducing individuals to contractual relations with capitalist economics and alienating them from their fellow man, family, job, and beliefs. Finally, critical theorists uncover the means by which the state inculcates mass beliefs, preventing people from seeing their true interests, a dominance over ideas and thoughts the Italian activist Antonio Gramsci labeled "hegemony."[35] Hegemony is the product of schoolhouses and universities. But it is also derived from the value placed by society on specific kinds of technocratic knowledge, activities obscure to regular people but nevertheless valorized and empowered, such as the role played by currency traders or public health commissioners. Some critical theorists refer to the power wielded by such people as "epistemic authority."[36]

Each of these moral systems offers a rigorous means by which to evaluate whether conduct by intelligence officers is ethical or not. However, some scholars have sought to develop a synthesis, mating deontology with the logic of consequences to offer a single, all-encompassing means by which to determine ethical choices.[37] This makes little sense, as the claims made by deontological moral theorists and utilitarians are mutually incompatible by design. Kant was explicitly arguing against Jeremy Bentham and other moral philosophers emphasizing a form of rational empiricism based on individual desires, while Mill rejected duty as the basis for ethical conduct, likening Kant's argument to religion. The same is true for critical theorists, who are reacting to (criticizing) *both* moral systems. Also, the ethical dilemmas facing intelligence officers are complex, perhaps uniquely so. We know from cognitive science that people learn more from people who have different opinions than their own. It is probably better to offer these professionals competing perspectives so they might determine for themselves the bases for proper conduct, rather than the illusion of a single answer.

## CASE STUDIES

In this section we briefly examine several areas of potential ethical concern as they relate to intelligence operations. This is by no means a large sample of the relevant

[33]Geuss, Raymond. *History and Illusion in Politics*. Cambridge, UK: Cambridge University Press, 2001, 3.

[34]Foucault, Michel. *Discipline and Punish: The Birth of the Prison*, translated by Alan Sheridan. New York, NY: Vintage Books, 1979.

[35]Gramsci, Antonio. *Selections From the Prison Notebooks*, edited and translated by Quentin Hoare. New York, NY: International, 1971.

[36]Geuss, *History and Illusion in Politics*, 38.

[37]Hatfield, "Ethical Defense of Treason by Means of Espionage."

issues and areas to be examined, which would fill several volumes. It is a group of cases that have been prominent in recent years and yet still raise important issues beyond the current context. We will not examine these case studies using the rigorous techniques of social science or intelligence analysis designed to explain causality, methods detailed at length in several earlier chapters. Our focus instead is on applying the three moral frameworks discussed earlier to analyzing the ethical domains of such conduct. The emphasis will be on weighing the various factors with which each moral system would be concerned, not on generating a final determination as to whether or not such activities are morally permissible. The objective is to allow students to make their own determination using these systems as to whether or not the conduct in question is ethical. However, one thing that should be readily apparent to anyone who takes these moral systems seriously is that many intelligence activities will not meet the ethical standards that these frameworks establish. This should give future intelligence officers pause. It should also form the basis for a critical reexamination of intelligence operations as they are currently conducted in democracies.

## Relationship With the Press and Other Nongovernment Actors

US intelligence officers have repeatedly **used nongovernmental organizations (NGOs) and press agencies as fronts** for information operations and/or intelligence collection, often without the knowledge or consent of these organizations. One prominent example of this activity occurred during the Cold War, when the CIA sponsored an influential literary magazine, the *Paris Review*, even installing as its founding editor a CIA officer.[38] The magazine served as a legitimate literary outlet, publishing the likes of Ernest Hemingway, Philip Roth, and Jack Kerouac. But it also functioned as an information operations organization against the Soviet bloc. The *Paris Review* was hardly the only cultural outlet subsumed into intelligence operations. There have even been rumors one of the most iconic "power ballads" of the late Cold War, the German heavy metal band Scorpions' "Wind of Change," was penned by the CIA.[39] But these activities are not limited to the use of culture as a weapon against America's enemies. More recently, the CIA created a fake vaccination program in Pakistan as part of its effort to establish whether Osama bin Laden was living in a house in Abbottabad.[40] Infiltration of such organizations by intelligence officers is accomplished as cover to conduct espionage overseas in denied areas, countries into which intelligence

---

[38]Whitney, Joel. "The Paris Review, the Cold War, and the CIA." *Salon*, May 27, 2012. https://www.salon.com/2012/05/27/exclusive_the_paris_review_the_cold_war_and_the_cia/.

[39]Chick, Stevie. "Wind of Change: Did the CIA Write the Cold War's Biggest Anthem?" *The Guardian*, May 15, 2020. https://www.theguardian.com/tv-and-radio/2020/may/15/wind-of-change-did-the-cia-write-the-cold-wars-biggest-anthem. See also the podcast that investigates these rumors as well as the history of the CIA's affiliation with a wide variety of artists, *Wind of Change*: https://www.newsroom.spotify.com/2020-05-12/cold-war-propaganda-meets-music-icons-on-new-investigative-podcast-wind-of-change/.

[40]Shah, Saeed. "CIA's Fake Vaccination Programme Criticised by *Médecins Sans Frontières*." *The Guardian*, July 14, 2011. https://www.theguardian.com/world/2011/jul/14/cia-fake-vaccination-medecins-frontieres.

agencies may have little ability to insert a human intelligence (HUMINT) collection program otherwise. The NGOs in question can be functioning businesses that provide deep cover for CIA operations officers[41] or even nonprofit organizations engaged in aid activities.

Adherents of deontology would reject this method out of hand, as it would likely undermine trust in the objectivity of the press and the neutrality of NGOs for a long time to come, perhaps forever. As this would sharply reduce the ability of these groups to operate in places in the world in which their services are most needed, this would result in more suffering for people who rely on the aid provided by NGOs and less accurate information flowing back to countries that might have interests in the region. A reduction in press efficiency would thus both harm innocent people and impede effective decision making by democratic publics. For all these reasons, the use of the press and NGOs as fronts for HUMINT collection and/or covert action would be considered unethical.

Utilitarians would likely draw attention to the danger posed to other members of the press or NGO if the targets find out that an intelligence organization used their media outlet as cover for espionage. Targets of intelligence collection might respond with violence directed at the front group or other similar, yet uninvolved, organizations. Such has been the case with *Médecins Sans Frontières* (**Doctors Without Borders**), an international NGO that deploys physicians to war zones and collapsed states to provide free medical care for civilians. Doctors Without Borders has been repeatedly targeted by insurgents in Afghanistan and Iraq. In 2016, the Syrian government claimed Doctors Without Borders was in fact a French intelligence operation.[42] However, this concern might be mitigated by the alternatives that would likely be used in the absence of such espionage. If this HUMINT collection operation might improve targeting or the ability of a law enforcement or intelligence organization to capture a terrorist or insurgent with little to no collateral damage, this might offset the risk posed to journalists or NGO members. Saving the lives of innocent people who would no doubt be killed by more "kinetic" activities might result in more happiness than the possibility that such organizations might be regarded with suspicion by hostile regimes or nonstate actors.

Critical theory's take on this situation is complicated. First, critical theorists would note the symbiotic relationship between the press and government sources, one that tends to reproduce the extant power structure and thus undermine potentially helpful change. Despite frequent protestations to the contrary, all news organizations are heavily dependent on government agencies or individuals for information that becomes proprietary content—the news. The press is a complex sector of business activity, not just

---

[41]See Carleson, J. C. *Work Like a Spy: Business Tips From a Former CIA Officer.* New York, NY: Portfolio, 2013.

[42]Spencer, Richard. "'*Médecins Sans Frontières* Run by French Intelligence,' Says Assad Regime." *The Telegraph*, February 17, 2016. https://www.telegraph.co.uk/news/worldnews/middleeast/syria/12161437/Medecins-Sans-Frontieres-run-by-French-intelligence-says-Assad-regime.html.

the provision of objective information. Moreover, journalists frequently employ anonymous or unauthorized government sources to reveal information that others cannot get, thereby benefiting on a personal (career) level from their position. Alternatively, journalists are also used as false flags for illegal conduct or a source of blame if an operation goes wrong, making them frequent victims of state power in the same manner as civilians on the ground. Lethal attacks on the press have grown considerably over the past two decades, with accusations of US forces even specifically targeting journalists in Iraq in 2007.[43] These accusations were recently echoed with some law enforcement personnel firing on and even arresting members of the press in the United States during the George Floyd protests in 2020.[44]

Thus the press can be both a source of state power and its victim. In addition, some critical theorists have noted the advantages of "panoptic surveillance" in protecting human rights, with NGOs and states operating hand in glove to prevent and/or prosecute genocide.[45] It is a difficult balancing act. Moreover, NGOs are not necessarily the disinterested actors they seem to be, as Doctors Without Borders "finds facts in the name of values" in the countries in which it operates, documenting human rights abuses.[46] Given the power disparity between states and nonstate actors, critical theorists would be loath to judge infiltration by intelligence organizations of the press or NGO community as ethical. Yet they would also not be blind to the sometimes willing involvement of these organizations in perpetuating power structures.

## Privacy and Surveillance

Perhaps the most far-ranging power possessed by the US IC and several of its allied systems and competitors is the ability to monitor voice, visual, and data communications. Since the 1970s, the National Security Agency (NSA) has had the ability to listen in on every phone call in the world.[47] Russia, China, and Great Britain possess similar capabilities. During the early 2000s, the NSA and the FBI initiated several controversial domestic communication monitoring programs in an attempt to catch potential terrorist communications. These programs analyzed the "metadata" of

---

[43]Reuters. "Leaked US Video Shows Deaths of Reuters' Iraqi Staffers." April 5, 2010. https://www.reuters.com/article/us-iraq-usa-journalists/leaked-u-s-video-shows-deaths-of-reuters-iraqi-staffers-idUSTRE6344FW20100406.

[44]Tracy, Marc, and Rachel Abrams. "Police Target Journalists as Trump Blames 'Lamestream Media' for Protests." *The New York Times*, June 1, 2020. https://www.nytimes.com/2020/06/01/business/media/reporters-protests-george-floyd.html; and Grynbaum, Michael M., and Marc Santora. "CNN Crew Arrested on Live Television While Covering Minneapolis Protests." *The New York Times*, May 29, 2020. https://www.nytimes.com/2020/05/29/business/media/cnn-reporter-arrested-omar-jimenez.html.

[45]Steele, Brent J., and Jacque L. Amoreaux. "NGOs and Monitoring Genocide: The Benefits and Limits to Human Rights Panopticism." *Millennium: Journal of International Studies* 34 (2004): 403–431.

[46]Redfield, Peter. "A Less Modest Witness: Collective Advocacy and Motivated Truth in a Medical Humanitarian Movement." *American Ethnologist* 33, no. 1 (2006): 3–26.

[47]Bamford, James. *The Puzzle Palace*. New York, NY: Penguin Books, 1983.

millions of phone calls originating in the United States to overseas numbers. Although these programs were eventually terminated due to several whistleblower complaints and additional congressional oversight, these activities have morphed into different forms of electronic surveillance that continue to this day. Spying on citizens is regularly practiced by authoritarian regimes. However, such practices have historically been heavily criticized in the United States, such as the FBI's COINTELPRO during the 1960s, which helped lead to the establishment of the congressional oversight regime of today. Are there conditions under which such surveillance is ethical?

The answer from deontologists would be an unequivocal "no." Although there is no specific right to privacy guaranteed in the US Constitution, one of the core tenets of deontology is the individual dignity accorded to each person. This dignity would be violated by government monitoring of what people believed to be private communications, often involving intimate conversations between people about which the government has no right to access. Moreover, knowledge that the government was monitoring all communications would have what US legal scholars call a "chilling effect." People would no longer discuss their true feelings, ideas, and/or opinions if they knew the government was listening, thereby fundamentally suppressing the speech rights of citizens. No matter the ostensible emergency condition under which such a program was employed, such a mass surveillance program would also clearly violate the categorical imperative—it is most definitely not something people would want to be implemented always and everywhere.

For utilitarians, the question is more complicated. Although they would acknowledge the potentially negative societal effects of discouraging speech via the chilling effect, utilitarians would also draw attention to the effect produced by the surveillance program. Would it make people feel safer? If it made people feel safer, and thus happier, than they would have been otherwise, then accepting the cost of the individual loss of privacy for the greater societal gain of increased happiness would make surveillance tolerable. Yet utilitarians would not be blind to the long-term consequences of the creeping intrusion of government power into the everyday lives of people. Government leaders might alter the definition of what constitutes security in the future, enabling even more intrusive monitoring of citizens, such as continuous monitoring of citizens' on-the-job conduct or even mandatory DNA sampling from childbirth. Utilitarians would be concerned that the previous permissibility of phone and data surveillance to increase security would lead to more of the same, thereby in the long term decreasing happiness via the establishment of tyranny.

Critical theorists would draw attention to mass surveillance as being part and parcel of the modern technocratic state. The very logic of modern state power is ever-increasing policing regimes as social control and regimentation to increase the efficiency of market dynamics. For critical theorists, what makes such a proposal even more dangerous is its routinization within the context of the private sector. Data companies like AT&T and Verizon would be enabled to serve as collectors of these data in cooperation with the government, drawing capital and state closer together and increasing the power of both. Critical theorists would be appalled by systems of mass surveillance, but not surprised by them.

## Whistleblowers

**Whistleblowers** are people who are employed by an intelligence organization who, motivated by clearly articulated principles, knowingly disclose wrongdoing by government officials and/or restricted materials to the world in an effort to stop unlawful and/or unethical conduct. In the US IC, whistleblowers have a specific legal status that is largely the legacy of **Daniel Ellsberg**, a Pentagon intelligence analyst who leaked thousands of pages of documents related to the Vietnam War to *The New York Times*. Ellsberg had grown dismayed by the pattern of lying by the Johnson and Nixon administrations regarding the causes, conduct, and prospects for a US victory in the conflict. The documents he leaked indicated that the US government had known for years that the war was not going well, the likelihood of winning was slight, and hundreds of thousands of people were being killed for little to no gain. Ellsberg was indicted for leaking the classified material, and the government sought a restraining order against the *Times* to prevent publication. In a landmark decision, the US Supreme Court ruled 6–3 that the paper had the right under the First Amendment to publish the top-secret material because publication did not pose a "grave danger" and was in the overriding public interest. The criminal case against Ellsberg was also dismissed. Combined, these court decisions provided the framework for protections for US IC whistleblowers and the subsequent Whistleblower Protection Act of 1989. To qualify for protection against prosecution, potential whistleblowers must first attempt to inform their chain of command, without corresponding action taken to address the problem. Next, US government employees are expected to contact the Merit Systems Protection Board (MSPB), although historically people granted whistleblower status have also reached out to their agency's inspector general and/or a member of Congress. Whistleblowers may choose to assume the risk of disclosing the classified material in the press, which itself has specific privileges afforded it under the First Amendment. But this is no guarantee—the probative value of the disclosed material must outweigh the potential damage to sources and methods and personnel. It must also meet the legal conditions set forth by the MSPB and the 1989 law.

Whistleblowing is a form of civil disobedience, and political philosophers have long held that people who commit such acts must be prepared to face consequences for their principled positions. Both the legal context outlined earlier and its position in political philosophy are important because a number of people have disclosed classified material and practices in recent years, disclosures that have materially damaged the US IC. Yet none of these people may be considered whistleblowers, in either the legal or the moral philosophical context of the term. In 2017, an intelligence contractor, Reality Winner, was arrested for leaking top-secret NSA documents regarding Russian efforts to interfere with the 2016 US presidential election. She offered no coherent ethical argument for leaking the material. In 2010, Chelsea Manning uploaded hundreds of thousands of classified State Department and military documents to the website **WikiLeaks**, an organization run by the Australian fugitive Julian Assange. WikiLeaks has been classified as a hostile intelligence organization by the US IC. Prior to her gender-reassignment surgery, Chelsea was then Bradley Manning, a recent US Army military intelligence recruit who was struggling with gender identity and mental health problems from the moment she was inducted. At her trial Manning offered no coherent ethical justification for the disclosure of the classified material. Indeed, her defense team argued mental illness as a mitigating circumstance for the disclosure. After she had served 7 years of a 35-year sentence, Manning's sentence was commuted by President Obama, and she was released. In perhaps the most damaging act of espionage in the history of the US IC, **Edward Snowden** stole as many as 1.7 million US IC documents,[48] including its most highly guarded secret, the IC's budget. Snowden began leaking these documents to a journalist from the British newspaper *The Guardian*, Glenn Greenwald. Styling himself a whistleblower, Snowden fled the United States for Hong Kong, where he met with Greenwald, who in cooperation with other news organizations began publishing some of these documents. Snowden subsequently fled to Russia, where he now resides under the sponsorship and protection of the Russian government.

Several factors mitigate against calling any of these three whistleblowers, either in the very specific legal sense of the term or more broadly from a moral perspective. First, none of them made any attempt to protect the identities of foreign nationals who have helped the US IC, placing all of their lives in danger with the exposure of this cooperation. Second, none of the leakers made any effort to selectively identify documents that made a specific case regarding wrongdoing on the part of the US IC—all three indiscriminately disclosed classified material, much of which was irrelevant to any post hoc attempted justification via IC wrongdoing. Once released, these documents nevertheless exposed intelligence sources and methods, many of which were and are legally and ethically defensible. Finally, the release of these documents aided foreign powers, particularly in the case of Snowden, who continues to actively cooperate with Russia against US interests. The secrets Snowden disclosed, including the IC's budget, revealed to the United States' adversaries a great deal regarding the IC's capabilities, as well as its weaknesses. Of the three, Snowden's case most closely resembles treason, not a misbegotten or poorly understood attempt at whistleblowing.

The specifics of these three criminals are important, as their moral failings point to criteria that are used in the ethical evaluation of whistleblowers in general. For deontology, perhaps the most important criteria in the ethical justification of the disclosure of secrets would be that they bring about no harm to innocent people or people who have

---

[48]Strohm, Chris, and Del Quentin Wilbur. "Pentagon Says Snowden Took Most Secrets Ever: Rogers." *Bloomberg News*, January 9, 2014. https://www.bloomberg.com/news/articles/2014-01-09/pentagon-finds-snowden-took-1-7-million-files-rogers-says.

cooperated in good faith. Thus, whistle-blowers must remain ethically consistent in their application of withering, though perhaps deserved, criticism of intelligence. They cannot charge the IC with immoral conduct while simultaneously committing that same conduct by endangering innocents—people cannot be used as a means to an end. In addition, deontologists would emphasize the relationship between exposure of these secrets and trust between countries. Kant loathed secret treaties, and his thinking on the matter strongly informed Woodrow Wilson's 14 Points, which included a ban on secret treaties. Yet recall deontology's emphasis on how intelligence activities affect trust between states. Exposure of intelligence coordina-tion between democracies by a potential

YouTube.com/user/TheWikiLeaksChannel

**PHOTO 13.1** Edward Snowden at an award ceremony in Moscow, 2013.[49]

whistleblower might place a great burden on the trust between these countries, thereby reducing the ability of their intelligence services to protect the "zone of peace" between these countries. Finally, recall the categorical imperative. If whistleblowers were to invoke it, then they would expect all rational people to behave the same way in this situation. That sets a very high bar for whistleblowers to meet. However, whistleblow-ing can clearly be ethically justified from the perspective of deontology if it meets these conditions. Kant was a great lover of truth, and whistleblowers clearly have the ability to dramatically increase the amount of information available to citizens about what their government is doing in their name.

At first glance, utilitarians would be much more inclined than deontologists to permit whistleblowing, as the primary criterion is the provision of happiness. Whistleblowers are deemed ethical if the secrets they expose increase the happiness of people who learned them. On the surface, this seems straightforward. However, it is not. First, how is a whistleblower necessarily to know the answer to this question prior to releasing a cache of classified documents? This seems almost impossible to deter-mine, particularly for some IC practices that are extremely technical and thus difficult to understand. Second, whistleblowers should also balance the increase in the level of happiness with its potential spillover into other moral goods. Specifically, although the disclosure of some practices by the IC might make people happier, as such activities

---

might be unpopular, their disclosure might reduce the provision of security, a condition that presumably promotes a great deal of overall happiness as well as many different kinds of happiness (Mill's quality criterion). The whistleblower would have to weigh the cost potentially imposed on other moral goods that might only be indirectly related, such as the willingness of both foreign governments and their citizens to cooperate with the United States. Exposure of secrets could easily damage trust, impacting everything from international trade to the future willingness of foreign agents to spy for the United States, thereby again impacting the provision of security. Finally, utilitarians would note the specific impact of each document or secret exposed; whistleblowers would have to perform the same ethical calculus for each.

Of the three moral systems we are using in these case studies, critical theory would be the most permissive regarding the role of whistleblowers. Indeed, many of the current justifications offered for whistleblowers are framed in the context of the expression "speaking truth to power." Ironically enough for the current context, this phrase is frequently invoked by IC leaders as one of the ethical duties of intelligence officers, particularly analysts, and is used in the 2019 National Intelligence Strategy.[50] Yet the modern origins of the expression lie clearly in critical theory, specifically the US civil rights movement, and in the writings of the French poststructuralist Michel Foucault. For many critical theorists, whistleblowers represent the ability, even the duty, of ordinary citizens to expose the actual exercise of state power, which is frequently concealed from view. In doing so, the whistleblower has the ability to disrupt or mediate the state's domination of individuals, exposing the technologies of oppression. For critical theorists, the specifics of what is exposed by whistleblowers is most important, rather than the symbolic importance of the act of whistleblowing itself. Whistleblowers interfere with the state's panoptic control of people, forcing the state to displace and move away from the practices that are exposed. For critical theorists, this intervention offers a fleeting possibility for the exercise of authentic democracy.

## Torture

Following the 9/11 attacks, the US IC went on a war footing. As part of this dramatic increase in operational activity, the national command authority directed the IC to more directly coordinate with US military units in combat theaters, first in Afghanistan and then subsequently in Iraq and dozens of other countries in which special operations forces (SOF) were hunting al-Qaeda. One of the unfortunate results of operational uptick was the use of intelligence assets in ways in which they had not been used in decades, specifically as a means to augment the initially meager counterinsurgency capabilities of the US military, particularly in Iraq. The line between intelligence operatives and SOF blurred considerably, a process that began with the very effective

---

[50]Office of the Director of National Intelligence, *National Intelligence Strategy of the United States*, 31.

prosecution of the CIA's plan to seize control of Afghanistan.[51] Within the span of a few weeks, SOF and CIA Special Activities Division (SAD) paramilitary forces had embedded with friendly Afghan rebels and driven the Taliban and al-Qaeda into the Hindu Kush mountains bordering the country and Pakistan. One of the results of these operations was the capture of thousands of Taliban and al-Qaeda members.

After a messy vetting of the captured al-Qaeda members, a process that resulted in the misidentification of dozens of terrorists, many of the prisoners identified as "high-value detainees" were moved to secret prison camps, known as **black sites**. Run in collaboration with the military, the black sites remained secret, with no public acknowledgment of their existence by the US government or even who had been detained. Other high-value detainees were moved to the Guantanamo Bay Naval Base, land leased from the Cuban government since 1903. Eventually, the secret prison program extended to black sites in Europe, Asia, and Africa. The numbers of prisoners at these sites continued to grow, as the CIA's **extraordinary rendition program** resulted in the addition of thousands of prisoners. Extraordinary rendition refers to the secret kidnapping without due process of law of suspected terrorists. Many of the people renditioned were seized in democratic countries, with hundreds, perhaps thousands, renditioned from North Atlantic Treaty Organization (NATO) member states. Although most of the people seized had confirmed ties to al-Qaeda and other terrorist organizations, an unknown number were misidentified—innocent people were kidnapped as part of this program. After the invasion of Iraq in 2003, a section of the former Iraqi prison Abu Ghraib was used in a similar manner.

Detainees at all of the black sites were tortured by both members of the US armed forces and intelligence officers. Initially, the torture was improvised on-site, with interrogators growing frustrated with the resistance of some of the more dedicated al-Qaeda fighters, many of whom had received training to resist US interrogation techniques. During the 1980s, a senior officer in al-Qaeda, Ali Mohamed, had worked at the John F. Kennedy Special Warfare Center and School at Fort Bragg, North Carolina. As part of its pre-9/11 training program, al-Qaeda used US Army manuals on guerrilla warfare, surveillance, counterintelligence, urban combat, survival, and assassination smuggled out by Mohamed.[52]

Later, the CIA attempted to develop a more systematic interrogation program. Utilizing two psychologists who had never conducted an interrogation before, the CIA contracted out its detainee interrogation program, despite the decades of knowledge on the subject at the CIA, FBI, and Department of Defense (DOD). The program created by these psychologists used the euphemism **enhanced interrogation techniques (EITs)** as

[51]See Biddle, Stephen. *Afghanistan and the Future of Warfare: Implications for Army and Defense Policy*. Carlisle, PA: Strategic Studies Institute, US Army War College, 2002.

[52]See Nasiri, Omar. *Inside the Jihad: My Life With al Qaeda*. New York, NY: Basic Books, 2006; Wright, Lawrence. *The Looming Tower*. New York, NY: Knopf, 2006, 179–181; and Lia, Brynjar. *The Architect of Jihad: The Life of al Qaeda Strategist Abu Mus'ab al-Siri*. New York, NY: Columbia University Press, 2008, 82–84.

means to conceal what was really happening. Military and CIA interrogators employed techniques specifically identified as torture in the 1984 Convention Against Torture, an international treaty sponsored by the United States, and in the US military's own training manuals. Interrogators denied detainees food and water, and subjected them to sensory deprivation, including extremely loud music and harsh lighting in their cells that lasted for days. Detainees were forced to remain naked, had human feces rubbed on their bodies, and were otherwise humiliated. Some prisoners were forced to remain in painful positions for days, while others were beaten, sodomized, and subjected to waterboarding, a technique that simulates drowning. An unknown number of detainees died as part of this program. A comprehensive probe by the US Senate, a process that took five years and involved millions of pages of documents, determined no useful intelligence was gleaned from this program that had not already been obtained via other means.[53]

US government copyright/Public domain/Wikimedia Commons

**PHOTO 13.2** Abu Ghraib torture victim.[54]

Much like its perspective on mass surveillance, the deontological view on torture would be a definitive prohibition against such activities. For deontologists, torture is one of the worst kinds of violations of an individual's human dignity. It is intrinsically cruel, both due to the pain it inflicts and because it occurs outside of the legal process. Torture is also a form of punishment, which can only be justly inflicted on the guilty. As the rationale for the IC's use of

[53]US Senate. "Report of the Senate Select Committee on Intelligence Committee Study of the Central Intelligence Agency's Detention and Interrogation Program." December 9, 2014. https://www.intelligence.senate.gov/sites/default/files/documents/CRPT-113srpt288.pdf.

[54]US Government. "File: AbuGhraibAbuse." Wikimedia Commons. Last modified July 27, 2020. https://commons.wikimedia.org/w/index.php?curid=581864.

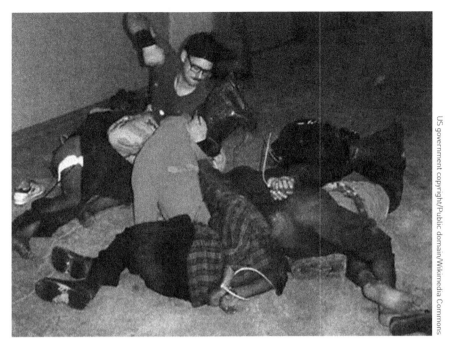

**PHOTO 13.3** Specialist Charles A. Graner punches handcuffed Iraqi prisoners.[55]

torture is to improve interrogation compliance, it is unethical because the accused have not been convicted of any crime. Moreover, as the IC's concern is only in finding out what secrets the terror suspect might possess, human beings are used as a means to an end, violating their dignity. Torture also undermines the basis of civil society, as citizens would have reason not to trust their government, given its wanton cruelty. This undermines the effectiveness of otherwise just sovereigns. Finally, the rendition program by which the torture program was carried out sometimes involved the kidnapping of people with the cooperation of foreign intelligence services. But it frequently did not. In an infamous incident in 2007, the German government indicted CIA officers who had kidnapped a German national, Khaled el-Masri, who they believed to be a terrorist but who was in fact innocent. The German government was also outraged that CIA aircraft had used air bases in Germany to transport people who had been renditioned without notifying the BND or BfV. Such incidents highlight how the torture and detention programs also interfere in the governance of other countries, which Kant inveighed against in *Perpetual Peace*.

---

[55]US Government. "File: AG-8 [Abu Ghraib]." Wikimedia Commons. Last modified July 31, 2020. https://commons.wikimedia.org/w/index.php?curid=579576.

For the logic of consequences moral system, the ethics of torture are more complicated. From one perspective, torture reduces the provision of happiness. This is a result of the pain inflicted on both the tortured and the people who learn about the true nature of these actions, the most benign of which are still appalling. However, utilitarianism might also permit torture, for if torture is used to obtain information that will save lives, it will thus reduce the torture victim's happiness, and probably some other people who learn of it as well. But it would likely result in a net increase in happiness from the lives saved. The most frequently cited situation in which utilitarians explore the ethical use of torture is the **ticking time bomb scenario**. With a limited amount of time to prevent the explosion of a hidden bomb by terrorists, some utilitarians believe the moral system provides the basis for the ethical use of torture, provided it meets four conditions.[56] First, torture can be used only to obtain information to save people's lives, not as a form of punishment or as a deterrent against future terrorist attacks. Second, torture must be used on subjects only if it is likely that they in fact possess the necessary information to save the aforementioned lives. Third, this information must reference a specific threat that will likely occur in the very near future, so much so that other means to obtain this information will probably fail. Finally, in order for the torture to be permissible, the interrogators must believe that it is likely the information they will gain will be sufficient to prevent the attack.

However, this utilitarian case for torture has significant logical problems within the context of the theory itself. First, it fails to take into account Mill's distinction between different kinds of pain and pleasure. Because it produces post-traumatic stress disorder (PTSD) in most of its victims, torture is a kind of pain very different from stubbing one's toe. It is the very feeling of helplessness, the belief that this pain may go on indefinitely without ending in death, that makes torture much worse than other forms of pain.[57] It is hard to believe that the happiness produced by saving people's lives from the ticking time bomb will qualitatively offset the deleterious effects of the brutality of torture for those who are its victims, those who inflict it (they frequently suffer from PTSD as well), and the publics that learn of it. Second, the utilitarian case for torture ignores the effect that knowledge of the practice of torture will have on the provision of other goods that increase happiness, such as international cooperation that promotes collective security and international trade. Such cooperation would decline as allies learn of the use of torture, particularly against their own citizens. The use of torture by democracies might also be used as a recruiting tool for terrorists, highlighting the ostensible hypocrisy of liberal human rights.[58] Thus

---

[56]The utilitarian case for torture is summarized in Allhoff, Fritz. "Terrorism and Torture." *International Journal of Applied Ethics* 17, no. 1 (2003): 105–118.

[57]Bellaby, Ross. "What's the Harm? The Ethics of Intelligence Collection." *Intelligence and National Security* 27, no. 1 (2012): 98.

[58]Johnson, Douglas A., et al. "The Strategic Costs From Torture." *Foreign Affairs* 95 (September 1, 2016): 121–126.

torture might prevent one ticking time bomb while producing more, thereby leading to a net decline in happiness. In short, utilitarianism provides a logical argument for the ethical use of torture. But using the same core tenets of the moral theory, it also provides a strong case against its use.

Critical theory would find no conditions under which torture might be ethical. Instead, consistent with its emphasis on revealing the hidden exercise of power over ideas and practices, the theory would attempt to explain the origins of the use of torture itself by the United States. Critical theorists would focus on what they would argue are the real reasons democracies might believe they "need" to use torture—the fear produced by the wanton exercise of such power of the state over an individual human being. Critical theorists would note the frequent emphasis on humiliating prisoners in the CIA's detainee program, humiliation that was frequently calibrated based on the majority of the detainees coming from very conservative Muslim societies. From this perspective, stacking up naked Muslim men in front of female military police at Abu Ghraib and then photographing them was the point of the torture, not information. The abject humiliation of Muslim men was designed less to elicit actionable intelligence—as was made clear from the Senate report, little to none was—than to demonstrate the power of the United States over the Muslim world.[59]

Critical theorists would also draw attention to the epistemic authority wielded by the psychologists who designed and ran the program, knowledge not possessed by the people who would carry out the torture or by the political actors who authorized it.[60] This cognitive distance enabled such activities to be viewed as legitimate or proper, particularly when they were consistently described with euphemisms or elliptical language. Torture became a legitimate act in a liberal democracy through its epistemic transformation into so-called EITs, thereby shielding even most intelligence officers from knowledge regarding what EITs really are.

## Assassination

Perhaps the most controversial ethical issue related to intelligence operations is whether or not intelligence organizations may use **assassination** as a policy tool. Assassination is defined as the killing of prominent political, economic, or social leaders with the aim of silencing them, removing them so as to replace them with someone more amenable to US interests, and/or intimidating their followers. Assassination can be committed with clear attribution—that is, the killing is public and violent—or covertly in a manner that makes the person seem to have died from natural causes. From a legal perspective, assassination was first banned by **Executive Order 11905**,

---

[59]The role of the punishment as a spectacle of power is explored at length in Foucault, *Discipline and Punish*.

[60]Risen, James. "Outside Psychologists Shielded US Torture Program, Report Finds." *The New York Times*, July 10, 2015. https://www.nytimes.com/2015/07/11/us/psychologists-shielded-us-torture-program-report-finds.html.

signed by President Gerald Ford in 1976 and subsequently expanded upon by President Jimmy Carter in Executive Order 12036. In the wake of the scandals revealed by the Church and Pike Committees during the early 1970s, both Ford and Carter sought to rein in the US IC and constrain its activities. During the early Cold War, the CIA had regularly participated in coups d'état that resulted in the deaths of political leaders, including the 1963 removal and killing of Ngo Diem, president of South Vietnam and a strong US ally. Even worse, the CIA had established the **Phoenix Program** during the Vietnam War, a covert assassination program that killed perhaps as many as 30,000 people in Indochina, some of whom were employed by the South Vietnamese government. The Phoenix Program was designed to surgically target North Vietnamese agents and members of the Viet Cong. But in the absence of a criminal investigation and trial, there is little guarantee the program didn't kill at least some innocent people. The CIA and US military programs also supported both government and far-right paramilitary killing squads in Latin America, organizations operating against communist infiltration of the region. When these practices came to light during the congressional investigations (see Chapter 9), the American public was appalled, which led of course to the system of oversight we have today. But assassination in particular troubled President Ford, who banned the practice with 11905. Carter extended the logic of 11905 to reduce many other covert action activities.

When Ronald Reagan assumed office in 1981, there was widespread dissatisfaction in the US IC regarding what many viewed were constraints on operations that were far too limiting, no matter the appropriateness of their original intent. Consequently, President Reagan signed **Executive Order 12333** in 1981, an order that reaffirmed the general ban on assassination. However, President Reagan also expanded the use of **Presidential Findings**, the legal power granted to the president under section 503 of the 1947 National Security Act and in Title 50 of the US Code (see Chapter 7). A Presidential Finding authorizes covert action. Since the mid-1980s, this has also included the explicit authorization of the "targeted killing" of terrorists, a euphemism for assassination. In practice, however, Reagan went even further. In 1986, he authorized the US military to bomb Libya in retaliation for the terrorist bombing of a Berlin nightclub in which a US Marine was murdered. Code-named Operation EL DORADO CANYON, the bombing runs also included an attempt to kill Libyan dictator Muammar Gaddafi, an attack that failed and resulted in the death of the strongman's infant daughter.

Following the 9/11 attacks, both the US military and the IC have operated targeted killing programs, primarily employing unmanned aerial vehicles (UAVs), more commonly referred to as drones.[61] However, the killing of Osama bin Laden by SEAL Team Six and members of the CIA's SAD during the raid on his Abbottabad complex in 2011

---

[61]During the 1980s, the Israel Defense Forces pioneered the use of UAVs in combat and ran a drone assassination program much like the DOD and CIA programs. But for simplicity's sake, we'll focus on US activities here.

may also be considered a targeted killing. Similar such raids occurred with regular frequency during the wars in Iraq and Afghanistan. Moreover, during the George W. Bush administration, the United States operated an SOF assassination squad, which reportedly was closed down in 2009 (see Chapter 9). When we discuss the use of assassination in the contemporary US IC, we are usually referring to drone strikes, although targeted killings have not been limited only to the use of UAVs. However, the bulk of the people killed by these activities have been through the drone programs, which have resulted in the deaths of hundreds of al-Qaeda and Islamic State terrorists. But they have also killed an unknown number of innocent civilians, probably thousands.[62] Moreover, drone strikes have been used on US citizens, including to kill the al-Qaeda propagandist Anwar al-Awlaki in 2011. Finally, there are some indications that in an effort to slow or stop Iran's nuclear program, the United States may have cooperated with Israeli intelligence organizations in the killing of five Iranian nuclear scientists.

Are such programs ethical? Deontologists would argue for the total prohibition of assassination, no matter how it is dressed up as "targeted killing." Such activities fundamentally undermine trust between nations, for if one country can legitimately employ such techniques to kill political leaders and terrorists, then all countries may do so. The result is the erosion of rule-governed relations between countries. Such practices also clearly violate the categorical imperative—rational people would not want governments to be able to kill people at will without judicial process or whenever they deemed it "necessary." This is the very definition of tyranny.

However, the deontonlogical case against assassination is not without some logical tensions. First, one of the primary reasons offered by the United States for engaging in targeted killings is self-defense—that is, the suspected terrorists being killed by these programs were plotting attacks on the United States and/or its allies. Kantians would likely counter this argument by noting that war is between states, not individuals, and targeted killings are thus not a form of warfare. The conditions of self-defense for states do not apply in the same way as they might for inter-state warfare. In addition, Kantians would similarly note that the definition of "self-defense" is far too flexibly applied by the United States. The net result would be an erosion in the willingness of other states to observe the previously understood basis for using violence in the international system—war. Indeed, there is already evidence that states are referencing the United States' preventative war rationale for all manner of state-sponsored violence.[63]

The second logical issue with the deontological position on assassination relates to revolution. Kant argued that revolution against government by its citizens was

---

[62]President Obama directed that civilian deaths should be accounted for when possible. However, on May 7, 2019, President Trump rescinded this order. For the most rigorous attempt at estimating total civilian deaths, see the methodology developed in 2011 by Columbia University's Human Rights Institute at https://web.law.columbia.edu/sites/default/files/microsites/human-rights-institute/files/COLUMBIACountingDronesFinal.pdf.

[63]Fisk, Kerstin, and Jennifer M. Ramos. "Actions Speak Louder Than Words: Preventative Self-Defense as a Cascading Norm." *International Studies Perspectives* 15 (2014): 163–185.

illegitimate, and that people would have to endure even the cruelty of authoritarian rule because revolution would unleash social forces that were much worse, specifically the condition of lawlessness.[64] Yet if the end goal of Kantian moral theory is the establishment of republican governments and the expansion of the zone of peace they create, it seems hard to believe that states could not ethically achieve regime change via assassination. The targeted killing and removal of tyrants must surely be preferable to the horrendous casualties incurred by the wars such leaders are prone to create. Similarly, one could argue from a Kantian perspective as a corollary that countries engaged in war with groups of people should use methods likely to limit casualties. Although they are far from the high-precision weapons they are frequently touted to be, drones are more precise than the large-scale deployment of US ground forces and/or the use of conventional airpower assets, both of which would incur considerably more firepower and thus casualties. To be clear, deontologists would never agree that assassination is ethical. But this argument is not without problems under the conditions set by the theory itself.

Utilitarians would be far more amenable to the use of targeted killings as a tool of state policy, provided of course several conditions were met. First, utilitarians would likely accept a broader definition of self-defense than the more rule-oriented deontologists. As always, the key criterion would center on the provision of happiness provided by drone attacks. In this context, utilitarians would weigh total deaths. Although the assassination of these terrorists might be accompanied by some civilian casualties, total deaths might in fact be lower than the likely terrorist attack that would have resulted. This sets up the criterion of **proportionality**, which is frequently cited in connection to the use of force. The level of the threat must be proportional to the amount of force used to limit that threat. Thus, if the net result was lives saved, then utilitarians would argue that the targeted killing was proportional and thus ethical. Proportionality may also be evaluated in terms of the use of drones versus the alternative weapons platforms or tactics that might be used, methods that would likely result in far more military and civilian casualties than the drone strikes.[65]

The second issue utilitarians would focus on relates to the first. If the net result was lives saved, meaning fewer people died as collateral casualties than would have died if the terrorists had successfully executed their attack, that is a big hurdle to clear. An even bigger hurdle, however, is whether or not the drone assassination generates additional consequences. Do drone attacks lead to more terrorist activity? This question was once posed, albeit outside of any moral context, by then secretary of defense Donald Rumsfeld, who reportedly asked his staff if the United States was killing terrorists faster than they were being recruited. If drone attacks may foil one attack but

---

[64]Beck, Lewis W. "Kant and the Right of Revolution." *Journal of the History of Ideas* 32, no. 3 (1971): 411–422.

[65]Keene, Shima D. "Lethal and Legal? The Ethics of Drone Strikes." *International Journal of Ethics* 12, no. 1 (2015): 90.

inspire several more terror plots, then the net result is not an increase in happiness. The fostering of blood feuds by Pashtun tribesmen is not an ethically acceptable outcome of otherwise successful targeted killings. If, however, the net result was a deterrent effect on terrorists, then utilitarians would deem them ethical. Put differently, utilitarians would examine whether or not drone attacks work.[66] If both the proportionality and effectiveness conditions were met, then utilitarians would likely deem targeted killings ethical.

Critical theorists would judge assassinations to be fundamentally unethical, in terms of the proximate act itself, the ulterior motives or purposes driving such violence, and the role such targeted killings play in expanding the power of the state. Noting the United States' reference to the technique "shock and awe" in its use of precision-guided weapons in the early days of the Iraq War, critical theorists would argue that targeted killings are anything but precision weapons. They kill hundreds, perhaps thousands, of civilians because the blast radius of Hellfire missiles ensures that people a hundred feet away may still be wounded by the missile. The original purpose of the AGM-114 missile was as an anti-tank weapon, and this lineage continues to result in the deaths of innocent people in so-called precision strikes. Other combat payloads used in drone strikes are even worse, as the casualty radius of the precision version of the Mark 82 gravity bomb is 200 feet.[67] Moreover, from the perspective of critical theorists, the real "target" of such violence is the Arab or Muslim street, not the individual terrorist. The effect of the violence inflicted by drones is deliberately diffuse, meant to terrify publics from whence international terrorist groups are predominantly based.

Yet most damning for critical theorists is the relationship of the drone program to state violence. Critical theorists would draw attention to two issues in this context. First, one of the "selling points" to the US public regarding their use is the lack of risk to US forces. For critical theorists, this lack of risk to US soldiers results in a disengagement of the American public to remote violence perpetrated in their name. This makes war easier, conducted with less oversight, and empowers the killing of thousands of faceless, nameless people. It creates the **illusion of bloodless conflict** because the pain inflicted is only one-way, a reality further suppressed by the technical debates regarding whether or not strikes are legal, thus diverting attention away from the agony visited on their victims.[68] Second, much like their views on torture, critical theorists would also view assassination as an outgrowth of modern state violence. States treat both torture and drones as similar instruments in support of the technology of

---

[66]This is, of course, a key debate in the security studies literature as well. See Jordan, Jenna. "Attacking the Leader, Missing the Mark: Why Terrorist Groups Survive Drone Strikes." *International Security* 38, no. 4 (2014): 7–38; and Mir, Asfandyar. "What Explains Counterterrorism Effectiveness? Evidence From the US Drone War in Pakistan." *International Security* 43, no. 2 (2018): 45–83.

[67]Hambling, David. "Why Was Pakistan Strike So Deadly?" *Wired*, June 24, 2009. https://www.wired.com/2009/06/why-was-pakistan-drone-strike-so-deadly/.

[68]Gregory, Thomas. "Drones, Targeted Killings, and the Limits of International Law." *International Political Sociology* 9, no. 1 (2015): 197–212.

domination. In the case of drones, increasing use of artificial intelligence in making targeting decisions further dissociates citizens from the consequences of decisions made in their name while increasing the state's technocratic domination of "bio-power"—control over bodies resulting from ostensibly rational, objective decisions that are in fact veiled forms of racism.[69]

## CONCLUSION: THE ETHICAL DEMANDS OF NATIONAL SERVICE

As we have seen in this chapter, the bar set by deontology, utilitarianism, and critical theory is high. The standards for ethical conduct established by these three moral systems may be impossible to meet, constraining the conduct of many intelligence operations. Yet ethical expectations for intelligence officers may be higher than those for members of any other organization in the federal government *precisely because* intelligence has always existed on the gray edges of the international and domestic law. Even in the best of times, conducting many intelligence operations in an ethical manner is difficult. However, such activities have been particularly difficult during the Trump administration. All presidents have their problems. All presidents attempt to politicize intelligence and national security affairs. But none have done so with such reckless disregard for the US national interest as Donald Trump. Due to both his character and his conduct, serving the 45th US president presents some unique ethical challenges.

Despite claiming that "there's nobody bigger or better at the military than I am" (whatever that even means), Trump is a draft dodger, receiving five deferments from military service during the Vietnam War via the dubious claim of "bone spurs."[70] He has repeatedly behaved in a dishonorable manner toward Gold Star families and criticized war hero and senator John McCain by remarking, "I like people who aren't captured," a particularly despicable attack considering the years of torture McCain endured in North Vietnam and Trump's avoidance of service in that conflict.[71] Even worse, during a state visit to France in 2018, Trump referred to American servicemen

---

[69]Allison, Jamie. "The Necropolitics of Drones." *International Political Sociology* 9, no. 2 (2015): 113–127.

[70]Fox News. "Donald Trump Running for President." Transcript from *The O'Reilly Factor*, June 16, 2015. https://www.foxnews.com/transcript/donald-trump-running-for-president; and Shane, Leo, III. "Trump Made Up Injury to Dodge Military Service, His Former Lawyer Testifies." *Military Times*, February 27, 2019. https://www.militarytimes.com/news/pentagon-congress/2019/02/27/trumps-lawyer-no-basis-for-presidents-medical-deferment-from-vietnam/.

[71]Raphelson, Samantha. "Trump Call Controversy Renews Spotlight on Gold Star Families." *National Public Radio*, October 23, 2017. https://www.npr.org/2017/10/23/559558075/trump-call-controversy-renews-spotlight-on-gold-star-families; Stied, Matt. "A Brief History of Trump's Feud With John McCain." *New York Magazine*, March 20, 2019. https://nymag.com/intelligencer/2019/03/an-abbreviated-history-of-trumps-feud-with-john-mccain.html; and Barrett, Ted, and David Cole. "Republican Senator Calls Trump's McCain Insults 'Deplorable.'" *CNN*, March 21, 2019. https://www.cnn.com/2019/03/20/politics/johnny-isakson-john-mccain/index.html.

who have made the ultimate sacrifice for their country as "suckers" and "losers."[72] The president's approach to race relations has been no better. Trump has consistently made incendiary statements, calling Hispanic immigrants "rapists" during the 2016 campaign, referring to a crowd dominated by neo-Nazis at the Charlottesville riot in 2017 as "very fine people," and cribbing the language of white supremacists with his remark during the 2020 George Floyd protests that "when the looting starts, the shooting starts."[73]

President Trump refuses to read intelligence reports, consider the relevant issues, or show even a modicum of respect for the professional standards of intelligence officers and other experts, many of whom have advanced degrees from the finest colleges and universities and decades of experience in their respective fields.[74] He frequently cites conspiracy theories while making policy decisions, referencing QAnon and other antigovernment alt-right groups and movements, and rejects the very existence of one of the most dangerous threats to the world: climate change.[75] He has often argued for bizarre, even dangerous, "solutions" to problems, including asking Department of Homeland Security and National Security Council officials in August 2017 to examine if they could use nuclear weapons on hurricanes.[76] During the pandemic he continually advocated the use of the dangerous and untested drug hydroxychloroquine to treat or prevent COVID-19 and even suggested that injecting bleach should be considered as a treatment for the virus.[77] After his inaccurate views about the world predictably don't pan out, Trump frequently tries to shift responsibility to the same experts

[72]Goldberg, Jeffrey. "Trump: Americans Who Died in War are 'Losers' and 'Suckers.'" *The Atlantic*, September 3, 2020. https://www.theatlantic.com/politics/archive/2020/09/trump-americans-who-died-at-war-are-losers-and-suckers/615997/.

[73]Scott, Eugene. "Trump Defends Inflammatory Remarks, Asks 'Who Is Doing the Raping?'" *CNN*, July 2, 2015. https://www.cnn.com/2015/07/01/politics/donald-trump-immigrants-raping-comments/index.html; Drobnic Holan, Angie. "In Context: Trump's 'Very Fine People on Both Sides' Remark." *PolitiFact*, April 26, 2019. https://www.politifact.com/article/2019/apr/26/context-trumps-very-fine-people-both-sides-remarks/; and Wines, Michael. "'Looting' Comment From Trump Dates Back to the Racial Unrest of the 1960s." *The New York Times*, May 29, 2020. https://www.nytimes.com/2020/05/29/us/looting-starts-shooting-starts.html.

[74]Barnes, Julian E., and Adam Goldman. "For Spy Agencies, Briefing Trump Is a Test of Holding His Attention." *The New York Times*, May 21, 2020. https://www.nytimes.com/2020/05/21/us/politics/presidents-daily-brief-trump.html.

[75]BBC. "Trump on Climate Change Report: 'I Don't Believe It.'" November 26, 2018. https://www.bbc.com/news/world-us-canada-46351940.

[76]Barnes, Thomas. "Trump 'Suggested Firing Nuclear Weapons at Hurricanes to Stop Them Hitting US,' Report Claims." *The Independent*, August 26, 2019. https://www.independent.co.uk/news/world/americas/us-politics/trump-nuking-hurricanes-nuclear-weapons-disrupt-storm-bomb-a9078796.html

[77]McDonald, Jessica, and Rem Rieder. "Trump Misleads on Hydroxychloroquine, Again." *FactCheck.org*, June 3, 2020. https://www.factcheck.org/2020/05/trump-misleads-on-hydroxychloroquine-again/; and Rogers, Katie, Christine Hauser, and Maggie Haberman. "Trump's Suggestion That Disinfectants Could Be Used to Treat Coronavirus Prompts Aggressive Pushback." *The New York Times*, April 24, 2020. https://www.nytimes.com/2020/04/24/us/politics/trump-inject-disinfectant-bleach-coronavirus.html.

he refused to listen to in the first place, including blaming a CIA briefer who warned of the danger of the coming pandemic in January 2020 in order to divert attention from his own incompetent response to the crisis.[78] He has demeaned the role of the president of the United States with his churlish behavior on Twitter, using language unbefitting the office. He constantly verbally assaults institutions and people that are fundamental to the US system of government, using the rhetoric of Nazi Germany and the Soviet Union to attack the press as "the enemy of the people" and repeatedly referring to members of the IC as "Nazis" who are part of the "Deep State" conspiracy out to destroy him. Finally, the president is an inveterate liar. No less of a figure as former secretary of state and chairman of the Joint Chiefs of Staff Colin Powell, a man devoted to national service and a lifelong Republican, has described Trump succinctly: "He lies all the time. He began lying the day of inauguration, when we got into an argument about the size of the crowd that was there . . . and I don't think that's in our interest."[79] Indeed, as of April 2020 President Trump has lied or made misleading statements 18,000 times in 1,170 days in office, over 15 public lies per day.[80]

In addition to Trump's base character, his conduct has frequently been inimical to the US national interest. Foremost among these problems is his solicitation of states and nonstate actors that are US adversaries. Beginning with his overt request for support from WikiLeaks—designated as a hostile intelligence organization by the US IC—in collusion with Russian government information operations during his 2016 campaign, Trump has consistently sought help from US foes. During the campaign, Trump's aides, including both the director of his campaign, Paul Manafort, and his future national security adviser, Michael Flynn, covertly communicated with members of the Russian government. Thirty people connected with the Trump campaign have lied about contacts between the campaign and the Russian government, while six of these people have been convicted of multiple felonies each in charges related to Special Counsel Robert Mueller's investigation of these activities. The **Mueller Report** indicated that the president himself could have been charged with at least 10 counts of obstruction of justice were it not for a Justice Department memorandum preventing Mueller from doing so.[81] Following the president's victory, his son-in-law, Jared Kushner, attempted to circumvent US IC SIGINT collection to establish a secure

---

[78]Barnes and Goldman, "For Spy Agencies, Briefing Trump Is a Test of Holding His Attention"; and Durkee, Alison. "Trump Was Warned About the Coronavirus More Than a Dozen Times in Daily Intel Briefings." *Vanity Fair*, April 28, 2020. https://www.vanityfair.com/news/2020/04/trump-received-coronavirus-warnings-daily-intelligence-briefings-pdb.

[79]CNN. "Colin Powell Criticizes Trump's Response to Protests in 'State of the Union' Interview." June 7, 2020. https://www.cnn.com/2020/06/07/politics/colin-powell-interview-donald-trump-protests/index.html.

[80]Markowitz, David. "Trump Is Lying More Than Ever: Just Look at the Data." *Forbes*, May 5, 2020. https://www.forbes.com/sites/davidmarkowitz/2020/05/05/trump-is-lying-more-than-ever-just-look-at-the-data/#2f47f3631e17.

[81]Mueller, Robert S., III. *Report on the Investigation Into Russian Interference in the 2016 Presidential Election*, Vol. II. Washington, DC: US Department of Justice, 2019.

communications system with the Russian government.[82] Trump has consistently undermined the US IC and national security communities by publicly stating he believes President Vladimir Putin's word over the overwhelming evidence of Russian election interference provided by the US IC.[83] Trump has also repeatedly disclosed classified material to the Russians, behavior that has caused so much concern in the US IC that its officers have chosen not to tell Trump about operations against Russia lest he reveal them.[84] The US IC even exfiltrated its most highly guarded Russian agent in 2017, fearing the president might reveal his identity to Putin.[85] In actions that ultimately led to his impeachment by Congress in 2020, Trump ordered the Pentagon to withhold **military aid to Ukraine** against Russia unless the government of Ukraine investigated the son of the president's primary political opponent, former vice president Joe Biden, making US foreign policy directly subordinate to Trump's reelection ambitions. There is no historical precedent for this pattern of conduct by a US president.

Repeatedly claiming that he knows more than his generals, President Trump has frequently interfered in military operations in a manner inconsistent with civil-military relations in a democracy and against the US national interest. He has meddled in the military justice process, pardoning several convicted war criminals and removing the secretary of the Navy for refusing to dismiss the charges against them.[86] Unable to obtain congressional funding for his border wall even when Republicans controlled both chambers, Trump subsequently diverted nearly $4 billion in DOD funds earmarked to build schools for soldiers' children and infrastructure improvements to his wall project.[87] Without consulting either the DOD or South Korea, Trump ordered the cancellation of joint US–Republic of Korea exercises so as to please North Korean dictator Kim Jong-un.[88] Against the advice of his entire national security team, Trump withdrew US forces from Syria, abandoning longtime US ally the Kurds to vicious

---

[82]Haberman, Maggie, Mark Mazetti, and Matt Apuzzo. "Kushner Is Said to Have Discussed a Secret Channel to Talk to Russia." *The New York Times*, May 26, 2017. https://www.nytimes.com/2017/05/26/us/politics/kushner-talked-to-russian-envoy-about-creating-secret-channel-with-kremlin.html.

[83]Bennett, John T. "Trump Takes Putin's Word for It on Russian Election Meddling." *Roll Call*, July 16, 2018. https://www.rollcall.com/2018/07/16/trump-takes-putins-word-for-it-on-russian-meddling-in-elections/.

[84]Sanger, David, and Nicole Perloth. "US Escalates Online Attacks on Russia's Power Grid." *The New York Times*, June 15, 2019. https://www.nytimes.com/2019/06/15/us/politics/trump-cyber-russia-grid.html.

[85]Ward, Alex. "CIA Reportedly Removed Top Spy From Russia Over Fear of Retaliation—and Maybe Trump." *Vox*, September 10, 2019. https://www.vox.com/2019/9/9/20856915/cnn-trump-russia-spy-putin-cia.

[86]Bell, Andrew M., and Thomas Gift. "War Crime Pardons and What They Mean for the Military." *War on the Rocks*, December 5, 2019. https://warontherocks.com/2019/12/war-crime-pardons-and-what-they-mean-for-the-military/.

[87]Myers, Meghann, and Joe Gould. "Trump Planning to Use Billions More in Military Funds to Build Border Wall." *Military Times*, January 14, 2020. https://www.militarytimes.com/news/your-military/2020/01/14/trump-planning-to-use-billions-more-in-military-funds-to-build-border-wall-per-report/.

[88]Cook, Nancy, Louis Nelson, and Nahal Toosi. "Trump Pledges to End Military Exercises as Part of North Korea Talks." *Politico*, June 12, 2018. https://www.politico.com/story/2018/06/12/trump-kim-meeting-press-conference-637544.

attacks by the Turkish Army.[89] In a temper tantrum related to German chancellor Angela Merkel's refusal to attend a G7 summit out of COVID-19 concerns and dismay over the president's invitation to Putin to attend, Trump ordered the removal of more than one-quarter of US troops stationed in Germany, thereby weakening NATO against Russia.[90]

Finally, during the civil unrest of the summer of 2020 following the death of George Floyd at the hands of the Minneapolis Police Department, Trump ordered federal law enforcement and National Guard troops to disperse a peaceful, constitutionally protected protest in Lafayette Square in front of the White House so he could have a photo opportunity at St. John's Episcopal Church.[91] Combined with his attempts to get active-duty US Army units to take control of US cities, this action prompted widespread criticism from retired generals and defense figures, including multiple former secretaries of defense and chairmen of the Joint Chiefs of Staff from four different presidential administrations.[92] There were some indications from the current leadership of the military that they would refuse such orders as unlawful.[93] The coda to the incident was Trump's former secretary of defense and retired Marine Corps general James Mattis, who resigned in protest over Trump's abandonment of the Kurds, releasing a letter condemning Trump's conduct. Mattis's language was searing.

> Donald Trump is the first president in my lifetime who does not try to unite the American people—does not even pretend to try. Instead he tries to divide us. We are witnessing the consequences of three years of this deliberate effort. We are witnessing the consequences of three years without mature leadership . . . We know that we are better than the **abuse of executive authority** that we witnessed in Lafayette Square. We must reject and hold accountable those in office who would make a mockery of our Constitution.[94]

---

[89]Barnes, Julian E., and Eric Schmitt. "Trump Orders Withdrawal of US Forces From Northern Syria." *The New York Times*, October 16, 2019. https://www.nytimes.com/2019/10/13/us/politics/mark-esper-syria-kurds-turkey.html.

[90]Herszenhorn, David M. "Trump Orders Large Withdrawal of US Forces From Germany." *Politico*, June 6, 2020. https://www.politico.eu/article/donald-trump-withdrawal-us-forces-from-germany-angela-merkel/.

[91]Baker, Peter, et al. "How Trump's Idea for a Photo Op Led to Havoc in a Park." *The New York Times*, June 2, 2020. https://www.nytimes.com/2020/06/02/us/politics/trump-walk-lafayette-square.html.

[92]Stracqualursi, Veronica. "The Prominent Former Military Leaders Who Have Criticized Trump's Actions Over Protests." *CNN*, June 5, 2020. https://www.cnn.com/2020/06/05/politics/military-leaders-trump-floyd-protests/index.html.

[93]Schmitt, Eric, et al. "Esper Breaks With Trump on Using Troops Against Protesters." *The New York Times*, June 3, 2020. https://www.nytimes.com/2020/06/03/us/politics/esper-milley-trump-protest.html.

[94]Quoted in Goldberg, Jeffrey. "James Mattis Denounces President Trump, Describes Him as a Threat to the Constitution." *The Atlantic*, June 3, 2020. https://www.theatlantic.com/politics/archive/2020/06/james-mattis-denounces-trump-protests-militarization/612640/.

Be they members of the armed forces or civilian employees, all federal civil servants take an oath of office requiring them to "defend the Constitution of the United States against all enemies, foreign and domestic."[95] The oath is not to the president or other leaders—it specifically references the document establishing the governing principles of US democracy. However, the US Constitution was not *sui generis*. Much of its substantive content was derived from Enlightenment philosophers such as Charles-Louis Montesquieu, John Locke, and Jean-Jacques Rousseau. Thus, although it is primarily a legal document, it does not exist in isolation from moral philosophy. Neither do the people who take the oath. US intelligence officers have a duty to both the US public and a higher moral purpose. In some circumstances, both might require obedience to President Trump or other leaders' lawful orders. However, in other situations, the president's authority to give an order might be unclear or ambiguously defined under the Constitution, despite the president's attempt to arrogate more authority. At that time, intelligence officers have little else to follow as a guide but their conscience and the ethical demands of their profession. They cannot merely consult the law. They must reference the principles from which laws are derived. To be an effective intelligence officer requires more than just knowledge and compliance of the law. It requires ethically informed action.

This chapter exposed students to some of the moral systems that guide ethical decisions. The objective was for students of intelligence to carefully consider how the operations of the US IC relate to these moral systems, accepting some ethical arguments while rejecting others. Such an activity will inevitably require a form of self-evaluation in light of the ethical requirements of such systems. Hopefully, this will help shed light on how students might confront the difficult challenges presented by the potential abuse of executive authority, now or in the future.

## KEY CONCEPTS

politicization  312
morality  313
ethics  313
patriotism  313
political realism  314
Just War theory  315
securitization  315
deontology  316

consequentialism  318
utilitarianism  318
critical theory  319
use of NGOs and the
    press as fronts  321
Doctors Without
    Borders  322
whistleblower  325

[95]Legal Information Institute, Cornell Law School. 5 US Code § 3331. Oath of Office. Accessed September 28, 2020. https://www.law.cornell.edu/uscode/text/5/3331.

## ADDITIONAL READING

Allhoff, Fritz. *Terrorism, Ticking Time Bombs, and Torture: A Philosophical Analysis.* Chicago, IL: University of Chicago Press, 2012.

Bean, Hamilton. "Rhetorical and Critical/Cultural Intelligence Studies." *Intelligence and National Security* 28, no. 4 (2013): 495–519.

Bellaby, Ross W. *The Ethics of Intelligence: A New Framework.* New York, NY: Routledge, 2016.

Erskine, Toni. "'As Rays of Light to the Human Soul'? Moral Agents and Intelligence Gathering." *Intelligence and National Security* 19, no. 2 (2004): 359–381.

Goldman, Jan, ed. *The Ethics of Spying: A Reader for the Intelligence Professional.* Lanham, MD: Scarecrow Press, 2006.

Hayden, Michael. *The Assault on Intelligence: American National Security in an Age of Lies.* New York, NY: Penguin, 2018.

Olson, James M. *Fair Play: The Moral Dilemmas of Spying.* Washington, DC: Potomac Books, 2006.

Omand, David, and Mark Phytian. *Principled Spying: The Ethics of Secret Intelligence.* Washington, DC: Georgetown University Press, 2018.

Velasco, Fernando, and Rubén Arcos. "Facing Intelligence Analysts With Ethical Scenarios." In *The Art of Intelligence: Simulations, Exercises, and Games*, edited by William J. Lahneman and Rubén Arcos. Lanham, MD: Rowman & Littlefield, 2014.

# 14

# THREATS TO THE UNITED STATES AND ITS INTERESTS

Jonathan M. Acuff, LaMesha L. Craft,
Christopher J. Ferrero, Richard J. Kilroy Jr.,
and Jonathan C. Smith

In this chapter we examine several strategic threats to the United States. Our discussion is not intended to comprehensively catalog all of the dangers to US interests, as such an effort would fill several volumes. Instead, we chose to focus on a varied set of the most important challenges emanating from nation-states, nonstate actors, and natural phenomena. Selecting which threats deserve coverage in this context is difficult. For example, how should one balance the threats of climate change versus the dramatic increase in the rate of species extinction? Within several decades, higher temperatures, more damaging storms, desertification, and rising sea levels will cost the United States hundreds of billions of dollars annually, imperil trillions of dollars of coastal real estate, and exacerbate a variety of regional conflicts and their attendant threats.[1] Yet the rapidly increasing rate of species extinction poses similarly devastating impacts. The potential collapse of entire ecosystems will produce enormous changes for the people inhabiting the regions in which ecosystem collapses occur, with spillover effects damaging the entire world.[2] A decline in biodiversity threatens everything from the global food system to the production of medicine. These two problems are clearly intertwined. However, in this case we chose to focus on climate change, as it is a driver of species extinctions and, particularly if global temperatures increase by two degrees Fahrenheit and "lock in" its effects, it poses longer-term and greater challenges to more people with specific political and economic impacts that can be readily analyzed.

We applied similar logic in selecting the other subjects to examine in this chapter. First, we balanced the relative time horizons and impacts of these threats. All of them require immediate action to successfully shape outcomes favoring US interests. Yet for some the effects are near-term, such as criminal gangs, while the dangers posed by others are medium- or longer-term and more impactful, such as climate change and strategic competitors. Others are higher priority, in terms of both the immediacy of their impact and the potential scale of the threat. Second, we included a mix of low-probability, high-impact events, such as inter-state wars or the use of weapons of

---

[1] US Global Change Research Program. *Fourth National Climate Assessment*, Vol. II. Washington, DC: US Global Change Research Program, 2018. https://nca2018.globalchange.gov/.

[2] Nuwer, Rachel. "Mass Extinctions Are Accelerating, Scientists Report." *The New York Times*, June 8, 2020. https://www.nytimes.com/2020/06/01/science/mass-extinctions-are-accelerating-scientists-report.html.

mass destruction, versus events with a relatively low impact yet high probability of occurring, such as the activities of criminal networks. Third, we attempted to distinguish between threats with domestic and international origins. For some threats, it is impossible to make the distinction between domestic and international causes and effects, such as the transnational implications of the problems posed by criminal gangs. However, as this volume is not primarily focused on homeland-security-related issues, coverage is heavily weighted toward threats of global significance.[3] Finally, we emphasized strategic threats—that is, threats that have the potential to alter the global **balance of power**, the relative ratio of military and economic power between states, in a manner less favorable to the United States.

## STRATEGIC COMPETITORS

**Jonathan M. Acuff**

Following the breakup of the Warsaw Pact alliance and the subsequent collapse of the Soviet Union in 1991, the United States emerged from the Cold War the sole remaining Great Power in the international system. Long before the end of the Soviet bloc, one could make the case that the United States had become the systemic **hegemon**, the nation-state that could unilaterally shape international outcomes in a manner no other state could.[4] However, this had clearly become the case by the early 1990s. The United States possessed largely unfettered power during the decade following the end of the Cold War, defeating Iraq's army in a one-sided contest during the Gulf War and then inflicting a similar thrashing of Serbia's military using only airpower in the 1998–1999 Kosovo War. During the 1990s, the United States experienced a decade of rapid economic growth and technological innovation, both of which increased the already enormous power disparity between the United States and other countries. Yet global power relationships rarely remain static for long, and the "unipolar moment" of US dominance would show signs of fading only two decades after the triumph of liberal capitalist democracy over Soviet communism.[5]

Relative to both other states in the system and the United States' own recent capabilities, US power has declined. The United States spends nearly $700 billion a year on its military. Yet it no longer has the most advanced weapon systems in a variety

---

[3]One of the ways homeland security scholars address these analytic challenges is via the "all hazards" approach. See Kilroy, Richard J., Jr., ed. *Threats to Homeland Security: Reassessing the All-Hazards Perspective*, 2nd ed. Hoboken, NJ: Wiley, 2018.

[4]Strange, Susan. "The Persistent Myth of Lost Hegemony." *International Organization* 41, no. 4 (1987): 551–574.

[5]Krauthammer, Charles. "The Unipolar Moment." *Foreign Affairs* (Winter 1990/1991).

of classes, from self-propelled artillery to hypersonic aircraft and missile technology.[6] Nearly 15,000 US military and contractor deaths and over $4.4 trillion spent on wars and in Iraq and Afghanistan not only yielded no strategic gains, but this expenditure of blood and treasure has left both Iran and China in stronger positions to influence the Middle East and Southwest Asia.[7] For all but the richest 10 percent of Americans, incomes have not increased in 40 years, economic inequality that has a variety of side effects from lower educational outcomes to reduced life expectancy.[8] US infrastructure has dramatically deteriorated, with one in three US bridges in need of complete replacement, deficient airports, and an antiquated railroad network.[9] Both US educational institutions and the US health care system have declined from 6th in the world in 1990 to 26th, sharply degrading the quality of available human capital and impeding innovation.[10] Nearly 43 percent of Americans are obese, with annual treatment and lost worker productivity costing over $155 billion annually.[11] Apart from reducing technological innovation and capital investment due to increased health care costs, the United States' poor education standards and high obesity rate have an additional, more direct effect on national security—just 29 percent of Americans 17–24 years of age are qualified to serve in the military while all others are disqualified due to obesity and/or poor educational achievement.[12] Both political and corporate corruption have also gotten much worse, with the United States falling from 15th in 1995 to 23rd in the world in 2019, behind such countries as Estonia, Uruguay, and the United Arab Emirates (UAE).[13] Finally, US public debt has sharply increased in the past 20 years and is now

---

[6]Hallman, Wesley. "Defense and Delusion: America's Military, Industry Are Falling Behind." *Defense News*, June 14, 2018. https://www.defensenews.com/opinion/commentary/2018/06/13/defense-and-delusion-americas-military-industry-are-falling-behind/.

[7]Watson Institute for International and Public Affairs. "Costs of War." November 2019. https://watson.brown.edu/costsofwar/.

[8]Desilver, Drew. "For Most US Workers, Real Wages Have Barely Budged for Decades." Pew Research Center, August 7, 2018. https://www.pewresearch.org/fact-tank/2018/08/07/for-most-us-workers-real-wages-have-barely-budged-for-decades/.

[9]American Road and Transportation Builders Association. "2020 Bridge Report." Accessed September 29, 2020. https://artbabridgereport.org/reports/ARTBA%202020%20Bridge%20Report%20-%20State%20Ranking.pdf.

[10]Lim, Stephen S., et al. "Measuring Human Capital: A Systematic Analysis of 195 Countries and Territories, 1990–2016." *The Lancet* 392, no. 10154 (2018). https://www.thelancet.com/journals/lancet/article/PIIS0140-6736(18)31941-X/fulltext#seccestitle160.

[11]Hales, Craig M., et al. "Prevalence of Obesity and Severe Obesity Among Adults: United States, 2017–2018." CDC National Center for Health Statistics, 2018. https://www.cdc.gov/nchs/products/databriefs/db360.htm.

[12]Phillips, Jeffrey E. "Here's Why Fighting Youth Obesity Is a Matter of National Security." *Military Times*, July 18, 2018. https://www.militarytimes.com/opinion/commentary/2018/07/18/commentary-heres-why-fighting-youth-obesity-is-a-matter-of-national-security/.

[13]Transparency International. "Corruption Perceptions Index 2019." Accessed September 29, 2020. https://images.transparencycdn.org/images/2019_CPI_Report_EN_200331_141425.pdf. Historical data are from https://www.transparency.org/en/cpi/1995.

approaching $27 trillion, over 132 percent of gross domestic product (GDP) compared to 58 percent in 2000.[14]

Let us be clear—the United States is not weak. The US GDP is still the largest in the world by far, at $21.4 trillion compared with its nearest competitor, China, at $14.3 trillion.[15] It still spends much more than any other country on its military, has the world's largest and most technologically sophisticated air force, and fields an array of weapons that in some areas remain dominant. Moreover, many of its problems are self-inflicted policy choices, with the US electorate unwilling to rein in entitlement spending while simultaneously supporting repeated rounds of tax cuts, both of which have sharply reduced the resources available for government support of infrastructure, research, and education. US antipathy toward international institutions during the George W. Bush and Donald Trump administrations may also have magnified the effects of questionable domestic policy choices, with the United States increasingly having to go it alone as it fails to generate support from its historical allies.[16] Regardless of the reasons, in relative terms the US advantage over some of its strategic competitors has narrowed considerably, so much so that within a few years one could make the case for the end of US hegemony and its replacement by a **multipolar international system**, a structure of global power in which several Great Powers of comparable strength compete.[17]

In this context it is important to distinguish between different forms of international competition, specifically hegemonic rivalries, regional rivalries, and nonrivalrous competition. **Hegemonic rivalries** are forms of military competition between two or more states for dominance over the international system. Such rivalries often result in catastrophic conflicts, with the Peloponnesian War, the Napoleonic Wars, and both world wars often characterized as hegemonic contests.[18] **Regional rivalries** are also forms of competition between states in which disputes often become militarized. However, unlike hegemonic rivalries, at least one of the participants lacks the capability to make a bid for global dominance. Finally, **nonrivalrous competition** occurs between states that are allies or relatively friendly toward each other and do not engage in militarized disputes. This form of state interaction usually takes the form of economic competition, although it may have military dimensions that result from technological advances spurred on by economic competition.

---

[14]US Debt Clock. Accessed July 7, 2020. https://www.usdebtclock.org/.

[15]World Bank. "GDP (Current US$)." Accessed September 29, 2020. https://data.worldbank.org/indicator/NY.GDP.MKTP.CD.

[16]Many analysts have argued the decline in American primacy is a result not of an increase in adversary capabilities but of poor policy choices, declining US will, and/or a lack of commitment to international institutions. See, for example, Lieber, Robert J. "Staying Power and the American Future: Problems of Primacy, Policy, and Grand Strategy." *Journal of Strategic Studies* 34, no. 4 (2011): 509–530.

[17]National Intelligence Council. *Global Trends 2025: A Transformed World.* Washington, DC: US Government Printing Office, 2008.

[18]Gilpin, Robert. *War and Change in World Politics.* Cambridge, UK: Cambridge University Press, 1983; and Mearsheimer, John J. *The Tragedy of Great Power Politics.* New York, NY: Norton, 2001.

In the contemporary international system, only one state is a potential hegemonic rival of the United States. China's rate of economic growth over the past 40 years, unprecedented in human history, has enabled a rapid program of **military modernization**. From 2000 to 2016, China's military budget increased an average of 10 percent a year, slowing to 5 to 7 percent per year since 2017. Nominally totaling over $170 billion, true military spending is probably in excess of $200 billion.[19] Presiding over an ambitious modernization program, China plans to complete comprehensive restructuring and reequipment of the People's Liberation Army (PLA), People's Liberation Army Navy (PLAN), and People's Liberation Army Air Force (PLAAF) by 2035, with the long-term result of a "world-class" military by 2049.[20] Although the quality of its senior leadership is unknown, after significant troop reductions over the past decade the PLA is now leaner, equipped with more modern weaponry, and likely better trained than at any time in its history.[21] The PLAAF has fielded two models of what it calls "stealth" aircraft, although the ability of these airframes to actually conceal their radar signatures remains questionable. China has executed the largest naval building program in history, including construction of new submarines and two aircraft carriers, and now possesses the world's largest navy.[22] The People's Republic of China (PRC) is currently developing a wide array of advanced weapon systems, from counter-space anti-satellite missiles to electromagnetic rail guns and directed energy beam weapons.[23] Finally, within one to two decades China plans to be able to wage a modern information war, project power out of its region, and fight and win a global conflict.[24]

In a clear departure from its historical focus on regional security, China has increasingly asserted itself in international politics, often in an aggressive manner. China has established the largest infrastructure construction program in history, the **Belt and Road Initiative**, which has indebted dozens of countries in Asia, Africa, and Eastern Europe and allowed China to acquire military basing rights as a form of payment.

---

[19]Defense Intelligence Agency. *China Military Power: Modernizing a Force to Fight and Win*. Washington, DC: Defense Intelligence Agency, 2019, 20–21. http://www.dia.mil/Portals/27/Documents/News/Military%20Power%20Publications/China_Military_Power_FINAL_5MB_20190103.pdf.

[20]Office of the Secretary of Defense. *Annual Report to Congress: Military and Security Developments Involving the People's Republic of China, 2019*. Washington, DC: US Department of Defense, May 2, 2019, 31. https://media.defense.gov/2019/May/02/2002127082/-1/-1/1/2019_CHINA_MILITARY_POWER_REPORT.pdf.

[21]Blasko, Dennis J. "What Is Known and Unknown About Changes to the PLA's Ground Combat Units." *China Brief* 17, no. 7 (2017). https://jamestown.org/program/known-unknown-changes-plas-ground-combat-units/.

[22]Maizland, Lindsay. "China's Modernizing Military." Council on Foreign Relations, February 5, 2020. https://www.cfr.org/backgrounder/chinas-modernizing-military.

[23]Nurkin, Tate, et al. "China's Advanced Weapons Systems." Jane's by IHS Markit, May 22, 2018. https://www.uscc.gov/sites/default/files/Research/Jane's%20by%20IHS%20Markit_China's%20Advanced%20Weapons%20Systems.pdf.

[24]Ibid.; and Cooper, Cortez A., III. "PLA Military Modernization: Drivers, Force Restructuring, and Implications." CT-488. Testimony Before US-China Economic and Security Review Commission, February 15, 2018. www.rand.org/content/dam/rand/pubs/testimonies/CT400/CT488/RAND_CT488.pdf.

Several of the recipients of Belt and Road loans are now effectively client states of the PRC. In violation of international law, it has deployed air and naval assets to the Spratly and Paracel Islands to increase its area denial capabilities within its defense perimeter and, potentially, to project power beyond it. It has abolished most of the freedoms guaranteed to Hong Kong by treaty. As a means by which to shape both its image and the policy positions of targeted countries, China has attempted to infiltrate the governments and nongovernmental organizations of several democracies, including Taiwan, Australia, the Philippines, New Zealand, Germany, and the United States.[25] It has executed a comprehensive cyber strategy to steal hundreds of billions of dollars of intellectual property from US and European firms, thereby enabling it to skip the time and development costs associated with technological innovation in both civilian and military industries.[26]

Negative rivalries have a tendency to "lock in" and acquire a logic of their own, independent of rational calculation of interests, and exacerbate the domestic politics of authoritarian states, which rely heavily on propaganda to support regime legitimacy.[27] For some analysts, this has already happened, with a hegemonic war a likely result of Sino-US competition.[28] Other scholars see the possibility of striking a "grand bargain," trading away Taiwan in exchange for Chinese accession to a continued US presence in the region and avoidance of a hegemonic conflict.[29] Still others argue that no such conflict is in the offing because the rivalry between the United States and China is different from previous hegemonic rivalries, with China much further behind the United States technologically than previous rivals.[30] Although Xi Jinping has taken steps to

---

[25]Mattis, Peter. "An American Lens on China's Interference and Influence-Building Abroad." The Asan Forum, April 30, 2018. http://www.theasanforum.org/an-american-lens-on-chinas-interference-and-influence-building-abroad/.

[26]Marcias, Amanda. "FBI Chief Slams Chinese Cyber Attacks on US." CNBC, July 7, 2020. https://www.cnbc.com/2020/07/07/fbi-chief-slams-chinese-cyberattacks-against-us-hudson-institute.html. Some scholars argue the gains from China's cyber espionage program are vastly overstated, as Chinese cyber operations do little to address the country's core weaknesses. See Lindsay, Jon R. "The Impact of China on Cybersecurity: Fiction and Friction." *International Security* 39, no. 3 (2015): 7–47.

[27]Thompson, William R. "Identifying Rivals and Rivalries Around the World." *International Studies Quarterly* 45, no. 4 (2001): 557–586; and Weiss, Jessica Chen, and Allan Dafoe. "Authoritarian Audiences, Rhetoric, and Propaganda in International Crises: Evidence From China." *International Studies Quarterly* 63, no. 4 (2019): 963–973.

[28]Friedberg, Aaron L. *A Contest for Supremacy: China, America, and the Struggle for Mastery in Asia.* New York, NY: Norton, 2011; Xuetong, Yan. *Ancient Chinese Political Thought, Modern Chinese Power.* Princeton, NJ: Princeton University Press, 2011; Liff, Adam P., and G. John Ikenberry. "Racing Towards Tragedy? China's Rise, Military Competition in the Asia-Pacific, and the Security Dilemma." *International Security* 39, no. 2 (2014): 52–91; Holslag, Jonathan. *China's Coming War With Asia.* Cambridge, UK: Polity Press, 2015; and Allison, Graham. *Destined for War: Can America and China Escape Thucydides' Trap?* New York, NY: Houghton Mifflin, 2017.

[29]Glaser, Charles L. "A US-China Grand Bargain? The Hard Choice Between Military Competition and Accommodation." *International Security* 39, no. 4 (2015): 49–90.

[30]Brooks, Stephen G., and William C. Wohlforth. "The Rise and Fall of the Great Powers in the Twenty-First Century: China's Rise and the Fate of America's Global Position." *International Security* 40, no. 3 (2016): 7–53.

consolidate his power, China's leaders are by no means unified in their confidence in China's ability to challenge the United States. However, there can be no doubt that China's power has increased markedly over the past two decades and that it is rapidly approaching parity with the United States.

Regional rivalries involving the United States are a more common, though far less dangerous, form of competition than a bid for hegemony from China. After failing to reach an accommodation regarding Russian acceptance of the post–Cold War order, the United States has become enmeshed in a regional rivalry with Russia as that country seeks to regain power and influence in Eurasia.[31] Since Vladimir Putin assumed the Russian presidency in 1999, his primary objective has been to return Russia to the prominence of the Soviet Union, to "re-establish the power of the [Russian] state."[32] Putin has sought to accomplish this not via reimposing Marxist–Leninist ideology but rather by co-opting or eliminating all rivals for domestic power and retaking the territory of the 14 countries formerly controlled by the USSR, such as his seizure of Crimea from Ukraine in 2014, or reducing them to client status.[33] Although the Russian Federation was a very weak state for the first decade of his rule, beset by sharply reduced life expectancy, alcoholism, inflation, corruption, and inadequate funding of its military and public institutions,[34] Putin has recently made significant progress on many of these issues. He has firmly consolidated his power, crushing all political opposition, and turned the previously pro-Western Russian public away from the United States and its allies.[35] Despite a punishing Western sanctions regime and widespread corruption, the Russian economy has improved. Recently, Putin has been able to embark on an ambitious program of **military modernization**, albeit one marked by gross exaggeration of the capabilities of new weapons and doubts as to the overall effectiveness of the entire effort.

Despite Putin's consolidation of domestic power and his ability to address some of Russia's demographic challenges in recent years, Russia's aggressive actions against Estonia, Georgia, and Ukraine have further alienated its neighbors, driving them toward, not away from, the West.[36] Russian meddling in the 2016 presidential election and Russia's overt support for the election of Trump have disrupted US domestic politics,

[31]Mastanduno, Michael. "Partner Politics: Russia, China, and the Challenge of Extending US Hegemony After the Cold War." *Security Studies* 28, no. 3 (2019): 479–504.

[32]Dyson, Stephen Benedict, and Matthew J. Parent. "The Operational Code Approach to Profiling Leaders: Understanding Vladimir Putin." *Intelligence and National Security* 33, no. 1 (2018): 93.

[33]Fish, M. Steven. *Democracy Derailed in Russia: The Failure of Open Politics.* Cambridge, UK: Cambridge University Press, 2005.

[34]McFaul, Michael, and Kathryn Stoner-Weiss. "The Myth of the Authoritarian Model." *Foreign Affairs* (January/February 2008).

[35]Sokolov, Boris, et al. "Anti-Americanism in Russia: From Pro-American to Anti-American Attitudes, 1993–2009." *International Studies Quarterly* 62, no. 3 (2018): 534–547.

[36]Driscoll, Jesse, and Daniel Maliniak. "With Friends Like These: Brinkmanship and Chain-Ganging in Russia's Near Abroad." *Security Studies* 25, no. 4 (2016): 585–607.

yet yielded little by way of concrete advantages that accrue to Russia. In spite of the American president's hostility toward the North Atlantic Treaty Organization (NATO) and his erratic trade and security policy shifts, similar efforts against Great Britain during the Brexit vote and against France and Germany during those countries' recent elections have not shifted their allegiance away from the alliance. Historically, **information operations** and propaganda have been employed in an attempt to compensate for fundamental Russian economic and military weakness relative to its competitors. This time is no different. Russia can exploit extant societal divisions in the West, which are considerable. But it cannot control the targeted countries, and its efforts may presage increased hostility toward Russia precisely because of Putin's actions.

In contrast with its predecessor, the Soviet Union, Russia lacks both the material resources and international legitimacy to become a hegemonic challenger. But it can act as a **spoiler**. For example, Russia has covertly provided financial support for a variety of far-right European political parties, while at the same time openly courting better diplomatic relations with the targeted countries. This has yielded favorable results in Austria, Hungary, and Italy, dislodging these countries from the mainstream of democratic practice and disrupting governance of the European Union (EU). A continued rightward shift in Poland might have similar results, despite the long history of Russo-Polish animosity. By attempting to break judicial opposition to his policies and displaying xenophobia, anti-Semitism, homophobia, and hostility toward Germany, Polish president Andrzej Duda's administration has had a fractious relationship with the EU. A Polish return to the Russian orbit would represent a significant shift in the power dynamics of Europe.

Similarly, Iran is a regional power that primarily poses a threat to the United States as a spoiler, not for its ability to project power out of the region. Iran's economy has been hobbled by decades of sanctions and mismanagement. Despite this, the Iranians have carefully husbanded their limited human capital and industrial manufacturing capabilities and built robust nuclear weapons and missile programs.[37] They have also benefited indirectly from US actions in the region. Iran's implacable enemy, the Sunni Baathist regime of Saddam Hussein, was destroyed by the United States in the Iraq War and replaced by a government dominated by Shiite political parties friendly toward the Islamic Republic. More recently, the US campaign to destroy the Islamic State in northern Iraq removed a potential menace from Iran's border, while broader US disengagement from the region has left Iran's ties to Bahrain and the UAE intact. Having funded and supplied **Hezbollah** for decades, Iran is one of the few remaining state sponsors of terrorism. It also operates a network of advisers and intelligence officers via the Islamic Revolutionary Guard Corps' Quds Force, which supports terrorist activities in Lebanon, the Palestinian Authority, Syria, Afghanistan, and Yemen.

---

[37]Nuclear Threat Initiative. "Iran." Accessed September 29, 2020. https://www.nti.org/learn/countries/iran/nuclear/.

From President George W. Bush listing Iran as part of the "axis of evil" to President Trump's unprovoked withdrawal from the 2015 nuclear agreement, the United States has frequently characterized Iran as a profound threat. In fact, the country is far from the power its own propaganda machine and the United States portray it as. Iran is **deeply divided** internally. Over the past decade, it has experienced repeated episodes of severe domestic political unrest as the conservative religious elite, supported by rural interests, have clashed with urban protesters, mainly educated young people.[38] The country is also in a dangerous neighborhood, with the failed state of Afghanistan on one border and historical enemies Turkey, Saudi Arabia, and Russia nearby. It has seen its primary ally, Syria, torn apart by a civil war. The 2019 drone attacks on Saudi oil fields by Iran and its support for a mob menacing the US embassy in Baghdad resulted in the US assassination of the leader of the Quds Force, Qassim Soleimani, in January 2020. Iran can menace states friendly toward the United States, as in the case of its proxy war with Saudi Arabia in Yemen and its ongoing support for Hezbollah against Israel. But it cannot fundamentally threaten US interests. For all the concern regarding the Iranian nuclear program, if Iran went nuclear, it would still be **deterred by the Israeli nuclear arsenal**. Moreover, it could not use its weapons against the Saudis or its other enemies lest it incur a US counterstrike that would destroy the country. Iran's support for terrorism, dormant nuclear program, cyber warfare capabilities, and cooperation with China are risks to US interests in the region.[39] But the Iranians do not represent the existential threat frequently attributed to them.

Often referred to as the Hermit Kingdom, the Democratic People's Republic of Korea (DPRK) is one of the world's most brutal dictatorships. North Korea's legitimating ideology, *juche*, is totalitarian and, despite its Maoist overtones, is in fact a form of fascism.[40] The DPRK is ruled by the Kim family, which has controlled the country in a multigenerational cult of personality since Kim Il-sung founded the state and initiated the Korean War in 1950. Despite repeated overtures to South Korea and the West, the current dictator, Kim Jong-un, has been at least as brutal as his father and grandfather. After assuming power, he moved to consolidate his rule by ordering the execution of his uncle and the assassination of his half-brother in Malaysia in 2017.[41] For decades, the Kim family has practiced a form of patronage directed at members of

---

[38]Kamalipour, Yahya R., ed. *Media, Power, and Politics in the Digital Age: The 2009 Presidential Election Uprising in Iran.* Lanham, MD: Rowman & Littlefield, 2010.

[39]Fassihi, Farnaz, and Steven Lee Myers. "Defying US, China and Iran Near Trade and Military Partnership." *The New York Times*, July 11, 2020. https://www.nytimes.com/2020/07/11/world/asia/china-iran-trade-military-deal.html.

[40]Myers, B. R. *The Cleanest Race: How North Koreans See Themselves—and Why It Matters.* New York, NY: Melville House, 2011.

[41]There are some indications his half-brother was connected to the US intelligence community. But this claim has not been widely reported. See Strobel, Warren P. "North Korean Leader's Slain Half-Brother Was a CIA Source." *The Wall Street Journal*, June 10, 2019. https://www.wsj.com/articles/north-korean-leaders-slain-half-brother-was-said-to-have-been-a-cia-informant-11560203662.

the North Korean Workers' Party, looting the country to cement control and to enrich themselves and their followers. Paired with pseudo-Marxist state planning and the end of subsidies from the USSR in the early 1990s, the result has been **economic collapse**, causing multiple famines that have killed millions. But for Western food aid, the famines would continue.

Some analysts claim the DPRK spends one-third of its GDP on its military.[42] If true, this would be by far the highest percentage of military spending in the world. The North Korean Army consists of 1.1 million men, making it the world's fourth largest, slightly larger than the US Army. It has thousands of artillery pieces and rocket launchers within range of Seoul, which in time of war would likely fire on the South Korean capital of nearly 10 million. However, despite its size and varied composition, much of the North Korean military is in decline, with outdated, poorly maintained equipment, weak leadership, and inadequately trained personnel.[43] To at least partially compensate for its crumbling conventional capabilities, the DPRK has invested heavily in special operations forces and has repeatedly used them to kill or kidnap South Korean civilians. Similarly, it has developed extensive **cyber capabilities**. One of the largest cyber attacks thus far was executed by North Korea against the Sony Corporation in 2014 over its film *The Interview*, which ridiculed the North Korean dictator. The DPRK regularly executes cyber attacks against US and other government websites, stealing roughly $1 billion annually, including nearly making off with $1 billion from the US Federal Reserve in 2016.[44]

The DPRK has a vast chemical weapons stockpile and likely also has biological weapons capability.[45] In 2006, in defiance of international agreements, North Korea successfully tested its first nuclear weapon. It has likely recently acquired the ability to manufacture hydrogen bombs as well.[46] For over a decade, Pyongyang has been attempting to build a true intercontinental ballistic missile (ICBM), capable of reaching the US West Coast. Its *Hwasong* series missiles have thus far failed most of their operational tests. Nevertheless, the DPRK seems determined to obtain a **nuclear weapon delivery system** capable of striking the United States. More recently, the North Koreans have been attempting to develop a submarine platform capable of launching such a weapon at a US target.[47]

---

[42]Hewitt, Kate. "Rethinking North Korean Sanctions: Lessons and Strategies for Long-Term Planning." *38 North*, January 16, 2018. https://www.38north.org/2018/01/khewitt011618/.

[43]International Institute for Strategic Studies. *The Military Balance, 2020*. London, UK: Routledge, 2020, 284.

[44]Sanger, David E., David D. Kirkpatrick, and Nicole Perlroth. "The World Once Laughed at North Korean Cyberpower. No More." *The New York Times*, October 15, 2017. https://www.nytimes.com/2017/10/15/world/asia/north-korea-hacking-cyber-sony.html.

[45]Nuclear Threat Initiative. "North Korea." Accessed September 29, 2020. https://www.nti.org/learn/countries/north-korea/.

[46]Ibid.

[47]International Institute for Strategic Studies, *Military Balance, 2020*, 223.

North Korea constantly menaces its neighbors, US allies the Republic of Korea and Japan. The very definition of a "rogue regime," it participates in a wide variety of aggressive activities, from its cyber attacks to its weapons programs. Over two decades, a wide variety of coercive policies, including the toughest sanctions regime in history, and diplomatic overtures have failed to bring the DPRK into the fold. In stark contrast with previous US presidents who have avoided legitimating the North Korean regime by meeting directly with it, President Trump held several summits with Kim Jong-un in Singapore, in Hanoi, and at the demilitarized zone between the two Koreas. Trump's policy of **engagement and flattery**, including referring to the dictator as a "friend" and characterizing Kim's brutality as a "great and beautiful vision for his country," has yielded no gains for the United States, quite the opposite in fact—North Korea resumed production of nuclear weapons and missile testing in 2019.[48] President Trump has proved no more capable than his four predecessors in getting the North Koreans to give up nuclear weapons.

Finally, some regional rivalries do not directly involve the United States but are nevertheless dangerous. For example, **Pakistan–India** is a regional rivalry with potential global implications, as both states are nuclear powers. Pakistan is China's client, and the PRC and India are similarly entangled in a regional rivalry of their own. Although the United States is not a party to these disputes, conflict escalation involving even a limited nuclear exchange would clearly have an enormous impact beyond the region. Similarly, the long-standing competition between NATO members Greece and Turkey over the island nation of Cyprus has resulted in one war and numerous armed disputes. A repeat episode could inadvertently drag the United States in, as regional instability could easily spread. Much the same is true regarding regional stability for both the rivalry between Bosnia, Kosovo, and Serbia over the borders of the former Yugoslavia and the competition involving Egypt, Sudan, and Ethiopia over the control of the flow of the Nile River. Other regional rivalries in Africa, Latin America, and Southeast Asia could also affect US interests in difficult-to-anticipate ways.

Nonrivalrous competition is the most common form of competition between the United States and other states. Although the United States has displayed a marked preference for unilateral action over international institutions in recent years, most states remain on friendly terms with the country.

Nonrivalrous competition is usually economic, with interfirm and intersector competition in the capitalist world market generating cross-national variation in GDP growth. Such differences by definition involve winners and losers, with shifts in employment patterns producing deindustrialization in highly developed countries like the United States and its European allies. These shifts can have political consequences,

---

[48]Buncombe, Andrew. "Trump Praises North Korean Dictator's 'Great and Beautiful Vision' for His Country." *Independent*, August 2, 2019. https://www.independent.co.uk/news/world/americas/us-politics/trump-kim-jong-un-north-korea-us-great-beautiful-latest-a9037186.html; and Albert, Eleanor. "North Korea's Nuclear Capabilities." Council on Foreign Relations, December 20, 2019. https://www.cfr.org/backgrounder/north-koreas-military-capabilities.

as the **rise of populism** is due in part to such shifts. Populist leaders are more protectionist, tend toward isolationism, and undermine or ignore international diplomatic efforts. The Trump administration's abandonment of the Iran nuclear framework and the Paris Agreement, agreements that all US allies strongly supported,[49] are examples of such populist disengagement.

Nonrivalrous competition may take on a military dimension in the form of some countries' military production capabilities being reduced by the decline and/or bankruptcy of some domestic defense firms, thereby sharply reducing their indigenous ability to manufacture weapons. For example, Boeing's announcement in early 2019 that it planned to acquire an 80 percent stake in aerospace firm Embraer would have left Brazil without a domestic military aircraft manufacturing capability, the very reason for the creation of Embraer by the military junta governing the country in the mid-1960s. However, the flip side of this competition is improved weapon systems and increased reliance on jointly developed military technology that is the inevitable byproduct of globalization. Such **interdependence in military production** probably reduces the likelihood of international conflict.[50] It does, however, pose a potential problem in terms of industrial espionage and proliferation of military technology to third world countries. China and Russia have clearly benefited in the more lax protection of some of the United States' allies with which it builds or trades weapons. For example, Turkey's recent purchase of Russian air defense systems the country would attempt to integrate with its F-35 fighters could result in the Russians gaining insight into to how to defeat the US-built aircraft.[51]

One constant thread running through each of the remaining threats we examine in this chapter is how the composition of interstate competition will shape how the United States and its allies respond to each. For example, strong multilateral cooperation on climate change would greatly amplify efforts undertaken by the United States, thereby dramatically reducing the danger posed by this threat. However, if the development of green technologies and monitoring of a carbon emission control regime continue to play out as a form of rivalry between US and Chinese tech firms, its primary manifestation to this date, both implementation of a carbon reduction plan and its effectiveness will be greatly diminished. Similarly, Chinese action during the initial stages of the COVID-19 pandemic sharpened the distrust of the United States and Western democracies at precisely the moment the PRC had been making headway in getting several NATO members to adopt Huawei's 5G infrastructure. Subsequent

---

[49]Israel was strongly opposed to the Iranian nuclear agreement. However, it is worth remembering that while the United States and Israel are on very friendly terms, there is no collective security agreement between these two countries.

[50]Brooks, Stephen G. "The Globalization of Production and the Changing Benefits of Conquest." *Journal of Conflict Resolution* 43, no. 5 (1999): 646–670.

[51]Gould, Joe. "US Could Buy Turkey's Russian-Made S-400 Under Senate Proposal." *Defense News*, June 29, 2020. https://www.defensenews.com/congress/2020/06/29/us-could-buy-turkeys-russia-made-s-400-under-senate-proposal/.

Chinese actions in Hong Kong have only amplified these problems. Thus the pattern of interstate competition between the United States and China has spilled over into international responses to both climate change and the COVID-19 pandemic.

## PANDEMICS

**Jonathan M. Acuff**

For over two decades, the US intelligence community (IC) has produced intelligence reports for consumption by the highest level of government that have consistently warned of the risk of the large-scale outbreak of communicable diseases.[52] Although these forecasts have varied widely in the relative emphasis placed on pandemics compared to other threats, **strategic warning** regarding the danger posed by mass outbreaks of infectious diseases was issued long before the COVID-19 pandemic. Moreover, very specific—and ultimately accurate, given what has occurred with the COVID-19 outbreak—factors were identified that would make pandemics hard to detect and respond to. Climate change and the poor state of health care infrastructure were both indicated as problems that would amplify the likelihood of outbreaks, weaken both multilateral and domestic responses, and increase the resulting death toll.[53]

Although the US IC offered accurate analysis of the emergent trend, it has experienced greater difficulty in improving its **point prediction** capability. This is a complex problem. Warning is heavily reliant on the quality of information emanating from the region initially affected by the disease. As demonstrated by the Chinese government's attempt to conceal the COVID-19 outbreak and falsify data regarding the scope of the outbreak, the United States cannot always rely on countries to provide accurate information to direct a response. Moreover, responsible international organizations often have conflicting agendas, seeking to balance their mandate with the requirement of respecting both the sovereignty and the power of organizational stakeholders. The World Health Organization was far too willing to accept transparently false reporting and restrictions on access to Wuhan, the site of the COVID-19 outbreak. But US IC intelligence analysts face additional barriers to providing precise disease forecasts. Medical intelligence is not an issue area that most IC analysts typically deal with

[52]National Intelligence Council. *Global Trends 2015. A Dialogue About the Future with Non-Governmental Experts.* Washington, DC: Central Intelligence Agency, 2000, 81. https://www.dni.gov/files/documents/Global%20Trends_2015%20Report.pdf; National Intelligence Council. *Mapping the Global Future: 2020.* Washington, DC: Office of the Director of National Intelligence, 2004, 30. http://www.dni.gov/files/documents/Global%20Trends_Mapping%20the%20Global%20Future%202020%20Project.pdf; National Intelligence Council, *Global Trends 2025*, 75; National Intelligence Council. *Global Trends 2030: Alternative Worlds.* Washington, DC: Office of the Director of National Intelligence, 2012, xi. https://www.dni.gov/files/images/buttons/pdf_2.png.

[53]National Intelligence Council, *Global Trends 2025*, 75; and National Intelligence Council. *Global Trends: Paradox of Progress.* Washington, DC: Office of the Director of National Intelligence, 2017, 25 and 170. https://www.dni.gov/files/images/globalTrends/documents/GT-Full-Report.pdf.

directly, as it is the business of epidemiologists at the **Centers for Disease Control and Prevention (CDC)**. Effective health surveillance and warning require extensive medical training, which is a challenge as most intelligence analysts lack even a background in elementary statistics, let alone epidemiology.

However, unlike many other examples of advance warning provided by the US IC to policymakers, the United States and its allies did respond to the warnings that began to appear during the 1990s regarding the danger of a pandemic. These efforts accelerated after 9/11, resulting in considerable buildup of public health capabilities and disaster response under the Bush administration, investments that paralleled efforts made by numerous EU members and Japan. Moreover, technological developments during this period were not static. The emergence of **dual-use biomedical technologies** expanded the nature of the threat posed by diseases and increased the potential for the deployment of bioweapons by terrorists.[54] Beginning in 2009, the Barack Obama administration expanded multilateral cooperation, efforts punctuated by severe disease outbreaks in Haiti, East Asia, and Africa as well as the Zika virus carried by mosquitoes in the United States and Latin America during 2015–2016. Following its uneven response to the Ebola outbreak in West Africa in 2014, the Obama administration also developed a 69-page **pandemic response playbook**, a set of protocols to be followed during an outbreak, and established a section of the National Security Council (NSC) to monitor and respond to pandemics.[55]

Despite these marked advances in forecasting and response capabilities at the federal, state, and local levels, these capabilities were squandered. At the state and local levels, public health capabilities eroded sharply following the Great Recession of 2008 due to massive budget cuts that were never made good once economic growth resumed in 2010. Some of the federal disease response capability was also eroded during the budget sequestration battles of the 2010s.[56] In short, **public health** at all levels of the US government has been chronically underfunded during the past decade. The United States' ongoing problems in providing efficient health care for its citizens also created a structural vulnerability.

In addition to funding issues, the United States has failed in several specific areas related to disease forecasting and response. Despite the reforms of the Obama and Bush administrations, the United States still lacks a specialized **response team** capability.[57] In contrast, following its experience with SARS, H1N1, and MERS outbreaks,

---

[54]Walsh, Patrick F. *Intelligence, Biosecurity, and Terrorism*. London, UK: Palgrave Macmillan, 2018.

[55]Executive Office of the President of the United States. *Playbook for Early Response to High-Consequence Emerging Infectious Disease Threats and Biological Incidents*. Washington, DC: Executive Office of the President of the United States, 2016; and Diamond, Dan, and Nahal Toosi. "Trump Team Failed to Follow NSC's Pandemic Playbook." *Politico*, March 25, 2020. https://www.politico.com/news/2020/03/25/trump-coronavirus-national-security-council-149285.

[56]Hatfill, Stephen J. "Rapid Validation of Disease Outbreak Intelligence by Small Independent Verification Teams." *Intelligence and National Security* 35, no. 4 (2020): 533.

[57]Ibid.

South Korea developed an extremely effective disease response system, with a single government agency making decisions and immediate response teams composed of epidemiologists, computer technicians, and laboratory personnel deployed to execute contract tracing.[58] The United States has also failed to effectively integrate the wealth of expertise in academia and the private sector. Johns Hopkins University's Bloomberg School of Public Health quickly became the standard for coronavirus statistics. The University of Washington's Institute for Health Metrics and Evaluation developed the most respected forecasting model to track the progression of COVID-19. As the nature of the threat posed by infectious diseases has evolved, the IC must do a better job of engaging academia, the private sector, and the think tank community to improve the quality of its forecasting and response.[59]

In response to COVID-19, the **US performance** has been far worse than that of most of the industrialized world (see Table 14.1). With only 4.25 percent of the world's population, as of August 2020 the United States accounted for more than 25 percent of the identified cases worldwide, 5 million of the 19 million total. Yet this figure is probably much lower than the actual number of infected people—six months after the onset of the pandemic, the United States was still not testing enough of its population. It is also noteworthy that many developing countries have performed significantly better than the United States in controlling the outbreak and reducing the death rate. For example, Vietnam, which modeled its response along US guidelines developed after SARS, has done much better than the United States with only 10 deaths and a per-case fatality rate of only 1.3 percent.

**TABLE 14.1 ■ COVID-19 Fatalities in Advanced Industrialized Countries[60]**

| Country | Total Deaths | Deaths per 100,000 | Deaths per Case |
|---|---|---|---|
| Argentina | 4,411 | 9.91 | 1.9% |
| Australia | 278 | 1.11 | 1.3% |
| Austria | 720 | 8.14 | 3.3% |
| Belgium | 9,866 | 86.38 | 13.6% |
| Brazil | 99,572 | 47.54 | 3.4% |

*(Continued)*

---

[58]Town, Jenny. "South Korea's Pandemic Response." Stimson Center, March 26, 2020. https://www.stimson.org/2020/south-koreas-pandemic-response/; and Lee, Heesu. "These Elite Contact Tracers Show the World How to Beat Covid-19." *Bloomberg*, July 27, 2020. https://news.bloomberglaw.com/health-law-and-business/these-elite-contact-tracers-show-the-world-how-to-beat-covid-19.

[59]Lentzos, Michael S., Michael S. Goodman, and James M. Wilson. "Health Security Intelligence: Engaging Across Disciplines and Sectors." *Intelligence and National Security* 35, no. 4 (2020): 465–476.

[60]Coronavirus Resource Center. "Mortality Analyses." Johns Hopkins University. Accessed August 8, 2020. https://coronavirus.jhu.edu/data/mortality.

| TABLE 14.1 ■ (Continued) | | | |
|---|---|---|---|
| Country | Total Deaths | Deaths per 100,000 | Deaths per Case |
| Canada | 9,017 | 24.33 | 7.5% |
| Chile | 9,958 | 53.17 | 2.7% |
| China* | 4,681 | .34 | 5.3% |
| Colombia | 12,250 | 24.67 | 3.3% |
| Czech Republic | 389 | 3.66 | 2.2% |
| Denmark | 617 | 10.64 | 4.2% |
| Estonia | 63 | 4.77 | 3% |
| Finland | 331 | 6 | 4.4% |
| France | 30,327 | 45.27 | 12.9% |
| Germany | 9,195 | 11.09 | 4.3% |
| Iceland | 10 | 2.83 | .5% |
| Ireland | 1,772 | 36.51 | 6.7% |
| Israel | 581 | 6.54 | .7% |
| Japan | 1,042 | .82 | 2.3% |
| Latvia | 32 | 1.66 | 2.5% |
| Lithuania | 81 | 2.9 | 3.7% |
| Mexico* | 51,311 | 40.66 | 10.9% |
| New Zealand | 22 | .45 | 1.4% |
| Norway | 256 | 4.82 | 2.7% |
| Poland | 1,787 | 4.71 | 3.6% |
| Russia* | 14,768 | 10.17 | 1.7% |
| Singapore | 27 | .48 | .05% |
| South Africa* | 9,909 | 17.15 | 1.8% |
| South Korea | 304 | .59 | 2.1% |
| Spain | 28,503 | 61 | 9.1% |
| Sweden | 5,763 | 56.59 | 7% |
| Switzerland | 1,986 | 23.32 | 5.5% |
| Turkey | 5,813 | 7.06 | 2.4% |
| United Kingdom | 46,596 | 70.08 | 15% |
| United States | 161,347 | 49.32 | 3.3% |

*Source:* Coronavirus Resource Center, Johns Hopkins University, August 8, 2020.

*Data from these countries are suspect.

COVID-19 has revealed serious structural problems in US global health surveillance, public health funding and health care infrastructure, and point prediction capabilities for disease forecasting in the IC. Yet leadership matters. Countries controlled by populists, such as Brazil, the United Kingdom, Mexico, and the United States, have generally done poorly, as their leaders failed to follow the advice of scientists and the medical community. In 2018, President Trump disbanded the NSC pandemic unit and rejected the Obama administration's epidemic response playbook when the pandemic began.[61] The US president ignored repeated warnings in January and February from both the Department of Health and Human Services and the US IC regarding a strange virus afflicting China.[62] Trump has publicly claimed at least 25 times that the virus would simply disappear on its own, refused to require masks to reduce transmission, touted a dangerous antimalarial drug, and suggested Americans inject disinfectant as a form of treatment.[63] He has re-tweeted assertions by a game show host that his own CDC is "lying," repeatedly falsely claimed that "99.9 percent" of infected people survive COVID-19, and praised the ability of a doctor to treat the virus who believes alien DNA is used in the manufacture of medicines and that demon insemination occurs through dreams.[64] President Trump's response has been incompetent. He has demonstrated neither the requisite intellectual ability to understand the basic features of the disease nor a willingness to listen to the experienced scientific experts whose guidance he should have followed. Invoking the thinking of witch doctors and game show hosts is simply not a serious response to a disease that has killed more than 160,000 Americans and over 700,000 people worldwide. The United States has been fortunate that the pandemic was not Ebola or a similar pathogen with a much higher mortality rate than COVID-19.

---

[61]Riechmann, Deb. "Trump Disbanded NSC Pandemic Unit That Experts Had Praised." Associated Press, March 15, 2020. https://apnews.com/ce014d94b64e98b7203b873e56f80e9a; and Diamond and Toosi, "Trump Team Failed to Follow NSC's Pandemic Playbook."

[62]Graham, David A. "Why Trump Was Deaf to All the Warnings He Received." *The Atlantic*, April 29, 2020. https://www.theatlantic.com/ideas/archive/2020/04/how-many-warnings-did-trump-ignore/610846/.

[63]Rieger, J. M. "24 Times Trump Has Said the Virus Would Go Away." *The Washington Post*, August 5, 2020. https://www.washingtonpost.com/video/politics/24-times-trump-said-the-coronavirus-would-go-away/2020/04/30/d2593312-9593-4ec2-aff7-72c1438fca0e_video.html; Chalfant, Morgan. "Trump Says He Won't Issue National Mask Mandate." *The Hill*, July 17, 2020. https://thehill.com/homenews/administration/507908-trump-says-he-wont-issue-national-mask-mandate; McDonald, Jessica, and Rem Rieder. "Trump Misleads on Hydroxychloroquine, Again." *FactCheck.org*, June 3, 2020. https://www.factcheck.org/2020/05/trump-misleads-on-hydroxychloroquine-again/; and BBC. "Outcry After Trump Suggests Injecting Disinfectant as Treatment." April 24, 2020. https://www.bbc.com/news/world-us-canada-52407177.

[64]Samuels, Brett. "Trump Retweets Game Show Host Who Said CDC Is Lying to Hurt Him Politically." *The Hill*, July 13, 2020. https://thehill.com/homenews/administration/507011-trump-retweets-game-show-host-who-said-cdc-is-lying-about-coronavirus; Rabin, Roni Caryn, and Chris Cameron. "Trump Falsely Claims '99 Percent' of Virus Cases Are 'Totally Harmless.'" *The New York Times*, July 5, 2020. https://www.nytimes.com/2020/07/05/us/politics/trump-coronavirus-factcheck.html; and Connolly, Griffin. "Trump Defends Doctor Who Claimed Medicine Is Made From Alien DNA and Walks Out of Briefing Amid Question." *Independent*, July 29, 2020. https://www.independent.co.uk/news/world/americas/us-politics/trump-stella-immanuel-alien-dna-hydroxychloroquine-press-briefing-today-a9643021.html.

## CLIMATE CHANGE AS A DRIVER OF INTERNATIONAL INSTABILITY

**LaMesha L. Craft**

In 2008, the National Intelligence Council's assessment on the implications of global climate change identified wide-ranging threats to US national security interests through the year 2030. Scientists and experts who have examined the impacts of climate change on international instability acknowledged that climate change *alone* will not trigger a major shift in stability. However, the **effects of climate change** wholly exacerbate and complicate international security threats.[65] Ultimately, climate change is a threat that shapes the entire geostrategic environment, which includes relationships between regional powers, fragile nations, and nonstate actors.[66] Furthermore, as noted in the 2019 Worldwide Threat Assessment, the impacts of the global environment, ecological degradation, and climate change are likely to fuel competition for resources, magnify economic distress, and sow social discontent.[67]

### Accelerant of Global Geopolitical Tensions

Nation-states have exploited the changing geography of oceans and landmass to expand or develop new territory, as observed over the last few years in the Arctic region[68] and the South China Sea (SCS). The change in geography has also created tensions in South Asia and Africa as nations vie for access to (and in some cases control of) food and water resources. The diminishing sea ice, declining snow coverage, and melting ice sheets have increased the level of uncertainty within the Arctic region. This is especially significant as the level of military and economic activity in the region has increased since the early 2000s.[69] The Arctic region consists of eight nations (Canada, the Kingdom of Denmark, Iceland, Norway, Finland, Sweden, the United States, and Russia) with sovereign territory in the Arctic. The diminishing sea ice has created new shipping lanes and has expanded access to some natural resources. It has also

---

[65]National Intelligence Council. "Global Food Security: Key Drivers—A Conference Report." NICR 2012-05. February 1, 2012. https://www.dni.gov/files/documents/nic/NICR%202012-05%20Global%20 Food%20Security%20Conf%20Rpt%20FINAL.pdf.

[66]Center for Climate and Security, "A Climate Security Plan for America." September 2019. https://climateand security.files.wordpress.com/2019/09/a-climate-security-plan-for-america_2019_9_24-1.pdf.

[67]Spratt, David, and Ian Dunlop. "Existential Climate-Related Security Risk: A Scenario Approach." May 2019. https://docs.wixstatic.com/ugd/148cb0_a1406e0143ac4c469196d3003bc1e687.pdf.

[68]White, Daniel. "The National Security Implications of Climate Change: Redefining Threats, Bolstering Budgets, and Mobilizing the Arctic." *Journal of International Affairs* 73, no. 1 (2020): 321–329. https://jia .sipa.columbia.edu/national-security-implications-climate-change-redefining-threats-bolstering-budgets-and-mobilizing.

[69]Konyshew, Valery, and Alexander Sergunin. "Is Russia a Revisionist Military Power in the Arctic?" *Defense & Security Analysis* 30, no. 4 (2014): 323–335. https://doi.org/10.1080/14751798.2014.948276.

facilitated Russian expansion in the region.[70] Russia is the largest Arctic nation by landmass, military presence, and population. Commercial and defense activities over the last few years suggest Russia views itself as a **polar great power**. In December 2014, Russian president Vladimir Putin established the Northern Fleet Joint Strategic Command to coordinate the renewed emphasis on the Arctic. Since then, Russia has gradually created new Arctic units, refurbished old airfields and infrastructure, and established military bases along its Arctic coastline. Experts continue to monitor Russian military activity, especially efforts to establish a network of air defense and coastal missile systems, early-warning radars, and a variety of sensors.[71]

China has also demonstrated economic, geopolitical, and military endeavors to expand its sphere of influence for years. Some efforts involve the SCS, a major sea line of communication that is rich with oil, natural gas, and fishery stocks. Recent SCS expansion, coupled with the effects of climate change in the Asia-Pacific region, will undoubtedly accelerate geopolitical tensions between regional competitors such as Vietnam, the Philippines, Indonesia, Malaysia, Brunei, and Taiwan.[72] For example, the 2018 super typhoon in the Philippines, the continuous sinking of Jakarta due to sea-level rise, and natural disasters in 2018 that have ruined parts of Indonesia create conditions of increased demand for food and water.[73]

## Increased Threats to Food and Water Stability

Similarly, the reduction of **water availability** has been a major contributor to conflict. The World Economic Forum's Global Risk Report listed water crises as one of the top-five risks since 2011.[74] In 2017 alone, water insecurity contributed to conflict within at least 45 countries, particularly in the Middle East and North Africa.[75]

---

[70]Office of the Under Secretary of Defense for Policy. "Department of Defense Arctic Strategy." June 2019. https://climateandsecurity.files.wordpress.com/2019/06/2019-dod-arctic-strategy.pdf; White, "National Security Implications of Climate Change"; and Taylor, P. C., W. Maslowksi, J. Perlwitz, and D. J. Wuebbles. "Arctic Changes and Their Effects on Alaska and the Rest of the United States." In *Climate Science Special Report: Fourth National Climate Assessment*, Vol. I, edited by D. J. Wuebbles, D. W. Fahey, K. A. Hibbard, D. J. Dokken, B. C. Stewart, and T. K. Maycock. Washington, DC: US Global Change Research Program, 2017, 303.

[71]Office of the Under Secretary of Defense for Policy, "Department of Defense Arctic Strategy."

[72]Askari, Muhammad Usman. "China's Territorial Disputes in the South China Sea: A Prologue From Past to Present." *Journal of the Research Society of Pakistan* 56, no. 1 (2019): 101–108; and Geib, Peter, and Lucie Pfaff. "The Dynamics of Chinese Expansion in the South China Sea." *Journal of Applied Business and Economics* 18, no. 1 (2016): 62–68. https://doi.org/10.33423/jabe.v18i1.828.

[73]Rezzonico, Andrea. "The South China Sea: A Potential Climate, Nuclear, Security Hotspot." Council on Strategic Risks, April 24, 2019. https://councilonstrategicrisks.org/2019/04/29/the-south-china-sea-a-potential-climate-nuclear-security-hotspot/; and Office of the Director of National Intelligence, "Global Trends 2030."

[74]Van Der Heijden, Kitty, and Callie Stinson. "Water Is a Growing Source of Global Conflict." World Economic Forum, March 2019. https://www.weforum.org/agenda/2019/03/water-is-a-growing-source-of-global-conflict-heres-what-we-need-to-do/.

[75]United Nations Office for the Coordination of Humanitarian Affairs. "World Humanitarian Data and Trends 2018." December 2018. https://www.humanitarianresponse.info/sites/www.humanitarianresponse.info/files/documents/files/whdt2018_web_final_singles.pdf.

Water insecurity, and the subsequent degradation of agricultural production, inevitably increases historic tensions between countries that compete for water and food resources. For example, India's control over Pakistan's supply of fresh water—which is influenced by the shrinking Himalayan glaciers—creates added tension between India and Pakistan.[76] By the year 2030, the problem of a growing world population, with an increased scarcity of resources, will amplify the demand for food by 30 percent, the demand for water by 40 percent, and the demand for energy by 50 percent. **Extreme weather events**, floods, wildfires, soil degradation, and sea-level rise will also compound global food and water insecurity and do have the potential to heighten social unrest.[77] For example, during the 2008 food-price spike, at least 61 countries experienced unrest because of price inflation; in 38 of these countries, protests were often violent.[78]

## Degradation of US Military Basing and Operations

The impact of climate change on **US military basing** and operations is multipronged. The competition for land and resources in the Arctic region threatens US homeland defense as well as regional cooperation among other Arctic nations. Specifically, US interests in the Arctic include maintaining flexibility for global power projection (e.g., freedom of navigation and overflight) and limiting nations such as China from leveraging the region as a corridor for competition.[79] Whereas the thawing permafrost, storm surges, and coastal erosion adversely affect Department of Defense infrastructure, such as military installations, DOD installations are essential in maintaining military readiness by providing a suitable environment for training and testing. Over the coming decades, installations will experience significant risks from climate-driven changes in the environment (such as rising sea levels and severe storms), which could compromise the capacity of these lands and waters to support the military mission.[80] In 2016, the Union of Concerned Scientists analyzed 18 military installations along the East and Gulf Coasts based on their respective strategic importance to the DOD mission. The majority of the installations are sites where the military tests weaponry, conducts training exercises, builds ships and other equipment, and

---

[76]Center for Climate and Security, "Climate Security Plan for America."

[77]Director of National Intelligence. "Worldwide Threat Assessment of the US Intelligence Community." February 13, 2018. https://www.dni.gov/files/documents/Newsroom/Testimonies/2018-ATA---Unclassified-SSCI.pdf.

[78]National Intelligence Council, "Global Food Security."

[79]Office of the Director of National Intelligence, "Global Trends 2030."

[80]Department of Defense. "Climate Adaptation for DOD Natural Resource Managers: A Guide to Incorporating Climate Considerations Into Integrated Natural Resource Management Plans." August 2019. https://climateandsecurity.files.wordpress.com/2019/08/dod-adaptation-guide-at-low-res-final-041519_508-compliant.pdf.

develops emerging technology.[81] The study demonstrated how sea-level rise already affects many of the installations. It also included scenarios that highlighted how if preventative measures are not taken, those installations will likely endure extensive tidal flooding, permanent loss of land, and destructive storm surges. According to the study, by 2100 nearly half of the 18 installations could lose between 25 and 50 percent of their land area.[82]

## CYBER THREATS IN THE 21ST CENTURY

### LaMesha L. Craft

As noted in Chapter 8, the future is plural, and many potential game-changers of global trends involve the application or exploitation of technology. This section will examine cyber threats in the 21st century, but inherent in that discussion should be the unstated acknowledgment that the creation of technology itself is not bad; mankind's nefarious use of technology is bad. The use of technology has solved many of the world's problems—it has also exacerbated others. There are several themes of emerging technology to explore, such as artificial intelligence (AI) and machine learning, big data analytics, ethical considerations in AI, and the likelihood of a "cyber 9/11."

### Artificial Intelligence, Machine Learning, and Big Data Analytics

The application of AI is not a *new* phenomenon. In 1955, John McCarthy and three colleagues coined the term *artificial intelligence* and defined it as "making a machine behave in ways that would be called intelligent if a human were so behaving."[83] Machine learning (a subset of AI) is the development of algorithms that facilitate machines learning and adapting through experience instead of explicit instructions.[84]

---

[81]Hall, J. A., S. Gill, J. Obeysekera, W. Sweet, K. Knuuti, and J. Marburger. "Regional Sea Level Scenarios for Coastal Risk Management: Managing the Uncertainty of Future Sea Level Change and Extreme Water Levels for Department of Defense Coastal Sites Worldwide." US Department of Defense, Strategic Environmental Research and Development Program, April 25, 2016. https://www.serdp-estcp.org/News-and-Events/News-Announcements/Program-News/DoD-Report-on-Regional-SeaLevel-Scenarios.

[82]Union of Concerned Scientists. "Executive Summary: The US Military on the Front Lines of Rising Seas: Growing Exposure to Coastal Flooding at East and Gulf Coast Military Bases," July 2016. https://www.ucsusa.org/sites/default/files/attach/2016/07/front-lines-of-rising-seas-key-executive-summary.pdf.

[83]McCarthy, John, Marvin Minsky, Nathaniel Rochester, and Claude E. Shannon. "Proposal for the Dartmouth Summer Research Project on Artificial Intelligence, August 31, 1955." *AI Magazine* 27, no. 4 (2006). https://aaai.org/ojs/index.php/aimagazine/issue/view/165.

[84]Vedder, Anton. "Why Data Protection and Transparency Are Not Enough When Facing Social Problems of Machine Learning in Big Data Context." In *Being Profiled: COGITAS ERO SUM: 10 Years of Profiling the European Citizen*, edited by Emre Bayamlıoğlu, Irina Baraliuc, Liisa Janssens, and Mireille Hildebrandt. Netherlands: Amsterdam University Press, 2018, 42–45. doi:10.2307/j.ctvhrd092.10; and Hao, Karen. "What Is Machine Learning?" *MIT Technology Review*, November 1, 2018. https://www.technologyreview.com/s/612437/what-is-machine-learning-we-drew-you-another-flowchart/.

The use of AI can yield various benefits such as improved communications, health care, education, disease control, agriculture, space exploration, and science.[85] Nevertheless, scientists have increasingly acknowledged the need to examine the prospect of humans losing control of AI systems, the vulnerabilities inherent in a growing dependence on AI, and the absence of international regulations and laws to counter AI used for nefarious purposes.[86]

This likely stems from the growing international emphasis on funding and developing AI capabilities. Over the last five years, at least 20 countries publicly announced plans to develop AI technology in the interest of maintaining a competitive advantage and leveraging the economic and social benefits of AI.[87] In 2017, China announced its Next Generation Artificial Intelligence Development Plan. In that same year, Russian president Vladimir Putin reportedly opined "whoever becomes the leader in AI will become the ruler of the world."[88] In 2018, French president Emmanuel Macron announced plans to invest 1.5 billion euros into AI over the next five years to catch up with China and the United States. In 2019, US president Donald Trump signed Executive Order 13859, *Maintaining American Leadership in Artificial Intelligence*, in which the opening statement identified AI as the driver of economic growth and national stability.[89]

As the interest in AI and machine learning expands, so too does the requirement to process the exponential amount of data using big data analytics. Experts in the Internet of Things estimate there will be billions of connected devices and embedded systems that will enable over 75 percent of the world's population to daily interact online by 2025. They also estimate that machine learning will continue to change the technological landscape to augment everyday operations and business processes.[90] Inherent in the expanse of technology is the growing threat to data protection and individual privacy, and the magnitude of cybersecurity threats to AI-dependent systems, like cloud computing.[91]

---

[85]Kavanaugh, Camino. *New Tech, New Threats, and New Governance Challenges: An Opportunity to Craft Smarter Responses?* Washington, DC: Carnegie Endowment for International Peace, 2019, 13–23. doi:10.2307/resrep20978.5.

[86]Yampolskiy, Roman, and M. S. Spellchecker. "Artificial Intelligence Safety and Cybersecurity: A Timeline of AI Failures." October 2016. https://arxiv.org/pdf/1610.07997.pdf; Vedder, "Why Data Protection and Transparency Are Not Enough When Facing Social Problems of Machine Learning in Big Data Context"; and Gill, Amandeep Singh. "Artificial Intelligence and International Security: The Long View." *Ethics & International Affairs* 33, no. 2 (2019): 169–179. doi:10.1017/S0892679419000145.

[87]Kavanaugh, *New Tech, New Threats, and New Governance Challenges*; Allison, Graham, and "Y." "The Clash of AI Superpowers." *The National Interest* 165 (2020): 11–16.

[88]Gill, "Artificial Intelligence and International Security."

[89]"Executive Order 13859 of February 11, 2019: Maintaining American Leadership in Artificial Intelligence." *Federal Register* 84, no. 31 (2019): 3967–3972. https://www.hsdl.org/?view&did=821398.

[90]Khvoynitskaya, Sandra. "The Future of Big Data: 5 Predictions From Experts for 2020–2025." *iTransition*, January 30, 2020. https://www.itransition.com/blog/the-future-of-big-data.

[91]Kavanaugh, *New Tech, New Threats, and New Governance Challenges*.

## Ethical Considerations: Who's Watching Whom?

The ethical application of technology in concepts of war, governance, and security requires a thorough understanding of both the power and the limits of technology. To be fair, technology has been used in warfare for decades.[92] However, the introduction of AI-enabled capabilities has driven research institutes and civil society groups to pursue the establishment of governance that will regulate the ethical, moral, and legal uses of technology. The need to account for such implications has become an agenda topic for organizations like the United Nations Conference on Disarmament, as well as the United Nations Educational, Scientific and Cultural Organization (UNESCO).[93] Some efforts include creating guiding principles for the use of lethal autonomous weapon systems and establishing the Asilomar Principles to deter AI development with malicious intent.[94] Most scientists believe it is unlikely that nations will fight wars solely with fleets of ghost ships and armies of robots in the next 20 years. However, it is likely that combat systems will have increased autonomy within that time frame.[95]

The development of increased autonomous systems (albeit for national defense, economic growth, or agricultural development) emphasizes the crux of vulnerabilities in technology. Increased autonomy and machine-based learning rely heavily on established trust in man-made algorithms. However, scientists have already discovered that algorithms can be limited in accuracy based on their respective features and designs. For example, some facial recognition software exhibits discriminatory and biased results based on flaws within the algorithm. In that same vein, some computer engineers and scientists believe nation-states have not done enough to examine how AI could be used/built for malevolent purposes, despite historic examples of (sometimes fatal) failures of AI systems due to faulty designs or safety programs.[96]

## The Likelihood of a "Cyber 9/11" Scenario

Over the last few years, government officials and military leaders have used terms like *cyber–Pearl Harbor* or *cyber 9/11* to describe a potential cyber attack that impacts US national interests. The reliance on technology and the history of previous cyber incidents has created a nearly endless list of "cyber 9/11" scenarios. Possible scenarios include the targeting of industrial control and SCADA systems to disrupt critical infrastructure; the corruption of financial data to create mass hysteria, as customers

[92]Gill, "Artificial Intelligence and International Security."

[93]Kavanaugh, *New Tech, New Threats, and New Governance Challenges*; and US Government Accountability Office. "Data and Analytics Innovation: Emerging Opportunities and Challenges." Report GAO-16-659SP. September 20, 2016. https://www.gao.gov/products/GAO-16-659SP

[94]Future of Life Institute. "Asilomar AI Principles." Accessed December 29, 2019. https://futureoflife.org/ai-principles/?cn-reloaded=1.

[95]Gill, "Artificial Intelligence and International Security."

[96]See Yampolskiy and Spellchecker, "Artificial Intelligence Safety and Cybersecurity," for examples of AI failures.

pull all of their money out of banks and the stock market; a coordinated ransomware attack that halts the international transportation of goods, services, and personnel; and a multipronged, well-orchestrated disinformation campaign that drives two or more countries to the brink of war.

However, strategists, psychologists, and political scientists challenge the notion that cyberspace operations will lead to war, because the thresholds for war in the cyberspace domain remain undefined.[97] Namely, unlike the traditional act of war, activity conducted in cyberspace is seldom kinetic and, to date, has not caused mass casualties. The daunting truth is cyberspace is literally changing at the speed of light and the full magnitude of cyber threats in the 21st century will continue to evolve. Intelligence professionals must remain agile and adaptive when analyzing adversary intent and capability in the cyberspace domain.

## INTER-STATE WAR

**Jonathan C. Smith**

The use of large-scale physical violence against an adversary is the ultimate expression of power. Particularly with the advent of nuclear weapons, inter-state war has the potential for the largest and most extensive destructive capabilities and represents a true existential threat to any nation-state. This was true even in the pre-nuclear age. For instance, Poland ceased to exist after the German invasion and occupation of that country at the start of World War II. Due to the magnitude of the consequences for a country, its intelligence organizations will often spend a great deal of time and resources attempting to understand the capabilities and intentions of hostile military powers. Indeed, many of the organizations in the US IC were created with the express purpose of understanding the potential military threat that the Soviet Union represented to the United States during the Cold War.

However, the **incidence of inter-state war** has declined over the past century. As Figure 14.1 notes, after the surge in the World War II time period (1939–1945), there has been a marked drop-off in the incidence of inter-state war.[98] Additionally, the death toll resulting from inter-state war is declining. Indeed, the United States has not participated in an inter-state war since the invasion of Iraq in 2003, more than 16 years ago. It is unlikely that the national security community of any country is now less interested in advocating for its interests than in previous periods of history. Instead, it is more likely that the rise of international institutions, democratic governance, and the economic benefits from international trade have reduced the incentives for inter-state

[97]Lewis, James A. "Thresholds for Cyberwar." Center for Strategic & International Studies, October 1, 2010. https://www.csis.org/analysis/thresholds-cyberwar.

[98]Sarkees, Meredith, and Frank Wayman. *Resort to War: 1816–2007*. Washington, DC: CQ Press, 2010.

war.[99] However, that does not mean that international competition has declined; it means only that nation-states are likely using different means to pursue their interests.

---

**FIGURE 14.1   ■   Pairs of States Involved in Inter-State War**

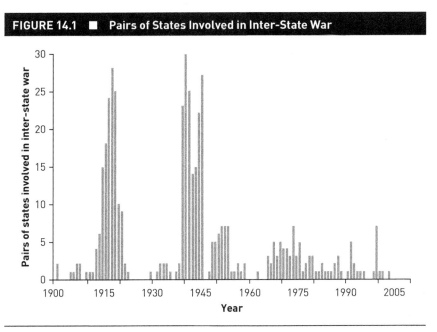

*Source:* Szayna, Thomas, et al. *What Are the Trends in Armed Conflicts, and What Do They Mean for US Defense Policy.* Washington: RAND Corporation, 2017, 3. Accessed on December 1, 2019, at https://www.rand.org/pubs/research_reports/RR1904.html.

---

It also does not mean that military power is irrelevant as a tool for advancing national security interests. Beyond counterinsurgency conflicts with internal sub-state actors, **hybrid war** is a growing strategy for utilizing military power. This type of conflict is "an amalgam of espionage, subversion, even forms of terrorism to attain political ends without actually going to war in any conventional sense."[100] Contemporary inter-state conflicts in Eastern Europe and the Middle East bear many of these traits. One result of this type of conflict is the difficulty in definitively identifying who is responsible for a given attack. For instance, Russia's use of unmarked special operations troops, known as Little Green Men, in the Crimean annexation in 2014 created sufficient plausible deniability to delay any international response. This type of conflict represents a growing challenge for intelligence organizations attempting to identify the start and progress of a conflict, let alone what actors are actually involved.

---

[99]Szayna, Thomas, et al. *What Are the Trends in Armed Conflicts, and What Do They Mean for US Defense Policy?* Santa Monica, CA: RAND Corporation, 2017, 3.

[100]Schindler, John. "We're Entering the Age of Special War." *Business Insider*, September 25, 2013. https://www.businessinsider.com/were-entering-the-age-of-special-war-2013-9.

**PHOTO 14.1** Little Green Men in Ukraine, 2014.

There is some concern that new technological innovations might reduce the human costs of war, thus making it more likely that countries would pursue conventional inter-state war to advance their national interests. With the growth in precision of targeting capabilities, the risk of large-scale civilian casualties has been reduced. For instance, thanks to GPS-guided weapons, a B-52 bomber in the Afghanistan War (2001–present) is more likely to be engaging in close air support missions (which require that weapons be deployed very precisely) than carpet bombing missions, which B-52s were utilized for during the Vietnam War (1965–1973). More recently, the growth of autonomous and semiautonomous weapon systems means that the attacking country does not have to risk the lives of its own personnel in the attack. For instance, the cruise missile attack that the United States conducted against a Syrian-controlled airfield in 2017 was able to damage the target and never risked the lives of any US military personnel. Both of these trends would appear to mitigate the human costs of war, thus making the use of military conflict more palatable. As the Confederate general Robert E. Lee (1807–1870) noted, "It is well that war is so terrible, otherwise we would grow too fond of it."

Regardless of whether incidents of inter-state war will continue to diminish in size and frequency, the potential for large-scale inter-state war still exists. For instance, the United States must be prepared for a North Korean invasion of South Korea. Regardless of how likely or unlikely that appears today, the fact that this country has an army of nearly a million men equipped with advanced weaponry is an adversary capability that cannot be ignored. Hence, while the most likely threat to US national security is not inter-state war, it is still the threat that poses the largest-possible consequences to the vital interests of the country.

The US national security establishment focuses much of its energy into this area. The defense department budget dwarfs other elements of national power that could be employed in international affairs. For instance, in 2018, the DOD budget was $649 billion; the State Department budget was $52 billion. When considering the various instruments of power that it could employ to advance its national security interests, the United States might look akin to a fiddler crab with its one oversized claw.

This focus on developing nuclear and conventional military capabilities comes at a cost but does provide a substantial advantage in capability. The **US military budget in 2018** was larger than that of the next seven countries *combined*—China, Russia, India, France, Germany, the United Kingdom, and Saudi Arabia spent a combined total of $609 billion in that year (see Figure 14.2).[101] But you get what you pay for. The US Navy has far more aircraft carriers than any other country. The US Air Force has more aircraft than Russia and China combined. It also maintains a network of bases in more than

**PHOTO 14.2** North Korean military parade.

70 foreign countries and has a transportation system that allows it to project substantial military power anywhere around the world in a short period of time.[102]

---

**FIGURE 14.2** ■ **US Defense Spending Comparison, 2018**

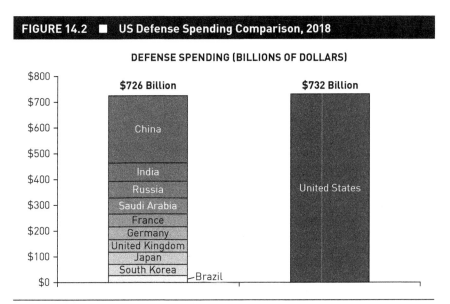

*Source:* Paul G. Peterson Foundation. "US Defense Spending Compared to Other Countries." Accessed on December 1, 2019, at https://www.pgpf.org/Chart-Archive/0053_defense-comparison& xid=17259,15700023,15700124,15700149,15700168,15700173,15700186,15700201.

---

[101]Paul G. Peterson Foundation. "US Defense Spending Compared to Other Countries." May 13, 2020. https://www.pgpf.org/chart-archive/0053_defense-comparison.

[102]Vine, David. "Where in the World Is the US Military?" *Politico*, July/August 2015. https://www.politico.com/magazine/story/2015/06/us-military-bases-around-the-world-119321.

Certainly, the maintenance of this capability is useful since even the threat of the use of force can help advance national security interests. Former secretary of state George C. Marshall once noted, "diplomacy not backed by military force is mere posturing."[103] For instance, the US nuclear weapons capability and its deployment of military forces to Europe were instrumental in supporting the larger national security policy of containment during the Cold War. However, the extent to which these capabilities may be useful in any future inter-state conflict is unknown. As the saying goes, generals always fight the last war.

## ETHNIC CONFLICT, REVOLUTION, AND STATE DESTABILIZATION

**Jonathan M. Acuff**

With the decline of inter-state war, what is the most common driver of international violence? Although the United States and its allies must continue to invest heavily in large conventional armies as an insurance policy and deterrent against Russian and Chinese arms, most political violence in the world now has little to do with bids for hegemony. Rather, most contemporary conflicts derive from ethnic and/or religious antagonisms, competition over resources, and weak or corrupt governance. These conflicts are fed by a combination of the weakness of less developed states and the legacy of European colonialism, which established state borders in Africa, the Middle East, and Asia that bore little resemblance to the human terrain of ethnic, tribal, and religious affiliation. In poorer countries, the highest-functioning institution is often the military, which leads to frequent military intervention in politics in the form of coups d'état or revolutions. The weakness of poor states also makes cross-border incursions by both state and nonstate actors more likely, either seeking unification with coreligionists or ethnic and tribal brothers across the border or simply plundering resources. These conflicts tend to spill over beyond the immediate regions in which they occur into other states, leading to what international relations scholars refer to as **shatter belts,** groups of states with related internal problems that are prone to conflict. Noting the "youth bulge" that has developed in parts of the world, the IC has expanded the regional definition of belts of instability into what it terms the "arc of instability . . . stretching from the Andean region of Latin America to Sub-Saharan Africa, across the Middle East and the Caucasus, and through the northern parts of South Asia."[104]

---

[103]Worley, Duane. *Orchestrating the Instruments of Power: A Critical Examination of the US National Security System*. Lincoln: University of Nebraska Press, 2015, 8.

[104]National Intelligence Council, *Global Trends 2025*, iv and 21–22.

## State Destabilization

**State destabilization** refers to a wide variety of both domestic and transnational activities that undermine governance. A state's fragility may increase because levels of political and private sector corruption so inhibit economic opportunity for its citizens that they lose all faith in the government, turning to private actors for assistance. This process may become so pronounced that state sovereignty breaks down, a phenomenon readily apparent in the fiction of central governments in places like Afghanistan, Haiti, and Zimbabwe. In contrast with work on state destabilization in the wake of the collapse of the communist bloc that emphasized how corrupt leaders and warlords would eventually build states so as to maximize their ability to extract rents, more recent research suggests many warlords are content exploiting chaos to simply steal.[105] The delegitimization of governments makes them vulnerable to **coups d'état** from their armed forces, which seek only to change who is doing the looting, and broader-based **social revolutions**, which seek to transform the entire structure of political and economic institutions.

More than 60 states on the Fragile States Index are listed as in imminent danger of state destabilization.[106]

## Irredentism

An additional challenge that may accompany destabilized states but that also may occur in otherwise well-governed nations is the danger of **irredentism**. This refers to attempts by religious, ethnic, and/or tribal groups who are separated from each other across international borders but nevertheless seek to unite. As most of Africa and the Middle East inherited borders drawn by the European empires during the 19th century, these regions are especially prone to irredentist conflicts. However, such violence is not limited to these regions. The ethnic wars that followed the breakup of Yugoslavia and persistent ethnic violence in Eastern Europe and the Caucasus region are also examples of irredentism.[107] Moreover, the instability created by irredentism often results in intervention by regional and/or international powers, which often increases the violence. Most contemporary conflicts in the world have an ethnic and/or religious dimension related to cross-border issues. And they will likely increase in frequency and severity. Several billion people live in the zone of what will become extreme heat by 2070. The societies in which they reside are already fractured. As climate change

---

[105]Olson, Mancur. "Dictatorship, Democracy, and Development." *The American Political Science Review* 87, no. 3 (1993): 567–576; and Chayes, Sarah. *Thieves of State: Why Corruption Threatens Global Security.* New York, NY: Norton, 2015.

[106]The Fund for Peace. *Fragile States Index: Annual Report 2019*, 7. Accessed September 29, 2020. https://fragilestatesindex.org/wp-content/uploads/2019/03/9511904-fragilestatesindex.pdf.

[107]Saideman, Stephen M., and R. William Ayres. *For Kin and Country: Xenophobia, Nationalism, and War.* New York, NY: Columbia University Press, 2015.

increases pressure on water and land resources, particularly in the sub-Saharan belt, the resulting mass migrations will exacerbate these conflicts.

## Transnational Social Movements

**Transnational social movements** are groups of people who, instead of using existing political institutions and processes, participate in mass protests to attempt to change their societies. Such movements are frequently organized and supported across borders, particularly through social media. Digital sharing of information about state violence, corruption, and other governance issues can occasionally have a cascade effect, generating protests that create a logic of their own.[108] Although the mass protests that broke apart the communist bloc in Eastern Europe were of obvious importance to US interests, on the surface most social movements do not seem to directly affect the United States. How might such events represent a strategic threat to the United States? Mass protests seeking a transition to democratic rule would seem to intrinsically favor US interests. However, as the breakup of the Soviet Union and the Arab Spring indicate, no matter the liberal intentions or rhetoric of a social movement, it can quickly collapse into a retrenchment of authoritarianism, with the social basis for a peaceful transition destroyed or bought off by security forces.[109] Moreover, as the revolutions of 1848 in Europe and 2011 in the Middle East demonstrate, revolutions can quickly go regional, with dramatic consequences.[110] The violence they spawn may destabilize countries friendly toward the United States, as was the case with Egypt following the Arab Spring. Such movements may also spawn international terrorism, particularly if democratic reform efforts fail. One of the ways to think about the rise of al-Qaeda in the late 1990s and early 2000s is the decades-long failure of Arab intellectuals and activists to reform the fundamentally corrupt autocracies of the Middle East. The security forces of Egypt, Syria, Iraq, and Saudi Arabia were competent enough to crush any peaceful attempts at reform, thus radicalizing opponents of these regimes.

## Assessing the Likelihood and Impact of Pressures on States

The US IC does not have a good recent track record of accurately forecasting coups, revolutions, social movements, or the outbreak of ethnic conflict.[111] The IC has

---

[108]Hussein, Muzammil M., and Philip N. Howard. "What Best Explains Successful Protest Cascades? ICTs and the Fuzzy Causes of the Arab Spring." *International Studies Review* 15 (2013): 48–66.

[109]Snyder, Jack L. *From Voting to Violence: Democratization and Nationalist Conflict.* New York, NY: Norton, 2000.

[110]Weyland, Kurt. "The Arab Spring: Why the Surprising Similarities With the Revolutionary Wave of 1848?" *Perspectives on Politics* 10, no. 4 (2012): 917–934.

[111]One notable exception was the breakup of the former Yugoslavia and its descent into ethnic warfare. See Treverton, Gregory F., and Renanah Miles. *Unheeded Warning of War: Why Policymakers Ignored the 1990 Yugoslavia Estimate.* Washington, DC: Center for the Study of Intelligence, 2015. https://www.cia.gov/library/center-for-the-study-of-intelligence/csi-publications/books-and-monographs/csi-intelligence-and-policy-monographs/pdfs/unheeded-warning-yugoslavia-NIE.pdf.

proven quite adept at identifying large trends, such as its spot-on prediction in 2004 that by 2020 the "third wave" of democratization will have reversed and its similarly consistent focus on the weakness of most of the states in the Middle East.[112] However, point predictions have proven more difficult. Forecasting such events may be intrinsically more difficult than the policy changes or actions of large states, even states as opaque as North Korea. As their origins and occurrence are often idiosyncratic, former assistant director of central intelligence at the Central Intelligence Agency (CIA) Mark Lowenthal terms them nonlinear events and thus more challenging to get ahold of.[113] As part of what are now commonly referred to as Black Swans, such events are not part of normalized distributions, and thus their probability is not easy to mathematically compute.[114] However, there is no consensus on this issue. Some scholars argue that the term is overused, applied to many events that are in fact not true Black Swans, and offers no help in dealing with the vast majority of important events that are predictable.[115] Other scholars contend that far from being "nonlinear," revolutions and the like may in fact be part of patterns of behavior by decision makers and thus readily predictable, were the US IC to more commonly employ even simple statistical and formal modeling methods.[116]

On the other hand, the consistent failure of the US IC to predict the occurrence or even correctly characterize the impact of these events may be indicative of a more general decline in its ability to produce strategic intelligence.[117] This may be a result of declining educational standards across the IC or simply the failure to devote sufficient funding to strategic issues in lieu of tactical and operational activities.[118] The CIA had a much better track record of predicting such events when it devoted adequate attention and resources to the analysis of political instability and the systematic tracking of warning indicators.[119] Regardless of the reason for this analytic shortcoming, social movements, ethnic conflict, coups, and other forms of domestic political violence have

---

[112]National Intelligence Council, *Mapping the Global Future: 2020*, 13.

[113]Lowenthal, Mark M. *The Future of Intelligence*. Cambridge, UK: Polity Press, 2018, 79.

[114]See Taleb, Nassim. *The Black Swan: The Impact of the Highly Improbable*. New York, NY: Penguin, 2007.

[115]Tetlock, Philip E., and Dan Gardiner. *Superforecasting: The Art and Science of Prediction*. New York, NY: Broadway Books, 2015, 237–244.

[116]Case in point is Bruce Bueno de Mesquita's use of a simple expected utility model to correctly predict the USSR would invade Afghanistan when almost every area studies analyst argued that it would not. See Bueno de Mesquita, Bruce. "An Expected Utility Theory of International Conflict." *The American Political Science Review* 74, no. 4 (1980): 917–931.

[117]Gentry, John A. "The 'Professionalization' of Intelligence Analysis: A Skeptical Perspective." *International Journal of Intelligence and Counterintelligence* 29, no. 4 (2016): 643–676.

[118]Ibid.

[119]Gentry, John A., and Joseph S. Gordon. *Strategic Warning Intelligence: History, Challenges, and Prospects*. Washington, DC: Georgetown University Press, 2019, 167.

been one of the defining features of the post–Cold War world. They show little sign of abating in the near future.

## WEAPONS OF MASS DESTRUCTION

### Christopher J. Ferrero

During the roughly three decades since the end of the Cold War, terrorism has been the most likely and immediate threat to most countries, including the United States. The attack of September 11, 2001, stands out as particularly bold, deadly, and significant. Yet some perspective is useful. The post-9/11 urgency to fight terrorism was largely fueled by concerns that the next attack could be much worse. As terrible as 9/11 was, it did not involve weapons of mass destruction (WMD). Whereas the 9/11 attack cost about 3,000 lives, a more horrifying and plausible scenario could involve millions of lives lost in an attack employing nuclear or other indiscriminate, mass-casualty weapons. Due to their unique destructive capacity, monitoring and countering the proliferation of WMD have long been priorities of the US policy and intelligence communities. After all, the improvised use of a passenger jet as a cruise missile, such as occurred on 9/11, does not threaten the very survival of the United States. The use of WMD could, however. The 2019 US National Intelligence Strategy ranks counterproliferation among its top-three topical mission objectives, alongside counterterrorism and the collection of cyber threat intelligence.[120]

**Weapons of mass destruction** include nuclear, chemical, and biological weapons. Many definitions of WMD also include ballistic missiles, which can be used as the delivery vehicles for nuclear, chemical, and biological warheads.

### Nuclear Weapons

Nuclear weapons were invented by the United States during World War II. They employ massive blast effects measured in tons of TNT equivalent. The largest nuclear weapon in the US arsenal today is equivalent to 1.2 million tons of TNT.[121] Nuclear weapons also produce thermal effects that can set fires over a wide radius and produce radiological fallout that can poison land and living beings long after the detonation. Nuclear weapons' only use in hostilities was against the Japanese cities of Hiroshima and Nagasaki in 1945, helping to hasten the end of the war. Though massively destructive, these bombs were small (15,000–20,000 tons of TNT equivalent) compared to the warheads deployed by the Great Powers today.

---

[120]Office of the Director of National Intelligence. "2019 National Intelligence Strategy." Accessed January 18, 2020. https://www.dni.gov/index.php/newsroom/reports-publications/item/1943-2019-national-intelligence-strategy.

[121]Brookings. "50 Facts About US Nuclear Weapons Today." April 28, 2014. https://www.brookings.edu/research/50-facts-about-u-s-nuclear-weapons-today/.

Though they have not been used in hostilities in over seven decades, nuclear weapons have been "used" ever since 1945 as a deterrent to further major war. The fact that the Cold War between the United States and the Soviet Union did not escalate to a third world war is perhaps attributable to the use of nuclear threats as a deterrent. Neither side wanted to risk a major war that would result in the destruction of both. This logic is known as **mutually assured destruction, or MAD.** It remains operative between the United States and Russia today; each side has the ability—even if struck first—to launch a devastating strike on the other. The outcome would be orders of magnitude greater than the death and destruction of the world wars and would unfold over a much shorter period. For example, a 1961 Joint Chiefs of Staff estimate of the effects of a first strike on the Soviet Union calculated 275 million deaths within hours. Over six months, depending on variables like weather, radiation fallout and lingering injury would cause as many as 600 million deaths across a stretch of territory from Europe to China—a toll equal to 10 Holocausts.[122]

Today, the United States and Russia retain by far the largest nuclear arsenals in the world. Each possesses approximately 6,000 nuclear weapons, though as of 2020 they are permitted to deploy only 1,550 each under a bilateral arms control treaty known as the **New Strategic Arms Reduction Treaty (New START).** Other possessors include China (an estimated 290 nuclear weapons), France (300), the United Kingdom (200), Pakistan (160), India (140), Israel (90), and North Korea (30). Altogether, there are about 14,000 nuclear weapons in the world.[123]

Concern over the proliferation—or spread—of nuclear weapons led to the 1968 **Nuclear Nonproliferation Treaty (NPT).** The NPT requires countries with nuclear weapons to make good-faith efforts toward disarmament and prohibits nonnuclear states from acquiring nuclear weapons. It further requires states that use nuclear energy for peaceful purposes to allow monitoring by an international body known as the **International Atomic Energy Agency (IAEA).** India, Pakistan, and Israel never signed the NPT, but most countries of the world did. North Korea signed but withdrew in 2003. International sanctions on Iraq under Saddam Hussein during the 1990s and against Iran during the 2000s have been based on evidence of NPT violations.

Though Iraq is no longer a nuclear threat, Iran has built an extensive nuclear infrastructure that could be used to produce a weapon within months of a policy decision to do so. The 2015 **Joint Comprehensive Plan of Action (JCPOA),** better known as the Iran Nuclear Deal, placed restrictions on the quantity of nuclear material that Iran could enrich and the level to which it could be enriched. A nuclear weapon can be made with the uranium isotope U-235 enriched to about 90 percent purity. For civilian nuclear applications, the U-235 concentration can be 3–5 percent. The JCPOA

---

[122]Ellsburg, Daniel. *The Doomsday Machine.* New York, NY: Bloomsbury Press, 2017, 2–3.

[123]Arms Control Association. "Nuclear Weapons: Who Has What at a Glance." Accessed January 17, 2020. https://www.armscontrol.org/factsheets/Nuclearweaponswhohaswhat.

allowed Iran to enrich uranium to only 3.67 percent U-235, ensuring that it could only be used for peaceful purposes like electricity generation and medical services. The deal also shut down Iranian facilities that could produce plutonium, another nuclear material useful in making a bomb. Iran abided by the agreement but engaged in other threatening behavior, leading the United States to withdraw from the JCPOA in 2018. In early 2020, Iran announced that it would no longer abide by any of the JCPOA restrictions, increasing the risk that it could acquire nuclear weapons.

Analysts disagree about the significance of countries like Iran and North Korea possessing nuclear weapons. Many assess that these countries have no intention of using these weapons except in extreme cases of self-defense. In other words, they want to use them as **deterrents**. Others fear that the radicalism of such countries' leaders could lead them to make offensive use of the weapons. In the aftermath of 9/11, concern arose that such "rogue states" might provide nuclear weapons to terrorists. Terrorist acquisition of nuclear weapons remains a low-probability, high-impact scenario of great concern to intelligence agencies worldwide. Extensive resources are devoted to monitoring the global traffic in dual-use technologies—technologies that can be used for legitimate industry but also for WMD. Civilian nuclear programs across the world are monitored by the IAEA, which serves as an international nuclear materials accounting and intelligence agency. The IAEA derives its authority to inspect countries from the NPT.

Terrorist organizations like al-Qaeda have expressed interest in acquiring nuclear weapons. Additional states may also proliferate. For example, Saudi Arabia has threatened to acquire nuclear weapons if Iran acquires them. The global nuclear nonproliferation regime is at a crossroads as of 2020. The major nuclear powers rejected a 2017 treaty completely banning nuclear weapons. This treaty was adopted by the United Nations General Assembly. Its main support came from small countries that are not nuclear powers and that are not covered by the US nuclear umbrella. Instead of banning nuclear weapons outright, the Great Powers prefer to maintain the NPT system whereby their arsenals remain legal as long as they engage in disarmament talks. For as long as this two-tiered system remains in place, countries will place high priority on monitoring each other's nuclear capabilities, preventing nonnuclear states like Iran from joining the nuclear ranks, and securing nuclear weapons and associated materials so that they are not acquired by terrorists or used accidentally.

## Chemical and Biological Weapons

Chemical weapons employ toxic chemicals to attack the blood, lungs, skin, or nervous systems of human beings. They can also be used to damage plant and animal life. One of the most common agents is the blister agent mustard gas, which chemically burns the surface of one's body as well as the lungs if inhaled, leading to difficulty breathing. It was used by European powers in World War I and by the Islamic State during its terrorist reign in Syria in the mid-2010s.[124] The most lethal chemical agents

[124]Nuclear Threat Initiative. "The Chemical Threat." December 30, 2015. https://www.nti.org/learn/chemical/.

are nerve agents. Sarin is the most common nerve agent. The Bashar al-Assad regime in Syria used sarin against its own people in 2013, nearly prompting a war with the United States. Subsequent chemical attacks by the Syrian regime employing sarin and more rudimentary, dual-use chemicals like chlorine led to precision US missile strikes as punishment and deterrence.

Chemical weapons were first banned under the 1925 Geneva Protocol. International law and norms against chemical weapons were greatly strengthened by the 1993 **Chemical Weapons Convention (CWC)**, which bans all production and use while providing verification through an international body known as the Organisation for the Prohibition of Chemical Weapons. However, the prominent role of chemicals in modern industry makes it hard to guarantee that no dual-use chemicals will be diverted for military or terrorist purposes.

Because of contagion effects, biological weapons risk greater and more widespread destruction than chemical weapons. Thankfully, they are more challenging to produce and use and are therefore much less common. Biological weapons employ natural toxins to sicken and kill their targets. Likely attack vectors are more surreptitious than delivery by missile. For example, Soviet assassins injected targets with the biological agent ricin. Terrorists could infect a food or water supply, or spray pathogens in liquid aerosol form from a drone. As gene editing and other biotechnology becomes more widely disseminated, the risk increases of terrorists concocting lethal pathogens in a covert laboratory. Fortunately, would-be users of biological weapons need to be concerned about blowback. Terrorists could contract and die from the illness before completion of their mission. States tempted to use biological weapons may not be able to contain the pathogen's spread, leading to sickness and death in their own populations. Biological weapons are banned under the 1972 **Biological Weapons Convention**, but the treaty lacks a verification mechanism like the NPT and CWC.

## Ballistic Missiles

**Ballistic missiles** are large and powerful missiles designed to carry conventional and WMD payloads over long distances. A short-range missile can fly about 600 miles. Longer-range intercontinental missiles, or ICBMs, can fly over 3,500 miles. Ballistic missiles employ rocket fuel and follow a ballistic trajectory, like a bullet shot from a gun. Shooting down a ballistic missile is frequently likened to shooting a bullet with a bullet. Smaller missiles are slower and are thus easier to shoot down with missile defenses. Reliable technology does not yet exist, however, to shoot down faster, longer-range missiles. For this reason, a country's acquisition of a long-range ballistic missile capability is of great concern, as it would allow a country on one side of the planet to strike a country on the other side of the planet with a conventional or WMD payload. Russia is developing hypersonic warhead technology that would make it all but impossible to defend against a ballistic missile attack due to the missile's high speed. Ballistic missiles have also grown in accuracy in recent years, making them more lethal and credible for use in many military scenarios where the parties wish to avoid collateral damage.

Ballistic missiles are most feared for their potential to deliver nuclear weapons. The United States, Russia, France, Great Britain, China, India, Pakistan, and Israel all deploy nuclear weapons on ballistic missiles. Growth in North Korean and Iranian nuclear capabilities since the 1990s has coincided with the development of ballistic missile capabilities. North Korea has tested missiles that may be able to strike as far as Washington, DC. Iran is further behind in developing an ICBM capability, but can strike targets within nearly 2,000 kilometers, which includes the entirety of the Middle East, southern and eastern portions of Europe, the Horn of Africa, and a large swath of the Indian Ocean. Iran has also shared its missile technology with terrorist allies, mainly Lebanese Hezbollah, which retains an arsenal of over 130,000 conventionally armed missiles and rockets for use against Israel and its allies.[125]

## TERRORISM

**Jonathan M. Acuff**

Although it has been a tactic pursued by the weak since the Old Testament, the US experience with terrorism was largely limited to a brief spate of anarchist activism following World War I, observing from afar the actions of terrorist groups overseas, and American activists funding foreign terrorist groups, such as the support afforded the Irish Republican Army (IRA). Following the Iran hostage crisis during the Jimmy Carter administration, newly elected president Ronald Reagan began to take more direct action in the Middle East than previous administrations had to date. A joint US-French attempt to end the Lebanese Civil War in 1982 precipitated a wave of terrorist attacks against US forces, including the bombing of the US embassy in Lebanon and a truck bomb that leveled the Marine Corps barracks and left hundreds dead. The United States subsequently withdrew from Lebanon, confining itself largely to retaliatory air strikes against state sponsors of terrorism and covert action against terrorists during the remainder of the Cold War. Following the collapse of the Soviet Union and the communist bloc, state-sponsored terrorism sharply declined.[126] Bereft of their generous subsidies from the USSR, most terrorist groups folded or entered into negotiations with their political opponents, as in the case with the IRA and the Palestinian Liberation Organization. What followed was the replacement of mostly state-supported, largely leftist organizations with a **new wave of terrorism**, defined this time not by secular ideology but by religious beliefs.[127] This new wave of religious

[125]Shaikh, Shaan. "Missiles and Rockets of Hezbollah." *Missile Threat*, June 16, 2018. https://missilethreat.csis.org/country/hezbollahs-rocket-arsenal/.

[126]Acuff, Jonathan M. "State Actors and Terrorism: The Role of State-Sponsored Terrorism in International Relations." In *Threats to Homeland Security: Reassessing the All-Hazards Perspective*, edited by Richard J. Kilroy Jr. Hoboken, NJ: Wiley, 2018.

[127]Juergensmeyer, Mark. *Terror in the Mind of God: The Global Rise of Religious Violence*, 4th ed. Berkeley: University of California Press, 2017.

terrorism took the form of both Sunni and Shia Islamic radicalism in the Middle East and Southwest Asia, far-right evangelical Christianity in the United States and Western Europe, and even Buddhist-inspired terrorism in Sri Lanka—the Tamil Tigers.

The 9/11 attacks perpetrated by **al-Qaeda** were part of this wave of terrorism, precipitating a radical shift in US foreign policy. The United States invaded Afghanistan in 2001, which had served as a training base and staging area for al-Qaeda for more than a decade. The 2003 invasion of Iraq was also ostensibly part of the George W. Bush administration's war on terror, despite the fact that Saddam Hussein's regime was neither involved in the 9/11 attack nor linked to al-Qaeda. The initial attack on Iraq included the widespread use of precision weapons, the so-called shock and awe campaign that while designed to decapitate the leadership of the Iraqi state was also clearly intended to cow the Arab street—to out-terrify existing terrorists and deter potential new recruits. It was a success in the former and a spectacular failure in the latter. The United States became bogged down in a counterinsurgency (COIN) campaign it did not plan for and was clearly not committed to waging with great resolve. While Iraq's streets burned and American soldiers deployed as many as six times to conflict zones, the Bush administration implemented tax cuts and a dramatic expansion in Medicare benefits, historically unprecedented policy decisions during wartime. Only with the creation of COIN doctrine from scratch in 2007 was the United States finally able to make a real effort against the Iraqi insurgency, which included elements of al-Qaeda but was clearly dominated by Indigenous groups.[128] But COIN doctrine probably had little to do with the reduction in violence in Iraq during the tail end of the US involvement—ethnic cleansing had tragically succeeded in separating Sunni and Shia urban enclaves that were the center of the violence. However, COIN and the increased operational tempo of US forces had a significant impact on al-Qaeda's involvement in Iraq. Following the "surge" of US forces in Iraq in 2007–2008, expansion of the drone assassination campaign against al-Qaeda's middle management, and the elimination of Osama bin Laden in the raid on his compound in Pakistan in 2011, the terrorist group had been decimated, its senior leadership gutted, and tens of thousands of its recruits killed or captured. Although al-Qaeda continues to pose a threat in Africa, particularly in Mali, its role in shaping the politics of the Middle East has sharply declined.

A more radical replacement for al-Qaeda, the **Islamic State (IS)**, emerged in northern Iraq and eastern Syria in 2014.[129] IS was built out of the cadre of an al-Qaeda

---

[128]Ricks, Thomas E. *The Gamble: General Petraeus and the American Military Adventure in Iraq*. New York, NY: Penguin, 2009. The new COIN manual employed by the US military was Petraeus, David H., James F. Amos, and John A. Nagl. *The US Army and Marine Corps Counterinsurgency Field Manual*. Chicago, IL: University of Chicago Press, 2007. Several prominent scholars who reviewed the manual noted its lack of innovation, ignorance of social science research from the past three decades, and even outright plagiarism of large passages of famous work by Max Weber and Anthony Giddens. See Biddle, Stephen, et al. "Review Symposium: The New US Army/Marine Corps Counterinsurgency Manual as Political Science and Political Practice." *Perspectives on Politics* 6, no. 2 (2008): 347–360.

[129]McCants, William. *The ISIS Apocalypse: The History, Strategy, and Vision of the Islamic State*. New York, NY: St. Martin's Press, 2015.

cell, the al-Nusra Front, and recruits from Iraqi and American prison camps used to house detainees from the COIN battlefield, some of whom became radicalized in these camps. IS became widely known as it rapidly conquered large swathes of Iraq in the summer of 2014, driving the demoralized, poorly led Iraqi Army before it and seizing large stocks of US equipment. As US combat forces had been withdrawn by President Obama in accordance with a treaty signed by the Bush administration, there seemed little prospect of arresting IS's ambition to establish a caliphate under which it would permanently establish its apocalyptic, extraordinarily cruel form of Islamic fundamentalism. But the Obama administration and US allies deployed significant air assets to the region, halted the collapse of Iraqi forces, and began to pound IS positions. In coordination with Kurdish forces, the only consistently effective military group in Iraq, the United States drove IS into a smaller and smaller perimeter. By the time the Trump administration took over, IS controlled very little of the territory it had seized. President Trump deployed US Marine Corps artillery units and expanded the ongoing air and special operations campaign. By December 2017, IS had lost its nominal capital, Raqqa, and been driven underground.

Both al-Qaeda and IS have lost their initial home bases. This has sharply reduced their ability to project power out of the Middle East. Yet they have managed to establish "franchises" in dozens of countries, from which they continue to conduct operations. IS in particular has inspired a series of bombings and other attacks in the Middle East and Western Europe and has participated in the insurgencies that have plagued Syria, Libya, and Nigeria. At one point, a significant section of the Sinai Peninsula was controlled by IS.[130] France in particular has suffered greatly from IS-inspired attacks (see Chapter 4). However, despite the ability of terrorist groups to destabilize weak states, the threat represented by international terrorism toward the United States was never existential. Terrorist groups by their nature are asymmetric threats—they cannot stand toe-to-toe with reasonably well-equipped and competently led military forces, to say nothing of their performance against Western militaries. When they do, the superior firepower possessed by state militaries invariably crushes them, no matter their skill level or training. After all, the nature of terrorist groups is to attack unarmed civilians, thereby engendering media attention to foster the belief that they are stronger or more popular than they really are. Historically, terrorist groups almost always fail to achieve their political objectives and disband in defeat.[131] As a tool for coercing states, terrorism is ineffective.[132] Support for terrorism has plummeted in the Middle East, and both IS and al-Qaeda are having a very difficult time recruiting. Americans are far more likely to die from household gun violence or in a traffic accident than at the hands

---

[130]Jones, Seth G., et al. *Rolling Back the Islamic State.* Santa Monica, CA: RAND Corporation, 2017, 140. https://www.rand.org/dam/rand/pubs/research_reports/RR1900/RR1912/RAND_RR1912.pdf.

[131]Cronin, Audrey Kurth. *How Terrorism Ends: Understanding the Decline and Demise of Terrorism Campaigns.* Princeton, NJ: Princeton University Press, 2009.

[132]Abrahms, Max. "Terrorism Does Not Work." *International Security* 31, no. 2 (2006): 42–78.

of an international terrorist group.[133] The United Kingdom spends "proportionately half as much [as the United States] on its counterterrorism efforts," yet enjoys a comparable level of safety.[134] International terrorism simply does not represent the strategic threat that many US politicians have characterized and continue to characterize it as.

To the extent international terrorism is a danger to the United States and its interests, the threat takes three forms. First, there is the ongoing willingness of terror groups to inspire either **small cells or lone wolves** to attack civilians. To date, the United States has seen comparatively little of this. Although al-Qaeda- and IS-inspired attacks have occurred, notably the Boston Marathon bombing in 2013 and a massacre in San Bernardino, California, in 2015, the casualties produced by these incidents have been low compared with similar such attacks in Europe. As painful as they are to witness, these kinds of attacks simply do not pose a strategic threat to the United States. Second, terror groups continue to wage campaigns against US allies and friendly countries. The result is **state destabilization** in Afghanistan, Iraq, Libya, Mali, Saudi Arabia, Nigeria, Kenya, Yemen, and Somalia. As one of the few state-sponsored terrorist groups in the world, the Shiite organization **Hezbollah** is now part of the Lebanese government. Though possessing little interest in projecting its power out of the region, Hezbollah poses an ongoing threat to Israel and cooperates with its sponsor, Iran, in destabilizing the region as a whole. Third, there have been intermittent efforts over the years by some terrorist groups to **acquire WMD**. The Taliban have repeatedly attacked Pakistani nuclear storage facilities, including an attack in 2012 at Minhas Airbase that penetrated all seven checkpoints before being stopped. A Belgian nuclear power plant was sabotaged in 2014 by an IS group, and no less than 13 French nuclear plants were overflown by drones of unknown origin that same year.

From the perspective of strategic threats, the prospect of international terrorists acquiring WMD is the most concerning. However, the threat is still relatively low compared to other dangers. If a terrorist group obtains fissile material or attempts to inflict damage on a nuclear plant, it is still unlikely to inflict mass casualties. Nuclear power plants are hardened structures with multiple redundancies, and it is exceedingly difficult to both manufacture a delivery device and successfully deploy it undetected. Yet no matter its low likelihood, the possibility of an attack on a nuclear plant or the detonation of either a dirty bomb or a captured nuclear device in a US city is a threat that continues to require attention and resources. Much the same can be said regarding other forms of WMD, as both the sarin gas attack by Aum Shinrikyo in 1995 and the poisoned ricin letters in the United States during 2003–2004 attest. Both of these attacks were with chemical agents, which are significantly easier to obtain and field than bioweapons. Even then, they caused few casualties and demonstrated the challenges even technically proficient terrorists experience in executing WMD attacks.

---

[133]Mueller, John, and Mark G. Stewart. "Hardly Existential: Thinking Rationally About Terrorism." *Foreign Affairs*, April 2, 2010. https://www.foreignaffairs.com/articles/north-america/2010-04-02/hardly-existential.

[134]Ibid.

The likelihood of terrorists successfully developing or deploying a biological agent is even lower than the danger posed by chemical weapons. Nevertheless, both deserve attention alongside fissile material as low-likelihood, potentially high-impact threats worthy of vigilance.

In contrast to the relative decline in the threat posed by international terrorist groups, the **threat of domestic terrorism** in the United States has risen sharply. In terms of the number of both attacks and resulting deaths, the threat now far exceeds the danger posed by international, principally radical Islamist terror groups. Such domestic terrorist groups are predominantly far-right, antigovernment organizations, frequently espousing neo-Nazi ideology and/or Christian evangelical beliefs. Although they are frequently portrayed as domestic terrorist groups by both conservative politicians and right-wing media, neither Antifa nor Black Lives Matter is a terror group—Antifa isn't even a unified organization.[135] Both President Trump and Attorney General William Barr have repeatedly described the people marching to protest police violence as "terrorists."[136] However, there is no evidence the violent rioting that occasionally occurred at these protests had any links to Antifa.[137]

Far-right groups present by far the greatest threat of domestic terrorism. The Southern Poverty Law Center identified 940 hate groups in the United States in 2019, up from 784 in 2014.[138] Most of these groups readily fit the definition of domestic terrorist groups, as their preferred method is to use violence to gain media attention to further their political objectives. Far-right terrorist groups have a presence in every state in the country and have infiltrated US law enforcement and military organizations. For example, the Atomwaffen Division terror group has cells in roughly 20 states and has members who are members of the US military.[139] As its name indicates, the group is neo-Nazi in orientation and seeks nuclear weapons as a means to further its genocidal objectives. The Federal Bureau of Investigation (FBI) has consistently failed to prioritize far-right extremist organizations as the primary threat posed by domestic terrorism. An egregious example of this is the fact that all 12 of the people listed as

---

[135]Kenney, Michael, and Colin Clarke. "What Antifa Is, What It Isn't, and Why It Matters." *War on the Rocks*, June 23, 2020. https://warontherocks.com/2020/06/what-antifa-is-what-it-isnt-and-why-it-matters/.

[136]Bertrand, Natasha. "Intel Report Warns Far-Right Extremists May Target Washington." *Politico*, June 19, 2020. https://www.politico.com/news/2020/06/19/intel-report-warns-far-right-extremists-target-washington-dc-329771.

[137]Beer, Tommy. "51 Protesters Facing Federal Charges—Yet No Sign of Antifa Involvement." *Forbes*, June 10, 2020. https://www.forbes.com/sites/tommybeer/2020/06/10/51-protesters-facing-federal-charges-yet-no-sign-of-antifa-involvement/#5a3eeb284138.

[138]Southern Poverty Law Center. "Hate Map: 2019." Accessed September 30, 2020. https://www.splcenter.org/hate-map.

[139]Thompson, A. C., Ali Winston, and Jake Hanrahan. "Inside Atomwaffen as It Celebrates a Member for Allegedly Killing a Gay Jewish College Student." *ProPublica*, February 23, 2018. https://www.propublica.org/article/atomwaffen-division-inside-white-hate-group; and Southern Poverty Law Center. "Atomwaffen Division." Accessed September 30, 2020. https://www.splcenter.org/fighting-hate/extremist-files/group/atomwaffen-division.

"Most Wanted" were associated with left-wing ideology; 8 of the 12 were people of color.[140] Yet since 1994, **right-wing terrorist attacks** far outnumber attacks by either international terrorists or attacks by left-wing associated groups.[141] Over 65 percent of the attacks in 2019, accounting for over 76 percent of all extremist-related murders (38 of 42) in the United States, were by far-right groups, and over 90 percent as of July 2020.[142] The FBI's emphasis on left-wing terrorism and President Trump and Attorney General Barr's characterizations are empirically indefensible.

Unfortunately, extreme-right groups have found a welcoming political climate in which to operate. The Trump administration has sought to blunt criticism of its links to the alt-right movement, groups President Trump described as "very fine people" following the neo-Nazi violence in Charlottesville, Virginia, in 2017. In 2018, the National Strategy for Counterterrorism specifically identified white nationalism as a significant threat.[143] Similarly, in 2020, for the first time a white nationalist group was specifically named as a terrorist group, the Russia-based Russian Imperial Movement, a group that has no ties to the far right in the United States.[144] Yet President Trump has repeatedly re-tweeted and praised far-right groups, ranging from Holocaust deniers to white supremacists. Trump frequently favorably references **QAnon**, a loose network that claims the Democratic Party is involved in a child sex-trafficking ring as part of the "Deep State" that secretly governs the United States. These accusations precipitated a terrorist attack by one of the followers of QAnon on a pizza restaurant in 2016 ostensibly associated with these bizarre claims.[145] More recently, President Trump's former national security adviser, Michael Flynn, took the QAnon oath of allegiance, and the Republican Party has run 11 candidates for House and Senate offices who openly associate themselves with QAnon.[146] It is difficult for the Trump administration to

---

[140]Federal Bureau of Investigation. "Most Wanted: Domestic Terrorism." Accessed August 3, 2020. https://www.fbi.gov/wanted/dt.

[141]Jones, Seth G., Catrina Doxee, and Nicholas Harrington. "The Escalating Terrorism Problem in the US." Center for Strategic and International Studies, June 17, 2020. https://www.csis.org/analysis/escalating-terrorism-problem-united-states.

[142]Center on Extremism. *Murder and Extremism in the United States in 2019*. New York, NY: Anti-Defamation League, February 2020. https://www.adl.org/media/14107/download; and Ibid.

[143]Office of the Director of National Intelligence. "National Strategy for Counterterrorism of the United States of America." October 2018, 9–10. https://www.dni.gov/files/NCTC/documents/news_documents/NSCT.pdf.

[144]Savage, Charlie, Adam Goldman, and Eric Schmitt. "US Will Give Terrorist Label to White Supremacist Group for First Time." *The New York Times*, April 6, 2020. https://www.nytimes.com/2020/04/06/us/politics/terrorist-label-white-supremacy-Russian-Imperial-Movement.html.

[145]Kennedy, Merrit. "'Pizzagate' Gunman Sentenced to Four Years." NPR, June 22, 2017. https://www.npr.org/sections/thetwo-way/2017/06/22/533941689/pizzagate-gunman-sentenced-to-4-years-in-prison.

[146]Cohen, Marshall. "Michael Flynn Posts Video Featuring QAnon Slogans." CNN, July 7, 2020. https://www.cnn.com/2020/07/07/politics/michael-flynn-qanon-video/index.html; and Rosenberg, Matthew, and Jennifer Steinhauer. "The QAnon Candidates Are Here. Trump Has Paved the Way." *The New York Times*, July 14, 2020. https://www.nytimes.com/2020/07/14/us/politics/qanon-politicians-candidates.html.

credibly assert it is addressing the danger posed by domestic terrorism when it so closely affiliates with the ideological beliefs espoused by the far-right extremist groups constituting the bulk of the threat.

Alone among industrialized democracies, the United States lacks a domestic **anti-terrorism statute**. In contrast with the robust legislative response following the 9/11 attacks, the United States has struggled to draft a domestic terrorism law. The structural, constitutional challenge that is frequently referenced is the First Amendment, which explicitly protects political speech. But neither sedition nor threatening violence is a form of protected speech. Dating from the Waco terrorist incident followed by the Oklahoma City bombing, four presidential administrations have failed to tackle the issue of domestic terrorism more directly. Yet the contrast between the lack of a law enforcement response to the heavily armed, frequently neo-Nazi protesters of the COVID-19 mask mandates and social distancing in several states and the level of violence police directed at the mostly peaceful demonstrators protesting George Floyd's death could not be starker. Much like its international counterpart, domestic terrorism does not constitute a strategic threat, as it cannot alter the balance of power. However, it is a security threat worthy of much more attention than it has hitherto been accorded, particularly in comparison with the trillions of dollars expended confronting international terrorism.

## CRIMINAL NETWORKS

**Richard J. Kilroy Jr.**

The end of the Cold War brought unique challenges to the US IC, with the spread of **transnational organized crime (TOC)**. While organized crime has existed for millennia, it was the vacuum created by the implosion of the former Soviet Union and the rise of new, more powerful **transnational criminal organizations (TCOs)** in the 1990s, primarily in Eastern Europe, that challenged new democratic states.[147] These criminal networks filled the void left by aging and corrupt communist regimes, by providing their own form of governing authorities, which controlled the political institutions, and economic means of production in many of these states. They often bridged both licit and illicit activities, not only by trafficking in drugs, arms, and people, but also by controlling commercial sectors such as energy production, transportation, shipping, and communications. Globalization and democratization actually helped to fuel the rise of these TCOs, enabling them to legitimize their activities. It is estimated today that TCOs control over $3 trillion of the global economy.[148]

---

[147]Glenny, Misha. *McMafia: A Journey Through the Global Criminal Network*. New York, NY: Knopf Doubleday, 2009.

[148]The Millennium Project. "Global Challenge 12." Accessed August 1, 2019. http://www.millennium-project.org/challenge-12/.

## Latin American Criminal Networks

One region that has received much attention by the IC, both internationally and domestically, has been Latin America, due to the presence of powerful **drug trafficking organizations (DTOs)**, often called cartels. Yet, calling them DTOs can obfuscate the fact that these TCOs are also trafficking arms, people, and many commercial goods across borders. In the 1970s and 1980s, drug cartels in Colombia, such as the Medellín Cartel (led by Pablo Escobar) and the Cali Cartel (led by the Orejuela brothers), captured much of the media attention due to their trafficking of cocaine into the United States. This was due not only to their power and influence in Colombia, but also to their connections to the Mexican mafia and criminal gangs in the United States, such as MS-13, Calle 18, Sureños, and others, which distributed the drugs. The breakup of the Colombian cartels in the 1990s gave rise to a power vacuum filled by new Mexican cartels, such as the Sinaloa, Gulf, Tijuana, Juarez, Los Zetas, and others, which fought for control of lucrative trafficking routes into the United States.

Due to the threat these powerful criminal organizations posed to Mexico's internal security, Mexican president Felipe Calderón declared a war on Mexican drug cartels. In 2009, Calderón declared martial law in parts of the country, such as Ciudad Juárez on the US border across from El Paso, Texas, ordering the military to take control of the city government and police in order to stem the violence and corruption. Yet, despite these policies, homicide rates in Mexico skyrocketed under Calderón. As a result, Mexicans voted out the ruling National Action Party (PAN) in 2012, bringing the Institutional Revolutionary Party (PRI) back into power under Enrique Peña Nieto, who promised to tackle the violence in the country. His kingpin strategy sought to emulate what had been successful in Colombia in targeting the leaders of the cartels. However, the result was a growth in new and more powerful cartels under new leaders. Six years later, homicide rates had not declined, reaching 29,000 in 2018 alone.[149] Mexicans again voted out the ruling party in favor a new political party, the National Regeneration Movement (MORENA), led by third-time presidential candidate Andrés Manuel López Obrador (AMLO), hoping for relief from the violence in their country.

Today, Mexico continues to experience insecurity from criminal organizations, whose operations have also spilled over into neighboring countries of the Northern Triangle (Guatemala, Honduras, and El Salvador). These countries have some of the highest homicide rates in the world.[150] People fleeing the violence in these countries primarily head for the United States, which has led to a spike in migration, creating a humanitarian crisis on the US-Mexico border. While the vast majority of these people

---

[149]Beitel, June. *Mexico: Organized Crime and Drug Trafficking Organizations*. Washington, DC: Congressional Research Service, June 3, 2018.

[150]World Bank. "Intentional Homicide Rates (per 100,000), 2019." Accessed August 1, 2019. https://data .worldbank.org/indicator/VC.IHR.PSRC.P5?most_recent_value_desc=true.

do not pose a threat to the United States, the **US Customs and Border Protection (CBP)** must still work to secure the border from both criminal and possibly terrorist threats who may seek to gain access to the United States trying to pose as refugees.[151]

## Intelligence Community Response to Criminal Networks

The US IC supports law enforcement agencies in their efforts to confront the threat posed by criminal networks, domestically and abroad. The FBI and the Drug Enforcement Administration (DEA) are members of the IC. Their intelligence analysts focus on criminal threats posed by TCOs and DTOs, providing threat assessments of criminal networks, to include identifying key personnel, organizations, tactics, and methods. Along the Southwest border, the **El Paso Intelligence Center (EPIC)** is a DEA-led organization that provides intelligence support to federal, state, and local law enforcement agencies. EPIC also coordinates its activities with the **US Northern Command's Joint Task Force South (JTF-S)**, also located in El Paso, Texas, which coordinates military support to the command's efforts to combat TCOs operating in North America. As a result of the Mérida Initiative, which was started under George W. Bush in 2008, the United States has provided military and law enforcement support to Mexico and Central American countries in their efforts to combat organized crime. One initiative included setting up an intelligence fusion center in the US embassy in Mexico City, in order to provide intelligence support to Mexican intelligence and law enforcement agencies.[152]

## CONCLUSION: OF THREATS AND PRIORITIES

In this chapter, we examined a variety of strategic threats the United States currently faces. This is not an exhaustive list. Moreover, some threats have been prioritized over others, based upon the danger posed by the threat, the relative probability of its occurrence, and the associated timeline. Yet not all experts in national security agree as to the relative rank-ordering of threats we provided. For example, while global climate change clearly poses a catastrophic threat to US security, some scholars or policy practitioners might argue that how much carbon is ultimately released into the atmosphere is meaningless if there is even a limited nuclear exchange between the United States and China, which would imperil all life on the planet. Regardless, the threats we have identified will figure prominently in important debates among decision makers as to how

---

[151]Schroeder, Robert D. *Holding the Line in the 21st Century*. US Customs and Border Protection. Accessed August 1, 2019. https://www.cbp.gov/sites/default/files/documents/Holding%20the%20Line_TRILOGY .pdf.

[152]Evans, Michael. "NSA Staffed US-Only Intelligence 'Fusion Center' in Mexico City." *Migration Declassified*, November 14, 2013. https://migrationdeclassified.wordpress.com/2013/11/14/nsa-staffed-u-s-only-intelligence-fusion-center-in-mexico-city/.

to deploy the resources of the United States and its allies to address these problems. No doubt they will provide for an equally robust discussion in your class.

## KEY CONCEPTS

## ADDITIONAL READING

Abrahms, Max. *Rules for Rebels: The Science of Victory in Militant History*. Oxford, UK: Oxford University Press, 2018.

Alba, Davey, and Ben Decker. "41 Cities, Many Sources: How False Antifa Rumors Spread Locally." *The New York Times*, June 22, 2020. https://www.nytimes.com/2020/06/22/technology/antifa-local-disinformation.html.

Arjomand, Said Amir. *After Khomeini: Iran Under His Successors*. Oxford, UK: Oxford University Press, 2009.

Avant, Deborah D. *The Market for Force: The Consequences of Privatizing Security*. Cambridge, UK: Cambridge University Press, 2005.

Beitel, June. *Mexico: Organized Crime and Drug Trafficking Organizations*. Washington, DC: Congressional Research Service, June 3, 2018.

Belton, Catherine. *Putin's People: How the KGB Took Back Russia and Then Took on the West*. New York, NY: Farrar, Straus & Giroux, 2020.

Blasko, Dennis J. *The Chinese Army Today*, 2nd ed. New York, NY: Routledge, 2012.

Bunn, Matthew, and Scott D. Sagan. *Insider Threats*. Ithaca, NY: Cornell University Press, 2016.

Cooley, Alexander. "Ordering Eurasia: The Rise and Decline of Liberal Internationalism in the Post-Communist Space." *Security Studies* 28, no. 3 (2019): 588–613.

Glenny, Misha. *McMafia: A Journey Through the Global Criminal Network*. New York, NY: Knopf Doubleday, 2009.

Goodwin, Jeff, James M. Jasper, and Francesca Polletta, eds, *Passionate Politics. Emotions and Social Movements*. Chicago, IL: University of Chicago Press, 2001.

Graff, Garrett M. "An Oral History of the Pandemic Warnings Trump Ignored." *Wired*, April 17, 2020. https://www.wired.com/story/an-oral-history-of-the-pandemic-warnings-trump-ignored/.

Greyson, George. *The Executioner's Men: Los Zetas, Rogue Soldiers, Criminal Entrepreneurs, and the Shadow State They Created*. Piscataway, NJ: Transaction, 2012.

Herspring, Dale R., ed. *Putin's Russia: Past Imperfect, Future Uncertain*, 3rd ed. Lanham, MD: Rowman & Littlefield, 2007.

Hoffman, Bruce. *Inside Terrorism*, 3rd ed. New York, NY: Columbia University Press, 2017.

Kaufman, Stuart J. *Nationalist Passions*. Ithaca, NY: Cornell University Press, 2015.

Leonhardt, David. "The Unique US Failure to Control the Virus." *The New York Times*, August 6, 2020. https://www.nytimes.com/2020/08/06/us/coronavirus-us.html.

Lieven, Anatol. *Climate Change and the Nation State: The Realist Case*. Oxford, UK: Oxford University Press, 2020.

Mattis, Peter. "So You Want to Be a PLA Expert." *War on the Rocks*, November 19, 2019. https://warontherocks.com/2019/11/so-you-want-to-be-a-pla-expert-2/.

Park, Kyung-Ae, and Scott Snyder, eds. *North Korea in Transition: Politics, Economy, and Society*. Lanham, MD: Rowman & Littlefield, 2012.

Ross, Robert S., and Zhu Feng, eds. *China's Ascent: Power, Security, and the Future of International Politics*. Ithaca, NY: Cornell University Press, 2008.

Rushton, Simon, and Jeremy Youde, eds. *Routledge Handbook of Global Health Security*. New York, NY: Routledge, 2015.

Sechser, Todd S., and Matthew Fuhrmann. *Nuclear Weapons and Coercive Diplomacy*. Cambridge, UK: Cambridge University Press, 2017.

Staniland, Paul. *Networks of Rebellion*. Ithaca, NY: Cornell University Press, 2014.

Tellis, Ashley J., Allison Szalwinski, and Michael Wills, eds. *Strategic Asia 2020: US-China Competition for Global Influence*. Seattle, WA: National Bureau of Asian Research, 2020.

Wulff, Stefan. *Ethnic Conflict: A Global Perspective*. Oxford, UK: Oxford University Press, 2006.

# INDEX

Note: Page numbers followed by "n" denote footnotes.